STATELY HOMES, MUSEUMS, CASTLES & GARDENS IN BRITAIN

Editor: Patricia Kelly
Designer: Turnergraphic Ltd
Illustrations by: Paul Fry
Compiled by: Publications Research Unit
Advertising: Peter Whitworth, Tel: Basingstoke 20123

Maps produced by the Cartographic Department of
the Automobile Association and based upon Ordnance
Survey maps with the permission of the Controller
of HM Stationery Office. Crown copyright reserved.

Castle Howard

(North Yorkshire) 18th century palace, the first creation of Sir John Vanbrugh. Unique collection of pictures, furniture, tapestries, porcelain and historic costume. 15 miles from York, off A64.

Harewood House

(West Yorkshire) 1759 Home of the Earl and Countess of Harewood. Seven miles north of Leeds on A61. Also Harewood Bird Garden and Butterfly House.

Warwick Castle

(Warwickshire) Magnificent medieval fortress. State Rooms. Armoury. Dungeon. Torture Chamber. Ghost Tower. Clock Tower and Barbican. Guy's Tower. Peacock Gardens.

Woburn Abbey

(Bedfordshire) Home of the Dukes of Bedford. Only one hour by road from London, Oxford, Cambridge, Stratford, Birmingham and Leicester.

Blenheim Palace

(Oxfordshire) Home of the 11th Duke of Marlborough, birthplace of Sir Winston Churchill. A gift from the nation to the victor of Blenheim.

Longleat House

(Wiltshire) Prime Elizabethan mansion, built 1566-1580, home of the Marquess of Bath. Longleat Safari Park. Restored Victorian Kitchens and many other summer attractions.

Beaulieu

(Hampshire) Palace House (1538) home of Lord and Lady Montagu of Beaulieu; Ruins of 13th century Beaulieu Abbey; The National Motor Museum.

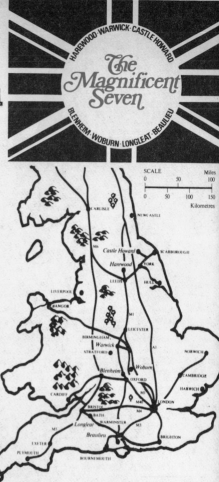

The Magnificent Seven

HAREWOOD · WARWICK · CASTLE HOWARD

BLENHEIM · WOBURN · LONGLEAT · BEAULIEU

The history of Britain is written into the landscape. It is in dark woods and green fields. It is in quiet villages. And, most dramatically of all, it is in the ancient castles and great country houses that tell their own story of kings and wars and the colourful life of past centuries.

Seven of these magnificent properties are presented here. They stretch from Castle Howard in North Yorkshire via Harewood, Warwick, Woburn, Blenheim, Longleat, to Beaulieu on the South Coast. Each House is a jewel in its own right; a truly magnificent living piece of history.

The owners of the 'Magnificent Seven' invite you to visit and enjoy their homes which are a key to Britain's History.

Contents

Produced by the Publications Division of the Automobile Association,
Fanum House, Basingstoke, Hants RG21 2EA.

Phototypeset by Vantage Photosetting Co Ltd, Southampton.
Printed by Fletcher & Son Ltd, Norwich, and bound by Richard Clay
(The Chaucer Press) Ltd, Bungay, Suffolk.
Colour printing by Camgate Litho Ltd, London.

Photographs by courtesy of Aerofilms Ltd, Borehamwood; Martin
Boddy; Morgan-Grampian (Professional Press) Ltd; Alan Rutter; Don
Squibb and Chris Taylor.

The contents of the publication are believed correct at the time of
printing but the current position may be checked through the AA. While
every effort is made to ensure that information appearing in
advertisements is correct, no responsibility can be accepted by the AA
for inaccuracies.

ISBN 0 86145 010 8   55877

Country House Outlook – '1980 is a crucial year'

by Marcus Binney, Chairman, Save Britain's Heritage

In recent years when owners have wanted to hand great houses and estates over in settlement of tax (as they may do) the critical problem has been one of endowment. In such circumstances, the Treasury almost invariably wants to hand the house on to the National Trust, or the National Trust for Scotland, but the Trusts understandably will rarely accept such houses without an endowment to cover the deficit in repairs and running costs. A protection against future fiascos like the break-up of Mentmore Towers should be provided by the establishment of the new National Heritage Fund. With its inauguration, the Inland Revenue will be able to accept a house in lieu of tax, and then the National Trust will be able to seek an endowment from the National Heritage Fund.

The new Fund's initial capital will be provided by transferring to it the assets of the existing Land Fund (over £17 million in July 1979) set up by Dr Dalton with the proceeds from the sale of surplus war stores as a memorial to the nation's war dead. 'For many years', Dr Dalton wrote in *Country Life* in 1946, 'I have felt real concern at the loss to the nation which was involved in the commercial sale, often piecemeal, of famous properties following the death of their owners . . . It has always seemed to me that the State should have had the means to prevent such desecration'. In addition, the new Heritage Fund will receive an annual grant (thought to be in the region of £3 million), though this is only partial recompense for the £50 million which on the advice of the Treasury was removed from the Fund in 1957.

The National Heritage Fund, one hopes, will only be the solution of last resort. Government ministers (of both parties) have repeatedly stressed that the best way of maintaining great houses is to allow their existing owners to continue to look after them. In response to one of the largest petitions ever presented to Parliament – with some 1.5 million signatures – the last government provided exemptions from Capital Transfer Tax for outstanding houses in return for public access: considerable, but by no means insoluble problems remain over providing funds for maintenance, and over allowing many of the smaller houses to set costs of upkeep against income as the larger ones are able to do.

Another key issue is the question of contents. An owner faced with a sudden repair bill which is well beyond his income, will inevitably consider whether there is not some piece of furniture or a work of art that can be sold to provide the necessary funds. Yet such sales inevitably undermine the very purpose of preserving the house.

The answer in some cases, at least, must be for a work of art to be accepted in lieu of tax and then, providing certain safeguards concerning security, conservation and access are met, for it to be loaned back to the house for display to the public. This is a proposal strongly supported by many museum directors and by the Museums Association and the Standing Commission on Museums and Galleries.

Then, of course, there is the difficulty of houses, fine architecturally, which have lost not only their contents but their owners as well. In the past such empty and decaying shells, even when they contain handsome panelling or plasterwork, have often seemed useless white elephants. The last few years, however, have seen an extraordinary upsurge of interest in such properties not only from incurable romantics but practical-minded businessmen and sober administrators. Large country houses are now sought for conversion into holiday apartments, hotels, offices, working communities and even spiritual retreats.

Kinmel Park in Clwyd, a remarkable Victorian house inspired by Wren's Hampton Court, stood roofless for three winters after a savage fire in 1975. Last year, it was acquired as a Christian Conference Centre, and acres of mansard roof have been entirely reconstructed. Within months Kinmel was receiving its first visitors.

At Dingley in Northampton, a young architect has bought a long derelict but beautiful 16th and 17th-century house and is converting it into eleven self-contained houses and apartments: all of these have been sold before completion. Boringdon in Devon, an Elizabethan house unoccupied for half a century, has been bought by a new owner who is restoring the main house to live in and converting the stables for holiday lets.

Other long-neglected houses have recently been bought back by their original owners. Robin Brackenbury and his wife bought Holme Pierrepont in Nottingham (see page 157), eleven years ago to prevent it leaving the family and have launched an enterprising and ambitious repair scheme with help from the Manpower Services Commission. Also in Nottinghamshire a young company director has bought back Winkburn Hall, a handsome early 18th-century house his father had been forced to sell the year before he was born.

Other important houses, however, do remain empty. Barlaston Hall in Staffordshire, a Grade 1 Georgian house which is a landmark for miles around, has been left closed and forlorn despite the offer of a substantial Historic Buildings Council repairs grant to the owners, Wedgwood Ltd. Pelwall Hall, near Market Drayton in Shropshire, one of the few surviving houses by Sir John Soane, is still deteriorating.

But while a house continues to exist, however abandoned, there is always a chance that it will be saved eventually. In the last decade the national preservation societies have fought and won a series of inquiries to prevent the demolition of a number of outstanding country houses – Barlaston Hall; Hylands Hall, Essex; Revesby Abbey, Lincolnshire and Llangoed, Powys.

Yet the curious British addiction to demolition remains. The Italians and the French appear happy to leave their villas and châteaux closed and falling gently and gracefully into decay, for decades if necessary. Here, a crisis lasting a matter of years can spell destruction for a lovely house that has perhaps stood for a century and a half or more, and which, with some attention, could last for generations.

In Britain a total of at least 628 notable country houses were demolished between 1945 and 1974 – 431 in England, 175 in Scotland and 23 in Wales. Since 1974 the number has happily fallen to a trickle – maybe two or three a year. There it must stay.

Marcus Binney

British Cathedrals

Cathedrals are usually open daily at all reasonable times and will be found in the following places:

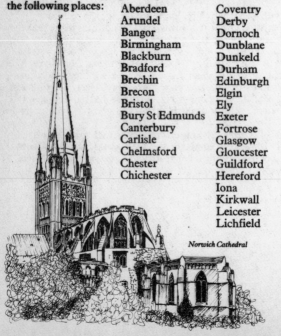

Norwich Cathedral

Aberdeen
Arundel
Bangor
Birmingham
Blackburn
Bradford
Brechin
Brecon
Bristol
Bury St Edmunds
Canterbury
Carlisle
Chelmsford
Chester
Chichester

Coventry
Derby
Dornoch
Dunblane
Dunkeld
Durham
Edinburgh
Elgin
Ely
Exeter
Fortrose
Glasgow
Gloucester
Guildford
Hereford
Iona
Kirkwall
Leicester
Lichfield

Lincoln
Liverpool
Llandaff
London
Manchester
Newcastle
Newport
Norwich
Oxford
Peel
Peterborough
Portsmouth
Ripon
Rochester
St Albans
St Andrews
St Asaph
St Davids
Salisbury
Sheffield
Southwell
Truro
Wakefield
Wells
Winchester
Worcester
York

The National Grid

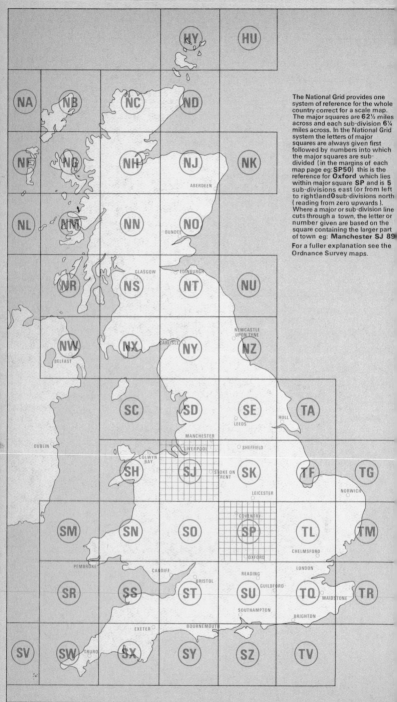

The National Grid provides one system of reference for the whole country correct for a scale map. The major squares are **62½** miles across and each sub-division **6¼** miles across. In the National Grid system the letters of major squares are always given first followed by numbers into which the major squares are subdivided (in the margins of each map page eg: **SP50**) this is the reference for **Oxford** which lies within major square **SP** and is **5** sub-divisions east (or from left to right) and **0** sub-divisions north (reading from zero upwards). Where a major or sub-division line cuts through a town, the letter or number given are based on the square containing the larger part of town eg: **Manchester SJ 89**

For a fuller explanation see the Ordnance Survey maps.

Key to Atlas

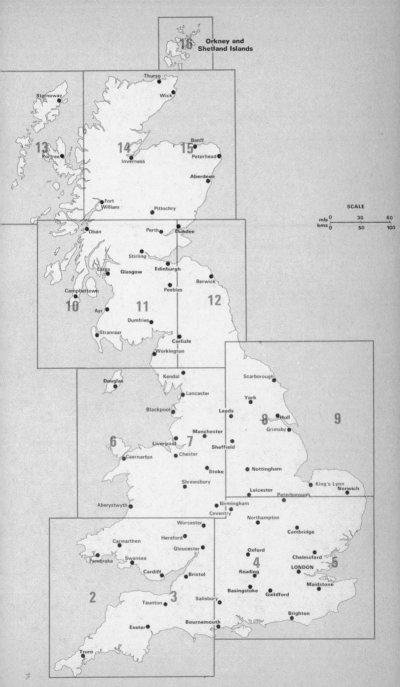

Orkney and Shetland Islands 16

Thurso
Wick
Stornoway

13 Portree
14 Inverness
15 Banff
Peterhead
Aberdeen

Fort William
Pitlochry

SCALE

mls 0   30   60
kms 0   50   100

Oban
Perth Dundee
Stirling
Largs
Glasgow Edinburgh
Campbeltown Peebles Berwick
10 Ayr 11 12
Dumfries
Stranraer
Carlisle
Workington

Douglas
Kendal
Scarborough
Lancaster
York
Blackpool Leeds
8 Hull 9
Manchester Grimsby
6 Liverpool 7 Sheffield
Caernarfon Chester
Stoke Nottingham
Shrewsbury
Leicester King's Lynn
Peterborough Norwich
Aberystwyth
Birmingham
Coventry
Worcester Northampton
Hereford Cambridge
Carmarthen Gloucester Oxford
Pembroke Swansea Chelmsford
Cardiff Reading LONDON 5
4 Maidstone
2 3 Bristol Basingstoke Guildford
Taunton Salisbury
Brighton
Bournemouth
Exeter
Truro

*This atlas is for location purposes Only:
see Member's Handbook for current road
and AA road services information*

Maps produced by

the AA Cartographic Department
(Publications Division), Fanum House,
Basingstoke, Hampshire RG21 2EA

*Based on the Ordnance Survey Map with
the Sanction of the Controller H.M.S.O.*

3 **4** **5** **6** **7** **8** **9** **0** **1** **2** **3** **4** **5** **6**

6

5 SM

4

3

2

1

0

9

8

7

6

5 SR

4

3

2

1

0

9

8

7

6

5 SW

4

3 ST JUST

ABERAERON
NEW QUAY

Plwmp

SN
LAMPETER

CARDIGAN
Newport
FISHGUARD
Cilgerran
Dre-Fach
Felindre
NEWCASTLE EMLYN
Talle

St David's
Bronwydd Arms
CARMARTHEN
LLANDEIL
Scolton
Dryslwyn

HAVERFORDWEST
Llawhaden
Picton
NARBERTH
Abergwili
AMMANFOR
Llanstephan

MILFORD HAVEN
NEYLAND
KIDWELLY
LLANEI
Pembroke Dock
St Florence
BURRY PORT

Lamphey
TENBY
GORSEINON
PEMBROKE
Manorbier
Llanrhidian
Mumble

SS
ILFRACOMBE

Lundy Island
Arlingto
Croyde
Appledore Instow
BARNSTAPLE
NORTHAM
BIDEFORD
GREAT
TORRINGTO

Shebbear
STRATTON
Thornbury Wornworn
BUDE A3072
HOLSWORTHY

OKEHAMPTON
Boscastle
Shelep
Tintagel
LAUNCESTON
Lydford
Delabole
Camelford
Trewin
PADSTOW
TAVISTOCK
Minjdi
Dupath
WasharVay
BODMIN
St Neot
St Chec Casto
A390
NEWQUAY
St Richi
BackandAbbe
Lanivet
LISKEARD
BUC
LOSTWITHIEL
Stormel
SALTASH
St Newly (at last)
SALTASH
St Agnes
ST AUSTELL
Plympe
Probus
FOWEY
TORPOINT
PLYMOUT
LOOE
SW
TRURO
Mevagissey
Polperro
SX
Yea
REDRUTH
Pen
CAMBORNE
Pock
St Mawes
ST IVES
Lelant
Hayle
PENRYN
Zenn
Chvester
Godolphin
FALMOUTH
Morvah
Madron
Cruwas
Cross
Mawnan Smith
Sancreed
Marazion
HELSTON
PENZANCE
Mullion

8 **9** **0** **1** **2** **3** **4** **5** **6**

3 **4** **5** **6** **7**

2

1

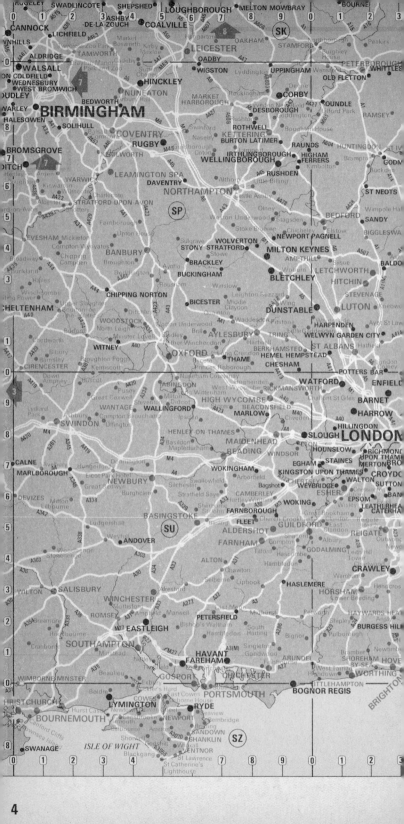

4

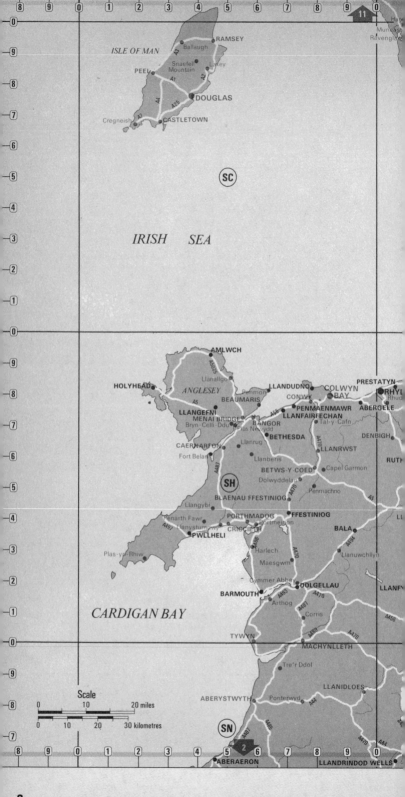

ISLE OF MAN

RAMSEY
Ballaugh

Snaefell
Mountain
PEEL
Laxey

DOUGLAS

Cregneish
CASTLETOWN

(SC)

IRISH   SEA

11

Ha
Muncast
Ravenglass

AMLWCH

HOLYHEAD

ANGLESEY

Llanallgo

Penmon

LLANDUDNO
COLWYN
BAY
CONWY

PRESTATYN

RHYL

BEAUMARIS

LLANGEFNI
MENAI BRIDGE

Bryn-Celli-Ddu
Plas Newydd

PENMAENMAWR
LLANFAIRFECHAN

BANGOR

Tal-y-Cafn

ABERGELE

DENBIGH

RUTH

CAERNARFON

Fort Belan

BETHESDA

Llanrug

Llanberis

BETWS-Y-COED
Dolwyddelan

LLANRWST

Capel Garmon

(SH)

Penmachno

BLAENAU FFESTINIOG

A5

Llangybi

Penarth Fawr

PORTHMADOG
Portmeirion

FFESTINIOG

LL

Llanystumdwy
CRICCIETH

PWLLHELI

Plas-yn-Rhiw

Harlech

BALA

Llanuwchllyn

Maesgwm

Cymmer Abbey

DOLGELLAU

BARMOUTH

LLANF

Arthog

CARDIGAN BAY

Corris

TYWYN

MACHYNLLETH

Tre'r Ddol

Scale
10   20 miles

0   10   20   30 kilometres

LLANIDLOES

ABERYSTWYTH

Ponterwyd

A44

(SN)

2

ABERAERON

LLANDRINDOD WELLS

6

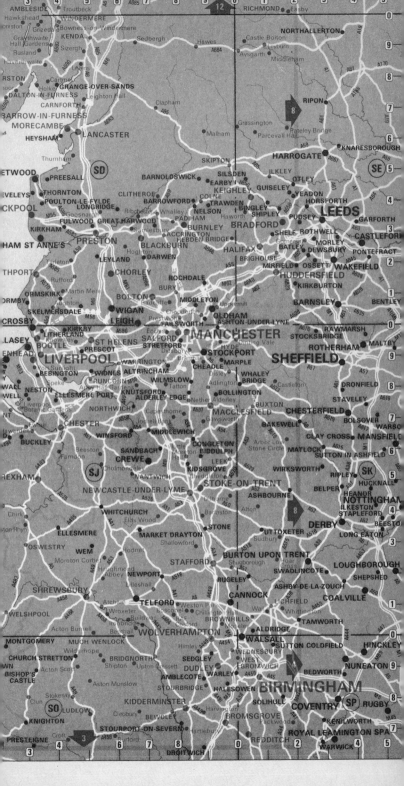

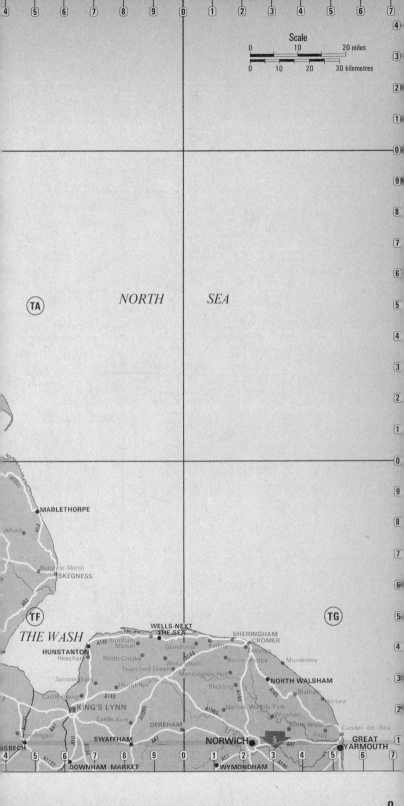

NORTH SEA

TA

NORTH SEA

THE WASH

TF

TG

MABLETHORPE

Alford

A52

Burgh-le-Marsh
SKEGNESS

A52

WELLS-NEXT-
THE-SEA

SHERINGHAM
CROMER

Burnham
Market
HUNSTANTON
Heacham
North Creake
Sandringham
Houghton
Castle Rising
A148
KING'S LYNN
Castle Acre
A1065
DEREHAM
SWAFFHAM
A47
Terrington
A47
WISBECH
A1122
DOWNHAM MARKET
A134
A10

A149

Glandford
Walsingham
Thursford Green
Mannington Hall
Blickling

Kelling
Bacton
Mundesley

NORTH WALSHAM
Stalham
Horsey
A140
Norfolk Wildlife Park
Wroxham
South Walsham
Filby
Caister-on-Sea

A149
A1065
A11
WYMONDHAM
NORWICH
5
A47
A146
GREAT
YARMOUTH

Scale

0   10   20 miles
0   10   20   30 kilometres

9

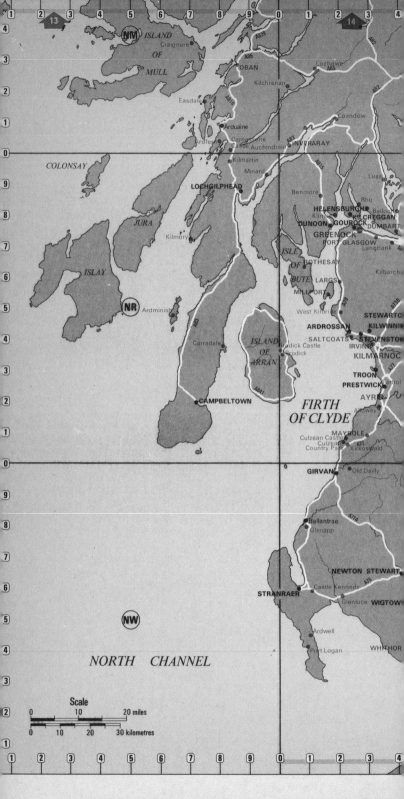

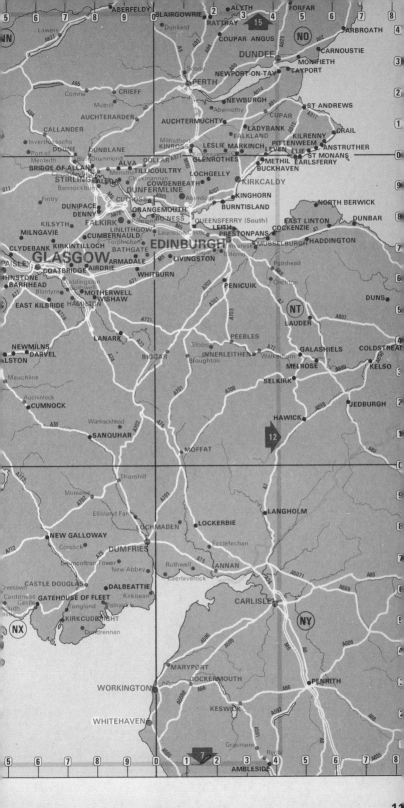

NORTH SEA

FIRTH OF FORTH

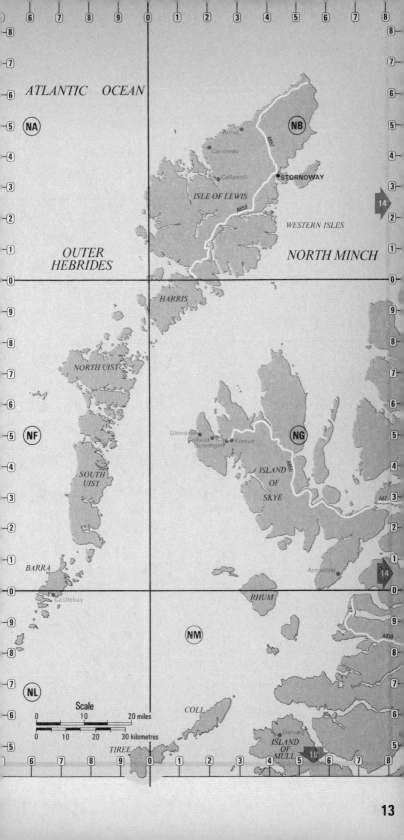

ATLANTIC OCEAN

NA

NB

Arnol
Carloway
Callanish
STORNOWAY

ISLE OF LEWIS

A857

A859

WESTERN ISLES

14

NORTH MINCH

OUTER
HEBRIDES

HARRIS

NORTH UIST

NF

SOUTH
UIST

Glendale
Colbost
Dunvegan
Kilmuir

NG

ISLAND
OF
SKYE

A850

A87

BARRA

Armadale

Castlebay

RHUM

14

NM

A830

NL

COLL

Scale
10
20 miles

0   10   20   30 kilometres

TIREE

Dervaig
ISLAND
OF
MULL

16

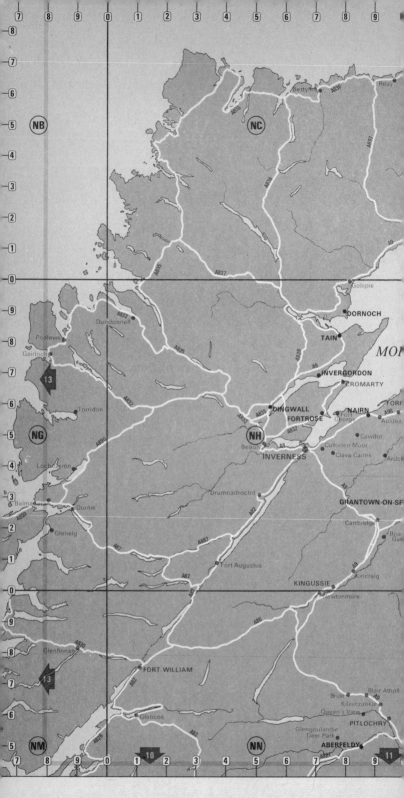

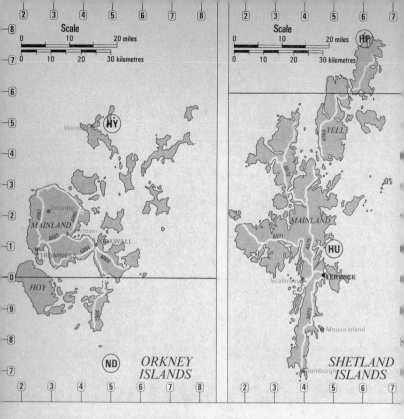

ORKNEY
ISLANDS

SHETLAND
ISLANDS

TOURIST INFORMATION CENTRES

Look for this sign:

Hever Castle Maze – aerial view.

The Mazes of England
by Adrian Fisher

The words 'maze' and 'labyrinth' are derived from different cultures, but both have the same meaning – complex network of paths. English mazes have a certain appeal all of their own, and can be traced back to rock carvings in Cornwall made 3,500 years ago.

There are two types of mazes. One type consists of a single path that leads in a meandering fashion to the middle of the maze and this is known as a Uni-cursal maze. The other type is a Multi-cursal maze. The uni-cursal form is much older, and was originally used to give protection from evil spirits, that reputedly weren't able to turn corners. Usually cut in turf, uni-cursal mazes have been known, for various reasons, by such names as Troy Town, Walls of Troy, Julian's Bower, Maiden's Bower, Shepherd's Race or Mizmaze. The traditional Cretan design found at Tintagel (see illustration page 30) was widely used, and in medieval times a Christan version also became popular. Many other turf mazes had unique designs.

About the author
Adrian Fisher developed his taste for uncharted three-dimensional passages while exploring caves in the Mendip Hills. He started his first hedge maze in Bournemouth in 1975. His work on the unravelling of turf maze designs enabled him to develop a new generation of maze design for the Pilgrimage Maze at St Albans Cathedral. An archaeological dig is planned for 1981, after which the site will become available for this new turf maze, the first in Britain for 200 years.

Designed in the shape of a rose, to symbolise the martyrdom of St Alban, it will take the theme of the Path of Life.

Adrian is currently participating in the Munich Labyrinth Exhibition, which continues until February 1980. At the moment he is also designing a maze as part of a Robin Hood Theme Park near Nottingham.

The author undertakes commissions to design mazes and is writing a book on British mazes. He is always pleased to hear from other maze enthusiasts.

Tintagel or Cretan design.

Medieval Christian design.

Uni-cursal mazes

You will find that most turf mazes are located in charming and quiet places that are well worth a visit. They have a fascinating history, although local legends have grown up, making it difficult to distinguish between fact and fiction. In Devon 'Maze Sunday' was a day set aside for feasting and drinking. In Nottingham, a three-day fair used a turf maze as one of its main attractions. The maze was called 'Robin Hood's Race'. Sadly it was ploughed up in 1797.

There were several examples of mazes known as 'Maiden's Bower', which probably recollected an ancient fertility rite; the young maidens were given a short start, before being chased by young men to the middle. The Minotaur legend springs to mind with its obvious similarities with the maidens fleeing along a single path, and only a closed goal to look forward to!

One Julian's Bower maze remains at Alkborough. The name could be derived either from Iulus, the son of Aeneas, or from Saint Julian. Aeneas and his son Iulus wandered for years around the Greek Islands after the fall of Troy and Aeneas is reputed to have drawn maze patterns in the sandy beaches to amuse little Iulus.

Not all mazes are made of hedges or turf. King Henry II kept his mistress, the 'Fair Rosamund', in a building called Rosamund's Bower, near his palace at Woodstock, Oxfordshire. His indignant Queen, Eleanor of Aquitaine, penetrated the maze of rooms and passages with its 150 doors, and forced Henry's mistress to drink poison. In 1870 Sir Gilbert Scott laid a pavement maze in stone at Ely Cathedral.

Since the Second World War, Greg Bright, a contemporary maze designer, spent a year in 1971 digging a trench maze at Worthy Farm, Pilton, in Somerset; Paul Edwards, another maze fan, has built a maze out of upright larch logs in a Birmingham Park; and the new maze at Ragley Hall is built of stone and concrete. Lord Eliot's new maze in Cornwall is a hedge maze with a difference. It also has a series of moveable gates, so that the maze can be arranged in billions of different ways.

Hampton Court is the earliest hedge maze in England, and the most famous. It was replanted in 1690, and possibly goes back to Cardinal Wolsey's time. The outer shape is fixed by the different paths that criss-cross the area of garden known as the Wilderness. This distinctive triangular shape, as well as the actual design, has been

Hampton Court Maze – aerial view.

copied over a dozen times, in England alone. The maze was immortalised in Jerome K Jerome's *Three Men in a Boat*, and the description still captures its spirit today.

Hedge mazes are expensive to build and to maintain, which is why they were originally found only in Royal or Baronial grounds. Formal grounds, which often included a maze, flourished until the 18th century, when Capability Brown introduced the Natural Landscape. He destroyed many of these in order to achieve his new look. Ironically, as the Royal Gardener for twenty years, Capability Brown lived alongside the maze at Hampton Court, but he was expressly ordered not to interfere with it.

The great upsurge in hedge mazes came in Victorian times. The second Earl Stanhope was an eminent mathematician, and he designed at least three mazes, including that at Chevening in Kent (see illustration, page 32). This maze, built in the 1820s, was the firs to use 'islands'. If you study the Chevening design, you will notice that the hedges have been shaded in different ways. The stippled hedges are separate 'islands', which could be removed without making much difference to the puzzle. The centre is also located within an island. The effect of islands is to prevent you from finding the centre of the maze by keeping left (or right) all the way round the edge. Chevening is now the private home of the Prince of Wales, and the maze is not open to the public, the Chevening design was highly respected and was copied in three other mazes, at Anerley, North Woolwich and Beauport.

With the growing prosperity of Victorian times, an increasing number of wealthy people built mazes for their private pleasure; for example, at Glendurgan, Somerleyton Hall, Worden Park and Hever Castle. However, the great majority of Victorian mazes were built as part of the Victorian leisure industry. Some were made in new public parks, laid out between newly-built Victorian suburbs, and many more were found in Pleasure Gardens, run for profit, whose attractions were provided within an hour's walk of Victorian cities. These mazes have mostly been covered by 20th-century suburbs, and no trace of them remains. In London an hotel occupies the site of a maze in Paddington, a council estate anonymously covers the Anerley maze, and in South Kensington, Prince Albert initiated a maze a stone's throw from the Albert Hall, financed from the profits of the

31

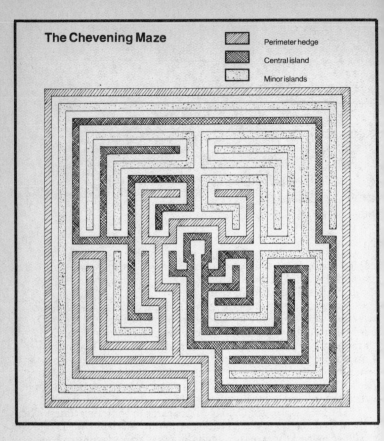

The Chevening Maze

Perimeter hedge

Central island

Minor islands

Crystal Palace Exhibition. This last maze, now covered by the Science Museum, was designed by William Nesfield, who also designed Kew Gardens and the Somerleyton Maze.

Between the two World Wars, few mazes were built. Indeed, both World Wars were a great threat to mazes; after five years of enforced neglect, mazes became overgrown beyond repair and had to be removed. The mazes at Arley Hall, Totteridge Park and Debdale Hall were all lost in this way. More dramatically, the Belton Maze was abruptly replaced by a Ministry of Defence building in 1939; the nearest parallel to this was the destruction of the Theobald's Maze by Parliamentary troops in 1643; during the English Civil War.

Since 1945 mazes have enjoyed a new lease of life. Seaside resorts have built mazes as an added attraction for their holiday visitors, in particular there is the maze at Blackgang Chine on the Isle of Wight, and there are two in Scarborough. The Stately Homes have opened their gates to ever increasing numbers of the public, offering gardens, wildlife parks, amusements and mazes, new mazes have been built at Longleat, Chatsworth and Ragley Hall.

The writer's private holly maze in Bournemouth, and Randoll Coate's work in Gloucestershire provide further diversity. The unique Maze of the Mysteries of the Gospel, at Wyck Rissington in Gloucestershire conveys the Christian gospel of Life, Death and Eternal Life to its visitors, an annual service is held each August when the church congregation processes through the maze.

There is a simple method to follow, when solving puzzle mazes. If the hedge that surrounds the goal also connects with the outside hedge, use the hand-on-wall method: simply follow the perimeter hedge in and out of each dead end until you reach the goal. The Chevening Maze defeats this method by placing the goal within a central island. Wall huggers now travel harmlessly around the perimeter and return to the entrance without finding the goal. For further confusion, the Chevening Maze also contains five minor islands, which are clearly visible.

The Longleat Maze opened in June 1978 brings us right up to date. It is the world's largest maze and Britain's first three-dimensional maze; and Greg Bright has used his latest ideas on partial values and Mutually Accessible Centres. After a few yards, the goal is seen just the other side of a hedge. Even in Chevening, by following the hedge round, you would reach the goal. Not so at Longleat: bridges and underpasses create a new pattern of logic, which is only beginning to be analysed. The end of the twentieth century promises to be a great time for mazes!

British Mazes
Open to the Public

Key:
■ Hedge Mazes
● Turf Mazes
▲ Miscellaneous

Scotland: ■ Hazlehead Park, Aberdeen

Victoria Park Esplanade (Scarborough)
● Brandsby
■ Worden Park
Alkborough ●
■ Tatton Park
■ Chatsworth
Wing ●   Somerleyton Hall ■
Ely ▲
Hilton ●   ▲ Bourn
Ragley Hall ▲
● Saffron Walden
■ Wyck Rissington
Hampton Court ■
■ Longleat   ■ Hever Castle
■ High Rocks
▲ Tintagel
Breamore ● ● Winchester
Blackgang Chine
Glendurgan

The following summary shows most of the exciting mazes open to the public: there are at least seventeen other mazes in private grounds, whose privacy must be respected.

BRITISH HEDGE MAZES

Date	Place	Material	Size	Designer	Remarks
Earlier than 1670	Hampton Court Palace East Molesey, Surrey	Yew	68×25 m	Unknown	The earliest hedge maze in Britain; receives ½ million visitors a year.
c.1670	High Rocks Hotel Nr. Tunbridge Wells, Kent	Laurel	57×21 m	Exact copy of Hampton Court Maze	Visited by James II, who used to attend the wells.
1833	Glendurgan Near Falmouth, Cornwall	Laurel	—	Alfred Fox	Only open on certain days during the summer. Owned by National Trust.
1846	Somerleyton Hall Nr. Lowestoft, Suffolk	Yew	75×49 m	William Nesfield	Central Pagoda on top of knoll.
1886	Worden Park Leyland, Lancs	Beech	—	A member of the Harington family	Worden Hall burnt down in 1943; now the maze is in a public park.
1905	Hever Castle Nr. Edenbridge, Kent	Yew	23×23 m	William Waldorf Astor	Maze used to recreate the Tudor setting where Henry VIII courted Anne Boleyn.
1935	Hazlehead Park Aberdeen	Privet	58×49 m	Sir Henry Alexander?	Given to the citizens of Aberdeen by Sir Henry Alexander.
1950	St. Laurence's Rectory Wyck Rissington, Glos.	Hawthorn and ivy	25×20 m	Canon H. S. Cheales	Maze of the Mysteries of the Gospels. More for the pilgrim than the sightseer.
1959	Victoria Park Scarborough, North Yorks	Privet	41×30 m	Scarborough Borough Council	—
1962	Chatsworth Bakewell, Derbyshire	Yew	40×35 m	D. A. Fisher	On the site of Joseph Paxton's Great Conservatory; design based on earlier maze of First Duke of Devonshire.
1962	Blackgang Chine Isle of Wight	Privet	27×25 m	John Dabell	Floodlit between June and September.
1963	Esplanade Maze Scarborough, North Yorks	Privet	32×22 m	Scarborough Borough Council	—
c.1930	Tatton Park Knutsford, Cheshire	Beech	—	4th Baron, Lord Egerton of Tatton	Maze in good condition and a great feature of the gardens.
1978	Longleat House Warminster, Wilts	Yew	116×54 m	Greg Bright	The world's largest maze. Britain's first three-dimensional maze.

BRITISH TURF MAZES

Date	Place	Material	Size	Designer	Remarks
Unknown	Breamore House Breamore, Hants	Turf paths in chalk	27 m diam	Monks?	'Mizmaze' Medieval Christian design.
1200	Alkborough Nr. Scunthorpe, Lincs	Turf paths	13 m diam	Benedictine monks	'Julian's Bower' medieval Christian design.
Unknown	Brandsby North Yorkshire	Turf paths	9 m diam	Unknown	'City of Troy' traditional Cretan design.
Earlier than 1710	St Catherine's Hill Nr. Winchester, Hants	Furrows within turf	26×26 m	A Winchester schoolboy?	'Mizmaze' built inside Roman Camp with view of city
Unknown	Village Green, Wing, Leics	Turf paths	12 m diam	Unknown	Medieval Christian design.
Earlier than 1699	The Common Saffron Walden, Essex	Brick path in turf	42 m diag	Unknown	The largest turf maze in Britain, with 4 Bastions.
1660	Village Green, Hilton, Cambs.	Turf paths	16 m diam	William Sparrow	Medieval Christian design, with unique sundial at centre.

MISCELLANEOUS BRITISH MAZES

Date	Place	Material	Size	Designer	Remarks
At least 1500 BC	Rocky Valley Tintagel, Cornwall	Rock carving	—	Unknown	The original maze design, and the earliest in Britain.
Presumed later than 1770	Church of SS Helena and Mary, Bourn, Cambs.	Red and black tiles	—	Based on Hampton Court design	Surrounds font beneath church tower.
1870	Ely Cathedral Ely, Cambs.	Black and white stone	6×6 m	Sir Gilbert Scott	Constructed during restoration to the cathedral in 1870.
1979	Ragley Hall Alcester, Warwickshire	Re-con. stone and concrete	—	Maurice Rich	—

These lists are almost certainly incomplete, any additions or corrections will be gratefully received.

Making the most of your guide

The **gazetteer section** of this book is divided into the following sections:

England; Isle of Man, Isles of Scilly, Isle of Wight and Channel Islands; Wales; Scotland and Scottish Islands.

For your convenience towns and villages are listed alphabetically by name within each section. As far as possible the places of interest situated within one mile or two of a town or village are placed under the nearest town or village heading. However, some places of interest are too far from any town or village; in this case, such places are listed under the name of the establishment.

This simple method of arranging entries allows you to make use of this book in several ways, either by:

Town
If you know the name of the town/village you want to go to, turn straight to the alphabetically-arranged gazetteer section.

or Place of interest
If you know the particular place of interest that you want to visit, refer to the index at the back of the book. This will give you the relevant page in the gazetteer.

or General area
If you are planning a day out, or a holiday in a particular area; look first at the key to atlas pages at the front of the two-colour map section. From this key you can locate the map that covers the area you require. Towns and places of interest are picked out in red on each map.
Alternatively, you can look up a known place of interest in the gazetteer section and refer to the map reference beside that entry. You will see from the relevant map page if there are any other places of interest in that area.

Telephone numbers

All exchange names are the same as the town/village heading unless shown otherwise.

Index

Please note that the index at the back of this book is an index to **establishments only**. You will not find any town or village names shown, as they are easy to find in the gazetteer which is in straight alphabetical order within each country section. Likewise, an establishment whose name begins with a town name (eg Chertsey Museum) is also omitted from the index.

Symbols The following symbols and abbreviations are used throughout the book:

Symbol	Meaning	Abbr.	Meaning
♿	Accessible to visitors in wheelchairs. All parts accessible	ex	except
		Free	Admission free
		10p	Admission 10p
♿ B	Ground floor and/or gardens only	ch 20p	Children 20p
		ch 15 20p	Children under 15 20p
(79)	Indicates 1979 information		
		Pen	Senior Citizens
BH	Bank Holidays	Party	Special or reduced rates for parties booked in advance
PH	Public Holidays (Scotland)		
⚠	Parking at establishment		
P.	Parking nearby	Party 30+	Special or reduced rates for parties of 30 or more booked in advance
⚠	No parking		
⍟	Refreshments and/or restaurant		

Zeichenerklärung: Die nachstehenden Zeichen und Abkürzungen werden in diesem Reiseführer verwendet.

&#9855;	für Rollstuhlfahrer zugänglich. Zutritt zu allen Teiler	ch 20p	Kinder 20p
		ch 15 20p	Kinder unter 15 Jahre 20p
♿ B	Nur einige Teile zugänglich/ bzw Garten	Pen	Rentner
		Party	Sondertarife bzw. Ermässigungen für im voraus bestellte Gesellschaften
(79)	1979 Angaben		
BH	Bankfeiertage		
PH	Feiertage (Schottland)		
&#9888;	Parken an Ort und Stelle	Party 30+	Sondertarife bzw. Ermässigungen für im voraus bestellte Gesellschaften von wenigstens 30 Personen
P.	Parken in der Nähe		
&#9888;	Parkenverbot		
&#9098;	Erfrischungen		
ex	ausser		
Free	Freier Eintritt		
10p	Eintritt 10p		

Symboles: Les symboles et abréviatons suivants sont utilisés dans tout le manuel.

&#9855;	Les invalides en fauteuils roulants pourront y accéder Le tout ouvert au public	Free	Entrée libre
		10p	Entrée 10p
		ch 20p	Enfants 20p
♿ B	Seulement certaines parties ouvertes et/en les jardins	ch 15 20p	Enfants de moins de 15 ans 20p
		Pen	Retraités
(79)	Indique des renseignements pour 1979	Party	Tarifs spéciaux ou réduits pour groupes réservés d'avance
BH	Jours fériés		
PH	Jours fériés en Ecosse	Party 30+	Tarifs spéciaux ou réduits pour groupes de 30 et plus réservés d'avance.
&#9888;	Stationnement à l'établissement		
P.	Stationnement dans le voisinage		
&#9888;	Stationnement interdit		
&#9098;	Rafraîchissements		
ex	sauf		

Verklaring der tekens: de volgende tekens en afkortingen worden in deze reisgids gebruikt.

&#9855;	toegankelijk voor bezoekers in rolstoel Alle gedeelten toegankelijk	ch 20p	kinderen 20p
		ch 15 20p	kinderen onder 15 jaar 20p
♿ B	Gedeeltelijk en/of tuinen	Pen	Gepensioneerden
(79)	1979 informatie	Party	speciale of gereduceerde prijs voor vooraf gemaakte boekingen voor gezelschappen
BH	Nationale officiële vakantiedag		
PH	officiele vakantiedag (Schotland)		
&#9888;	parkeerplaats bij gebouw	Party 30+	speciale of gereduceerd prijs voor vooraf gemaakte boekingen voor gezelschappen van 30 of meer person.
P.	nabijgelegen parkeerplaats		
&#9888;	Parkeerverbod		
&#9098;	verfrissingen		
ex	uitgezonderd		
Free	toegang gratis		
10p	toegand 10p		

ENGLAND

P.K.F

ABBOTSBURY *Dorset* Map 3 SY58
Abbotsbury Gardens Beach Road. Stone
walled garden set in wild garden in 16 acres of
grounds. Peacocks, fine trees, and notable
collection of flowering shrubs. Plant sales.
Open mid Mar to Oct, Mon to Sat 10–5, Sun
2–5.30. 40p (ch 15 20p). Under revision for
1980. ⚠ *(Tel 387)* &
Abbotsbury Swannery New Barn Road.
Famous breeding ground for swans and a
home or port of call for a great many species
of wild birds. Open mid May to mid Sep 10–5
daily. 40p (ch 20p). Admission prices for 1979
not yet decided. P. & **(79)**

ABINGDON *Oxfordshire* Map 4 SU49
Town Museum County Hall. Built 1678 by
Christopher Kempster, one of Wren's master-
masons; described as the grandest Market-
House in England. Local history museum;
archaeological finds, charters, two 18th-C
uniforms, smocks; changing exhibitions.
Open all year, daily (ex BH) 2–5p (ch 16 2p).
P. *(Tel 23703)*

ACCRINGTON *Lancashire* Map 7 SD72
Haworth Art Gallery Manchester Road.
Constructed in 1909 for the Haworth family,
the building was given to the Corporation of
Accrington in 1921 for use as an art gallery.
Fine wood panelling, plaster ceilings and
fireplaces, plus collection of Early English
water-colours and oil paintings, also one of
the world's finest collections of Tiffany Glass.
Art exhibitions change monthly. Brass
Rubbing Centre and Nature Trail. ⚲ Open all
year (ex 4 Apr, 25/26 Dec and 1 Jan), Mon to
Sat 2–5; Sun Apr to Sep 2–7, Sun Oct to Mar
2–5. Free. ⚠ *(Tel 33782)* & B

ACTON BURNELL *Salop* Map 7 SJ50
Acton Burnell Castle Ruined 13th-C fortified
manor house. First English Parliament said to
have met here in 1283. Open at all reasonable
times. Free. *(AM)*

ACTON SCOTT *Salop* Map 7 SO48
Acton Scott Working Farm Museum 3m S
of Church Stretton off A49. Important site
museum sited on the centre of a 1,200-acre
estate in south Shropshire used to
demonstrate agricultural practice as it was at
the turn of the century. The farm is stocked
with rare breeds of farm animals, and the work
is largely done by hand or horse. The site is
unique in that visitors may actively participate
in several of the jobs that need to be done
throughout the farming year. Shop illustrating
and selling Shropshire crafts.
Demonstrations of the various crafts are
given throughout the season at weekends
(details on application). Shop (refreshments).

Picnic area open after 12 noon. Open Apr to
Oct Mon to Sat 1–5, Sun & BH 10–6 (last
admission 30 mins before closing time).
Parties at other times by appointment. 25p (c
5–16 10p). Guide free for school parties
booked in advance. Guide for adult parties
booked in advance an additional £2.
Admission prices under revision for 1980. Nc
dogs. ⚠ *(Tel Marshbrook 306/7)* &

ADLINGTON *Cheshire* Map 7 SJ98
Adlington Hall W of Adlington Sta. Tudor
banqueting hall, Elizabethan 'black-and-
white' portion, 18th-C south front, and
'Bernard Smith' organ, restored in 1959 and
associated with Handel. Gardens include ye
walk and lime avenue. ⚲ Open 4 Apr to end
Sep, Sun and BH weekends 2.30–6 (also
Wed and Sat during Jul and Aug); parties on
weekdays by arrangement. 70p (ch 35p).
Party 25+. ⚠ *(Tel Prestbury 829206)*. *(Mr C
Legh)* & B

ALBURY *Surrey* Map 4 TQ04
Albury Park Former home of Duchess of
Northumberland. A country mansion which
was re-fashioned in 1846 by Pugin. Open
May to end Sep, Wed, Thu 2–5. 40p (ch 25p
⚠

ALCESTER *Warwickshire* Map 4 SP05
Pleck Gardens 2m NW on B4090. Over thre
acres of roses, heather, azaleas,
rhododendrons, etc, with formal garden, thre
ponds, and budgerigars. Open 1 Apr to 1 Oc
daily 10–6.30. 30p (ch 14 and pen 10p).
Admission prices under revision for 1980. ⚠
(Tel 2553). *(Miss Evelyn C Chapman)* &
Ragley Hall 2m SW. 17th-C home of
Seymours, with splendid great hall by James
Gibbs, featuring baroque plasterwork and
wealth of English and French pictures,
furniture and porcelain. Fine gardens. Park,
including adventure wood, country trail and
lakeside picnic places. ⚲ House and garden
open Easter to Sep, Tue, Wed, Thu, Sat and
Sun (including BH) 1.30–5.30, last admissic
5. See local press for opening times of park.
Admission prices not yet decided. ⚠ *(Tel
2090)*. *(Marquess of Hertford)* &

ALDBOROUGH *North Yorkshire* Map 8 SE4
Roman Town Remains of northernmost
Roman town (though not northernmost
military station). Portions of boundary wall,
two tessellated pavements, and small
museum. Open Apr to Sep, see inside front
cover. Museum closed Mon and Tue. 15p (cl
16 and pen 5p). Remains free. *(AM)*

ALDEBURGH *Suffolk* Map 5 TM45
Moot Hall Restored, two-storey, early 16th-C
timber-framed building. Council chamber on
upper floor, reached by external staircase,
contains old maps and prints, objects of loca

terest. Open Easter to May, Sun 2.30–6; un and Oct 2.30–5 (6 Sun); Jul to Sep 11–1 nd 2.30–5 (6 Sun). 10p (ch and pen 5p). (limited). *(Tel 2158)*

LDERSHOT *Hampshire* Map 4 SU85
irborne Forces Exhibition Browning arracks, Queen's Avenue. One of Army's nest museums in newly erected barracks. n display are weapons, including briefing odels from 1939–45 War and captured nemy arms, airborne vehicles, dioramas of ctions, many scale models, parachutes and quipment, photographs and medals cluding VC and GCs. Open daily (ex 25 ec) Mon to Fri 9–12.30, 2–5. Sat .30–12.30, 2–5 Sun 10–12.30, 2–4.30. 0p (ch and pen 10p). Party 20+. P. *(Tel 4431 ext 619)* ♿
oyal Corps of Transport Museum Buller arracks. Uniforms and badges of Royal orps of Transport and predecessors, and odels and photographs of vehicles used om 1795 to present day. Open all year. Mon Fri (ex BH) 9–12 and 2–4. Free. Ⓟ *(Tel 4431 ext 2417)* ♿

LFORD *Lincolnshire* Map 9 TF47
lford Manor House c1540. Museum cludes period shops, school room, maid's edroom, dairy, agricultural and transport alleries. ☕ (Tue & Fri). Opening times and ates not yet decided. 15p (ch 5p). Under evision for 1980. Ⓟ *(Tel 6247)*
lawthorpe Collection of Bygones Voodlands', Mawthorpe 2m S. A collection of ings from most aspects of the Bygone Era of oth house and farm including rural crafts. team engines are in steam on open days, 8 nd 29 Jun, 20 Jul, 10 and 31 Aug, also 5 Oct, 7, 28 Sep steam threshing. 11–6. Vintage rm tractors on display, also farm nplements undergoing restoration. Large ollection of farm machinery including horse-rawn implements. Departments in large hed depict rural crafts and farming tools, rocer's shop, war-time dept and washday ept. Another collection of household bygone quipment from cooking range to clothes. oyalty section, chemist's shops and many ore items of interest. ☕. Ⓟ *(Tel 2336)* ♿

LFRISTON *East Sussex* Map 5 TQ50
lergy House Mid 14th-C half-timbered atched priests' house. Open Apr to end Oct aily 11–6 (or dusk if earlier). 1 Nov to 23 Dec Medieval Hall and shop only) Wed, Fri, Sat nd Sun 11–sunset. Last admission ½hr efore closing. Medieval Hall, exhibition oom, garden and shop 30p (Nov and Dec no harge as Hall and shop only open). *(NT)*

Drusillas Zoo Park One of the best small zoos in the south, with greatly varied collection of breeding groups including, capuchin and diana monkeys, racoons, coati mundis, rare breeds of cattle and sheep, also penguins, parrots and flamingo lagoon. Children's adventure playground and railway, working pottery, Sussex craft shop and bakery, antique shop and Bennett collection of tropical moths and butterflies. ☕ Open Apr to end Oct daily 11–6 (or dusk if earlier), winter Sat and Sun 11–dusk. Grounds free, Zoo Park 70p (ch 12 and pen 35p). Ⓟ *(Tel 870234)* ♿

ALLINGTON *Kent* Map 5 TQ75
Allington Castle Former home of Lord Conway of Allington, on banks of River Medway. A 13th-C moated castle with later alterations by the Wyatts, it retains castellated curtain wall, gatehouse, and great hall. Medieval market 14 Jun. ☕ May to Sep. Open all year, (ex 25 Dec) daily 2–4. 50p (ch 12, 25p). Ⓟ *(Tel Maidstone 54080). (The Order of Carmelites)* ♿ B

ALNWICK *Northumberland* Map 12 NU11
Alnwick Castle Norman border stronghold of Percy family, restored by Salvin. Keep, armoury, museum (10p, ch 5p. 1979 charge) and main apartments containing pictures by Titian, Canaletto, Van Dyck, and other famous artists, Meissen china, and historic heirlooms are shown. Open 4 May to 26 Sep, daily (ex Sat) 1–5 (no admission after 4.30pm). 80p (ch 16 40p); Party 70p (ch 30p) No dogs. Ⓟfree *(Tel 2722 or 2207). (Duke of Northumberland)*

ALRESFORD *Hampshire* Map 4 SU53
Mid Hants Railway (Watercress Line), Alresford Station. Steam railway runs on three miles of the old Winchester to Alton line between Alresford and Ropley. Beautiful Hampshire countryside with views of hills and watercress beds, after which the railway is named. At Ropley a variety of steam locomotives are in various stages of restoration. ☕ (Alresford Station). Open 24 Mar to 28 Oct Sat 1.05–5.55, Sun 11.30–5.55 (leaflet available giving details, times of trains etc). Fares 1st class return £1 (ch 3–14 50p); 3rd class return 80p (ch 3–14 40p). Party 20+. All under revision for 1980. Ⓟ (Alresford Station). *(Tel 3810)* ♿ parties welcome; special coach and toilets should be available for 1980.

ALTHORP *Northamptonshire* Map 4 SP66
Exit 16 on M1. House redecorated 1790 by Henry Holland. Magnificent collection of pictures, furniture and china. Arboretum and

pleasure grounds. Home of the Spencer family since 1508. ℒ Open 15 Apr to end Sep, Tue, Thu and Sun. Daily in Aug (ex Mon) 2.30–5.30. Also Sun in winter and BH 11.30–5.30. Pleasure grounds, gift shop and tearoom open all year Sat and Sun. House £1 (ch 50p), Grounds only 30p. House not suitable for young children. ⚠ *(Tel East Haddon 209)* ⌖

ALTON *Hampshire* Map 4 SU73
Curtis Museum Contains local collections of geology, botany, zoology, archaeology and history; also craft tools, dolls, toys and games. Annexe and Allen gallery contains exhibition of paintings by W H Allen (1863–1943), loan exhibitions and English pottery. Open all year (ex Sun) Mon to Sat 10–5. Free. Parties by arrangement. P. *(Tel 82802). (Hampshire County Museum Service)* ⌖ B

ALTON *Staffordshire* Map 7 SK04
Alton Towers Ruined early 19th-C mansion, former home of Charles Earl of Shrewsbury, set in beautiful grounds. Numerous lakes and pools were created with various fountains, foremost of which is the Chinese Pagoda Fountain. Also amusements including cable cars, boating lake, amusement park, planetarium and pottery studio. Large touring caravan park. ℒ Open Easter to mid Oct, daily grounds 9.30–dusk, towers ruins 11–6. Admission prices under review. ⚠ *(Tel Oakamoor 702449)* ⌖ B

ALVINGHAM *Lincolnshire* Map 8 TF39
Water Mill An 18th-C Water cornmill restored as a working museum. There has been a mill on this site since domesday and it was once worked by the monks of Alvingham Abbey. The present machinery was probably installed in 1782 and is powered by one of the few remaining breast wheels. Open Aug and Sep Mon and Thu 2–5, 2nd and 4th Suns 2–5.30, BH Sun and Mon 11–5.30. 25p (ch 15 15p). ⚠ *(Tel South Cockerington 544)*

AMBLESIDE *Cumbria* Map 7 NY30
Stagshaw Gardens 1m S on A591. A garden created in mature woodland on a fell side overlooking Windermere lake. A magnificent and unique collection of species and hybrid rhododendrons, azaleas, camellias and other flowering shrubs. Open daily at all reasonable hours. 30p (ch 15p) *(NGS) (NT)*

AMPFIELD *Hampshire* Map 4 SU42
Hillier Arboretum Jermyn's Lane. Over 115 acres of trees and shrubs from most countries of the world. Large collections of alpines and herbaceous perennials. An all year round collection containing many rarities. Open all year Mon to Fri 9–4.30; 6 Apr to 26 Oct Sun

and BH 10–5. 50p (ch 20p). No dogs or picnicing. Parties by prior arrangement. ⚠ *(Tel Braishfield 68787)* ⌖ (dry weather only)

AMPTHILL *Bedfordshire* Map 4 TL03
Houghton House N off A418. Associated with the Countess of Pembroke, sister of Sir Philip Sidney, and possibly 'House Beautiful' of Bunyan's *Pilgrim's Progress*, ruined 17th-C mansion dismantled in 1794. Open, see inside front cover. Free. ⚠ *(AM)*

ANSTY *West Sussex* Map 4 TQ22
Legh Manor 16th-C house, with interesting furnishings and attractive gardens. Open Apr to Oct, second and third Weds and second Sat in each month. 2.30–5.30. ⚠ (ex coaches) *(Tel Haywards Heath 413428). (Sussex Archaeological Society)*

APPLEDORE *Devon* Map 2 SS43
North Devon Maritime Museum Odun House, Odun Road. Exhibitions and display on North Devon's maritime history. Models in authentic settings together with photographs and paintings illustrate seafaring, trade, shipbuilding, fishing and coastal craft, pilotage navigation, wreck and rescue. Also full size reconstruction of an Appledore kitchen c1900. Open Easter to 30 Sep daily 2.30–5.30 also Tue to Fri 11–1. 30p (ch 10p). Coaches and parties welcome. ⚠ *(Tel Bideford 6042)*

ARBORFIELD *Berkshire* Map 4 SU76
Royal Electrical and Mechanical Engineers' Museum Moat House. Devoted to REME history and equipment; models, photographs, uniforms, etc. Open all year, Mon to Fri (ex BH) 9–5 (4.30 Fri). Free. ⚠ (limited). *(Tel Arborfield Cross 760421 ext 220)*

ARBOR LOW STONE CIRCLE *Derbyshire* Map 7 SK16
Circle of 40 stones enclosing others, forming megalithic structure within ditch and rampart. Open, see inside front cover. Free. ⚠ *(AM)*

ARBURY HALL *Warwickshire* Map 4 SP38
Unique Elizabethan and 18th-C Gothic house, seat of the Newdegates since the 16t C. 18th-C alterations were made by Sanderson Miller and Henry Keene. Fine plaster ceilings, furniture, pictures, and china; 17th-C stable block, porch designed by Wren; housing museum of veteran cycles. ℒ Open Easter Sun to 1 Oct, Sun and BH 2.30–6; parties by special arrangement with *Administrator, Arbury Estate Office, Windm Hill, Astley.* 80p (ch 14 35p); gardens and park only 60p subject to possible increase for 1980. ⚠ *(Tel Fillongley 40529)*

ARDINGLY *West Sussex* Map 4 TQ32
Wakehurst Place 1½m N. A great Elizabethan
mansion restored, with gardens noted for
exotic plant species, rare trees, and flowering
shrubs. A picturesque water course links a
series of ponds and lakes. The gardens are
administered by the Royal Botanical
Gardens, Kew. Gardens only open daily (ex
25 Dec, 1 Jan, and 5 May), Nov to Jan 10–4;
Feb and Oct 10–5; Mar 10–6; Apr to Sep
10–7. 75p (ch 35p) Party Mon to Fri 50p (ch
25p) No dogs. ⚠ Ch 10 only admitted if
accompanied. *(NT)* &

ARLEY HALL GARDENS *Cheshire*
Map 7 SJ68
6m W Knutsford and 5m from M6 junc 19 and
20; M56 junc 9 and 10. These 8 acres of
private gardens have belonged to one family
for 500 years and provide great variety of style
and design. Fine herbaceous border, unusual
avenue of clipped ilex trees, walled gardens,
yew hedges, shrub roses, azaleas,
rhododendrons, and 15th-C 'cruck' barn. In
1975 these gardens gained a premier award in
the British Tourist Authority's Landscape
Heritage Competition. ⚓ Open (gardens
only) Easter to mid Oct daily (ex Mon but open
BH) 2–6.30 (last admission 6pm). 55p (ch
28p). Under revision for 1980. Hall and private
chapel open to organised parties by prior
arrangement. ⚠ *(Tel Arley (Northwich) 353)*.
(Viscount and Viscountess Ashbrook) &

ARLINGTON *Devon* Map 2 SS64
Arlington Court 7m NE of Barnstaple, off
A39. Mansion of 1822 in large wooded estate
with terraced garden and lake. House
contains collection of model ships, pewter,
and seashells, and the stables a large
collection of horse-drawn vehicles. ⚓ Open 1
Apr to 31 Oct, daily 11–6, (house only closed
on Mon). £1.50, gardens open also Nov to
Mar, during daylight hours. Grounds, garden,
park and stables £1; gardens and park free
(Nov to Mar). *(NT)*

ARUNDEL *West Sussex* Map 4 TQ00
Arundel Castle Entrance at Lower Lodge in
Mill Road. Norman stronghold restored in
18th and 19th C in magnificient grounds. Fine
portraits by Van Dyck, Gainsborough,
Reynolds, etc, and furniture from 15th C. Also
Fitzalan Chapel. Open Apr to Oct. Opening
times, dates and admission prices for 1980
not yet known. No dogs. ⚠ cars 20p *(Tel
883136 or 882173)* &
Museum of Curiosity 6 High Street. The life
work of the Victorian naturalist and
taxidermist, Walter Potter, formerly housed at
Bramber. First opened in 1861. Has a good
collection of natural history and also the

famous animal tableaux – Kittens Wedding,
Rabbits Village School, Death of Cock Robin,
Guinea Pigs Cricket Match etc. Also curios,
toys, dolls, from all over the world. Open
Easter to end Oct 10.30–5.30. 35p (ch 4–16
and pen 15p). P. *(Tel 882420)*
Wildfowl Trust Mill Road. 55 acres of well
landscaped pens, lakes and paddocks with
more than 1,000 ducks, geese and swans
from all over the world. Hides overlook ponds,
reed beds and a wader scrape which are
sanctuaries for numerous species of wild
birds. Open all year (ex 25 Dec) daily
9.30–6.30 (dusk in winter). 65p (ch 16 30p,
pen 50p). Party 20+. ⚠ *(Tel 883355)* & **(79)**

ASHBOURNE *Derbyshire* Map 8 SK14
Hamilton House Toy Museum 27 Church
Street. Houses a wide range of dolls and
associated items, toy trains and model
railways covering the period 1790s to 1950s.
Open Tue to Sat 11–5.30, Sun and BH Mon
2–5.30. *(Tel 5343)*

ASHBURTON *Devon* Map 3 SX77
Ashburton Museum West Street. Exhibits
include local antiquities, weapons, American
Indian antiques, geology specimens. Open
May–Sep Tue, Thur, Fri, Sat 2.50–5. Free.
P. *(Tel 52298)*

ASHBURY *Oxfordshire* Map 4 SU28
Ashdown House 2½m SE on B4000. 17th-C
mansion in lonely downland, built of chalk
blocks and rising to four storeys. Built by 1st
Lord Craven for Elizabeth of Bohemia.
Paintings from Craven Collection hang in hall
and on staircase. Open (grounds and roof
only) Apr (Wed only), and May to Sep, Wed
and first and third weekend in month 2–6.
Conducted tours to roof 2.30, 3.30, 4.30 and
5.30. 50p (grounds only 30p). *(NT)*

ASHBY-DE-LA-ZOUCH *Leicestershire*
Map 8 SK31
Ashby-de-la-Zouch Castle Mainly 14th-C,
but Hastings Tower added in 1474 by Lord
Hastings. Royalist strongholds in Civil War,
later slighted. Open, see inside front cover,
but closed Wed and Thu. 15p (ch 16 and pen
5p) ⚠ *(AM)*

ASHCHURCH *Gloucestershire* Map 3 SO93
Dowty Railway Preservation Society
Northway Lane. Five sidings in which are
preserved several steam locomotives and
some rolling stock, including GWR restaurant
car. Extensive narrow gauge system with
steam and diesel locomotives plus varied
rolling stock. Open all year Sat and Sun 2–6.
10p (ch 5p, ch 8 and pen free) ex. steam days
then as advertised. ⚓ ⚠. May move during

Arley Hall Gardens,
Cheshire

In 1975 these privately-owned gardens
of 8 acres gained a premier award in the
British Tourist Authority's Landscape
Heritage Competition. Principal features
are twin herbaceous borders (among the
first to be established in England), a
most unusual avenue of large clipped ilex
trees, an avenue of pleached lime trees,
walled gardens, yew hedges, shrub roses,
azaleas and rhododendrons.

1980. Please phone first to avoid a wasted journey. *R Wilcox, Publicity Manager DRPS, 27 Quail Park Drive, Heronswood Park, Kidderminster. (Tel Kidderminster 743079)* &

ASHFORD *Kent* Map 5 TR04
Godinton Park 2½m NW Gabled house, dating from 1628, with fine panelling and carving, portraits, furniture, and china, and 18th- and 19th-C garden layout, including topiary work. Open Easter Sat, Sun, Mon and 1 Jun to 30 Sep, Sun and BH 2–5, or by appointment. 50p (ch 16 25p). Admission prices under revision for 1980. No dogs. ⚠ *(Tel 20773). (Mr A Wyndham Green)* & B
Intelligence Corps Museum Templer Barracks. Items concerning the corps from two World Wars and other articles up to the present day. Open all year (ex BH), Mon to Fri 10–12 and 2–4. Free. ⚠ *(Tel 25251 ext 206)* & B

ASHLEWORTH *Gloucestershire* Map 3 SO82
Tithe Barn 15th-C building, 120ft long with porch bays and queen-post roof. Open daily until sunset. 10p. No dogs. *(NT)*

ASHTON *Hereford and Worcester* Map 3 SO56
Berrington Hall 3½m N Leominster. Built 1778–83 by Henry Holland. Fine interior decoration, including painted and plaster ceilings, much of it unaltered, and recently restored stonework. 455-acre park, laid out by 'Capability' Brown in 1780, includes 14-acre 'pool', fine trees, shrubs, and plants. Wide views towards Wales. ⚲ (teas Sat and Sun). Open Apr to end Sep, Wed, Thu, Sat, Sun, BH Mon; Oct, Sat and Sun only 2–6; other times by written appointment with estate office. 85p. Joint ticket with Croft Castle £1.50. No dogs. *(NT)*

ASHWELL *Hertfordshire* Map 4 TL23
Village Museum Early Tudor timber-framed house, once tithe office of abbots of Westminster. Now a scheduled ancient monument. Contains collection showing life of village from Stone Age to present day. Open all year Sun 3–5.30; other times by appointment in writing to the *Hon Curator*. 10p *(Tel 2176)*

ASTON MUNSLOW *Salop* Map 7 SO58
The White House Museum of Buildings and Country Life 6m NE of Craven Arms on B4368. The Stedman Homestead, four houses in one, continuously inhabited. Undercroft of the manor house to which the dovecote was granted in 1250; 14th-C Cruck Hall; 16th-C cross-wing with 18th-C addition. Another open bay dwelling-house of 16th-C. Stable of 1680, with original cobbled floor and other stone buildings of various functions and periods. Rooms and buildings equipped with domestic utensils, farming tools and implements in their functional setting. Open Easter to 30 Oct. Other details under review. Schools and parties 20+ by prior arrangement. ⚠ Picnic area. No dogs. *(Miss J C Purser) (79)*

ATCHAM *Salop* Map 7 SJ50
Attingham Park 3m SE Shrewsbury. House dates from 1758 and was designed by George Steuart; fine interior containing Nash pictures and furnishings. Stands in 1,159-acre Humphrey Repton Park. Open 6 Apr to end Sep, Tue to Thu, Sat, Sun and BH Mon 2–5.30. 80p (grounds only 20p) *(NT)*

ATHELHAMPTON *Dorset* Map 3 SY79
Athelhampton On A35 1m E of Puddletown. Family home for 500 years, one of finest medieval houses in Southern England. 15th-C Great Hall, Tudor Great Chamber, fine staircase, interesting furnishings. Ten acres of formal and landscape gardens, and 15th-C dovecote. River gardens. ⚲ teas. Open Wed before Easter to 1st Sun in Oct, Wed, Thu, Sun BH and also Tue and Fri in Aug 2–6. Admission prices for 1980 not yet known. Plants and antiques for sale. No dogs. ⚠ *(Tel Puddletown 363). (Sir Robert Cooke) (NGS)*

AUBOURN *Lincolnshire* Map 8 SK96
Aubourn Hall 16th-C house with fine Jacobean staircase and panelled rooms. Open 27 Apr, 25 May, Jul and Aug. Wed 2–6 other times by appointment. 50p. No dogs. ⚠ *(Tel Bassingham 224). (Mr H N Nevile)*

AUDLEY END *Essex* Map 5 TL53
17th-C house, only part of original, built by Thomas Howard, Earl of Suffolk, with some work by Robert Adam, and standing in fine park. Pictures and furnishings in state rooms, miniature railway in grounds. ⚲ Open Apr to early Oct, daily (ex Mon) and BH 10–5.30 (grounds close 6.30pm). 70p (ch 16 and pen 30p). ⚠5p. *(AM)*

AUGHTON *Lancashire* Map 7 SD30
Cranford Unusually planned, modern ½-acre garden, with rare trees, shrubs and roses. Open Apr to mid Oct, daily 10 to dusk. *(Mr T J C Taylor). (NGS)* &

AVEBURY *Wiltshire* Map 4 SU06
Avebury Manor Fine example of Tudor Manor on edge of largest prehistoric megalithic circle in Europe. Open May and Sep, Sat and Sun and daily Jun, Jul and Aug 2.30–5.30. BH 10–6. 60p (ch 12 30p). Under revision for 1980. No dogs. P. *(Tel 203). (Marquess and Marchioness of Ailesbury)* & B
Avebury Museum Alexander Keiller Museum. Finds from late Neolithic Age site and nearby Neolithic Windmill Hill site. Near museum a circle of sarsen stones is enclosed by bank and ditches. Open*, see inside front cover. 15p (ch 16 and pen 5p). ⚠ *(AM and NT)*

AXBRIDGE *Somerset* Map 3 ST45
King John's Hunting Lodge Market Place. Restored early Tudor house with old photographs, and exhibits of local interest including coins, flint items, and animal bones. Town stocks and constables' staves also on show. Open Apr to end Sep, daily 2–5. Free. ⚠ *(NT)*

AYLESBURY *Buckinghamshire* Map 4 SP81
Bucks County Museum Church Street. Housed in former grammar school built in 1720 and two 15th-C houses, which were completely altered in the mid 18th-C. There is a fine plaster ceiling dating from 1760. The displays relate to the geology, natural history, archaeology and history of the county and include costume and a Rural Life Gallery. Open all year daily (ex 4 Apr; 25, 26 Dec; 1 Jan) Mon to Fri 9.30–5, Sat 9.30–12.30, 1.30–5. Free. *(Tel 82158 and 88849)*

AYLESFORD *Kent* Map 5 TQ75
Priory Restored 13th- to 14th-C Carmelite house with fine cloisters; now conference centre and place of pilgrimage and retreat. Sculpture and ceramics by modern artists, pottery, and rose garden. Souvenir shop, pottery shop, ⚲ open 10.30–12.45 and 2–5 daily (closed Mons Nov to Easter). Open all

year, daily 9am to dusk. Donations. (guided tours by arrangement). △ *(Order of Carmelites) (Tel Maidstone 77272)* ♿

AYNHO *Northamptonshire* Map 4 SP53
Aynhoe Park 6m SE Banbury. 17th-C mansion. The interior was largely remodelled in the 19th-C by Sir John Soanes. Open May to Sep Wed and Thu 2–5. 40p (ch 25p). △ *(Tel Croughton 810636)*

AYOT ST LAWRENCE *Hertfordshire* Map 4 TL11
Shaw's Corner At SW end of village. Dates from this century and was the home of George Bernard Shaw between 1906 and his death in 1950. He donated the house in 1944 and the contents are as in his lifetime. His ashes were scattered in the garden. Open Mar and Nov Sat and Sun, also Apr to Oct daily (ex Mon and Tue, but open BH Mon) 11–1 and 2–6 or sunset. 80p *(NT)*

AYSGARTH *North Yorkshire* Map 7 SE08
National Park Centre Permanent interpretation centre for the Aysgarth Falls area with display, books, maps etc. Aysgarth mini trail starts here. Open Apr to end Sep daily, mid morning to late afternoon. Free. △ *(Tel 424)*
The Old Mill, The Yorkshire Museum of Carriages and Horse-Drawn Vehicles ¾m E adjacent to bridge on unclass road N off A684. In an old stone mill at Aysgarth Falls. This mill now houses approximately 50 horse-drawn vehicles including some splendid coaches, carriages and much impedimenta of the Era of Horse-Drawn Transport. Open Easter to late Oct (if closed during this period, apply at cottage next to office). 10–12 and 1.30–6. 25p (ch 10p). P. *(Tel Richmond, Yorks 3325)*

BACONSTHORPE *Norfolk* Map 9 TG13
Baconsthorpe Castle Late 15th-C moated, semi-fortified house, incorporating gatehouse and range of curtain walls with towers. Open, see inside front cover. 10p (ch 16 and pen 5p). △ *(AM)*

BADMINTON *Avon* Map 3 ST88
Badminton House Off B4040. 17th- to 18th-C Palladian mansion, partly by Kent, with fine paintings and furnishings. Situated in great park where famous Badminton Horse Trials are held (17–21 Apr) and home of Dukes of Beaufort since 17th C. ☕ in orangery. Open each Wed from 4 Jun to 3 Sep, 2.30–5. 50p (ch 10p, pen 25p). Church, stables and kennels open to visitors. △ *(Tel 202). (Duke of Beaufort KG PC GCVO)* ♿

BAKEWELL *Derbyshire* Map 8 SK26
Magpie Mine 3m W. The surface remains are the best example in Britain of a 19th-C lead mine. Open 22 Jul to 9 Sep daily (ex Sat) from 2.30. Free. Further information can be obtained from Peak District Mining Museum, Matlock Bath *(Tel Matlock 3834)*
The Old House Museum Off Church Lane. Early Tudor house with original wattle and daub interior walls, and an open timbered chamber. Exhibition of costumes, kitchen and household utensils, tools, etc. Open Easter Sat to end Oct, daily (ex Bakewell Show Day) 2.30–5; 25p (ch of school age 15p). Party bookings: E T Goodwin, 32 Castle Mount Crescent, Bakewell. *(Tel 3647)*

BALSALL COMMON *Warwickshire* Map 4 SP27
Berkswell Windmill Windmill Lane. Also known as Balsall Windmill. A fine example of a Warwickshire tower mill complete in both machinery and fittings, including tools. Open 6 May to end Sep, Sun only, 11–1 and 2.30–5.30. All other days by appointment. 20p (ch and pen 10p). △ limited. *(Tel Berkswell 33403)*

BAMBURGH *Northumberland* Map 12 NU13
Bamburgh Castle Restored Norman castle in splendid North Sea coast setting. Impressive hall, and armoury with large weapon collection, also loan collection of armour from HM Tower of London. Guided tours of interior when conditions permit. Open Apr to Sep, daily from 1pm. 60p (ch 30p), subject to possible review. Party rates for morning or afternoon tours. △ *(Tel 208). (Lord Armstrong)*
Grace Darling Museum Pictures, documents, and various relics of the heroine, including boat in which she and her father, keeper of Longstone Lighthouse, Farne Islands, rescued nine survivors from wrecked 'SS Forfarshire' in 1838. Open 1 Apr to 1 Oct, daily 11–7. Free. P. ♿

BANBURY *Oxfordshire* Map 4 SP44
Banbury Museum and Globe Room Marlborough Road. Due to move to 8 Horsefair, Banbury summer 1980. A small museum with exhibits of local history and folk life. Permanent exhibition of the history of Banbury and the Cherwell Valley. Changing exhibitions. Bookshop. Open all year, daily (ex Sun) Mon, Wed–Fri 10–1, 2–5, Tue, Sat 10–1. Free. P. *(Tel 2282)*

BANHAM *Norfolk* Map 5 TM08
Banham International Motor Museum at Banham Zoo. Lord Cranworth's collection of cars, racing cars, motorcycles and children's pedal cars from the 1920s to the 1960s are on display in a new and imaginative setting. Now enlarged with over 40 vehicles, also large

BAMBURGH CASTLE

Impressive citadel set upon a basalt crag with fine original Norman Keep and other apartments largely restored during the late 19th century. Public rooms — Museum, King's Hall, Cross Hall, Fayre Chamber, Armoury and Keep Hall, also loan collection of armour from HM Tower of London. Open to the public from 1pm, variable closing. Guiding when conditions permit. Parties by arrangement morning or afternoon. Custodian — Bamburgh 208.

collection of dolls. A vehicle adventure ground for children to climb and play on. Open daily in summer 11.30 – 5. 60p (ch 30p). Party 50p (ch 25p). ⚠ *(Tel Grundisburg 202)* &

P.K.F.

Banham Zoo and Monkey Sanctuary The Grove. Situated in over 20 acres of grounds, this zoo which specialises in monkeys and apes, contains a world-wide collection of animals and birds. The collection includes gibbons, chimps, bears, otters, seals, penguins, llamas, wallabies, ostriches, pelicans, cranes, flamingoes, macaws, etc. Fruit, farm and dairy produce on sale in Grove Farm Barn opposite. ⚓ (licensed). Open all year, daily 10.30 – 6.30 or dusk if earlier. Party. ⚠ *(Tel Quidenham 476)* &

BARDON MILL *Northumberland*
Map 12 NY76
Vindolanda (Chesterholm) Remains of 3rd- and 4th-C Roman fort and frontier town. Replicas of Hadrian's turf wall and stone wall. Large museums. Also ornamental garden. Main excavations take place Apr to end Sep, annually. ⚓ licensed. Open all year (ex 25 Dec) daily 10 – 6.30. 50p (ch 18 and pen 25p). ⚠ *(Tel 277). (Vindolanda Trust)* & **(79)**

BARLASTON *Staffordshire* Map 7 SJ83
Wedgwood Museum and Visitor Centre Traditional skills in the production of Wedgwood can be seen in the craft demonstration area, and the museum

contains a comprehensive collection of the works of Josiah Wedgwood from 1750, and includes a film show and shopping facilities are also available. Open all year Mon to Fri 9 – 5, last complete visit 3.30, appointment preferred. 50p (ch 25p). Ch 5 not admitted, ch 5 – 15 must be accompanied by an adult. P. *(Tel 3218 or 4141)* &

BARNARD CASTLE *Co Durham*
Map 12 NZ01
The Bowes Museum Splendid French-style château, built in 1869 and situated in the countryside of upper Teesdale. Houses a collection of fine and decorative arts of international importance: paintings, tapestries, furniture, porcelain, silver etc. Series of English period rooms 1570 – 1870, galleries of costume, textiles, Gothic art, music and other subjects. Children's Room, local history, temporary exhibitions. ⚓ Open all year (closed 25 – 26 Dec and 1 Jan), May to Sep Mon – Sat 10 – 5.30, Sun 2 – 5. Closes 4 Nov to Feb and 5 Mar, Apr and Oct. 45p (ch and pen 10p). Admission charges under revision for 1980. ⚠ *(Tel Teesdale 37139)* &
The Castle 11th- to 13th-C ruin with circular three-storeyed keep. Open*, see inside front cover. 15p (ch 16 and pen 5p). *(AM)* &
Egglestone Abbey 1 m SW. Picturesque remains of Premonstratensian Abbey on right bank of River Tees. Open, see inside front cover. Free. *(AM)*

BARNSLEY *Gloucestershire* Map 4 SP00
Barnsley House Garden Old Garden, completely re-designed since 1962. Laburnum walk (early June), Lime walk, Knot garden, herb garden and borders with use of ground cover, kitchen garden laid out as decorative potager. Two 18th-C summerhouses, one Gothic, the other

Classical. Garden open Wed Apr to Oct 10–6, 1st Sun in May Jun, Jul and Aug 2–7 (every Wed throughout year for plant sales). House not open. 40p (pen 25p). ⚠ (coaches in village). *(Tel Bibury 281)* ⅄

BARNSLEY *South Yorkshire* Map 8 SE30
2m E of M1 (junction 37).
Monk Bretton Priory 1½m E. An important Cluniac house with considerable remains of the church and claustral buildings. Open, see inside front cover. 10p (ch 16 5p). ⚠ *(AM)*
Worsborough Mill Museum Worsborough. 2½m S of Barnsley on A61. The corn mill is a working industrial site museum. It consists of a 17th-C water-powered mill and an adjoining 19th-C mill powered by a rare 1911 hot bulb oil engine. Both mills are built of local sandstone and are set in the wooded valley of the river Dove. The mill is a central feature of the Worsborough Country Park. The water mill works whenever the museum is open and there are frequent special exhibitions and displays relating to milling, agriculture and local history. Open all year, Wed to Sun 10–6 or dusk if earlier. Special openings and working steam engines and craft displays. 10p (ch 5p, pen free). ⚠ *(Tel 203961)* ⅄ (by arrangement with attendant staff).

BARNSTAPLE *Devon* Map 2 SS53
St Anne's Chapel Museum 14th-C former chapel, now small but interesting museum of largely local interest. Historical records of industry and social life. Open 1 Jun to 20 Sep, Mon to Sat 10–1 and 2–5. 10p (ch free). Catalogues 5p. P. *(Tel 72511 ext 272 for enquiries)*
The North Devon Athenaeum The Square. The museum contains a collection of local antiquities and North Devon earthenware, ceremonial spoons, geological and fossil collections, Roman pottery excavated at Trentishoe, butterfly collection, coin collection, maps, etc. The reference library also housed here was established by William Frederick Rock in 1888 and has a special collection of books on local history, geography, geology, biology, classical literature, topography and travel. Open all year, Mon to Sat (ex Sat pm and Sun) 10–1, 2.15–6. Free. Ch 14 must be accompanied by an adult. P. *(Tel 2174)*
Marwood Hill 8–10 acres of rare trees and shrubs, rose garden, quarry garden with alpine plants, 2 small lakes and a bog garden. Greenhouses include a Camellia house and Australian house. Plants for sale. Open all year 20p (ch 5p). ⚠ *(Tel 2528)*
Youlston Park 4½m NE on A39. Former 18th-C Chichester residence. Fine ceilings, staircase and Chinese Room. Woodland garden and lake. ⚏ Opening times 2–6 (closed Mon). Prices not available. ⚠ *(Tel Shirwell 200)* ⅄ B

BARRINGTON *Somerset* Map 3 ST42
Barrington Court 3m NE of Ilminster, on B3168. Beautiful Tudor mansion of Ham Hill stone, built 1514–20 by Lord Daubeny. Nearby is converted stable building of 1670. Open Apr to Sep, Wed 10.15–12.15 and 2–6; Oct to Easter, Wed 2–4; last guided tour 5.30. Admission to house and gardens 40p. Special charity days house 40p, gardens 40p. No dogs. No picnics. *(NT)*

BARROW-IN-FURNESS *Cumbria*
Map 7 SD26
Furness Abbey 1½m NE on unclass road. Cistercian Abbey with extensive remains of the church, sited in the 'Glen of Deadly Nightshade' near Barrow. Open, see inside front cover. 20p (ch 16 and pen 5p). ⚠ *(AM)*
The Furness Museum Ramsden Square. Museum of Furness district with finds from late Stone Age sites. Also Vickers-Armstrong ship models and Lake District bygones. Various monthly exhibitions. Open all year, Mon to Sat 10–5 (ex Thu 10–1). Closed Sun, BH and Public Hols. Free *(Tel 20650)*

BASILDON *Berkshire* Map 4 SU67
Child Beale Wildlife Trust Riverside walks, and lakes with ornamental pheasants, peacocks, wildfowl, flamingoes, cranes, Highland cattle and Soay sheep. Children's playground and paddling pool. Open Easter to mid Sep, Wed, Thu, Sun and BH 10–6. ⚠ cars 50p, minibuses £1, coaches £3; Sat free (closed Mon, Tue and Fri). Times and charges for 1980 under review. *(Tel Pangbourne 2386, Upper Basildon 325)* ⅄
Basildon Park 2½m NW of Pangbourne on W side of A329. Classical 18th-C house by John Carr of York in a magnificent setting overlooking the Thames valley. There is some fine plasterwork and an Octagon room, also pictures and furniture. Open Apr to Oct (ex 4 Apr) Wed to Sun 2–6 (Oct 2–5.30), BH Mon 11–1, 2–6. Last admission to house 30 mins before closing. House and grounds £1.10. *(NT)*

BASING *Hampshire* Map 4 SU65
House Ruins of a great Tudor palace built in 1530's on the site of a former Norman Castle. All the Tudor Kings and Queens visited here. The house was destroyed in 1645 during the civil war by Cromwell's troops after a three-year siege. Exhibitions. Outdoor trail and tape recorded guides tell the story of the house. ⚏ Open Easter to Sep, Tue to Sat 2–5.30, Sun and BH 11–5.30. Prices for 1979 not yet available. ⚠ *(Tel Basingstoke 67294)* **(79)**

BASINGSTOKE *Hampshire* Map 4 SU65
Willis Museum and Art Gallery Contains local collections of archaeology, geology, natural history, Basingstoke Canal, horology, watch and clock makers' tools. Displays of recent accessions and temporary exhibitions in the Art Gallery, also a new Town History Gallery. Open all year (ex Sun and Mon morning) Mon 1–5, Tue to Sat 10–5. Free. Parties by arrangement. *(Tel 65902)*. *(Hampshire County Museum Service)* ⅄ B

BATH *Avon* Map 3 ST76
American Museum in Britain Claverton Manor. 2½m E. Built in 1820 by Sir Jeffrey Wyatville, overlooks Avon valley, and now museum of American decorative arts and gardens from 17th, 18th and 19th C. Winston Churchill delivered his first ever political speech in the grounds in 1897. ⚏ Open 29 Mar to 2 Nov daily (ex Mon) 2–5, BH Mon and preceding Sun 11–5. House and grounds £1.20 (ch 14 and pen £1). Grounds only 40p. Reduced rates 1st Fri in month and whole Oct. Parties of ch not admitted during normal opening hours. ⚠ *(Tel 60503)* ⅄ B
Assembly Rooms Bennett Street. Designed c 1771 by John Wood the Younger. Redecorated in 1979. Associated with novels by Charles Dickens and Jane Austen. ⚏ (Easter–Sep). Open all year (ex 25 Dec), weekdays 9.30–6, Sun 10–6, last admission ½hr before closing time. ⚠(limited) *(Tel 61111)(NT)* also ***Museum of Costume*** housed in the assembly Rooms. Based on the internationally famous collections built up by Doris Langley-Moore OBE. The collections have been enriched by donations and loans from many sources and are amongst the

largest and most comprehensive in the world. Also on display are toys and dolls and an important collection of jewellery. Modern fashions include costumes from Dior and Yves St Laurent Couture Houses, also the 'Dress of the Year'. Fashions from the Regency to the 1920s are displayed in period rooms and settings, many based on well known scenes in Bath. ℘ Open all year, Mar to Oct Mon to Sat 9.30–6, Sun 10–6; Nov to Feb Mon to Sat 10–5, Sun 11–5. 80p (ch 16 25p). P. *(Tel 61111 ext 324)* ⓰

Bath Carriage Museum Circus Mews. Finest and most comprehensive collection of horse-drawn carriages in the country. Large exhibition of harnesses etc from the coaching era. Housed in Circus Mews, built in 1759 by John Wood the Younger. Carriage rides available daily throughout the season. Open all year (ex Fri) 9.30–6 (Sun 10–6) Summer; 10–5 (Sun 11–5) winter. Admission price not available. P. *(Tel 25175)* ⓰

Beckford's Tower and Museum Lansdown. Built in 1827 by H E Goodridge for William Beckford of Fonthill, in a striking Neo-Classical style. Fine views from Belvedere, 156 steps. Small museum of Beckfordiana on 1st floor. Open Apr to Oct, Sat and Sun only 2–5. 15p (ch 14 and pen 10p). ⚠ *(Tel 858106)*

Camden Works Industrial Museum Housing the Bowler collection, the entire stock-in-trade of a Victorian Brass Founder, General Engineer and Areated Water manufacturer, displayed in settings that capture the atmosphere of the original premises. Open all year, daily (ex Fri, 6 Apr also 24 and 25 Dec) 2–5. 40p (ch 16 and pen 25p). *(Tel 318348)*

Holburne of Menstrie Museum (University of Bath) Gt Pulteney Street. Outstanding collection of paintings, porcelain, silver, miniatures and furniture housed in an 18th-C building. The Crafts Study Centre shows work by 20th-C British craftsmen. ℘ May to Sep. Open all year (ex Christmas) Mon to Sat 11–5, Sun 2.30–6. 40p (ch, students and pen 20p). ⚠ *(Tel 66669)*

No. 1 Royal Crescent Stone-built Georgian house in perhaps best known of Bath's terraces and crescents. House restored to original condition and furnished with fine examples of 18th-C furniture. Open first Tue in Mar to last Sun in Oct, Tue to Sat 11–5, Sun 2–5. 40p (ch, students and pen 20p). Street P. limited to 2 hours. Admission charges under review for 1980. *(Tel 28126)*

Prior Park College Overlooking city, Georgian mansion built c1735 by John Wood

the Elder for Ralph Allen, now Roman Catholic public school, run by the Christian Brothers. Well-known Palladian bridge in grounds. Chapel and grounds open all year, daily 11–4, by kind permission of President; mansion open May to Sep, Tue, Wed; Aug Mon to Thu 2–6. 20p (ch 14 10p, pen free). ⚠ *(Tel Combe Down 832752)* ⓰ B

Roman Baths and Pump Room Abbey Churchyard. Remains of Roman baths of 'Aquae Sulis', with museum devoted to the Roman history of Bath and containing important archaeological finds from the City. Britain's only hot water springs and largest Roman bathing complex. Open all year, Apr to Oct daily 9–6, Nov to Mar, Mon to Sat 9–5, Sun 11–5. 80p (ch 16 25p). Party 20+ 65p (ch 35p). ℘ (Apr to Nov). Under revision for 1980. P in City. *(Tel 61111)*

BATLEY *West Yorkshire* Map 8 SE22
Art Gallery Market Place. Permanent collection of British oil paintings, water colours, drawings and sculpture from mid 19th C onwards. Temporary loan and special exhibitions throughout the year. Open all year daily (ex Sun) 10–7 (Sat 9–4). Free. ⚠ *(Tel 473141)*

Bagshaw Museum Wilton Park. 19th-C building housing museum of local history, archaeology, geology, ethnography and Oriental arts, natural history, and folk life opened in 1911. Best approached from Upper Batley Lane. Open all year Apr to Oct, Tue to Sat 10–6 (Sun 1–5); Nov to Mar, Tue to Sat 10–5. Coal mine open weekdays by special appointment. Free ⚠ *(Tel 472514)* ⓰

BATTLE *East Sussex* Map 5 TQ71
Battle and District Historical Society Museum Langton House. Diorama of Battle of Hastings and reproduction of Bayeux Tapestry. Exhibits show local history, including Romano-British and Sussex ironwork. Open Easter to Oct, Mon to Sat 10–1 and 2–5 (Sun only 2.30–5.30). 10p (ch 5p). Under revision for 1980. P. *(Tel 2722)*

BEACONSFIELD *Buckinghamshire* Map 4 SU99
Bekonscot Model Village Off A40. Well laidout rock gardens, with model village and large model railway. Model trains run frequently from 10–5.30 Easter to Oct (weather permitting). Gardens open all year (ex Christmas hols) daily. Easter to Oct Mon to Fri 10–4.45, Sat and Sun 10–5.30; Winter 10–3.45. 50p (ch 3–16 25p). Reduction in winter. Party 20+ (weekdays only) 40p (ch 20p). P. *(Tel 2919)* ⓰ (small wheelchairs only, narrow paths)

Holburne of Menstrie Museum

(University of Bath)

Great Pulteney Street, Bath.

Outstanding collection of paintings, porcelain, silver, miniatures and furniture housed in an 18th century building. The Crafts Study Centre showing work by 20th Century British craftsmen.

BEAMINSTER *Dorset* Map 3 ST40
Parnham House Impressive Tudor mansion set in 14 acres of traditional gardens and formal terraces. Home of the John Makepeace Furniture Workshop and the School for Craftsmen in Wood. Great Hall has exhibition of unique furniture. Riverside picnic area. Open Apr to Oct (ex Sun 15 Jun) Wed, Sun and BH 10 – 5. 90p (ch 16 50p). ⚠ *(Tel 862204)* ♿

Mapperton Gardens 2m SE off A356 and B3163. Extensive terraced and hillside gardens with formal borders and specimen shrubs and trees, 18th-C stone fish-ponds and summer-house, Orangery. ⚲. Open 10 Mar to 10 Oct, Mon to Fri 2 – 6. Admission prices not yet available. ⚠

BEAMISH *Co Durham* Map 12 NZ25
North of England Open-Air Museum
Beamish off A693 and A6076. England's first open-air museum. Beamish is about Northern people and their way of life. On a 200-acre site, buildings of all kinds have been rebuilt and furnished with the contents they once held. Already on the site is a railway area with station, goods shed, weighbridge house and signal box. At Home Farm can be seen exhibitions on harvests and farm animals, as well as old farm tools, implements, farm animals and a fine collection of North Eastern farm carts. A Colliery has been rebuilt with steam locos working and a full scale replica of Locomotion No. 1 is demonstrated. Also at the Colliery can be seen a row of rebuilt fully furnished pitmen's cottages. Visitors can ride behind steam locos and in trams across the site. Transport collection and demonstrations of traditional crafts. Open all year daily Apr to end Aug 10 – 6, Sep to Mar (closed Mon) 10 – 5. Last admission 1 hour before closing

time. 70p (ch and pen 35p). Subject to revision for 1980. *(Tel Stanley (0207) 31811)* &

BEAULIEU *Hampshire* Map 4 SU30
Beaulieu Abbey*, *National Motor Museum and Palace House On B3054. 70,000 sq ft of exhibition floor space, and large library, in National Motor Museum containing over 300 veteran and vintage cars, motor cycles, and pedal cycles. Abbey was founded in 1204 and refectory now parish church. Palace House, once Abbey gatehouse, has large additions from 1870. Monorail, veteran bus rides, model railway, Transporama and other features. Special events include rallies and steam fairs. Gift shops. ⬭ (licensed). House, Motor Museum, Abbey and gardens open all year (ex Dec 25) daily summer 10 – 6 (5 winter). Inclusive admission charged, (ch and pen half price). ⚠ *(Tel 612345)*. *(Lord Montagu of Beaulieu)*. & (ex Palace House). See also **BUCKLER'S HARD**, ***Maritime Museum.***

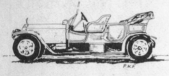

P.K.F.

BEDALE *North Yorkshire* Map 8 SE28
7m SW of Northallerton
Bedale Hall On A684; 1½m W of A1 at Leeming Bar. Georgian house with ballroom wing and museum room. Open May to Sep, Tue 10 – 4, other days by appointment. Free. P. *(Tel 3131)* & B

BEDFORD *Bedfordshire* Map 4 TL04
Bunyan Museum Mill Street. In Bunyan Meeting House (1850), on site of barn, where John Bunyan preached. Contains all surviving personal relics, and world-famous collection of over 400 foreign language editions of his works, including *The Pilgrim's Progress* in over 165 languages. Open Apr to Oct Tue – Sat 2 – 4 20p. P. *(Tel 58627)* &
Cecil Higgins Art Gallery Castle Close. New extension contains outstanding collections of ceramics, glass, water-colours, prints. Late Victorian style room settings in adjoining house. Costume and lace by appointment only. Special arrangements for group visits, evening parties. Open Tue to Fri 12.30 – 5.00, Sat 11.00 – 5.00 Sun 2.00 – 5.00, BH. Closed Mon and Christmas. Admission charges during summer months and opening hours under revision. *(Tel Bedford 211222)* &

BEER *Devon* Map 3 SY28
Beer Heights Light Railway and Peco Modelrama Situated on a hillside at the back of the village exists Modelrama featuring Beer Heights Light Railway, a steam-operated passenger carrying line which runs through the Peco Pleasure Park, with interesting scenic features and delightful views across the bay. Miniature putting green. The main building houses an exhibition of Model Railways in various small gauges displayed in typical locations around the house and garden. Souvenir and model railway shops. Snacks at Beer Victoria Station buffet. ⬭ Main meals in Orion Pullman Car. Indoor Exhibition open all year. Outdoor amenities open after Spring BH to mid Oct, Mon to Fri 10 – 5, Sat 10 – 12.30 (closed Sun and BH). Grounds and exhibition 40p (ch 5, free,

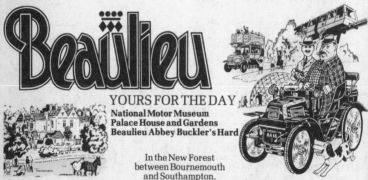

Beaulieu

YOURS FOR THE DAY

**National Motor Museum
Palace House and Gardens
Beaulieu Abbey Buckler's Hard**

In the New Forest
between Bournemouth
and Southampton.

5–11 15p, 12–17 30p). Drive a train 5p. Rides on railway 15p (all ages). ⚠ *(Tel Seaton 21542 ext 36)*

BEESTON *Cheshire* Map 7 SJ55
Beeston Castle Off A49. 13th-C stronghold built by Earl of Chester in almost inaccessible position on steep hill. Open Mon to Fri 9.30–4.30. Free. Closed Sat and Sun. ⚠ *(AM)*

BEKESBOURNE *Kent* Map 5 TR15
Howletts Zoo Park Off A257. Famous collection of wild animals, including breeding groups of gorillas, tigers, wolves, free-running deer and antelope, also snow leopards, tapirs, and wild boar. ☕ Open all year 10–6 (1 hour before dusk winter). Prices not yet available. ⚠ *(Tel Hythe 60618)* ♿ B

BELTON *Lincolnshire* Map 8 SK93
Belton House Park and Gardens On A607.

Attributed to Wren, home of Lord Brownlow's family since built in 1685. Magnificent carvings by Grinling Gibbons, pictures, silver, furniture, tapestries and souvenirs of Duke of Windsor. Fine gardens and 700-acre deer park. Children's Adventureland, Museum of Horse and Nature Trails. Special events on most Sundays. ☕ Open 29 Mar to 5 Oct daily from 11am. £1.20 (ch and pen 60p) all inclusive tickets. ⚠ *(Tel Grantham 66116)*. *(Lord Brownlow)* ♿ B

BELVOIR *Leicestershire* Map 8 SK83
Belvoir Castle Between A52 and A607. Home of the Duke of Rutland. Palatial early 19th-C reconstruction by James Wyatt, on hilltop overlooking Vale of Belvoir, with notable *objets d'art*, armoury and museums of 17th/21st Lancers and Grenadier Guards. Many special events on Sundays at no extra charge. ☕ (also waitress service for booked

parties Wed, Thu and Sat only). Open 26 Mar
to 28 Sep Wed, Thu, Sat and BH Tue also 4
Apr 12–6, Sun 2–7. Sun Jun, Jul and Aug
12–7. Oct, open only on Sun 2–6. BH Mon
11–7 (last admissions ½hr before Castle
closes). Party 30+ (Adults and pen).
Admission charges on enquiry. No dogs. *(Tel
Knipton 262)* ჱ B

BENINGBROUGH *North Yorkshire*
Map 8 SE55
Beningbrough Hall Off A19. Entrance at
Newton Lodge. Built about 1716, this
attractive house stands in a wooded park. In
the principal rooms are 100 pictures from the
National Portrait Gallery. The Victorian
laundry is open and exhibitions describe
domestic life of the period, also gardens.
Open Apr to Oct, daily 12–6. £1 *(NT)*

BENTHALL *Salop* Map 7 SJ60
Benthall Hall On B4375. 16th-C house with
fine panelling, carved oak staircase, and
17th-C ceilings, on a much older site. Housed
Royalist garrison during Civil War, but later
taken by rebels. Garden contains shrubs and
plants. Open 5 Apr to end Sep, Tue, Wed, Sat,
BH Mon 2–6. 60p (garden only 20p). *(NT)*

BERKELEY *Gloucestershire* Map 3 ST69
Berkeley Castle On B4509, 1½m W of a A38.
Home of the Berkeleys for over 800 years,
splendid 12th-C and later castle, in which
Edward II was murdered in 1327. Keep,
dungeon, great hall, state apartments and
medieval kitchens shown. Elizabethan
terraced gardens include bowling alley, and
nearby is an extensive deer park. ♔ Open Apr
and Sep, daily (ex Mon) 2–5, May to Aug Tue
to Sat 11–5, Sun 2–5. Oct, Sun only 2–4.30,
BH Mon 11–5.80p (ch 40p). Admission
prices for 1980 under review. No dogs. ⚠ *(Tel
Dursley 810332). (Mr R J Berkely MFH)* ჱ B
Jenner Museum Commemorates Edward
Jenner (1749–1823), who discovered
smallpox vaccine. The museum is housed in
the cottage he erected for the first boy he
vaccinated. Open 1 Apr to 30 Sep, daily (ex
Mon) and BH 2.30–6. 10p (ch 14 5p). Parties
can be booked out of hours if necessary. *(Tel
631)* ჱ

BERKHAMSTED *Hertfordshire* Map 4 SP90
Berkhamsted Castle Remains of 11th-C
motte and bailey castle with later circular
keep. Former home of Black Prince and
prison of King John of France. Open Mon to
Fri 9–4.15. Closed weekends and BH. Free.
(AM)

BERNEY ARMS WINDMILL *Norfolk*
Map 5 TG40
Access by boat from Gt Yarmouth or by rail to
Berney Arms station; road to mill unmade,
gated, rough, and unsuitable for cars. Tall,
late 19th-C marsh windmill in lonely part of
Halvergate Marshes, near where River Yare
is joined by River Waveney. Open Apr to Sep,
daily 9.30–7. 15p (ch 16 and pen 5p). *(AM)*

BERWICK-UPON-TWEED *Northumberland*
Map 12 NT95
Castle and Town Walls Remains of 12th-C
stronghold incorporating three towers and
west wall. Medieval town walls reconstructed
during Elizabethan period. Open see inside
front cover. Free. P. *(Tel 7881). (AM)*
Museum and Art Gallery Marygate. Local
antiquities, ceramics and brasswork, and
pictures, including representative display of
French school. Open Jun to Sep, Mon to Fri
2–5. Sat 10–1. Free. P. *(Tel 7320)*
*Museum of the King's Own Scottish
Borderers* The Barracks. Designed by
Vanbrugh in 1717, said to be oldest barracks

in Britain. Open all year (ex BH and Suns)
Mon to Fri 9–12 and 1–4.30, Sun 9–12; other
times by prior arrangement with *Curator, Lt-
Col D C R Ward*. 10p (ch 16 5p). P. *(Tel
7426/7)* ჱ B
Town Hall Fine 18th-C building on site of
three previous structures. Council chamber
assembly room, and old town gaol. Open by
prior arrangement with *Clerk of the Trustees*.
10p ⚠ *(Tel 6332 ext 50) (79)*

BEVERLEY *Humberside* Map 8 TA03
Art Gallery and Museum Champney Road.
Local antiquities, Victorian bygones and
china, pictures by F W Elwell of Beverley and
others, and bust of Sir Winston Churchill by
Bryant Baker of New York. Various solo Art
Exhibitions. Open all year (ex Sun) Mon, Tue,
Wed and Fri 9.30–5.30, Thu 9.30–12 noon,
Sat 9.30–4. Free. P. *(Tel Hull 882255)*
Lairgate Hall Dates from 1710–80, now
used as council offices. Interesting late 18th-
C stucco ceiling, marble mantelpiece.
Chinese room with hand-painted wallpaper.
Open all year. Mon to Thu 8.45–5.30, Fri
9–4. Free. ⚠ *(Tel Hull 882255)*
*The Museum of the East Yorkshire
Regiment* (The Prince of Wales Own
Regiment of Yorkshire) 11 Butcher Row. The
exhibits are arranged in six rooms which
include one recalling the warmth and comfort
of an Officers' Mess, one which houses the
Library and another full of uniforms as well as
having two dioramas. Open Tue–Fri (ex BH)
2–4 Free. Party. *(Tel Hull 882157)*

BEWDLEY *Hereford and Worcester*
Map 7 SO77
Bewdley Museum The Shambles, Load
Street. A folk museum, situated in a row of
18th-C shops. The crafts and industries of the
Bewdley area are illustrated, including
displays on charcoal burning, basket making,
and coopering. Craftsmen's workshops within
the museum and demonstrations of pottery
throwing, glass blowing and the making of
traditional straw corn-dollies can often be
seen. Open 1 Mar to 30 Nov, Mon–Sat
10–5.30, Sun 2–5.30. 12p (ch and pen free).
P. *(Tel 403573)*
West Midland Safari and Leisure Park On
A456 to Kidderminster. 200-acre wildlife and
leisure park. All-inclusive price includes
animal reserves, pets corner, sea lion show,
amusement park rides, splash pack, rowing
boats, canoes, skate park, picnic and leisure
areas and the 'Rio Grande' railway. ♔ Open
mid May to Oct daily 10–5. Admission prices
not available. ⚠ free. *(Tel 402144)* ჱ

BEXHILL-ON-SEA *East Sussex* Map 5 TQ70
Bexhill-on-Sea Museum Egerton Park.
Local archaeological and natural history
collection. Open all year, Mon–Sat (ex Fri)
10–4.30, Sun Jul to Sep 2–4.30. 10p (ch 4p).
P. *(Tel 211769)*
Bexhill Manor Costume Museum Set in
small gardens, the manor contains a display
of costumes, 1740–1960 accessories, toys
and dolls. Open Easter to 30 Sep, Tue to Fri
and BH 10.30–1 and 2.30–5.30, Sat and Sun
2.30–5.30 (closed Mon, ex BH Mon). 25p (ch
5–16 15p). Admission prices under revision
for 1980. ⚠ *(Tel 215361)* ჱ

BIBURY *Gloucestershire* Map 4 SP10
Arlington Mill On A433. 17th-C corn mill on
site on River Coln mentioned in 'Domesday
Book'. Now a museum with working
machinery, agricultural implements and
bygones. Open daily Mar to Oct and winter
weekends 10.30–7 (dusk in winter). 50p (ch
20p, pen 30p). ⚠ *(Tel 368)*

BICKLEIGH *Devon* Map 3 SS90
Bickleigh Castle Off A396. Take A3072 from Bickleigh Bridge, then fork left. Medieval romantic home of the heirs of the Earls of Devon. Great Hall, Armoury, Guard Room, thatched Jacobean Wing. Early Norman Chapel. Moat and Gardens. Open Easter to Sep, Wed, Sun, and BH Mon, also from Jul to 1st week Sep daily (ex Sat) 2–5. 80p (ch 40p, pen 60p). Prices subject to alteration for 1980. *(Tel 363). (Mr O N Boxall)* & B
Bickleigh Mill Craft Centre and Farm A picturesque old working watermill adapted to the production of craftwork (pottery, glass engraving, woodturning, jewellery making, corn dollies etc). One of the largest and most comprehensive working craft centres in the West Country adjacent to a heritage farm with rare breeds of animals and poultry where cows and goats are milked by hand and the farm worked by shire horses complete with its own museum. A British Tourist Authority Award Winner. Open all year daily (ex 25 Dec to 5 Jan incl). 6 Jan to 21 Mar 2–5; 22 Mar to 24 Dec 10–6. Admission prices under review for 1980. ⚠ *(Tel 419)*

BICTON *Devon* Map 3 SY08
Railway, Countryside Museum, Hall of Transport and Gardens On A376 N of Budleigh Salterton. Large countryside museum. Narrow-guage railway. Italian garden laid out in 1735. Collection of veteran and vintage motor vehicles. Exotic greenhouses, children's adventure playground. Picnic areas. Vintage bus rides. Pinetum. ⬤. Open 1 Apr to 31 Oct daily 10–6. Admission prices for 1980 not yet decided. ⚠ *(Tel Colaton Raleigh 68465)*. (Clinton Devon Estates) &

BIDDENDEN *Kent* Map 5 TQ83
Baby Carriage Collection Bettenham
Manor. A unique collection of 350 baby
carriages (prams) displays examples of the
craftsmanship of a bygone era. Exhibits
portray the history of the pram up to the
present day and include 18th-C stickwagons,
Victorian perambulators and mailcarts,
Edwardian bassinettes, Victorias and large
coachbuilt prams of twenties. The museum, in
a Kentish oast house, adjoins a 15th-C
moated manor house of historical and
architectural interest and is set in a 15-acre
garden. Collection open all year, house and
garden May to Sep, both by appointment only.
Free. *(Tel 291343). (Mr J Hampshire)* ⅃

BIDEFORD *Devon* Map 2 SS42
Burton Art Gallery Victoria Park, Kingsley
Road. Built in 1951, to house a collection of
pictures and *objets d'art*. Other gifts and
loans have been made. Visiting exhibitions.
Open all year daily (ex Sun) Mon to Fri 10–1
and 2–5; Sat 9.45–12.45. Free. P. *(Tel 6711)*
⅃ **(79)**

BIDFORD-ON-AVON *Warwickshire*
Map 4 SP15
Domestic Fowl Trust Dorsington Manor. 8m
W of Stratford-upon-Avon on unclass road off
B4085. Unique collection of domestic ducks,
geese, hens and turkeys, with over sixty breeds in
all, covering some 4 acres. Many species to
be seen are in danger of extinction. ⌑ picnic
area and giftshop. Steam/vintage rally end of
May. Open Apr to Oct daily 10.30–6 (closed
Mon ex BH). 50p (ch 14 30p). ⚠ *(Tel 2442)* ⅃
(79)

BIGGLESWADE *Bedfordshire* Map 4 TL14
*Shuttleworth Collection of Historic
Aeroplanes and Cars* Old Warden
Aerodrome 2m W from roundabout on (A1)
Biggleswade bypass. A highly interesting
collection of historical aircraft, cars, bicycles
and other items of transport. Open all year,
daily (except for one week at Christmas)
10–5. 75p (ch and pen 40p, ch 5 free). ⌑ and
shop. Special Flying Days (historic aircraft) on
last Sun in month, May to Sep. 2 Special
pageant days Jul and Sep; £5 per vehicle incl
occupants. Cyclists and pedestrians £1, ch
50p. Prices for flying days to be announced.
⚠ £1. *(Tel Northill 288)* ⅃

BIGNOR *West Sussex* Map 4 SU91
Roman Villa and Museum Between A29 and
A285. Occupied in 2nd and 4th C, first
discovered in 1811; preserves some of finest
mosaic pavements in Britain, new mosaic
recently uncovered. Open 1 Mar to 31 Oct
(closed Mon ex Aug and BH) 10–5 (6.30 Apr
to Sep). Admission charges for 1980 not
available. ⚠ *(Tel Sutton 259)* ⅃

BILLINGFORD MILL *Norfolk* Map 5 TM17
Built in 1860 as a replacement for a former
post mill destroyed in a storm. The five-
storeyed brick tower still contains most of the
original machinery and equipment. Open all
year 9–dusk, key available (see notice on
mill). Free. Parking on common. *(Tel Norwich
611122 ext 5224)*

BIRCHINGTON *Kent* Map 5 TR36
Powell-Cotton Museum Quex Park. 1m SE
of village, off B2048. Ethnography, and
natural history of Africa and Asia. Also on view
are furnished rooms in Quex house and the
gardens. Museum open Thu all year;
museum, house and gardens open 6 Apr to
28 Sep Wed, Thu, Sun and BH; 15 Jul to 5
Sep daily (ex Sat and Mon). 2.30–6. 45p (ch
25p). Party. *(Tel Thanet 42168)* ⅃ B

BIRKENHEAD *Merseyside* Map 7 SJ38
Birkenhead Priory Priory Street. Founded in
1150, the Priory provided accommodation for
a prior and 16 monks of the Benedictine
Order. Most of the buildings were neglected
after the Dissolution of the Monasteries and
only the ruins remain. Open all year May to
Sep, Tue to Fri, 10–1, 2–4; Oct to Apr, Tue to
Fri 10–1 (Sat all year 10–12). Free ⚠ *(Tel
051–6524177)* ⅃ B
Williamson Art Gallery and Museum Slatey
Road. Exhibits include: major collection of
work by English water-colourists and
Liverpool school of painters; sculpture;
decorative arts; ceramics (English,
Continental, Oriental wares); glass, silver and
furniture. Also a large collection of paintings
by P Wilson Steer, as well as approximately
25 special exhibitions throughout the year. A
local history and maritime museum
containing model ships, adjoins. Open all
year (ex 25, 26 Dec and BH) 10–5 (ex Thu
10–9, Sun 2–5). Free. ⚠ *(Tel 051–652 4177)*

BIRMINGHAM *West Midlands* Map 7 SP08
Aston Hall Aston. Jacobean mansion built by
Sir Thomas Holt, now museum. Panelled long
gallery and marble chimney pieces. ⌑ Open
daily 1 Apr to 31 Oct, Mon to Sat 10–1, 2–5,
Sun 2–5. 30p (ch and pen 15p, school parties
booked in advance free). ⚠
Birmingham Railways Museum Warwick
Road, Tyseley (SE of city, off A41); near
Tyseley station. Live steam depot with well-
known express passenger locomotives,
reproductions of historic coaches, and former
working machinery. Special opening days
featuring traction engines, vintage cars, etc.
Open all year (ex BH), Sun 2–5.30. 20p (ch
14 10p). Conducted parties by arrangement.
(Tel Northfield 3934). **(79)**
Blakesley Hall Yardley (6m SE). A timber-
framed yeoman's farmhouse, built c1575,

**MUSEUM OF SCIENCE AND INDUSTRY
BIRMINGHAM — Newhall Street B3 1RZ**

(city centre)   **Tel: 021-236 1022**

Aeroplanes, locomotives, road transport,
steam and IC engines, machine tools,
replica workshops, small arms, applied
science.
*Open until 9pm on first Wednesday of
each month.
Hours of opening: Monday to Friday
10—5pm, Saturdays 10—5.30pm.
Admission free.   Sundays 2-5.30pm.*

ow partly furnished as a period house of the
7th C. Displays on the history of the house,
ocal crafts and the ancient parish of Yardley.
Open all year (ex 4 Apr, Christmas) Mon to
Sat 1.30–5.30. 15p (ch and pen 5p). (Tel
021–783 2193)

Cannon Hill Nature Centre At the SW
entrance to Cannon Hill Park, opposite
Pebble Mill Road. The Nature Centre displays
living animals of the British Isles and Europe
in both outdoor and indoor enclosures.
Conditions have been created to resemble
natural habitats also to attract wild birds and
butterflies etc, forming a miniature wildlife
park. Open all year (ex Tue, 4 Apr and 25. 26
Dec) 10–6 (4 winter; also closes 5 Fri,
summer). (Tel 021–472 7775)

Museum and Art Gallery Chamberlain
Square. Important archaeological exhibits,
collection of modern sculpture, and paintings
including large pre-Raphaelite section,
numerous major works by Bellini, Guercino
and Canaletto, English water-colour
landscapes, and representatives of French
and Dutch schools). ☕ Open all year (ex 4 Apr
and Christmas) Mon to Sat 10–5.30, Sun
2–5.30. Free. P. (Tel 021–235 2834) 占 See
also **Sarehole Mill**

Museum of Science and Industry Newhall
Street (close to Post Office Tower). Industrial,
technological and scientific displays from the
Industrial Revolution up to the present.
Engineering hall is architecturally interesting
(formerly a Victorian plating works) and
contains machine tools, electrical equipment,
working steam, gas and hot air engines.
Locomotive hall has steam locomotives,
including Pacific locomotive 'City of
Birmingham', steam road locomotives, and
working machinery. Transport section
contains veteran cars, motorcycles, John
Cobb's world speed record car, fire engine,
Birmingham tramcar. Science section has
working demonstrations of many aspects of
science and electronics. Pen room displays
writing instruments from all parts of the world.
Music room with organs, musical boxes,
pianola and various mechanical musical
instruments. In the aircraft section is a World
War II Spitfire and Hurricane, and collection of
aircraft engines, including early jet, also
displays of bicycles, small arms, clocks and
watches. Steam weekends Mar and Oct,
Traction Engine Rally May. Engines steamed
1st and 3rd Wed each month. Open all year
(ex 4 Apr and Christmas) Mon to Fri 10–5
(9pm 1st Wed in month), Sat 10–5.30, Sun
2–5.30. Free. P. (Tel 021–236 1022)

Sarehole Mill Well-restored
18th-C water mill, last surviving in district.
Opened as branch of Birmingham City
Museum in Jul 1969, with exhibits on
agricultural history and rural crafts. Milling
parts on view include items from Pinto
Collection. South wheel of mill operational.
Open 1 Apr to 30 Nov, (ex 4 Apr) Wed to Sat
1.30–5.30. 20p (ch must be accompanied
and pen 10p). ⚠ (Tel 021–777 6612)

Selly Manor and Minworth Greaves
Sycamore Road, Bournville. Off A38. Two
13th- and early 14th-C timbered houses re-
erected in Bournville. Collection of old
furniture and domestic equipment. Open mid
Jan to mid Dec, Tue, Wed, Fri 2–5 (ex BH).
Parties by arrangement with curator. Free. P.
Tel 021–472 0199)

Weoley Castle Selly Oak, off A38. Remains
of a fortified 13th-C manor house, with small
site museum displaying finds from
excavations. Open all year (ex 4 Apr,

Christmas also Mons and Tues), Wed, Thu,
Fri, Sat 10–5. 10p (ch and pen 5p). P.
(roadside). (Tel 021–427 4270)

BISHOP'S STORTFORD Hertfordshire
Map 5 TL42
**Rhodes Memorial Museum and
Commonwealth Centre** South Road. Early
19th-C house with exhibits illustrating life of
Cecil Rhodes, also aspects of his life and
work in Africa. Open all year (ex Sun & BH)
Mon to Sat 10–4, Free⚠ (Tel 51746) 占 B

BISHOP'S WALTHAM Hampshire
Map 4 SU51
Bishop's Waltham Palace On A333. Dates
from 12th C and consists of state apartments
around cloister court, with great hall and four-
storeyed tower. Surrendered to
Parliamentary forces in 1644 during Civil War.
Open, see inside front cover but closed Mon
(ex BH) and Sat. 10p (ch 16 and pen 5p). ⚠
(AM)

BLACKBURN Lancashire Map 7 SD62
Lewis Museum of Textile Machinery Noted
for series of period rooms portraying
continuous development of textile industry
from 18th C onwards. Open all year, Mon to
Sat 9.30–6, closed Sun. Free. P. (Tel
667130)
Museum and Art Gallery Library Street.
Local history, militaria, coins, ceramics, fine
books and manuscripts, paintings, water-
colours, and Japanese prints. Open all year,
Mon to Sat 9.30–6. Closed Sun. Free. P. (Tel
667130)

BLACKPOOL Lancashire Map 7 SD33
Grundy Art Gallery Queen Street.
Established 1911, this gallery exhibits a
permanent collection of paintings by 19th-
and 20th-C artists. Also touring exhibitions,
one man shows, and group exhibitions. Open
all year (ex BH) Mon to Sat 10–5. Free. ⚠
(Tel 23977)
Tower Buildings and Circus The tower
stands 518ft high. The buildings at its base
contain a spacious ballroom with bar. Ocean
room cabaret lounge, children's daytime non-
stop entertainment, tropical gardens and free
flight aviary, aquarium, butterfly gardens,
children's fun farm. ☕ Open May to Oct Mon
to Sun 9.30–11pm. Admission prices not yet
known. P. (Tel 25252) 占
Zoopark East Park Drive. An interesting
collection of 660 large and small mammals
and birds. New house and enclosure for
Lowland Gorillas. Miniature railway. Shop,
picnic area. Open all year, daily (ex 25 Dec)
from 10 onwards. 80p (ch 40p). ⚠ (20p).
Prices subject to revision for 1980. Free ⚠ for
coaches. Zoo bus service to and from
Blackpool town centre, 1¼m. (Tel 65027) 占 B

BLANDFORD FORUM Dorset Map 3 ST80
Royal Signals Museum Blandford Camp.
New museum of history of army signalling
methods. Also photographs, paintings, and
uniforms. Open all year (ex 4 Apr, Christmas
holiday) Mon to Fri 10–1 and 2–5; Sat 10–12
by appointment. BH Sat 10–12. Free. P. (Tel
2581 ext 248)

BLICKLING Norfolk Map 9 TG12
Blickling Hall On B1354. Early 17th-C red-
brick house in fine park. Dutch gables, state
rooms with fine pictures and furnishings, fine
Jacobean plaster ceiling in gallery. Formal
gardens laid out in 1793 and re-designed in
1930, and park with crescent-shaped lake,
and mausoleum of 1793 by Bonomi.
Orangery and Temple designed by Ivory of

Norwich. Open Apr to 12 Oct, Tue to Thu, Sat, Sun, BH Mon Apr to 22 May and 1 to 12 Oct 2–6; 24 May to 30 Sep 11–6 (last admissions 5.30). House closed 12.30–1.30. £1.10. Gardens only Mon–Fri 24 May to 30 Sep 70p. Party 15+ 24 May to 30 Sep. No dogs. *(NT)*

BODIAM *East Sussex* Map 5 TQ72
Bodiam Castle Off A229. Picturesque moated structure, built 1386 and dismantled 1643, with gatehouse, and 37 fireplaces inside. Open Apr to end Oct, daily 10–7; Nov to end Mar, Mon to Sat 10–sunset. 60p ⚠ (fee) *(NT)*

BODMIN *Cornwall* Map 2 SX06
Military Museum The Keep, Victoria Barracks. The Duke of Cornwall's Light Infantry. Open 1 Apr–28 Feb, Mon to Fri 9–12.30 and 2–4.45 (ex BH and Mar). Free. ⚠ ♿

BOLDRE *Hampshire* Map 4 SZ39
Spinners School Lane. Gardens entirely made and maintained by owners; azaleas, rhododendrons, camellias, magnolias etc. interplanted with primulas, blue poppies and other choice woodland and ground cover plants. Rare plants and shrubs for sale. Open 21 Apr to 14 Jul daily (ex Mon) 2–7. Other times by arrangement. 20p ⚠ No dogs. *(Mr and Mrs P G G Chappell). (Tel Lymington 73347). (NGS)* ♿ B

BOLSOVER *Derbyshire* Map 8 SK47
Bolsover Castle On A632. Norman, but rebuilt and enlarged in 1613, partly by John Smythson. Fine fireplaces and ornate panelling, and range of buildings added after 1617, including remarkable 170ft-long Riding School and Gallery, with rows of dormer windows carrying pediments. Fine views. Open*, see inside front cover, 25p (ch 16 and pen 10p). ⚠ *(AM)*

BOLTON *Gt Manchester* Map 7 SD71
Hall I'th'Wood Museum 16th- and 17th-C house, partly half-timbered, associated with Crompton. Open all year (ex Thu, 25 & 26 Dec, 1 Jan & 13 Apr also Sun in winter) 1 Apr to 30 Sep weekdays 10–5.45, Sun 2–5.45; 1 Oct to 31 Mar 10–5. Free. P. *(Tel 51159)* **(79)**
Tonge Moor Textile Museum Tonge Moor Road. Includes Arkwright's waterframe (1768), Crompton's spinning mule (1779), and Hargreave's original spinning jenny. Open all year (ex Sun and BH) Mon, Tue, Thu 9.30–7.30, Wed 9.30–1, Fri 9.30–5, Sat 9.30–12.30. Free. P.(street) *(Tel 21394)* ♿

BOOTLE *Merseyside* Map 7 SJ39
Bootle Library Stanley Road. This new library (opened Sep 1979) holds a continuous programme of exhibitions of paintings by

Merseyside and regional artists. Additionally selections from the Bootle permanent collections, notably English pottery and porcelain (particularly Liverpool pottery) are on display. Open normal Library hours Mon, Wed, Fri 10–7; Tue 10–5; Thu and Sat 10–1 P. ♿

BOROUGHBRIDGE *North Yorkshire* Map 8 SE36
Devil's Arrows Off A1 to SW of town, famous trio of probably Bronze Age monoliths, 16–22ft high, spanning some 360ft, probably part of what may have been a double alignment.

BOROUGH GREEN *Kent* Map 5 TQ65
Great Comp Off B2016. 7-acre garden replanned and maintained by owners for many years. Shrubs, heathers herbaceous plants, and fine lawns and paths. Early 17th-C house (not open). Open 1 May to 15 Oct, Fri, Sun and BH between these dates. ⚐ on Sun. 50p (ch 20p). No dogs. *(Mr and Mrs Cameron). (NGS)* ♿

BOSCASTLE *Cornwall* Map 2 SX09
Museum of Witchcraft and Black Magic Illustrates the past and present customs of witches and their implements in the South West. Open Easter to 24 Oct, daily 10–7. 30p. Under revision for 1980. Dogs on leads only. ⚠ *(Tel Buckfastleigh 3452)*

BOSCOBEL *Salop* Map 7 SJ80
Boscobel House Off A5. House, c 1600, which preserves place where Charles II hid in 1651. Descendant of Royal oak in grounds. Open, see inside front cover (closed daily 1–2). 25p (ch 16 and pen 10p). ⚠ *(AM)*
Whiteladies Priory (St Leonard's Priory) Remains of an Augustinian nunnery, dating from 1158. Largely destroyed in the Civil War. Charles II stayed here on his way to Boscobel House. Open any reasonable time. Free. Guide book available at nearby **Boscobel House**. *(AM)*

BOSTON *Lincolnshire* Map 8 TF34
Fydell House South Square. Georgian house, dating from 1726, now Pilgrim College. Open during term time, weekdays 10–5; other times by appointment with Warden. Free. P. *(Tel 63116)*
Guildhall South Street. Borough art gallery and museum in fine 15th-C building. Cells in which first Pilgrim Fathers were held prisoner in 1607 still here. Open all year Mon to Sat 9.30–12.15 and 1.15–5 (Oct to Apr, 9.30–12 and 1.30–4.30 Mon to Fri, Sat 9.30–12 only). 10p (ch 16 free). P. *(Tel 64601)*

BOUGHTON HOUSE *Northamptonshire* Map 4 SP98
15th-C monastery greatly enlarged between

BODIAM CASTLE
East Sussex

This exciting castle, most advanced in design, was built in 1386 for the defence of the Rother valley. It is surrounded by a moat and inside access has recently been extended to the entrance tower. NT property.

For admission please refer to the gazetteer entry.

1530 and 1695. Celebrated collection of paintings, furniture, tapestries, carpets, porcelain and painted ceilings. State rooms. Beautiful grounds, picnic area, woodland adventure playground. Open Easter, Spring holiday weekends, and Aug, Sep and Oct afternoons. Telephone for detailed dates, times and admission prices. P. *(Tel Kettering 82248)* &

BOUGHTON MONCHELSEA *Kent*
Map 5 TQ74
Boughton Monchelsea Place Off A229. Battlemented Elizabethan and Regency manor house still inhabited, with breathtaking views of its 18th-C deer park and the Kentish Weald. Records preserved since 1570. Also collection of dresses and ancient vehicles. Open Easter to 7 Oct, Sat, Sun, BH (each Wed in Aug) 2.30 – 6. Parties by arrangement anytime. House and grounds 70p (ch 14 30p). Grounds only 35p (ch 10p). Under revision for 1980. No dogs in house. ⚠ *(Tel Maidstone 43120).* (Mr M B Winch) & B (gardens)

BOURN *Cambridgeshire* Map 5 TL35
Bourn Windmill Off B1046. Old post mill dating from 1636 – probably earliest example to have survived. Open during reasonable daylight hours. Notice re local keyholders displayed at mill. Free. P. (roadside only)

BOURNEMOUTH *Dorset* Map 4 SZ09
Big Four Railway Museum Dalkeith Hall, Dalkeith Steps, rear of 81A Old Christchurch Road. Contains over 1,000 railway items, including one of the largest collections of locomotive nameplates, work plates etc, in the country. A large working model railway is in operation. Also models, book and relic shop. Open all year 10 – 5, 1 Jun to 30 Sep daily (1 Oct to 31 May, Wed and Sat only) 50p (ch 16 30p). P. *(Tel 27995)*
British Typewriter Museum Now situated in the Rothesay Museum, almost opposite Bournemouth Pier. There are over 300 typewriters on display which were collected by Mr W A Beeching, author of 'Century of the Typewriter' and donated to Bournemouth Corporation. This is the only museum in the world devoted to typewriters and it is open daily (ex Sun). P. (3 municipal). *(Tel 21009)*
Bournemouth Mobile Museum A double-decker bus built in 1960 and converted into a mobile museum in 1976 – 77. Bournemouth's Open-Air Museum illustrating 10,000 years of history. The museum is parked at different areas in the town during the week. Open all year as and when advertised. 15p (ch 5p, ch 5 free). The museum may be hired at a daily block charge of £10 plus transit charge outside Bournemouth area. Prices under revision for 1980. *(Tel 21009)*

Rothesay Museum 8 Bath Road. Lucas collection of early Italian paintings and pottery, English china and furniture, New Zealand room, armoury room and marine room including relics from Sir Cloudesley Shovell's flagship, *HMS Association*, sunk in 1707. The British Typewriter Museum (Beeching Collection) now occupies part of the first floor of this museum. Open all year (ex 4 Apr, 25 and 26 Dec and Sun) Mon to Sat 10.30 – 5. 20p (ch 5 – 14 5p) 1 Nov to 31 Mar free (ex Thu 20p). Admission charges under review for 1980. P. *(Tel 21009)*
Russell-Coates Art Gallery and Museum Built in 1894 as East Cliff Hall, contains period rooms, section on Oriental art, Henry Irving theatrical collection, freshwater aquarium. ⚐ Open all year (ex 4 Apr, 25 & 26 Dec, and Sun), Mon to Sat 10.30 – 5. Free 1 Nov to 31 Mar (ex Thu 10p); 1 Apr to 31 Oct. 20p (ch 14 5p, ch 5 free). Subject to alteration in 1980. P. *(Tel 21009)*

BOURTON-ON-THE-WATER
Gloucestershire Map 4 SP12
Birdland Zoo Gardens and Wildlife Art Gallery On A429. 4-acre garden with over 600 species of foreign and exotic birds. Ponds, groves, aviaries and tropical house. Open daily (ex 25.Dec) Mar to Nov 10 – 6; Dec, Jan and Feb 10 – 4. 60p (ch 14 30p, pen 50p). Party. Dogs on lead (at owner's risk). Art gallery open daily 11 – 5. P. *(Tel 20689)* &
Model Village In garden of old New Inn, built to scale of one ninth original. Includes miniature replica of River Windrush, and working model waterwheel, and churches, shops, and New Inn faithfully portrayed in Cotswold stone. ⚐ in Hotel. Open all year, summer 9.30 – 6.30 (9.30 – dusk winter). 30p (ch 14 20p). Under revision for 1980. *(Tel 20467)* &
Motor Museum 30 cars and motorcycles ranging from vintage to the 1950s, also large collection of old advertising signs together with a vast number of other interesting items from yester-year. All housed in an 18th-C water mill on the River Windrush in beautiful Cotswold country. Open all year, Jun to Sep 9.30 – 7; Sep to May 10 – 6. 45p (ch 16 30p, ch 5 free). Max family price £1.50. Party. P. *(Tel 21255)* &

BOVINGTON CAMP *Dorset* Map 3 SY88
The Tank Museum (Royal Armoured Corps and Royal Tank Regiment) Off A352. Over 140 armoured fighting vehicles (wheeled and tracked) dating from 1915 onwards. Separate displays of armament, power plant, and associated equipment. ⚐ Open all year (ex Christmas week), Mon to Fri 10 – 12.30 and 2 – 4.45 Sat, Sun and BH 10.30 – 12.30 and 2 – 4. Times may change for 1980. 20p ⚠ *(Tel Bindon Abbey 462721 ext 463)* &

BOWES *Co Durham* Map 12 NY91
Bowes Castle On A66. Norman keep, built
between 1171 and 1187, in angle of Roman
fort of 'Lavatrae'. Open, see inside front
cover. Free. *(AM)*

BOWNESS-ON-WINDERMERE *Cumbria*
Map 7 SD49 (see also WINDERMERE)
Belle Isle Beautiful 38-acre island situated in
the middle of Lake Windermere. The unique
house was the first completely round house
built in England and contains portraits of the
Curwen family, views of Lake Windermere by
Philip de Loutherburg and specially designed
furniture by Gillow of Lancaster. Nature trail.
Children's playground. Motor launch runs
continuously from far end of Bowness
promenade. ⚲ Open May to Sep, Sun, Mon,
Tue, Thu 10.30–5. 60p (ch 30p) boat trip to
island. Guided tour of house 11.15, 12.30,
2.30 and 4pm, 30p P. *(Tel 3353)*
Hill Top 2m SW. Here Beatrix Potter wrote
many of the Peter Rabbit books. The 17th-C
house contains some of her original drawings,
furniture, china and pictures. Owing to the
small size of this house it may be necessary to
restrict the numbers visiting at any one time.
Visitors are warned that considerable delays
may occur at peak visiting times and that
there is no electric light in the house. Shop.
Open Apr to end Oct daily (ex Fri) 10–5.30,
Sun 2–5.30 or dusk if earlier. 80p (ch 40p).
No indoor photography. Enquiries to the
Curator *(Tel Hawkshead 334)*

BRADFORD *West Yorkshire* Map 7 SE13
Bolling Hall Bowling Hall Road. Period
house dating from 15th-C containing local
history museum with fine furniture including
rare Chippendale bed, heraldic glass and
'ghost room'. Open all year daily (ex 25/26
Dec and 4 Apr) 10–5, (enquire for summer
opening times). Free. P. *(Tel 23057)*
Cartwright Hall Lister Park. Contains
permanent collections of European and
British paintings, sculpture, drawings,
modern prints and ceramics. Recent
acquisition Joshua Reynolds' painting 'The
Brown Boy'. Also temporary exhibitions of
natural history, geology and archaeology. ⚲
Open, as Bolling Hall above. Free. ⚠ *(Tel
493313)* ⅋
Industrial Museum Moorside Mills,
Eccleshill. Museum of Industrial Archaeology
featuring the growth of the worsted industry of
the area. Textile, Motive Power and Transport
galleries. Tank locomotive, veteran and
vintage cars. Trolleybus and tram shed. Mill
house furnished early 1900. ⚲ Open all year
daily (ex 25/26 Dec and 4 Apr) 10–5. Free. ⚠
*(Tel 631756, school visits may be booked on
this number)* ⅋

BRADFORD-ON-AVON *Wiltshire*
Map 3 ST86
Barton Tithe Barn 14th-C building, once
property of Shaftesbury Abbey, since
presented to Wiltshire Archaeological
Society. Open any reasonable time. Free.
(AM)
The Hall Grounds of Elizabethan house, c
1600, formerly known as Kingston Hall, used
as model for British exhibit at 1900 Paris
Exhibition. Grounds only open all year 9–5.
Free. ⚠ No dogs. ⅋
Great Chalfield Manor 2½ NE. Restored
stone-built 15th-C house, with moat and great
hall. Small 13th-C church adjacent. Open 16
Apr to 24 Sep, Wed 12–1 and 2–5. 70p. *(NT)*

**BRADGATE PARK and SWITHLAND
WOODS** *Leicestershire* Map 8 SK51
850-acre country park with Old John Tower
(1786), and ruins of Bradgate House, brick
mansion, completed c 1510 by son of 1st
Marquis of Dorset, birthplace of Lady Jane
Grey (1537–54). Open all year to
pedestrians; no cars, except those carrying
invalids – special arrangements can be made.
Ruins open Apr to Oct, Wed, Thu, Sat
2.30–5, Sun 10–12.30. Free. (5 car parks,
Park and Swithland woods). ⚠ 10p. *(Tel
Leicester 871313 The Ranger)* ⅋
Also *Marion's Cottage* Newtown Linford.
Contains exhibitions and information, shop,
bookstall. Open all year, Apr to Oct, Wed,
Thu, Sat, Sun 2–6 (Sat, Sun 2–5 Nov to Mar)
⚠ ⅋

BRADWELL-ON-SEA *Essex* Map 5 TL90
Bradwell Lodge Off B1021, S of town. Early
16th-C house of Tudor and Georgian periods
with wing (1785) by Robert Adam. Bow-
windowed belvedere used by Gainsborough
in 18th C. Saxon St Peter's Church (AD654)
on sea-wall 1¾m E of house. House open by
appointment only. 50p (ch 12 25p). ⚠ *Mr and
Mrs J Mann)*

BRAMBER *West Sussex* Map 4 TQ11
Bramber Castle Formerly owned by Dukes
of Norfolk, ruined Norman stronghold on
South Downs ridge with wide views. Open
always. Free. *(NT)*
House of Pipes Museum with 25,000
exhibits covering 150 countries and 1,500
years, believed to be the only 'smokiana'
exhibition in the world. It is a fascinating study
of social history in everyday life, set in a
19th-C shopping arcade. Awarded a British
Tourist Authority Commendation. Open all
year daily (ex 25 Dec) 9–8 (6.30 Oct to Apr).
20p (ch 4–14 10p). Under revision for 1980.
Party. ⚠ ⅋

BRAMHALL *Gt Manchester* Map 7 SJ88
Bramhall Hall S of Stockport off A5102. 14th

BRAMALL HALL
STOCKPORT, CHESHIRE

For over 500 years, the home of the Davenport
family, and now owned and administered by the
Metropolitan Borough of Stockport. This magpie-style
building is outstanding in its parkland setting. Some
2 miles south-east of the centre of Stockport, the Hall
is open April to Sept. Daily 10am-12 noon. Schools and
other organised parties (by appointment). 12 noon-5pm
general public. Closed Mondays. Sat & Sun & Bank
Holidays 12 noon-5pm. Oct-March. Daily 10am-12 noon.
Schools and other organised parties (by appointment).
12 noon-4pm general public. Closed Mondays and
December. Sat, Sun & appropriate Bank Holidays
12 noon-4pm.

Admission 30p Adults: 15p Children and subject to price review. Free parking.

and 15th-C house with fine timber and plaster work. Extensive restoration work is in hand. Open Apr to Sep Tue to Sun and BH 12 – 5, Oct to Mar, Tue to Sun and BH 12 – 4. 30p (ch 15p) plus VAT. Parties 10 – 12. ⚠ *(Tel 061 – 485 3708)* ⅋ B

BRAMHAM *West Yorkshire* Map 8 SE44
Bramham Park On A1 4m S of Wetherby. This Queen Anne House, containing fine furniture, pictures and porcelain, is the home of Mr and Mrs George Lane Fox, decendants of the builder, Robert Benson (Lord Bingley). The gardens, landscaped in the French style, extend to 65 acres and contain ornamental ponds and cascades, temples and beech avenues. Gift shop. ☕ Open Easter BH then 1 May to end Sep, Sun, Tue, Wed, Thu and BH Mon. Closed 27 May to 3 Jun during Bramham Horse Trials. Grounds 11 – 6, House 1.15 – 5.30. Admission price for 1980 not yet decided. ☕ Open Easter BH then 1 party rates from *House Administrator, Estate Office, Bramham Park, Wetherby, West Yorkshire. (Tel Boston Spa 844265)*

BRAMHOPE *West Yorkshire* Map 8 SE24
Puritan Chapel On A660. In grounds of former hall, well-restored, almost unique chapel (1646 – 49), with many 17th-C fittings, such as box pews and a two-decker pulpit. Illustrated pamphlet and post cards available. Open 1 Apr to 31 Oct, Wed, Sat, Sun, BH, 10 – 12 and 1 – 4 (5, Jun to Sep). P. *(Tel Leeds 678791)*

BRAMPTON *Cambridgeshire* Map 4 TL27
Pepys' House On A141. Old gabled cottage where parents of Samuel Pepys once lived, and where famous diarist once buried his gold for fear of Dutch invasion. He owned house from 1664 until his death in 1703. Open all year, Mon to Sat (ex BH) by prior appointment only. ⚠ for one car only (no coaches). *(Tel Huntingdon 53431)*

BRAMPTON *Cumbria* Map 12 NY56
Lanercost Priory 2½m NE. Was a house of Augustinian Canons founded about 1166 by William de Vaux. Remains of quire and transepts. Open, see inside front cover. 15p (ch 16 and pen 5p). ⚠ *(AM)*

BRASTED *Kent* Map 5 TQ45
Emmetts 4-acre hillside shrub garden. Open Apr and Jul to Oct, Wed and Sun, May and Jun Tue to Thu and Sun, 2 – 6 (last admissions 5). 40p. *(NT)*

BRATTON *Wiltshire* Map 3 ST95
Bratton Camp and White Horse Off B3098. 18th-C White Horse below Iron Age Camp. Open at all reasonable times. Free. ⚠ *(AM)*

BREAMORE *Hampshire* Map 4 SU11
Breamore House, Countryside and Carriage Museums On A338. Elizabethan Manor House (1583), with fine collection of works of art, including paintings, china and tapestries. Countryside Museum displays rural arts and agricultural machinery, and Carriage Museum with old coaches. ☕ (teas). Open 1 Apr to 30 Sep, Tue to Thu, Sat, Sun and all BH 2 – 5.30. Admission to house £1 (ch 50p), Countryside Museum 70p (ch 35p), Carriage Museum 50p (ch 25p), combined ticket £1.30 (ch 65p). ⚠ *(Tel 270). (Sir Westrow Hulse)* ⅋

BREAN *Somerset* Map 3 ST35
Brean Down Bird Garden Situated at the base of Brean Down, adjacent to the sea and 7 miles of sand. The Downs is NT property and a bird sanctuary. The garden was built in 1972 and there are 250 – 300 birds from all parts of the world kept in very long flights. ☕ Open Apr to Oct daily 10 – 6. 35p (ch 20p). P. *(Tel 209)*

BRENDON *Hereford and Worcester* Map 3 SO93
Tithe Barn 14th-C building with fine porches and outside staircase. Open all year, daily until sunset. 10p. *(NT)*

BRENZETT *Kent* Map 5 TR02
Brenzett Aeronautical Museum Ivychurch Road. Founded in 1972. Exhibits relics of many famous aircraft including: Focke-Wulf FW190, Zeppelin, Messerschmitt 109E/410, Junkers 88, Spitfire and many more. Also aero engines, aircraft armaments and other aeronautical items. Open Easter to 31 Oct, Sun and BH 11 – 6; Jul and Aug, Tue, Wed and Thu 2 – 5. 25p (ch 10p). ⚠ *(Tel Tenterden 3197)* ⅋

BRESSINGHAM *Norfolk* Map 5 TM07
Bressingham Gardens and Live Steam Museum On A1066. 6 acres of informal gardens near live steam museum. There are three steam-hauled trains: a 9½-inch gauge, a 15-inch gauge running through two miles of the wooded Waveney Valley and a 2ft-gauge through two miles of Europe's largest hardy plant nursery. Also collection of 40 road and rail engines, mostly restored to working order. Voigt street organ. Exhibition hall. Steam roundabout. ☕ Open early May to late Sep, Sun 1.30 – 6; late May to mid Sep also Thu 1.30 – 5.30; Aug also Wed 1.30 – 5.30; also 15 Apr and BH (ex winter) from 1.30pm. Admission prices for 1980 not yet available. ⚠ *(Tel 386). (Mr Alan Bloom)* ⅋

BRIDGNORTH *Salop* Map 7 SO79
Midland Motor Museum Stanmore Hall, 1½m on A458 Stourbridge Road. A collection of

very well restored sports cars and sports and racing motor cycles, housed in the converted stable of Stanmore Hall and surrounded by beautiful grounds. 8-acre bird garden set around 1½-acre lake. ⚲ Open all year, daily (ex 25 Dec) 10–6, dusk if earlier. Admission prices not yet decided. (ch and pen approx half price). ⚠ *(Tel 61761)* ₷

Severn Valley Railway The leading Standard Gauge Steam Railway, with one of the largest collections of locomotives and rolling stock in the country. Services from Bewdley to Bridgnorth through 12½ miles of picturesque scenery along the river Severn. Intensive services of passenger trains every weekend from the beginning of Mar to end Oct and most weekdays from May to Sep, in addition to all P & BH. Special events planned for Apr, Jun and Sep. Family tickets available in addition to special party discounts. 1980 charges not yet decided. *(Tel Bewdley 403816 and Bridgnorth 4361)* ₷

BRIDGWATER *Somerset* Map 3 ST33
Admiral Blake Museum Blake Street. 15th-C house, birthplace in 1598 of Admiral Blake, now museum of relics of admiral's time, exhibits of local interest, and items relating to Battle of Sedgemoor. Exhibition of watercolours by John Chubb, Mayor of Bridwater 1788. Open all year (ex BH), Tue to Sat 11–4. Free (no ch 14 unless with adult). P. *(Tel 56127)* **(79)**

BRIDLINGTON *Humberside* Map 8 TA16
Sewerby hall, Park and Zoo Georgian House dating from 1714–20 and 1808, now Art Gallery and Museum of history and archaeology, Amy Johnson Trophy Room. Gardens of botanical interest, especially the Old English walled garden. Miniature Zoo and Aviary in gardens. Band concerts, Sun May to Aug. ⚲ Clock Tower Tavern. 'Sewerby Trains' operate from Limekiln Lane, Bridlington to Park Gates. Grounds open all year 9–dusk, 25p (ch 10p) to Park from Spring BH to mid-Sep when games facilities are available to public. Prices under revision for 1980. Party. Enquiries to Director of Parks and Recreation *(Tel 73769 enquiries, 78255 for booking)* ₷ B

BRIDPORT *Dorset* Map 3 SY49
Museum and Art Gallery South Street. Housed in a Tudor building, thought to have once been the house of the chantry priests of the oratory of St Leonards. Its exhibits concentrate on the local trade of nets, ropes and twines, and old 'Jumper' net making loom, which has been in use since 1830. There are also exhibits of archaeology, geology, natural history, former domestic and agricultural tools, Victorian costume, a dolls house and a collection of dolls in native and historical dress. The art gallery contains paintings from the collection of the donor of the building Capt A P Codd. Open all year, daily (ex Sun and Thu also Sat pm) 10.30–1; Jun–Sep also 2.30–4.30. 20p (ch 12 10p). P. *(Tel 22116)* ₷

BRIGHOUSE *West Yorkshire* Map 7 SE12
1m NW of M62 (junc 25)
Brighouse Art Gallery Halifax Road. Contains a permanent collection of work by mainly 19th-C English artists, but also shows temporary exhibitions throughout the year. Open all year (ex 25, 26 Dec and 1 Jan) Mon to Sat 10–5 Sun 2.30–5 (closed Sun Oct to Mar). Free. ⚠ *(Tel 719222)* ₷

BRIGHTON *East Sussex* Map 4 TQ30
Aquarium and Dolphinarium Marine Parade. Dolphins may be seen performing in a massive pool. Their show culminates in a

The full 12½ miles length of the Severn Valley is here seen at its best and most varied. The line runs from Bridgenorth to Bewdley through many colourful village stations and over the Great Victoria Bridge.
Light refreshments always available. Full catering on request Station pub and shops. Party catering at special rates. Business or pleasure March to October. ASK FOR DETAILS.

BEWDLEY (0299) 403816 ·BIGGEST STANDARD GAUGE STEAM RAILWAY

Preston Manor, Preston Park, Brighton BN1 6SD

There has been a house on the site of Preston Manor since about 1250, but the present form of the house dates from 1739, with extensive additions in 1905. Preston Manor today presents the appearance of an opulent Edwardian country house, and houses a notable collection of furniture, portraits and family memorabilia.
The house is open from Wednesday to Saturday from 10.00 am to 5.00 pm, Sundays 2.00-5.00 pm. Closed Good Friday, Christmas Day, Boxing Day and New Year's Day.
Admission: Adults 35p, OAP's 25p, Children 15p. Joint admission ticket with the Royal Pavilion 90p (excluding Regency Exhibition). Parties of 20 or more 30p per head.

leap of 18ft. Also an aquarium of 80 large tanks containing marine life. ⚇ and licensed bar. Open all year 9 – 6.30. 80p (ch 40p). P. *(Tel 604233)* ♿ (by arrangement)
Booth Museum of Natural History Dyke Road. Contains British birds mounted in natural settings, evolution gallery and temporary exhibitions. New Gallery 'The Unnatural History of an English County'. Bookshop with extensive stock of books on Natural History, especially birds. Open all year, Mon to Fri 10 – 5, Sun 2 – 5. (Temporarily closed Thu). Free. P (in street). *(Tel 552586/603005 ext 64)* ♿

Museum and Art Gallery Church Street. The collections include Old Master Paintings, watercolours, Sussex archaeology and folklife, ethnography and musical instruments. Also the Willet Collection of pottery and porcelain and display of 20th-C fine and applied art, including Art Nouveau and Art Deco. Also various special exhibitions. ⚇ Open all year (ex 4 Apr, 25 & 26 Dec and Mons) Tue to Sat 10 – 5.45, Sun 2 – 5 (6 in summer). Free. Parking meters outside main entrance. *(Tel 603005)* ♿ B
Preston Manor Off A23. Georgian house with additions in 1905. Houses a notable collection of furniture, portraits, and family memorabilia. Open all year, (ex 4 Apr, 25/26 Dec, 1 Jan also Mon and Tue), Wed to Sat 10 – 5, Sun 2 – 5. Party (ch 15p, pen 25p). Party 20+ 30p. Joint admission ticket with Royal Pavilion 90p. ⚠ in drive. *(Tel 552101)*
Royal Pavilion Marine Palace of the Prince Regent (George IV). Henry Holland's Palladian villa (1787) transformed by John Nash with an Indian-style exterior and fantastic Chinoiserie internal decorations. Now restored to former splendour. Important collection of furniture, some returned on loan by HM the Queen. Regency exhibition Jul to end Sep. ⚇ Easter to early Nov. Open all year Oct to 28 Jun daily 10 – 5 (8, 1 Jul to 30 Sep). Closed 25, 26 Dec, 29, 30 Jun. Admission varies according to season. 70/90p (ch 25.35p). Charges from Apr 1980 under review. P. *(Tel 603005)* ♿ B
Volks Railway First electric railway in Great Britain. Opened in 1883. Runs along sea front from Aquarium to Black Rock Marina (1¼ miles, 2ft 8½in guage). Open Easter to end Sep. Daily 11 – 6.30. P. *(Tel 681061)*

BRILL *Buckinghamshire* Map 4 SP61
Boarstall Duck Decoy and Nature Reserve Exhibition hall, collection of wildfowl, woodland walk, incorporating seven numbered stops where certain features, trees and plants will be of particular interest. Many different types of birds have been recorded at the Decoy. Demonstrations Sun 4, BH 11, 12, 2 and 4. Picnic area. Open 1 Mar to 28 Aug, Tue to Sun 10 – 5, also open BH Mons. 40p (ch 20p, ch 5 free). ⚠ *(Tel 237488)*
Brill Windmill Off B4011. One of the oldest post mills in England, with parts dating back to c1680. Worked until 1916 and now owned by the Buckinghamshire County Council. Open Apr to Sep, Sun 2.30 – 5.30, and other times by appointment. 20p (ch 14 5p). *(Tel Aylesbury 22171)*
Dorton House Off B4011. 17th- to 18th-C house with later alterations, now Ashfold School. Open May to Jul, and Sep, Sat, Sun 2 – 5. 40p (ch 14 and pen 20p). ⚠ *(Tel 237)* ♿ B

BRIMHAM *North Yorkshire* Map 8 SE26
Rocks Off B6265. Grotesquely shaped rocks on heathery moorland at height of 950ft.

Described in Victorian guide-books as 'a place wrecked with grim and hideous forms defying all description and definition'. Old shooting lodge being converted into information point and shop. Always accessible. ⚠ 50p *(NT)*
BRINKBURN *Northumberland* Map 12 NZ19
Priory Church Off B6344. Well-restored Augustinian priory church, founded 1135 in bend of River Coquet, fine example of period. Roof replaced in 1858, but remaining medieval fittings include font, double piscina and some grave slabs. Open* see inside front cover. 15p (ch 16 and pen 5p). ⚠ *(AM)*
BRISTOL *Avon* Map 3 ST57
Blaise Castle House Henbury. 4m NW of city, off B4957. 18th-C mansion, now folk museum, situated in extensive grounds. Open all year (ex 1 Jan, 4 Apr, 5 May, 26, 27 May, 25 – 27 Dec). Mon to Sat 2 – 5. Free. ⚠ *(Tel 506789)* ♿ B
Bristol Industrial Museum Prince's Wharf, Prince Street. A converted dockside transit shed in the heart of Bristol, 400yd from SS Great Britain. Display of vehicles, horse-drawn and motorised, from the Bristol area, locally built aircraft, aero engines, railway exhibits include full size industrial locomotive Henbury steamed *c.* once a month. Various kinds of machinery illustrating local trade and manufacturing. Open all year Sat to Wed incl, 10 – 12 and 1 – 5 (closed Thu, Fri also 1 Jan, 4 Apr, 25 – 27 Dec). Free. P. *(Tel 299771 ext 290)*
Cabot Tower More than 100ft high and dating from 1897 – 8, commemorates quatercentenary of Cabot's discovery of North America on 24 Jun 1497. Fine viewpoint. Open all year, daily 9 – dusk. 5p. P. (meters) **(79)**
City Museum and Art Gallery Queen's Road. Fine collections of archaeological, geological, natural history, scientific, and transport exhibits, and also pictures, ceramics, sculpture, fine art, and an aquarium. There will be numerous special exhibitions. Museum shop, coffee shop. Open all year, Mon to Sat (ex 1 Jan, 4 Apr, 5, 26, 27 May, 25 – 27 Dec). 10 – 5. Free. ⚠ *(Tel 299771)* ♿
John Wesley's Chapel Broadmead. The oldest Methodist Chapel in the world, built 1739, rebuilt 1748, in each case by John Wesley. Living rooms added above in 1748 and both chapel and living rooms are preserved in their original form. John Wesley frequently resided in the rooms, also used as headquarters of his work in West and Midlands. Charles Wesley looked after chapel and rooms and lived nearby 1739 – 71. Wesley Day celebrations 24 May. Open all year, daily (ex Sun, Wed and BH) 10 – 4. Free. ⚠ *(Tel 24740)*
Red Lodge Park Row. 16th-C house altered in the early 18th C, with fine oak carvings and furnishings of both periods. Open all year (ex Sun and 1 Jan, 4 Apr, 5, 26, 27 May, 25 – 27 Dec). Mon to Sat 2 – 5. Free. *(Tel 299771)*
SS Great Britain In floating harbour off Cumberland Road. Designed by I K Brunel, she was the first iron, screw-propelled ocean-going ship; launched in 1843, her long career, with many vicissitudes, ended after a ship-wreck in the Falkland Islands, from where she was raised and towed back in 1970 to the dock in which she was built. ⚇ and gift shop. Museum, dockside displays. Open all year (ex 24 and 25 Dec), daily 10 – 6 (5 in winter). 60p (ch and pen 30p). Prices under revision for 1980. Party. ⚠ *(Tel 20680)*

St Nicholas Church Museum St Nicholas Street. Contains the history of Bristol from its beginning until the Reformation including Bristol church art, especially silver of all periods. Also a changing display of water-colours and drawings showing topographical features of the city mainly during the 18th/19th C, and the Hogarth altar piece originally painted for St Mary Redcliffe. Brass rubbing centre. Open Mon to Sat (ex 1 Jan, 4 Apr, 5, 26, 27 May, 25 – 27 Dec). 10 – 5. Free. P. &

The Georgian House 7 Gt George Street. Georgian house with 18th-C furniture and fittings. Open all year Mon to Sat 10 – 5 (ex Sun, and 1 Jan, 4 Apr, 5, 26, 27 May, 25 – 27 Dec). Free. Street parking (meters). *(Tel 299771)*

Vine House Henbury (3m NW of city, off B4055 next to Salutation). Planted by resident family since 1946, 2-acre garden with trees, shrubs, water and naturalised garden. Open all year by arrangement. 25p (ch 16 and pen 10p). *(Tel 503573). (Professor and Mrs T F Hewer). (NGS)* &

Westbury College Westbury-on-Trym (3m N of city, off B4055). 15th-C gatehouse of 13th-C Priest's College. Key with *Vicar, 12 Eastfield Road. (NT)*

Zoological Gardens Clifton Down. Extensive gardens, and varied collection of animals, reptiles, and fishes. ☑ & licensed bar. Open daily (ex 25 Dec), Mon – Sat from 9am, Sun from 10am (closing times vary with season). Admission prices not yet decided. No dogs admitted. P. *(Tel 38951)*

BROADSTAIRS *Kent* Map 5 TR36
Bleak House Overlooks town, noted for associations with Charles Dickens also Coastal Maritime Section in Garden. Open Easter weekend than 14 May to 30 Sep, daily 2 – 5. 50p (ch 12 25p). Party. P. *(Tel Thanet 62224)*

Dickens House Museum Immortalised by Charles Dickens in 'David Copperfield' as the home of Betsey Trotwood. Contains Dickens' letters and former possessions, local and Dickensian prints, costumes and Victoriana. The parlour is refurbished as described in 'David Copperfield'. Open Apr to Oct, daily 2.30 – 5.30. (Tue, Wed, Thu evenings 7 – 9, Jun to Sep.) Parties by arrangement. Prices of admission under revision for 1980. P. *(Hon Curator Tel Thanet 62853)*

BROADWAY *Hereford and Worcester* Map 4 SP03
Broadway Tower Country Park 65ft tower built in 18th C by the 6th Earl of Coventry, housing an observation room, history of the tower 'period exhibitions' and a shop (selling books, souvenirs, etc). A countryside

exhibition is located in the 150-year-old Tower barn. Tower Barn Natural History Centre with live and static displays on British mammals, birds, deer, sheep etc. Nature walks and picnic areas. ☑ Open Apr to end Sep 10 – 6. 40p (ch 20p). Party. ⚠ *(Tel 2390)* & B

BROCKHAMPTON *Hereford and Worcester* Map 3 SO65
Lower Brockhampton 3m E Bromyard. On high ground, north side of A44; entrance by Bromyard Lodge. Half-timbered 14th-C house with a rare 15th-C gatehouse. Medieval hall open all year (ex Jan and 4 Apr), Mon, Wed, Fri, Sat and BH Mon 10 – 1 and 2 – 6, Sun 10 – 1. 60p (ch 30p). *(NT)*

BROKERSWOOD *Wiltshire* Map 3 ST85
Phillips Countryside Museum and Woodland Park Off A361. 88 acres of natural woodlands, with nature walks, lake, wildfowl, etc, and a Natural History Museum opened in 1970. Forestry exhibition in museum. Guided walks. Collection of birds' eggs of the world can be inspected on prior application. ☑ and shop. Open all year, daily 10 – dusk. 50p (ch 14 20p, accompanied, free). Special rates for parties and youth organisations. ⚠ *(Tel Westbury 822238)* &

BROMSGROVE *Hereford and Worcester* Map 7 SO97
The Norton Collection Museum Davenal House, 28 Birmingham Road, Bromsgrove. A wide selection of Victorian musical boxes, gramophones, wireless and crystal sets, organs, kitchenware, lamps and Victoriana can be seen. Crafts and Industries Room. Costume and Chemist's Shop. Local History also Boar Coffee House. Open Mon to Sat 10 – 5, Sun 12 – 6. *(Tel 77934)* & (prior notice)
Avoncroft Museum of Buildings Redditch Road, Stoke Heath. Open-air museum displaying old buildings saved from demolition and re-erected. Exhibits include 18th-C windmill operational on certain days, a granary and thatched barn; timber framed houses, medieval roofs, a cock pit theatre and nail and chainmakers' workshops. Museum shop. Picnic site. Open 1 Mar to 30 Nov, daily 10.30 – 5.30 (or dusk if earlier). Admission prices for 1980 not available. ⚠ *(Tel 31886)* & B

BROOK *Kent* Map 5 TR04
Wye College Museum of Agriculture 4m ENE of Ashford on unclass road. An exhbition of old farm implements and machinery housed in a fine old tithe barn dating from the 14th C. Display of hop cultivation in old oast house. Open May to Sep, Wed 2 – 5 and Sat in Aug. Free. Parties by arrangement. ⚠ limited. *(Tel Wye 812401 ext 239)* & B

BROOMY HILL *Hereford and Worcester*
Map 3 SO43
Herefordshire Waterworks Museum The
museum is housed in a Victorian Pumping
station of 1856, near the banks of the River
Wye. The first phase of the museum was
opened in Apr 1975 and contains two steam
pumping engines built in 1895 and 1906.
These have now been restored to working
order. The rest of the museum is expected to
be ready within the next 2–3 years where a
number of very old pumping engines and
other waterworks equipment from
Herefordshire will be displayed. There are
also plans for a narrow-gauge waterworks
railway. Open first Sun in each month Apr to
Sep also every Sat & Sun, Jul/Aug 1–5;
dates and times for 1980 not yet available.
Party ⚠ Enquiries to *The Secretary HR
Penhale, 87 Ledbury Road, Hereford
HR1 2TR (Tel Hereford 4101)* ⅃

BROUGH *Cumbria* Map 12 NY71
Brough Castle On A66. Dates from 12th to
13th C, repaired in 17th C by Lady Anne
Clifford. Stands on site of Roman 'Verterae'.
Open, see inside front cover. 10p (ch 16 and
en 5p). ⚠ *(AM)*

BROUGHAM *Cumbria* Map 12 NY52
Brougham Castle Off A66. 12th- to 14th-C
castle, repaired in late 16th C by Lady Anne
Clifford. Open*, see inside front cover. 15p
(ch 16 and pen 5p). ⚠ *(AM)*

BROUGHTON *Oxfordshire* Map 4 SP43
Broughton Castle 2m W of Banbury on
B4035. Originally owned by William of
Wykeham later passing into hands of first
Lord Saye and Sele, early 14th- and mid
16th-C house with moat and gatehouse, 16th-
C ceilings and mantelpieces. Period furniture
and paintings and Civil War relics. ⅃ Open
Wed and Sun 1 Jun to 14 Sep also Thu Jul
and Aug and BH Sun and Mon 2–5. Party (all
year). Admission probably 90p (ch 10 50p). P.
Tel Banbury 2624). (Lord Saye and Sele)

BROUGHTON POGGS *Oxfordshire*
Map 4 SP20
Filkins and Broughton Poggs Museum On
A361. Domestic articles (including cooking
utensils), village lock-up, and example of
mantrap. Usually open all year, Fri, Sat and
Sun 9–6. *(Apply Mr Foster, Filkins 365)* ⅃

BROWNHILLS *West Midlands* Map 7 Sk00
Chasewater Light Railway Chasewater
Park. On unclassified road, off A5. Society,
founded in 1959, has preserved collection of
small relics, as well as mainly Victorian rolling
stock and several industrial locomotives.
Some 2m of track. Steam-operated trains run
second and fourth Sun in each month, Apr to
Sep. ⅃ Open all year, Sat and Sun from
–dusk. ⚠ *(Tel 5852)*

BROWNSEA ISLAND, Poole Harbour
Dorset Map 4 SZ08
500 acres of heath and woodland, with nature
reserve, two lakes, mile of bathing beach and
fine views of Dorset coastline. First scout
camp held here under Lord Baden-Powell in
1907. ⅃ Throughout the day in Villano
cafeteria. Open Apr to 30 Sep, daily 10–7 (or
dusk), by boat from Poole Quay or
Sandbanks. 50p (ch 25p). *(NT)*

BROXBOURNE *Hertfordshire* Map 5 TL30
Broxbourne Zoo White Stubbs Lane. 2m W
of Broxbourne on unclass road. This zoo
covers some 22 acres housing over 250
animals and birds, which are continually
being added to. ⅃ Open all year (ex 25 Dec)
10–6 (5 winter). 60p (ch 30p , ch 2 free). ⚠
(Tel Hoddesdon 62852) ⅃ **(79)**

BRYMPTON *Somerset* Map 3 ST51
Brympton d'Evercy Mansion House Stuart
and Tudor mansion in superb setting. Also
Priest House Country Life Museum. State
rooms, Felix dress collection. Parish church
alongside. Extensive grounds. ⅃ teas. Picnic
area, vineyard, cider and wine available.
Open 1 May to 26 Sep, daily (ex Thu and Fri)
2–6. Admission prices for 1980 not yet
decided. ⚠ *(Tel West Coker 2528)* ⅃

BUCKDEN *Cambridgeshire* Map 4 TL16
Buckden Palace Off A1. Remains of ancient
palace, once residence of Bishops of Lincoln.
Fine Tudor tower and inner gatehouse of red
brick, dating probably from *c*1490, and
modern house in grounds. Open Jul, Aug,
Sep, Sun 3–7; exterior always viewable.
Admission charges to be decided. ⚠ *(The
Claretian Missionaries)*

BUCKFAST *Devon* Map 3 SX76
The Museum of Shellcraft Off A38. Large
collection of shellcraft from all over world, and
shows art of the shellcraft workers. Open
Easter to 24 Oct, daily 10–7. Admission
charges not avilable. Dogs on lead only. P.
(Tel Buckfastleigh 3452)

BUCKFASTLEIGH *Devon* Map 3 SX76
Dart Valley Railway Steam locomotive
hauled trains run between Buckfastleigh and
Totnes Riverside. **Note** Passengers cannot
leave or join trains at Totnes. Store of ex
Great Western rolling stock, including a
number of locomotives. ⅃ Bookshop, **also
Riverside Miniature Railway** A passenger-
carrying miniature railway round the Dart
Valley station area ½m ride. Open Easter then
mid May to mid Sep, daily (ex Sat), 11–5.
Access from Dart Valley Railway. P. *(Tel
2338)*

BUCKLAND *Gloucestershire* Map 4 SP03
Buckland Rectory Off A46. England's oldest
rectory, medieval house with 15th-C great hall

BROWNSEA
ISLAND

Poole Harbour, Dorset

The Get-away beach from
Bournemouth.
See Gazetteer for details.

with open timber roof and contemporary glass. Associated with John Wesley. Also earlier half-timbered house and spiral stone staircase. Open May, Jun, Jul, Sep, Mon 11–4; Aug, Mon and Fri 11–4. Free. ⚠ *(Tel Broadway 2479). (Rev Michael Bland MA)*

BUCKLAND ABBEY *Devon* Map 2 SX46 3m W of Yelverton, off A386. Original house altered by Grenvilles, former owners and present house sold to Sir Francis Drake in 1581. Now partly Drake Museum, including legendary Drake's Drum. Also shrub and herb gardens, and tithe barn. Refreshments in afternoon. Open Good Fri to end Sep, Mon–Sat and BH 11–6, Sun 2–6; Oct to Wed before Easter, Wed, Sat, Sun 3–5, last admission ½ hour before closing. 80p (ch 40p) *(NT)*

BUCKLER'S HARD *Hampshire* Map 4 SZ49 *Maritime Museum* Off B3054. Small museum, opened by the late Earl Mountbatten of Burma in 1963, in village where wooden warships, including vessels for Nelson's fleet were once built from New Forest oak. Village Festival in July. ⚌ Open all year (ex 25 Dec). Easter to Spring BH. 10–6. Spring BH to Sep 10–9, Oct to Easter 10–4.40. Admission prices not yet known. ⅋

BUDLEIGH SALTERTON *Devon* Map 3 SY08 *Fairlynch Arts Centre and Museum* Fore Street. In 18th-C house, museum with exhibits of mainly local interest. Entirely new exhibitions annually. Costume display. Local history exhibition. Smuggler's Cellar. Open Easter to end Oct 2.30–5; Jul to end Aug also 10.30–12.30 (ex Sun mornings) 20p (ch 10, pen and students 10p). Honiton Lace making demonstrations, Sat and Sun afternoons. *(Tel 2666)*

BUILDWAS *Salop* Map 7 SJ60 *Buildwas Abbey* A beautiful ruined Savignac Abbey founded in 1135 standing in picturesque setting. Vaulted Chapter House dates from end of 12th C or early 13th C. Open, see inside front cover. 10p (ch 16 and pen 5p). *(AM)*

BUNGAY *Suffolk* Map 5 TM38 *Bungay Castle* On A144. Dates from 12th C, with restored late 13th-C gatehouse and drawbridge leading to keep and curtain wall. Large outer bailey, and views across Waveney valley. Open all year; guide book and keys available 9–1, 2.15–4.30 at *Sayer's shop or Council Office both in Earsham Street.* Free. P. *(Tel 2176)*
Otter Trust Earsham. A 23-acre site bounded by the River Waveney, including three lakes. World's largest collection of otters in semi-natural conditions for captive breeding for

release and research purposes. Mobile Interpretative Centre and a fine collection of waterfowl on the lakes. The Trust's main aim is to help save the world's otters from extinction. Shop and ⚌. Open 1 Mar to 30 Nov daily 10.30–6 (dusk if earlier). 80p (ch 16 40p). ⚠ *(Tel 3470)* ⅋

BURFORD *Oxfordshire* Map 4 SP21 *Cotswold Wildlife Park* 2m S off A361. Landscaped open plan zoological park with exotic mammals, tropical birds, etc in landscaped enclosures. Also large reptile collection, aquarium and insect house. Other attractions include woodland walks, formal gardens, adventure playground, train and pony rides. ⚌ (Parties up to 30, menus on request). Open all year daily (ex 25 Dec) 10–6 (or sunset Oct–Mar). £1 (ch 14 and per 60p, ch 3 free) (subject to change). ⚠ *(Tel 3006)* ⅋ (wheelchairs available)
Tolsey Museum Local crafts museum of charters and seals of Burford dating from 16th-C, old manuscripts, Burford craftsman's model 17th-C dolls house, furnished and dressed in Regency style. Open Easter to late Oct, daily 2.30–5.30. 20p (ch 5p). P. *(Tel 2168, Hon Sec)*

BURFORD *Salop* Map 7 SO56 *Burford House Gardens* Off A456. Near River Teme, house (1720) with gardens designed by John Treasure, featuring trees, shrubs, clematis, herbaceous plants, roses and 18th-C summer house. The ground floor of Burford House is open and flower arrangements are displayed on antique furniture. Permanent exhibition by the 'Teme Painters' local artists. Garden shop. ⚌ Gardens open mid Apr to mid Oct daily 2–5. Admission prices not available. Reduced rates for parties. ⚠ No dogs. *(Tel Tenbury Wells 810777)*

BURGH CASTLE *Norfolk* Map 5 TG40 *The Castle* Off A143. Massive walls from former 3rd-C fort of the Saxon shore system, guarded by six pear-shaped bastions, Accessible any reasonable time. Free. *(AM)*

BURGHCLERE *Hampshire* Map 4 SU46 *Sandham Memorial Chapel* Off A34. Built 1926–7, and presented to NT in 1947, the walls are covered with paintings by Stanley Spencer and depict war scenes from the Salonika front in 1914–18 War. Open all year (ex 4 Apr, 25 Dec and 1 Jan) daily until 7 pm or sunset; key at adjacent almshouses. Free. *(N*

BURGH-LE-MARSH *Lincolnshire* Map 9 TF56 *Burgh-le-Marsh Windmill* On A158. Five-sailed tower windmill (c 1833), in working order, with four floors for inspection. Completely overhauled. Shop. ⚌ Open all

ear, daily during daylight. Free. ⚠ *(Tel
urgh 281 due to alter to Skegness 810281).
Lindsey County Council)* 🚹 **(79)**
unby Hall 2½m NE off A158. Red-brick
ouse built c 1700 by Sir William
assingberd, with oak staircase, wainscoted
oms, and Reynolds portraits. Formal
ardens and herbaceous borders. House
oen by prior written appointment with *J
Vrisdale, Gunby hall, Gunby, Grantham,
incs.* Garden open Wed afternoons. 70p.
ardens only 50p (ch half-price). *(NT)*

URGHLEY HOUSE *Cambridgeshire*
Map 4 TF00
ngland's greatest Elizabethan house.
ontains painted ceilings, silver, fireplaces,
rgest private collection of Italian Old
asters, Verrio's masterpiece, the Heaven
oom, a miracle of perspective. Burghley
orse trials held in Sep. ⚿ Open 1 Apr to 5
ct, Tue to Thu, Sat, BH 11 – 5, Sun 2 – 5.
dmission prices not yet decided. No dogs. ⚠
Tel Stamford 52451). (Marquess of Exeter).
earby Barnack Church has Saxon Tower
nd 13th-C font. 🚹 park only

URNHAM MARKET *Norfolk* Map 9 TF84
armelite Friary ½m NE Burnham Market on
nclass road, Gatehouse and remains of
armelite Friary founded in 1241 with some
riginal windows and interesting flint and
one panelling. The adjoining farmhouse
corporates a 14th-C doorway and a large
uttress. Open all year. Accessible at all
nes. Free. P. *(Tel Norwich 611122 ext
224)*

URNLEY *Lancashire* Map 7 SD83
*owneley Hall Art Gallery and Museum
nd Museum of Local Crafts and
dustries* 14th-C house with later
odifications. Collection of oil paintings, early
nglish water-colours, period furniture,
ories, 18th-C glassware, archaeology and
atural history. Loan exhibitions from Apr to
ep. Large park with playing fields. Nature
ail. ⚿ Open all year (ex 25 & 26 Dec & 1 Jan
Sat all year), summer Mon – Fri 10 – 5.30,
un 12 – 5; winter Mon – Fri 10 – 5.15, Sun
2 – 5. Free. ⚠ *(Tel 24213)* 🚹 B

URROW BRIDGE *Somerset* Map 3 ST32
umping Station Museum 10m SE of
ridgwater, off A361; approach by turning off
361 opposite King Alfred Hotel, down
nclassified road to River Authority sign by
ver past Lyng farm. Steam pumping engines
1864 and 1869 preserved in excellent
ondition in small museum on River Parrett.
lso antique hand pump and other items.
pen, subject to attendant being available,
on to Fri 9 – 5. Free. ⚠ *(Tel Bridgwater
7333 or Burrow Bridge 324)*

URTON AGNES *Humberside* Map 8 TA16
urton Agnes Hall On A166. Built in 1598,
agnificent Elizabethan house with five
enturies of furniture, pictures, china, and
pestries. Old gatehouse. Woodland
ardens and herbaceous borders on view. ⚿
pen 1 Apr to 31 Oct, daily (ex Sat) 1.45 – 5
, Sun). Hall and gardens 60p (ch 40p).
ardens and grounds only 40p. ⚠ *(Tel 324).*
Mr M Wickham Boynton)* 🚹 B

orman Manor House Dates from 1170 and
eserves original Norman piers and groined
of of a lower chamber. Upper room,
obably 15th-C, and old donkey wheel. Open
y reasonable time. Free. ⚠ *(AM)*

BURTON COURT *Hereford and Worcester*
Map 3 SO45
14th- to 18th-C house with original 14th-C
great hall, and other interesting work. Notable
collection of Chinese and European
costumes, and model fairground exhibition.
⚿ *(teas).* Open Spring BH to mid Sep, Wed,
Thu, Sat, Sun, BH Mon 2.30 – 6. 40p (ch 20p,
coach parites 30p per person). ⚠ *(Tel
Pembridge 231). (Mrs R M Simpson)* 🚹

BURTON UPON TRENT *Staffordshire*
Map 8 SK22
The Bass Museum Horninglow Street.
Housed in the Company's ex joiners shop
dated 1866, a permanent exhibition traces the
development of brewing in Burton from
earliest times up to the present. External
exhibits include a steam locomotive, an
experimental brewhouse and a maltings
engine. Museum shop. ⚿ Open all year (ex
25, 26 Dec) Mon to Fri 10.30 – 4.30, Sat, Sun
and BH 11 – 5. 35p (ch and pen 15p). Party. ⚠
(Tel Burton 42031 during opening hours) 🚹 B
Museum and Art Gallery Guild Street.
Mainly devoted to local history with exhibits
on the area from prehistoric times to the
present day. Also a comprehensive exhibition
of British birds which has been recently
redisplayed. Open all year, daily (ex Sun)
11 – 6, Sat 11 – 5. Free. P. *(Tel 63042)*

BURWASH *East Sussex* Map 5 TQ62
Bateman's 1m SW. Lovely 17th-C house,
once home of Rudyard Kipling (*Puck of
Pook's Hill* was written here). Study remains
as it was during his time here (1902 – 36).
Attractive gardens. Water-mill recently
restored. ⚿ Open Mar to end May and Oct,
daily (ex Fri), 2 – 6; Jun to end Sep, Mon to
Thu 11 – 6, Sat and Sun 2 – 6. 80p. No dogs.
Indoor photography by permission only. *(NT)*

BURY *Gt Manchester* Map 7 SD81
Bury Art Gallery and Museum Moss Street.
Contains a fine collection of 19th-C British
paintings including works by Turner,
Constable and Landseer. The museum
outlines the social history of the town and the
natural history of the area. Open all year ex
Sun and BH. Mon to Fri 10 – 6, Sat 10 – 5.
Free. P. *(Tel 7644110)* 🚹 by appointment.
*Regimental Museum XX The Lancashire
Fusiliers* Wellington Barracks, Bolton Road.
Covers the history of XX The Lancashire
Fusiliers from 1688 to the present day,
including: period uniforms, relics of Napoleon
Bonaparte, who was guarded by the
Regiment at St Helena; relics of Major-
General James Wolfe of Quebec fame and of
Major-General Robert Ross who captured
Washington in the American Wars. There is a
special VC section (this Regiment won more
VCs than any other in the British Army in the
1914 – 18 war), and a collection of
campaigning medals and decorations. Open
all year daily (ex Thu, Sun) 9 – 5. 5p (ch 15 2p).
⚠ *(Tel 2208)* 🚹 B
Transport Museum East Lancashire
Railway Preservation Society. Number of
railway items from the steam age on display,
and it is hoped to operate a train service on
the Bury – Rawtenstall line, now closed by
British Rail. Road exhibits include preserved
buses, fire engines and steam roller. Model
railway, operating and engine in steam last
Sun in each month Mar to Sep, 6/7 Apr,
Spring and Summer BH. ⚿ on steam days.
Open all year Sat, Sun, 7 Apr, Spring and late
Summer BH 11 – 5. 20p (ch 10p). Party. ⚠
Helpers in work of preservation welcomed.
(Tel 061 – 764 7790 during open hours) 🚹 B

BURY ST EDMUNDS *Suffolk* Map 5 TL86
Angel Corner Queen Anne house containing
Gershom-Parkington collection of clocks and
watches. Open all year, daily (ex Christmas
and New Year holidays, also 4 Apr and Sun).
10 – 1 and 2 – 5 (4 Nov to Feb inclusive). Free.
Moyse's Hall Cornhill. Rare 12th-C house,
now museum of Suffolk local history,
archaeology, and natural history. Open all
year, Mon to Sat 10 – 1 and 2 – 5 (4, Nov to
Feb). 20p (ch 15 10p; if accompanied by adult
free, pen 10p, organised school parties 5p
each). P. *(Tel 63233 ext 236)* **(79)**
Norton Bird Gardens A very interesting
collection of foreign birds and waterfowl etc.
Aviaries well designed and planted to create
natural conditions for the birds. Set in 4-acre
garden with flowering bulbs, roses,
herbaceous beds, shrubs and trees. ⚑ Open
all year daily 11 – 7 or dusk. Admission prices
for 1980 not yet available. ⚠ *(Tel Pakenham
30957)* &

BUSCOT *Oxfordshire* Map 4 SU29
Buscot Park Off A417. 18th-C house with
fine collection of paintings and notable water
garden layout. Apr to end Sep, Wed to Fri,
second and fourth Sat and following Sun in
month 2 – 6. (Last admission to house 5.30).
80p (grounds only 40p). No dogs; no indoor
photography. *(NT)*

BUXTON *Derbyshire* Map 7 SK07
Museum and Art Gallery Terrace Road.
Local history, archaeology, and extensive
collections from local caves; local fossils,
minerals, and ornaments of Blue John and
Ashford Marble; ceramics and glass; 19th and
20th-C oil and watercolour paintings, local
maps, prints and photographs. Open all year
Mon to Fri 9.30 – 6 (5, Sat). Free. *(Tel 4658)* &

BYLAND ABBEY *North Yorkshire*
Map 8 SE57
Considerable remains of the church and
monastic buildings dating from late 12th C
and early 13th C. Well preserved glazed tiles.
Open, see inside front cover. 15p (ch 16 and
pen 5p). *(AM)*

GREAT WESTERN

P.K.F.

CADEBY *Leicestershire* Map 4 SK40
Cadeby Light Railway In grounds of Cadeby
Rectory. Probably the smallest of Britain's
narrow gauge railways. Engine normally
running is a 1919 steam saddle tank
locomotive. Other exhibits include a 1927
Foster Traction Engine and three steam
rollers from 1903 onwards. Exhibition model
railway in 4mm scale representing the Great
Western Railway in South Devon of about
1935. Music Festival in Nov. Catering by prio
arrangement. Open all year on second Sat of
each month 2 – 5.30. Free. P. (Roadside). *(Te
Market Bosworth 290462)* &

CAISTER-ON-SEA *Norfolk* Map 9 TG51
*Caister Castle, Motor Museum, Tower, an
Grounds* Off A1064. Purpose-built Motor
Museum contains vehicles of all ages from
1896 to present day, set out in easy to view
'arena' type building. Moated castle ruins
(home of Shakespeare's Sir John Falstaff an
where many of the 'Paston Letters' were

The Mighty Engine . . .

Hurrah for the mighty engine:
As he bounds along his track;
Hurrah for the life that is in him,
And his breath so thick and black.
And hurrah for our fellows,
    who in their need
Could fashion a thing like him –
With a heart of fire, and a soul
    of steel
And a Samson in every limb.

Alexander Anderson (19th-century navvy poet)

Railway preservation has come a long way since the pioneer days of the Bluebell and Festiniog lines twenty years ago. Today, it is difficult to estimate the total number of railway enthusiasts, but it is certain that interest in railways and preservation has been growing steadily. In Britain, almost every county has its own preserved railway or steam centre. The numbers of visitors can be measured in millions each year, and the value of assets in land and equipment runs into tens of millions of pounds. Even British Rail, whose elimination of steam in 1968 and total ban on movement of preserved locomotives in steam represented the nadir of preservationists' hopes, has passed through a relaxation of the ban to positive indulgence by the passing of nearly 1,000 miles of secondary lines for regular steam-hauled railtours and

Steam hauled railtour: LMS Jubilee Loco 5596 Bahamas at Ludlow Station.

even the hiring back of some of its former locos for its own steam tours.

Preservation takes many forms – standard gauge, narrow gauge and miniature; as museum exhibits, working at a steam centre or on a preserved railway, or on a BR line hauling railtours. It is not confined solely to steam, as there is considerable interest in diesel locos and a fair number are preserved with the prospect, as they are withdrawn by BR, of more to come. Nor is it confined to locos, either. Rolling stock, civil engineering and railway architecture, and signalling are equally important and all are well represented. In fact, because the enthusiast interest is there, it will (subject to continued public interest), in the years to come, be the preserved railways rather than the museums which will maintain the historic traditions and atmosphere of Britain's long, varied and pioneering railway industry.

As most people are likely to visit and travel on a preserved standard gauge railway, it is worthwhile giving an examination of the main components of such a line. Of greatest concern to the passenger will be the steam or diesel motive power, followed closely by the appearance and comfort of the rolling stock. Less obvious, but vitally important, is the signalling while also in the background will be the

Locomotive scrapyard at Barry, South Wales.

civil engineering element. Lastly, and the key to the entire operation, will be the organisation itself and its management of paid staff and volunteers.

There is a good chance that whichever standard gauge line or steam centre you visit you will see at least one loco from the now world-famous Woodham's scrapyard at Barry in South Wales. Of more than 250 ex BR steam locos preserved in Britain, over 100 have been rescued from this yard and many are now in working order.

Restoration problems of an ex Barry loco well illustrate the standard of mechanical overhaul required if it is to haul public passenger trains or pass the critical examinations of BR inspectors for operating on steam railtours. The boiler has to be lifted out of the frames for examination of the firebox, and all flue and steam tubes replaced before hydraulic pressure testing of the shell. Bogies, wheel tyres, axleboxes, brakes, cylinders and valve gear have to be checked and overhauled, and all essential parts such as missing coupling rods, gauges, safety valves, injectors etc obtained or manufactured. Sometimes this work is done in purpose-built workshops such as at Sheffield Park (Bluebell), but usually, for lack of facilities, carried out in the open. Restoration takes up to five years and can cost between ten and thirty thousand pounds.

Passenger rolling stock is of two distinct types. Firstly, there are the ex-BR Mark 1 main-line and suburban coaches of a standard design dating from the late 1950s. These are available in large numbers and require relatively little restoration. Secondly, are the historically more interesting coaches of pre-Nationalisation origin, such as the Stanier straight-sided type (LMS), Gresley varnished teak coaches of the LNER, Collett and Hawksworth coaches of the GWR in chocolate and cream, and the Maunsell and later Bulleid malachite green coaches of the Southern. Almost all were scrapped by the late 1960s, but a few still survive.

For these older coaches, restoration is a daunting task which can take skilled volunteers up to a year to complete and add several thousand pounds to the original cost. Body panels, roof, floor, bogies and all timber framing have to be examined and possibly replaced, and seats (upholstered in the correct material), compartments, wiring, plumbing and all the other fittings which go into a 40-year-old carriage have to be re-instated. Finally, there is the repetitive job of painting, lining and varnishing. Some of the finest examples of restored coaching stock in this group may be seen at Didcot (GWR) and on the Severn Valley Railway (GWR and LMS) and Bluebell Line (Southern).

Restored coach.   Severn Valley Railway. ▶

In addition, there are many contemporary and earlier miscellaneous passenger vehicles (4- and 6-wheelers, dining and sleeping cars etc) undergoing restoration to complement the historic collection on display at the National Railway Museum, York.

The track, or permanent way, has to be maintained to a high standard and this requires regular attention to rails, chairs, sleepers, ballast and drainage. Replacement of rotten timber sleepers is a frequent task and where possible is done with second-hand concrete sleepers. The North York Moors Railway, Britain's second largest preserved line at 18 miles, has 38,000 sleepers, and a replacement programme extending over eight or nine years. The ballast must be maintained in good condition to prevent any movement of the track and it, as well as embankments and cuttings, have to be well-drained to prevent water-logging or earth slips.

The civil engineering aspect of a preserved railway will cover the stations, goods and locomotive sheds, workshops and carriage sheds, over- and underline bridges, viaducts and tunnels. Over-bridges are sometimes the responsibility of the county council, but underline structures are the owning railway's responsibility and the cost of replacing a life-expired wrought iron bridge with steel or concrete is considerable. Several lines have substantial stone or wrought iron viaducts, notable examples being the massive single-span of the Victoria Bridge across the River Severn (Severn Valley Railway) and the Swithland Reservoir viaducts on the Main Line Steam Trust, south of Loughborough.

Tunnels can be found on the Keighley and Worth Valley, North York Moors, Dart Valley Railway (Torbay Section) and Severn Valley Railway. The most spectacular of any line for engineering works is the Festiniog which has completed the 'Deviation' route from Dduallt up to Tan-y-Grisiau. Involving the construction of a spiral (a unique feature in Britain), a 300-yard tunnel (17 months' work) and a new route and bridges behind the CEGB power station, it has cost over a million pounds, (the direct cost to the Festiniog being far less as a result of compensation, grants and volunteer labour).

Stations are a most important feature and have a character of their own as each railway company had its own special style of architecture. British Rail has found this out to their cost, with several hundred station buildings listed as being of architectural or historical interest. Often preservation companies will try to maintain the pre-Nationalisation or even pre-Grouping character of their lines with locos and rolling stock in, for example, Great Western or LNER livery and will select one or more stations for restoration in a Victorian or Edwardian setting. Outstanding examples are Sheffield Park (Bluebell), Highley (Severn Valley), Rothley (Main Line Steam Trust), Ropley (Mid-Hants) and on the North York Moors Railway, which will re-create throughout an early 20th-century North Eastern setting.

Signalling and all traffic movements have to be operated under DoT regulations and so the signalling visible on a line is definitely not there as a colourful decoration. However, decoration is present because of the individuality of design of the original railway companies' signalling equipment. Signal posts can be of wood, tubular steel, steel lattice, concrete or double rail bolted together, and each can be topped off with an elaborate company finial. Signal boxes varied in design and construction from one company to another, and could be built of timber, a combination of timber and brick or stone, or entirely of brick or stone. Two of the largest so far preserved are at Loughborough (MLST) and Wansford (Nene Valley Railway).

All railways require a great number of staff to run them. Drivers, firemen, guards, ticket inspectors, station managers and car park, ticket office, refreshment and sales attendants are in the fore-front, but, in the background and not to be forgotten, are the carriage and wagon, permanent way and signalling and telegraph staff and the loco fitters and restorers as well as the general administration and publicity people. At first most of these jobs were undertaken by volunteers, but with the increasing professionalism that is needed by commercial pressures, administration and sheer volume of work, an increasing number of full-time staff is being employed. Some preserved railways started off being owned by volunteers in a society, and partly

...rough choice have remained unaltered, resisting to this day, the commercial pressures which have transformed others. This is revealed in the difference between the Talyllyn Railway and the Festiniog. The latter, like the Severn Valley Railway, has developed into a commercial company and will carry out whatever modifications are necessary in order to handle the maximum number of passengers.

The third type of preserved railway is the one where enforced closure of a line by BR after a long fight by protesters has led to the forming of a society and company at the same time, with the intention of purchasing through public subscription the entire line and reopening it to fulfill a social need, with steam operation as a profit-making attraction at weekends. Two lines in this category are the Mid-Hants which has, so far, raised an incredible £120,000 of public money (but regrettably because of British Rail's valuation of the Alton-Winchester route at over £300,000 have had to considerably reduce their ambitions and operate a weekend steam service only) and the West Somerset Railway, who are in the relatively fortunate position of leasing the entire route from the Somerset County Council who bought the track bed. They have been more successful in providing a service for the local community with regular daily diesel multiple unit trains.

Most railway companies have in addition to their own paid staff the backing of their own railway preservation societies who cater for the railway enthusiasts and co-ordinate the volunteer labour. Membership of individual societies varies, but can be up to six or even thousand. Drivers, firemen, guards etc have to be rostered and therefore give up a lot of time. Others will give up entire summer holidays to help out, and subject to interest and qualification, can be put under supervision, usually from current or ex-BR staff, to do any job on the line. However, that does not mean that any enthusiastic amateur can be put in charge of a locomotive. In fact, the opposite is the case. All standard gauge railways conveying the general public have to be examined by the Railway Inspectorate of the Department of Transport before a Light Railway Order is granted for them to operate passenger trains. This limits train speeds to a maximum of 25 mph and, in addition, locos, rolling stock, track, signalling and structures with public access have to be up to the required standards of safety, and the operation of passenger trains has to meet requirements very similar to those on British Rail. Drivers, firemen, guards and signalmen have to undertake the same type of training as on BR, pass the same examinations and operate with the same rule books.

The railway preservation movement as a whole is now regarded as a major tourist attraction, and therefore we will now attempt to list what there is to be seen and where it can be found. England contains too many locations to be covered geographically, so the places will be categorised, but Wales, Scotland and the Isle of Man, will be covered individually.

Starting in England with the operational ex-BR lines, there are, firstly, in the North, the Lakeside and Haverthwaite Railway (Lake District) (p 116), Keighley and Worth Valley Railway which passes through the Brontë town of Haworth (p 116), and the North Yorkshire Moors Railway from Grosmont to Pickering (p 162). In the Midlands there is perhaps the 'premier' line, the Severn Valley Railway from Bridgnorth to Bewdley (p 58), at Loughborough the Great Central Railway Ltd (Main Line Steam Trust) which operates

Welshpool and Llanfair Railway

North Yorks Moors Railway rolling stock.

from Loughborough to Rothley (p 146), and at nearby Shackerstone, the Market Bosworth Light Railway (p 149). In East Anglia there are the Nene Valley Railway from Peterborough westwards to Wansford (p 196), and at Sheringham near Cromer, the North Norfolk Railway running to Weybourne (p 177).

There are no working lines in the London area, but in the South-East are the Mid-Hants Railway (Watercress Line) from Ropley to Alresford near Winchester (p 39), the Bluebell at Sheffield Park near East Grinstead (p 176), and the Kent and East Sussex line at Tenterden (p 191). Southern and South-West England have four lines – the Isle of Wight Steam Railway (Haven Street to Wootton) (p 209), the West Somerset (Britain's longest preserved line at 23 miles) from Minehead almost into Taunton (p 151) and the two scenically magnificent sections of the Dart Valley Railway in Devon (p 61) from Buckfastleigh to Totnes, and Paignton to Kingswear.

Moving on to steam depots and preservation centres, these can be found in the North-West at Carnforth ('Steamtown' is the largest

BR loco depot in private ownership, and provides motive power
British Rail and other railtours) (p 83), Southport ('Steamport' is
ther ex-BR depot) (p 181), Bury (East Lancs RPS) (p 63) and in
Manchester area at the Dinting Railway Centre near Glossop
other railtour depot) (p 99). In the West Midlands there are the
lmer Railway Centre, Hereford (railtour depot) (p 118) and the
mingham Railway Museum, Tyseley (railtour depot) (p 52).

In Central, Southern and South-East England, there are the
wty Railway Preservation Society, Ashchurch near Tewkesbury
41); the Great Western Society's Didcot Railway Centre (ex GW
o-depot) (p 99), Quainton Railway Centre near Aylesbury (p 165),
Stour Valley RPS at Chappel and Wakes Colne Station near
lbury (p 85) and the Bressingham Steam Centre at Diss in Norfolk
57).

The next major group are the societies and companies intending
elay track or who have not yet obtained a Light Railway Order.
is includes the Yorkshire Dales Railway at Embsay near Skipton;
mbrian Railway Society at Oswestry; Peak Railway Society at
tlock; North Staffordshire Railway Society at Cheddleton, near
ek; Midland Railway Centre at Butterley near Nottingham; Dean
rest Railway at Lydney (p 147), the East Somerset Railway at
nmore near Shepton Mallet (p 95); the Bitton Railway Centre at
stol; the Colne Valley Railway Society at Castle Hedingham in
sex (p 85) and the Swanage Railway Society in Dorset.

Of mainly industrial interest are the Bowes and Tanfield
ilways near Gateshead, the North of England Open-Air Museum at
amish, Co Durham (p 47), the Middleton Colliery Railway in
eds (p 129), the Foxfield Light Railway near Cheadle (p 99) and
Chasewater Light Railway near Brownhills (p 61), both in Staffs.
the South, steam is to be found at the Bristol Industrial Museum
59), at Quainton, which has the greatest number of industrial

t Valley Railway (Torbay Section)   Midland Railway 2–4–0 loco at
gswear Station loco 4588.   Butterley.

steam locos, and at the Cornish RPS depot at Bugle.

In addition to the world-famous National Railway Museum at York (p 207) which also acts as a steam centre for BR railtours, the following museums contain locos:
The Science Museum, London (p 139); Great Western Railway Museum, Swindon (p 53); Birmingham Science Museum (p 188); North Road Station Museum, Darlington (p 97) which houses Stockton and Darlington Railway relics and the Tiverton Museum, Devon (p 192).

For anyone interested in standard gauge railway relics, there are the following: Winchcombe Railway Museum, near Cheltenham; P Four Railway Museum, Bournemouth (p 55); Monkwearmouth Station Museum, Sunderland (p 187) and the South Devon Railway Museum, Dawlish Warren Station (p 98).

Diesel motive power is to be found on the North Yorkshire Moors line which has five, the Severn Valley Railway (two), West Somerset (one), Didcot Railway Centre (one), and BR Engineering Swindon Works (on open days only) (two). They consist mainly of the famous 'Western' class. These and other lines are likely to take on

Didcot Steam Centre.

re types as they are withdrawn from British Rail. The NYMR,
ighley and Worth Valley and West Somerset also operate diesel
ltiple units and railbuses.

For narrow gauge enthusiasts, the following will be of interest:
e Motive Power Museum, Lytham St Annes; Cadeby Light
lway, Cadeby (p 64); Whipsnade and Umfolozi (Whipsnade Zoo)
200) and Leighton Buzzard Narrow Gauge Railways (p 130),
colnshire Coast Light Railway, Cleethorpes (p 91); Sittingbourne
l Kemsley Light Railway, Kent; Brockham Museum, near
rking; Hollycombe Steam Museum, near Liphook (p 133); Bicton
odland Railway, Bicton Gardens, near Sidmouth (p 51); Lappa
ley Railway near Newquay (p 172) and the Bressingham Steam
itre at Diss which also has narrow gauge and miniature railways.

Miniature railways (18-inch gauge down to 7¼-inch) fans should
t the following: Ravenglass and Eskdale (Lake District) (p 165)
l Romney, Hythe and Dymchurch Railway, Kent (p 155), which
iough of only 15-inch gauge are in a class of their own and more
nparable to the Welsh two-foot gauge lines; Hilton Valley Railway
Veston Park (p 199); Stapleford Park Miniature Railway (p 183),
cestershire; Oakhill Manor Railway near Shepton Mallet (p 158);
orama at Beer, (p 48) and the unique Forest Railway at Dobwalls
)9).

tored locomotive (diesel) D1062 Western Courier (now in operation on SVR).

Finally, for devotees of trams, there are, in addition to the Blackpool line, the Crich Tramway Museum, Derbyshire (p 95); the Beamish Open-Air Museum system (p 47) and the narrow gauge tramway from Seaton to Colyton, Devon.

The eight Welsh narrow gauge lines (see *AA Touring Guide to Wales*) are as healthy and as popular as ever and are being joined by the Welsh Highland Railway at Porthmadog. The Festiniog has reached Tan-y-Grisiau and is now within $1\frac{1}{2}$ miles of its destination at Blaenau Festiniog, where, under a joint scheme with British Rail and local councils, it will run into a new station providing a unique cross-Snowdonia rail-link from Porthmadog to Llandudno Junction.

Other developments include the first standard gauge line in Wales, the Gwili Railway, north of Carmarthen (p 215), and the restoration of Llangollen Station by the Flint and Deeside group and their relaying of track westwards along the beautiful Dee Valley towards Corwen. Elsewhere, locos and railway items are to be found at the industrial museums in Cardiff and Swansea, the Corris Railway Museum, Corris (p 218), the Conwy Valley Railway Museum, Betws-y-Coed (p 214); the Caerphilly Railway Society; the Great Orme Tramway, Llandudno, and Penrhyn Castle Museum, Bangor (p 214).

Dduallt Station, Festiniog Railway.   Llanberis Lake Railway

In Scotland the Strathspey Railway (p 233) has opened up five miles of line along the lovely Spey valley from Aviemore to Boat of Garten. Having obtained the original steam shed at Aviemore, they are now concentrating on completing the new passenger station then Scotland's other major steam organisation, the Scottish Railway Preservation Society, now have approval for an ambitious new steam centre and passenger line at Bo'ness on the Firth of Forth which will involve withdrawal in the near future from their present headquarte at Falkirk. Also in Scotland is the smaller Lochty Railway in Fife, a of a static nature is the historic collection of Scottish railway companies' locos in the Glasgow Transport Museum (p 242).

Lastly, and in a 'world of its own' is the Isle of Man which has three separate systems: the three-foot gauge steam IoM Railway (no reduced to Douglas–Port Erin) and the two electric tramway system the Manx Electric and Snaefell Mountain Railways.

A brochure and timetable covering the Welsh narrow gauge lin and called *The Great Little Trains of Wales* is available from the Narrow Gauge Railways of Wales Joint Marketing Panel, c/o Wharf Station, Tywyn, Gwynedd.

Further information on any of the railways mentioned may be obtained from the Association of Railway Preservation Societies (Sheringham Station, Norfolk, Tel 0263 822045), who publish a brochure entitled *The 1980 Guide to Steam Trains in the British Isles*, you could consult the map-guide *Steam in Britain* published by the BTA.

1980 is a momentous year for railway preservation, as it will se the 150th anniversary of the opening of the Liverpool and Manchester Railway in 1830. Events planned throughout the year will include permanent exhibitions at Rainhill and Earlestown until October, tours of the original station facilities and exhibitions at Edg Hill, Liverpool and Liverpool Road, Manchester, steam-hauled railtours between Liverpool and Manchester on Sundays from June August, and the highlight will be the re-enactment at Rainhill near S Helens of the Locomotive Trials of 1829 on each of the three days of the Spring Bank Holiday, in which newly constructed replicas of Stephenson's 'Rocket' and other early locos will take part. This will followed by a grand cavalcade of preserved steam, diesel and electric locos.

Further details should be available from main BR stations (or direct from 'Rocket' 150, BR, Room 405, Rail House, Lord Nelsor Street, Liverpool), Tourist Info Centres and the railway press.

written), 98ft-tower. 1951 Festival of Britain
Tree Walk removed from Battersea Park. ⚲
Museum, grounds and tea-rooms open mid
May to end Sep, daily (ex Sat) 10.30–5.
Admission prices not yet known for 1980.
Dogs on lead only. ⚠ *(Tel Wymondham 251).*
(Dr P R Hill JP CC D Tech)
Roman Town On A1064. South gateway,
town wall built of flint concrete with brick
bonding courses, and part of what may have
been a seaman's hostel. Open, see inside
front cover. Free. *(AM)*

CALNE *Wiltshire* Map 3 ST96
Bowood 2m W off A4. Georgian house of
magnificent proportions dating from Henry
Keene (1754), including additions by Robert
Adam, C R Cockerell and Sir Charles Barry.
Rooms open to visitors include the laboratory
where Dr Joseph Priestley discovered
oxygen (1774), Orangery/picture gallery,
Chapel, Sculpture Gallery and three newly
converted exhibition rooms. Pleasure
grounds and gardens extend over 100 acres
and include Capability Brown's lake, cascade
and grottos. Adventure play area, shop ⚲ and
restaurant. Open 4 Apr to end Sep daily (ex
Mon) but including BH 2–6, Sun and BH
12–6. £1.15 (ch and pen 60p).
Rhododendron walks off A342. 50 acres open
mid May to mid Jun, daily (ex Mon) but
including Spring BH 2–6. 70p (ch and pen
35p). ⚠ *(Tel 812102). (The Earl of
Shelburne)* ⅁ B

CALSTOCK *Cornwall* Map 2 SX46
Cotehele House 2m W on W bank of Tamar.
8m SW of Tavistock, off A390. Granite house
of 1485 to 1627 built around two courts,
formerly home of Earls of Mount Edgcumbe.
Beautiful gardens on different levels,
including Victorian terraces, shrub garden,

and medieval dovecote. There is restored
Morden Mill, the manorial watermill in valley
below. House contains 17th- and early 18th-C
armour, furniture, and tapestry. ⚲ Open 1 Apr
to end Oct, Tue to Sun (house only closed
Mon ex BH Mon) 11–6 (last admissions
5.30); Nov to Mar garden only open during
daylight hours. House, garden and mill £1.50;
garden, grounds and mill 90p. *(NT)*
CAMBERLEY *Surrey* Map 4 SU86
Camberley Museum Knoll Road. Contains
exhibits on local history, archaeology,
costume, flora and fauna, and notable
persons including Bret Harte, Ethel Smythe,
Sir Arthur Sullivan and Admiral John Sturdee.
Open all year Tue to Fri 2–5, Sat 10–12 and
2–4. Free. ⚠ *(Tel 64483)* ⅁
**National Army Museum, Sandhurst
Departments** RMA Sandhurst. The Indian
Army Memorial Room and the Hastings
Room house collections of uniforms, medals,
weapons, silver and paintings connected with
the army of the East India Company and the
Indian Army from their early days up to 1947.
A similar collection devoted to the Irish
regiments disbanded in 1922 is located
nearby in the Blenheim wing of Old College.
Open by appointment (closed 24 to 26 Dec; 1
Jan; 4 Apr and certain ceremonial occasions)
10–5 (Sun 11–5). Free. ⚠ *(Tel 63344 ext
485)* ⅁ B
CAMBO *Northumberland* Map 12 NZ08
Wallington 1m S on B6342. 17th- and 18th-C
house with rococo plasterwork, and a central
hall added in the 19th C, situated in a great
moorland estate of over 12,000 acres rising to
an altitude of over 1,000ft. Additional rooms
opened up 1968/69. Magnificent fuchsias in
conservatory in walled garden. ⚲ Open:
House Apr to end Sep daily ex Tue, 1–6; Oct,
Wed, Sat and Sun 2–5. Grounds open all

year. House and grounds £1.20. Grounds Apr to Sep 50p, Oct, Sat and Sun 50p. Free remainder of year. *(NT)*

CAMBRIDGE *Cambridgeshire* Map 5 TL45
Ancient University city on the River Cam. Many of the colleges line the East bank, overlooking the Backs: sweeping lawns set with willow trees, on the opposite side of river transformed from rough marshland by Richard Bently (Master of Trinity College from 1699 to 1734). The colleges are open to the public on most days during daylight though there are some restrictions during term time.
Cambridge and County Folk Museum
Castle Street. Formerly White Horse Inn, exhibits include domestic objects, toys, furniture and agricultural tools, and large collection of pictures and photographs relating to county. Open all year (ex BH), Tue to Fri 10.30–5, Sat 10.30–1 & 2–5, Sun 2.30–4.30. 25p (ch 16 and pen 10p). P street (meters). Coach car park (free) at top of Castle Street. *(Tel 355159)*
Fitzwilliam Museum Trumpington Street. Exhibits extensive art and archaeological collections including Egyptian, Greek and Roman antiquities, coins, medals, European paintings, Medieval and literary manuscripts, ceramics, textiles, Medieval and Renaissance *objets d'art*, arms and armour and a library. ⚓ Tue to Sat 10.30–4. Upper or lower floor open all year Tue to Sat 10–5, Sun 2.15–5. Closed Mon (ex 7 Apr, 26 May, 25 Aug) 4 Apr and 24 Dec to 1 Jan inclusive. Free. P. *(Tel 69501)* ⅏ (advance notice)
Jesus College Founded in 1496 by Bishop Alcock of Ely in the former Benedictine nunnery of St Radegund, which he had suppressed and taken over. Several of the buildings retained their former uses (the chapel remaining a chapel, the refectory became the dining room) but were also improved and added to, including an extra storey on the living quarters.
King's College A complex of buildings overlooking the banks of the Cam. The magnificent chapel is the only complete medieval part of this college built in 1441–1515 in Perpendicular style. It retains all its original stained glass and contains Rubens' Adoration of the Magi. Subsequent buildings belong mainly to the 19th C, apart from the Gibbs Building, a fine Classical addition begun in 1723
St John's College Founded 1511 by Lady Margaret Beaufort, mother of Henry VII. It consists of three red-brick courts with a fine gate-tower, 17th-C library and chapel designed by Sir Gilbert Scott
Museum of Archaeology and Anthropology Downing Street. Covers prehistoric archaeology of the world in general, with section on Cambridge area from Stone Age to Middle Ages, and cultures of the peoples of the Americas, Africa, the Pacific and South-East Asia. Open all year (ex Christmas, Easter week and Suns), Mon to Fri 2–4, Sat 9.30–12.30. Free. P. *(Tel 59714)*
Scott Polar Research Institute Lensfield Road. Museum of Polar exploration and research. Contains relics, manuscripts, paintings, photographs, etc relating to Arctic and Antarctic expeditions, with special emphasis on the expeditions of Captain Scott. Also contains displays illustrating polar native peoples, Eskimo art, and modern scientific exploration. Open all year Mon to Sat 2.30–4. Free. ⚠ *(Tel 66499)*
Trinity College The early college comprised two adjacent elements, King's Hall founded

by Edward II 1317 and Michaelhouse founded 1323. They were consolidated into one unit in 1546, when Henry VIII disbanded Michaelhouse at the Dissolution. Remnants of these buildings are still visible. The various buildings of differing dates were converted into two quadrangles by further additions in 1593–7 by Thomas Nevile. The library, begun in 1676 to designs by Sir Christopher Wren, formed a fourth side to Nevile's Court, the smaller of the two quadrangles.
University Botanic Garden Trumpington Road. Original site of 5 acres founded in 1762, present area of 40 acres being acquired in 1831. Fine botanical collections. Open all year (except Christmas Day and Boxing Day), weekdays 8–7.30 (dusk in winter); Sun 10–6.30 (key holders) 2.30–6.30 (non-key holders May to Sep only); glasshouses 2–5 (or dusk). Free (£1 returnable deposit charged for keys on Sun; keys issued on professional reference only – particulars from Director). No dogs or bicycles. P (limited street). *(Tel 350101)* ⅏

CAMELFORD *Cornwall* Map 2 SX18
North Cornwall Museum and Gallery The Clease. Museum of rural life with sections on agriculture, slate and granite quarrying, blacksmith's and wheelwright's tools, cobbling, dairy and domestic scene including a collection of bonnets. The gallery holds various exhibitions. Open 1 Apr to 30 Sep, Mon to Sat 10.30–5. Closed Sun. 30p (ch 16 5p). P. *(Tel 3229)*

CANFORD CLIFFS *Dorset* Map 4 SZ08
Compton Acres Gardens On B3065. Rock and water gardens, and heather, Japanese, Roman, English and Italian gardens covering 15 acres, with fine views over Poole Harbour and Purbeck Hills. ⚓ Open 1 Apr to end of Oct, daily 10.30–6.30 (Jun to Aug, Thu until dusk). 60p (ch 35p). No dogs or radios. Picnic area. ⚠ *(Tel 708036)* ⅏

CANTERBURY *Kent* Map 5 TR15
Eastbridge (St Thomas's) Hospital 25 High Street. Dating from 12th C, one of the oldest buildings in city, used partly as almshouses since 16th C. Flint-faced façade has 14th-C windows, refectory has 13th-C mural. There are two chapels and a vaulted undercroft noted in the Norman Heritage Trail 'in the steps of the Conqueror'. Open all year (ex 4 Apr and 25 Dec), 10–1 and 2–5, Sun 11–1 and 2–5. Free.
Greyfriars Friary Off Stour Street. By River Stour. Recently restored 13th-C remains of first friary of Franciscan movement. Open in summer, Mon to Sat 12–1 and 2–5. 10p (ch and pen 5p). Parties by arrangement. *(Tel 622292)* ⅏
Howe Barracks Contains exhibits of all the former county regiments of Kent, Surrey, Sussex and Middlesex from which the Queen's Regiment was formed on 31 Dec 1966. Open all year Mon to Fri (ex BH) 10–12 and 2–4, other times by appointment. Regimental shop. Free. ⚠ *(Tel 65281 ext 30)*
Roman Pavement Butchery Lane. Part of a Roman town house, with mosaic floor and hypocaust, excavated after war damage and incorporated into rebuilding. Displays of Roman finds, mainly local, of pottery, coins, jewellery and small objects. Open Apr to Sep, weekdays 10–1 and 2–5; Oct to Mar, weekdays 2–4. 15p (ch 10p). Under revision for 1980. *(Tel 52747)*
Royal Museum, Art Gallery and Buffs Regimental Museum High Street. The archaeology of east Kent, including the

Roman silver spoon hoard, Roman coin hoard, Anglo Saxon glass and jewellery with the silver 'Canterbury Cross'; paintings include works by local artist Sidney Cooper, engravings and photographs; collections of medals, uniforms, weapons and trophies of the Royal East Kent Regiment. Monthly changing exhibitions. Open all year, weekdays 10–5. Free. *(Tel 52747)*

St Augustine's Abbey Founded by St Augustine on land given by King Ethelbert in 598 foundations of a 7th-C church. Remains of 11th-C round church underlie extensive ruins of medieval Benedictine abbey. Open, see inside front cover, Sun all year from 9.30. 15p (ch 16 and pen 5p). *(AM)*

West Gate Museum 14th-C gateway, last of city's gates to survive: displays and material relating to the gatehouse in the city wall system, and to its use as a gaol, with cells, handcuffs, manacles, etc. Open Apr to Sep, weekdays 10–1 and 2–5; Oct to Mar, weekdays 2–4. 15p (ch 10p). Under revision for 1980. *(Tel 52747)*

CANVEY ISLAND *Essex* Map 5 TQ78
Dutch Cottage Museum A130. One of two early 17th-C thatched, octagonal cottages of Dutch design, probably erected when Vermuyden was reclaiming the island with a sea-wall. Exhibits of furnishings and models of shipping used on Thames from earliest times. Also small but fine collection of corn dollies. Open Spring BH to end Sep, Wed, Sat, and Sun 2.30–5, BH 10–1 and 2–5. Parties by arrangement. Free. ⚠ limited. *(Tel South Benfleet 52368)* **(79)**

CAPESTHORNE *Cheshire* Map 7 SJ87
Capesthorne Hall On main London–Manchester road (A34), near Jodrell Bank radio telescope. The home of the Bromley-Davenport family, built in 1722 and altered later by Blore and Salvin, with pictures, ancient vases, furniture, silver and Americana. The adjoining chapel is believed to be by John Wood of Bath, and if this is so, it appears to be his earliest surviving work. ⊡ 3–6 on open days. Open 25 Mar to Sep Suns 2–5; May to Sep Wed and Sat 2–5; 24 Jul to 13 Sep Tue & Thu 2–4. Parties at other times by arrangement. 80p (ch 40p), gardens only 40p (ch 20p). Dogs allowed in park only. ⚠ Further information from *Hall Manager, Capesthorne Hall, Macclesfield, Cheshire SK11 9JY. (Tel Chelford 221). (Lt-Col Sir Walter H Bromley-Davenport TD DL)*

CARLISLE *Cumbria* Map 11 NY45
Carlisle Castle Restored castle and dungeons built by William II in 1092, but dating mainly from 12th-C. Open*, see inside front cover. 50p winter 25p (ch 16 and pen

20p winter 10p). ⚠ *(AM)* Also **The Border Regiment and King's Own Royal Border Regiment Museum** Queen Mary's Tower. 300 years of the Regiment's history depicted in trophies, models, weapons, medals, silver, documents, pictures and prints, together with the story of Cumbria's part-time soldiers. Open as castle. No extra admission charge. ⚠ *(Tel 32774)*

The Guildhall Greenmarket. A splendid and recently renovated early 15th-C timbered building containing displays about Guild, Civic and local history. Open May to Aug Mon to Fri 10–6, Sat 10–5. Winter Mon to Sat 10–4. Free

Museum and Art Gallery Castle Street, Housed in Tullie House, a 17th-C town house, is the Regional Collection of Cumbrian Archaeology (especially Roman) and Natural History; British paintings (19th and 20th-C); English porcelain, costume, toys and dolls, musical instruments. Temporary Exhibitions. Open Apr to Sep Mon to Fri 9–7 (5 winter), Sat 9–5, Sun 2.30–5 Jun to Aug only. Free. *(Tel 34781)*

The Prior's Room Prior's Tower, Cathedral grounds. The 13th-C tower has a first-floor room domesticated by Prior Senhouse *c* 1510, with remarkable painted ceiling of 45 panels bearing devices of Cumbrian families. Also interesting bosses and inscriptions. Admission from Cathedral. Open Mon to Sat 2–5 (May to Sep 10–9) Suns by appointment. 10p (ch 14, 5p). P

CARNFORTH *Lancashire* Map 7 SD47
Steamtown Railway Museum Former British Rail motive power depot. A complete large engine shed housing 30 steam locomotives of all sizes, from Great Britain, France and Germany. Home of the famous 'Flying Scotsman'. Gift shop and ⊡ Open daily (ex 25 Dec) 9–5. Steam days Sun Easter to Oct, daily Jul, Aug and BH. 50p (ch and pen 25p), rises to 70p (ch and pen 30p) when locos are in steam, for rides in vintage coaches. ⚠ *(Tel 4220)*

CARRAWBROUGH *Northumberland* Map 12 NY87
Roman Wall (Mithraic Temple) On B6318. Remains of Mithraic temple measuring only 35ft by 15ft, dating from 3rd C but with later alterations, on line of Roman Wall near fort of 'Procolitia'. Excavations in 1950 revealed three dedicatory altars to Mithras and figure of the Mother Goddess. Open any reasonable time. Free. ⚠ *(AM)*

CARTMEL *Cumbria* Map 7 SD37
Priory Gatehouse Off B5277. Only remaining fragment, apart from the church, of 14th-C Augustinian Priory, formerly a school,

now a local craft shop. Open daily. Christmas at reasonable hours. Free. *(NT)*

CASTLE ACRE *Norfolk* Map 9 TF81
Earthworks of former castle, slight remains of keep, and 13th-C Bailey from fortified borough. Admission free at any reasonable time. Remains of late 11th-C priory, including 12th-C church noted for its arcaded west front, 11th-C Prior's Lodging, and early 16th-C gatehouse. 20p (ch 16 and pen 5p). Priory open*, see inside front cover. ⚠ *(AM)*

CASTLE ASHBY *Northamptonshire*
Map 4 SP85
Castle Ashby House Off A428. In fine grounds, 16th- to 17th-C mansion with interior noted for pictures, furnishings, and 17th-C woodwork, including chimney pieces and moulded ceilings; outstanding private

collection of Greek vases. South front added by Inigo Jones. Lettered stone parapet (1624) surrounds house, and grounds and terraces date largely from 1860. Gift shop. ⬛ Open 4 to 13 Apr then 1 Jul to 31 Aug daily 2–5. Sun and BH 11–5. Admission prices not available. *(Tel Yardley Hastings 332). (The Marquess of Northampton)*

CASTLE BOLTON *West Yorkshire*
Map 7 SE09
Dates from 1379–97, part restored to original state this century, in pretty Wensleydale setting. Former stronghold of the Scropes, prison of Mary, Queen of Scots, 1568–69, and besieged and taken in 1645 by Parliament forces. Copy of original Dales kitchen. ⬛ (licensed). Open all year, daily (ex Mon) during daylight hours. 30p (ch 15p) ⚠ *(Tel Wensleydale 23408)*

ASTLE DONINGTON *Leicestershire*
ap 8 SK42
e Donington Collection Houses the
orld's largest collection (over 80) of single-
ater racing cars and over 60 vehicles
vering the development of Leyland cars
d many other transport exhibits. Also
itain's newest motor racing circuit. ♫ Open
 year (ex Christmas week) daily 10–6.
.65 (ch 15 5o p, ch 7 free). ⚠ *(Tel Derby
0048)* Ᏹ

ASTLE HEDINGHAM *Essex* Map 5 TL73
olne Valley Railway and Museum* Access
site is on A604 between Castle Hedingham
d Great Yeldham. Stock includes six steam
comotives and items of rolling stock.
iginal Colne Valley and Halstead railway
ildings are being rebuilt on the site.
comotives in steam every BH (ex
ristmas) and other weekends as
vertised. Book and souvenir shop. ♫ Open
 year Sat, Sun and BH 9–dusk. Non steam
ys 20p (ch 16 and pen 10p, ch 3 free). On
eam days 45p (ch and pen 30p, ch 3 free).
 rides free. Prices under revision for 1980.
(Tel Hedingham 61174)
e Castle Off A604. Norman keep
erlooking attractive village. Open 1 May to
d Sep, Tue, Thu, Sat 2–6, BH (ex 13 Apr)
–6. 15p (ch 10p). P on Castle Hill. *(Tel
dingham 60435). (Miss M Majendie and
Margery Blackie)* **(79)**

ASTLE HOWARD *North Yorkshire*
ap 8 SE76
agnificent 18th-C house, designed by
nbrugh and built in 1699–1726 for Charles
ward, 3rd Earl of Carlisle; still lived in by
ward family. Contains famous collection of
rcelain, paintings and furniture.
rrounding the house are extensive grounds
th lakes and fountain. Hawksmoor's great
ausoleum and Vanbrugh's restored Temple
the Four Winds. Costume galleries in 18th-
stable court, house Britain's largest private
llection of 18th- to 20th-C costume. Steam
ir Aug. ♫ licensed. Open 4 Apr to end Oct,
ily. Grounds and restaurant from 11, House
d Costume Galleries 11.30–5. Admission
ces not yet decided for 1980. ⚠ *(Tel
neysthorpe 333)* Ᏹ

ASTLE RISING *Norfolk* Map 9 TF62
stle Rising* Off A149. Fine Norman keep,
obably built by Earl of Arundel, within
pressive earthworks. Open*, see inside
nt cover. 20p (ch 16 and pen 5p). ⚠ 5p.
M)
inity Hospital* Almshouses founded 1616
 Earl of Northampton, building with towered
tehouse, and courtyard leading to hall, resi-
nces, and rebuilt chapel. Original fireplace
d refectory in common room. Open all
ar, Tue, Thu and Sat 10–12 and 2–6 (4, Oct
May). Free. P (roadside). *(Tel 241)* Ᏹ

ASTLETON *Derbyshire* Map 7 SK18
ue-John Caverns and Mine* Over two
les long, with chambers 200ft high, the best
the local caves. Contains rare deposits of
aethystine spar. ♫ Open all year, daily (ex
 Dec) 9.30–5.30 (dusk winter). 80p (ch
p). P. *(Tel Hope Valley 20638)*
ak Cavern* On A625. One of the most
ectacular natural limestone caves in
strict. Underground walk (half a mile) is
ectrically lit. There is running water, and
any grotesque shapes are visible. Grand
trance Hall, where ropes have been made
 over 500 years, and traces of a row of
ttages can be seen. Open 4 Apr to mid Sep,
ily 10–5. 60p (ch and pen 30p). Party 20+

48p (ch 24p). P. *(Tel Hope Valley 20285)*
Peveril (or Peak) Castle Ruined keep
erected originally by Henry II. Later portion
has vanished. Open*, see inside front cover.
20p (ch 16 and pen 5p). ⚠ *(AM)*
Speedwell Cavern Floodlit cavern with
illuminated canal and bottomless pit. One
mile underground boat trip. ♫ Open all year,
daily (ex 25, 26 Dec) 10–6 90p (ch 45p). ⚠
(Tel Hope Valley 20512)

CAWTHORNE *South Yorkshire* Map 8 SE20
Cannon Hall On A635. Built c 1765, mainly
by John Carr of York, the museum set in 70
acres of parkland is owned by Barnsley
Metropolitan Borough Council. Contains
furniture, paintings, and glassware. Also
Regimental Museum of the 13th/18th Royal
Hussars (Queen Mary's Own). The Harvey
Collection of Dutch and Flemish paintings
(formerly the National Loan Collection) is now
on permanent display. Open all year (ex 4
Apr, 25/26 Dec), 10.30–5, Sun 2.30–5. Free.
⚠ *(Tel Barnsley 790270)*

CHADDERTON *Gt Manchester* Map 7 SD80
Foxdenton Hall Foxdenton Lane, off B6189.
Dates from 1665 and c 1700, restored in 1965.
Open all year, Sun, Apr to Sep, Tue 2–dusk.
(Park daily until dusk). Free. ⚠

CHALFONT ST GILES *Buckinghamshire*
Map 4 SU99
Milton's Cottage Half-timbered 16th-C
cottage and the only existing home in which
John Milton lived and worked. Whilst in the
cottage he completed 'Paradise Lost' and
commenced 'Paradise Regained'.
Mementoes of Milton on display. Cottage
garden. Open 1 Feb to 31 Oct daily (ex Sun
am and Mon) 10–1 and 2–6. Nov weekends
only. closed Dec and Jan. 40p (ch 15 10p).
Party 20+. P. *(Tel 2313)* Ᏹ

CHAPPEL *Essex* Map 5 TL92
Chappel Steam Centre Chappel Station. Off
A604 by Viaduct. Ten steam locomotives plus
historic rolling stock, restored railway
buildings and associated equipment.
Chappel is not just a museum but a centre
where every aspect of railway preservation
can be seen at close quarters, down to the
smallest detail. Open every weekend (ex 25
Dec) 11–dusk. Steam days 2 Mar, 5–7 Apr,
4–5 and 25–26 May, 1 Jun, 6 Jul, 3 and
24–25 Aug, 7 Sep, 5 Oct and 2 Nov. 60p (ch
and pen 30p), includes admission, parking
and unlimited steam hauled rides. ⚠ Ᏹ

CHARD *Dorset* Map 3 ST30
Forde Abbey 12th-C Cistercian monastery,
with notable gatehouse, enlarged by Abbot
Chard, and converted to house in 17th C by
Cromwell's Attorney-General. Inhabited by
present family since 1864, contains set of five
famous Mortlake tapestries. 20 acres of
grounds, with water and rock gardens. ♫
Open May to Sep Wed, Sun and BH 2–6. 75p
Admission charges for 1980 not yet decided.
⚠ *(Tel South Chard 20231). (Mr Geoffrey D
Roper)* Ᏹ

CHARLECOTE *Warwickshire* Map 4 SP25
Charlecote Park On B4086. Fine restored
Elizabethan house (1558), built originally for
Lucy family, with picturesque gatehouse.
Museum on first floor of house, and in Great
Hall, Shakespeare was said to have been
brought before Sir Thomas Lucy for poaching
in 228-park deer park. ♫ Open 14 Apr to end
Apr and Oct, Sat and Sun, May to Sep, daily
(ex Mon, but including BH) 11.15–5.45 (last
tour 5.15). £1.10, deer park and garden 75p;
school parties on Thu mornings only by prior
arrangement. *(NT)*

CHARLWOOD *Surrey* Map 4 TQ24
Gatwick Garden Aviaries and Garden Zoo
¾m SW at Russ hill. Colourful collection of
birds varying from macaws, flamingoes,
penguins and waterfowl. Colonies of
monkeys, some totally free. Otters, wallabies
etc. In natural setting, lawns and lakes. ⲣ
Open Easter to end Sep daily 10.30–6. 45p
(ch 3–14 and pen 30p, ch 3 free). ⚠ *(Tel
Crawley 862312)* & *(79)*

CHARTWELL *Kent* Map 5 TQ45
2m SE of Westerham. Former home of Sir
Winston Churchill, now Churchill memorial
Museum with many relics of the famous
statesman. House open 1 Mar to end Nov,
Tue, Wed, Thu (closed Mon and Fri) but open
BH Mon, 2–6 or sunset. Sat, Sun and BH Mon
11–6 or sunset. Garden and studio Apr to mid
Oct same times. Admission to house and
gardens £1.20, gardens only 60p (ch half

price); studio 30p extra. Entrance by
numbered ticket at times in summer to avoid
delay; waiting time can be spent in the
gardens. ⲣ licensed, 10.30–5.30 on open
days. *(NT)*

CHATSWORTH *Derbyshire* Map 8 SK27
Built largely by Talman and Wyatville, 17th-
and 19th-C palatial home of Dukes of
Devonshire in magnificent park and water
gardens. Wood carvings by Samuel Watson,
ironwork by Tijou, paintings by Verrio and
Laguerre, Old Master drawings, and fine
collection of pictures, books, and furniture.
Farming and Forestry Exhibition. ⲣ House
open late Mar to early Oct Tue, Wed, Thu and
Fri 11.30–4, Sat and Sun 1.30–5, BH Mon
and Tue 11–5. Farmyard open daily 30 Mar
9 Oct Subject to alteration. Admission prices
for 1980 not yet decided. ⚠ *(Tel Baslow 220*
(The Trustees of the Chatsworth Settlement

CHATSWORTH

HOME OF THE DUKE AND DUCHESS OF DEVONSHIRE
1980 season   April 1st-November 2nd

HOUSE open each day except Monday 11.30am-4.30pm.
GARDEN open daily 11.30am-5pm.
FARMYARD open until October 5th only Monday-Friday 10.30am-4.30pm
Saturday & Sunday 1.30pm-5.30pm, Bank Holidays till 5.30pm.
Winter opening of house & garden till the end of December.
Further information from The Comptroller, Chatsworth,
Bakewell, Derbyshire. Telephone:0246 882204
The Trustees reserve the right to alter the opening times.

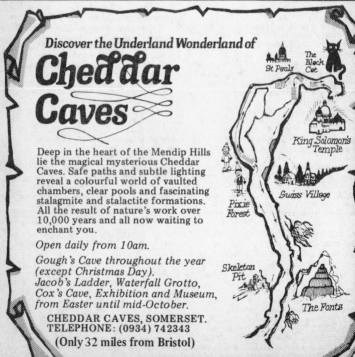

Discover the Underland Wonderland of

Cheddar Caves

Deep in the heart of the Mendip Hills
lie the magical mysterious Cheddar
Caves. Safe paths and subtle lighting
reveal a colourful world of vaulted
chambers, clear pools and fascinating
stalagmite and stalactite formations.
All the result of nature's work over
10,000 years and all now waiting to
enchant you.

Open daily from 10am.

*Gough's Cave throughout the year
(except Christmas Day).
Jacob's Ladder, Waterfall Grotto,
Cox's Cave, Exhibition and Museum,
from Easter until mid-October.*

CHEDDAR CAVES, SOMERSET.
TELEPHONE: (0934) 742343
(Only 32 miles from Bristol)

HAWTON *Hampshire* Map 4 SU73
Jane Austen's House In the village street,
now a museum. Visitors are allowed to picnic
in the garden. Open all year, daily (ex Mon
and Tue Nov to Mar and 25, 26 Dec) 11–4.30.
50p (ch 14 10p). Party 20+ ⚠ *(Tel Alton
3262)* ₰ B

CHEDDAR *Somerset* Map 3 ST45
Cheddar Caves Museum The Cliffs. A
natural museum on archaeology and zoology
containing Paleolithic – Pleistocene finds. A
burial of the last phase of the Ice Age together
with flint and bone implements of this period
found in Gough's Cave are preserved in the
museum. Evidence of Iron Age and Romano-
British occupation has also been found. ⚏
Open Easter – Oct daily 10 – 5.30. 25p (ch
5p) P. *(Tel 742343)*

CHEDDLETON *Staffordshire* Map 7 SJ95
Flint Mill Beside Caldon Canal. Two mills are
preserved here with their low-breast wheels in
working order. The original 17th-C south
watermill ground corn but the 18th-C north
mill was built to grind flint for the pottery
industry. Museum collection includes
examples of motive power (100HP Robey
steam engine and model Newcomen engine)
and transport (miller's cart and restored 70ft
horse-drawn narrow boat 'Vienna' moored on
the Caldon Canal). Open all year, Sat, Sun
afternoons. Application in advance for
weekday visits to Mr Underwood, 4 Cherry Hill
Avenue, Meir, Stoke-on-Trent. Free. ⚠

CHEDWORTH *Gloucestershire* Map 4 SP01
Roman Villa Fossebridge, off A429. In
Chedworth Woods, dating from AD 180–350,
with mosaic pavements. One of the best-
preserved examples in England. Open Mar to
Oct, Tue to Sun and BH (closed 4 Apr), Feb
and Nov to 16 Dec, Wed to Sun 11 – 4 (or
sunset). 85p, school parties 40p. No dogs or
picnics. *(NT)*

CHELMSFORD *Essex* Map 5 TL70
Chelmsford and Essex Museum Oaklands
Park, Moulsham Street. Collections of
Prehistoric and Roman Essex, bygones,
coins, costumes, paintings, British birds and
mammals, glass, ceramics, geology and local
industries display. Also Victorian room,
gunstill collection of glass and temporary
exhibition programme. Incorporates Essex
Regiment Museum brought here from
Warley. Open all year (ex 4 Apr; 25, 26 Dec;
Jan), Mon to Sat 10–5, Sun 2–5. Free. ⚠
*(Tel 353066, Essex Regiment Museum
0614)* ₰ B

CHELTENHAM *Gloucestershire* Map 3 SO92
Art Gallery and Museum Clarence Street.
Dutch and British paintings, Cotswold
furniture, English and Chinese ceramics,
pewter, glass, furniture, modern art and
craft exhibitions. Local history. Temporary
exhibitions throughout the year. Open all year
(ex Suns and BH) Mon to Sat 10 – 5.30. Free.
P. *(Tel 37431)*
Gustav Holst Museum Clarence Road.
Holst personalia. Contains Regency and
Victorian room settings, also working
Victorian kitchen and basement. Open all
year (ex BH) Tue to Sat 11 – 5.30. Free. *(Tel
24846)*
Pittville Pump Room Probably finest
building in town, and masterpiece of 19th-C
Greek revival, built between 1825 and 1830
by Forbes and Papworth, and bought by
borough in 1890. Notable colonnaded
façades, portico, and pillared and balconied
hall. Pump Room restored and spa fountain
repositioned in 1960. Now used for
receptions, concerts, dances, and other
functions. Open Mon to Sat 10–4 (closed
1–2), Sun and BH 2–5. Free. May be closed
when caretaker not available. ⚠ *(Tel 21621)*
₰

CHERTSEY *Surrey* Map 4 TQ06
Chertsey Museum Windsor Street. A late
Georgian house, The Cedars, Museum
opened in 1972 contains Matthews collection
of costumes and accessories, local history
collection, and silver. Exhibitions 'Family
History' 26 Feb to 15 Mar; 'Fluid & Flow' 17
May to 7 Jun. Open all year, Tue and Thu
2–5, Wed, Fri and Sat 10–1 and 2–5. Free.
P. *(Tel 65764)*

CHESSINGTON *Surrey* Map 4 TQ16
Chessington Zoo On A243. Set in 65 acres
of lovely Surrey countryside. Large and varied
collection of animals and birds including
gorillas and orangutans. Children's zoo. Bird
garden. World of Mechanical Music
Exhibition. During the summer there is a
funfair, model railway and circus. ⚏
(licensed). Open daily (ex 25 Dec) 10–5 (7
summer hol period; 4 Oct to Mar). £1.30 (ch
60p). Under revision for 1980. ⚠ *(Tel Epsom
27227)* ₰

CHESTER *Cheshire* Map 7 SJ46
The British Heritage Vicars Lane (opposite
Roman Amphitheatre). Home of World
Champion Town Crier. An exhibition telling
over 2,000 years of Chester history. Audio-
visual theatre, map and print room, showing
the development of Chester since Roman
days. A unique life size reconstruction of the
Rows as they might have been in early

CHEDDLETON FLINT MILL
Staffordshire

Specialises in the history of pottery raw
materials. Original buildings and equipment
restored to running order, many items
having been collected to show the related
processes. Two of the working exhibits -
Robey steam engine, model Newcomen
engine. The restored narrow boat "Vienna"
is moored permanently on the Caldon
Canal at the wharf. Cheddleton Flint Mill
Industrial Heritage Trust is a registered
Charity.

Victorian days. The Cobbled Street contains six shops which include cooper, blacksmith and pharmacy. A Brass Rubbing Centre is on the ground floor. Admission to Brass Rubbing Centre free. 25p (to rub various brasses including instruction and equipment). Craft Shop specialising in British made goods. Guided tours of City at 11 and 3 (May to Sep). Open from 9 daily. 70p (ch and pen 35p). Please telephone for winter opening hours. *(Tel 42222)*
Cheshire Military Museum Chester Castle, Castle Street. Mainly 19th C. Museum is located in 'A' block and has exhibits from Cheshire Regiment, Cheshire Yeomanry, 5th Inniskilling Dragoon Guards and 3rd Carabiniers. Open daily, Apr to Sep 9.30–6; Oct to Mar 9.30–5; Sun Apr to Sep 12–6, Oct to Mar 1–5. 10p (ch 5p). P. *(Tel 27617)* **(79)**
Chester Heritage Centre St Michael's Church, Bridge Street. Exhibition of Chester' architectural heritage, including 20-minute audio-visual shows and displays relating to the city's history and the large-scale conservation programme now in operation. Open all year 1 Oct to 31 Mar, daily (ex Wed) 1.30–4.30; 1 Apr to 30 Sep, weekdays (ex Wed) 10–5, Sun 2–5. 30p (ch 18 and pen 15p). Party 10+ 10% reduction. *(Tel 317948)*
Grosvenor Museum Grosvenor Street. Contains one of finest collections of Roman remains in Britain, including special Roman Army gallery and many inscribed and sculptured stones excavated in Chester. Natural History gallery. Temporary exhibitions. Period house closed for renovation. Open all year (ex 4 Apr; 25, 26 Dec), Mon to Sat 10–5, Sun 2–5.30. Free (Schools should book in advance). *(Tel 21616/313858)*

CHELTENHAM
borough council

ART GALLERY & MUSEUM SERVICE
CLARENCE STREET

Dutch Paintings, Cotswold Furniture, Ceramics and Metalwork. Temporary Exhibitions.
Open Monday-Saturday (Closed Bank Holidays).
10-5.30pm. Free Admission. Tel: 0242 37431

GUSTAV HOLST BIRTHPLACE MUSEUM
4 CLARENCE ROAD

House where composer was born in 1874, containing rooms with period furnishings, paintings, music, photographs, music instruments, and working Victorian kitchen. Parties welcome by arrangement.
Open Tuesday-Saturday. (Closed Bank Holidays).
11-5.30pm. Free Admission. Tel: 0242 24846.

CHESTER ZOO

One of the world's foremost Zoos.
Animals exhibited in spacious outdoor enclosures.
Their welfare is our first consideration.
DELIGHTFUL GARDENS,
TROPICAL HOUSE, AQUARIUM
Plenty of cover if wet.
Catering facilities.
FREE PARKING
Open daily throughout the year from 9am
(with the exception of Christmas Day)
Free coloured brochure on request to:
Dept Y4, Chester Zoo, Chester.

Stanley Palace Watergate Street. Dating from 1591, restored in 1935, half-timbered former home of the Stanleys, Earls of Derby. Now local headquarters of English-Speaking Union. Open all year Mon to Fri (ex BH) 10–4.30. Free.⌾ *(Tel 25586) (79)*
Zoo and Gardens Interesting collection of animals in open-air enclosures amid fine gardens. Tropical House, aquarium, and walk-through aviary. ⚲ (licensed). Open all year daily (ex 25 Dec) 9–dusk. £1 (ch 14 50p). Party 25+. Tropical House 15p. Aquarium 5p, Waterbus trips 15p (ch 10p). Under revision for 1980. ⌾ *(Tel 20106)* ♿

CHETTLE *Dorset* Map 3 ST91
Chettle House Early 18th-C baroque house in red brick, designed by Thomas Archer, with staircase of same period. Open all year, exterior daily 10.30–sunset, interior by appointment. Admission free. Limited parking. *(Tel Tarrant Hinton 209). (Mr Bourke)* '79)

CHICHELEY *Buckinghamshire* Map 4 SP94
Chicheley Hall Built for Sir John Chester between 1719 and 1723. It is one of the finest and least altered 18th-C houses in the country. Fine Georgian craftsmanship: brickwork, stone and wood carving, joinery and plasterwork. ⚲ Open 4 Apr to 26 May Sat, Sun and BH 2.30–6, then Wed, Thu, Sat, Sun and BH until 28 Sep. 70p (ch 12 and pen 30p). Prices under revision for 1980. Party 20+. ⌾ *(Tel North Crawley 252)* ♿

CHICHESTER *West Sussex* Map 4 SU80
District Museum In former 18th-C corn store, with local history, archaeological, and Royal Sussex Regiment relics. Open all year, Tue to Sat 10–6 (5, Oct to Mar). Free. P. *(Tel 784683)* ♿ B

Guildhall Museum Priory Park. Branch of District Museum, containing archaeological finds from district. Open Jun to Sep, Tue to Sat 1–5. Free. P. ♿
St Mary's Hospital Refounded *c*1240, with interesting hall with wagon roof supported by oak posts, and a notable chapel screen. Open all year, Tue to Sat 11–12 and 2–5 (4, Oct to Mar) (closed BH and staff holidays). Admission not less than 3p per person. P (charge). *(Tel 783377)* ♿

CHIDDINGSTONE *Kent* Map 5 TQ54
Chiddingstone Castle Off B2027. In a park, mainly 17th- to 18th-C house containing pictures, furnishings, rare Oriental art treasures, including largest collection of Japanese lacquer on show outside Japan, and Royal Stuart and Jacobite, and Egyptian collections. Fishing in lake £2 per day, onlookers (one only per £2 ticket). Open 1 Apr to 26 Oct Tue to Fri 2–5. Sat, Sun and BH Mons 11.30–5. 50p (ch 12 25p). ⌾ *(Tel Penshurst 347). (Mr Denys E Bower)* ♿ B

CHILHAM *Kent* Map 5 TR05
Chilham Castle Impressive hexagonal Jacobean castle and massive Norman flintstone keep (neither open) on site of ancient Saxon fortifications and manor house overlooking the valley of the River Stour. Extensive garden, woodland and lakeside walks with wildfowl and peacocks. Free flying eagles and falconry display. Medieval Jousting Sundays. Woodwings Flying Circus (radio controlled planes) BH Suns and Mons. *Also The Kent Battle of Britain Museum* A registered charity. Fine collection of relics including Spitfire and Messerschmitt engines, propellers, airframes, photographs, uniforms, badges and swords. ⚲ Garden and museum

open Easter to Oct (closed Mon and Fri ex BH
Mon) afterwards only. Provisionally £1 (ch
50p). ⚠ (free). *(Tel 319). (The Viscount
Massereene and Ferrard)* &

CHILLINGHAM *Northumberland*
Map 12 NU02
Chillingham Wild Cattle (Castle *not* open to
public). Off B6348. Park containing herd of
some 50 remarkable wild white cattle.
Viewable 1 Apr to 31 Oct, weekdays (ex Tue)
and BH 10 – 12 and 2 – 5, Sun 2 – 5; Tickets
50p (ch 14 20p) from keeper's cottage. ⚠ *(Tel
Chatton 213 or 250)*

CHILLINGTON HALL Staffordshire
Map 7 SJ80
Home of the Giffards since 1178, present
house dates from 1724 and 1785 (when Sir
John Soane was architect), and grounds are
by 'Capability' Brown. Fine saloon, and
association with flight of Charles II after Battle
of Worcester in 1651. Open 1 May to 11 Sep,
Thu 2.30 – 5.30; also 6 Apr, Sun before Spring
and Summer BH and all Sun in Aug. Party
(other days). Admission prices for 1980 not
yet decided. ⚠ *(Tel Brewood 850236). (Mr P
Giffard)* &

CHIPPENHAM *Wilts* Map 3 ST97
Sheldon Manor Plantagenet Manor House,
13th-C porch 15th-C detached Chapel.
Beautiful terraced gardens, roses, water
garden, ancient yew trees and hedges.
Historic Houses Festival 'Festival of Gardens'
21 May to 8 Jul. ⚤ (teas). Open 30 Mar to 28
Sep, Thu, Sun and BH 2 – 6. 65p (ch 15 30p),
ch 5 free). Under revision for 1980. ⚠ *(Tel
3120)*

CHIPPING CAMPDEN *Gloucestershire*
Map 4 SP13
Campden Car Collection High Street.
Twenty two immaculate sports, and sports
racing cars 1927 to 1963, each of distinctive
history, together with a number of engines
and a display of photographs of motor sport.
Open Easter then daily 2 – 6. 25p
(ch 10p). Under review for 1980. P. (street).
(Tel Evesham 840289). (Curator) &
Market Hall Gabled, Jacobean structure,
built on open arches, and standing in main
street of most beautiful of stone-built
Cotswold towns. Open regularly. Free. *(NT)*
Woolstaplers Hall High Street. Building
c1340, with interesting collection of bygones.
Open Easter then May to Sep daily 11 – 6. 35p
(ch 10p). Under revision for 1980. P (street).
(Tel Evesham 840289)

CHOLMONDELEY *Cheshire* Map 7 SJ55
Cholmondeley Castle Gardens 7m W of
Nantwich on A49. The gardens were
originally laid out in the beginning of the 19th
C and have shrub and water gardens

with walks and picnic areas by the lake, also
an ancient Chapel in the park and the farm
has a collection of rare breeds of farm
animals. The castle is **not** open to the public.
Various events, Band concerts, Morris
dancing etc as advertised in local press. Gift
shop. ⚤ Open 15 Apr to 7 Oct Sun and BH
1 – 6. 35p (ch 10p). ⚠ *(Tel 202). (Marquess of
Cholmondeley)* & **(79)**

CHORLEY *Lancashire* Map 7 SD51
Astley Hall Timbered and richly plastered
16th-C and later house in some 99 acres of
park and woodland. Fine furnishings, pottery,
ceilings, and pictures. Special exhibitions. ⚤
Open daily afternoons only. 20p (ch 10p). ⚠
(Tel 2166) & B

CHRISTCHURCH *Dorset* Map 4 SZ19
Christchurch Castle and Norman House
Rare example of ruined Norman house
(c1160). Stands in bailey of 11th-C house, of
which part of this stands. Open, see inside
front cover. Free. *(AM)*
Red House Museum and Art Gallery Quay
Road. Local history, archaeology, bygones,
Victoriana, dolls and costumes, wildlife, and
natural history contained in Georgian
building. Gardens with old roses, herbs and
trees. Open all year (ex Mons, 25 Dec), Tue to
Sat 10 – 5, Sun 2 – 5. 10p (ch 10 and pen 5p).
P. for 30 mins at roadside, 100yd, 2hrs 10p.
*(Tel 2860). (Hampshire County Museum
Service)* & B
Tucktonia Stour Road. Best of Britain in
miniature (exhibits to 1/24th scale. Including
buildings of London, Industrial Britain,
Cornish fishing village plus many more. The
exhibits are illuminated and animated. Also
leisure complex with features for all ages. ⚤
Open Mar to Oct (details can be checked
before visiting with *tel no* given below), from
10. Admission 85p (ch and pen 65p). Party.
Prices may be subject to alteration. ⚠ *(Tel
485100/482710)* &

CHURCH CROOKHAM *Hampshire*
Map 4 SU85
The Gurkha Museum Queen Elizabeth's
Barracks. Contains a record of the Gurkha's
service to the crown from 1815. Open all year
Mon to Fri (ex BH and certain Gurkha Hols)
9.30 – 4.45. Free. ⚠ *(Tel Fleet 3541 ext 63)* &

CHYSAUSTER ANCIENT VILLAGE
Cornwall Map 2 SW43
Eight drystone masonry houses leading off a
courtyard and incorporating characteristic
Cornish underground chamber, or 'fogou'.
Adjoining dwellings are byres for cattle, giving
foretaste of so-called later 'long-house'.
Inhabited between 1st and 3rd C AD. Open*,
see inside front cover. 15p (ch 16 and pen 5p).
⚠ *(AM)*

Sheldon Manor
near CHIPPENHAM

Plantagenet Manor-House dating from 1282, still a family home with a warm
welcome, a delicious home-made cream tea, and many ancient and beautiful things
to see. Connoisseur gardens with roses, water and very old yew trees.
Open: Sundays, Thursdays and Bank Holidays from 2-6pm, Easter to October.
Also Wednesdays in August, 2-6pm.
Approach: 1½ miles west of Chippenham, signposted from A420, eastbound
traffic signposted from A4. M4 (Exit 17) 4 miles.
Participating in West Country Festival of Gardens, May, June, July 1980.

CIRENCESTER *Gloucestershire*
Map 4 SP00
Corinium Museum Park Street. Contains
one of the country's most comprehensive
collections of Roman remains – mosaic floors,
Romano-British sculpture, and items of
everyday life, plus a remarkable example of a
five-letter square palindrome. Considerably
enlarged and modernised in 1974 to become
a regional museum for the Cotswolds.
Temporary exhibitions throughout the year.
Open all year May to Sep, Mon to Sat 10 – 6,
Sun 2 – 6; Oct to Apr (closed Christmas), Tue
to Sat 10 – 5, Sun 2 – 5. 25p (ch 5p, students
and pen 15p). Party (adults) 15p. P. *(Tel 5611)* &

CLANDON *Surrey* Map 4 TQ05
Clandon Park On A247, near West Clandon.
18th-C house, built by Leoni for 1st Lord
Onslow, with fine plasterwork, furniture, and
pictures. Famous collection of valuable
furniture added in 1970. ♉ Open Apr to 19
Oct, BH Mon, Tue (ex following BH), Wed,
Thu, Sat, Sun 2 – 6. £1 *(NT)*

CLAPHAM *North Yorkshire* Map 7 SD76
*Yorkshire Dales National Park Information
Centre* Permanent exhibition centre for
region, with photographs, maps, teaching
aids, etc. Reginald Farrer Trail commences
here. Open Apr to end Sep daily mid mornings
to late afternoon. Free. ⚠ *(Tel 419)*

CLEARWELL *Gloucestershire* Map 3 SO50
Clearwell Caves Ancient Iron Mines
Ancient iron mine with exhibits of local mining
and geological interest from Forest of Dean
area, including several vintage stationary
engines. Large picnic area. Open Easter to
end Sep, Tue to Fri, Sun and BH 10 – 5. 50p

(ch and pen 25p). Under revision for 1980.
Educational parties at other times by
arrangement with proprietor, *Mr Ray Wright,
The Bungalow, Heywood Road, Cinderford,
Glos*. ⚠ *(Tel Cinderwood 23700)* & B
Clearwell Castle A 'mock' Gothic castle
reputed to be the oldest in Britain with a
Regency interior. There are 8 acres of formal
gardens on five different levels which are still
being restored. Bird Park. ♉ Open 4 Apr to 1
Oct, Tue to Fri 2 – 6, Sun and BH 11 – 6
(closed Mon and Sat). Closed at certain times
for special functions. 75p (ch and pen 50p).
Party. Admission prices under revision for
1980. ⚠ *(Tel Coleford 2320)*

CLEETHORPES *Humberside* Map 8 TA30
Lincolnshire Coast Light Railway North
Sea Lane Station, Humberston. Historic
narrow-gauge passenger-carrying light
railway. Open Spring BH week, daily then Sat
and Sun until 12 Jul, then daily until 7 Sep.
Single fare 7½p (ch 3 free). ⚠ &
Zoo and Leisure Park a 27-acre site with
lions, tigers, elephants, camels, chimps,
seals, reptile house, monkey house, large
free-flight aviary, emu, deer, cattle, wolves
and a pets corner. Play areas for children and
fairground. Colussus Day 1 Apr. Picnic areas.
♉ Open all year daily (ex 25 Dec) 10 – dusk.
50p (ch and pen 30p). Under revision for
1979. *(Tel 813533)* & **(79)**

CLEOBURY *Salop* Map 7 SO67
Clee Hill Bird and Animal Garden Contains
birds, poultry and waterfowl from 6
continents. Also mammals including deer,
Llamas, wallabies, sheep, etc. Gift shop. ♉
(licenced). Open all year (ex 25 Dec) Summer
10 – 6, winter 10 – 4. 45p (ch 25p, ch 3 free). ⚠
(Tel Cleo Hillstone 274) & **(79)**

CLEVEDON *Avon* Map 3 ST47
Clevedon Court Off B3130. 14th-C manor house, associated with Tennyson and Thackeray, with 14th-C chapel and 18th-C terraced garden. ℒ Open Apr to end Sep, Wed, Thu, Sun, BH Mon 2.30–5.30 (last admission 5). 70p (*NT*)
Clevedon Craft Centre and Country Museum Moor Lane. Turn off B3130 opposite Clevedon Court, cross M5. Wood carving and woodturning every Sun afternoon when craftsmen are available for discussion. Ten studios, and Countryside Museum. Exhibition gallery, countryside Museum at Whitsun and Summer BH. ℒ Open May to Dec 10–5.30 Tue to Sun and BH Mon. Tea room and museum closed Mon to Fri from end of Oct to Easter. Free. ⚠ *(Tel 872867)* &

CLIFFORD *Hereford and Worcester* Map 3 SO24
Clifford Castle Remains of 11th-C castle, traditional birthplace of 'Fair Rosamund', comprising gatehouse, hall, and round towers. Open with permission from *Mr and Mrs Parkinson*; apply at house by castle entrance. Free. P. (in lane by entrance). *(Tel 230)* (79)

CLITHEROE *Lancashire* Map 7 SD74
Clitheroe Castle Museum Contains important collection of carboniferous fossils and many items of local interest. It adjoins the remains of the castle, one of the oldest structures in Lancashire with the smallest Norman Keep in England. The Castle grounds command magnificent views over the Ribble Valley. Open Easter to Sep, Tue, Thu, Sat and Sun 2–4.30, last two weeks Jul and whole Aug daily. 10p (ch free if accompanied). P. *(Tel 24635)* & B
Browsholme Hall Bashall Eaves. 2½m NW. Home of Parker family, Bowbearers of the Forest of Bowland. Tudor with Elizabethan front, Queen Anne Wing and Regency additions. Portraits, furniture, antiquities. Open 5–13 Apr, 24 May–1 Jun, 16–31 Aug daily 2–5. House and grounds 80p (ch 40p). Parties by written arrangement throughout the year. No dogs. ⚠ *(Tel Stoneyhurst 330/538)* & B

CLIVEDEN Buckinghamshire Map 4 SU98
Extensive and historic gardens overlooking Cliveden Reach of Thames. Present house, third to be constructed on the same site, is now let to Stanford University. ℒ Gardens open all year, daily 11–6.30. House Apr to end Oct, Sat and Sun 2.30–5.30. House and grounds £1.20. Grounds only £1. No dogs in house, on lead in grounds. *(Tel Burnham 61406)*. *(NT)*

CLOUDS HILL Dorset Map 3 SY89
4m SW of Bere Regis. Former home of T E Lawrence (Lawrence of Arabia). Open all year, Apr to end Sep Wed–Fri, Sun and BH 2–5, Oct to end Mar, Sun 1–4. 60p. No photography. *(NT)*

CLUMBER PARK AND CHAPEL Nottinghamshire Map 8 SK67
2½m SE Worksop. The Chapel built (1886–1889) for the 7th Duke of Newcastle is open after restoration work. Described as 'a cathedral in miniature' the architect was G F Bodley RA (1827–1902). A superb example of the Gothic Revival based on 14th-C Decorated Style. The mansion was demolished in 1938 although the footings have recently been exposed. The remainder of this 3,800-acre park survives including the longest double lime tree avenue in Europe,

stables with a tower clock dated 1763, Classical bridge over lake, lodges, pleasure gardens etc. Shops, bicycle hire, day fishing, ferry. Park open all year. ℒ Open weekends and BH also Mon to Thu, Apr to Oct. Small vehicle charge only. *(NT)*

CLUN *Salop* Map 7 SO28
Clun Town Trust Museum In town hall, original court house to Clun Castle; court was moved to market square in 1780. Flint tools, maps of earthworks, etc, domestic and farming relics, and exhibits of local geological and mineralogical interest. Open Easter until Nov, Tue and Sat 2–5. Other times by request, and parties by arrangement only. School parties welcome. Free. P. *(Enquiries Mrs F Hudson, Florida Villa, Tel 247)*

COBHAM *Kent* Map 5 TQ66
Cobham Hall Off B2009. 16th-C and later mansion, with work by Inigo Jones and Wyatt, situated in large park with fine trees; now girls' public school. ℒ Open 3–7 Apr then every Wed, Thu and Sun from 30 Jul to 4 Sep also 25 Aug, 2–6 (last tour 5.30 pm). 50p (ch and pen 25p). Party 15+. Admission prices under revision for 1980. ⚠ *(Tel Shorne 3371)* & B
Luddesdown Court Norman manor house dating from the 11th C, claimed to be the oldest continuously inhabited house in Britain. Most of original structure still remains. Open by appointment with owner. Free. *(Tel Meopham 814359)*. *(Mr J A Williams)*
Owletts 17th-C house with contemporary staircase and ceiling. Open Apr to Oct, Wed and Thu 2–5. 40p *(NT)*

COBHAM *Surrey* Map 4 TQ16
Cedar House 15th- to 18th-C house overlooking River Mole, with open-timbered roof to hall. Open on application to tenant. Free. *(NT)*

COCKERMOUTH *Cumbria* Map 11 NY13
Wordsworth House Built 1745, birthplace in 1770 of William Wordsworth. Original staircase and fireplaces. ℒ Open Apr to Oct, daily (ex Thu) 10.30–2.30 and 2–5. 70p (ch 30p). *(NT)*

COCKLEY CLEY *Norfolk* Map 5 TF70
Iceni Village and Museum Full-scale reconstruction on original site of Iceni encampment, showing how tribe lived 2,000 years ago. 200yd away is historical museum in cottage built 1450, with models and exhibits of local life from prehistoric times to present day. Agricultural and carriage museum. Early Saxon church (c620) in grounds. Open Easter to Sep, Sun 1.30–5.30. School parties by appointment. Admission charge for 1980 not yet decided. ⚠ *(Tel Swaffham 21339)*

COGGESHALL *Essex* Map 5 TL82
Paycocke's Early 16th-C house with notable panelling. Open Apr to Sep, Wed, Thu, Sun, BH Mon 2–5.30. 70p. No dogs. *(NT)*

COLCHESTER *Essex* Map 5 TM02
Bourne Mill Dutch-gabled fishing lodge (1591) erected from materials from St John's Abbey. Open Apr to Sep, Wed, Sat, Sun, BH Mon 2–6. Other times by appointment. No unaccompanied children. 40p *(NT)*
Colchester and Essex Museum North of High Street. The Castle, massive 11th-C keep built largely of Roman bricks around vaulted base of Roman temple, now houses extensive collection of Roman and other antiquities. Open all year (ex 4 Apr, 25–27 Dec), weekdays 10–1, 2–5 (4 Sat Oct to Mar), Sun (Apr to Sep only) 2.30–5. 25p (ch and pen free); conducted tours of vaults and cells weekdays Jul and Aug, tours 20p (ch 10p). P. *(Tel 77475)* & B

Colchester Zoo Stanway Hall, 3m W of town, off B1022. Hall, rebuilt in 16th C, and 14th- to 17th-C church in 40-acre park. Zoo, founded in 1963, includes large cats (lions, tigers, leopards etc), Nocturnal House, aquarium and birdland. Model railway. Picnic areas. ⏚ Open all year, daily 9.30 – 7.30. 70p (ch 2 – 14 30p); Party 25+. ⚠ *(Tel 330253)* ₺ **(79)**

Hollytrees Fine Georgian house, dating from 1718, with collection of costumes and antiquities. Open all year (ex 4 Apr and 25 – 27 Dec) weekdays 10 – 1, 2 – 5. Free. *(Tel 77475)*

Museum of Social History Holy Trinity Church, Trinity Street. Historical displays of County life and crafts, with some bicycles etc. Open all year Mon to Sat 10 – 1, 2 – 5 (4 Sat, Oct to Mar). Free. P. *(Tel 77475)* ₺

Natural History Museum High Street. Formerly 15th-C All Saints Church, with fine flint tower. Natural History of Essex with special reference to the Colchester area. Dioramas and aquarium. Open all year (ex 4 Apr, 25 – 28 Dec), weekdays 10 – 1 and 2 – 5 (4 Sat Oct – Mar). Free. P. *(Tel 76071 ext 344)*

The Minories Victor Batte-Lay Trust, 74 High Street. Georgian house, rebuilt in 1776 from original Tudor buildings. Opened as art gallery and centre for visual arts in 1958; continuous programme of exhibitions of contemporary fine and applied art, also lectures, concerts etc. ⏚ Open all year Tue to Sat 11 – 5, Sun 2 – 6. 20p (ch, students and pen 5p). P. *(Tel 77067)* ₺ B

White Barn House 4m E on A133 at Elmstead Market. The garden, begun only 20 years ago, has a variety of contrasting plantings. The Dry garden, on gravel soil and full sun, contains plants adapted to drought. The Shade garden has plants with fine foliage, eg, hostas and ferns as well as flowering plants. A spring fed ditch has been dammed to make 5 large pools, full of fish and surrounded by exotic bog plants. The nursery adjoining contains over 1,000 different plants. Open all year (ex Sun and BH) 9 – 5. 25p, subject to review for 1980. ⚠ *(Tel Wivenhoe 2007)* ₺

COLNE *Lancashire* Map 7 SD83
British in India Museum Sun Street. Dioramas, working model railway, coins, medals, stamps, and other items relating to British in India up to 1947. Open 1 May to 30 Sep, Sat and Sun only, 2 – 5. 25p (ch 15 and pen 10p). P. *(Tel Nelson 63129)* ₺ B

COMPTON *Devon* Map 3 SX86
Compton Castle Off A380 near Marldon. Restored 14th- to 16th-C house with courtyard, hall, chapel, and old kitchen open to public. ⏚ Open 1 Apr to Oct, Mon, Wed, Thu 10 – 12 and 2 – 5. 70p *(NT)*

COMPTON *Surrey* Map 4 SU94
Watts Picture Gallery Memorial gallery with about 150 paintings by G F Watts, who is buried above the nearby Watts Mortuary Chapel. Gallery open all year, daily (ex Thu) 2 – 6 (2 – 4 Oct to Mar), also 11 – 1 Wed and Sat; chapel open all year, daily. Free. ⚠ *(Tel Guildford 810235)* ₺ B

COMPTON BEAUCHAMP *Oxfordshire* Map 4 SU28
Wayland's Smithy A gallery-grave chamber, excavated in 1920 from a large prehistoric mound, and re-excavated and restored in 1962 – 3. Lies near the ancient ridgeway at about 700ft on the northern slopes of the Berkshire Downs. Accessible any reasonable time. Free. *(AM)*

COMPTON WYNYATES *Warwickshire* Map 4 SP34
Tudor mansion built 1480 – 1520 largely by Sir William Compton, a lifelong friend of King Henry VIII who stayed several times. Interior largely unaltered. In steep hillside setting below the Cotswold Scarp with beautiful topiary garden. Picnic area. Gift shop and ⏚. Open 4 to 13 Apr then 1 to 31 Aug daily 11 – 5. Admission prices not yet decided. ⚠ *(Tel Tysoe 229)*. *(The Marquess of Northampton)*

CONISBROUGH *South Yorkshire* Map 8 SK59
Conisbrough Castle Unique example of circular six-buttressed keep, built in late 12th C. Curtain walls with solid round towers. Open*, see inside front cover. 15p (ch 16 and pen 5p). ⚠ *(AM)*

CONISTON *Cumbria* Map 7 SD39
Brantwood 2½m SE off B5285. On unclass road east side of Coniston Water. Former home of John Ruskin, with garden, one of the finest nature trails in the Lake District, also deer trails. Memorial exhibition to John Ruskin on display, including pictures, coach boat and personal possessions. Picnics permitted. Open Easter to mid Oct, Sun to Fri 11 – 5.30. House and Nature Trails 65p (ch 16, pen and disabled 30p). Family Ticket (Mother, Father and ch 16) £1.50. Nature Trail only 25p (ch 10p). ⚠ Toilets for the disabled. *(Tel 396)* ₺

CORBRIDGE *Northumberland* Map 12 NY96
Roman Station Remains of Roman 'Corstopitum', cAD210, including granaries, portico columns, and probable site of legion headquarters. Excavated finds in museum on site. Open*, see inside front cover. 40p, winter 15p (ch 16 and pen 15p, winter 5p). ⚠ *(AM)*

Hunday National Tractor and Farm Museum West Side. 3m E off A69. The collection is housed in original stone buildings from 1806. Over 250 vintage tractors and engines, showing the development of agriculture from 1900 to the Post-War period. The collection includes small hand tools, barn equipment, joiners tools, harness, farm and dairy equipment, an 1835 Bingfield steam engine and thresher, also a 1903 lvel which won a 1st prize at the Royal show in 1903. ⏚ Open 30 Apr to 30 Sep weekdays (ex Fri) 10 – 6, Sun 12 – 6, last admission 5 pm. 70p (ch 35p, ch 4 free, pen 25p). Party. ⚠ *(Tel Stocksfield 2553)* ₺ B

CORBY CASTLE *Cumbria* Map 12 NY45
On unclassified road from A69 at Warwick Bridge. Ancient pele tower in 17th- and early 19th-C house. Early 18th-C grounds with forest trees by River Eden. Grounds only open 1 Apr to 31 Oct, daily 10 – 7. 20p (ch free). ⚠ *(Tel Wetheral 60246)*. *(Mr J P Howard)*

CORFE CASTLE *Dorset* Map 3 SY98
Corfe Castle 12th- to 16th-C stronghold in Purbeck Hills, besieged in 1646 during Civil War and later slighted. Open Mar to Oct, daily 10 – dusk, Nov to Feb afternoons only, weather permitting. 30p (ch 16 20p). Party 20+ by arrangement. P. *(Tel 442)*

Corfe Castle Museum Tiny rectangular building, partly rebuilt in brick after fire in 1680. Small museum with old village relics. Dinosaur footprints 130 million years old. Council chamber on first floor accessible by staircase at one end, and Ancient Order of Marblers meets here each Shrove Tuesday (open by appointment only). Museum open all year, summer 9 – 9, winter 9 – 6. (Times are approximate). Free. P. ₺

CORSHAM *Wiltshire* Map 3 ST86
Corsham Court Elizabethan manor with additions by 'Capability' Brown and Nash. Georgian state rooms with furniture by Chippendale, Adam, Cobb, and Johnson, famous Methuen collection of Old Masters, garden with flowering shrubs, herbaceous borders, Georgian bath house, peacocks and 15th-C gazebo. Open all year, Sun, Wed and Thu; mid Jul to mid Sep, daily (ex Mon and Fri); and during Bath Festival and BH Mon 11–12.30 and 2–6 (4.30 in winter). 80p (ch 40p). Party 15+ 50p each. Gardens only 25p (ch 15p). Under revision for 1980. ⚠ *(Tel 712214). (Lord Methuen)* ♿

COSFORD RAF *West Midlands* Map 7 SJ70
Aerospace Museum Extensive collection of aircraft, aircraft engines, rockets and missiles. The British, German and Japanese aircraft collection includes Spitfire, Mosquito, Javelin, Messerschmitt, Avro, Bristol, and many more. Rocket collection includes V1, V2, Messerschmitt, Henchel, Rheinmettal and others. Amateur radio station in operation. ⚑ Open Sat, Sun and BH Apr to Oct 10–5. 1980 charges not yet decided. ⚠ *(Tel Albrighton 4872)* ♿

COTON *Northamptonshire* Map 4 SP67
Coton Manor Wildlife Gardens A beautiful old garden surrounding 17th-C stone manor house. Rare wildfowl, cranes and flamingoes add greatly to the attraction of the lakes and water gardens. ⚑ Gift shop. Large variety of unusual plants for sale. Open Easter or Apr 1 to end of Oct, Sun, Thu and BH 2–6 also Wed Jul–Aug. 50p (ch 14 25p). Admission prices under revision for 1980. ⚠ *(Tel Northampton 740219)*

COUGHTON *Warwickshire* Map 4 SP06
Coughton Court 16th-C and later house, with imposing stone gatehouse (1509), two Elizabethan half-timbered wings, and Jacobite relics. Associated with Gunpowder Plot. ⚑ Open Apr and Oct Sat and Sun; May to end Sep Wed, Thu, Sat and Sun, BH Mon and following Tue 2–6 (or sunset if earlier). 70p. No dogs. *(NT)*

COVENTRY *West Midlands* Map 4 SP37
Coventry Cathedral 7 Priory Row. The present cathedral was designed by Sir Basil Spence and consecrated in May 1962. Contains outstanding modern works of art, including the Sutherland altar tapestry, the West Screen (a wall of glass engraved by John Hutton with saints and angels) and stained glass unequalled in modern times. Also treasury and ruins, including 14th-C tower. Open all year, daily 7–7.30 (summer) –5.30 (winter) ex during services. Admission: Treasury 20p (ch 10p); Tower 20p (ch 15p). ⚑ (licensed) daily (ex Sun) 10.30–5. Party. P. *(Tel 27597)* ♿

Coventry Zoological Gardens Whitley Common. Includes lions, pumas, leopards, monkeys, apes, etc. Children's amusements and leisure park. ℉ (licensed). Picnics. Open all year daily 10 – dusk. 20p (ch 14 10p). Family ticket 50p. Restaurant for hire. ⚠ *(Tel 301772)* ♿

Herbert Art Gallery and Museum Jordan Well. Collections include industry and technology, social history, archaeology and folk life, natural history, visual arts. Of special interest is the Iliffe collection of Graham Sutherland's sketches for the 'Christ in Glory' tapestry in Coventry Cathedral, a social history gallery with changing displays and the natural history room. Open all year (ex 4 Apr and part of Christmas period) Mon to Sat 10 – 6, Sun 2 – 5. Free. P. *(Tel 25555 ext 2662)* ♿

Lunt Roman Fort Baginton. On S side of city, off Stonebridge highway, A45. Reconstruction of Roman fort, which stood on this site AD 60 – 80, with interpretive centre housed in reconstructed granary. Other features include gateway and gyrus. Open 24 May to 28 Sep (ex Mon and Thu) Tue 1 – 6 (advisable to telephone). 45p (ch and pen 25p). ⚠ *(Tel 25555 ext 2662)* ♿ B

Museum of British Road Transport The museum will open in Oct 1980 and will show the part Coventry and the West Midlands area in general, have played in the development of transport throughout the world. Displays will include motor cars, commercial vehicles, motor cycles and cycles, together with associated relevant materials. ℉ Open Oct 1980 Tue to Fri 10.30 – 5, Sat 10 – 6, Sun 12 – 6. Admission prices not yet available. P. *(Tel 465488)* ♿

St Mary's Guild Hall Between Bayley Lane and Earl Street. Medieval guildhall, begun in 1340 and completed in 1550, with minstrels' gallery, restored hall with portraits and Flemish tapestries, and Caesar's watchtower. Open Easter then 1 May to 31 Oct, Mon to Sat 10 – 5, Sun 12 – 5 (subject to civic requirements – enquiry advised before visiting). Free. P. *(Tel 25555 ext 2874)*

Vehicle Building and Automotive Museum 63 Holyhead Road. Following the amalgamation of the National Union of Vehicle Builders with the Transport and General workers Union 1972, it was decided to preserve the historical records of the vehicle builders in a small museum, which would also trace the progress of the vehicle from the early coach days to the modern motor car. Four rooms containing preserved documents and articles related to the union. Also displays following the production in various stages of latter day and modern vehicles. Open all year Mon to Fri 9 – 5, other times by appointment. Free. ⚠ *(Tel 29628)* ♿ B

COXWOLD *North Yorkshire* Map 8 SE57

Shandy Hall Medieval house associated with Laurence Sterne, whose books, *Tristram Shandy* and *Sentimental Journey* were mostly written here, between 1760 and 1768. Now a Sterne Museum. Open Jun to Sep, Wed 2 – 6, all other times by previous appointment. 50p (ch accompanied 25p). Admission for 1979 not yet decided. ⚠ *(Tel 465)(79)*

CRANBORNE *Dorset* Map 4 SU01

Cranborne Manor Private Gardens and Garden Centre Private gardens, laid out in 17th C, preserved Elizabethan mount and knot gardens, herb and river gardens. Gardens only open, Apr to Oct, first Sat and Sun in month, BH and some other weeks advertised locally. Sat 9 – 5, Sun 2 – 5. Garden Centre open all year, Mon to Sat 9 – 5, Sun 2 – 5. 50p (ch 10p). Under revision for 1980. ⚠ *(Tel 248 or 289). (Marquess of Salisbury)*

CRANBROOK *Kent* Map 5 TQ73

Angley House Garden 12 acres containing large collection of trees, rhododendrons and other shrubs in woodland setting with lake. Open Apr to Jul and Oct daily 11 – 7. 25p (ch 12 10p). No dogs because of peacocks. No coaches because of access and parking. *(Tel 2291)(79)*

CRANHAM *Gloucestershire* Map 3 SO81

Prinknash Abbey On A46 between Cheltenham and Painswick. Situated in a large park, this 14th- and early 16th-C house was the residence of Benedictines and guests of Gloucester Abbey; Henry VIII and Anne Boleyn came here in 1535. The house was in private ownership from 1539 to 1928 and became a priory (later abbey) for Benedictine monks from Caldey in 1928 who completed the new buildings in 1972. ℉ 9.30 – 5.30. Open all year daily. Abbey Church 5 – 8.30. Pottery Mon to Fri 10 – 5 also Sat am, Sun pm (Pottery shop 9 – 6). Viewing gallery 20p (ch 14 free). Guides available. ⚠ *(Tel Painswick 812239)* ♿ B

Prinknash Bird Park Set in nine acres of beautiful parkland with lakes and wood now leading to restored 16th-C Haunted Monks Fishpond. Views of Gloucester Cathedral, and the Welsh mountains beyond. Flock of snow geese. Demoiselle Cranes, pheasants, peacocks, White and Indian Blue, Black and Mute Swans, geese and other water fowl, most free. Pygmy goats and Jacob sheep. Open 1 Mar to 31 Oct daily 10 – 6, Nov to Feb weekends only 11 – 4 (or 1hr before dusk). 35p (ch 25p pen 30p). Party (5p reduction of all classes). ⚠ *(Tel Painswick 812727)(79)*

CRANMORE *Somerset* Map 3 ST64

East Somerset Railway At Cranmore Railway Station is an exhibition of steam locomotives and rolling stock, with locomotive engine shed and workshops, engine in steam Suns and BH, Mar to Oct for brake van rides. Approx 1m country ride due to open 1980. Signal box art gallery. Souvenir shop ℉. Open all year daily (ex Christmas) 9 – 5.30 (4 winter). 50p (ch 15 and pen 25p), admission prices under revision for 1980. *(Tel 417)*

CREWKERNE *Somerset* Map 3 ST40

Clapton Court Gardens 3m S on B3165. One of Somerset's most beautiful gardens with rare and unusual trees and shrubs, rhododendrons, azaleas and magnolias of botanical interest in formal and woodland gardens. Outstanding Springtime display of daffodils. Garden centre. Cream teas Sun and BH. Other meals by arrangement for booked parties (not Sun or BH). Open 23 Mar to 20 Oct daily (ex Sat) 2 – 5. 50p (ch 16 25p). ⚠ *(Tel 73220 or 72200)* ♿

CRICH *Derbyshire* Map 8 SK35

Tramway Museum Matlock Road. Off B5035. Old tramcars from many parts of Britain, and from abroad, preserved in former quarry. Many are in working order, and visitors may ride on them along a 1m tramway with views over Derwent Valley. Also reconstructed Georgian Assembly rooms façade from Derby, with Victorian street furniture and an exhibition also display relating to Derbyshire lead mining, at the terminus. ℉. Admission prices and opening times not yet known. ⚠ *(Tel Ambergate 2565)* ♿

CRICKET ST THOMAS *Somerset* Map 3 ST30
Wild Life Park and Country Life Museum Home of the National Heavy Horse Centre. Historic and beautiful park, with 9 lakes and collection of wild animals and birds. Tropical walk-through aviary. New penguin enclosure. Large children's fort. Picnic area. ☕ (licensed). Garden shop and gift shop. Open all year daily. Admission prices under revision. ⛺ *(Tel Winsham 396)* ♿

CROFT *Hereford and Worcester* Map 7 SO46
Croft Castle Off B4362. Restored, partly 14th-C mansion, with 16th- 17th-, and 18th-C alterations, including Georgian staircase and ceilings. Four round towers, and original 14th- or 15th-C walls can be seen. 1,636-acre estate includes fine oaks, beeches, and Spanish chestnuts lining the avenues. Notable Iron Age fort of Croft Ambrey nearby. Open Apr to end Sep, Wed, Thu, Sat, Sun, BH Mon 2.15–6 (or sunset); Oct, Sat and Sun 2.15–6 (or sunset). 85p. joint ticket with Berrington Hall £1.50. *(NT)*

CROMER *Norfolk* Map 9 TG24
Cromer Zoo Well-situated, overlooking the sea and covering approximately 5-acres with animals including lions, leopards, bears, monkeys, tigers, etc. ☕ Open all year, daily 10–7 (4 in winter). 80p (ch 40p) ⛺ *(Tel 2947)* ♿
Cromer Museum Tucker Street. Three 19th-C Fishermens' Cottages. One furnished as a cottage of *c*1900, also pictures and collections of Victorian Cromer. Collections illustrate the natural history and archaeology of the area. Open all year Mon to Sat 10–5, Sun 2–5, 15p (ch 5p, ch accompanied and pen free). P. *(Tel 513543)*
Lifeboat Museum Situated in No. 2 boathouse at the bottom of The Gangway. Covers both local lifeboat history and general RNLI history. Open 1 May to 30 Sep daily 10–5. Free. P. ***also Lifeboat Station*** on Pier. Open as above. School parties accepted at Lifeboat Station. ♿

CROWLAS *Cornwall* Map 2 SW53
Age of Steam Rospeath Lane, on A30 between Penzance and Hayle. An 18-acre steam park with over a mile of 10¼" gauge passenger-carrying steam railway. Also children's boating lake with island. Self-drive slot model steam paddle boats and trains. Large, indoor model railway, museum and gallery. Traction engines and steam organs etc sometimes on view. Gift shop. Picnic and play areas. ☕ Open Easter to Oct daily from 10.30. Admission prices not available. ⛺ *(Tel Cockwells 631)* ♿ (free)

CROYDE *Devon* Map 2 SS43
Croyde Gem Rock and Shell Museum A unique museum and craft workshop of gemstones and shells. Displays of the world's gemstones in the natural and polished state. Demonstrations of cutting and polishing. Shop for jewellery, equipment and materials. Daily 1 Mar to 31 Oct 10–5.30, Jul to Aug 10–10, restricted winter opening please phone. 10p (ch and pen 5p). Party. P. *(Tel 890407)* **(79)**

CUSWORTH *South Yorkshire* Map 8 SE50
Cusworth Hall Museum House (1741 and 1750) with fine chimney pieces, chapel in south-west wing. Museum of South Yorkshire life. Sections of interest to children. Extensive grounds open all year, with fishing in ponds, cricket and football pitches. Children's study base; research facilities. House open all year, daily 11–5 (4 Nov to Feb), Sun 1–5. Free. ⛺ *(Tel Doncaster 61842)* ♿ B

DACRE *Cumbria* Map 12 NY42
Dalemain The oldest part of this historic house is medieval. Originally a pele tower, added to in Tudor times and the imposing Georgian façade was completed in 1750. Splendid oak panelling, Chinese wall paper, Tudor plasterwork, fine Queen Anne and 18th-C furniture. Rooms recently opened include the Victorian nursery and the housekeeper's work room. The tower contains the Westmorland and Cumberland Yeomanry Museum. Countryside Museum in 16th-C cobbled courtyard. Historic gardens. Gift shop. ☕ (home-made teas). Open 5 Apr to end Sep, daily (ex Fri) 2–5.15. House and garden 80p (ch 14 and registered disabled 40p); gardens only 20p (ch 14 and registered disabled 5p). Under revision for 1980. ⛺ and picnicking free. *(Tel Pooley Bridge 450)* ♿ B

DALTON-IN-FURNESS *Cumbria* Map 7 SD27
Castle Standing in main street, 14th-C tower built originally by Furness Abbey monks as a court room. Owned by Duke of Buccleuch's family since 1660. Open at all reasonable hours; key from ***Mr I J Whitehead, 18 Market Place.*** 20p *(NT)*
Tytup Hall A small early 18th-C country mansion in Palladian style. Wood panelling preserved in three of first floor rooms and hall. Father West wrote his 'Antiquities of Furness', a study of the area, here. Open all year by appointment only. 50p ⛺ *(Tel 62929). (Dr J R Edge)*

DALWOOD *Devon* Map 3 ST20
Loughwood Meeting House Mid 17th-C Nonconformist place of worship, in remote

wooded setting, with plastered barrel ceiling. In almost original condition. Open all year. Free. *(NT)*

DANBY *North Yorkshire* Map 8 NZ70
Danby Lodge National Park Lodge Lane. The former shooting lodge offers full information and countryside interpretation service to visitors to the North York Moors National Park. The grounds include riverside meadow, woodland and terraced gardens. Slides and films shown daily. Exhibition about the North York Moors. Bookshop information desk. Guided walks Suns and daily Jul and Aug. ⚲ Open 1 Apr to 31 Oct daily 10–6, Nov, Feb, Mar weekends 10–5. 30p (ch 18 10p, pen 20p). Under revision for 1980. ⚠ *(Tel Castleton 654)* ⅋ B

DARLINGTON *Co Durham* Map 8 NZ21
Art Gallery Crown Street. Contains a permanent collection of pictures but also has temporary loan exhibitions throughout the year. Open all year, daily (ex Sun and BH) 10–8 (5.30 Sat). Free. P. *(Tel 62034)* ⅋
Darlington Museum Tubwell Row. Local social and natural history, archaeology and bygones. Observation beehive and beekeeping exhibits (approx May to Sep) each year. Open all year (ex 4 Apr, 25 and 26 Dec, 1 Jan) Mon to Sat (ex Thu afternoon) 10–1 and 2–6 (5.30 Sat). Free. P. *(Tel 63795)*
North Road Station Railway Museum Opened in 1975, this museum is housed in what is probably the oldest railway station in Britain (1841), still in use and carefully restored. It contains exhibits and models connected with the Stockton and Darlington and the North Eastern Railway Companies, including an early railway coach (c1845), a chaldron wagon and five 19th-C locomotives,

one of which is the original 'Locomotive No. 1' built by George Stephenson in 1825 also the Derwent built 1845. A model railway. Souvenir shop. ⚲ Open all year daily Easter to end Oct, Mon to Sat 10–5, Suns 2–4; Nov to Easter, Mon to Sat 10–3. 20p (ch 16 and pen 10p). Party. ⚠ *(Tel 60532)* ⅋

DARTINGTON *Devon* Map 3 SX76
Dartington Hall Only 14th-C banqueting hall of house shown. Large gardens, with trees and shrubs, courtyard, and terraces. Research, education, agriculture, and other commercial enterprises on the estate are controlled by Dartington Hall Trust. ⚲ Open all year, daily. Gardens and hall occasionally closed for special events. Free. ⚠ *(Tel Totnes 862271)* ⅋ B *(NGS)*

DARTMOUTH *Devon* Map 3 SX85
Agincourt House Lower Ferry. Built 1380, and restored 1671 and 1966, partly timbered house, one of the oldest in town. Formerly rich merchant's house, now antique shop and museum with two of its four floors open to public. Open all day all year (ex week after Christmas). Free. P. *(Tel 2472)* **(79)**
Bayard's Cove Castle Low, circular ruined stronghold, built by townspeople in 1537, with gunposts as at Dartmouth Castle (see below). Accessible at all reasonable times. Free. ⚠ *(AM)*
Butterwalk Museum Half timbered 17th-C house, part of restored colonnaded arcade, with small maritime and nautical museum (over 100 ship models). Open end Oct to end Apr, Mon–Sat 2–4; May to Oct, Mon–Sat 11–5. 10p (ch 15 5p, ch 5 free). P. *(Tel 2923)*
Dartmouth Castle Tudor stronghold, dating from 1481, with some remains of earlier structure. Stands on estuary of River Dart facing Kingswear Castle on opposite shore, to

which it was attached by chain in times of war. Timber-framed opening for the chain can still be seen. Open*, see inside front cover. 25p (ch 16 and pen 10p). ⚠ *(AM)*

Newcomen Memorial Engine In Royal avenue Gardens by River Dart, this glass-fronted building commemorates the 300th anniversary of Newcomen's birth, and houses his atmospheric pressure steam pumping engine of 1725. Possibly the oldest of its type in world, it may be seen working. Open to view Easter to end Oct Mon–Sat 11–5, Sun 2–5. Special opening times in winter for pre-arranged parties. 10p (ch 15 5p, ch 5 free). P. *(Tel 2923)*. 18-page booklet is available, 25p incl postage. ⚹

DAWLISH WARREN *Devon* Map 3 SX97
South Devon Railway Museum and Model Railway Dawlish Warren Station A large collection of smaller railway relics including locomotive name/number plates, station signs, notices, tickets, documents, etc and model railway ('oo' scale). Shop stocking railway books, records, photographs, model equipment etc. Open daily Sun before Easter to Sun after Easter, Sun only until Spring BH then daily to end Sep 10–dusk. 50p (school child 25p). P. *(Tel 862131)* ⚹

DEAL *Kent* Map 5 TR35
Deal Castle Built by Henry VIII, with massive central citadel, houses exhibits of Iron Age weapons, early pottery, and relics of Deal's history. Open*, see inside front cover. 25p (ch 16 and pen 10p). ⚠ *(AM)*

Maritime and Local History Museum 22 St George's Road. Opened 1972 with exhibits including local boats, model sailing-ships, 'bygones', maps, old photographs, etc. Annexe where land and sea finds are examined, treated and classified. Local booklets, postcards etc on sale. Open Spring BH to end Sep daily 2–5. 20p (ch 5p, accompanied free). Under revision for 1980. P. *(Tel 4524)* ⚹ B

Walmer Castle 1m S, on coast. Built in 16th C, official residence of the Lord Warden of the Cinque Ports. Open*, see inside front cover, but closed always between 1 pm and 2 pm and also on Mons, ex BH. Gardens closed in winter. 40p (ch 16 and pen 15p), winter 15p (ch and pen 5p). Closed for a period, usually in Aug, when the Lord Warden is in residence. ⚠ *(Tel 01-734 6010 ext 448) (AM)*

DEDDINGTON *Oxfordshire* Map 4 SP43
Deddington Castle Mainly earthworks from outer bailey and inner ward. Excavations have revealed portions of 13th-C chapel. Piers Gaveston (favourite of Edward II) taken prisoner here before being executed in 14th-C. Open any reasonable time. Free. *(AM)*

DEDHAM *Essex* Map 5 TM03
Castle House Former home and studio of the late Sir Alfred Munnings KCVO, PRA. Contains paintings, drawings, sketches, and other works. Open 11 May to 12 Oct, Wed, Sun, BH, Thu and Sat in Aug 2–5; parties by arrangement. 40p (ch 15, 10p). Under review for 1980. ⚠ *(Tel Colchester 322127)*

DEENE *Northamptonshire* Map 4 SP99
Deene Park Mainly 16th-C house of great architectural importance and historical interest. Large lake and park. Extensive gardens with old fashioned roses, rare trees and shrubs. ⚏ Open 6, 7 Apr; 25, 26 May, Suns Jun and Jul, also 24, 25 Aug, 2–6. Admission prices not available. ⚠ *(Tel Bulwick 223 or 278)* ⚹

Kirby Hall 1½m W. Fine, partially restored house, begun in 1572, but altered in mid 17th C for Sir Christopher Hatton, Lord Chancellor, by John Thorpe, and later portion ascribed to Inigo Jones. Attractive garden layout. Open, see inside front cover. 20p (ch 16 and pen 5p). ⚠ *(Tel Corby 3230) (AM)*

DEERHURST *Gloucestershire* Map 3 SO82
Odda's Chapel Off B4213 near River Severn. Rare Saxon chapel, dating back to 1056, and erected originally by the Lord of the Manor. Attached to old half-timbered house. Open, see inside front cover. 10p (ch 16 and pen 5p). *(Tel Tewkesbury 292663) (AM)* ⚹

DELABOLE *Cornwall* Map 2 SX08
Delabole Slate Quarry and Museum Ancient slate quarry, worked continuously since 1555. Over 500ft deep and 1⅛ miles round. Featured in the Guinness Book of Records as being the largest man-made hole in England (possibly Europe). Museum and craft shop. Open 2 week Easter and May to Sep Mon–Fri 10–6. 25p (ch 15p). Under revision for 1980. ⚠ *(Tel Camelford 2242)*

DENVER MILL *Norfolk* Map 5 TF60
Large tower built in 1835, with 6 storeys and a complex of buildings formerly containing a steam mill. Steam gave way to diesel power and the engine and equipment is still in place, together with much of the wind-driven machinery. Open all year (by appointment) 9–dusk (closed Sun). Free. P. *(Tel Downham Market 2285)*

DERBY *Derbyshire* Map 8 SK33
Derby Museum and Art Gallery Antiquities, social history, natural history, militaria, Bonnie Prince Charlie room (1745 rebellion), scaled working layout of the former Midland Railway. Paintings by Joseph Wright of Derby (1734–1797), Derby porcelain, costume. Open all year, daily (closed Sun, Mon, and BH) Tue to Fri 10–6, Sat 10–5. Free. Parking in town. *(Tel 31111 ext 782)* ⚹

Industrial Museum Silk Mill, off Full Street. Housed in an early 17th-C silk mill substantially rebuilt in 1910. The Rolls-Royce aero engine occupies the ground floor gallery, alongside the history of aviation from the Wright Brothers to the present day. 'An Introduction to Derbyshire Industries' occupies the first floor gallery. Open all year (closed Sun, Mon and BH) Tue to Fri 10–5.45, Sat 10–4.45. Free. *(Tel 31111 ext 740)* ⚹

DEREHAM *Norfolk* Map 9 TF91
Bishop Bonner's Cottages Row of restored cottages, with coloured East Anglian pargeting (1502), now a museum, with local archaeological discoveries, and exhibitions of rural crafts during summer months. Open mid May to Sep, Tue, Thu, and Fri 2.30–5, Sat 3–5.30; contact *Mrs Webb, 6 Sandy Lane*. Free. P. *(Tel 2789)* **(79)**

Norfolk Rural Life Museum 2½m NW on unclass road at Gressenhall. A Museum of Norfolk rural life to show history of the County of Norfolk over past 200 years with particular emphasis on agriculture. Open daily (ex Mon) 10–5, Sun 2–5.30. 30p (ch and pen free) ⚠ *(Tel Gressenhall 563)*

DEVIZES *Wiltshire* Map 4 SU06
Devizes Museum Exhibits from prehistoric, Roman, and medieval periods in Wiltshire, including 1st-C Belgic 'Marlborough Bucket'. Open all year, Tue to Sat 11–1, 2–5. 25p (ch 16 free, students and pen 10p). Under revision for 1980. P. *(Tel 2765)* ⚹ B

DIDCOT *Oxfordshire* Map 4 SU58
*Great Western Society Didcot Railway
Centre* Access through main entrance of
Didcot station. Largest collection of ex-Great
Western rolling stock assembled in GWR
engine shed, including 20 steam locomotives,
a diesel railcar, and large selection of
passenger and freight rolling stock. ⚏ and gift
shop. Open Sun also BH Mon Apr to Oct.
Steam days first and last Sun of each month
also BH Mon and Sun in Aug, 11–5. GWR
steam train in operation. BH weekends and
Enthusiasts' Day 80p (ch 40p) otherwise 60p
(ch 30p). Special rates for family parties.
Prices under revision. P. Enquiries to *Great
Great Western Society, Didcot Railway
Centre, Oxon*

DIDSBURY *Gt Manchester* Map 7 SJ89
Fletcher Moss Museum Wilmslow Road.
New displays, due to open in 1980, of art and
design in Manchester. Drawings and
watercolours by the Pre-Raphaelites and
20th-C artists. Temporary exhibitions during
the summer. Open Mon to Sat 10–6 (4 Nov to
Feb); Sun 2–6 (4 Nov to Feb) 12–6 May to
Aug. Free. *(Tel 061-445 1109)*

DILHORNE *Staffordshire* Map 7 SJ94
Foxfield Light Railway Society New
museum of industrial steam locomotives,
under auspices of Foxfield Light Railway
Society. There are twelve steam locomotives,
two or more which may be in steam on an
open day. The former mineral line on which
they run passes over 3½ miles of track through
undulating rural scenery. ⚏ Souvenir shop.
Open Apr to Sep, Sun and BH 2–6. Day
membership of society essential 60p (ch 14
and pen 30p), subject to possible increase. ⚠
(Tel Stoke-on-Trent 313920) ⚅

DINMORE *Hereford and Worcester*
Map 3 SO45
Dinmore Manor 12th- to 14th-C Chapel of
the Knights Hospitaller of St John of
Jerusalem, with cloisters and music room.
Chapel and gardens open all year (ex 25
Dec), daily 10–6. 40p (ch 16 and pen 20p). ⚠
(limited). *Tel 061-943 2313)*. *(Mr J S Murray)*
⚅

DINTING VALE *Derbyshire* Map 7 SK09
Dinting Railway Centre Off A57 in Dinting
Lane. One engine is always in steam Mar to
Oct, Sun and BH. Large picnic area. ⚏.
Steam weekends 1 Jan, 4–7 Apr, 3–5 and
25/26 May also 23–25 Aug. Open all year,
daily (ex 24 May and 25/26 Dec) 10.30–5.
30p (ch 16 15p) subject to confirmation. Party.
⚠ *(Tel Glossop 5596)* ⚅

DISLEY *Cheshire* Map 7 SJ98
Lyme Park Of Elizabethan origin, enlarged in

1726 by Leoni and in 1817 by Lewis Wyatt,
with fine Palladian façade, Jacobean rooms,
and collection of pictures and furnishings. A
park of more than 1,300 acres, contains herd
of deer.Hall shown Mar to Oct, daily (ex Mon)
Apr to Sep, Sun and BH 1–6, Tue to Sat 2–5.
Mar and Oct Sun 1–4.30 and Tue to Sat 2–4.
House 37p. Park and gardens open all year,
daily 8–sunset. Free. Prices subject to
revision for 1980. ⚠ 30p. *(NT)*

DITCHLEY *Oxfordshire* Map 4 SP32
Ditchley Park 18th-C mansion by James
Gibbs, now Anglo-American conference
centre, in landscaped park. Interior
decoration includes rooms by Flitcroft and
Kent. Open 21 Jul to 1 Aug daily 2–5. 60p P.
(Tel Enstone 346). No photography except by
prior permission. ⚅ B (gardens)

DOBWALLS *Cornwall* Map 2 SX26
Forest Railroad Park Very extensive
miniature railway based on the era of steam
on the American railroad. A mile ride
modelled on the Cumbres Pass route of the
Denver and Rio Grande railroad, and another
spectacular mile of track based on the
Sherman Hill route of the Union Pacific
railroad. Forest, tunnels, embankments,
canyons and the steepest gradients on a
miniature railway anywhere. Large picnic
areas; railway walk; indoor railway exhibition;
children's play areas; radio controlled boats;
⚏ Open 4 Apr to 14 Apr then 1 May to end
Sep daily 10.30–6. Admission prices not yet
decided. ⚠ *(Tel 20325)*
Thorburn Museum and Gallery The unique
world renowned permanent memorial
exhibition of paintings, sketches, prints,
books, letters, photographs etc, by Britain's
greatest bird painter – Archibald Thorburn
(1860–1935). Over 120 original paintings
(many of major importance) on display in the
collection which is housed in a large
converted barn. Award winner in the 'Museum
of the year' award 1977 also British Tourist
Authority's 'Come to Britain' competition.
Open Easter 10 days then 1 May to end of
Sep, daily 10.30–6. At other times by
appointment only. Admission charges not yet
decided for 1980. P. *(Tel 20325)*

DODDINGTON *Lincolnshire* Map 8 SK87
Doddington Hall Romantic Elizabethan
mansion with Tudor gatehouse, walled rose
garden. Fine furniture, porcelain, textiles and
pictures. Souvenir and gift shop. ⚏ (tea)
Open 2–6, Wed May to Sep also Sun, Jun,
Jul and Aug, and 7 Apr, 5 and 26 May, 25 Aug.
Parties at other times by arrangement. School
project. Prices for 1980 not yet decided. *(Tel
227. (Mrs A Jarvis)*

DODINGTON *Avon* Map 3 ST77
Dodington House, Park and Carriage Museum 200yds N of M4 junction 18. 18th-C classic house, built by James Watt and approached by a mile-long drive through 700 acres of parkland laid out by 'Capability' Brown. Furniture, paintings, *objets d'art*, and unusual fireplaces by Wyatt can be seen in the house. **Carriage Museum** Horses and over 30 carriages, **Family Museum** aviation scale model collection. Children's adventureland, children's farm, antique agricultural implements exhibition and nature trails. ⚐ and bar. Open Apr to Sep, daily 11–5. Admission prices not yet decided. Train and carriage rides extra. Dogs on lead only (not in house). ⚠ *(Tel Chipping Sodbury 318899)* ♿

DONCASTER *South Yorkshire* Map 8 SE50
Museum and Art Gallery Chequer Road. Prehistoric and Romano-British archaeology, British natural history, local history and costumes, British and European Art Collection, paintings, sculpture, ceramics, glass and silver. ⚐ Open all year (ex 25 and 26 Dec) and 1 Jan), Mon–Fri 10–5, Sun 2–5. Free. ⚠ *(Tel 62095)* ♿

DONINGTON-LE-HEATH *Leicestershire* Map 8 SK41
Donington-le-Heath Manor House Near Coalville. Medieval manor house of c1280 with very few alterations. 2 Apr to 1 Oct Wed to Sun also BH Mon and Tue 2–6. Free. ⚠ *(Tel Coalville 31259)*

DONNINGTON *Berkshire* Map 4 SU46
Donnington Castle Late 14th-C gatehouse, with earthworks from Civil War sieges of 1644–46. Open at any reasonable time (exterior only). Free. ⚠ *(AM)*

DORCHESTER *Dorset* Map 3 SY69
Came House 2m SE of Dorchester, off A352 near Winterbourne Came. 18th-C house with columned 7 bay entrance façade, and interior with good fireplaces and plasterwork. Open only by appointment to Major N D Martin. 50p ⚠

Dorset County Museum High West Street. Fine County collection of prehistoric and Roman antiquities, geology, natural history, rural crafts, and relics of both Thomas Hardy and William Barnes. Hardy's manuscripts for *The Mayor of Casterbridge*, and his reconstructed study can be seen. concerts, lectures, films. Open all year (ex Sun, 4 Apr, 25/26 Dec), Mon to Fri 10–5, Sat 10–1 and 2–5. 30p (ch and pen 15p), ch 5 free). ⚠ *(Tel 2735)*

Dorset Military Museum The Keep. Covers nearly 300 years of military history, with exhibits of Dorset Regiment, Militia, Volunteers, Queen's Own Dorset Yeomanry and Devonshire and Dorset Regiment (from 1958). Also well-stocked reference library. Open all year (ex Sun, 13 and 16 Apr, 25 and 26 Dec), Mon to Fri 9–1 and 2–5, Sat 9–12 (Jul to Sep 9–1 and 2–5). 20p (ch 10p). ⚠ *(Tel 4066)*

Hardy's Cottage 3m E, off A35 near Higher Bockhampton. Thatched house, birthplace in 1840 of Thomas Hardy. Cottage open only by appointment with tenant. *(Tel Dorchester 2366)*; exterior viewable Mar to Oct, daily 11–6 (or sunset). 60p. P in woods 10 min walk from house. *(NT)*

Old Crown Court In 1834, in the Court Room of the Old Shire Hall, the Tolpuddle Martyrs were sentenced to transportation to Botany Bay in Australia for demanding a wage increase. Building is now a Tolpuddle

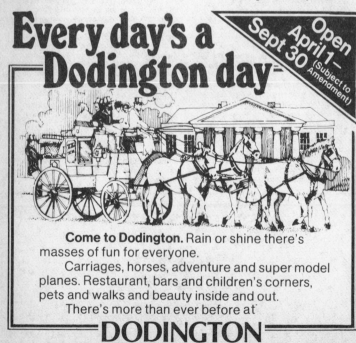

Memorial. Open all year, Mon to Fri 10–12 and 2.30–4 (Nov to Apr 10–12); other times only by arrangement at adjacent West Dorset District Council. Free. P. *(Tel 5211)*

Maiden Castle 1m SW. Prehistoric earthworks, the name being derived from Celtic 'Mai-Jun' (the stronghold by the plain)' Huge, oval, triple-ramparted camp, with extensive plateau on summit. Complicated defensive system of ditches and ramparts. Open at any reasonable time. Free. ⚠ *(AM)*

Wolfeton House 1½m NW on A37. A fine medieval and Elizabethan manor house with magnificent stonework, great stairs, fire places and ceilings. 17th-C furniture and pictures. Gatehouse chapel and cider house. ⚏ for parties by appointment. Open 1 May to 10 Sep Sun, Tue, Wed and BH plus daily Aug (ex Sat) 2.30–6. Parties throughout the year by appointment. 75p. ⚠ *(Tel 3500)*

DOVER *Kent* Map 5 TR34

Crabble Watermill Lower Road. A six-storey building erected in about 1812 to provide flour for the troops stationed in the area when Britain was threatened with invasion by Napoleon. The mill gradually ceased to function and finally went out of use in about 1890. The mill was restored to full working order by the Cleary Foundation in 1973. Open Easter, then Spring BH to end Sep, Wed and Sat 2–5, Sun and BH 10–1 and 2–6. When machinery working ch 14 not admitted. Ch 14 admitted Wed and Sat, if accompanied by a parent. 15p (ch 10p). Party. *(Tel Dover 201066)* &

Dover Castle Norman castle with keep (1181–87) containing 242ft deep well. Roman 'Pharos', or lighthouse, and restored Saxon St Mary de Castro's church nearby. Keep* grounds and underground passages, see inside front cover. ⚏ Admission to keep 40p, winter 25p (ch 16 and pen 20p, winter 10p); underground passages 25p (ch 16 and pen 10p). Grounds free. ⚠ 10p. *(AM)*

Roman Painted House New Street. Large part of an exceptionally preserved Roman town house 1,800 years old containing the best preserved and oldest Roman wall paintings north of the Alps. Also substantially complete underfloor central heating systems, part of later Roman fort wall, stone tower, extensive display panel on Roman Dover and some recent finds. Free guided tours for parties. Open Mar to Nov, Tue to Sun 10–5. 20p (ch and pen 10p). ⚠ *(Tel 203279)* & B

Town Hall Includes 13th-C Hall of Maison Dieu, part of former pilgrim's hostel founded by Hubert de Burgh. Museum, founded 1836, contains exhibits of local history, archaeology, ceramics, coins, natural history,

geology. There is a monthly programme of temporary exhibitions. Open 10–4.45 (closed Wed and Sun). Free. *(Tel 201066)* &

DOWN AMPNEY *Gloucestershire* Map 4 SU09

Down Ampney House and Art Exhibition 6m SE of Cirencester, 3m NW of Cricklade, off A419. Tudor and later house with well restored mid 15th-C hall. Exhibition of paintings by local artists held annually. Open 28 Jul to 5 Aug. Daily 10–7. 10p. ⚠ **(79)**

DOWNE *Gt London* Map 5 TQ46

Down House Contains the Darwin Memorial. Gardens also open. Open 1 Mar to 31 Jan (ex Mon, Fri, 24–27 Dec and all Feb) 1–6 (last visitor 5.30). Open BH Mons. 50p (ch 15 20p). ⚠ *(Tel Farnborough, Kent 59119, Tue to Thu 10–6)* &

DRAYTON MANOR PARK AND ZOO
Staffordshire Map 4 SK10
On A4091 1m S of junction with A5(T). 1½m S of Tamworth. 160 acres of parkland with 15-acre zoo, including lions, pumas, tigers, monkeys, reptile house, birds, paddocks and farm section. Jungle cruise on the lower lake. Miniature railway, cable cars, amusement park, boats, garden centre, Dinosaurs in the 'Lost World'; shops. ⚏ (licensed) (party tearoom). Open Easter to Oct, daily 10.30–7. Admission prices as advertised. Reduced rates for parties. ⚠ (Parked on parkland). *(Tel Tamworth 68481)* &

DREWSTEIGNTON *Devon* Map 3 SX79
Castle Drogo 2m NE of Chagford, turn off A382 at Sandy Park. A granite castle built between 1910 and 1930, one of the most remarkable works of Sir Edwin Lutyens. Standing at 900ft it overlooks the wooded gorge of the River Teign. Open 1 Apr to Oct, daily 11–6 (last admission 5.30). £1.30, gardens and grounds only 90p *(NT)*

DUDLEY *West Midlands* Map 7 SO99
Black Country Museum Tipton Road
(opposite Dudley Guest Hospital). An open-
air museum of the region with buildings re-
erected to form a village representing the way
of life in this area. The village has a 19th-C
canal boat dock with a range of narrow boats
on display. A chainmaker's house with its
brewhouse has been re-erected and in the
garden, the chainshop stages regular
demonstrations of chainmaking. At weekends
trips into the famous Dudley Tunnel start from
the site. Also a coal mine, chemist's shop and
chapel are on display. Open from 1 May to 30
Sep. Admission charges not available. ⚠ *(Tel
Birmingham 557 9643)*
Central Museum and Art Galley St James's
Road. Permanent collection of fine art and a
wide variety of temporary exhibitions
throughout the year. Fine geological gallery.
Reconstructed Black Country Nail Forge, also
the Brooke Robinson Museum. The Brierley
Hill Glass collection will be on display until
amalgamation with the Stourbridge Glass
collection at Kingswinford in 1980. Open all
year, Mon to Sat 10 – 6. Free. *(Tel 55433)*
Dudley Zoo Situated in 40 acres of
attractively wooded grounds, the great variety
of animals, birds, reptiles and fish includes a
white tiger, okapis, ring-tailed lemurs and
silvery marmosets. Children's corner, a chair-
lift and part of the ruins of Dudley castle can
be explored. Picnic area. ⚏ Open daily,
weekdays from 9.30, Sun from 10. ⚠ No pets
admitted.

DUNGENESS *Kent* Map 5 TR01
Dungeness Lighthouses Old lighthouse,
standing slightly inland, was replaced in 1961
because its light had been obscured by the
nuclear power station. Ground floor of new
lighthouse open all year daily (ex Sun and
during fog) 1 pm to 1 hr before sunset (at
visitors' own risk). Free. P. *(Tel Lydd 20236)*
'A' Nuclear Power Station Building open
throughout the year for organised group tours
by pre-arrangement, and to the general public
Jun – Sep, Wed 2 – 4. Ticket obtainable from
the local South Eastern Electricity Board
shops. Ch 14 not admitted. Free. ⚠ *(Tel Lydd
20461)* **(79)**

DUNSTER *Somerset* Map 3 SS95
Dunster Castle Restored 11th-C and later
castle, with rare portraits, hall leading to
famous carved staircase; banqueting hall
containing leather hangings. Open Apr to Sep
daily (ex Fri and Sat) 11 – 5, Mar, Oct and Nov,
Tue, Wed and Sun 2 – 4. £1 (ch 14 50p). Party
15+. ⚠ *(Tel 314) (NT)*

Old Dovecote 12th-C dovecote, part of
former priory, retaining rare original potence
(revolving ladder for reaching nesting boxes).
Open Easter to mid Oct, daily 10 – dusk. Free;
leaflet 5p

DUNWICH *Suffolk* Map 5 TM47
Dunwich Museum St James Street.
Contains the history and relics of the ancient
city of Dunwich, also flora and fauna of the
area. Open all year (ex Christmas and New
Year) Sat and Sun 2 – 4.30, also Tue and Thu
May to Jul and Sep and Oct 2 – 4.30, and daily
Aug 2 – 4.30. Free. ⚠ *(Tel Westleton 218 or
276)*

DUPATH *Cornwall* Map 2 SX37
Holy Well Dedicated to St Sampson of
Guernsey and erected c1500, one of best
known ancient Holy Wells of Cornwall.
Viewable at any reasonable time. Free. *(AM)*

DURHAM *Co Durham* Map 12 NZ24
Durham Castle Norman structure, utilised
since 1832 by University of Durham. Open
first three weeks of Apr and 1 Jul to 30 Sep,
Mon – Sat 10 – 12 and 2 – 4.30; rest of year,
Mon, Wed, Sat 2 – 4; closed at times owing to
university functions. 60p (ch 14 and pen 30p).
Guides are available at no extra cost and
guide books are on sale at the Porter's Lodge.
P. *(Tel 65481)*
**Durham Light Infantry Museum and Arts
Centre** Aykley Heads. History of famous
regiment, including armaments, medals, and
uniforms, in modern setting. Also Arts centre
on first floor of building. Exhibitions, films and
family activities. Military Vehicle Rally Aug
BH. ⚏ Open all year Tue to Sat 10 – 5, Sun
2 – 5 (closed Mon ex BH). 20p (ch and pen
5p). P. Free brochure. *(Tel 67798)* ⚐
Gulbenkian Museum of Oriental Art
University of Durham, Elvet Hill. Contains
Egyptian and Mesopotamian antiquities;
Chinese and Japanese pottery, porcelain,
jades, ivories, textiles and paintings; Indian
and Tibetan paintings and sculpture; and
works from the Near East. Open Mon to Fri
9.30 – 1, 2.15 – 5; Sat 9.30 – 12, 2.15 – 5, Sun
2.15 – 5 (closed Sat and Sun Christmas to
Easter). 30p (ch, students and pen 15p). P.
(Tel 66711)
St Aidan's College Grounds Windmill Hill.
The college was designed by Sir Basil
Spence, architect of Coventry Cathedral, and
built in the early sixties. The spacious and
well-stocked grounds were landscaped by
Professor Brian Hackett and are at their best
during July, when the shrub beds are in
flower. Features of interest include a
laburnham walk and a reflecting pool, well

stocked with aquatic plants and fish. Open all year, daily from 9 – dusk. Free, but donation to NGS. ⚠ *(Tel 65011)* & B

DUXFORD *Cambridgeshire* Map 5 TL44
Duxford Airfield 2m W of village on A505. This former Battle of Britain fighter station with hangars dating from the First World War now houses most of the Imperial War Museum's collections of military aircraft, armoured fighting vehicles and other large exhibits. The airfield has changed little in outward appearance since the Second World War. There are more than sixty historic aircraft on the airfield including a B-17 Flying Fortress, P-51 Mustang, Junkers 52, Lightning, Javelin, Super Sabre and Victor. Also on display is the Duxford Aviation Society's civil aircraft collection including Concorde 01. Details available from *Imperial War Museum, Lambeth Road, London SE1 6HZ*. Open 15 Mar to 2 Nov, daily 11 – 5 (or dusk). Admission/parking fee charged, telephone for details. *(Tel 01-735 8922 or Cambridge 833963)* &

DYMCHURCH *Kent* Map 5 TR02
Martello Tower (No. 24) One of a series of circular towers designed to repel expected Napoleonic invasion in early 19th C, with rooftop mounting for heavy gun. Open*, see inside front cover (Apr to Sep only). 15p (ch 16 and pen 5p). ⚠ *(AM)*

DYRHAM *Avon* Map 3 ST77
Dyrham Park 17th-C mansion, designed partly by William Talman in 1698, with contemporary Dutch-style furnishings. Garden front of 1692 by Hauduroy. ⚐ Open house and garden Apr, May and Oct daily, except Thu and Fri, 2 – 6; Jun to Sep daily, except Fri, 2 – 6. £1 *(NT)*

EAGLESCLIFF *Cleveland* Map 8 NZ41
Preston Hall Museum Museum illustrates social history of Stockton, and collections include ceramics, personalia, arms and armour, and period rooms. ⚐ Open all year Mon to Sat 10 – 6. Sun 2 – 6. Free. ⚠ *(Tel 871184)* & B

EASBY *North Yorkshire* Map 7 NZ10
Easby Abbey Sited on banks of River Swale, a Premonstratensian Abbey dedicated to St Agatha, founded 1155. Considerable remains of monastic buildings. Open, see inside front cover. 15p (ch 16 and pen 5p). Free Mon and Tue, Apr to Sep only. ⚠ *(AM)*

EAST BERGHOLT *Suffolk* Map 5 TM03
Flatford Lock Similar in appearance to the lock shown in many of John Constable's paintings, the unique lock has been restored

by voluntary workers of the River Stour Trust and is now used by non-powered craft. Demonstrations can be arranged for parties. Contact *F Batten, Wissington Grove, Nayland*. A restored Stour Lighter is also available for inspection on request. Open at all times. Free. ⚠ &
Flatford Mill and Willy Lott's Cottage 18th-C water mill and mill house once owned by Constable's father, subject of *The Hay Wain* and other famous pictures by the painter. 17th-C Willy Lott's Cottage stands nearby. Both in full time use by Field Studies Council. Exteriors only viewable. *(NT)*

EASTBOURNE *East Sussex* Map 5 TV69
Eastbourne Circular Redoubt Royal Parade. Extensive fortification built in 1804 during Napoleonic Wars against the threat of invasion. Now the home of the Sussex Combined Services Museum which illustrates the military history of Sussex. Access to the gun platform and aquarium. Open May to Sep, daily, Oct to Apr Mon to Fri, 10 – 6. 25p (ch 16 and pen 15p). Under review for 1980. ⚠ *(Tel 33952)*
Coastal Defence Museum Tower 73 (The Wish Tower), King Edward's Parade. One of the Martello Towers erected to combat threatened Napoleonic invasion in early 19th C now restored as museum displaying defence methods and equipment of that period. Open Easter to Sep, daily 10 – 5.30. 12p (ch 14 and pen 8p). Prices under review for 1980. ⚠ *(Tel 35809)*
Towner Art Gallery Borough Lane. Georgian manor house (1776) with later alterations, in pleasant gardens, containing collection of 19th and 20th-C British paintings, contemporary artists' prints and Georgian caricatures. Art exhibitions. Open all year (ex 4 Apr, 25 and 26 Dec) Mon to Sat 10 – 5 (closed 1 – 2), Sun 2 – 5. Free. ⚠ *(Tel 21635)* & B

EAST CLANDON *Surrey* Map 4 TQ05
Hatchlands 18th-C house, with interiors of 1759, including plaster drawing room ceiling and library by Robert Adam. Open 1 Apr – 30 Sep, Wed and Sat 2 – 5.30 (last entries at 5pm). 40p (ch 12 20p). ⚠ (limited). *(Tel Guildford 222787)*. See also **Clandon Park**.

EAST GRINSTEAD *West Sussex* Map 5 TQ33
Sackville College Early Jacobean almshouse, with hall and chapel, built round a quadrangular courtyard, and founded in 1609 by 2nd Earl of Dorset. Contains fine oak furniture. Open May to Sep, daily (ex Sat) 2 – 5. 25p (ch 14 15p). P. *(Tel 21639)* & **(79)**

Standen 1½m S signposted from B2110.
Designed in 1894 by Philip Webb with original
William Morris textiles and wallpapers.
Hillside garden. Open Apr to end Oct, Wed,
Thu and Sat 2 – 5.30 (last admission 5pm).
80p. Garden only 30p. Dogs on lead in garden
only. *(NT)*

EAST LAMBROOK *Somerset* Map 3 ST41
*East Lambrook Manor, Gardens & Margery
Fish Nursery* 15th- and 16th-C house, with
old panelling and a well-known garden with
rare plants – a memorial to Margery Fish.
Garden and Nursery open all the year daily
9 – 5, house open every Thu 2 – 5 1 Mar to
31 Oct. Admission to house 15p (ch 10p)
garden and Nursery 15p (ch 10p). Party. ⚠
House and garden open first Sun in Jul for
Gardeners Royal Benevolent Society. *(Tel
South Petherton 40328). (Mr F Boyd-
Carpenter)* ⚼ (garden)

EAST MEON *Hampshire* Map 4 SU62
Court House 14th-C ecclesiastical court hall,
solar, etc, in walled gardens, in unspoilt
village. Open by appointment only with Mr A D
Gill. 25p (ch 10p). ⚠ *(Tel 274)*

EASTNOR *Hereford and Worcester*
Map 3 SO73
Eastnor Castle Built by Sir Robert Smirke for
1st Earl Somers in early 19th C, contains fine
furnishings, pictures, and armour. Grounds
have specimen trees. ⚲ Open Sun, 20 May to
end Sep also Wed and Thu Jul and Aug, also
BH Mons. Other times by appointment for
parties only. Admission prices not yet known,
ch and pen half price. ⚠ *(Tel Ledbury 2304).
(The Hon Mrs Hervey-Bathurst)* **(79)**

EASTON *Suffolk* Map 5 TM25
Easton Farm Park Rare breeds of farm
animals, Victorian Dairy, pets paddock and
adventure playpit. Visitors can watch the
cows being milked each afternoon. Country
bygones, picnic area, Bee keeping exhibition,
coarse fishing, Craft shop. ⚲ Open 4 Apr to 5
Oct daily 10.30 – 6. ⚠ *(Tel Wickham Market
746475)* ⚼

ECCLES *Gt Manchester* Map 7 SJ79
Monks Hall Museum Wellington Road. 16th-
C building with later additions, with
permanent collection of Nasmyth machinery,
paintings, ceramics, and local bygones, and
frequent temporary exhibitions. Small toy
museum in part of building. Open all year (ex
Sun, 4 Apr, 24/25 Dec and 1 Jan) Mon to Fri
10 – 6, Sat 10 – 5. Free. P. *(Tel 061-789 4372)* ⚼

EDNASTON *Derbyshire* Map 8 SK24
Ednaston Manor A Lutyens house with
garden of botanical interest. Large collection
of shrubs, shrub roses, clematis and unusual
plants; most varieties in containers for sale. ⚲
Sun. Gardens open 15 Apr to 30 Sep, Wed,
Thu 1 – 4.30. Sun 2 – 6. Parties weekdays,
meals by arrangement. Coach parties
welcome. 40p (ch 10p). ⚠ *(Tel Brailsford
325). (Mr S D Player) (NGS)* ⚼ **(79)**

ELCOT PARK HOTEL Berkshire
Map 4 SU36
5½m W Newbury off A4. 16-acre garden
overlooking the Kennet Valley with extensive
views. Mainly lawns and woodland laid out by
Sir William Paxton in 1848. Magnificent
displays of daffodils, rhododendrons and
other shrubs in spring. ⚲ Open all year 10 – 6.
Free (ex on National Gardens Scheme Suns).
⚠ *(Tel Kintbury 276 or 421). (NGS)* ⚼ B

*ELDS WOOD, THE WILLOUGHBRIDGE
GARDEN TRUST Staffordshire* Map 7 SJ73
200-year-old gravel quarry converted into
woodland garden, with daffodils,
rhododendrons, and azaleas. Water and rock
gardens. Gardens open Mar to Nov, 11 – 7.30
(or dusk). *(Tel Pipe Gate 237)* ⚼

ELSHAM *Humberside* Map 8 TA01
Elsham Hall Country Park With domestic
animals, bird sanctuary, carp feeding, craft
shop, open-air gallery for local artists, walk
round a trail and attempt a country quiz, pony-
trekking and fly fishing (by appointment, *Tel
Barnetby 698*). Wrawby Moor art gallery,
Pottery, Blacksmith. Air museum
(Preservation Society). Craftsmen at work
when advertised. ⚲ all year. Parties by
appointment. Hi-fi music by volunteers on
Sun during summer, 3 – 6.30. Open all year
(ex 4 Apr, 25 Dec), daily 1 – 8 (or dusk); Sat
and Sun and BH 11 – 8 (or dusk). 45p (ch
30p). Prices under revision for 1980. Trails
with warden Suns 2.30 (summertime). ⚠ *(Tel
Barnetby 738 or Barnetby 689 Caravan Club
Site)* ⚼

ELSTOW *Bedfordshire* Map 4 TL04
Moot Hall 1½m SW of Bedford on A6. 15th-C
market hall with 17th-C collection portraying
life and times of John Bunyan. Open all year,
daily (ex Mon, but incl summer BH) 10 – 1 and
2 – 5 (dusk in winter), Sun 2 – 5.30 (dusk in
winter). 10p (ch 5p, School parties up to 40 ch
£1.50). Family ticket 25p. ⚠ *(Tel Bedford
66889)* ⚼ B

ELVASTON *Derbyshire* Map 8 SK43
Elvaston Castle and Country Park Mansion
built by Wyatt in 1817, remains of 17th-C
house incorporated in the fabric, standing in
attractive grounds landscaped by William
Barron. Small agricultural museum in stable
yard and display of restored horse-drawn
caravans and wagons in courtyard. Family
history, Estate and Countryside museums
now being developed. Park, with lake, formal
gardens and Old English garden, includes
140 acres of woodland and facilities for
caravanning/camping, horse riding, field
studies and nature trail. House contains
information centre, shop and ⚲ (Easter to
Oct). Park open all year; Castle and Old
English garden 10 – 5. Free. ⚠ 30p weekends
and BH, other times free. *(Tel Derby 71342
Park Supervisor, 73735 Caravan/camp site
Warden)* ⚼ B

EMBLETON *Northumberland* Map 12 NU22
Dunstanburgh Castle 1½m E. Ruins of early
14th-C castle, facing North Sea, and built
partly by John of Gaunt. Open*, see inside
front cover (incl 13 Apr). 15p (ch 16 and pen
5p). *(AM and NT)*

EPWORTH *Humberside* Map 8 SE70
Old Rectory Birthplace and former home of
John and Charles Wesley built in 1709 after a
previous Rectory had been destroyed by fire,
restored in 1957. Open Mar – Oct Mon – Sat
10 – 12 and 2 – 4, Sun 2 – 4, winter months by
arrangement. Donations requested.
Accommodation available, meals by
arrangement. ⚠ *(Tel 872268)* ⚼ B

ESHER *Surrey* Map 4 TQ16
Claremont Entrance by Claremont Lane
A244, designed 1772 for Clive of India by
Henry Holland and 'Capability' Brown,
replaced former early 18th-C house built by
Vanbrugh for himself. Façade has columned
portico, and there are good fireplaces and
plaster ceilings. Now school for sons and
daughters of Christian Scientists and others.
Open Feb to Nov, first Sat and following Sun
in month 2 – 4.30. 50p (ch and pen 25p). ⚠
(Tel 67841)

Claremont Landscape Garden On S edge of Esher, E of A307. The earliest surviving English landscape garden, recently restored. Lake, island with pavilion, grotto and turf amphitheatre, viewpoint and avenues. House not NT property. Open every day Apr to end Oct, 9–7 or sunset if earlier; Nov to end Mar 9–4. 20p. *(NT)*

ETON *Berkshire* Map 4 SU97
Eton College World-famous public school, founded by Henry VI in 1440, with beautiful chapel. Chapel open 2–5 (10.30–12.30 in school hols, closed Sun in school hols). School Yard and Cloisters open weekdays 2–5 (6 during summer term); 10.30–12.30 in school holidays. 30p. Guided tours pm. May to Oct, 60p. ⚠ *(Tel Windsor 66461)* ♿ B

EUSTON *Suffolk* Map 5 TL87
Euston Hall 16th-C house with fine collection of paintings, including Stubbs, Van Dyck and Lely. 'Pleasure grounds' gardens by John Evelyn. Picnic area. Also 17th-C parish church in Wren style. ☕ Open 3 May to 27 Sep. Thu 2.30–5.30. 50p (ch 15 and pen 25p). ⚠ *(Tel Thetford 3281). (Duke of Grafton)* **(79)**

EVESHAM *Hereford and Worcester* Map 4 SP04
The Almonry Vine Street. 14th-C stone and half-timbered building, associated with former Benedictine abbey, containing museum of local history covering culture and industry of Vale of Evesham since prehistoric times. Open 4 Apr to end Sep, daily (ex Mon and Wed) 2.30–6.30; open BH. 15p (accompanied ch free). P. *(Tel 6944)*

EWELL *Surrey* Map 4 TQ26
Bourne Hall Cultural Centre Spring Street. 18th-C house replaced by cultural centre, museum, art centre, library, and also theatre hall and banqueting rooms. Collections embrace the human and natural history of the Epsom and Ewell area, and include costumes, dolls, toys, early photography and some finds from Nonsuch Palace. The Art Gallery has a continuous temporary Exhibitions programme. Other services include the identification of objects brought in by visitors. Open all year (ex Sun and Mon) Wed and Thu 10–5 (8 pm Tue & Fri); Sat 9.30–5. Free. ⚠ *(Tel 01-393 9573)* ♿

EXBURY *Hampshire* Map 4 SU40
Exbury Gardens Woodland gardens with azaleas, rhododendrons, and other flowering shrubs. ☕ Open early Apr to mid Jun, daily 2–6.30. 60p (ch 30p) coaches 50p per person. Prices under revision for 1980. ⚠ *(Tel Fawley 891203). (Mr E L de Rothschild) (NGS)* ♿

EXETER *Devon* Map 3 SX99
Custom House The Quay. Brick building (1681), illustrates first use of brickwork in city. Contains some fine plasterwork ceilings. Visitors shown interior by arrangement with HM Customs and Excise, casual visitors usually accepted. *(Tel 74021)*
The Devonshire Regiment Museum Wyvern Barracks. The exhibits cover the history of the Devonshire Regiment from its formation in 1685 to 1958 when the Regiment amalgamated with the Dorset Regiment. Exhibits include, uniforms, weapons, medals, historical documents and military souvenirs collected by the Regiment over the years. Open all year (ex Sat, Sun and BH) Mon to Fri 9–4.30. Free. ⚠ *(Tel 76581 ext 268)*
Guildhall High Street. Dates from 1330, partially rebuilt 1446, arches and façade added 1592–5. Open all year, Mon to Sat 10–5.30 except when used for meetings. P. Free. *(Tel 77888)* ♿ B

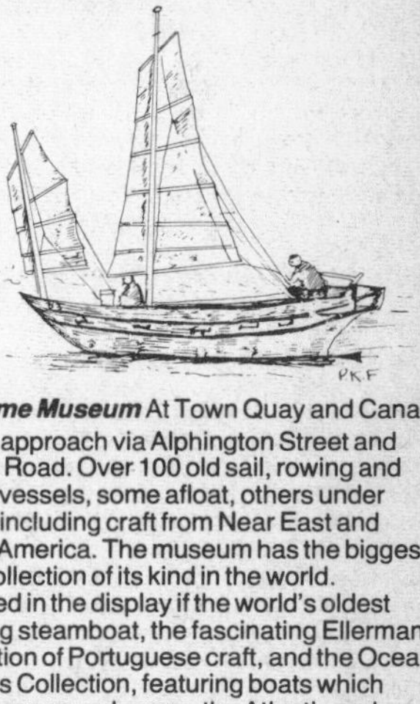

Maritime Museum At Town Quay and Canal Basin; approach via Alphington Street and Haven Road. Over 100 old sail, rowing and steam vessels, some afloat, others under cover, including craft from Near East and South America. The museum has the biggest boat collection of its kind in the world. Included in the display if the world's oldest working steamboat, the fascinating Ellerman Collection of Portuguese craft, and the Ocean Rowers Collection, featuring boats which have been rowed across the Atlantic and Pacific Oceans. The museum's buildings and boats have featured in the TV series *The Onedin Line*. Quays and old warehouses, and the oldest pound lock canal in England. Maritime book and gift shop. Steam launch trips in summer. ☕ Easter then Jun to Sep. Open all year daily (ex 25/26 Dec) 10–6

summer (5 winter). £1 (ch 50p and pen 75p). Under revision for 1980. Party 20+. Rowing boats for hire. ⚠ free. *(Tel 58075)* ㅎ B
Rougemont House Museum Castle Street. Georgian town-house, now museum of Devon and Exeter prehistoric, Roman and medieval archaeology. Open all year, Tue–Sat 10–1 and 2–5.30. Free. P. *(Tel 56724)*
Royal Albert Memorial Museum Queen Street. Founded in 1865, and extended several times. Large permanent displays of fine and applied art, natural history and ethnography, local industry. Of particular interest are collections of Devon paintings, Exeter silver, glass, local and foreign natural history. Museum shop and programme of temporary exhibitions. Open all year, Tue to Sat 10–5.30. Free. P. *(Tel 56724)*
St Nicholas' Priory Off Fore Street. Remains of 11th- to 16th-C Benedictine priory, with Norman undercroft, Tudor room, and 15th-C kitchen. Only complete monastic western range in England to have survived the dissolution and be restored. Displays of pewter, furniture and wood carving. Open all year Tue to Sat 10–1 and 2–5.30. 25p (ch 10p). Under revision for 1980. P. *(Tel 56724)*
Tuckers Hall Fore Street. Old Hall of the Weavers, Fullers, and Shearmen, occupied since 1471 by their incorporation which was granted Royal Charter in 1479–81. Wagon roof and panelling of 1638. Open all year Tue, Thu, Fri 10.30–12.30 (Oct to May, Fri only). ⚠ *(Tel 36244)*
Underground Passages Princesshay Medieval aqueducts which once supplied water to the city. Open all year, Tue to Sat 2–4.30. 25p (ch 10p). P. Under revision for 1980. *(Tel 56724)*
EXMOUTH *Devon* Map 3 SY08
A la Ronde Summer Lane, 2m N on A377. Curious 16-sided (hexadecaponal) house, dating from 1798, belonging to the Parminters. Regency gallery and interesting furnishings. The gallery and approaching staircase are covered in thousands of shells, the work of the 'Parminter Ladies'. There are unique collages of sand and seaweed, and a feather frieze around the drawing room. Wide coastal views from the house. ⚓ Open Easter to Oct, Mon–Sat 10–6, Sun 2–7. 60p (ch 14 30p). Under revision for 1980. ⚠ *(Tel 5514)*. *(Mrs Tudor-Perkins)* ㅎ
The Steam and Countryside Museum Sandy Bay, 1m SE. A museum for all the family. One of the largest working museums in the country. Hundreds of exhibits. Thatched Devon cottage, Shire horses, ponies and many other friendly animals.

Open 4 Apr to 28 Sep, from 10.30 am. 80p (ch 5–16 30p). ⚠ *(Tel 74533)* ㅎ

EYE MANOR *Hereford and Worcester* Map 3 SO46
4m N of Leominster. Built in 1680 by Ferdinando Gorges, and noted for its nine magnificent plaster ceilings. Contains exhibitions of decorative straw-work, dolls period costumes, needlework, etc. Students can sometimes be seen making corn dollies in August. Picnic area. Open 25 May to 14 Sep, Wed, Thu, Sat, Sun 2.30–5.30 also every afternoon Aug and 26/27 May. 50p (ch 19 20p). Party. ⚠ *(Tel Yarpole 244)*. *(Mr and Mrs C Sandford)* ㅎ B

EYNSFORD *Kent* Map 5 TQ56
Eynsford Castle Remains of 12th-C castle, including rectangular hall, walls, and ditch. Open*, see inside front cover. 15p (ch 16 and pen 5p). ⚠ *(AM)*
Lullingstone Castle 1m SW off A225. Mainly 18th-C house with fine 16th-C gate tower, the first large scale building to be of brick throughout with cut brick for detail. Other notable features include; The Great Hall, State Dining Room, Grand Staircase, State Drawing Room, State Bedroom and the Ante Room. Open Apr to Sep, Wed, Sat and Sun, also public hols 2–6. 75p (ch 13 15p, pen 25p). Party 30+. ⚠ *(Tel Farningham 862114)* ㅎ B
Lullingstone Roman Villa ½m W off A225. Remains of Roman villa, with a fine tessellated pavement. Now completely roofed with additional exhibits in lighted gallery. Open*, see inside front cover. 40p, winter 15p (ch 16 and pen 15p, winter 5p). ⚠ Summer coaches 20p, car 10p, motor cycles 5p. *(AM)*

FALMOUTH *Cornwall* Map 2 SW83
Pendennis Castle One of coastal forts erected c1540 by Henry VIII, with Elizabethan and later additions. Exhibition of coastal defences of the Tudor period. ⚓ Open*, see inside front cover. 30p (ch 16 and pen 15p). ⚠ *(AM)*
Penjerrick Gardens 3m SW of Falmouth, off B3291 near Budock. Beautiful sub-tropical gardens, including display of flowering shrubs. Open 1 Mar to end Sep Wed and Sun 1.30–4.30. 30p in box in garden. ⚠ *(Tel Mawnan Smith 659)*. *(Mrs J M K Fox)*

FARLEIGH HUNGERFORD *Somerset* Map 3 ST85
Farleigh Castle Ruined 14th-C castle with chapel containing monuments to the Hungerfords. Open*, see inside front cover. 20p (ch 16 and pen 5p). ⚠ *(AM)*

FARNBOROUGH *Warwickshire* Map 4 SP44
Hall 17th- and 18th-C house with wide views across Warwickshire plain towards Edgehill. Temples in fine grounds. Open Apr to Sep, Wed and Sat 2–6. 80p, grounds only 50p. *(NT)*.

FARNDON *Cheshire* Map 7 SJ45
Stretton Mill A water-powered corn mill with two wheels dating from 16th to 19th C, recently restored by the County Museum Service. Exhibition in stables. Open Easter to end Sep, 2–6 (ex Mon). 30p (ch 15p). ⚠ *(Tel Tilston 276)*

FARNHAM *Surrey* Map 4 SU84
Birdworld, Zoological Bird Gardens and Aquarium Holt Pound. 3½m SW of town, on A325 beyond Wrecclesham. Large variety of birds including parrots, flamingoes, hornbills, kestrels, penguins and waterfowl, also Aquarium housing tropical, fresh water and marine fish and invertebrates. 🍴 Open all year (ex 25 Dec), daily 9.30–6 (or 1 hr before dusk whichever comes first). Party. Children must be accompanied. No dogs. ⚠ *(Tel Bentley, Hants 2140)* &
Farnham Castle Keep Ruined shell keep of castle originally erected 1129–71 by Bishop Henry de Blois. Open, see inside front cover (Apr to Sep only). 15p (ch 16 and pen 5p). ⚠ *(AM)*
Willmer House Museum 38 West Street. Geology, archaeology, local history and art in Willmer House, a fine example of Georgian brickwork. Open all year (ex 25 & 26 Dec), Tue to Sat 11–1 and 2–5, Sun and BH 2.30–5 (closes ½ hr earlier in winter). Free. P. *(Tel 715094)*

FARWAY *Devon* Map 3 SY19
Farway Countryside Park 1½m S on unclass road. AA signposted on B3174. A collection of rare breeds and present day British farm animals can be seen in a beautiful farm setting with magnificent views over the Coly Valley. 130 acres of natural countryside. 'Guide Dogs for the Blind' dog show last Sun in Jun. Pony and donkey cart rides, daily Easter hols, then, Sun only until 27 May then daily to 10 Sep. Open 4 Apr to 30 Sep daily (closed Sat but open BH Sat) 10–6 (last admission 5 pm). 80p (ch 3–14 45p, pen 40p). Under revision for 1980. ⚠ *(Enquiries Mrs J M Forbes, Farway Countryside Park, Colyton, Devon. Tel 224)*

FAVERSHAM *Kent* Map 5 TR06
Chart Gunpowder Mills, Westbrook Walk. Town was once the centre of the gunpowder industry, and one of former mills dating from the late 18th C, believed to be oldest of their kind in the world, has been preserved and

restored. Also remains of others on site. Exterior on view at all times, interior open on request. Free. ⚠ (limited). *(Tel 4542)*
Fleur de Lis Heritage Centre Preston Street. History and architecture of a thousand years vividly illustrated by displays, audio visual programme and actual bygones in former 16th-C coaching inn. Open all year Mon to Sat 9–1 and 2–5 (Thu 9–1, BH 2–5). 40p (ch 14, students and pen 20p). P. *(Tel 4542)*
Maison Dieu Ospringe, 1m SW off A2. Timber-framed 15th-C house, with collection of Roman pottery and small museum of local history. Open, see inside front cover but closed all day Mon and Tue pm. 15p (ch 16 and pen 5p). *(AM)*

FELBRIGG *Norfolk* Map 9 TG23
Felbrigg Hall Early 17th- and mid 18th-C house. Jacobean south range has tall parapet, and over three protruding bays are carved the words *Gloria Deo in excelsis*. West wing is 17th-C and drawing room has fine plaster ceiling of 1687. Park with fine trees, woodland and lakeside walks. 🍴 Open (principal rooms and gardens) Apr to 12 Oct. Tue to Thu, Sat, Sun, and BH 2–6 (last admission 5.30). £1. Party 15+. No dogs. *(NT)*

FILBY *Norfolk* Map 9 TG41
Thrigby Hall Wildlife Gardens On unclass road off A1064. Selection of Asian mammals, birds and reptiles displayed in the landscaped gardens of the Hall. Features include 250-year-old summer-house, tropical house, bird house, ornamental waterfowl lake, yew walk. Stable, gift shop. 🍴 Open all year, daily 9.30–dusk. 80p (ch 5 and pen 40p). ⚠ *(Tel Fleggburgh 477)* &

FINCHALE PRIORY *Durham* Map 12 NZ24
Considerable remains of the 13th-C church of the Benedictine priory in picturesque position on banks of the River Wear. Open, see inside front cover. 15p (ch 16 and pen 5p). ⚠ *(AM)*

FINCHINGFIELD *Essex* Map 5 TL63
Finchingfield Guildhall and Museum Late 15th-C building comprising four Almhouse flats, library, meeting hall and museum. The museum exhibits items of local history from Roman times onwards. Art and Craft exhibition Spring BH week. Open Easter then 28 May to Sep, Sun and BH, 3–6. Free. ⚠ *(Tel Great Dunmow 810412)* **(79)**
Spains Hall 1m NW on unclass road. Elizabethan Manor house with some panelled rooms, 18th- and 19th-C furniture, also works of art. There are two fine tapestries and the Chippendale chairs are embroidered with the arms of the County and 14 Districts of Essex. Flower and Kitchen gardens each with

a greenhouse, and in the flower garden, a large 17th-C Cedar of Lebanon. ♨ (teas). Open 3 May to 3 Aug Sat and Sun, also 5 and 26 May, 2–5.30. House and garden £1 (ch 50p). Party. ⚠ *(Tel Great Dunmow 810266). (Sir J Ruggles-Brise)* ᕯ B

FIRLE *East Sussex* Map 5 TQ40
Firle Place Mainly Georgian house, with Tudor core. South Downs home of the Gage family for 500 yrs, containing connoisseurs' collection of European and English Old Masters, Sèvres porcelain and fine furniture. Shop and ♨ Open Jun to end Sep Sun, Wed and Thu, also Easter, 5, 25/26 May, and 24/25 Aug 2.15–5.30. Conducted tours 75p (ch 30p). 1st Wed in month unguided tour £1.10 (no reduction for ch). Party 30+. Admission prices under revision for 1980. ⚠ *(Tel Hailsham 843902 or Glynde 256)*

FISHBOURNE *West Sussex* Map 4 SU80
Roman Palace Salthill Road. Occupied 1st to 4th C, largest Roman Palace in Britain, with numerous mosaic pavements. Open Mar and Apr daily 10–5; May to Sep 10–6; Oct 10–5; Nov 10–4. 65p (ch 10p, students 35p). Under revision for 1980. *(Tel Chichester 785859). (Sussex Archaeological Society)*

FLADBURY *Hereford and Worcester* Map 3 SO94
Delamere Bird Gardens Hill Furze off B4084. A collection of birds, pet animals and model railways. Picnic area. Open all year, daily 9.30–dusk. 30p (ch 14 15p). ⚠ *(Tel Evesham 860580)* ᕯ

FLIMWELL *Kent* Map 5 TQ73
Bedgebury National Pinetum 1½m N off A21. Established by Forestry Commission in 1925, 160 acres of trees, including the most comprehensive collection of conifers in Europe, planted round old hammer pond. Over 100 research plots. ♨ weekdays during summer. Open all year, daily 10–8 or dusk (whichever is earlier). 25p (schoolchildren 10p). ⚠ *(Tel Goudhurst 392)*

FOLKESTONE *Kent* Map 5 TR23
Museum and Art Gallery Grace Hill. Local history, archaeology, and natural science. Temporary art exhibitions. Open all year (ex BH), weekdays 10–1 and 2.30–5.30 (5 Sat). Free. P. *(Tel 57583)*

FORD *Northumberland* Map 12 NT93
The Lady Waterford Hall Once the village school, it is now famous for the late, 19th-C mural pictures painted by Lady Waterford depicting members of the Ford Estate characters in Bible story scenes. Open all year 10–6. 10p (ch 5p). ⚠ *(Tel Crookham 224)* ᕯ Also

Heatherslaw Mill Dating back to the 13th C, but probably largely rebuilt in the 18th C, one of the oldest water-driven flour mills, with its machinery still intact. The mill was last used in 1946. ♨ Open Apr to Oct, daily 11–6. 30p (pen 10p). ⚠ *(Tel Crookham 338, caretaker)*

FORDWICH *Kent* Map 5 TR15
Old Town Hall Timber-framed building overlooking River Stour, one of the smallest of such buildings in Britain. Contains ducking stool, reputedly used to duck malefactors in river. Open Easter week and Whitsun to 30 Sep, Mon to Sat 10.30–12.30, 2.30–5.30. (Other times by arrangement.) 10p (ch 5p). ⚠

FOREST ROW *East Sussex* Map 5 TQ43
The Spring Hill Wildfowl Park Over 1,000 exotic birds including flamingos, cranes, peacocks, swans and rare species of geese and ducks, in a ten-acre Ashdown forest garden, around a 15th-C farmhouse. ♨ in Aviary Gift Shop. Open all year daily (ex 25 Dec) 10–6. Admission prices for 1980 not available. *(Tel 2783)* ᕯ

FOWEY *Cornwall* Map 2 SX15
St Catherine's Castle Ruined stronghold, erected in 16th C by Henry VIII to defend coast, and restored in 1855. Open all year, daily 9–dusk. Free. *(AM)*

FRAMLINGHAM *Suffolk* Map 5 TM26
Framlingham Castle Built by Roger Bigod between 1177 and 1215. Fine curtain walls, thirteen towers, array of Tudor chimneys, and almshouses built within inside walls by Pembroke College, Cambridge, in 1639. Open*, see inside front cover. 20p (ch 16p and pen 5p). ⚠ *(AM)*

FRITTON *Norfolk* Map 5 TG40
Fritton Lake Country Park Rare plants, shrubs, and herbaceous borders, and paths through wood to lake noted for fishing. Fishing in season, fishing and row boats for hire. Children's playground. ♨ and picnic areas. Gardens and grounds open 1 Apr to 15 Jun 11–6, 16 Jun to 30 Sep 7–7. 35p Prices under revision for 1980. Dogs on lead only. ⚠ *(Tel 208)* ᕯ

GAINSBOROUGH *Lincolnshire* Map 8 SK88
Old Hall Parnell Street. 15th-C and later, with great hall, period rooms, and medieval kitchen. ♨ Tue afternoons. Open all year (ex 25, 26 Dec, 1 Jan) weekdays 2–5; Easter to Oct, Sun also 2–5. Admission prices not yet decided. ⚠ *(Tel 2669 afternoons)*

GAWSWORTH *Cheshire* Map 7 SJ86
Gawsworth Hall Tudor black and white manor house associated with Mary Fitton possibly the 'Dark Lady' of Shakespeare's

Entrance Front of Firle

FIRLE PLACE

Nr. Lewes on A27
Eastbourne road

In parkland setting under South Downs, beautiful home of the Viscount Gage. Connoisseurs' collection of European and English Old Masters, Sèvres and English porcelain and furniture, is considered one of the most important in SE England. Historic American connections.

See gazetteer for opening times and admission prices.

sonnets, with rare tilting ground, pictures, armour and furniture. Carriage Museum. Open mid Mar to end Oct, daily 2–6. Party 20+. Dogs in grounds on lead only. Admission prices not available. △ free. *(Tel North Rode 456) (Roper-Richards family)*

GEDDINGTON *Northamptonshire* Map 4 SP88
Eleanor Cross Perhaps most beautiful of the many crosses erected by Edward I in memory of his dead Queen Eleanor on the route of her last journey to Westminster Abbey. Set up in 1294, best preserved of surviving trio. Accessible at any time. Free. *(AM)*

GILLING EAST *North Yorkshire* Map 8 SE67
Gilling Castle 14th-, 16th-, and 18th-C house, now preparatory school for Ampleforth College, with Elizabethan great chamber noted for panelling, painted glass, and ceilings. Fine gardens. Great chamber and hall, open weekdays 10–12 and 2–4; gardens open Jul to Sep, Mon to Sat. Great chamber free, Gardens 10p. △ *(Tel Ampleforth 238)* ♿

GILLINGHAM *Kent* Map 5 TQ76
Royal Engineers Museum Brompton. Includes relics of General Gordon among other exhibits. Open all year, Mon to Fri (ex BH) 9.30–12.30, 2–4. Free. △ *(Tel Medway 44555)* ♿ B

GLANDFORD *Norfolk* Map 9 G04
Shell Museum Small museum with Dutch gables built 1915 to house collection of seashells and curios from all corners of the world, collected by the late Sir Alfred Jodrell of Bayfield Hall. Open May to Sep, Mon to Fri 9–1, 2–5 Sat and Sun 2–5; Oct to Apr, Mon to Fri 9–1, 2–4 Sat 2–4. 2½p. Admission prices and opening times under revision for 1980. P. *(Tel Cley 349)* ♿

GLASTONBURY *Somerset* Map 3 ST43
Glastonbury Abbey Well-preserved 12th- and 13th-C ruins, with St Joseph's Chapel, Abbot's Kitchen, and flowering thorn tree nearby, on site of first Christian church in British Isles. West of England Pilgrimage last Sat in Jun, miracle plays twice weekly Jul and Aug. New Abbey Museum open in the ancient gatehouse with a model of the Abbey as in 1539. Open all year daily, Jun, Jul and Aug 9–7.30, rest of year 9.30–4.30 (Dec), 5 (Jan and Nov), 5.30 (Feb), 6 (Mar, Apr and Oct), 7 (May and Sep). 40p (ch 16 20p, ch 5 free) Parties. P. *(Tel 32267)* ♿ B
Somerset Rural Life Museum Abbey Barn and Abbey Farmhouse. Late 14th-C barn of Glastonbury Abbey contains relics of farming in Somerset in the horse age, cider making, peat cutting, withy cutting, etc. The adjoining farmhouse displays life of 19th-C Somerset peasant as shown by the things he used, and a typical farmhouse kitchen. Open all year Easter to 31 Oct, Mon to Fri 10–5 (8 Thu). Sat and Sun 2–7. 1 Nov to Easter Mon to Fri 10–5, Sat, Sun 2.30–5. 35p (ch 16 10p, pen free).
Tribunal 15th-C Court house of Abbey officials containing finds from late prehistoric Lake Village. Open, see inside front cover. 15p (ch 16 and pen 5p). △ *(AM)*

GLEMHAM HALL *Suffolk* Map 5 TM36
17th-C house, in 350 acres of grounds, with panelled rooms, pictures, and Queen Anne furniture. ☕ Open 7 Apr to 28 Sep Wed, Sun, BH 2–5.30. Admission prices for 1980 not available. △ *(Tel Wickham Market 746219) (Lady Blanche Cobbold)*

GLOUCESTER *Gloucestershire* Map 3 SO81
Bishop Hooper's Lodging Folk Life Museum, Westgate Street. Group of three timber-framed buildings, traditionally associated with the martyrdom in 1555 of Bishop John Hooper, containing relics of Siege of Gloucester (1643), and collections illustrating crafts and industries of the county. Open all year, Mon to Sat 10–5 (ex BH) Free. *(Tel 26467)*
City Museum and Art Gallery Brunswick Road. Archaeology, natural history, and geology of county, and period furnishings, glass and silver. Temporary art exhibitions throughout year. Open all year, Mon to Sat 10–5 (ex BH). Free. *(Tel 24131)*
City Wall and Bastion Kings Walk. Roman and medieval city defences in an underground chamber. Open May to Sep, Wed, Fri and Sat 2–5. 16p (ch 5p).

GLYNDE *East Sussex* Map 5 TQ40
Glynde Place Elizabethan manor substantially altered in the mid 18th-C. ☕ Open 15/16 Apr; then 6 May to 30 Sep, Wed, Thu and Sun 2.15–5.30. 80p (ch 12 40p). △ *(Tel 337 or 224)* **(79)**

GODALMING *Surrey* Map 4 SU94
Borough Museum Old Town Hall. Dates from 1814. On site of earlier building, and now museum of local antiquities. Open all year, Tue, Fri (ex 4 Apr), Sat 3–5; other times by appointment with Kathy Callow. *(Tel 4104)*

GODOLPHIN CROSS *Cornwall* Map 2 SW63
Godolphin House Between Townshend and Godolphin Cross, on unclass road. Partly early Tudor house, former home of Earls of Godolphin, with notable granite colonnades added in 1635. Painting of the 'Godolphin Arabian' by John Wooton. ☕ Open May and Jun, Thu 2–5, Jul, Aug and Sep, Tue and Thu 2–5. 50p (ch 20p). Admission prices under

GLASTONBURY ABBEY
The Abbey Gatehouse, Glastonbury

First Christian Sanctuary in the British Isles. Most important archaeological remains in the West Country.

Holy Thorn, Unique Abbots' Kitchen, New Museum in Medieval Gatehouse contains exquisite model of the Abbey as it stood in 1539, and remains of the Original Wattle and Daub Church which legend suggests was, in AD61, founded by Joseph of Arimathea.

Burial Place of King Arthur.

revision for 1980. Party 20+. No dogs. ⚠ *(Tel
Germoe 2409). (Mrs S E Schofield)*

GOMERSAL *West Yorkshire* Map 7 SE22
Off M62 (junc 26)
Red House Built 1660 of red brick, which
because of its rarity at that time gave rise to its
name. Additions by succeeding owners.
Associations with the Brontës, particularly
Charlotte, who often spent weekends here
with here schoolfriend Mary Taylor. She
immortalised it in her novel '*Shirley*', where it
is described under the name of 'Briarmains'.
Open Apr to Oct Tue to Sat 10–6, Sun 1–5;
Nov to Mar Tue to Sat 10–5. Free. ⚠ *(Tel
Cleckheaton 872165)* & B

GOODRICH *Hereford and Worcester*
Map 3 SO51
Goodrich Castle 12th to 14th C, originally
founded in 11th C, castle was slighted after
Civil War. Open*, see inside front cover. 25p
(ch 16 and pen 10p). ⚠ *(AM)*

GOODWOOD *West Sussex* Map 4 SU80
Goodwood House Three-sided flint faced
Wyatt Mansion (1780–1800) with Jacobean
core with notable pictures and interior
furnishings. Open all year for booked parties
with lunch or dinner and for commercial
events. Please write for leaflet giving 1980
prices and event dates. Open May to Sep,
Sun and Mon 2–5. &

GOOSNARGH *Lancashire* Map 7 SD53
1½m E of M6 (junc 32)
Chingle Hall Standing within its own moat.
Chingle Hall is a sturdy, white-walled
cruciform structure built in 1260 by Adam de
Singleton. It contains a chapel and four priest
holes and is reputedly the most haunted
house in Britain. Open Tue, Wed, Thu, Sat,

Sun and BH, 1 Jan to 24 Dec 2–6. 30p (ch 14
10p). Party. Admission prices under review
for 1979. ⚠ *(Tel 216)* **(79)**

GOSFIELD *Essex* Map 5 TL73
Gosfield Hall Tudor and later mansion, twice
visited by Queen Elizabeth I, with fine Tudor
gallery. Open May to Sep, Wed, Thu 2–5. 40p
(ch 25p). ⚠ *(Tel Halstead, Essex 2914)*

GOSPORT *Hampshire* Map 4 SZ69
Submarine Museum HMS *Dolphin* and, on
shore after Spring 1980, HMS/M *Alliance*.
Comprehensive display of submarine history
and development with models, trophies,
medals, pictures and the actual X-Craft that
twice raided Bergen. Open all year Mon to Sat
9–4 but only by previous arrangement with
Visits Office, HMS Dolphin, Gosport. Free.
(Tel Portsmouth 22351 ext 41868)

GRANTHAM *Lincolnshire* Map 8 SK93
Grantham Museum St Peter's Hill. Housed
within Public Library, the museum contains
collections of local antiquities, Grantham
history and items relating to Sir Isaac Newton.
Changing exhibitions. Open all year (ex Sun,
BH and Library holidays) Mon to Sat 9.30–5.
Free. P. *(Tel 3926)*

GRASMERE *Cumbria* Map 11 NY30
Dove Cottage and Wordsworth Museum
Former home of Wordsworth and Thomas de
Quincey, with rooms furnished as in
Wordsworth's time. The exhibition has been
enhanced by newly discovered manuscripts
of letters and poems, also by important loans,
including portraits of the Wordsworth Circle
from the National Portrait Gallery. Open Mar
to Oct daily (ex Sun) 9.30–1 and 2–5 (4.30
Mar and Oct). Last admission half hour before
closing. Admission and opening times under
revision for 1980. *(Tel 464 or 418)* &

GRASSINGTON *North Yorkshire*
Map 7 SE06
National Park Centre Hebden Road. Display
features conservation and the management
operations of the National Park Authority.
Open Apr to end Sep daily mid morning to late
afternoon. Free. ⚠ *(Tel 752748)*

GRAYS *Essex* Map 5 TQ67
Thurrock Museum Orsett Road. Local
history, agriculture, trade and industrial
collections. Palaeolithic to Saxon
archaeology of borough. Open all year (ex
XH), weekdays 10–8 (5, Sat). Free. P. *(Tel
5827)* ⑁

GRAYTHWAITE HALL GARDENS *Cumbria*
Map 7 SD39
m N of Newby Bridge on W side of Lake
Windermere.
-acre landscape garden with shrubs,
azaleas, and rhododendrons. Open 1 Apr to
0 Jun, daily 10–6. 20p (ch 15 5p). P. *(Tel
Newby Bridge 333 or 248). (Major M E M
andys)*

GREAT AYTON *North Yorkshire* Map 8 NZ51
Captain Cook Schoolroom Museum
xhibits relating to the explorer, incl maps,
books, pictures, etc. Open all year, May to
ep 10.30–12 & 2–4.30; Oct to Apr 2 to 4 or
y arrangement. 15p (ch 5p). P. *(Tel 2094)*

GREAT BARDFIELD *Essex* Map 5 TL63
ardfield Cottage Museum Dunmow Road.
5th-C thatched cottage with exhibitions of
ssex farming history, books, and pottery,
nd corn dollies for sale. Open Apr to Sep, Sat
nd Sun 2–6, or by written appointment.
ree. P. **(79)**

GREAT BEDWYN *Wiltshire* Map 4 SU26
edwyn Stone Museum Open air museum
the mason whose mark appears on
tonehenge, the Kennet and Avon Canal.
he Croft Pumps, countless churches, the
Willow Pattern Plate, the secret brains behind
e great architects of the last century. There
e plaster casts, headstones and other
orks set out in a humorous vein to decode
tonehenge and other works in the manner
ey control the behaviour of man. Open all
ear. Free. ⚠ Information and tours of the
urch, adjacent, ideal for coach parties on a
et day (60 min). *(Tel 234 Mr Lloyd)* ⑁
rofton Beam Engines 1½m SW. Now
ique, the 1812 Boulton and Watt, and the
845 Harveys of Hayle Beam Engines pump
ater 40ft to the top level of the Kennet and
on Canal. Operating in steam at Easter,
pring and August BH and three other
eekends in summer and autumn. 50p (ch
d pen 25p), family rate £1.25. Admission
ices under revision for 1980. Public canal
ps on narrow boat, *Jubilee*, during steaming
eekends. ⚠ Open but not working every
un (ex Christmas) at no charge. Write to *The
rofton Society* for further details – *273 East
rafton, Burbage, Wilts. (Tel Burbage
0474)*

GREAT BOOKHAM *Surrey* Map 4 TQ15
olesden Lacey 1m S. Designed by Thomas
ubitt in 1824, houses Greville collection of
ctures, tapestries and furnishings. Beautiful
ounds. ⚏ (licensed) open from 11 am on
ays when house is open. House open Mar
d Nov, Sat and Sun 2–5 (or sunset if
rlier); Apr to end Oct daily (ex Mon and Fri)
–6; open BH Mon, closed following Tue; last
dmission ½ hr before closing time; gardens
en all year, daily 11–sunset. Gardens only
p, house 60p extra. No dogs in house and
ly in garden if on lead *(NT)*

GREAT COXWELL *Oxfordshire* Map 4 SU29
Great Coxwell Barn Stone-built 14th-C barn,
possibly finest in England, with fine timber
roof. Open at all reasonable times. Free. *(NT)*

GREAT TORRINGTON *Devon* Map 2 SS41
Rosemoor Garden Charitable Trust 1m SE
of town. A garden of medium size with species
and hybrid rhododendrons, species roses
and ornamental trees and shrubs planted
since 1959. Scree and raised beds. Unusual
plants for sale. Teas for groups of 20 or more
persons by prior arrangement. Open Apr to
Oct daily, all day. 40p (ch 8 free, 8–15 20p).
Party. ⚠ *(Col J E and Lady Anne Palmer).
(NGS)* ⑁

GREAT WITCOMBE *Gloucestershire*
Map 3 SO91
Witcombe Roman Villa A large courtyard
Roman Villa in which a hypocaust and several
mosaic pavements are preserved. Open at
any reasonable times. Keys at farmhouse
adjoining. Free. *(AM)*

GREAT YARMOUTH *Norfolk* Map 5 TG50
Anna Sewell House Church Plain. This 17th-
C Tudor-fronted building, which is adjacent to
England's largest parish church, was the
birthplace of the authoress of *Black Beauty* on
30 Mar 1820. Guided tours. Souvenirs. Open
all year, Mon to Sat 10–4 (Thu 10–12 noon).
Admission charges not yet decided. ⚠ *(Tel
3372)*
Elizabethan House Museum built by a
wealthy merchant in 1596. It has a late
Georgian front, and contains panelled 16th-C
room, one with a magnificent Elizabethan
plaster ceiling. Other rooms have features
from later periods, some containing
contemporary furniture and exhibits
illustrating domestic life in the 19th-C.
Displays of Victorian children's toys,
Lowestoft porcelain and a collection of 18th-
19th-C drinking glasses. Open all year (ex 4 to
7 Apr, 25, 26 Dec and 1 Jan) Jun to Sep daily
(ex Sat) 10–1 and 2–5.30; Oct to May (Mon
to Fri) 10–1 and 2–5.30. Free. *(Tel 55746)*
The House of Wax Regent Road. A varied
and up-to-date exhibition of wax figures
contained in a fine Victorian house and
stables. Our Royal Family, past and present,
statesmen, screen and sports stars etc, a
'Murderers Gallery' depicting infamous
crimes and the basement contains macabre
'Torture Cellars'. Also a traditional Hall of
Funny Mirrors. Open Apr to Sep daily
10–dusk. 50p. Party. P. *(Tel 4851)*
Maritime Museum For East Anglia Marine
Parade. Maritime history of East Anglia
including the herring fishery, the wherry, life-
saving and the oil and gas industry. Open all
year (ex 4 to Apr, 25, 26 Dec, 1 Jan), Jun to
Sep 10–1 and 2–8; Oct to May Mon to Fri
10–1 and 2–5.30. 15p (ch 5p, free if
accompanied; pen free). Admission prices
under revision for 1980. ⚠ *(Tel 2267)*
Merrivale Model Village Near Wellington
Pier, Comprehensive village layout including
2¼in-gauge model railway, radio-controlled
boats and many models on scale of 1:12, set
in an acre of landscaped gardens and
illuminated after dusk from Jun to mid Sep.
Also indoor 'oo' gauge model railway. ⚏
Open May to Sep, daily from 9.30am. P. *(Tel
2097)*
Museum Exhibition Galleries Central
Library. Travelling and local art exhibitions.
Open all year (ex 4 and 7 Apr, 25/26 Dec and
1 Jan) Mon to Fri 9.30–5.30, Sat 9.30–1.
Free. *(Tel 58900)*

Norfolk Pillar South Beach Parade.
Monument to Nelson built in 1819. The
column is 144ft high, capped by a figure of
Britannia, and the summit is reached by an
internal staircase of 217 steps. Open Jul and
Aug daily (ex Sat) 2–6. 10p (ch 5p). P. *(Tel
55746)*
Old Merchant's House Row 117. Restored
300-year-old house with examples of 17th- to
19th-C local building craftsmanship, situated
in one of the old narrow lanes, or Rows,
leading from town wall to quay. Open Apr to
Sep Mon to Fri by guided tour only starting
from Row 111 Houses at 9.45, 11.20, 2.15
and 3.45. 15p (ch 16 and pen 5p). Ticket
includes Row 111 Houses and Greyfriars
Cloister. *(Tel 57900) (AM)*
Tolhouse Museum Tolhouse Street. Late
13th-C building with old dungeons and
exhibits on local history. Open all year (ex 4 to
7 Apr, 25, 26 Dec, 1 Jan) Jun to Sep, daily (ex
Sat) 10–1 and 2–5.30; Oct to May, Mon to
Fri. Free. ⚖ *(Tel 58900)*

GRIMES GRAVES *Norfolk* Map 5 TL88
Neolithic flint mines worked from
underground galleries. Roughly worked flints
were once exported for finishing elsewhere.
Re-opens 1980, see inside front cover for
open times. 15p (ch and pen 5p). Torch is
useful. ⚖ *(AM)*

GRIMSBY *Humberside* Map 8 TA20
Doughty Museum Town Hall Square. Will be
transferred to Welholme Galleries, Hainton
Avenue early 1980. Collection of 18th- and
19th-C ship models, pictures, and china
bequeathed to town in 1941 by late Mr Wilfred
Vere Doughty. Open all year, Tue to Sat
10–12.30 and 2–5.30. Free. P. *(Tel 59161)*
⚖

GRIZEDALE *Cumbria* Map 7 SD39
Visitor and Wild Life Centre Operated by
Forestry Commission in Grizedale Forest,
deer museum with large-scale photographic
dioramas illustrating animal life, Forest
Information office, Theatre in the Forest with
various events covering classical, folk,
natural history, jazz, drama, and dance, and
mile-long Millwood Forest nature trail and
other walks nearby. New Visitor Centre, Hotel
and restaurant nearby. Open all year daily
Easter to Oct 10–5; Oct to Easter 11–4. 10p
(ch 14 5p). ⚖ *(Tel Satterthwaite 273, theatre
bookings 291)*

GUILDFORD *Surrey* Map 4 SU94
Guildford Castle Castle Street. Early 12th-C,
rectangular, three-storeyed keep with fine
views. The castle ditch has been transformed
into a flower garden, seen at its best in May.
⚖ Open daily Mon to Fri; grounds all year
7.30–dusk; keep Apr to Sep 11–6. Grounds
free; keep 12p (ch 6p). P. *(Tel 71111)*
Guildford House Gallery 155 High Street.
Built 1660, and acquired by Corporation in
1957, timber-framed building containing
richly carved elm and oak staircase and finely
decorated plaster ceilings. Frequently
changing art exhibitions. Open all year, Mon
to Sat 10.30–5 (ex for a few days prior to each
exhibition). For details and dates of
exhibitions, apply for leaflet. Free. P. *(Tel
32133)*
Guildford Museum Castle Arch, Quarry
Street. Local history, archaeology, and
needlework. Open all year, Mon–Sat 11–5
(ex Sun, 4 Apr, and Christmas). Free. P. *(Tel
66551)*
Loseley House 2½m SW. Elizabeth house,
built of stone from Waverley Abbey, with fine

panelling, furniture, ceilings, carved chalk
chimney piece, and tapestries. Farm tours. ⚖
Farm shop. Open Jun to Sep, Wed, Thu, Fri,
Sat also 26 May, 25 Aug 2–5. 70p (ch 40p).
Party 20+. Admission prices under revision
for 1980. P. *(Tel 71881)* ⚖ B
**Hospital of the Blessed Trinity (Abbot's
Hospital)** High Street. Tudor brick building,
magnificent Doric arched gateway with four
turrets and enclosed courtyard. Notable
Flemish painted Chapel windows and
moulded chimneys. Open May to Oct Mon,
Wed and Sat; Sat only Nov to Apr; 11–12 ane
3–4. Applications for conducted parties to the
Master *(Mr H G Taylor)*. Free. ⚖ *(Tel 62670)*
⚖ B
Sutton Place Gardens 4m NE, off A3. A very
beautiful 16th-C house in red brick and
terracotta. There is a large and picturesque
garden layout. Gardens only open 3, 10, 17,
24 Apr; 1, 8, 15, 22 May. 2.30–5.30. 30p (ch
14 15p), in aid of local charities. ⚖ *(Tel
32055)* ⚖ *(NGS)*

GUILSBOROUGH *Northamptonshire*
Map 4 SP67
Guilsborough Grange Bird and Pet Park
West Haddon Road. Collection of birds,
waterfowl and animals set in beautiful natural
surroundings in grounds of 19th-C country
house. Also children's playground, pets
corner and rides. Gift shop. Country stroll. ⚖
Picnic area. Open 1 Mar to 2 Nov daily 11–7.
Admission prices not available. ⚖ Dogs
admitted on leads. *(Tel 740278)* ⚖

GUISBOROUGH *Cleveland* Map 8 NZ61
Chapel Beck Gallery Fountain Street. A
varied programme of changing exhibitions
with particular emphasis on local history of
Cleveland and the work of locally-based
artists and craftsmen. Regular travelling
exhibitions. Special events and
demonstrations. Open all year (ex 4 Apr, 25
Dec, 1 Jan) Mon to Sat 10–5.30. Free. ⚖ *(Te
35240)*
Gisborough Priory Fine remains of east end
of church of 14th C. The priory, founded in firs
half of 12th C, was of Augustinian canons.
Accessible any reasonable time. Free. ⚖
(AM)

GUITING POWER *Gloucestershire*
Map 4 SP02
Cotswold Farm Park 3½m NE on unclass
road. An exhibition of the development of
British livestock breeding on a typical
Cotswold farm. Rare farm animals. Local
handcrafts on sale. Pony-trap rides. ⚖ Open
May Day to 1 Oct, daily 10.30–6. 60p (ch 14
35p, pen 45p). ⚖ and picnic area. *(Tel 307)*
GWEEK *Cornwall* Map 2 SW72
Seal Sanctuary Hospital caring for all sea
creatures such as seals, birds, dolphins,
porpoises and turtles which are washed up
around the Cornish coast. There are five
hospital pools situated on the banks of the
beautiful Helford River, surrounded by
woodlands. Magnificent views. Always plent
of seals to see. Open all year daily
9.30–sunset. 60p (ch 16 30p, pen 40p).
Under review for 1979. ⚖ *(Tel Mawgan 361)*
⚖ *(79)*

HADDON HALL *Derbyshire* Map 8 SK26
2m SE Bakewell. 12th- to 15th-C house with
notable chapel and hall, terraced rose
gardens, the romantic associations with
Dorothy Vernon. ⚖ Open 1 Apr to 30 Sep,
Tue to Sat and BH Mon 11–6, BH Sun 2–
90p (ch 40p). Admission prices under revisio
for 1980. No dogs. ⚖ 10p. *(Tel Bakewell
2855). (Duke of Rutland)*

HADLEIGH *Essex* Map 5 TQ88
Hadleigh Castle Founded in 1231 by Hubert de Burgh and rebuilt by Edward III in 14th C, walls are of Kentish rag; and castle retains two of original towers. Accessible any reasonable time. Free. *(AM)*

HADLEIGH *Suffolk* Map 5 TM04
Guildhall Partly timbered building, extended in the 14th C with superb beams and King posts. Further extended in the 18th C with assembly room. Facing church and 15th-C Deanery all make a unique collection of early building styles. Open all year, daily, 10.30 – dusk. Free. *(Tel 823576)*

HAILES *Gloucestershire* Map 4 SP02
Hailes Abbey Museum Remains of Cistercian house founded by Earl of Cornwall in 1246. Roof bosses, tiles, and other relics in Museum. Open, see inside front cover. 15p (ch 16 and pen 5p). ⚠ *(AM and NT)*

PKF

HAILSHAM *East Sussex* Map 5 TQ50
Michelham Priory 2½m W. Augustinian Priory, founded in 1229 on earlier moated site. 14th-C gatehouse and 16th-C Tudor house; 17th-C furniture, stained glass, tapestries, and Sussex ironwork. Art exhibitions in Tudor great barn. Sussex crafts shop. Folk night held 20, 21 Jun; Rural Industries exhibition 6 to 10 Aug; Archery May to Sep, last Sun in each month. ⬤ (licensed). Open 4 Apr to 19 Oct, daily 11 – 5.30 (house closed 1 – 2). 70p (ch 30p). ⚠ *(Tel 844224)*. *(Sussex Archaeological Society)*

HALIFAX *West Yorkshire* Map 7 SE02
Shibden Hall 15th-C half-timbered house with old barns and collection of horse-drawn vehicles. Now Folk Museum of West Yorkshire. ⬤ Open Apr to Sep, Mon to Sat 11 – 7, Sun 2 – 5; Oct, Nov and Mar, Mon to Sat 11 – 5, Sun 2 – 5; Feb, Sun only 2 – 5. 20p (ch 16 and pen 10p). P. *(Tel 52246)* ♿ B

HALLAND *East Sussex* Map 5 TQ51
Bentley Wildfowl House, extensive grounds and major wildfowl collection of over 100 species of wildfowl. Also flamingoes, cranes, peacocks and ornamental pheasants. Picnic area, woodland walk. ⬤ Open daily Easter to end Sep 11 – 6; (last admission 4.30) 10.30 – 6.30 Sun (last admission 5); weekends only Oct to Easter 11 – 5.30 (last admission 4), house by appointment only during winter. 80p (ch 16 35p, pen 65p). Party. Prices under revision for 1980. No dogs in wildfowl enclosures. ⚠ free. *(Tel 573)* ♿

HAMBLEDON *Hampshire* Map 4 SU61
9m SW of Petersfield, on B2150.
Vineyard and Winepress Mill Down. Unusual example of vineyard and press house. On slopes of Windmill Down. Wine-

making briefly explained. ℒ Open last Sun in
Jul to first Sun in Oct, Sun 2.30–5.30, also 6,
9, 16 and 25 Aug, 3, 6, 13, 27 Sep and 1 Oct.
Booked parties 31 Jul, 28 Aug, 9, 11, 17 and
20 Sep. 70p (ch 18 30p, pen 50p) price
includes a taste of wine for persons over 18
years. Wine on sale (ex Sun). ⚠ *(Tel 475).*
*(Maj Gen Sir Guy Salisbury-Jones GCVO
CMG CBE MC)* ⅃

HAMBLEDON *Surrey* Map 4 SU93
Feathercombe 2m from Milford station on
Hambledon road. Attractive gardens with
flowering shrubs and wide views. Plants for
sale. Open 20, 27 Apr; 4, 5, 11, 18, 25, 26
May; 1, 8 Jun; 24, 25 Aug; 2–6. 20p (ch free).
(Mrs Wieler and Miss Parker) ⅃ *(NGS)*

HANBURY *Hereford and Worcester*
Map 3 SO96
Hanbury Hall Pedimented, red-brick, Queen
Anne period house, dating from 1701, noted
for hall and staircase painted by Sir James
Thornhill. Good plaster decoration in Long
Room, contemporary orangery and Watney
collection of porcelain. ℒ Open Apr to Sep,
Wed to Sun and BH Mon and following Tue
2–6, Oct Sat and Sun 2–6. 85p *(NT)*

HANDCROSS *West Sussex* Map 4 TQ22
Nymans Garden Thirty acres of gardens
featuring flowering shrubs and roses in large
estate. Open Apr to Oct, Tue Wed, Thu and
Sat 2–7; Sun, Bh Mon 11–7 (or sunset); last
admission 1hr before closing. 70p. *(NT)*

HARDKNOTT CASTLE ROMAN FORT
Cumbria Map 7 NY20
On Hardknott Pass above Eskdale, 375ft-
square fort with three double gateways
enclosing walled and ramparted area of
almost 3 acres. Situated above western end
of steep and narrow pass (maximum gradient
1 in 3), fort was occupied in mid 2nd C.
Accessible any reasonable time. Free. *(AM)*

HARDWICK HALL *Derbyshire* Map 8 SK46
2m S M1 Junc 29
Elizabethan mansion, built 1597 by Robert
Smythson for famous Bess of Hardwick
(Dowager Countess of Shrewsbury).
Remarkable vast area of windows, fine
tapestries, needlework, Cavendish portraits,
High Great Chamber, and walled courtyard
gardens. ℒ teas Apr to end Oct, Mon.
Lunches May to Sep (on days when Hall is
open). Open Apr to end Oct, Wed, Thu, Sat,
Sun, BH Mon 1–5.30 (or sunset); gardens
open during season, daily 12–5.30. Park
open all year daily. Hall and gardens £1.20;
gardens only 60p; Country Park 20p parking.
(NT) (NGS)

HAREWOOD *West Yorkshire* Map 8 SE34
*Harewood House, Bird Garden and
Butterfly World* The house, home of the Earl
and Countess of Harewood, was designed
1759 by John Carr of York and Robert Adam,
with 19th-C alterations by Sir Charles Barry. It
contains splendid Chippendale furniture,
English and Italian paintings and Chinese and
Sèvres porcelain. The Park, landscaped by
'Capability' Brown, now includes 4-acre bird
garden with species from all over the world.
Adventure playground and shops. ℒ party
catering. All facilities open daily 1 Apr to 31
Oct from 11 am. Limited opening Nov, Feb
and Mar. House Tue, Wed and Thu only 11
am. Bird garden as house, plus Sun.
Harewood closed Dec/Jan ex Bird Garden
and Adventure playground special opening
10 am daily 26 Dec to 3 Jan inclusive. ⚠
(24-hr information service, Tel 886225) ⅃

HARROGATE *North Yorkshire* Map 8 SE35
Harlow Car Gardens Crag Lane, Otley
Road. 60 acres of ornamental and woodland
gardens, and the Northern Trial Grounds.
Plant Bring and Buy Sat 3 May. Open all year
dawn to dusk. 60p (ch 20p). Party 50p. ⅃
Rudding Park Gardens Extensive
landscaped gardens, enclosing the early
19th-C Regency Country House. The
gardens are especially noted for their
magnificent beech and rare oak trees, vast
parkland and lawns, shrubberies of
rhododendrons, magnolias, and azaleas (of
which the celebrated Rhododendron Walk is
an outstanding example). The exterior of the
house, in Grecian style is remarkable for its
symmetry, lack of ornament and constant use
of bow windows. Aug BH, Rudding Park
Antiques Fair. ℒ Open daily Apr to Sep,
11–5.30. ⚠ 50p (occupants free). *(Tel
871350)* ⅃

HARTLEBURY *Hereford and Worcester*
Map 7 SO87
Hereford and Worcester County Museum
Hartlebury Castle. County crafts and
industries, horse-drawn vehicles, gipsy
caravans, period furnishings, costumes, toys
and dolls, and forge and wheelwright's shop.
ℒ Picnic area available. Open 1 Feb to 30
Nov, Mon to Thu 10–5, Sat and Sun 2–5. 25p
(ch and pen 10p); students and school parties
free. Under revision for 1980. ⚠ *(Tel 416)* ⅃
B

HARTLEPOOL *Cleveland* Map 8 NZ53
Gray Art Gallery and Museum Clarence
Road. Permanent collection of pictures.
Museum collections feature local history,
archaeology, engineering, Indian idols,

orcelain, British birds, working blacksmith's
shop in museum grounds. Open all year (ex 1
Jan, 4 Apr, 25 & 26 Dec) Mon–Sat 10–5.30,
Sun 3–5. Free. ⚠ *(Tel 68916)* &

Maritime Museum Northgate. Collections
feature the maritime history of the town and
shipbuilding industry. Also reconstructed
fisherman's cottage, a ship's bridge and an
early lighthouse lantern. Open all year (ex 1
Jan, 25 & 26 Dec) Mon to Sat 10–5. Free. ⚠
(Tel 72814)

HARTLEY WINTNEY *Hampshire*
Map 4 SU75
West Green House 1½m W on unclass road.
18th-C house, with a series of busts on the
outside walls. It belonged once to General
Hawley, of Culloden ill-fame. Attractive
garden. Open Apr to Sep: garden Wed, Thu
Sun 2–6; house Wed 2–6 by appointment in
writing with the tenant (minimum notice 7
days). Admission: house and garden 70p;
garden only 50p. *(NT)*

HARTWELL *Buckinghamshire* Map 4 SP71
Hartwell House E-shaped Jacobean
mansion with east façade of 1759–61 and
early 17th-C staircase. Now Hartwell House
Independent College of Further Education for
Young Women. Louis XVIII spent part of exile
here 1807–14. House and gardens open 14
May to 16 Jul, Wed only 2–5. 50p (ch 8 25p,
⚠ *(Tel Aylesbury 748355)*

HARVINGTON *Hereford and Worcester*
Map 7 SO87
Harvington Hall Moated Elizabethan manor
house with secret hiding places. ⚐ Open 1
Feb to 30 Nov, Tue to Sat 2–6 (or dusk if
earlier); also Easter to Sep 11.30–1, Sun 2–6
or dusk if earlier). Other times by
appointment. Last admission ½hr before
closing time. 50p (ch 14 25p). ⚠ *(Tel
Chaddesley Corbett 267)*

HARWICH *Essex* Map 5 TM23
The Redoubt 180ft diameter circular fort
surrounded by dry moat, built 1808 to defend
port against Napoleonic invasion. Walls are
8ft thick, and 18 rooms were provided to
contain stores, ammunition, and quarters for
300 men. Now being restored by Harwich
Society and part will be museum. Special fête,
spring BH. ⚐ Open Easter to end Oct, Sun
10–12 and 2–5. Free. P.

HASCOMBE *Surrey* Map 4 SU94
Winkworth Arboretum 1m NW on B2130. A
hillside of nearly 100 acres planted with
shrubs and rare trees; bluebells; two lakes.
Displays are best in May and end of Oct.
Views towards the North Downs. Open
always. Free. *(NT)*

HASTINGS *East Sussex* Map 5 TQ80
Fishermen's Museum Rock a Nore Road.

Former fishermen's church, now museum of
local interest, including last of Hastings
luggers built for sail. Open Easter to 30 Sep,
daily (ex Fri) 10–6. Free. P. &
Hastings Castle Castle Hill. Remains of
Norman castle on cliffs. Excavations were
made 1825 and 1968, and old dungeons were
discovered 1894. Open Easter to Sep daily
10–5. 22p (ch 11p) (prices may be subject to
increase). P. &
Hastings Museum and Art Gallery
Cambridge Road. Collections of natural
history of Hastings area, archaeology and
history of Hastings and neighbouring areas,
Sussex ironwork and pottery. Fine and
applied art. Durbar Hall (Indian Palace).
Extensive collection of pictures. Special
Exhibition Gallery. Open all year (ex 4 Apr, 25
and 26 Dec) Mon to Sat 10–1, 2–5, Sun 3–5
including BH. Free. ⚠ *(Tel 435952)* & B
Museum of Local History Old Town Hall,
High Street. Archaeology of Hastings area.
History of Hastings, especially Fishing
Industry and the Cinque Ports. Open Easter
(ex 4 Apr) to Oct 10–12.30 and 1.30–5.30
Mon to Sat. Free. *(Tel 425855)* & B
St Clement's Caves West Hill. Cut into
slopes of West Hill, extending over 4 acres,
and associated with smugglers. Open all year
daily, summer 10.30–5.30; winter
10.30–12.30 and 2–5. 32p (ch 16p) (prices
may be subject to increase). P. *(Tel 422964)*

HATFIELD *Hertfordshire* Map 4 TL20
Hatfield House The historic home of the
Marquess of Salisbury, a magnificent
Jacobean house built 1607–11 by Robert
Cecil, standing in a great park and gardens.
Special exhibition of Fashion through the
Ages plus the National Collection of Model
Soldiers, open one hour before house.
Guided tours weekdays. Dogs not admitted to
house, must be on lead in gardens. ⚐ in Old
Palace Yard. Open 25 Mar to 12 Oct (ex 4 Apr
and Mon, but open BH Mons) Tue to Sat and
BH 12–5 (Sun 2–5.30) Garden open
10.30–6 daily. Admission: House, Park and
Gardens £1 (ch 5–15, 55p). Exhibition extra
25p (ch 5–15, 20p); Park and Gardens only
45p (ch 5–15, 25p). Under revision for 1980.
Party 20+ ⚠ *(Tel 62823, Catering 62055)*.
(Marquess of Salisbury) &
The Old Palace Hatfield House. Standing
within the gardens is the surviving wing of the
Royal Palace in which Queen Elizabeth I
spent much of her childhood. Elizabethan
banquets held throughout the year. Tue, Thu,
Fri, and Sat evenings, also Wed May to Sep;
other evenings and luncheons for privately
booked parties. ⚠ *(Tel 62055 or 62030)* & B

HATHERN *Leicestershire* Map 8 SK42
Whatton House Gardens $4\frac{1}{2}$m NW of Loughborough on A6 between Hathern and Kegworth. The 25-acre gardens display flowering shrubs and have water, rose and Chinese gardens. A dog cemetery and Dutch garden, also a Bogy Hole, a curious garden ornament, built *c*1885. Garden Centre and ☕. Open Easter Sun to end Sep Sun only, also BH Mon 2–7. 25p (ch 10p, pen 15p). Under revision for 1980. Party. 🅿 *(Tel Loughborough 842225)* ♿

HAUGHLEY *Suffolk* Map 5 TM06
Haughley Park Newly restored house, dating from 1620, built on E-plan with crow-stepped gables and octagonal chimneys. Fine park and gardens. Open May to end Sep, Tue 3–6. 50p (ch 16, 25p). 🅿 *(Tel Elmswell 40205). (Mr A J Williams)* ♿ B

HAUGHMOND ABBEY *Salop* Map 7 SJ51
Extensive remains of a house of Augustinian canons founded about 1135. Chapter House has fine Norman doorway and the abbot's lodging is exceptionally well-preserved. Open, see inside front cover but closes 4.30 Tue and Wed. 10p (ch 16 and pen 5p). 🅿 *(AM)*

HAVERTHWAITE *Cumbria* Map 7 SD38
Lakeside and Haverthwaite Railway
Preserved here are two 2–6–4 class 4 Fairburn tank engines and nine other locomotives together with diesel locomotives and passenger and freight rolling stock. ☕ at Haverthwaite station. Open 4 Apr to 8 Apr (incl), Sun only to 27 April. Daily May to 5 Oct, then Sun only to 26 Oct. Sun to Fri 11–5.30, Sat 11.30–5. Standard gauge steam-hauled passenger trains operate hourly 11–5, when open, and most connect with the Lake Windermere steamers at the lakeside. Fares as published. 🅿 at Haverthwaite (20p). *(Tel Newby Bridge 594)* ♿

HAWES *North Yorkshire* Map 7 SD89
National Park Centre Station Yard. Interpretative display relating the Wensleydale railway line to the social and economic history of the area as part of a National Park. Open Apr to end Sep, mid morning to late afternoon. Free. 🅿 *(Tel 450)* ♿

Upper Dales Folk Museum Museum of life in the Upper Dales, opened in 1979. Open 1 Apr (or Easter) to 30 Sep Mon to Sat 11–1, 2–5, Sun 1–5; Oct Tue, Sat and Sun only. 30p (ch and pen 15p). 🅿 *(Tel 494)* ♿ B

HAWKSHEAD *Cumbria* Map 7 SD39
Courthouse Relic of pre-Reformation priory. Houses Folk Museum of Rural Crafts, with forestry, textile, and farm exhibits, a branch of the Museum of Lakeland Life and Industry. Open Easter, then May to Oct, daily (ex Mon) 2–5. 20p (ch 10p) *(NT)*

HAWORTH *West Yorkshire* Map 7 SE03
Brontë Parsonage The parsonage was the home of the three gifted 19th-C novelists, Charlotte, Emily and Anne. Contains Brontë relics. Open daily 11–5.30 (11–4.30 Oct–Mar) Sun 2–5.30 (2–4.30 Oct–Mar). Closed last 3 weeks in Dec. 20p (ch 16 10p). P. *(Tel 42323)*

Keighley and Worth Valley Railway and Museums Keighley, Haworth and Oxenhope. 32 steam engines, 7 diesels. Weekend service and daily Jul, Aug and Spring BH week of trains from Keighley (connections with BR) to Oxenhope via Haworth, 90p (ch and pen 45p, ch 5 free; reduced fares for shorter journeys). 15p (ch 16 10p) includes entry to Haworth yards and Oxenhope displays. 🅿 small charge at Haworth; free at Oxenhope, Oakworth and Ingrow. (24-hour Talking Timetable *Tel Haworth 43629;* or enquiries *45214)* ♿

HAXTED *Surrey* Map 5 TQ44
Watermill Museum Late 16th-C mill on 14th-C foundations, weather-boarded, with a mansard roof and adjoining tile-hung mill house, standing on Eden Water. Museum contains mill machinery, two working water-wheels, and picture gallery. Also exhibition by Wealden Iron Research Group. ☕ Open Easter to end Sep, Sat and Sun 11–6, also daily 2–6 (ex Mon) during summer holiday period. 25p (ch 14 and pen 15p). 🅿 ♿ B

HAYLE *Cornwall* Map 2 SW53
Bird Paradise A collection of colourful and exotic birds, including some rare and endangered species. Among these are the St Vincent Parrot, Thick-billed Parrot from Mexico, Hyacinthine Macaw, Great African Wattled Crane and Toco Toucans. There are also a Children's Zoo. Miniature steam railway, Craft village, pub and restaurant. ☕ Open all year, daily 10–dusk. £1.20 (ch 3–14 70p, pen 90p, ch 3 free). 🅿 *(Tel 753365)* ♿ The Craft Village and pub can be visited without payment of parking or admission fees.

HAYWARDS HEATH *West Sussex* Map 4 TQ32
Borde Hill $1\frac{1}{2}$m N on Balcombe Road. A large garden with woods and parkland. Many rare trees and shrubs of considerable botanical interest. ☕ Open 15 Mar to 28 Sep, Wed, Sat and Sun and BH 10–6. 50p (ch 20p). Party 12+40p. Dogs on lead only. 🅿 with picnic area. *(Tel 50326)* ♿

EACHAM *Norfolk* Map 9 TF63
orfolk Lavender Caley Mill. Largest
owers and distillers of lavender in Britain.
arvest during Jul to mid Aug. Shop for
vender, lavender products and herb plants.
(from May). Open all year, Sep to May,
on to Fri 9–4, Jun to Aug 9–6. Distillery 20p
h and pen 10p). ⚠ Parties should be
ooked in advance. Individuals call at Caley
ll for directions. *(Tel 70384)* ⑤

EATHFIELD *East Sussex* Map 5 TQ52
eathfield Wildlife Park Hailsham Road. A
riety of attractions which include wildlife,
rd City, 200 acres of woodland. 'Fab One'
d 'Chitty-Chitty-Bang-Bang' on permanent
splay, and the Figes Museum of Agricultural
chaeology in Queen Victoria's Royal
avilion. Among the wildlife exhibits are deer,
ltures, monkeys, sealions, chimpanzees,
d ostriches. The Gibraltar tower was built in
792 as a memorial to Lord Heathfield,
rmerly General George Eliot, defender of
braltar 1779–83, and is classified as a
chedule building. Special events include
action Engine Rally 18/19 Aug also
onthly events. ⚏ Open all year (ex 25 & 26
ec) daily 10–6 (or dusk if earlier). 80p (ch 14
d pen 60p, ch 3 free). ⚠ *(Tel 4656 and
~48)* ⑤ **(79)**

EBDEN BRIDGE *West Yorkshire*
ap 7 SD92
eptonstall Grammar School Museum 1 m
W on minor road. A 17th-C village school
uated in a churchyard with the ruins of a
edieval church and a 19th-C church. The
hool contains the original desks etc and folk
hibits from the surrounding area. Open all
ar (ex 1 Jan, 25 and 26 Dec) Apr to Sep, Sat
d Sun 2–6; Oct to Mar Sat and Sun 1–5.
pen BH. Free. P. *(Tel 3738)* ⑤ B

HECKINGTON *Lincolnshire* Map 8 TF14
Heckington Windmill Well-restored tower-
mill of 1830, with eight sails formerly used on
mill at Boston, and machinery still in working
order. Only one of its kind to have survived.
Open all year Mon to Fri 9–5, Sat 9–12;
enquiries to *Mr J Pocklington* at mill house
adjacent. Free. ⚠ (small fee). 14th-C village
church nearby. *(Tel 241)* **(79)**

HELMINGHAM *Suffolk* Map 5 TM15
Helmingham Hall Gardens Home of Lord
and Lady Tollemache, moated house with two
drawbridges which are raised every night.
Moated gardens in ancient deer park with
ornamental waterfowl, Highland cattle, large
herd of over 500 red and Fallow deer and
safari rides. Fresh vegetables and flowers
from garden on sale in addition to East
Anglian crafts from stable shop. Coach house
tea-rooms and picnic area. Gardens open 4
May then every Sun from 25 May to 28 Sep,
2–6. 80p (ch 40p, pen 50p). Party. ⚠ *(Tel
363)* ⑤

HELMSLEY *North Yorkshire* Map 8 SE68
Helmsley Castle Ruined 12th- to 13th-C
stronghold with domestic buildings added in
14th C. Open*, see inside front cover. 20p (ch
16 and pen 5p). *(AM)*

HELSTON *Cornwall* Map 2 SW62
Cornwall Aero Park See actual aeroplanes
used in Yorkshire Television's successful
Flambards also *Flambards* period room
settings. Wall Gallery. Sit at the controls of a
Shackleton and other historic aircraft or climb
aboard the flight deck of Concorde. Beautiful
landscaped grounds. Historic Wheels and
Wings exhibition 1980. Fun amusements.
Free crazy golf for children. Shop and ⚏.
Open Easter to early Nov, daily, 10–5 (6 Jul

and Aug). £1 (ch 60p). Party. ⚠ *(Tel 3404/4549)* &

Helston Museum Old Butter Market. Folk museum covering local history and articles from Lizard district. Open all year, Mon–Sat (ex Wed closed noon) 10.30–12.30 and 2–4.30. Touring Schools and visiting groups welcome by prior arrangement. Free. P. *(Hon Curator Lt Cdr A E Simmonds RN MBE Tel 2480)*

HENLEY-IN-ARDEN *Warwickshire*
Map 4 SP16

Guildhall Gabled, timber-framed building of 1448, restored in 1915, with outside staircase leading from Dutch-style garden to hall with fine roof timbering. Many relics and town records on display. Open any reasonable time on application to *Caretaker, Guild Cottage*. Free. Under revision for 1980. *(Tel 2309) (Mr E W Berry)*

Henley Bird Gardens High Street. Situated in the 4-acre grounds of an Elizabethan Manor House is a fine collection of over 400 foreign birds. Open Apr to Oct. 60p (ch 16 30p) P. *(Tel 2562)* &

HENLEY-ON-THAMES *Oxfordshire*
Map 4 SU78

Greys Court 2m W. Gabled Elizabethan house with fine chimney-pieces and plasterwork and interesting English and Swiss furniture. Medieval fortified courtyard with three towers and a keep, remains from former 13th-C house, and there is 200ft-deep well with 19ft-wide wooden donkey wheel. ⚏ Sat and BH and for booked parties. Open Apr to Sep, grounds and Carlisle Collection Mon to Sat, house Mon, Wed, Fri 2.15–6. Gardens 60p, house 30p extra, Carlisle Collection 30p extra. *(NT)*

HEREFORD *Hereford and Worcester*
Map 3 SO54

Bulmers Railway Centre Whitecross Road. On site of the former Midland Railways Goods Yard, operated by the 6000 Locomotive Association for and on behalf of H P Bulmer Ltd. Additional attractions on open days. ⚏ Open first weekend in Apr to last weekend in Sep for static display 2–5. Open days with engines in steam Easter and Spring BH weekends, small engine in steam one Sun per month (enquire before visit). Party. Weekend steamings of small locomotives (enquire before visit). All admission prices under review for 1980. ⚠ *(Tel 4791)* &

Churchill Gardens Museum and Brian Hatton Art Gallery 3 Venn's Lane. Branch Museum located in Regency house with fine grounds. Victorian nursery, butler's pantry and parlour. Costumes, furniture and

watercolours. Also the Hatton Gallery primarily devoted to works by the local artist Brian Hatton. Open all year, daily 2–5. Free ⚠ *(Tel 68121 ext 207)*

St John's and Coningsby Museum 110 Widemarsh Street. Early 13th-C hall arrange with armour and other subjects connected with the Order and Chapel of Knights of St John, with almshouses added in 1614 by Sir Thomas Coningsby of Hampton Court. Unique Friars' Preaching Cross in adjoining public gardens. Open Apr to Oct daily (ex Mo and Fri) 1–5. 15p (ch 5p). Party. ⚠ *(Tel 283. mornings)* &

Hereford Museum and Art Gallery Broad Street. Roman remains (*ie* tessellated pavements), natural history, English watercolours, local geology, and county's archaeology, also folk life and folklore material. Exhibitions at City Art Gallery change every month. Open all year, Mon to Sat 10–6 (5, Thu); 1 Sep to 1 Apr Sat 10–5. Free. P. *(Tel 68121 ext 207)* &

The Old House High Town. Restored half-timbered house, dating from 1621 with Jacobean furniture. Open all year Mon to Fri 10–1 and 2–5.30, Sat 10–1, Sun 2–5 (closed Sun Oct to Mar). 15p (ch 5p). Free admission Thu. *(Tel 68121 ext 207)*

HERSTMONCEUX *East Sussex* Map 5 TQ6
Royal Greenwich Observatory (Herstmonceux Castle) Entry off Wartling Road. Public exhibition and grounds only of castle. ⚏ Open from Easter to end Sep, Mo to Fri 2–5.30, Sat, Sun and BH 10.30–5.30. 55p (ch and pen 25p). Under revision for 1980. ⚠ Castle **not** open to the public. *(Tel 3171 ext 320)* &

HERTFORD *Hertfordshire* Map 4 TL31
Hertford Castle Early 16th-C brick gatehouse, much altered *c* 1800, partly by Henry Holland, with slight remains of original Norman castle. Interior now used as municipal offices. Open May to Sep, first Sat in each month 10–1, grounds open all year, daily until dusk. Free. P (limited). *(Tel 54977* & B

Hertford Museum 18 Bull Plain. Local archaeology, history, geology, and natural history. Open all year (ex 4 Apr, 25/26 Dec and Suns). Mar to Oct Mon to Fri 11–5 (10–Sat); Nov to Feb Mon to Fri 11–4 (Sat 10–4) Free. ⚠ *(Tel 52686)* & B

HEVER *Kent* Map 5 TQ44
Hever Castle and Gardens 3m SE Edenbridge off B2026. 13th-C moated castle where Henry VIII courted Anne Boleyn. Larg gardens and grounds including lake, Italian garden, fountains and topiary work. Open 3

DINMORE MANOR
MANOR HOUSE,
CLOISTERS, MUSIC ROOM AND GARDENS

Open throughout the year. Splendid views as far as the Malverns.

The Chapel is one of only three in England, dedicated to the Knights Hospitallers of St. John of Jerusalem.

Beautiful flowers in bloom throughout the season, with a magnificent panorama over the gardens from the walkway on top of the cloisters.

Situated to the west of the A49, south of Dinmore Hill, which is midway between Hereford and Leominster.

See gazetteer entry for further details.

ar to 28 Sep (ex 4 Apr) Tue, Wed, Fri, Sun
d BH. Gardens 1–7, castle 1.30–6 or 7
pending on day (last entry ½hr before
osing). Tue and Fri extra rooms on show.
rounds only 80p (ch 12 30p); castle
dditional £1 (ch 50p), Tue and Fri £1.50.
ogs on lead in grounds only. ⚠ *(Tel
denbridge 862205 ext 1, 865224 ext 4)* ⅋ B

EVINGHAM *Suffolk* Map 5 TM37
eveningham Hall 4m SW of Halesworth.
eorgian house by Sir Robert Taylor and
mes Wyatt, with famous entrance hall.
uscan room, library, etc; original furniture;
rk laid out by 'Capability' Brown; orangery
Wyatt. Gift shop, picnics, ⚲ and fishing
kets. Open 2 Apr to 12 Oct, Wed, Thu, Sat,
n, BH Mons. May to end Sep, Tue also,
use 2–6 (last entry 5.30) park and gardens
–6 (12–6, Sun and BH). 90p (ch 15 40p). ⚠
el Ubbeston 355)* ⅋

GHDOWN *West Sussex* Map 4 TQ00
off A259 halfway between Worthing and
tlehampton. Gardens laid out in chalk pit on
ghdown Hill, with rock plants, flowering
rubs, and daffodils. Also Miller's tomb and
cellent views. Open all year. Mon to Fri
–4.30 (Sat and Sun Apr to Sep). Free. ⚠
el Worthing 204226)* ⅋

GH WYCOMBE *Buckinghamshire*
ap 4 SU89
*ycombe Chair and Local History
useum* Castle Hill House, Priory Avenue.
ne house set in gardens with museum of
airs, old tools, and chair making apparatus.
pen all year, Mon (ex BH), Tue, Thu, Fri, Sat
–1, 2–5. Free. P. *(Tel 23879)* ⅋ B

MLEY *Staffordshire* Map 7 SO89
mley Hall 6m S of Wolverhampton off
49, 4m N of Stourbridge off A449.
tensive parkland, trout and coarse fishing

(extra charge). ⚲ Grounds only open all year,
daily 8–8 (or ½hr before dusk). Free. Cars
20p. *(Tel Dudley 56321)* ⅋
HINTON CHARTERHOUSE *Avon*
Map 3 ST75
Hinton Priory Carthusian priory founded
1232, with remains of chapter house and
refectory. 15th-C gatehouse forms part of
16th-C manor house on site. Open 1 Apr to 1
Oct, Wed, Sat, and BH 2–6. 20p ⚠ *(Tel
Limpley Stoke 3596)*
HITCHIN *Hertfordshire* Map 4 TL12
Hitchin Museum and Art Gallery Paynes
Park. Contains new displays of local history
collections, natural history and tropical fish.
Regimental Museum of the Hertfordshire
Yeomanry, costume and Victoriana. Special
temporary exhibitions changed monthly.
Good reserve collection of water-colours,
especially those by local Quaker artist
Samuel Lucas Snr 1805–1870, photographs
and costume, which can be seen by
appointment. Open all year (ex Sun and BH)
10–5. Free. ⚠ *(Tel 4476)* ⅋ B
HOAR CROSS *Staffordshire* Map 7 SK12
Hoar Cross Hall Off A515 near Newborough.
Elizabethan-style mansion, built 1871 and
modelled in part on Elizabethan Temple
Newsam in Leeds, with fine plasterwork on
ceilings and private chapel. Restored
gardens contain fine trees and shrubs, yew-
tree walks, and ponds. Picnic/play area. ⚲
Open Spring BH to Late Summer BH, Sun
2–6, BH Mon and Tue 12.30–6; other times
by appointment only. Hall and gardens 50p
(ch 20p). ⚠ (10p). *(Tel 427)*. *(Mr W A
Bickerton-Jones)* ⅋
HODNET *Salop* Map 7 SJ62
Hodnet Hall Gardens 6m SW Market
Drayton, 12m NE Shrewsbury. Re-designed
Elizabethan-style Victorian house (not open

to public), with 60-acre landscape garden. Collection of big-game trophies in 17th-C tearooms. Gift shop, plants for sale in Garden Centre featured on TV and radio. ☾ Sun and BH then daily May to Aug, picnicking allowed. Open 4 Apr ro 28 Sep, Mon to Sat 2 – 5 (gardens cleared 6pm), Sun and BH 12 – 6 (gardens cleared 8pm). Party. Dogs only on lead. ⚠ (Tel 202). (Mr and Hon Mrs Heber-Percy) ♿

HOGHTON Lancashire Map 7 SD62
Hoghton Tower 5m SE Preston on A675. 16th-C fortified Hilltop Mansion with magnificent Banqueting Hall where, in 1617, the 'Loin of Beef' was knighted by James I, also the King's Bedchamber, Audience Chamber, Ballroom and other state rooms, and the Tudor Well House with its horse-drawn pump and oaken windlass and the Stone Cells which housed malefactors and cattle thieves of bygone days. Walled gardens, lawns and Old English Rose Garden. Walks and grounds with views of sea, moors, hills of Lake District and Welsh mountains. Permanent Dolls House and Dolls collection and various other exhibitions. Open 5 Apr then every Sun until end Oct, also Sat Jul and Aug and all BH. 2 – 5. 75p (ch 25p). ⚠ 10p (Tel 2986) ♿ (gardener)

HOLKER Cumbria Map 7 SD37
Holker Hall Near Grange-over-Sands. 16th-to 19th-C country house with beautiful woodcarvings, home of Cavendish family. 22 acres of gardens, and deer park with fallow, sika and red deer. Regular equestrian, dog and airsport events during season. Horse driving trials end Apr. Sheep dog trials 21 Jun. Lakeland Rose show 14 & 15 Jul. Equestrian championships 3 Sep. (These dates are provisional.) Children's play area, newly opened Motor Museum, exhibition centre. Art Gallery gift shop. ☾ Licensed. Open 6 Apr to 30 Sep, daily (ex Sat) 11 – 6. £1 (ch 50p). Party. Motor museum extra 70p (ch 45p). Party. Admission prices under revision for 1980. ⚠ (Tel Flookburgh 328). (Mr and Mrs Hugh Cavendish) (NGS)

HOLKHAM Norfolk Map 9 TF84
Holkham Hall 1½m W of Wells-next-the-Sea off A149. Entrance by Almhouses Gate in Holkham village. Palladian mansion, built 1734 by William Kent and former home of Coke of Norfolk. Marble hall and state apartments with pictures and furnishings, terraces, Holkham Pottery, also Holkham bygones collection of agricultural and rural craft tools. Garden centre. Large Park. ☾ Open 26 May and 25 Aug also 29 May; Thu Jun to Sep also Mon Jul and Aug 11.30 – 5.

50p (ch 25p, pen in parties 25p). Admission prices under revision for 1980. No dogs. ⚠ 25p. (Tel Wells 227). (Earl of Leicester)
HOLLINGBOURNE Kent Map 5 TQ85
Eyehome Manor SW of village, 15th-C half-timbered house with 17th-C additions. Laundry museum. Also herb garden. ☾ Ope 4 Apr to 30 Sep, Sat and Sun, 2 – 6; Tue, We Thu, Sat and Sun Aug also BH 2 – 6. Parties other times by arrangement. 70p (ch 35p). ⚠ (Tel 514) (Mr and Mrs Simmons)
HOLT Wiltshire Map 3 ST86
The Courts House dates from c1700. Topiary gardens, with lily pond and arboretum, open Apr to end Oct, daily (ex Sa and Sun) 2 – 6. 30p (NT)
HONITON Devon Map 3 ST10
Allhallows Museum High Street (next to church). Honiton lace on display, also lace-making demonstrations. Historical documents etc. Locally excavated prehistor animal bones and artifacts. Open May to Sep 10 – 5. 20p (ch 16 5p). P. (Tel Farway 307, Hon Sec)
HORNSEA Humberside Map 8 TA24
Hornsea Pottery Rolston Road. Factory tours, seconds shop, gift shop, holiday shop country crafts centre, ☾ picnic area, mini-zo and 28 acres of landscaped gardens with lake. Open all year daily from 10am. Factory tours 35p (ch and pen 20p). Parties. 'Minida model village open early May to end Sep, 30 (ch and pen 15p). ⚠ (Tel 2161) ♿
HORRINGER Suffolk Map 5 TL75
Ickworth 2½m SW of Bury St Edmunds. Elliptical rotunda (1794 – 1830), with 18th-C and Regency French furniture, silver, and pictures, and formal garden with fine trees. ☾ Open Apr to 12 Oct, Tue, Wed, Thu, Sat, Su BH Mon 2 – 6 (last admission 5.30) park ope all year, daily. £1. Party 15+. Park free. No dogs in house or garden, on lead in park. (N
HORSEY Norfolk Map 9 TG42
Drainage Windmill Erected in 1912 on foundations of earlier mill, restored after bein struck by lightning in 1943, and ceasing to work. Accessible during summer. Free (NT)
HORSHAM West Sussex Map 4 TQ13
Horsham Museum 9 The Causeway. 16th-C black and white timbered house, showing collections of local history, costume, jewelle (The Grundy Collection), toys, early bicycles domestic and rural life, crafts and industries Sussex. Including a period Sussex kitchen, blacksmith's forge, wheelwright's and saddler's shops, prehistoric and geology room. Frequent temporary exhibitions throughout the year. Open all year (ex BH), Tue to Fri 1 – 5, Sat 10 – 5. Free. P. (Tel 4959

A day to remember
at Hornsea Pottery

Come and visit our leisure parks at Hornsea on the East
Yorkshire Coast and at Lancaster on the West coast. You
can browse over the award winning ranges of Hornsea
Pottery and buy it at much less than suggested retail prices.
But do try to find time for some of the other attractions.

Hornsea
At our Hornsea leisure park we have *Guided Factory
Tours, a Children's Playground, Mini-zoo, Gift Shop, Tea
Garden, Cafe, Picnic Area, Country Craft Centre and a
Model Village, 'Minidale', all set in 28 acres of landscaped
gardens.
Hornsea Pottery Co Ltd, Hornsea, Yorkshire HU18 1UD
Telephone : 040 12 (Hornsea) 2161

Lancaster
At our Lancaster leisure park (only 15 minutes off the M6,
exits 33 or 34) we have *Guided Factory Tours, Children's
Farmyard and Playground, Cafe, Tea Garden, Gift Shop
and a Rare Breeds Survival Unit all set in 42 beautiful acres
of parkland.
Hornsea Pottery Co Ltd, (Lancaster), Wyresdale Road,
Lancaster LA1 3LA Telephone : 0524 (Lancaster) 68444

*Our Factory Tours are in such great demand that we advise you to
come early and avoid disappointment. Don't forget we make no
charge for parking.

HORNSEA POTTERY
Open daily from 10 am

HORTON *Avon* Map 3 ST78
Horton Court Restored Cotswold house,
altered in 19th-C, with rare Norman halt. Hall
and perpendicular ambulatory. Open Apr to
Oct, Wed and Sat 2–6; other times by written
application to tenant. 20p *(NT)*

HOUGHTON *Norfolk* Map 9 TF72
Houghton Hall 1¼m off A148 between Kings
Lynn (12m) and Fakenham (8m). One of the
finest examples of Palladian architecture in
England, Houghton Hall designed by Colen
Campbell and Thomas Ripley was built in the
18th-C for Sir Robert Walpole. State rooms
have interior decorations and furniture by
William Kent and contain paintings and china.
Stables with heavy horses and Shetland
ponies, harness room and coach house.
Beautiful parkland and pleasure grounds. ⚑
and picnic area. Opening times and
admission prices not available for 1980. Party
20+. ⚠ *(Tel East Rudham 247)* &

HOUSESTEADS *Northumberland*
Map 12 NY76
Roman Wall (Housesteads Museum) Near
Bardon Mill. Roman fort of 'Vir covicium', with
mile-castles and 3-mile stretch of wall.
Museum has finds excavated in vicinity.
Open*, see inside front cover. 40p, winter 15p
(ch 15p winter 5p). ⚠ *(AM and NT)*

HOVE *East Sussex* Map 4 TQ20
Brighton and Hove Engineerium off Nevill
Road. Beam pumping engines of 1876 and
French Corliss horizontal engine, traction
engines, railway engines, fire engines etc.
The exhibition hall contains many hundreds of
full size and model engines, machines and
hand tools, household and cooking machines
which relate the progress of steam power and
its development from the 1780s'. Periodic
special exhibitions. Boiler house and steam
driven workshops also open. Easter and 12,
13 Aug, Steam and Craft Fairs. ⚑ weekends
only. Open all year (ex 23, 24, 25 Dec) daily
10–5. 70p (ch and pen 30p) when in steam;
weekdays (not in steam) 50p (ch and pen
20p). Prices under revision for 1980. No dogs.
P. *(Tel Brighton 559583)* & B

HOWICK *Northumberland* Map 12 NU21
Howick Hall Gardens and Grounds
Entrance by East Lodge. Late 18th-C
mansion with fine gardens and grounds.
Gardens and grounds only open 1 Apr to 30
Sep, daily 2–7, 20p (ch 15 10p). ⚠ *(Howick
Trustees Ltd) (Tel Longhoughton 285)*

HUDDERSFIELD *West Yorkshire*
Map 7 SE11
Art Gallery Princess Alexandra Walk.
Contains a permanent collection of British oil
paintings, watercolours, drawings, sculpture
from mid 19th-C onwards. Temporary loan
exhibitions throughout the year. Scherer
gallery of Bamforth photographs, lantern
slides and postcards. Open all year daily (ex
Sun) 9–7.30 (4 Sat). Free. P. *(Tel 21356)* &
Colne Valley Museum Cliffe Ash, Golcar.
Restored weaver's cottage, with living room
c 1860, weaver's workshop with working
looms, and local history display. New
clogmaker's workshop. Craft weekends Apr
to Oct. ⚑ shop – books of local interest and
industrial history. Open all year, Sat, Sun and
BH 2–5. 15p (ch 16 10p, pen free). P. Golcar.
(Tel 659762) **(79)**
Museum of Hand Tools Banney Road
Teacher's Centre, Halifax Road. Collection
includes trades equipment from joiners,
coopers, blacksmiths, plumbers, clog makers
etc, and special feature of 500 joiners'

moulding planes, hand tools only, all of which
can be examined. Many of the tools used by
the custodian to demonstrate the older crafts.
Open all year first Sat of each month
1.30–5.30 or by special appointment. Free.
⚠ *(Mr D Broadbeat) (Tel 39531 school hours
only)* & B
Tolson Memorial Museum Ravensknowle
Park. Geology, natural history, archaeology,
folk life, toys, development of cloth industry,
and collection of horse-drawn vehicles. Open
all year, Mon to Sat 10.30–5, Sun 2–5
(closed 25, 26 Dec). At weekends only 5p (ch
2½p, pen free). ⚠ *(Tel 30591)* &

HUGHENDEN *Buckinghamshire*
Map 4 SU89
Hughenden Manor 1½m N High Wycombe.
Disraeli's old home, remodelled by him in
1862, in 169-acre estate, with funiture and
books of the statesman. Open Apr to Oct.
House and garden Wed to Sat 2–6; Sun and
BH Mon 12.30–6; Mar and Nov Sat and Sun
only 2–5 or sunset. 90p. *(NT)*

HULL *Humberside* Map 8 TA02
Ferens Art Gallery Queen Victoria Square.
Contains a collection of works by European
Old Masters; 19th-C marine paintings from
Humberside; 20th-C English art and a regular
programme of visiting exhibitions. ⚑ (closed
Sun) 10.45–4. Open all year (ex 4 Apr, 24, 25
and 26 Dec) Mon to Sat 10–5, Sun
2.30–4.30. P. *(Tel 223111 ext 2750)*
Malster House 160 High Street. Georgian
house (1743), with stone and wrought iron
staircase and balustrade, some ornate stucco
work, and finely carved doors. Staircase and
entrance hall only shown all year. Mon to Fri
(ex BH) 10–4. 20p (incl guide book). *(NT)*
Town Docks Museum Queen Victoria
Square. Displays include 'Whales and
Whaling', 'Fishing and Trawling', 'Hull and the
Humber', 'Ships and Shipping', plus Victorian
Court Room. Open all year (ex 4 Apr, 24, 25 &
26 Dec) Mon to Sat 10–5, Sun 2.30–4.30.
Free. P. Osbourne Street. *(Tel 22311 ext
2737)* &
Transport and Archaeological Museum 36
High Street. Development of road transport
through the ages. Archaeology of
Humberside and Roman mosaics including
the Horkslow Pavement. Open all year (ex 4
Apr 24, 25 and 26 Dec) Mon to Sat 10–5, Sun
2.30–4.30. Free. P at Wilberforce house. *(Tel
223111 ext 2737)*
Wilberforce House 23–25 High Street. Early
17th-C mansion, where William Wilberforce
was born, with Jacobean and Georgian
Rooms, Slavery collection. Secluded garden.
Open all year (ex 4 Apr, 24, 25, 26 Dec),
weekdays 10–5, Sun 2.30–4.30. Free. ⚠
(Tel 223111 ext 2737)

HUNGARTON *Leicestershire* Map 4 SK60
Quenby Hall 7m NE Leicester on unclass
road. A Jacobean mansion built about 162
and extensively restored in 1974–5.
Excellent panelling, ceilings and furniture.
Fine view of cedars from library, walled
garden with lawns and flowers. ⚑ Hall open
Sun, Jun to Sep also 6/7 Apr, 4/5 and 25/26
May, 24/25 Aug, 2–6. ⚠ *(Tel 224)*

HUNGERFORD *Berkshire* Map 4 SU36
Littlecote House 2m NW on unclass road S
of River Kennet. Tudor manor with unique
collection of Cromwellian armour. Chapel,
haunted bedroom and a fine collection of oak
furniture. Roman excavations and Orpheus
mosaic. Beautiful gardens in Kennet Valley.
Walled garden and trout stream. ⚑ Sat, Sun

plus pre-booked parties. Open 1 Apr to 1 Oct Sat, Sun and BH 2 – 6. Party (weekdays). Prices not available for 1980. *(Tel 2509). (Mr D S Wills)* ᜒ B

HUNTINGDON *Cambridgeshire* Map 4 TL27
Cromwell Museum Market Square. Restored Norman building, once a school where Oliver Cromwell and Samuel Pepys were taught, now museum of Cromwellian relics. Open all year Tue to Sat 11 – 1 and 2 – 5 (4, Sat), Sun 2 – 4, closed BH ex 4 Apr. Free. P. *(Tel 52181 or outside office hours 52861)*
Hinchingbrooke House ½m W on A141. Tudor and later mansion, incorporating medieval Benedictine Nunnery. Former home of the Cromwells and Earls of Sandwich and now restored and used as a school. ⚓ Open Mar, Apr, May, Jun, Jul. Sun 2 – 5. Also Easter, BH Mon. 40p (ch 14 20p) Party 30p. P. *(Tel 51121)* ᜒ B

HURST CASTLE *Hampshire* Map 4 SZ38
On peninsula 4m S of Lymington. Erected 1544 by Henry VIII, occupied during Civil War by Cromwell's forces and restored in 1873. Accessible on foot or by boat from Keyhaven (weather permitting). Open*, see inside front cover. 15p (ch 16 and pen 5p). Nearest car park on beach. 1½m. *(AM)*

HURSTPIERPOINT *West Sussex* Map 4 TQ21
Danny Elizabethan E-shaped house dating from 1593. Early in the 18th C the South front was faced with a Queen Anne elevation. Open May to Sep, Wed and Thu 2 – 5. 40p (ch 25p). ⚠ *(Tel 833000)*

HUTTON-LE-HOLE *North Yorkshire* Map 8 SE78
Ryedale Folk Museum Ryedale antiquities from prehistoric times to beginning of this century, including reconstructed cruck houses, barn, wheelshed and Elizabethan furnace in grounds. Open day (21 Jun) all crafts in operation. Open Easter to end Sep daily 2 – 5.30 (11 – 5.30, mid Jul and Aug). 30p (ch 14 15p, pen reduced) may be subject to increase. P. *(Tel Lastingham 367)* ᜒ B

HYDE *Gt Manchester* Map 7 SJ99
Newton Hall ½m N of town centre in Dukinfield Road (A627). Restored 14th-C manor hall with original cruck beams, spurs and side-walls, set in two acres of parkland. Open all year, weekdays 9 – 4.30. Free. ⚠ *(Tel 061-308 2721)* **(79)**

HYTHE *Kent* Map 5 TR13
Saltwood Castle On N edge of Saltwood. Murderers of Thomas-à-Beckett rode from here. Grounds and parts of castle, including battlement walk, undercroft, armoury and

torture chamber. Open Sun and BH from 25 May to 27 Jul. Then daily in Aug (ex Mon and Sat) 2 – 5.30 but open 25 Aug. By appointment on other days for parties of fifteen or more, when guided tours of private rooms may be arranged (extra charge). ⚓ (teas). 50p (ch 12 25p). ⚠ *(Tel 67190, Secretary)*

ILFRACOMBE *Devon* Map 2 SS54
Chambercombe Manor 1m E off A399. One of England's oldest inhabited houses, parts of which are 800 years old. Haunted room, chapel, period furniture, armour and porcelain. Open Easter Su to end Sep, Mon to Fri 10.30 – 5, Sun 2 – 5 (closed Sat). A charge will be made for admission to the house only. ⚠ *(Tel 62624)*
Hele Mill 1m E. This mill dates back to 1525. It has been restored to full working order and is producing wholemeal flour. There is an 18ft overshot water wheel and inside are many interesting items of mill machinery. Open Easter to end Sep, Mon to Fri 10 – 5, also Sun 2 – 5. Admission prices not available. ⚠ *(Tel 63162)*
Ilfracombe Museum Natural history, Victoriana, archaeology, geology, photographs. Open daily 10 – 5 (10 – 1 winter), other times by arrangement. 20p (ch 10p). ⚠ *(Tel 63541)*

ILKLEY *West Yorkshire* Map 7 SE14
Manor House Castle Yard, Church Street. Elizabethan Manor House built on site of Roman fort, showing exposed Roman wall and collections of Roman material. Special art exhibitions each month. Ilkley Literature Festival. Open daily (ex 4 Apr, 25, 26 Dec) 10 – 5, enquire for summer opening hours. Free. ⚠ *(Tel 600066)* ᜒ B

INGATESTONE *Essex* Map 5 TQ69
Ingatestone Hall Brick-built house (c1545), with portraits and armorial china in long gallery, and annual exhibitions of documents and pictures. An exhibition on 'Industry in Essex' will be displayed in 1980. Open 5 Apr to 4 Oct, Tue to Sat and BH Mon 10 – 12.30 and 2 – 4.30. Free. No dogs. ⚠ *(Tel 3340). (Lord Petre and Essex County Council)* ᜒ B

INSTOW *Devon* Map 2 SS42
Tapeley Park House and Gardens 1½m W on A39 Bideford – Barnstaple Road. Italian-style gardens and woodland walk to lake. Pets and putting green. ⚓ Conducted tours for parties of part of the house. Open Easter to Oct, BH and daily (ex Mon) 10 – 6. Admission charges not yet decided. ⚠ *(Tel 860528). (NGS)* **(79)**

IPSDEN *Oxfordshire* Map 4 SU68
Wellplace Bird Farm Over 100 varieties of birds, pet lambs, goats, monkeys, foxes,

badgers, donkeys, otters, ponies, racoons, etc. ☒ Open Fec to end Nov, Sat and Sun from 10am; Easter to Sep also Mon to Fri from 1pm. 45p (ch 20p, ch 2 free). Party. ⚠ *(Tel Checkendon 680473)* ⅄

IPSWICH *Suffolk* Map 5 TM14
Ancient House Butter Market. A superb example of 16th-C English domestic architecture. The exterior is richly ornamented in pargetting and carved oak-frame windows. Inside is an 'Oak' room with panelling, beams and a Jacobean mantelpiece. Above the main doorway is the Royal Coat of Arms of Charles II, and it is claimed that he hid in a secret chapel within the house after the Battle of Worcester. It is now converted into a busy bookshop, but visitors are always welcome. Open all year, daily (ex Sun and BH) 9–5.30. Free. *(Tel 57761)*
Christchurch Mansion South side of Christchurch Park. 16th-C country house. Art Gallery attached. Period rooms, pictures, pottery, ship models and costume. Open all year (ex some BH) Mon to Sat 10–5 (or dusk), Sun 2.30–4.30. Free. P. Written enquiries to main museum below. *(Tel 53246). (Borough of Ipswich Dept of Recreation Amenities)*
The Museum High Street. Local geology, prehistory, Roman to medieval archaeology in eastern counties, and natural history collection. Ethnography. Art gallery with temporary exhibitions. Open all year (ex BH), Mon to Sat 10–5. Free. P. *(Tel 213761/2). (Borough of Ipswich Dept of Recreation & Amenities)*

IRONBRIDGE *Salop* Map 7 SJ60
Blists Hill Open Air Museum Coalport Road, Madeley, Telford. Buildings and machines illustrating industrial and social history of Ironbridge area, on 42-acre site. Part of Ironbridge Gorge Museum Trust (see below for details of opening times, etc). Also *Tar Tunnel* an 18th-C tunnel under Blists Hill with access to artificial 'wells' which collect natural bitumen. Part of Ironbridge Gorge Museum Trust. Open at variable hours. ⅄ B
Coalbrookdale Furnace and Museum of Iron Iron-founding museum and site of original furnace built by Abraham Darby, where first smelting of iron by coke was carried out in early 18th C. Outdoor exhibits and indoor museum open all year, daily 10–6 (5, Nov to Mar). Admission prices not yet known for 1980. ⚠ *(Tel 3522)*. Part of Ironbridge Gorge Museum Trust. ⅄. Also *Coach House Gallery* Coalbrookdale. Prints, drawings etc from Elton collection on display and special exhibitions. See above for details of opening.
Coalport China Works Museum Original buildings, workshop and social history displays about Coalport China Company, active here from c1790 to 1926. Part of Ironbridge Gorge Museum Trust (see above for details of opening times etc). ⅄
Severn Warehouse Visitor Centre Dale End. Exhibits displays and slide show introducing the historic Ironbridge Gorge. *See Coalbrookdale Museum for details of opening times etc.* ⅄

IXWORTH *Suffolk* Map 5 TL97
Abbey Extensive remains of monastic claustral buildings incorporated within later 17th-C house. Also remains of monastic church in grounds. Special exhibition. ☒ by prior arrangement. Open 1 May to 16 Aug, also Spring BH; Tue and Sun only 2.30–5; other times throughout the year by prior arrangement. 60p. ⚠ limited. *(Tel Pakenham 30374)*

Ironbridge Gorge Museum

Museum of Iron Coalbrookdale

Coalport China Works Museum

The dawn of the Industrial Revolution. Here 200 years ago the first Iron Bridge symbolised the birth of a new age. Today the Ironbridge Gorge Museum presents the story of this unique valley, its people and products.

Ironbridge is thirty minutes from junction 12 on the M6. Follow the signposts to Telford. The Museum is open daily from 10.00. Come early in the day to see it all.

Ironbridge Gorge Museum Trust
Ironbridge, Telford
Salop. TF8 7AW
Telephone: Ironbridge
(095 245) 3522

JARROW *Tyne and Wear* Map 12 NZ36
*St Paul's Church, Monastery and Jarrow
Hall* Church Bank. Standing in a conservation
area on the south bank of the River Tyne, St
Paul's Church (AD685) is famous as the
home of the Venerable Bede. During his
lifetime the monastery of St Paul was world
famous as a centre of learning and culture.
The chancel of the present building is the
church in which he worshipped. Excavation
on south side of church has revealed plan of
the monastery in which he lived and has
produced important archaeological finds, now
housed in Jarrow Hall. The Hall, c1785, has
been restored as a visitor centre and contains
the Bede Monastery museum, information
centre, craft shop and changing exhibitions.
🆓 Open Easter to Oct, Tue to Sat 10–5.30,
Sun 2.30–5.30 (closed Mons ex BH). Winter:
open weekdays 11–4.30. Church open as
Hall but including Mons. Hall 20p (ch and pen
5p). Church free. ♿ *(Tel 892106 or 897402)*
JODRELL BANK (Nuffield Radio Astronomy
Laboratories) *Cheshire* Map 7 SJ77
Mark 1 (250ft) radio telescope is one of the
largest fully steerable radio telescopes in the
world, and the Mark II (125ft by 85ft) has
advanced form of digital control. Display
material and working models on view. Also
arboretum. 🆓 Open 22 Mar to 31 Oct, daily
2–6; 1 Nov to 17 Mar weekends only 2–5
(closed Christmas and New Year). Jodrell
Bank Concourse building 60p (school ch 30p.
ch 5 free). Planetarium shows 40p (school ch
20p, infants not admitted). Prices under
revision for 1980. No dogs. ♿ *(Tel Lower
Withington, Cheshire [04777] 339)* ♿
KEDLESTON HALL Derbyshire Map 8 SK33
Adam mansion, standing in 500-acre park
with lakes, home of the Curzon family since
1100. Magnificent marble hall, State rooms,
collection of fine pictures. 12th-C church.
Indian museum. Canada goose colony in
park. Gift shop. 🆓 Open Easter then Sun from
27 Apr to 28 Sep (also open BH Mons). Also
open for private parties by arrangement.
House and museum 2–6; park gardens and
church 12.30–6. Admission charges for 1980
not yet decided. ♿ *(Tel Derby 840396)* ♿
(park only)
KEIGHLEY West Yorkshire Map 7 SE04
Cliffe Castle NW of town on A629. Mansion
of c1878 given by Sir Bracewell Smith.
Contains collections of natural and local
history, dolls and ceramics. Also craft
workshops. Aviary, and play area in adjacent
park. Suite of furnished rooms with French
furniture from Victoria and Albert Museum. 🆓
Open all year daily (ex 4 Apr, 25/26 Dec)
10–5, enquire for summer opening times.

Free. ♿ approach via Spring Gardens Lane.
(Tel 64184)
East Riddlesden Hall 1m NE. Stone-built
17th-C house, with curious wheel windows
typical of certain West Riding manors.
Furniture, pictures, armour, and fine tithe
barn. Open Apr to Oct, Wed to Sun and BH
Mon and Tue, 2–6. Jun, Jul and Aug
10.30–6. 60p. *(NT)*
KELLING *Norfolk* Map 9 TG04
Kelling Park Aviaries Weybourne Road.
Situated in 14 acres of beautiful gardens is
this fine collection of European and tropical
birds, including ornamental pheasants,
cockatoos, macaws and flamingoes. 🆓
(licensed). Picnic area, children's playground.
Open all year, daily 10–dusk. 70p (ch 35p). ♿
(Tel Holt 2235)
KELMSCOTT *Oxfordshire* Map 4 SU 29
Manor House Old gabled Cotswold manor
house, once home of William Morris. Open
Apr to Sep, first Wed in month 11–1 and 2–5;
also sometimes on written application to
resident giving two weeks notice. 60p. Under
revision for 1980. ♿ limited. *(Society of
Antiquaries)*
KENDAL *Cumbria* Map 7 SD59
Abbot Hall Art Gallery Fine house designed
by Carr of York in 1759. Ground floor rooms
restored to period decor with 18th-C pictures,
furniture and *objets d'art*. Modern galleries
displaying contemporary and period, fine and
decorative arts. Various changing exhibitions.
🆓 (Mon to Fri 10.30–4). Open all year (ex 4
Apr and 2 weeks Christmas/New Year) Mon
to Fri 10.30–5.30, Sat and Sun 2–5. 35p (ch
10p, pen 20p). Art gallery and museum (see
below) 55p (ch 20p). ♿ *(Tel 22464)* ♿
*Abbot Hall Museum of Lakeland Life and
Industry* Housed in stable block designed by
Carr of York in 1759 with displays of Lakeland
life, trade, social and economic history,
Museum of the Year 1973. Various changing
exhibitions. Craft shop. 🆓 (Mon to Fri
10.30–4). Open all year (ex 4 Apr and 2
weeks Christmas/New Year) Mon to Fri
10.30–12.30 and 2–5. Sat and Sun 2–5. 35p
(ch 10p, pen 20p). Museum and Art gallery
(see above) 55p (ch 20p). ♿ *(Tel 22464)*
Kendal Museum Station Road. Museum of
natural history, local history and archaeology
gallery and world-wide mammal collection.
New Lake District natural history exhibition in
course of construction. Open all year. Mon to
Fri 10.30–4, weekends 2–4. 10p (ch 16 5p).
♿ *(Tel 21374)*
KENILWORTH *Warwickshire* Map 4 SP27
Kenilworth Castle Keep dates from
1155–70, with later great hall by John of

Gaunt. Further additions, including gatehouse, now known as Lord Leicester's Buildings, built by the Dudleys during the 16th C. Open, see inside front cover. 30p, winter 15p (ch 16 and pen 15p, winter 5p). ⚠ *(AM)*

KESWICK *Cumbria* Map 11 NY22
Castlerigg Stone Circle 1m W on unclass rd. In picturesque mountain setting, prehistoric circle of 38 stones with oblong space containing 10 additional stones. Open any reasonable time. Free. *(AM and NT)*
Fits Park Museum and Art Gallery
Outstanding among the exhibits are many manuscripts and various relics of Hugh Walpole and Robert Southley, two manuscripts of Wordsworth, a geological collection, and a fine scale model (1834) of the Lake District. Good park surrounding museum. Open 1 Apr to 30 Oct, Mon to Sat 10–12, 2–5 (7, Jul and Aug). 15p (ch 16 10p), subject to alteration. P. (Roadside). *(Tel 73263)*
Lingholm Turn off A66 for Portinscale and continue on the road to Grange 1m. Formal and woodland gardens with a large collection of rhododendrons, azaleas, and other interesting shrubs. Woodland walk of 1½m. Open Apr to Oct, daily (ex Sun) 10–5. 50p (ch, accompanied, free). No dogs. ⚠ *(Tel 72003). (The Viscount Rochdale)* ᕦ

KETTERING *Northamptonshire* Map 4 SP87
Alfred East Art Gallery Sheep Street. Exhibitions, approximately twelve per year, visit the gallery, each lasting for about 3 weeks. Open all year, daily (ex Thu and Sun) 10–5. Free. P. *(Tel 85215)* ᕦ

KIDDERMINSTER *Hereford and Worcester* Map 7 SO87
Kidderminster Art Gallery and Museum Market Street. Exhibitions include work by local artists and art schools, and a permanent collection of prints by Frank Brangwyn as well as temporary exhibitions of a more general interest. Displays of local archaeology and history are also on view. Open all year, daily (ex Wed, Sun and BH) 11–4. Free. ⚠ *(Tel 66610)* **(79)**

KILLERTON HOUSE AND GARDEN Devon Map 3 SS99
5m NE of Exeter on B3185 off B3181. 18th-C house containing the Paulise de Bush collection of costume, shown in a series of room settings furnished in different periods, ranging from the second half of the 18th C to the present day. 15 acres of gardens with rare trees and shrubs. The estate covers more than 5,000 acres. Shop ⚌ licensed 11–6 (last admission 5.30). House and garden £1.30 (ch

5–15 65p), garden only 90p. Party (morning). Garden open all year during daylight. ⚠ *(Tel Hele 345). (NT)* ᕦ

KILVERSTONE *Norfolk* Map 5 TL98
'Latin American' Wildlife Park 50-acre wildlife park and miniature horse stud, specialising in South American animals and birds, including 7 species of South American cats, also 14 species of monkeys, grissons, maned wolves, tapirs, parrots, penguins, and semi-tropical birds. Pets corner, patting area, English walled garden, deer park, riverside walk, adventure playground and picnic areas. ⚌ Open all year, daily 10–6.30 (dusk in winter). Admission prices not available for 1980. Party. ⚠ *(Tel Thetford 5369). (Lord and Lady Fisher)* ᕦ

KIMBOLTON *Cambridgeshire* Map 4 TL06
Kimbolton School 11m SW of Huntingdon, on A45. Partly Tudor and 17th-C, and partly 18th-C by Vanbrugh with fine mural paintings in chapel and on staircase by Pellegrini and gatehouse by Robert Adam. State rooms and grounds open to the public. Open 6/7 Apr, 25/26 May, and Sun 12 Jul to 31 Aug. 25p (ch 16 5p). ⚠ *(Tel 505)*

KIMMERIDGE *Dorset* Map 3 SY97
Smedmore ⅞m SE. Jacobean, Queen Anne and Georgian house with a collection of antique dolls and walled gardens. Fine coastal views on attractive approach from Wareham. Open Jun, Jul and Aug, Wed 2.15–5.30 also first 2 Wed Sep. 60p (ch 14 30p). Subject to revision for 1980. ⚠ *(Tel Corfe Castle 717). (Major J C Mansel)* ᕦ

KINGSBRIDGE *Devon* Map 3 SX74
Cookworthy Museum Fore Street. Commemorates William Cookworthy, Quaker 'father' of English china clay industry, born in Kingsbridge. Exhibition of his history and porcelain is shown in this old former grammar school, utilising original schoolrooms of 1670. Victorian kitchen and scullery also shown. Costume room and comprehensive local history collection. New farm gallery illustrates farming history of the area. Open Easter to mid Oct, Mon–Sat 10–5 (last admission 4.30). 25p (ch 10p, pen 15p). Admission prices under revision for 1980. *(Tel 3235)*
Kingsbridge Miniature Railway The Quay. A 7¼ inch gauge passenger carrying miniature railway, ½m trip. Open Easter, then mid May to mid Sep daily 11–5.

KINGSDON *Somerset* Map 3 ST52
Lytes Cary Home of Lyte family for 500 years, preserving 14th-C chapel and 15th-C Great Hall. Open Mar to end Oct, Wed, and Sat 2–6 (last admission 5.30). 70p. No dogs. *(NT)*

KING'S LYNN *Norfolk* Map 9 TF62
Lynn Museum Market Street. Exhibits on local archaeology, geology and natural history. Medieval Pilgrims badges of special interest. Temporary exhibitions throughout year. Open all year (ex 4 Apr, 25, 26 Dec, 1 Jan and all BH) Mon to Sat 10–5. 10p (ch and pen free). P. *(Tel 5001)* ⑀
Museum of Social History At 27 King Street displays costume, ceramics, glass, toys and domestic material. Open all year (ex BH) Tue to Sat 10–5. Free. *(Tel 5004)*
St George's Guildhall Kings Street. Early 15th-C, largest surviving English medieval Guildhall, now used as a theatre. Open all year, daily when not in use (ex 1 Jan, 4 Apr, 25, 26 Dec, Sat afternoon, Sun), 10–12.30 and 2.30–5. 10p. *(NT)* ⑀

KINWARTON *Warwickshire* Map 4 SP15
Dovecote A stone-built 14th-C dovecote with ogee-shaped doorway, conical roof, and 600 nesting boxes. Open daily until sunset; key at adjacent Glebe Farm. 10p. *(NT)*

KIRBY MISPERTON *North Yorkshire* Map 8 SE77
Flamingoland At Kirby Misperton Hall. Late 18th-C house and 350 acres of Zoo and Pleasure Park. 1,000 animals, birds and reptiles. Jungle Cruise, Children's Farm, Gnomeland, Fairground. Model Railway and Caravan Village. ⟐ (licensed). Open Easter–Sep daily 10–4. £1.20 (ch 14 75p) (under review) ⚠ *(Tel 287)* ⑀

KIRBY MUXLOE *Leicestershire* Map 4 SK50
Kirby Muxloe Castle Off B5380. Ruined moated 15th-C fortified manor house, built of brick. Open, see inside front cover but closed Tue pm and all day Wed. 15p (ch 16 and pen 5p). *(AM)*

KIRKHAM *North Yorkshire* Map 8 SE76
Kirkham Priory Beautifully situated by River Derwent, with a particularly fine sculptures 13th-C gatehouse. Open*, see inside front cover. 15p (ch 16 and pen 5p). ⚠ *(AM)*

KIRKSTALL *West Yorkshire* Map 8 SE23
Kirkstall Abbey House Museum Original Gatehouse of the ruined Cistercian Abbey, which was occupied continuously for 800 years, now an interesting museum of local archaeology and folk studies, including three streets of craft workshops, houses, shops, Victorian parlour and public house, Abbey Fold, Stephen Harding Gate, and Harewood Square. Collection of costumes and toys. ⟐ Open daily (ex 25, 26 Dec, 1 Jan) Mon to Sat 10–5, Sun 2–5. 25p (ch 16 5p, ch 5 and pen free). ⚠ *(Tel Leeds 755821)* ⑀ B

KNARESBOROUGH *North Yorkshire* Map 8 SE35
Knaresborough Castle Remains of 14th-C stronghold, including the keep, two baileys, and gatehouse. Situated high above the River Nidd. Open Easter to end Sep, daily 10–7. Guided tours on request. Parties of schoolchildren *(apply to Director, Resort Services, Council Offices, Harrogate) Old Court House Museum* now open in castle grounds. Admission prices not yet decided. ⚠ *(Tel Harrogate 504684)* **(79)**
Zoological Gardens Conyngham Hall grounds. Lions, tigers, pumas, black panthers, sea lions, llamas, and wallabies. The world's largest snakes in captivity, snake handling shows Easter to Sep by Nyoka who trains the animals for films and TV. ⟐ Gift shop. Open all year (ex 25 Dec), daily 10–7 (4 in winter). 60p (ch 30p). Under revision for 1980. P. *(Tel Harrogate 862793)* ⑀

KNEBWORTH *Hertfordshire* Map 4 TL22
Knebworth House and Country Park Direct access from A1 (M) at Stevenage (South) roundabout. Home of Lytton family from 1492 to the present day, with magnificent Tudor banqueting hall, and furniture, paintings and other treasures covering 500 years of English history. In a country park with skate park, picnicking, riding, narrow-gauge railway, spectacular children's adventure playground. ⟐ (licensed). Open Apr to Sep, daily (ex Mon) BH and Sun in Oct. Park 11–6, House 11.30–5.30. Knebworth Park 75p covers unlimited access to all park facilities. Knebworth House and Park £1 includes House, gardens, exhibition and park facilities (no reduction for ch). Skate park, for details Nov to Easter please telephone. ⚠ *(Tel Stevenage 812661)* ⑀ B

KNIGHTSHAYES COURT *Devon* Map 3 SS91
19th-C house in large woodland gardens of interest at all seasons, with flowering shrubs and rhododendrons. ⟐ Open 1 Apr to Oct daily Garden 12.30–6, House 1.30–6. £1.30; garden and grounds only 90p *(NGS)*. *(NT)*

KNOWSLEY *Merseyside* Map 7 SJ49
Safari Park Lions, tigers, cheetahs, elephants, rhinos, monkeys, giraffes, zebras, buffaloes, and many other animals displayed in drive-through game reserves. Picnic areas. Open all year 10–5 summer (3.30 winter). £3.50 per Saloon car (incl all passengers). No soft-topped cars (Safari bus available). No dogs permitted in game reserves (kennels

available). Extra attractions Easter to Sep, dolphinarium, children's amusement park, pets corner. ☕ (licensed). Souvenir shops. △ *(Tel Prescott 9009)* ♿

LACOCK *Wiltshire* Map 3 ST96
Lacock Abbey 13th-C cloisters, house dating from 1540 and later, octagonal Tudor tower, half-timbered gables in courtyard, and 17th-C 'Gothick' hall by Sanderson Miller. Fox Talbot conducted photographic experiments here in 1835 and a museum of his work is now open at the entrance gate. Shop and information room. House and grounds open Apr, May and Oct, Wed to Sun and BH Mon 2–6; Jun to Sep daily 2–6; Nov to Mar closed except to historical and other societies by previous written arrangement. £1 (ch 50p). No dogs. *(NT)*. Village is also *NT* property.

LAMBERHURST *Kent* Map 5 TQ63
Bayham Abbey 2m W in East Sussex. In wooded River Teise valley on Kent border, ruins dating back to 13th C and including parts of church, cloistral buildings, and gatehouse. Preservation work still in progress, and museum to be opened with other facilities for visitors. Accessible any reasonable time. Free. △ *(AM)*
Owl House Gardens 1m NE. 13 acres of romantic walks, spring flowers, azaleas, roses, rhododendrons. Rare shrubs, woodland lakes. Setting of Marchioness of Dufferin & Ava's 16th-C 'Owlers' or smugglers' haunt. Open all year daily (ex Tue, Thu and Sat, but open BH weekends), Sun 3–6, 50p (ch 20p) subject to revision. △ *(Tel 01-235 1432). (Marchioness of Dufferin and Ava)* ♿
Scotney Castle 1m SE. A partly ruined 14th-C and later moated castle in a picturesque landscape garden of trees and flowering shrubs. Open Apr to Oct, Wed to Sun and BH 2–6 (5, Apr and Oct) 80p (ch 40p). No dogs. Exhibition in old castle 26 May to 31 Aug, times and days as above. Gardens and exhibition 90p (ch 40p). △ *(NT)*

LAMBTON *Co Durham* Map 12 NZ25
Lambton Pleasure Park 200 acres, drive-through Safari section with lions, elephants, zebra, white rhinos, etc, and 'Walkabout Area' with fenced enclosures, cages, etc. Enlarged pets corner, adventure playground, kiddies' playground, 'The Magic Castle' and Miniature Railway. Astroglide and roundabouts in castle grounds. ☕ and licensed. Open Mar to Oct, daily 10–5. Bus service for non-motorists £1 (ch and pen 50p). Under revision for 1980. No soft-top cars, no pets in Safari Park (free kennels at entrance). Telephone for current details. △ *(Tel Fencehouses 3311)* ♿

LAMPORT *Northamptonshire* Map 4 SP77
Lamport Hall 8m N of Northampton on A508. The house, most of which dates from the 17th and 18th Cs, is set in an attractive park, the garden contains one of the earliest Alpine rock gardens in England and has been in the Isham family home since 1560. The South-West Front is the work of John Webb, pupil and son-in-law of Inigo Jones, and was built in 1655, with wings added in 1732 and 1740. The lofty music hall contains Webb's stone chimney piece and 18th-C plaster work by John Woolston. There is a fine collection of family portraits and some of the Stuarts – supported by the Ishams – together with other 17th-C paintings, including work by Van Dyck, Guido Reni, Mierevelt, Maratti, Lely, etc and a collection of china and furniture. ☕ Open Easter to end Sep. Sun, and BH Mon and Tue, also Thu Jun to Aug 2.15–5.30. 70p (ch 14 35p). P. *(Tel Maidwell 272)* ♿

LANCASTER *Lancashire* Map 7 SD46
City Museum Old Town Hall, Market Square. Georgian building with local archaeology, history and museum of the King's Own Royal Lancaster Regiment. Open daily (ex Sun, 25, 26 Dec, 1 Jan) 10–5. Free. P. *(Tel 64637)*
Hornsea Pottery Co Ltd Wyresdale Road. Set in 42 acres of landscaped parkland includes new 19-acre Rare Breeds Survival Unit, picnic area, and children's playground. Self-service cafe and pottery shop. ☕ Open all year, Jul to Sep Mon to Sat 10–5.30, Sun 10–6, Easter and BH 9–6. All other times Mon to Fri 9–5, Sat and Sun 10–5. Factory tours should be booked in advance. *(Tel 68444)* ♿

LANHYDROCK *Cornwall* Map 2 SX06
Lanhydrock Restored 17th-C mansion in richly-wooded setting, with a fine gatehouse and picture gallery with plaster ceiling and 17th- to 20th-C family portraits. ☕ Open 1 Apr to end Oct, daily 11–6 (last admissions ½hr before closing). £1.50. Gardens only 90p. Winter, gardens Nov to Mar during daylight hours. Shop and ☕ Nov to 23 Dec. *(NT)*

LAUNCESTON *Cornwall* Map 2 SX38
Launceston Castle Formerly known as Dunheved, and the one-time seat of William the Conqueror's brother, fine round keep forms part of the 12th- to 13th-C remains. Open*, see inside front cover. 15p (ch 16 and pen 5p). △ *(AM)*
Lawrence House Mid Georgian house part of which is now museum of local interest. Open Apr to Sep, Mon to Sat (ex BH), 2.30–4.30, also Mon, Wed and Thu 10.30–12.30, Oct, Nov, Feb, Mar, Wed only. Free. *(NT)*

LACOCK ABBEY

Near Chippenham, Wiltshire

Medieval village and home of the Talbots.
See also the Fox Talbot Museum of Photography.
Refreshments in village.
See gazetteer for details.

Trecarrel Manor 4m S off A388, near Lezant. Restored Hall and Chapel from 1488. On view all year by appointment only. Admission prices under review for 1980. *(Tel Coads Green 286)* &

LAVENHAM *Suffolk* Map 5 TL94
Guildhall Picturesque, restored timber-framed building, built in 1529, the former hall of the Guild of Corpus Christi. Open Mar to Nov regularly, 10.30–12.30, 2–5.30 (closed Fri Mar and Nov). 60p. No dogs. *(NT)*
Little Hall 15th-C 'Hall' house is the only furnished house open to the public in Lavenham. Belonging to the Suffolk Preservation Society, it contains the Gayer-Anderson collection of antique furniture, pictures, ceramics, books, sculptures etc. Open Easter to mid Oct, Sat, Sun and BH 2–6. Parties by appointment. 30p (ch 15p). & *(Tel 247179)*

LAXFIELD *Suffolk* Map 5 TM27
Laxfield and District Museum The Guildhall. Housed in 16th-C building the museum contains hundreds of items relating to village life, mostly of the last century. Displays change from year to year and include a village shop, domestic interior, odd job man's workshop, costume, agricultural implements, the archaeology of Laxfield and photographs. Open May to Sep, Sat, Sun and BH 3–5.30, also Wed Jul and Aug. Midweek school parties by prior arrangement. Free. & *(Tel Ubbeston 312 and 464)*

LAYER MARNEY *Essex* Map 5 TL91
Layer Marney Tower Off B1022. Magnificent early 16th-C brick and terra-cotta tower, entrance gate-tower to Lord Marney's mansion. West wing has similar architectural detail; southside incorporates two-storeyed long gallery in black and red diapered brickwork. Long gallery, swimming pool and tennis court may be hired by written arrangement. & (by appointment). Gallery, tower and garden open 1 Apr to 30 Sep, Sun and Thu (Tue also in Jul and Aug) 2–6; BH Mons 11–6. 50p (ch 15 10p). & *(Tel Colchester 330202). (Major and Mrs Gerald Charrington)* & B

LEA *Derbyshire* Map 8 SK35
Rhododendron Gardens Attractive woodland gardens of three acres featuring rhododendrons, azaleas and rock garden. Gardens open Easter to mid Jun, daily 10–8. 30p (ch 10p). & *(Tel Dethick 380 or 374). (Mrs Tye and Miss Colyer). (NGS)* &

LEAMINGTON SPA *Warwickshire* Map 4 SP36
Warwick District Council Art Gallery and Museum Avenue Road. The art gallery specialises in British, Dutch and Flemish paintings and water-colours of the 16th–20th-C. The museum contains ceramics, Delft, Saltglaze, Wedgwood, Whieldon, Worcester, Derby Ware, etc, and an 18th-C glass collection. Open all year (ex 4 Apr, 25, 26 Dec, 1 Jan) Mon, Tue, Thu, Fri, Sat 10.45–12.45, 2.30–5. Thu also 6–8; Wed 10.45–12.45. Free. & limited. *(Tel 26559)*

LEEDS *Kent* Map 5 TQ85
Leeds Castle 5m ESE of Maidstone on B2163 off A20. Described by Lord Conway as 'the loveliest Castle in the world'. Named after Led, Chief Minister of Wthelbert IV, King of Kent, in AD857. Built on two islands in the middle of a lake, the Castle was originally a stronghold until converted into a Royal Palace by Henry VIII. Beautifully furnished and lovingly restored, a Royal Residence for over three centuries. Museum of Medieval Dog Collars. Water and woodland gardens, duckery and aviary. & (restaurant). Open 1 Apr to 30 Oct Tue, Wed, Thu, Sun and BH Mon and daily throughout Aug, grounds, & and bar 12 noon, Castle 1–5. Grounds 85p (ch and pen 50p); Castle extra £1 (ch and pen 50p extra). Admission prices under revision for 1980. & *(Tel Maidstone 65400)*. 9-hole golf course open every day.

LEEDS *West Yorkshire* Map 8 SE33
Middleton Colliery Railway Garnet Road. First railway authorised by Act of Parliament, in 1758, and first to succeed with steam locomotives in 1812. Number of industrial locomotives and examples of rolling stock are in use. Trains, normally steam, for visitors. & Open Easter to end Sep, Sat, Sun, and BH Mons, 2–4.30. Steam trains each weekend of season, from Tunstall Road roundabout (junct 45 on M1) to Middleton Park which includes picnic area, boating pool, swings etc and cafe. Fares, single 15p, return 30p (ch ½ price). Prices for 1980 under revision. & Enquiries to *Middleton Railway Trust Ltd, Garnet Road, Leeds LS11 5JY* &
Temple Newsam House and Park On south-east outskirts of city. Splendid Tudor and Jacobean house, standing in over 900 acres of parkland, landscaped by 'Capability' Brown. Georgian rooms and a collection of furniture, decorative arts, and paintings. Lord Darnley was born here, and later the house was owned by Lord Halifax, who, in 1922, sold it to the Corporation of Leeds. Gardens have magnificent rhododendrons and azaleas in spring. & Open all year, Tue to Sun (closed Mon but open BH Mon) 10.30–6.15 or dusk (Wed until 8.30, May to Sep). Closed 25, 26 Dec. 30p (ch and pen 10p). & *(Tel 647321)*

LEEK *Staffordshire* Map 7 SJ95
Brindley Mill Mill Street A523. Designed by
James Brindley 1752, and used as a corn-mill
until the late 1940s. Between 1970 and 1974
a preservation trust restored the derelict
building and put the old machinery, which had
remained intact, into working order. A
delightful garden is at the rear of the mill. The
James Brindley Museum due to open during
the early season. Open 5 Apr to end Oct, Sat,
Sun and BH Mon 2–5. 20p (ch 5p). P. *(Tel
384195). (Hon Sec, 5 Daintry Street)*
LEICESTER *Leicestershire* Map 4 SK50
Belgrave Hall Fine early 18th-C house, now
museum with furnishings. Stables with
coaches, and agricultural collection. Also
gardens. Open all year (ex 4 Apr, 25/26 Dec)
Mon to Sat 10–5.30, Sun 2–5.30. Free. P
roadside. *(Tel 554100)* &. B
Guildhall Guildhall Lane. Medieval Guildhall
and later Town Hall of Leicester. Great Hall,
Mayors Parlour, Library and police cells.
Open all year (ex 4 Apr, 25/26 Dec), Mon to
Sat 10–5.30, Sun 2–5.30. Free. P. *(Tel
554100)* &. B
Jewry Wall Museum and Site St Nicholas
Circle. Museum of archaeology from
prehistoric times to 1500. Remains of Roman
baths and Jewry Wall. Open all year (ex 14
Apr, 25/26 Dec), Mon to Sat 10–5.30, Sun
2–5.30. Jewry Wall open any reasonable
time. Free. P. *(Tel 554100)* &.
John Doran Museum East Midland Gas,
Leicester Service Centre Aylestone Road.
Housed in a historic building, a part of the
Aylestone Road Gasworks, a collection of all
aspects of the history of the gas industry. This
includes the history of the manufacture,
distribution and utilisation of gas, with
documentary material as well as old
appliances and equipment. Open all year Tue
to Fri 12.30 to 4.30. Free. ⚠ *(Tel 549414 ext
2192)*
Leicestershire Museum and Art Gallery
New Walk. Collections of 18th- to 20th-C
English paintings and drawings, unique
collection of 20th-C German art, especially of
Expressionism, ceramics, silver, Egyptology,
new geology and natural history
environmental galleries in preparation.
Extensive reference and study collections in
Art and Natural Sciences with a very active
educational programme. Closed 4 Apr, 25/26
Dec. Weekdays 10–5.30, Sun 2–5.30. Free.
P. *(Tel 554100)*
Leicestershire Museum of Technology
Abbey Pumping Station, Corporation Road.
Under development. Power gallery, new
knitting gallery, transport items, steam
shovel. Originally beam engines of 1891.
Open all year (ex 4 Apr, 25/26 Dec) Mon to
Sat 10–5.30, Sun 2–5.30. Free, except for
special events. ⚠ *(Tel 61330)* &.
Leicestershire Record Office 57 New Walk.
Extensive collection of official and private
archives, both rural and urban, relating to the
County of Leicestershire. Open all year Mon
to Thu 9.15–5; Fri 9.15–4.45; Sat
9.15–12.15. *(Tel 554100)*
*Museum of Royal Leicestershire
Regiment* Oxford Street. Housed in
Magazine Gateway is Museum of the
Leicestershire Regiment. Open all year (ex 13
Apr, 25/26 Dec) Mon to Sat 10–5.30, Sun
2–5.30. Free. P roadside. *(Tel 554100)*
Newarke Houses The Newarke. Social
history of the city from 1500 to present day.
19th-C street scene, 17th-C room, local
clocks, musical instruments. Open all year (ex
13 Apr, 25/26 Dec) Mon to Sat 10–5.30, Sun

2–5.30. P (roadside). *(Tel 554100)*
University Botanic Gardens Stoughton
Drive South (on SE side of city). Rock
gardens; pools; herbaceous, shrub and
woodland borders; rose beds; systematic
beds; herb garden; heather garden. Cool and
warm glasshouses. Open all year Mon to Fri
(ex BH) 10–5 (or dusk if earlier). Free. P. *(Tel
717725)*
Wygston's House Museum of Costume St
Nicholas Circle. Displays of English costume
from 1769 to 1924. Reconstruction of
draper's, milliner's, and shoe shops of 1920s.
Open all year (ex 4 Apr, 25/26 Dec), Mon to
Sat 10–5.30, Sun 2–5. Free. P. *(Tel 554100)*
LEIGH *Kent* Map 5 TQ54
Hall Place Outstanding gardens with
rhododendrons, specimen trees and shrubs
(labelled), Dutch and rose gardens, and 11-
acre lake. ⚲ (tea pavilion). Open Sun 6, 13,
20, 27 May; 3, 10, 17 Jun 2.30–6.30. 30p (ch
14 10p). Dogs on lead only. ⚠ *(Lord
Hollenden)* &. **(79)**
LEIGHTON BUZZARD *Bedfordshire*
Map 4 SP92
Narrow Gauge Railway Pages Park.
Original light railway was built to carry sand in
1919, and after its redundancy in 1967 the
railway society obtained permission to
operate over its 3½-mile length. 13 diesel,
steam and petrol locomotives, and others
from Spain and India. ⚲ Open Suns 23 Mar to
28 Sep also 4, 5, 7 Apr; 3, 5, 24, 26 May; 23,
25 Aug 11–5 (ex Sat 2–5). Trains run to
Vandyke Junction. Return journey time 45
mins. Fare 60p (ch 5–16 30p). Postal
enquiries and further information from
LBNGRS Ltd, Pages Park Station, Billington
Road, Leighton Buzzard, Beds LU7 8TN. *(Tel
373888)* &.
LEIGHTON HALL *Lancashire* Map 7 SD47
3m N of Camforth off A6, through Yealand
Conyers village. Neo-Gothic mansion with
fine interior, including early Gillow furniture.
Extensive grounds. Collection of Birds of
Prey. Eagles flown each afternoon, weather
permitting. ⚲ Open May to Sep, Tue to Fri
and Sun 2–5; Grounds and birds only Tue
and Fri, or by arrangement for parties of over
25. Admission to house and grounds 60p (ch
15 40p). Grounds and tea-room only 40p (ch
15 30p). Admission prices under revision for
1980. No dogs. ⚠ *(Tel Camforth 2729)*.
(Major and Mrs Reynolds)
LEISTON *Suffolk* Map 5 TM46
Leiston Abbey Remains of this 14th-C abbey
include choir and transepts of church, and
ranges of cloisters. Georgian house built into
the fabric. Accessible any reasonable time.
Free. ⚠ *(AM)*
LEITHHILL TOWER *Surrey* Map 4 TQ14
4½m SW of Dorking on unclass road. Leith Hill
(965ft) is highest point in the south-east. View
from the tower (1,029ft) includes many
counties, and in clear weather, both St Paul's
Cathedral and the English Channel near
Shoreham can be seen. Tower approachable
by foot only. ⚲ Open 1 Mar to 31 Oct, on fine
days 12–6. 5p (ch 3p). ⚠ *(NT)*
LELANT *Cornwall* Map 2 SW53
Lelant Model Village Model village built to
scale and portraying in miniature a selection
of Cornwall's most interesting buildings. The
delightfully landscaped grounds also include
a museum, water gardens, art gallery, tin
mining exhibition, junior commando assault
course, playground, craft shop. Also included
is an exhibition of smuggling and another
special exhibition of Cornwall's colourful
characters. Open Easter to end Oct, daily

10–5 (high season) 10–10). 75p (ch 16 and pen 40p, ch 5 free). Prices under revision for 1980. △ *(Tel Hayle 752676)*

LEOMINSTER *Hereford and Worcester* Map 3 SO45

Leominster and District Folk Museum Etnam Street. Contains a fine display of smocks, coins, farm implements, corn dollies, tools, and maps. Local history exhibits all given or lent to the museum by local people. The museum is housed in a building of 1855, on site of two old malt houses recently extended to provide two additional large exhibits rooms. Works of John Scarlett Davis, born in town 1804, including album of sketches and drawings. Open all year Apr to Oct, weekdays 10–1, 2–5, Sun 2–5; Nov to Mar, arrangements with *Hon Secretary, Norman Davis, Leominster Museum*. 10p (ch 16 5p). P. *(Tel 2567 or 2520)* ♿

LETCHWORTH *Hertfordshire* Map 4 TL23

First Garden City Museum 296 Norton Way South. Thatched house with new extension, containing the original offices of the architects of the Garden City, Barry Parker and Raymond Unwin. Displays explain the concept and development of Letchworth as the first Garden City of 1903. Open Mon to Fri 2–4.30, Sat 10–1 and 2–4 (closed Sun and BH). Free. *(Tel 3149)* ♿

Museum and Art Gallery Broadway. Museum contains archaeological material of North Hertfordshire, and natural history. Monthly art exhibitions. Open all year, weekdays (ex Suns, BH) 10–5. Free. P. *(Tel 5647)* ♿

LETHERINGHAM *Suffolk* Map 5 TM25

Watermill and Gardens On River Deben and near Easton village. Domesday Book mentions a mill in this site. Mill is some 250 years old and house is Tudor. The machinery was dismantled 60 years ago. 4 acres of gardens and woodland park with stream. Visitors may picnic in gardens or by river. ☕ (3–5.30). Plants and pottery for sale. Mill and gardens open Easter to end Sep, Sun Apr to mid May; Wed, Sun and BH mid May to Sep 12.30–6. 30p (ch 15 15p, ch 5 free). △ *(Tel Wickham Market 746349)* ♿ B

LEVENS *Cumbria* Map 7 SD48

Leave M6 from exit 36. On A6 5m S of Kendal.

Levens Hall Elizabethan mansion added to 13th-C pele tower. Fine pictures and Charles II furniture, etc. Unique steam collection in steam on house open days, traction engines in steam on Suns and BH Mon. The famous topiary garden, laid-out in 1692 still adheres to the original plan. Plant centre. Gift shop. ☕ (licensed) open when house open. House open 6 Apr to end Sep, Tue, Wed, Thu, Sun and BH Mon 2–5. Garden and plant centre open daily 10–5. Admission charges for 1980 not yet decided. No dogs. △ *(Tel Sedgwick 60321). (Mr C H Bagot)* ♿ B

LEVERINGTON *Cambridgeshire* Map 9 TF41

Leverington Hall Part of this Elizabethan house was rebuilt in second half of 17th C. There have been 18th-C alterations, notably the hall fireplace. Open all year by written appointment only. Donation to charity. △ *(Tel Wisbech 2055). (Mr S Graham Thompson FRCS)* ♿ B

LEWES *Sussex* Map 5 TQ41

Anne of Cleves House Southover. Dates from 16th C, now folk museum with extensive collections of domestic bygones, Sussex ironwork and Lewes gallery. Open mid Feb to Nov 10–5.30 (last entries 5pm); also Sun afternoons Apr to Oct. 35p (ch 20p). P

roadside. *(Tel 4610). (Sussex Archaeological Society)*

Castle and Barbican House Museum of Sussex Archaeology High Street. Norman castle, with shell keep and 14th-C barbican. Open all year, weekdays 10–5.30, Apr to Oct, Sun also 2–5.30 (last entries 5pm). Admission to castle 30p (ch 20p, students 25p) **also** museum as above; combined ticket 45p (ch 25p). P. *(Tel 4379). (Sussex Archaeological Society)*

The Military Heritage Museum Regency House, Albion Street. Displays of military uniforms, weapons and related items covering the period 1640–1914. *Room 1* contains a brief history of the British Army, *Room 2* features the Cavalry and Artillery, including a fine cavalcade of headdress. Open all year Tue to Sat 10–5. 25p (ch 15 and pen 10p, service personnel in uniform free). P. *(Tel 3137)*

LEYBURN *North Yorks* Map 7 SE19
Constable Burton Hall Gardens 3½m E on A684. Large informal garden, extensive borders, alpines, roses, walks amongst fine trees, small lake. Open 1 Apr to 1 Aug daily 9–6. 30p (ch 10 and pen free). ⚠ *(Tel Bedale 50428)*

LICHFIELD *Staffordshire* Map 7 SK10
Johnson Birthplace Museum Breadmarket Street. Birthplace of Dr Johnson in 1709, now Johnson Museum. Open all year (ex public and BH, other than 27 Aug) Mon to Sat, and 27 Aug 10–5 (4, Oct to Apr); Sun also May to Sep. 2.30–5.25p (ch 16 10p). Under revision for 1980. P. *(Tel 24972)*

LILFORD PARK *Northamptonshire* Map 4 TL08
On A605 between Oundle and Thrapston. 240-acre Park with interests for all the family, including birds, children's farm with pony rides, adventure playground, gift shop, crafts/museum centre, antiques centre and log cabin cafeteria. Special events include Crafts Market at Easter and East of England Motor Show at Spring BH. Lilford Hall, a 17th-C Jacobean building, stands in the Park but is not at present open to the public except for some events. 40p (ch 16 20p, ch 3 free). Sun 50p (ch 16 25p, ch 3 free) (ex BH and events). Admission prices under revision for 1980. Party 15+. P *(Tel Clopton 648 or 665)*

LILLESHALL *Salop* Map 7 SJ71
Lilleshall Abbey 1½m SW off A518 on unclass rd. An abbey of Augustinian canons established shortly before the middle of 12th C. Considerable remains of 12th-C and 13th-C church with aisleless nave. Accessible any reasonable time. Free. ⚠ *(AM)*

LIMPSFIELD *Surrey* Map 5 TQ45
Detillens 15th-C Wealden Hall House with kingpost roof. Contains collections of

furniture, china, porcelain, militaria and guns. Largest collection of orders and decorations in UK. Open 1 May to 30 Jun, Sat; 1 Jul to 30 Sep, Wed and Sat also BH 2–5. Parties at other times by arrangement (including BH). 75p (ch 40p). Under revision for 1980. ⚠ *(Tel Oxted 3342)* ⎣ B

LINCOLN *Lincolnshire* Map 8 SK97
Lincoln Castle Castle Hill. 11th-C and later structure, founded by William the Conqueror and retaining Norman bailey and two motte mounds. Parapet walk on walls. Open all year (ex Christmas), Mon to Sat 10–6 (4, Oct to Apr); Apr to Oct, Sun 2–5 (7.30, May to Sep). 25p (ch 14 12½p). Prices under revision for 1980. ⚠ *(Tel 25951)* ⎣

Greyfriars City and County Museum Broadgate. Former friary, dating from 13th C, with fine barrel roof in upper room. Now museum of local antiquities and natural history. Open all year (ex 24 Mar, 25, 26 Dec), Mon to Sat 10–5.30, Sun 2–5. Free. P. *(Tel 30401)*

Museum of Lincolnshire Life Lincolnshire Museums, Burton Road. This museum has been designed to give a picture of all aspects of county's life from Elizabethan times to present day and features horse-drawn and passenger vehicles, farm implements, and industrial machinery. Open 1 Feb to 30 Nov, Mon to Sat 10–5.30; Sun 2–5 (6, Jun to Aug). 15p (ch 18 and pen 10p). Party ch 5p. Admission prices under revision for 1980. ⚠ *(Tel 28448)*

Museum of the 10th Foot Royal Lincolnshire Regiment Sobraon Barracks, Burton Road. Regimental collection of military items including weapons, uniforms and medals. Exhibits dating from late 18th C. Open all year (ex BH) Mon to Fri 9–4.30. Free. P. *(Tel 25444)* ⎣

Usher Gallery Lindum Road. Collection of water-colours by Peter de Wint, miniatures, glass, ceramics and watches. Open all year (ex 4 Apr, 25, 26 Dec), weekdays 10–5.30, Sun 2.30–5. Free. ⚠ *(Tel 27980)*

LINDISFARNE (Holy Island) *Northumberland* Map 12 NU14
Lindisfarne Castle 16th-C castle, restored in 1900 by Sir Edwin Lutyens, with gardens designed originally by Gertrude Jekyll. Open only when tidal conditions permit, Apr to end Sep, daily (ex Fri) 11–1 (last admission 12.30) and 2–5; Oct Sat/Sun 2–5 (not accessible two hours before and four hours after high tide); other times by previous arrangement with Caretaker. £1 (ch 50p). *(NT)*

Lindisfarne Priory The cradle of English Christianity in the north, situated on Holy Island which is accessible at low tide across a causeway. Tide tables are posted at ends of causeway or telephone *Custodian (Holy*

sland 200). Open*, see inside front cover.
?0p (ch 16 and pen 5p). ⚠ *(AM)*

LINDSEY *Suffolk* Map 5 TL94
St James's Chapel Rose Green. Small,
hatched flint and stone chapel, built in the
13th C. Open, see inside front cover. Free. *(AM)*

LINGFIELD *Surrey* Map 5 TQ34
Greathed Manor 1m SE off B2028. Spacious
Victorian house, with pool in grounds. Open 1
May to 30 Sep, Wed and Thu 2 – 5. 40p (ch
25p). ⚠ No dogs. *(Tel 832577)* ൭ B (Gardens)

LINTON *Cambridgeshire* Map 5 TL54
Linton Zoological Gardens Mortimer
House, Hadstock Road. Established in 1972,
his zoo has concentrated on breeding
animals to increase the already large
collection which includes big cats, bears,
wolves, llamas, parrots, macaws, birds of
prey, emu, snakes, spiders and insects etc.
Baby animals can usually be seen. Animals
and birds are housed in landscaped
enclosures, covering 10 acres, as similar as
possible to their natural habitats. Flower
beds, shrubberies and exotic trees provide
botanical interest. Children's play area. Gift or
Souvenir Shop. ⚼ 1 Mar to 31 Oct. Picnic
area. Open all year (ex 25 Dec) 10 – 7 or dusk.
70p (ch 14 35, pen 45p), subject to alteration.
Party. ⚠ *(Tel Cambridge 891308)* ൭

LIPHOOK *Hampshire* Map 4 SU83
Bohunt Manor Medium-sized woodland
gardens, with lakeside walk, water garden,
roses, herbaceous borders, and collection of
over 100 ornamental ducks, geese and
cranes. Property has been given to World
Wildlife Fund. Open Apr to Sep, Mon to Sat
12 – 5. 25p (ch 5p). Open at weekend on
application. No dogs. ⚠ *(Tel 722208). (Lady
Holman)* ൭

*Hollycombe House Steam Collection
Railways and Woodland Gardens* In West
Sussex about 1½m SE on Midhurst Road
(unclass) off A3. Collection of steam-driven
equipment, including 2ft-gauge railway, in
woodland setting of azaleas, rhododendrons,
trees planted at turn of century, and downland
views. Roundabout with own steam organ,
steam swing yacht 'Neptune', road loco
'Princess Mary', Cake-walk and only Razzle
Dazzle and Steam Swings still in existence.
Demonstrations of ploughing, threshing and
steam rolling, traction engine rides, and other
items. ⚼ Open Easter to early Oct, BH and
Sun, garden and picnic areas 12 – 6 rides
2 – 6. 75p (ch and pen 40p) subject to
alteration. Dogs in car park only. ⚠ *(Tel
723233)* ൭

LITTLE BILLING *Northamptonshire*
Map 4 SP86
Billing Aquadrome 19th-C water mill
converted into a Mill Museum with a
photographic gallery of all the well-known
Mills of the Nene Valley in 300 acres of
parklands, lawns and lakes providing facilities
for camping, fishing, boating and swimming.
Children's playground. ⚼ (licensed). Shop.
Open 16 Mar to 7 Oct, 24hrs per day. £1 per
car (including occupants). ⚠ *(Tel
Northampton 890849)* ൭ **(79)**

LITTLE GADDESDEN *Hertfordshire*
Map 4 SP91
Ashridge Management College Large
Gothic Revival mansion (1808 – 14) by James
Wyatt, with porch by Wyatville and 13th-C
crypt. Main hall has hammer-beam roof and
there is fan-vaulting in main tower and chapel.
House became residential college in 1929
and was emergency hospital during 1939 – 45
War. Since 1959 it has been college for
management education. Park *(NT)*
landscaped by 'Capability' Brown, and
gardens by Humphrey Repton. Open,
gardens only Apr to Oct, Sat, Sun 2 – 6; house
and gardens 5 to 8 Apr, 2 – 4; 24 and 27 May
2 – 4, 25 and 26 May 2 – 6; 26 to 30 Jul 2 – 4.
30p (ch 7 15p); gardens only 20p (ch 10p). ⚠
(Tel 3491) ൭ B

LITTLEHAMPTON *West Sussex*
Map 4 TQ00
Littlehampton Museum 12A River Road.
Devoted mainly to exhibitions of old marine
and sailing items together with a number of
paintings of local interest. Open 1 Jan to 9 Apr
and 25 Oct to 31 Dec Wed only; 10 Apr to 30
Jun and 21 Sep to 24 Oct Mon, Wed and Fri; 1
Jul to 20 Sep Mon, Wed, Fri and Sat, 10.30 – 1
and 2.15 – 4.30. Opening times are under
review for 1980. Free. ⚠ *(Tel 5149)*
LITTLE MORETON HALL *Cheshire*
Map 7 SJ85
1m N of Kent Green. Splendid example of
16th-C half-timbering, with moat and
gatehouse, chapel, great hall, long gallery,
collection of oak furniture. Open Mar to 31
Oct, Mar, Sat, Sun 2 – 6 (or sunset); Apr to 31
Oct daily (ex Tue) 2 – 6 (or sunset) 80p (ch
35p) *(NT)*
LITTLE SODBURY *Avon* Map 3 ST78
Little Sodbury Manor 15th-C house with fine
Great Hall and Queen Anne wing, associated
with William Tyndale, translator of the New
Testament. Open 1 Apr to 30 Sep, by
appointment only. 80p. Under revision for
1980. ⚠ *(Tel Chipping Sodbury 312232)*
LIVERPOOL *Merseyside* Map 7 SJ39
Croxteth Country Park Formerly the family
seat of the Earls of Sefton, Croxteth Hall and
Park are now being developed for public use.
A modern Visitor Centre with large exhibition;
walled garden; woodland nature trail; picnic
areas. Park open all year daily 9 – dusk. Free.
Visitor Centre 10 – 5 Mon to Sat, 12 – 5 Sun; 1
Oct to 31 Mar 10 – 5 Mon to Sat; 12 – 5 Sun;
Walled garden, guided tours weekends only

1–5. Tours at other times on request, small charge for facilities. ⚠ *(Tel 051-228 5311)* ⅃ B

Liverpool City Libraries William Brown Street. One of the oldest and largest public libraries in the country, with a bookstock of over two million, Commercial, Technical, Arts and Recreations, Philosophy and Religion Departments; the International Library; the Local History Library, Music Library; and the Hornby Library containing 8,000 fine and rare books, fine bindings, 8,000 prints, and more than 4,000 autograph letters, as well as a permanent exhibition on 'The Art of the Book, manuscript and print'. Guided tours by prior arrangement. ⚐ Mon to Fri 10.30–11.30, 4–5.30. Open all year daily (ex Sun and BH) Mon to Fri 9–9 Sat, 9–5. Free. P. (meter) *(Tel 051-207 2147)* ⅃ **(79)**

Merseyside County Museums William Brown Street. Displays include, gallery of world natural history, an aquarium and vivarium, humanities gallery devoted to antiquities (Egypt, Near East, Cyprus, Greece, Celtic, Anglo-Saxon and Viking) and ethnology (Africa, Oceania, and the New World) including section on primitive art; basement gallery devoted to land transport (trains, coaches, cycles and cars) of the Merseyside area; gallery showing the development of Liverpool, particularly as a port. Displays illustrating history of time-keeping and space exploration are associated with the Planetarium (programmes twice daily, ex Mon). ⚐ Mon to Fri 10–2, 3–4.15. Open all year daily (ex 1 Jan, 4 Apr, 24–26 Dec) Mon to Sat 10–5, Sun 2–5. Free; planetarium 30p (ch and pen 15p). P. *(Tel 051-207 0001)* ⅃

Sudley Art Gallery Mossley Hill Road. Contains the Emma Holt Bequest of 18th- and 19thC British paintings including works by Reynolds, Gainsborough, Wilkie, Mulready, Holman Hunt and Turner, as well as a few French 19th-C paintings. Also displayed is some 19th-C British sculpture. Special exhibitions. Open all year daily (ex 4 Apr 24–26 Dec, 1 Jan) 10–5 (Sun 2–5). Free. ⚠ *(Tel 051-227 5324)*

Walker Art Gallery William Brown Street. Permanent collection of European paintings, sculpture and drawings dating from 1300 to the present day, including early Italian and Netherlandish paintings and 18th- and 19th-C British paintings. Loan exhibitions include John Moores' Liverpool Exhibitions and Peter Moores' Liverpool Projects. Open all year daily (ex 4 Apr, 24–26 Dec, 1 Jan) 10–5 (Sun 2–5). Free. P. *(Tel 051-227 5234 ext 2064)* ⅃

LIVERPOOL UNIVERSITY BOTANIC GARDENS *Cheshire* Map 7 SJ37 Off A540, near Ness-on-Wirral. Included in these gardens are rock gardens noted for very large collection of alpines, and the best known heather garden in country. Also herbaceous borders, roses, and rhododendrons. There is a fine herb garden, and scented plant garden for the blind. Open all year (ex 25 Dec) daily 9–sunset. Free. ⚠ 20p, coaches £1. *(Tel 01-336 2135)* ⅃

LODE *Cambridgeshire* Map 5 TL56 **Anglesey Abbey** 5m NW of Cambridge on B1102. Remodelled c1600, house incorporates 13th-C monastic undercroft. 100 acres of gardens, laid out this century, include long avenues of trees, flower beds and sculptures. Abbey and gardens open Apr to 12 Oct, Tue, Wed, Thu, Sat, Sun, and BH Mon 2–6; garden only open Mon and Fri 2–6 (last admission 5.30). £1, garden only 60p. Party 15+. No dogs. *(NT)*

LONDON–INNER Map I–V precede main atlas

AGNEW'S GALLERIES Map 11 2980 43 Old Bond Street, W1. Opened in 1876 as part of the Vittori Zanetti art business which originated in Manchester. Thomas Agnew, who entered the business in 1810, later became a partner. In 1932 a limited company Thomas Agnew and Sons was formed. Annual exhibitions include a water-colour exhibition devoted to English water-colours and drawings of the 18th and 19th Cs in Jan, Feb and a selling exhibition of Old Master paintings from the 14th–19th Cs. There are also exhibitions of French and English drawings from c1800 to the present day, work by English painters of this century, and loan exhibitions in aid of charity. Many oil paintings, drawings, water-colours and engravings pass through their hands, many on their way to famous art galleries and museums. Open all year Mon to Fri 9.30–5.30 (7, Thu, Oct to Jul) closed BH. Free, ex for some loan exhibitions. *(Tel 01-6296176)*

BANQUETING HOUSE Map 11 3080 Palace of Whitehall, SW1. Built in 1619, to a design by Inigo Jones, to replace the former home of Cardinal Wolsey, which had been destroyed by fire. It is in severe classical style, with a flat roof surrounded by a balustrade and the interior is enriched by Rubens' paintings. During the 17th-C London court life was centred here and many historic events took place here, including the execution of Charles 1 in 1649, restoration of Charles II, and the offer of the throne to Prince William of Orange and Princess Mary. It was converted into a royal chapel by Sir Christopher Wren for George I, and enlarged a century later by James Wyatt. In 1894 it was granted to the Royal United Service Institution as a museum but in 1964 it was restored to its original function. Open all year, daily (ex Mon, Oct to Mar and 13 Apr; open 16 Apr) Mon to Sat 10–5, Sun 2–5 (may be closed at short notice for government functions). 15p (ch 16 and pen 5p). ⚠ *(Tel 01-2124785)*. *(AM)*

BEAR GARDENS MUSEUM AND ARTS CENTRE Map 111 3280 It has recently been enlarged and is devoted to the influence and development of the Elizabethan and Jacobean theatre, and of course, Shakespeare. The Museum stands on the site of the last bear-baiting ring on Bankside, close to the site of the Hope Theatre and 100 yds from Shakespeare's Globe. The permanent exhibition takes the form of models of the Bankside theatres, together with information on the plays, players and history of each, which creates an awareness of the ambience and atmosphere of 16th C Southwark both as it reflects local and national history. Open all year, daily Mon to Fri 10.30–5.30, Sat and Sun 11–5. 50p (ch, students and pen 20p). Party. Under revision for 1980. P. *(Tel 01-928 6342)* ⅃ B

HMS BELFAST Map III 3380 Symons Wharf, Vine Lane, SE1. This 11,000-ton cruiser, which is now part of the Imperial War Museum, is permanently moored in the Pool of London as a floating naval museum. ⚐ (summer only). Open all year, daily (ex 1 Jan, 4 Apr, 5 May, 24–26 Dec) from 11 am. £1.40 (ch 16 and pen 70p). P in Potter's Fields, 100yds. *(Tel 01-407 6434)*

BRITISH CRAFTS CENTRE Map II 3081
43 Earlham Street, WC2. The British Crafts
Centre's object is to promote and sell work by
British craftsmen. Exhibits change rapidly and
cover a wide variety of crafts, including fine
examples of silver and jewellery, metalwork,
glass, ceramics, furniture and woodwork,
textiles, bookbinding, embroidery and
calligraphy. Open all year, (ex Sun) 10 – 5.30
Mon to Fri; 10 – 4 Sat. Free. &. *(Tel 01-
836 6993)* &. B

BRITISH MUSEUM Map II 3081
Great Russell Street, WC1. Founded 1753,
based on the collection of Sir Robert Cotton,
antiquary and book collector, who died in
1631, and on the collection of scientific books
and manuscripts bequeathed to the nation by
Sir Hans Sloane, 18th-C physician. Today it
contains vast archaeological collections,
many thousands of prints and drawings
illustrating the history of graphic art from the
15th C onwards, as well as many other
exhibits. Not all the collections are exhibited
at once. Each year, special exhibitions focus
more detailed attention on certain aspects of
the collections. Programmes on request.
Reserve collections are available for study by
scholars. ⚏ Open all year, daily (ex 1 Jan, 4
Apr, 5 May, 24 – 26 Dec) 10 – 5, Sun 2.30 – 6.
Free. &. *(Tel 01-636 1555 ext 525)* &.

COURTAULD INSTITUTE GALLERIES
Map II 2982
Woburn Square, WC1. The galleries of
London University contain the most important
collection of Impressionist paintings in Britain,
including work by Manet, Renoir, Degas,
Cezanne, Van Gogh, Gaugin and Toulouse-
Lautrec. Also Old Master paintings, especially
Italian primitives. Exhibitions of British
landscape water-colours in Spring, and in the
summer an exhibition of Impressionist
drawings and water-colours. Open all year
(ex Christmas and most BH) Mon to Sat
10 – 5, Sun 2 – 5. Free. Meter P. *(Tel 01-
580 1015)* &.

CRICKET MEMORIAL GALLERY
Map I 2682
Lord's Ground, NW8. Founded about 1865,
with collections of cricket bygones and 18th-C
paintings of cricket. Collection of pictures and
other exhibits and a library of cricket literature,
enriched by the notable book collections of A
L Ford and Sir Julien Cahn. In 1953, the
present gallery and museum was opened as a
memorial to cricketers of all nations, who
gave their lives in the two World Wars. Open
on match days Mon to Sat 10.30 – 5, other
times by appointment. 30p (ch and pen 15p).
Library open free of charge to students by
appointment with the Curator. &. (limited).
(Tel 01-289 1611) &. B

CUMING MUSEUM Map III 3278
155/157 Walworth Road, SE17. Contains
Roman and medieval finds from the nearly
2,000-year-old suburb of Southwark, south of
London Bridge. Examples from the local
'Delft' pottery industry, items associated with
Dickens, personal relics of Michael Faraday
(born locally in 1791), the equipment of a
family dairy firm which served the
neighbourhood for over 150 years, and a
collection of London superstitions. Open all
year Mon to Fri 10 – 5.30 (7, Thu), Sat 10 – 5.
Free. Limited street P. *(Tel 01-703 6514).*
(London Borough of Southwark)

DICKENS' HOUSE Map II 3082
48 Doughty Street, WC1. Dickens lived here
during his twenties and here completed
Pickwick Papers and wrote *Oliver Twist* and
Nicholas Nickleby. Pages of the original
manuscripts of his early books and others are
on view, together with valuable first editions in
the original paper pages of his works, his
special marriage licence; his family Bible
which contains a personal record of his sons
and daughters, and many other personal
relics. Entrance includes the Suzannet
Rooms. Open all year, daily (ex Sun, BH,
Christmas week and 13 Apr) 10 – 5. 60p (ch
15 25p, students 50p). Party. Under revision
for 1980. *(Tel 01-405 2127)*

*EMBANKMENT GALLERY, PADDLE
STEAMER TATTERSHALL CASTLE*
Map II 3080
Victoria Embankment, SW1. Gallery and arts
centre contained within a restored paddle
steamer, first commissioned in 1934.
Changing exhibitions are shown including:
established artists, public interest topics, and
facilities for aspiring and unknown artists.
Bookshop and functions facilities. Open all
year, Tue to Sun 10 – 6. 20p (ch 14 and pen
10p). P (charge) also across the river. *(Tel
01-839 6548/9)*

GEOLOGICAL MUSEUM Map I 2679
Exhibition Road, South Kensington.
Established 1935, its exhibitions include a
piece of the Moon and the largest exhibition
on basic earth science in the world – The
Story of the Earth. This is split into four main
sections: The Earth in Space which includes
an exhibit showing that an observer 150
million light years away, looking through an
immensely powerful telescope, would see
dinosaurs roaming around in a Jurassic
landscape; The Earth's Interior and Crust;
Geological Processes; and Geological Time.
There is also a famous collection of fine gem
stones, showing them in their parent rock, in

natural crystal form and in their final cut state. The regional geology of Great Britain and the ore deposits of the world are also displayed. A new permanent exhibition 'Britain Before Man' provides much fascinating information about 3,000 million years of pre-history. Open all year (ex 4 Apr, 5 May, 24–26 Dec and 1 Jan) Mon to Sat 10–6, Sun 2.30–6. Free. *(Tel 01-589 3444)* &

GUILDHALL Map III 3281
EC2. Rebuilt in 1411 but only the walls of the great hall porch and crypt survive from the medieval building. It was severely damaged in the Great Fire and the Blitz. Restoration work, completed in 1954 was carried out to designs by Sir Giles Scott. Here the Court of Common Council, which administers the city, meets and entertains. Open all year Mon to Sat 10–5 (Sun, May to Sep and Bh 2–5). The **Guildhall Library** contains an unrivalled collection of books, manuscripts, and illustrations on all aspects of London. Open all year, daily (ex Sun, BH) 9.30–5. The **Guildhall Clock Museum** with 700 exhibits illustrating 500 years of time keeping. Open Mon to Fri 9.30–5 (ex BH). Free. ⚠ *(Tel 01-606 3030)* &

HOUSES OF PARLIAMENT Map II 3079
SW1. A mid 19th-C building in Gothic style, based on a design by Sir Charles Barry, with additional detail by Augusta Pugin. It replaced the previously mainly medieval structure, destroyed by fire in 1834. The two chambers are set either side of a central hall and corridor, the House of Lords to the south and the House of Commons to the north, with identical projecting pavilions at either end of the river façade. The clock tower, 320ft high, contains Big Ben, the hour bell weighing 13½ tons, and the Victoria tower stands 340ft high. The House of Commons Chamber was burnt out in 1941 by incendiary bombs, and a new chamber was constructed to the design of Sir Giles Gilbert Scott and opened in 1950. During sessions, admission to the Stranger's Gallery, House of Commons Mon to Thu from 4.15 pm, Fri from 11.30 am by joining queue at St Stephen's Hall entrance; alternatively on application in advance to an MP Mon to Thu from 2.30, Fri from 11 am. Admission to Stranger's Gallery, House of Lords Mon to Wed from 2.30 pm, Thu from 3 pm, Fri from 11 am by joining queue at St Stephen's entrance (Old Palace yard side) or alternatively applying in advance to a Peer. Palace of Westminster open to a limited number of the public every Sat (ex one immediately preceding State opening) and 7 & 8 Apr, 5 & 26/27 May, 25/26 Aug; Mon, Tue and Thu in Aug; Thu in Sep providing neither house is sitting. 10–4.30. Free, although Guides require payment if employed. ⚠ *(Tel 01-219 3000)* & also
Westminster Hall Built 1097–99 by William Rufus, it is the oldest remaining part of Westminster. The glory of the hall is the cantilever or hammerbeam roof, the earliest and largest roof of its kind in existence, built between 1394 and 1401. Open during Session: Mon to Thu 10–1.30, providing neither House is sitting at the time. Sat 10–5. During Recess: Mon to Fri 10–4, Sat 10–5. Free. ⚠ & (by arrangement)

IMPERIAL WAR MUSEUM Map III 3179
Lambeth Road, SE1. Founded 1917 and established 1920 by Act of Parliament, this museum illustrates and records all aspects of the two World Wars and other military operations involving Britain and the Commonwealth since 1914. A wide range of weapons and equipment is on display, including aircraft, armoured vehicles, field guns and small arms, together with models, decorations, uniforms, posters, photographs and paintings. Also various reference departments, open by appointment only. ⚐ Open all year, daily (ex 1 Jan, 4 Apr, 5 May, 24 to 26 Dec) Mon to Sat 10–5.50, Sun 2–5.50. Free (except special exhibitions which have a small entrance fee). P meters only. *(Tel 01-735 8922)* & *(by appointment)* **(79)**

DR JOHNSON'S HOUSE Map III 3181
17 Gough Square, EC4. Gough Square was built c1700 and the timber used in the construction of the building is American white and yellow pine. Dr Johnson lived here 1749–1759 and here he compiled his famous English dictionary (a first edition is on display and wrote *The Rambler* and *The Idler*. The house was opened as a museum in 1914 and contains a fine collection of prints as well as letters and other relics. Open all year, daily (ex Sun, BH) May to Sep 11–5.30; Oct to Apr 11–5. 40p (ch, students and pen 20p). ⚠ *(Tel 01-353 3745)*

KENSINGTON PALACE, STATE APARTMENTS Map I 2579
W8. Kensington Palace was acquired by King William III in 1689 and remodelled and enlarged by Sir Christopher Wren, and is today still a Royal residence. Queen Victoria was born here, and a suite of rooms is devoted to her memory. Contained within the state apartments are picture and furniture from the royal collection. The redecorated Victorian rooms and the room devoted to the Great Exhibition are now open. Open all year (ex 1 Jan, 3 & 4 Apr, 24/25 & 26 Dec). Mar to Sep, Mon to Sat 10–6, Sun 2–5; Oct and Feb, Mon to Sat 10–5, Sun 2–5; Nov to Jan, Mon to Sat 10–4, Sun 2–4. 30p (ch 16 and pen 15p). Party 11+ 10% discount on arrival. *(Tel 01-937 9561 ext 2)*. Nearest car park in Bayswater Road. *(AM)*

LANCASTER HOUSE Map II 2979
Stable Yard, SW1. Built in the 19th C by the 'Grand Old Duke of York' and originally called 'York House'. It is now used as a centre for government hospitality. Open Easter Eve to mid Dec (ex during government functions) Sat, Sun and BH 2–6. 25p (ch 16 and pen 10p). ⚠ *(AM)*

THE LONDON DUNGEON Map III 3280
28/34 Tooley Street, SE1. A fantasy Medieval History exhibition/experience. Vast dark vaults house strange and horrifying scenes of Man's Inhumanity to Man in Britain's dark past. Awarded the British Tourist Authority award for Outstanding Tourist Enterprise. Open all year Apr to Sep 10–6, Oct to Mar 10–4.30. £1.25 (ch and pen 75p). Under revision for 1980. ⚠ *(Tel 01-403 0606)*

LONDON TRANSPORT MUSEUM Map II 3080
Housed in the former Flower Market in Covent Garden. Due to open Spring 1980. The museum aims to tell the story of the development of London's transport from its earliest beginnings right up to the present day. Vehicles include steam locomotives, trams, trolleybuses, railway coaches and horse buses, there are also extensive displays using working and static models, posters, and audio-visual material. A reference library is also available by appointment. Souvenir shop. ⚐ Open daily (ex 25/26 Dec) 10–6.

Entrance off the Piazza, clearly signposted. For further information contact the Head of Administration. Admission prices not available. *(Tel 01-935 6688 ext 48)* ⅃ B

MADAME TUSSAUD'S Map I 2882
Marylebone Road, NW1. Founded in Paris in 1770, Madame Tussaud's Wax Exhibition came to England in 1802, and settled in London in 1835. Exhibits include the Chamber of Horrors; historical figures, including kings and queens of the French and English royal families; 'Heroes'; The Battle of Trafalgar; and the Conservatory. ⚏ Open all year daily (ex 25 Dec) Oct to Mar 10–5.30; Apr to Sep 10–6. Please telephone for admission prices. P. *(Tel 01-935 6861)* ⅃ (Oct to Mar preferred)

MALL GALLERIES Map II 2980
The Mall, SW1. The exhibition galleries of the Federation of British Artists, where most of the Art Societies administered by this organisation hold their annual exhibitions. Open all year, daily (ex Sun, BH) 10–5 (1pm, Sat). 20p (ch and pen 10p). P. *(Tel 01-930 6844)*

MARLBOROUGH HOUSE Map II 2980
Pall Mall, SW1. Built 1709–11 by Wren for Sarah, Duchess of Marlborough, and renowned for the series of murals by Laguerre depicting Marlborough's battles. In 1817 it became a royal palace, of which the last occupant was Queen Mary. It is now used as a Commonwealth conference centre. Open by appointment only. 5p ⚠ *(Tel 01-930 9249)*. The **Queen's Chapel** designed by Inigo Jones for Charles I, stands in the grounds. Open Mon, Wed and Thu by prior arrangement only. **(79)**

MIDDLE TEMPLE HALL Map II 3180
The Temple, EC4. A fine example of Tudor architecture built during the reign of Queen Elizabeth I and completed about 1570. Hall features fine double hammer beam roof (only 2 or 3 other examples believed to exist in England). Also stained glass showing shields of past treasurers. The most treasured possession is the 29ft-long high table, made from a single oak tree of Windsor Forest. Another table was made from timbers of the Golden Hind, in which Sir Francis Drake, a member of the Middle Temple, sailed around the world. Portraits of George I, Elizabeth I, Anne, Charles I, Charles II, James, Duke of York and William III line the walls behind the high table. Open all year (ex Sun, BH) 10–12, 3–4.30. Free. ⚠ *(Tel 01-353 4355)*

THE MONUMENT Map III 3280
Monument Street, EC4. Erected by Wren and Hooke 1671–77 to commemorate the Great Fire of 1666, which is reputed to have started in nearby Pudding Lane. It stands 202ft-high and from the railed-in summit, a climb of 311 steps, there is an extensive view over London. Open all year, daily (ex Sun 1 Oct to 30 Mar, 13 Apr, 25, 26 Dec) Mon to Sat 9–4 (5.40, 1 Apr to 30 Sep) Sun 1 Apr to 30 Sep 2–5.40. 30p (ch 15p). *(Tel 01-626 2717)*. These times and prices are provisional for 1979. **(79)**

MUSEUM OF LONDON Map III 3281
London Wall. The museum was formed by amalgamating the former London Museum and the Guildhall Museum. The present purpose-built building was opened in 1976 and the museum is devoted entirely to London and its people. Everything on show contributes to the story of London during the past 2,000 years. Included are Royal relics and treasures from the City, a barber's shop from Islington, sculptures from the Temple of Mithras, a 1930 Ford, Selfridge's lift, medieval hen's egg together with a Roman Bikini and the experience of the Great Fire. Awarded the title 'Museum of the Year 1978'. ⚏ Open all year Tue to Sat 10–6, Sun 2–6. (Closed Mon incl BH Mon also 25/26 Dec). Parties by arrangement. Free. P. (NCP opposite in Aldersgate Street). *(Tel 01-600 3699)* ⅃ Please telephone ext 265 for information. **(79)**

MUSEUM OF MANKIND Map II 2980
6, Burlington Gardens, W1. Houses the exhibitions, library and offices of the ethnography department of the British Museum. Its collections embrace the art and material culture of tribal, village and other pre-industrial societies, from most areas of the world excluding Western Europe. Also archaeological collections from the Americas and Africa. A few important pieces are on permanent exhibition, but the museum's policy is to mount a number of temporary exhibitions lasting for at least a year. A separate store in Shoreditch contains the reserve collection which can be made available for serious study by arrangement. Open all year (ex 4 Apr, 24, 25 and 26 Dec and 1 Jan) Mon to Sat 10–5, Sun 2.30–6. Free. *(Tel 01-437 2224)*

NATIONAL ARMY MUSEUM Map I 2777
Royal Hospital Road, SW3. Contains a permanent chronological display of the history of the British, Indian and Colonial forces from 1485. Among the exhibits are uniforms, weapons, prints and photographs,

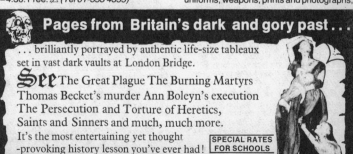

silver, glass and china, manuscripts and letters, relics of British commanders and mementos of Britain's soldiers. There is a special display of the orders and decorations of the Duke of Windsor and also those of five great field marshals – Lords Roberts, Gough, Kitchener and Wolseley and Sir George White VC. The picture gallery includes portraits by Reynolds, Gainsborough, Romney and Lawrence, battle scenes and pictures of Indian regiments. The reading room is open to holders of readers' tickets, obtainable by written application to the Director. Open all year, daily (ex 1 Jan, 4 Apr, 5 May, 24 to 26 Dec) 10 – 5.30, Sun 2 – 5.30. Free. ♿ *(Tel 01-730 0717)* ♿ (prior arrangement)

NATIONAL GALLERY Map II 2980
Trafalgar Square, WC2. Founded by vote of Parliament in 1824, but was first opened in the present building in 1838. Collection includes van Eyck's *Arnolfini Marriage*, Velazquez's *The Toilet of Venus*, Leonardo da Vinci's *Cartoon: The Virgin and the Child with SS Anne and John the Baptist*, Rembrandt's *Belshazzar's Feast*, Titian's *Bacchus and Ariadne*, and many more. ☕ Open daily (ex 1 Jan, 13 Apr, 7 May, 24 – 26 Dec) Mon to Sat 10 – 6, Sun 2 – 6. Free. Accessible to wheelchairs by Orange Street entrance. For information about exhibitions during 1980 contact the Press Office *ex 252. (Tel 01-839 3321)* ♿ (Orange Street entrance).

NATIONAL PORTRAIT GALLERY
Map II 3080
2 St Martin's Place, WC2. Contains national collection of portraits of the famous and infamous in British history, including paintings, sculpture, miniatures, engravings, photographs, and cartoons. Special exhibitions several times a year. Gallery shop. Exhibitions are also held at the new exhibition rooms at 15 Carlton House Terrace, London SW1. Open all year, daily (ex 1 Jan, 4 Apr, 5 May, 24 – 26 Dec) 10 – 5, Sat 10 – 6, Sun 2 – 6. Free (ex special exhibitions). ♿ *(Tel 01-930 1552)* ♿

NATIONAL POSTAL MUSEUM Map III 3181
King Edward Street, EC1. Contains probably the finest and most comprehensive collection of postage stamps in the world. Included are: the R M Philips collection of 19th-C Great Britain (with special emphasis on the One Penny Black and its creation); the Post Office Collection; a world-wide collection including practically every stamp issued since 1878; and the philatelic correspondence archives of Thomas de la Rue and Co who furnished stamps to over 150 countries between 1855 and 1965. Within these collections are thousands of original drawings and unique proof sheets of every British stamp since 1840. Special exhibitions. Visits for parties up to 40 may be arranged with a guide and film show. Open all year, daily (ex Sat, Sun, BH) Mon to Fri (10 – 4.30. Free. Meter parking in adjacent streets. *(Tel 01-432 3851)*

NATURAL HISTORY MUSEUM Map I 2679
Cromwell Road, South Kensington SW7. Three new exhibitions are now open: *Dinosaurs and their living relatives* features a spectacular display of fossil skeletons and a series of special exhibits producing a new way of looking at dinosaurs. In the *Hall of Human Biology* visitors can learn more about the way their bodies work, while *Introducing Ecology* uses an oak woodland and a rocky seashore to introduce a new way of looking at our natural surroundings. A new exhibition,

opening in the summer of 1980, takes a fresh look at man's place in evolution. In other parts of the Museum there are many traditional displays of living and fossil plants and animals, minerals, rocks and meteorites from the national collections. Exhibits of special interest include a lifesize model of a blue whale, the Cranbourne meteorite, a specimen of a coelacanth (a fish known as a living fossil) and the British bird pavillion where visitors can hear recordings of many different bird songs. As the museum is currently reorganising its public displays, some of the galleries may be temporarily closed. The museum's educational services provide some public lectures. Childrens centre open Sat afternoons and Tue to Sat during school hols. ☕ (open 10 – 5.30). Open everyday (ex 4 Apr, 5 May, 24 – 26 Dec and 1 Jan) Mon to Sat 10 – 6, Sun 2.30 – 6. Free. Meter P. Access for wheelchair-bound visitors by rear entrance. *(Tel 01-589 6323)* ♿

PERCIVAL DAVID FOUNDATION OF CHINESE ART Map II 2982
53 Gordon Square, WC1. Houses collection of Chinese ceramics from Sung Dynasty (960 – 1279) to 18th C including many inscribed and documented pieces important to the study of Chinese art history. The collection is famous for a pair of blue and white temple vases known as 'David vases', dated 1351, which are the earliest dated pieces of this ware in existence. Open all year (ex Sun, BH, including 1pm 3 Apr until Tue following) Mon 2 – 5, Tue to Fri 10.30 – 5, Sat 10.30 – 1. Free. P. (meters). *(Tel 01-387 3909)*

PLANETARIUM Map I 2882
Marylebone Road, NW1. Here the night skies are projected in all their beauty onto the inside of the dome from the two-ton Zeiss instrument, to an accompanying commentary. The skies are seen not only from Britain, but from Africa and Australia and even from outer space or the future. ☕ Open all year, daily (ex 25 Dec), presentations Apr to Sep 11 – 6; Oct to Mar 11 – 4.30. Please telephone for admission prices. P. *(Tel 01-486 1121)*

PUBLIC RECORD OFFICE MUSEUM
Map II 3181
Chancery Lane, WC2. The Public Record Office contains records of central government dating from the Norman conquest to the present day. The museum contains a small selection of the several million separate documents kept in the Office including the Domesday Book, Shakespeare's will, various royal letters and other documents of wide historical interest. Open Mon to Fri 1 – 4 (ex official holidays, first two weeks Oct). Parties at other times by arrangement. Free. ♿ *(Tel 01-405 0741)* ♿ (prior arrangement only)

QUEEN'S GALLERY Map II 2979
Buckingham Palace, SW1. Items from the Royal collection are housed in a building of 1831, originally designed as a conservatory by John Nash and later converted by Blore into a chapel in 1843. After suffering severe bomb damage in 1940, the building was eventually reconstructed in 1962, partly as the Private Chapel of Buckingham Palace and partly as an art gallery. Exhibits display various aspects of the Royal Collection. Open all year, daily (ex Mon, and for short periods between exhibitions) Tue to Sat, BH 11 – 5, Sun 2 – 5. 40p (ch 16 and pen 20p, also students on production of valid student card). ♿ *(Tel 01-930 3007)*

ROYAL ACADEMY OF ARTS Map II 2980
Piccadilly, W1. Founded in 1768 by George
III. The summer exhibition, from May to Aug,
shows works by living artists, and loan
exhibitions are held throughout the rest of the
year. Treasures of the academy include the
Michelangelo *Tondo*. ℱ Licensed (10.30 – 5
Mon to Sat, 12.30 – 5 Sun). Open daily 10 – 6
(incl Sun). Admission prices vary but
generally are 60p – £1 (ch, students, pen and
group visitors half price). ⚐ *(Tel 01-734 9052)*
&

ROYAL MEWS Map II 2879
Buckingham Palace, SW1. Designed by John
Nash and completed in 1825, the Royal Mews
contain the state coaches including the Gold
State Coach made in 1762, with panels
painted by the Florentine artist Cipriani, which
has been used for every coronation since that
of George IV, the Irish State Coach, the
Scottish State Coach, together with private
driving carriages and royal sleighs. In the
stables are kept the Windsor Greys and
Cleveland Bay carriage horses. Open Wed,
Thu 2 – 4 every week (ex certain times) and at
other times when published. 25p (ch and pen
10p). *(Tel 01-930 4832)* &

ST KATHARINE by the TOWER Map III
3380
Maritime Trust's Historic Ship Collection
comprises a number of British sailing and
steam-powered vessels of the 19th and early
20th C. Individual display in each ship. Open
all year Spring and Autumn 10.30 – 6; summer
10 – 7; winter 11 – 4.30. £1 (ch and pen 50p).
⚐

SCIENCE MUSEUM Map I 2679
Exhibition Road, South Kensington, SW7.
Extensive collections, including aero engines;
agriculture, astronomy; atomic and nuclear
physics; rail; road; sea and air transport; civil,
electrical, marine and mechanical
engineering; telecommunications, domestic
appliances, 'Gas Industry' gallery, etc. New
galleries on Printing, Paper making and
Lighting. Also a children's gallery with many
working demonstrations. Exhibition
'Exploration' continued during 1980. ℱ Open
all year, daily (ex 4 Apr, 5 May, 24 – 26 Dec
and 1 Jan) 10 – 6, Sun 2.30 – 6. Meter P. *(Tel
01-589 3456)* &

SIR JOHN SLOANE'S MUSEUM Map II 3081
13 Lincoln's Inn Fields, WC2. The home of Sir
John Sloane (1753 – 1837), the architect, built
in 1812 and containing his collections of
antiquities, sculpture, paintings, drawings
and books. The most famous are the
Sarcophagus of Seti I (1292 BC), *Rake's
Progress* and the *Election* series by William
Hogarth. Open all year (ex BH) Tue to Sat
10 – 5. Free. *(Tel 01-405 2107)*

STOCK EXCHANGE Map III 3281
EC2. The centre of industrial finance, where
stocks and shares in individual companies
are bought and sold. The scene on the trading
floor may be viewed from the gallery and a
guide is present to describe the scene. A
colour film may be seen. Open every working
day (ex 24 Dec) 9.45 – 3.15 (last guided tour
2.30). Party. Free. P. (meters). *(Tel 01-
588 2355)* &

TATE GALLERY Map II 3078
Millbank, SW1. Opened in 1897 the gallery
houses two national art collections of British
works from the 16th C to c1900, and modern
works by British artists born after 1850
together with foreign works from the
Impressionists onwards. Hogarth, Blake,

Turner, Constable and the pre-Raphaelites
are particularly well-represented in the British
Collection and the Modern Collection has
recently been enhanced by Henry Moore's
magnificent gift of 36 of his sculptures, a
selection of which will always be on view. The
development of art is traced from
Impressionism to postwar European and
American art including Abstract
Impressionism and Pop. A major extension
increasing the size of the Tate by 50%,
opened in May 1979. The new galleries are
fully airconditioned. Free lectures are
provided every day and free films and Guided
Tours Mon to Fri. ℱ Licensed. Restaurant
Mon to Sat 12 – 3; Coffee shop Mon to Sat
10.30 – 5.30, Sun 2 – 5.30. Open all year daily
(ex 1 Jan, 4 Apr, 5 May, 24 – 26 Dec) 10 – 6,
Sun 2 – 6. Free, ex for special exhibitions.
Meter P. *(Tel 01-821 1313, 01-821 7182
recorded information)* & *(Atterbury
entrance)*

TOWER OF LONDON Map III 3380
EC3. Begun by William the Conqueror in the
11th C in the south-east angle of the wall of
Roman Londinium. The keep or White Tower,
which was built soon after the conquest, now
contains the **Royal Armouries**. These
consist of the national collection of arms and
armour based on the great arsenal of Henry
VIII. Four of Henry VIII's personal armours
may be seen together with the finest products
of the Greenwich School of Armourers. There
are also displays of tournament and sporting
arms, arms and armour from the Middle Ages
to the 17th C, oriental armour (including an
elephant armour) and cannon. ℱ and picnic
area. Open all year, daily (ex 1 Jan, 4 Apr,
24 – 26 Dec) Mar to Oct 9.30 – 5 Mon – Sat,
Sun 2 – 5, Nov to Feb 9.30 – 4 Mon – Sat
(closed Sun). Admission: Mar to Oct (ex Jul,
Aug) £1 (ch 16 and pen 50p); Nov to Feb 50p
(ch 16 and pen 30p), Jul and Aug £1.50 (ch 16
and pen 50p). Also the **Jewel House** where
the crown jewels are displayed. Open as for
the Tower. Admission: 50p (ch 16 and pen
20p). Also the **Royal Fusiliers Museum**,
containing uniforms, including those worn by
George V as colonel-in-chief, regimental
silver and china, four dioramas of famous
battles and campaign medals, among them
10 Victoria Crosses, including the prototype
approved by Queen Victoria. Opening times
as for Tower. 10p. All admission prices for
1980 are under revision. *(Tel 01-709 0765)* & B

VICTORIA AND ALBERT MUSEUM Map I
2679
Cromwell Road, South Kensington SW7.
Queen Victoria laid the foundation stone for
the present building in 1899 and the building
designed by Sir Aston Webb was opened in
1909 by Edward VII. In it were placed the art
treasures from the South Kensington
Museum, which had been built under the
direction of Prince Albert from money derived
from the Great Exhibition of 1851. It now
contains one of the world's outstanding
collections of fine and applied arts. Special
exhibitions include Constable paintings, the
Raphael Cartoons and the Great Bed of
Ware. Open all year, daily (ex 1 Jan, 4 Apr, 5
May and 24 – 26 Dec and **Fridays**) 10 – 5.50,
Sun 2.30 – 5.50. Free. ℱ licensed weekdays
10.30 – 2.30, 3 – 5.30 Sun 2.30 – 5.30. ⚐ *(Tel
01-589 6371)* & B (Tel in advance)

WALLACE COLLECTION Map I 2881
Hertford House, Manchester Square, W1. An
outstanding collection of works of art
bequeathed to the nation by Lady Wallace in

1897, displayed in the house of its founders. Includes pictures by Titian, Rubens, Gainsborough and Delacroix together with an unrivalled representation of 18th-C French art including paintings, especially by Watteau, Boucher and Fragonard, sculpture, furniture, goldsmiths work and Sèvres porcelain. Also valuable collections of maiolica, European and oriental arms and armour. Open all year (ex 24–26 Dec, 1 Jan, 4 Apr and 5 May) Mon to Sat 10–5, Sun 2–5. Free. P meters. *(Tel 01-935 0687)* ⸜ During 1980 only half no. of rooms on show due to building works.

WELLINGTON MUSEUM Map I 2879 Apsley House, 149 Piccadilly, W1. Apsley House was designed by Robert Adam, built 1771–8 and extended by Benjamin Wyatt in 1828–1830, under the direction of the Duke of Wellington who purchased it in 1817. It was presented to the nation by the 7th Duke of Wellington in 1947, and opened to the public in 1952. Exhibits include famous paintings, silver, porcelain, orders and decorations and personal relics of the first duke (1769–1852); also Canova's great marble figure of Napoleon Bonaparte. An amusing collection of political caricatures on display. Open all year, daily (ex Mon and Fri also 4 Apr, 5 May, 24–26 Dec and 1 Jan) 10–6, Sun 2.30–6. Opening hours under review for 1980. Free. Underground P 400yds in Hyde Park. *(Tel 01-499 5676)*

WESLEY'S HOUSE AND MUSEUM Map III 3282 47 City Road, EC1. The house in which John Wesley lived and died is now a museum, containing a large collection of his personal possessions, etc. Open all year (ex Sun and BH) Mon to Sat 10–1, 2–4 and by arrangement. 20p. *(Tel 01-253 2262)*. Also *Wesley's Chapel* built 1778, completely restored 1978. Open daily. Main service 11am Sun. ⸜ B

LONDON—GREATER Maps I–V precede main atlas.

BECONTREE *Gt London* Map V TQ48 *Valence House Museum* Becontree Avenue. Off A112. Partly moated 16th- to 17th-C house, with Fanshawe portraits and museum of local history. Open all year by appointment only. Free. ⚠ *(01-592 2211)*

BETHNAL GREEN *Gt London* Map V TQ38 *Bethnal Green Museum* Cambridge Heath Road. A branch of the Victoria and Albert Museum. Its chief exhibits are toys, dolls and dolls' houses; model soldiers, Rodin bronzes; 19th-C Continental decorative arts, and costume from the mid 18th C with a special emphasis on the wedding dress, children's costume and Spitalfield Silks. Open all year, daily (ex 24 to 26 Dec, 1 Jan and 4 Apr and Fridays) 10–6, Sun 2.30–6. Free. ⚠ *(Tel 01-980 2415/4315)* ⸜ (Please telephone first) ⸜ (by appointment)

BEXLEY *Gt London* Map V TQ47 *Hall Place* Near junction of A2 and A223. 16th- to 17th-C house with contrasting elevations of chequered flint and brick. Ornamental gardens, with topiary in form of 'Queen's Beasts', roses, rock, water, herb, and peat gardens, and conservatory. House open all year, Mon to Sat 10–5, Sun 2–6; gardens open all year Mon to Fri 7.30–dusk, Sat and Sun 9–dusk. Free. ⚠ *(79)*

BLACKHEATH *Gt London* Map V TQ37 *Rangers House* Chesterfield Walk. Suffolk collection of Jacobean and Stuart portraits

housed in 18th-C villa, former home of Philip Stanhope, 14th Earl of Chesterfield. Collection contains a set of portraits by William Larkin, one of the finest to survive from this period, and a small collection of Old masters including *The Falconer* by Ferdinand Bol, *The Holy Family in the Carpenters Shop* by Carracci, a portrait of The Grand Duchess of Tuscany by Justus Sustermans, and royal portraits from Charles I to William and Mary, including a Van Dyck studio portrait. *The Three Eldest Children of Charles I.* Chamber concerts during 1979. Open all year daily (ex 4 Apr & 25 Dec). 10–5 (4 Nov–Feb). Free. ⚠ *(Tel 01-853 0035)*

BRENTFORD *Gt London* Map IV TQ17 *Kew Bridge Pumping Station* Kew Bridge Road entrance in Green Dragon Lane. London's living steam museum containing four beam engines working in steam plus three others. Model engines and other steam engines all working in steam, plus traction engines and a museum for London's water supply. Step back into the 19th C and see a site which worked from 1820–1945; old workshop, forges etc. ⚓ Souvenirs. Open all year Sat and Sun from 11, last admission 5pm, Fri by arrangement. 60p (ch 16 and pen 30p), family rate *ie* 2 adults and up to 3 children £1.50. Under review for 1980. ⚠ *(Tel 01-568 4757)* ⸜ B

Musical Museum High Street. 7m W of London, off A315. A musical menagerie of pianos, organs, violins, orchestrations, dulcimers, phonographs, musical boxes and the only self-playing Wurlitzer in Europe. Instruments played during tours well over 1 hour during which time silence must be maintained. Open Apr to Oct, Sat and Sun 2–5. 70p (ch 14 50p). Under revision for 1980. Nearest P in North Road, first turning to N on W side of museum. *(Tel 01-560 8108)*

CAMBERWELL *Gt London* Map V TQ37 *South London Art Gallery* Peckham Road. Presents ten exhibitions a year. Exhibits include Victorian paintings and drawings; a small collection of contemporary British Art; 20th-C original prints; and a comprehensive collection of topographical paintings and drawings of local subjects. Open only when exhibitions are in progress, daily 10–6, Sun 3–6. Free. P. *(Tel 01-703 6120)*. *(London Borough of Southwark)*

CHEAM *Gt London* Map IV TQ26 *Whitehall* 1 Malden Road. Built c1500 as a farmhouse. In the 17th-C Cheam school was started here and permanent displays feature the school, the building of timber framed houses, medieval Cheam pottery, and Nonsuch Palace. ⚓ Open all year (ex 24 Dec to 2 Jan), Apr to Sep, Tue to Fri and Sun 2–5.30, Sat 10–5.30; Oct to Mar, Wed, Thu and Sun 2–5.30, Sat 10–5.30; BH as Sat. 25p (ch 10p). P. *(Tel 01-643 1236)*

CHELSEA *Gt London* Map V TQ27 *Carlyle's House* Cheyne Row, SW3. Built in 1708, it is a fine example of an 18th-C town house now owned by the National Trust. Here Thomas Carlyle and his wife Jane lived from 1834 to 1865 and entertained among others Dickens, Thackeray, Browning and Tennyson. Many of Carlyle's letters, personal possessions and furniture are preserved, including an early piano which Chopin played and the desk where Carlyle wrote his books. Open Apr–Oct daily (ex Mon and Tue, open BH). 70p. No parties over 20 persons. Meter P only. *(Tel 01-352 7087)*. *(NT)*

CHINGFORD *Gt London* Map V TQ39
Queen Elizabeth's Hunting Lodge Rangers Road, Epping Forest. Picturesque old-timbered house, dating from c1510 now museum relating the life of animals, birds and plants in Epping Forest, and Man's association with them. Open all year Wed to Sun and BH Mon 2–6 (or dusk). 10p (accompanied ch free). ⚠ *(Tel 01-529 6681)* & B

CHISWICK *Gt London* Map IV TQ27
Chiswick House Domed mansion, considered to be the finest example of Palladian architecture of Great Britain. Built 1725–30 for the 3rd Earl of Burlington, Robert Boyle with interior decoration by William Kent. Well restored by the Department of the Environment. ♨ Open Mar, Apr and Oct 9.30–5.30, May to Sep 9.30–7, Nov to Feb 9.30–4. (Closed Mon and Tue Oct to Mar). Closed 1–2 daily for lunch. 20p (ch and pen 5p). ⚠ *(AM)*
Gunnersby Park Museum Popes Lane. Early 19th-C former Rothschild mansion, in fine park, now museum of local interest, including Rothschild coaches. ♨ summer only. Open all year, daily (ex 4 Apr, 24–26 Dec) Apr to Sep Mon to Fri 2–5, Sat and Sun 2–6; Oct to Mar daily 2–4. Free. ⚠ *(Tel 01-992 1612)* &
Hogarth's House Hogarth Lane, Great West Road. 17th-C house where Hogarth lived for 15 years, with paintings, drawings, and other relics. Open all year (ex 1 Jan, 4 Apr, 25 and 26 Dec) Mon to Sat (ex Tue Oct to Mar) 11–6 (4, Oct to Mar), Sun 2–6 (4, Oct to Mar). 10p (ch 5p). ⚠ *(Tel 01-994 6757)*

CRYSTAL PALACE *Gt London* Map V TQ37
Crystal Palace Zoo Crystal Palace Park. A children's zoo with monkeys, birds (including foreign species), otters, sheep, pygmy goats, penguins, deer and Welsh Mountain and Shetland ponies. Pony rides, pony-trap rides. Open School Easter hol to Sep, weather permitting, Mon to Fri 1–6. Sat, Sun and school hols, BH 11–6. Free. ⚠ *(Tel 01-778 4487)* &

DULWICH *Gt London* Map V TQ37
Dulwich Picture Gallery College Road. Housed in building designed in 1814 by Sir John Soane, restored and re-opened after severe damage during 1939–45 War. Notable collection of European Old Masters, particularly of the Dutch school. Open 16 Mar to 15 Oct Tue to Sat 10–5 (6, May to Aug) (4, 16 Oct to 15 May) Sun Apr to Sep 2–5 (6, May to Aug). 25p. P in College Road and Gallery Road. *(Tel 01-693 5254)* &

ELTHAM *Gt London* Map V TQ47
Eltham Palace Noted for great hall with 15th-C hammer-beam roof. Old bridge spans moat. Open Nov to Mar, Thu and Sun 10.30–4; Apr to Oct, Mon, Thu, Fri, Sat and Sun 10.30–6. Opening arrangements subject to possible alteration, advisable to contact Admin Officer. *Tel 01-859 2112 ext 255* before visit. Free. *(AM)*
Winter Gardens Avery Hill Park. About 750 species of tropical and temperate plants in cold, temperate and tropical houses, a collection second only to Royal Botanical Gardens at Kew. ♨ (Mar to Sep). Open all year Mon to Fri 1–4 Sat, Sun and BH 11–4 (6 summer). Closed 1st Mon each month and 25 Dec. Free. P. *(Tel 01-850 2666)* &

ENFIELD *Gt London* Map V TQ39
Forty Hall Built 1629 for Sir Nicholas Raynton, Lord Mayor of London, and altered 1700 and later. Contemporary plaster ceilings and screen, 17th- and 18th-C furniture, and pictures, ceramics, and glass. Temporary exhibitions. ♨ (Apr to Oct). Open all year (ex 4 Apr, 24–26 Dec) Tue to Fri 10–8 (5, Oct to Easter), Sat and Sun 10–6 (5, Oct to Easter). Free. P. *(Tel 01-363 8196)* & B

FOREST HILL *Gt London* Map V TQ37
Horniman Museum London Road. Ethnographical and zoological exhibits, with large natural history collections including vivaria and aquaria. Exhibition of musical instruments from all parts of the world. Special exhibitions. Also extensive library and lectures and concerts in spring and autumn. Education Centre programmes for ch and adults. ♨ (open daily 2.30–5.30, Sat from 11 am). Open all year (ex 24, 25 and morning 26 Dec – special arrangements Boxing Day afternoon) Mon to Sat 10.30–6, Sun 2–6. Free. P in Sydenham Rise opposite. *(Tel 01-699 1872/2339/4911)* &

GREENWICH *Gt London* Map V TQ37
Cutty Sark Clipper Ship Greenwich Pier. The Cutty Sark is a famous Tea and Wool Clipper built in 1869 and preserved in dry dock since 1957. Open daily (ex 24 and 25 Dec, 1 Jan), 11–5 (2.30 Sun and 26 Dec) (6 during summer). 50p (ch 14 25p). Party 12+ (ex Sat and Sun). P. *(Tel 01-858 3445)* **(79)**
Gipsy Moth IV Greenwich Pier. The yacht in which Sir Francis Chichester sailed single-handed round the world 1966–67, starting the fashion for 'Round the World' sailing races. Open daily (ex 24, 25 Dec and 1 Jan) Oct to Mar 11–5; Apr to Sep 11–6, Sun and 26 Dec 2.30–6. 20p (ch 14 10p). P. *(Tel 01-858 3445)* **(79)**

National Maritime Museum Romney Road.
Fine collection of items relating to British seafaring. Navigation Room is outstanding.
Queen's House designed by Inigo Jones
1616–35, first English house in Palladian
style. ⚏ Open all year, daily (ex 4 Apr, 24–26
Dec and 1 Jan) Mon to Fri 10–5 (6 in
summer), Sat 10–6, Sun 2.30–6. Free. P.
(Tel 01-858 4422) ⅃ B
Old Royal Observatory In Greenwich Park,
which was laid out by Le Nôtre, famous
French gardener of time of Louis XIV, and part
of National Maritime Museum, with exhibits of
astronomical, horological and navigational
interest. Actual work of observatory now
carried out at Herstmonceux Castle. Open all
year, daily (ex 4 Apr, 5 May, 24–26 Dec and 1
Jan) Mon to Fri 10–5 (6 in summer), Sat
10–6, Sun 2.30–6. Free. Planetarium gives
viewing during school holidays, Mon, Tue,
Thu, Fri 2.30 and 3.30; special educational
programmes on Sat (information from
Education section). 15p (ch 5p). P. *(Tel 01-
858 4422)*
Royal Naval College Group of buildings
designed by Webb (late 17th C) and Wren
(early 18th C), with additions by Hawksmoor,
Vanbrugh, and Ripley. Formerly Naval
Hospital, becoming College in 1873. Chapel
rebuilt in 18th C, and Painted Hall has ceiling
by Sir James Thornhill. Souvenir shop.
Painted Hall and Chapel only open all year,
daily (ex Thu) 2.30–5. Free. ⚠ within college
grounds. *(Tel 01-858 2154)*
HACKNEY *Gt London* Map V TQ38
Geffrye Museum Kingsland Road. A
collection of period furniture and woodwork
from the Elizabethan period to 1939, including
panelling and staircases from demolished
London houses, contained in the former
almshouses built *c*1713 with a bequest from
Sir Robert Geffrye (Lord Mayor of London
1685–6). Also temporary exhibitions. Open
all year Tue to Sat, BH (ex 4 Apr, 25 and 26
Dec) 10–5, Sun 2–5. Free. P in nearby
streets. *(Tel 01-739 8368)* ⅃ B
HAM *Gt London* Map IV TQ17
Ham House Historic Jacobean mansion
(1610 and later), facing River Thames, now
annexe of Victoria and Albert Museum with
collection of late Stuart furniture. Shop. Open
daily (ex Mon but open most BH Mon) Apr to
Sep 2–6, Oct to Mar 12–4. Closed 4 Apr, 5
May and 24, 25, 26 Dec. 50p (ch and pen
20p). Children under 12 must be
accompanied by an adult. Grounds free. No
dogs. *(NT and Victoria and Albert Museum)*
HAMPSTEAD *Gt London* Map IV TQ28
Fenton House Hampstead Grove. A William
and Mary house, built *c*1693, set in walled
garden. Collections include notable Oriental,
Continental and English china, needlework,
furniture and the Benton Fletcher Collection
of early keyboard instruments. Some
concerts in summer. Open Feb, Mar and Nov,
Sat and Sun; Apr to Oct daily (ex Mon and
Tue, but open BH Mon) 11–5, Sun 2–5 or
sunset. £1.20 (ch 15 60p). *(Tel 01-435 3471)*.
(NT)
Keats House Keats Grove. Regency house,
former home of the poet; *Ode to the
Nightingale* was written in garden.
Manuscripts and relics preserved. Open all
year (ex 4/5 Apr, 5 May, 25 & 26 Dec and 1
Jan) Mon to Sat 10–6, Sun 2–5, other BH
2–5. Free. P on Heath. *(Tel 01-435 2062)* ⅃
B
Kenwood House Iveagh Bequest
Hampstead Lane, Mansion built *c*1765 by
Robert Adam, and fine grounds, bequeathed
to nation in 1927 by Lord Iveagh. Notable
library, furniture, and works of art including
paintings by Rembrandt, Hals, Vermeer,
Reynolds and Gainsborough. Summer
Exhibition. Orangery and lakeside concerts.
⚏ Old Kitchen and Coach house. Open all
year (ex 4 Apr and 24/25 Dec) daily 10–7
(dusk in winter). Free. ⚠ P. *(Tel 01-348 1286)*
⅃ B

HAMPTON COURT *Gt London* Map IV TQ16
Hampton Court Palace Built by Cardinal
Wolsey in early 16th C, with notable
gatehouse, clock court, and great hall, and
large additions by Sir Christopher Wren,
including Fountain Court (*c*1689). Fine state
apartments and banqueting houses,
orangery housing Mantegna Cartoons, and
Great Vine, kitchen, and maze of special
interest. Fine gardens with banqueting house
and park near River Thames. State
apartments open all year May to Sep, Mon to
Sat 9.30–6, Sun 11–6; Mar, Apr and Oct Mon
to Sat 9.30–5, Sun 2–5; Nov to Feb Mon to
Sat 9.30–4. Sun 2–4. £1, winter 50p (ch 16
and pen 40p, winter 20p). Cars 25p (m/cycles
10p). *(AM)*

HARMONDSWORTH *Gt London*
Map IV TQ07
Manor Farm Tithe Barn 14th to 15th-C tithe
barn, 190ft long and 36ft wide, situated by
farm adjacent to parish church. Accessible at
all reasonable times. Free. ⚠

HARROW *Gt London* Map IV TQ18
Kodak Museum Wealdstone. Covers 150
years of photography, including largest
collection of historical photographic
equipment in country. Closed at present, re-
opens early 1980, Mon to Fri, Sat and Sun
afternoons. Times and further information on
application. ⚠ free, but limited weekdays.
(Tel 01-427 4380 ext 76 enquiries)

HENDON *Gt London* Map IV TQ28
Church Farm House Museum Greyhound
Hill. Old gabled house, dating from 1688, now
museum of local interest. Open all year (ex 4
Apr, 25 and 26 Dec, 1 Jan) Mon to Sat
10–12.30 and 1.30–5.30 (Tue 10–1 only),
Sun 2.30–6. Free. ⚠ *(Tel 01-203 0130)*
Royal Air Force Museum Entrance via M1,
A41 (Aerodrome Road, off Watford Way) or
A5 (Colindale Avenue off Edgware Road).
The Museum, on the former Hendon airfield,
covers all aspects of the history of the RAF
and its predecessors. Over forty aircraft are
on display from the *Bleriot XI* to the
'Lightning'. Twelve galleries depict over 100
years of military aviation history and include
displays of photographs, documents, bombs,
guns, and uniform equipment. The Battle of
Britain Museum has been built on a site
adjacent to the main Museum. It contains a
unique collection of British, German and
Italian aircraft which were engaged in the
great air battle of 1940. ⚏ licensed, shop and
cinema. Open all year (ex 4 Apr, 5 May,
24–26 Dec and 1 Jan) Mon to Sat 10–6, Sun
2–6. RAF Museum Free. Battle of Britain
Museum 60p (ch and pen 30p). ⚠ *(Tel 01-
205 2266)* ⅃

ISLEWORTH *Gt London* Map IV TQ17
Syon House Founded in 1415 as a
monastery and remodelled in the 18th-C with
splendid interiors by Robert Adam, in
particular the superbly coloured ante-room
and the gallery-library. Fine portraits and
furniture. Exterior refaced *c*1825.
'Northumberland' lion on east front. Notable

arden layout by 'Capability' Brown. House oks across River Thames. Open Easter en Sun to Thu until 30 Sep (closed Fri and at) 12–5 (1 Sun, 11 BH). Last tickets 4.15. . Approach via Park Road off Twickenham oad. No dogs. ℗ licensed bar. *(Tel 01-60 0884 during opening hours only)*. The use is separate from the **Syon Park ardens** (see below)and a combined ticket is vailable. *(The Duke of Northumberland KG)*
yon Park Follow A315 of A310 to Busch orner, and enter via Park Road, Isleworth trance. In grounds of Syon House, 55 acres gardens on bank of River Thames opposite ew Gardens, only 9 miles from Central ndon. Laid out in mid 16th C, it is said to be e first place in which trees were planted rely for ornament, and it owes much of its esent beauty to 'Capability' Brown, who laid it most of the present gardens around the ke. The Great Conservatory, built 1820 by wler, was the first large glass and metal nstruction of its kind in the world, and was e inspiration for the Crystal Palace at the eat Exhibition of 1851. It now houses a agnificent display of house plants, as well a walk-through aviary, and an aquarium. e 6-acre rose garden has over 12,000 ses. Syon Park has one of the largest rdening centres in England, and this itself is rth a visit. Gardens Apr to Sep, daily 10–6; t to Mar (ex Christmas week) 10–5 or dusk hichever is earlier). Admission prices not t decided. ℗ and children's play area. ⚠ el 01-560 0882) ⅋

(lease also see page 207 for advertisement)
ENSINGTON *Gt London* Map IV TQ27
mmonwealth Institute and Art Gallery ensington High Street. Contains exhibitions picting life in the countries of the mmonwealth. Films are shown daily, and exhibitions, featuring the finest works of mmonwealth painters and sculptors are ld frequently. The institute has its own rary. ℗ Open all year (ex 4 Apr, 5 May, –26 Dec and 1 Jan) Mon to Sat 10–5.30, n 2.30–6. Free. ⚠ *(Tel 01-602 3252)* ⅋
ighton House Art gallery and museum, lland Park Road. An essentially Victorian- rled house built in 1866, to a symmetrical sign by George Aitchison, which now forms e central part of the building. The Arab Hall the western side is decorated with applied s, fine examples of the oriental tile makers' rk of the 13th, 16th and 17th Cs, originating m Rhodes, Damascus, Cairo and ewhere, and a mosaic frieze by Walter ane in the Persian style. Within the house is ermanent exhibition of Victorian art, luding works by Lord Frederick Leighton as ll as paintings, drawings, sculpture, pottery d furniture by other artists and craftsmen of s period. Temporary exhibitions are also 'd throughout the year in the Winter Studio d Upper Perrin Gallery of the house, Open year, daily (ex Sun, BH) 11–5 (6, during nporary exhibitions). Garden open Apr to c 11–5. Free. Meter P 30yds. *(Tel 01- 2 3316)* ⅋ B
W *Gt London* Map IV TQ17
w Gardens Royal Botanical Gardens of 0 acres, with plants, trees, and flowers. seums and glasshouses, with rare hids, ferns, and cacti. Exotic Pagoda was rk of Sir William Chambers in 1761. Open year, daily (ex 25 Dec and 1 Jan and May y); gardens from 10am to between 4pm d 8pm (depending on season); museums m 10am; glasshouses from 11am. Closing es vary according to season, but not later

than 4.50pm Mon to Sat, 5.50pm Sun. May Day closing under revision, also admission prices for 1980. ⅋
Kew Palace Dutch-gabled 17th- to 18th-C house, with souvenirs of George III. Queen Charlotte died here in 1818. Stands in the Royal Botanical Gardens of Kew. Open Apr to mid Oct daily 11–5.30. 20p (ch 16 and pen 5p). Free. ⚠ *(AM) and* **Queen Charlotte's Cottage** Built in 1772 for the Queen, wife of George III. The interior remains as it was in the 18th-C when royalty were in residence. Open Apr to mid Oct 11–5.30 Sat, Sun and BH. 15p (ch 16 and pen 5p) ch5 free. *(AM)*

NEASDEN *Gt London* Map IV TQ28
The Grange Museum Neasden Lane NW10 (centre of roundabout). The building dating from around 1700 originally formed part of the outbuildings of a large farm and was later converted into a Gothic cottage. Permanent collections tell the story of the area that is now the London Borough of Brent. Changing temporary exhibitions, local history library, display on the British Empire Exhibition for which Wembley Stadium was built. Two period rooms of late 19th C and the 1930s. Open all year (ex BH) Mon to Sat 10–5 (8 Mon and Wed). Free. ⚠ *(Tel 01-452 8311)* ⅋ B

NORTH PECKHAM *Gt London* Map V TQ37
Livesey Museum 682 Old Kent Road. Museum displays two exhibitions every year, dealing mainly with Southwark's past and present. Permanent exhibition of Southwark's street furniture in the courtyard. Open when exhibition in progress. Mon to Sat 10–5. Free. Limited street P. *(Tel 01-639 5604)* ⅋ B

OSTERLEY *Gt London* Map IV TQ17
Osterley Park House Off B454 (Syon Lane). Originally dates back to c1575, with alterations of 1711. Splendid decoration by Robert Adam (1763 and 1767), and hall, staircase, Etruscan room, and tapestry room outstanding. Contemporary furniture bought by Victoria and Albert Museum. ℗ Open Apr to Sep Tue to Sun and BH 2–6 (closed Mon); Oct to Mar Tue to Sun 12–4 (closed 4 Apr, 5 May, 24–26 Dec, 1 Jan). 40p (ch and pen 15p). Under review for 1980. *(Tel 01-560 3918). (NT and V and A Museum)*

REGENT'S PARK *Gt London* Map V TQ28
London Zoo Part of the world-famous Zoological Society of London which was founded in 1826 by Sir Stamford Raffles with the aim of 'the advancement of Zoology and Animal Physiology and the introduction of new and curious subjects of the Animal Kingdom'. The zoo was opened in 1828. In 1865 London Zoo received its first African elephant called 'Jumbo' whose name has become immortalised as a name for giant things. Two of the more interesting acquisitions are a pair of giant pandas, Ching-Ching and Chia-Chia presented to the zoo after Edward Heath's visit to China during 1974. Among the world firsts that the zoo can claim are a reptile house in 1849, aquarium 1853, and insect house in 1889. The zoo contains today over 6,000 creatures, many of which were born at the zoo, covering 1,450 species, including breeding colonies of the rare orang-utans, chimpanzees and many other rare or endangered species. In recent years new pavilions have been built for apes, lions, tigers and monkeys, elephants and rhinos, small mammals (the largest collection under one roof in the world) and a giant walk-through aviary designed by Lord Snowdon.

The London and Whipsnade Zoos are supported by the most professionally complete veterinary and research services to maintain animal management standards at the Society's uniquely high level. ⏛ Licensed. Open all year, daily (ex 25 Dec) 9 (10 Nov to Feb) – 6 (7 Sun and BH) or dusk whichever is earlier. £2 (ch 90p). Under revision for 1980. P. outer circle of Park after 11 and in car park 600yds from main gate after 10. *(Tel 01-722 3333)* ₳

SOUTHGATE *Gt London* Map V TQ39
Broomfield Museum Broomfield Lane. This is located at Broomfield House, a timbered 17th-C house, with wall-paintings and a ceiling by Gerard Lanscroon. It stands in a small park. Special exhibitions of local interest throughout the year. Natural history room. Fresh painting exhibitions every month. ⏛ summer. Open all year, daily (ex Mon) Easter to Sep 10 – 8 (6, Sat and Sun); Oct to Easter 10 – 5. Free. ₳ *(Tel 01-882 1354)* ₳ B

TOTTENHAM *Gt London* Map V TQ39
Bruce Castle Museum Lordship Lane. An E-shaped Elizabethan, Jacobean and Georgian building, with an adjacent circular 16th-C tower, which stands in a small park. The museum contains three distinct collections on: Local History; Postal History – a private school was run by the family of Rowland Hill in this building during the 19th C; and the Middlesex Regiment, known also as the 'die-hards'. Open all year, Mon (ex BH), Tue, Thu, Fri, 10 – 5, Sat 10 – 12.30, 1.30 – 5. Free. ₳ *(Tel 01-808 8772)* ₳

TWICKENHAM *Gt London* Map IV TQ17
Marble Hill House Marble Hill Park. Home of Countess of Suffolk, mistress of George II, and begun in 1724 to a design by Roger Morris. Standing in a public park near the River Thames and with a notable hall and great room, with Georgian paintings and furniture. Special summer exhibitions. ⏛ in stable block. Open all year (ex 24 and 25 Dec and Fri) daily 10 – 5 (4, Nov to Jan). Free. P. 200yds. *(Tel 01-348 1286)* ₳
Orleans House Gallery Riverside. Original Orleans House, in which Louis Philippe, Duc d'Orleans, King of the French 1830 – 48, lived in early 19th C. It was originally built for Queen Anne's Secretary of State for Scotland, and was demolished in 1927. Surviving octagonal room, designed by James Gibbs in 1720, has exquisite plasterwork by Artari and Bagutti. Open all year, Tue to Sat 1 – 5.30 (4.30 Oct to Mar), Sun 2 – 5.30 (4.30 Oct to Mar); BH (ex 4 Apr, 25/26 Dec) 2 – 5.30, 1 Jan 2 – 4.30. Free. Woodland gardens open all year, daily 9 – dusk. ₳ *(Tel 01-940 0031)* ₳ B

WALTHAMSTOW *Gt London* Map V TQ38
Vestry House Museum of Local History Vestry Road, near Hoe Street. A small museum located in a former 18th-C workhouse standing in the conservation area 'Walthamstow Village', the historic centre of the parish. Historical items of local interest from the Stone Age onwards are displayed, including a reconstructed Victorian parlour and a Gallery of Costume. Also displayed is a porcelain hand-painted topographical tea service with scenes of area. Local archives are also available for consultation. The Bremer, Britain's first internal combustion engined car, built 1892 – 1894, can be seen. Lectures on various historical themes Oct to Mar 1st Wed in each month at 8.15 pm. Open all year Mon to Sat 10 – 5 (8, Mon and Wed). Free. ₳ *(Tel 01-527 5544 ext 391)*

William Morris Gallery Lloyd Park, Forest Road. William Morris lived in this house, known as 'Water House' from 1848 – 56. There are exhibits of his fabrics, wallpapers and furniture. The Century Guild Collection and the Brangwyn Gift. Open all year Mon to Sat 10 – 5 (10 – 8 Tue and Thu, Apr to Sep); first Sun in each month 10 – 12 and 2 – 5. Closed 1 Jan, Easter weekend, 25 Dec, and all BH. Free. ₳ *(Tel 01-527 5544 ext 390)* ₳ B

WEMBLEY *Gt London* Map IV TQ18
Wembley Stadium The world's number one stadium built in 1923, it holds 100,000. Home of the England football team – venue for annual Cup Final and World events. Tour comprises 10-minute audio-visual slide show, visit to dressing rooms, Royal Box and retiring rooms, a walk up Player's tunnel to pitch complete with sound effects. Admission includes free tea, coffee or soft drink. Open all year (ex 25 and 26 Dec, Thu and days before and after a match) tours on the hour 10 – 4 (ex 1 pm). £1 (ch 15 and pen 70p). Under revision for 1980. Party 20+. ₳ *(Tel 01-902 8833 ask for Guided Tours)* ₳

WEST HAM *Gt London* Map V TQ38
Passmore Edwards Museum Romford Road. Collections of Greater London and Essex archaeology, biology, geology and history. Open all year, daily (ex Sun and BH) Mon, Tue, Wed, Fri 10 – 6, Thu 10 – 8, Sat 10 – 1, 2 – 5. Free. P in streets. *(Tel 01-534 4545 ext 376 and 01-519 4296)*

WHITECHAPEL *Gt London* Map V TQ38
National Museum of Labour History Limehouse Town Hall, Commercial Road. The visual history from late 18th C to 1945 is portrayed in two sections from autocracy to democracy, and the turn to socialism 1881 to 1945. Its prime concern (through its large and rare collection) is to portray the development of democracy over the last 200 years. Open all year (closed 20 – 30 Dec, BH) Tue to Fri 9.30 – 5. Free. *(Tel 01-515 3229)* ₳

WIMBLEDON *Gt London* Map IV TQ27
Lawn Tennis Museum The museum, within the grounds of the All England Tennis Club, is the only one of its kind in the world and shows something of the games which preceded and helped in the conception of lawn tennis. Traces the development of the game over the last century. Also includes Library, the archives of which comprise collections of photographs, film, documents, postcards, autographs and other ephemera. Museum shop (gifts and souvenirs). Open all year (ex Mon, BH and Sat and Sun prior to the Championships) Tue to Sat 11 – 5, Sun 2 – 5. During Championships open daily 12 – 1, 1.30 – 2.30, 3 – 4, 4.30 – 5.30, 6 – 7.75p (ch and pen 35p). ₳ *(Tel 01-946 2244)*

WOOLWICH *Gt London* Map V TQ47
Museum of Artillery in the Rotunda Replica of circular structure designed by John Nash, which stood at one time in St James's Park. It contains a very interesting collection of artillery recently re-displayed. Open all year Apr to Oct, Mon to Fri 12 – 5, Sat and Sun 1 – Nov to Mar, Mon to Fri 12 – 4, Sat and Sun 1 – 4. Free. Closed 4 Apr, 25 and 26 Dec and Jan. ₳ *(Tel 01-856 5533 ext 3385)* ₳

London section ends

.ONDON COLNEY *Hertfordshire*
Map 4 TL20
Salisbury Hall and de Havilland Mosquito Aircraft Museum 5m S of St Albans on A6. Moated hall, dating from Charles II's reign. Interesting fireplaces and famous early English medallions of Roman emperors. ☕ from Whitsun. Hall and garden open Easter to end Sep, Sun 2–6; BH Mon 10.30–12.30 and 2–5.30, also Jul to end of Sep, Thu 2–6. 50p (ch 15 25p, ch 5 free). De Havilland Mosquito Mk B35, Vampire and Venom aircraft on show. 25p (ch 10p). Under revision for 1980. Party Tue to Fri. Dogs in grounds on leads. ▲ *(Tel Bowmans Green 23274). (Mr W J Goldsmith)* ♿ B

LONG CRENDON *Buckinghamshire*
Map 4 SP60
Court House 2m N of Thame. Partly half-timbered 14th-C building, probably at one time a wool store. Upper storey open Wed 2–6, Sat & Sun 11–6. 20p. *(NT)*

LONGLEAT HOUSE *Wiltshire* Map 3 ST84
Entrance on Warminster–Frome road, A362. Built for Sir John Thynne in 1580 and decorated in the Italian Renaissance fashion in the 19th C, with fine library, state rooms, ceilings, pictures and furniture. Europe's first Safari Park with hundreds of wild animals. Shearwater lake and viewpoint from Heaven's Gate are all outstanding. Victorian kitchens, Maze, Garden Centre, BBC 'Dr Who' exhibition and new Paddington Bear exhibition open Easter to Oct. ☕, picnic areas. Open all year daily (ex 25 Dec). House £1.10 (ch and pen 50p) extra for Victorian kitchens, 19th-C dolls houses, family by-gones, exhibitions, railway and maze, also road toll inclusive of grounds, picnic area and gardens 50p (not applicable to coaches). Safari Park (hard topped cars only) £3.50 per car, extra for safari boats and pets corner. Toilet for disabled in the stable yard. Prices and times under revision for 1980. *(Tel Maiden Bradley 55). (Marquess of Bath)*

LONG MELFORD *Suffolk* Map 5 TL84
Kentwell Hall A mellow redbrick Elizabethan manor with almost perfect original E-plan exterior elevations, completely surrounded by a broad moat in a tranquil setting. Restoration work can be seen in progress. ☕ on open days, full catering for parties by arrangement. Open Mar to Oct Sun, also Wed and Thu May to Sep, Fri and Sat 18 Jul to 20 Sep, 4–10 Apr incl, BH weekends Sat to Mon, 2–6. 85p (accompanied ch 14 45p; pen 45p on Thu only). Admission prices under revision for 1980. Party 20+. ▲ *(Tel 207)* ♿
Melford Hall Tudor and 18th-C mansion home of Hyde Parkers since 1781. Fine porcelain, furniture, and paintings. Open Apr to 30 Sep, Wed, Thu, Sun, and BH Mon 2–6 (last admission 5.30). 90p. Party 15+. No dogs. *(NT)*

LONG WITTENHAM *Oxfordshire*
Map 4 SU59
Pendon Museum 3½m N of Didcot on unclass road off B4016. A small but expanding museum depicting, in miniature, rural scenes of the 1930s. Also the late John Ahern's famous Madder Valley layout, and railway relics from 1812 onwards. ☕. Open Mar to Oct, Sat, Sun and BH 2–6. Nov to Feb Sat and Sun 2–5 (closed Christmas). 50p (ch 15 and pen 30p, ch 4 free). ▲ (limited). *(Tel Clifton Hampden 7365, weekends only)*

LOOE *Cornwall* Map 2 SX25
Cornish Museum Lower Street, East Looe. Folklore, fishing, mining, early fire fighting and many other local exhibits of historical interest. Open Spring BH to 30 Sep, daily 10–1, 2–5.30. 15p (ch 10p). P. ♿ **(79)**
Looe Aquarium Local marine aquarium containing specimens which can be caught within a mile of Banjo pier. Shark museum with exhibits of blue, porbeagle and mako sharks. Open 1 Jun to 30 Sep daily 10–6 (9 mid Jun to mid Sep). 20p (ch 10p). Under revision for 1980. P. *(Tel 2423)* ♿
The Monkey Sanctuary Murrayton. 3m ENE, off B3253. Sanctuary for rare Amazon woolly monkey species which are bred here. They can be watched in the trees and in the grounds. Talks given morning and afternoon. Indoor meeting in rainy weather. Visitors advised to bring children under 4 on dry days only. ☕. Open daily 30 Mar to 13 Apr then 11 May to 5 Oct 10.30–5.30. Monkeys actually meet the visitors. Admission charges not yet decided. ▲ *(Tel 2532)* ♿ (individuals only)

LOTHERTON HALL *North Yorkshire*
Map 8 SE43
10m E of Leeds, off B1217, near Aberford.
Built around earlier 18th-C house. Now a
country house museum, with furniture,
pictures, silver and ceramics from Gascoigne
collection, and works of art from Leeds
collections. Gallery of Oriental art. Fashion
galleries. ⟶. Open all year, daily (ex 25, 26
Dec) Tue to Sun 10.30 – 6.15 or dusk
(10.30 – 8.30, Thu, May to Sep). 25p (ch 5p,
pen and students free). △ *(Tel Aberford 259)*
(79)

LOUGHBOROUGH *Leicestershire*
Map 8 SK51
Great Central Railway Great Central Road.
Operational private steam railway running
over five miles from Loughborough Central to
Rothley, all trains calling at Quorn and
Woodhouse. Museum and locomotive depot
at Loughborough Central. Buffet car on trains,
restaurant as advertised. ⟶ at Loughborough
Central and Rothley. Open all year Sat, Sun
and BH Mon and Tue, also Wed and Thu
during Jul and Aug (closed 4 Apr and 25 Dec).
Return fare from any station £1.20 (ch and
pen 60p). △ at Quorn (Leisurerail Centre –
picnic area, children's railway, adventure
area, crazyrail golf etc). *(Tel 30726 or
216433)*

LOUND HALL MINING MUSEUM
Nottinghamshire Map 8 SK77
5½m S of East Retford on B6387. Exhibits
include locomotives, underground canal
barge, coal face machinery, headgear, hand
tools, lamps and electrical equipment. The
modern Bevercotes Colliery is adjacent to
museum. Open first Sun in each month, May
to Oct 2 – 5.30, Nov to Mar 2 – 4 (Mon to Fri
1.30 – 4 by prior arrangement for parties). 10p
(accompanied ch 16 free). △

LOWER BEEDING *West Sussex*
Map 4 TQ22
Leonardslee Gardens 1m S off A281.
Renowned spring garden, camellias, azaleas
and rhododendrons in valley, and 15th-C
hammer ponds. Tea weekdays. Open 20 Apr
the 27 Apr to 8 Jun, Wed, Thu, Sat and Sun
also Mon 5 and 26 May. Autumn tints all Sat
and Sun Oct. 10 – 6. 80p (ch 40p). No dogs. △
10p. *(Tel 212 or 305)*. *(Sir Giles Loder)* &

LOWESTOFT *Suffolk* Map 5 TM59
East Anglia Transport Museum Chapel
Road, Carlton Colville. The Museum
premises are situated on a 3-acre site and
contain a range of historic cars, commercial
vehicles, trams, buses and trolleybuses, in
addition to various items of transport interest.
A tram service operates during opening hours
also a narrow-gauge railway. ⟶. Open
Easter, weekends and BH from May to end
Sep, Sat 2 – 4, Sun and BH 11 – 5, also Aug
Tue to Fri 2 – 4. 35p (ch 15p). Party. △ *(Tel
Ubberston 398)*

LOWTHER *Cumbria* Map 12 NY52
Wild Life Country Park 5m S of Penrith off
A6. Deer, cranes, and rare breeds of cattle
and sheep can be viewed in a wild and natural
setting. Many European species housed in
special enclosures including otters, badgers,
wild pigs, etc. Picnic areas. ⟶. Open Apr to
Sep 10 – 5 (6, Jul and Aug). Admission not yet
decided for 1979. Gift shop and garden
centre. Dog kennels. △ *(Tel Hacklethorpe
392)* & **(79)**

LUCTON *Hereford and Worcester*
Map 3 SO46
Mortimer's Cross Water Mill 18th-C

undershot-type watermill which was working
until 1940. Open May to Sep, Thu 12 – 6; Mar,
Apr and Oct, Thu 12 – 4.30; Nov to Feb, Thu
12 – 3.30. 15p (ch 16 and pen 5p). *(AM)*

LUDGERSHALL *Wiltshire* Map 4 SU25
Ludgershall Castle 7m NW of Andover on
A342. Norman motte and bailey castle,
retaining large earthworks and flint walling of
later royal castle. Open all reasonable times.
Free. *(AM)*

LUDLOW *Salop* Map 7 SO57
Ludlow Museum Butter Cross. This
museum, housed in the Butter Cross of 1744,
has prehistoric, Roman and medieval
exhibits, examples of arms and armour,
Georgian and Victorian domestic items, local
history, biology and geology. Open Easter to
30 Sep, Mon to Sat 10.30 – 12.30 and 2 – 5,
Sun (Jun, Jul and Aug only) 10 – 1, 2 – 5. 30p
(ch 10p). P. County Museum Service reserve
collections open by appointment only. *(Tel
3857)*

LUNDY ISLAND *Devon* Map 2 SS14
In Bristol Channel. Tiny granite island, NT
property since 1969, and leased to Landmark
Trust. Puffins and other seabirds breed in
large numbers on cliffs around coastline.
Near quay are slight remains of Marisco
Castle, stronghold of early piratical ruling
family. Shutter Rock figures in Charles
Kingsley's *Westward Ho!* Open always,
landing fee 75p. Steamers from Ilfracombe
Quay *(Tel 62687)* from May to end Sep. No
cars. *(NT)*

LUTON *Bedfordshire* Map 4 TL02
Museum and Art Gallery Wardown Park.
Museum has collections illustrating natural
history, culture, and industries of Luton and
Bedfordshire with particular reference to
straw hat and pillow lace trade. 'Luton Life'
gallery includes a reconstructed 'street'
display. Also temporary exhibitions. Open all
year daily (ex 25, 26 Dec, 1 Jan and Sun in
Dec and Jan) Mon to Sat 10 – 6 (5 winter) Sun
2 – 6 (5 winter). Free. △ *(Tel 36941)* & B
Luton Hoo Entrance at Park Street gates, on
A6129. Magnificent Wernher Collection of art
treasures including tapestries and pictures;
also Russian Fabergé jewellery, in a country
mansion designed originally by Robert Adam.
Large park by 'Capability' Brown. ⟶. Open 4
Apr to 28 Sep, Mon, Wed, Thu and Sat (also
Apr) 11 – 6; Sun 2 – 6. House and gardens £1
(ch 40p). Gardens only 35p (ch 15p). Under
revision for 1980. No dogs. △ *(Tel 22955)*.
(NGS) &

LYDDINGTON *Leicestershire* Map 4 SP89
Bede House Former home of Bishops of
Lincoln, converted into hospital, or bede
house, by Lord Burghley in 1602. Open, see
inside front cover, Apr to Sep only. 15p (ch 16
and pen 5p). *(AM)*

LYDFORD *Devon* Map 2 SX58
Lydford Castle Midway Okehampton –
Tavistock off A386. Remains of mid 12th-C
stone keep altered a century later. Lower floor
was once a prison and the upper floor became
Stannary Court to administer local tin mines.
Open all reasonable times. Free. △ *(AM)*
Lydford Gorge 8m N of Tavistock on unclass
road. Scooped into succession of potholes by
River Lyd the gorge emerges into steep, oak-
wooded valley and is joined by a stream at
90ft-high White Lady waterfall. Open Apr to
Oct, daily 9 – 1hr before sunset. 70p. *(NT)*

LYDIARD PARK *Wiltshire* Map 4 SU18
1m N of M4 (Junc 16) on unclass road. Fine
Georgian mansion set in pleasant park,

ogether with the adjoining parish church of St
Mary, which contains fascinating memorials
o the St John family. Small agricultural
museum in the Stable block, as mansion,
ree. Open all year (ex 4 Apr, 25/26 Dec).
Weekdays 10–1, 2–5.30, Sun 2–5.30. 22p
ch and pen 11p). Party 20+. Grounds free. ⚠
*Tel Swindon 26161 ext 522 or Purton
♯70401)* ⅃ also **Agricultural Museum** 1½m
NE on unclass road at Shaw. Houses larger
tems of farming equipment, wagons, carts,
loughs, drills etc. Open Easter to Oct Sun
♯–5. Free. ⚠ free.

YDNEY *Gloucestershire* Map 3 SO60
Dean Forest Railway Society Ltd 1m N at
New Mills on B4234. A number of
ocomotives, coaches, wagons and railway
equipment on show at Norchard just outside
ydney on B4234. Steam days BH Sun and
Mon, every Sun Aug. ⚐. Open Sat and Sun
1–5 (closed Christmas). 10p–50p
Jepending on activities also subject to
alteration. P. *(Tel 3423)* ⅃

YME REGIS *Dorset* Map 3 SY39
Philpot Museum Bridge Street. Small
museum preserving old fire engine of 1706,
prints, documents, old lace exhibition, an
extensive collection of geological specimens
and local history exhibits. Also fossils from the
Blue Lias rock nearby where, in 1811, 12-
year-old Mary Anning discovered the remains
of an ichthyosaurus, of which a specimen is in
he museum. Open Easter to 30 Sep, daily
0.30–1, 2.30–5; Oct to Apr, Tue
0.30–12.30, Thu 2.30–4.30, Sat and Sun
0.30–12.30 and 2.30–4.30. 15p (ch 16 5p).
Jnder revision for 1980. P (charge). ⅃ B

YMPNE *Kent* Map 5 TR13
ympne Castle Restored Norman to 15th-C
tructure, modernised in 1905, once owned
y Archdeacons of Canterbury. Gardens
ave extensive views over Romney Marsh
nd across Channel to French coast. ⚐ BH
nly, or for parties by arrangement. Open
Easter to Oct Sun 2.30–6, other times by
rrangement. 1 Jul to 30 Sep and all BH daily
0.30–6. 50p (ch 14 15p). ⚠ *(Tel Hythe
♯7571). (Mr H Margary)*
Port Lympne Zoo Park and Gardens Many
ifferent animals including, Indian elephants,
rolves, rhinos, African leopards, Siberian
nd Indian tigers, monkeys etc. The mansion
vas built by Sir Herbert Baker, famous
rchitect of his time. Many of the original
nternal features have survived, the most
otable being the recently-restored 'Rex
Vhistler Tent Room', Moroccan patio,
exagonal library (where the Treaty of Paris

was signed after the First World War), and the
long hall with concentric patterned marble,
mosaic floor. 15 acres of spectacular gardens
with elaborate terracing. ⚐. Open all year (ex
25 Dec) daily 10–6 (or sunset). Admission
charges for 1980 not yet decided. ⚠ *(Tel
Hythe 60618/9)*

LYNTON *Devon* Map 3 SS74
Lyn and Exmoor Museum History of life of
Exmoor, housed in St Vincent Cottage, one of
oldest in resort, with unique slab roof, 16th-C
building now completely restored. Special
exhibition of scale models and photographs of
old Lynton–Barnstaple railway 1895–1935,
donated to museum. Open Apr to Sep, Mon to
Fri 10–12.30, 2–5, Sun 2–5. 20p (ch 14
10p). P.

LYVEDEN NEW BIELD *Northamptonshire*
Map 4 SP98
4m SW Oundle. Shell of unfinished two-
storeyed Greek-Cross house, designed
c1600 by Sir Thomas Tresham to symbolise
the Passion. Open daily. Party (arrangement
with custodian). *(NT)*

MACCLESFIELD *Cheshire* Map 7 SJ79
Macclesfield Museum and Art Gallery
West Park, Prestbury Road. Contains a
notable collection of Egyptian antiquities, oil
paintings, and sketches including work by C F
Tunnicliffe ARA and Landseer, and drawings
and prints of a topographical nature. Also a
small silk exhibition and a stuffed Giant
Panda. Open all year (ex Easter, BH and day
following, 25 Dec and Mons) Tue to Sat
10–12 & 1–5, Sun 2–5. Free. P. *(Tel 24067)*

MADRON *Cornwall* Map 2 SW43
Trengwainton Garden 2m W of Penzance,
on B3312. Gardens displaying a magnificent
collection of shrubs, including magnolias and
rhododendrons. Walled garden containing
tender and sub-tropical plants not grown
elsewhere in England. Open Mar to Oct, also
BH, Wed, Thu, Fri, and Sat 11–6. 70p *(NT)*

MAIDENHEAD *Berkshire* Map 4 SU88
The Courage Shire Horse Centre Set in
attractive Berkshire countryside. Up to twelve
Shire horses, each weighing around a ton,
can be seen in the timber-built stables.
Comprehensive display room giving history of
the Shire horse and showing prizes won by
the horses. Farrier's shop, pets corner,
playground and picnic area. ⚐. Open 1 Mar to
31 Oct daily (ex Mon unless BH) 11–5 (last
admission 4). ⚠ Licensed PH adjacent with
restaurant. For admission charges telephone
Littlewick Green 3917, and restaurant
reservations 5335. ⅃

Henry Reitlinger Bequest Oldfield, Riverside. Collection of pottery, sculpture, paintings, drawings, ceramics, and glass. Open Apr to 30 Sep, Tue and Thu 10 – 12.30 and 2.15 – 4.30, first Sun in each month 2.30 – 4.30. Other times by prior arrangement in writing. Free. ⚠

MAIDSTONE *Kent* Map 5 TQ75
Museum and Art Gallery Chillington Manor, St Faith's Street. Rebuilt in 1562, with medieval wing brought from East Farleigh. Now museum and art gallery, containing Japanese room. Museum contains Anglo-Saxon jewellery, glass and volume II of the Lambeth Byelaw (c1170). Exhibitions by local and national artists. Open all year, Mon (ex BH) to Sat 10 – 6 (5, Oct to Mar). Free. P. *(Tel 54497)*
Tyrwhitt Drake Museum of Carriages The Archbishop's Stables, Mill Street. Late medieval tithe barn or stables, containing interesting museum of horse-drawn carriages and vehicles. Near Archbishop's Palace. Open all year, weekdays (ex BH) 10 – 1 and 2 – 5. 20p (ch 10p). Party (by appointment). P. *(Tel 54497)* ♿ B

MALHAM *North Yorkshire* Map 7 SD86
Yorkshire Dales National Park Centre Permanent interpretation centre for the Malham area with displays, books, maps, teaching aids, etc. Open Apr to end Sep daily mid morning to late afternoon. Free. ⚠ *(Tel Airton 363)* ♿

MALTON *North Yorkshire* Map 8 SE77
Roman Museum Adjoining Milton Rooms, Market Place. Contains extensive Romano-British collections from the Roman Fort of Derventio and the settlements and villas in the vicinity. In addition there are displays of prehistoric and medieval material from Malton and district. Open all year Spring BH to 30 Sep, Mon to Sat 11 – 5, Sun 2 – 5; 1 Oct to 28 May, Mon to Sat 2 – 4.30, Sun 2 – 5. 10p (ch and students 5p). Questionnaires available for children. P. *(Tel 4941 ext 67)*

MANCHESTER *Gt Manchester* Map 7 SJ89
The City Art Gallery Mosley Street. British and Continental paintings before 1900 including Old Masters, Gainsborough, Stubbs, Turner, The Pre-Raphaelites and Impressionists. Sculpture, English and Continental silver, pottery and porcelain. Information about exhibitions, identifications, photographs etc, please write or telephone. Open Mon to Sat 10 – 6, Sun 2.30 – 6. Free. P *(Tel 061-236 9422)*
The Gallery of Modern Art Athenaeum, Princess Street (next door to City Art Gallery). From Sickert to Hockney. European painting, sculpture, drawings, prints and decorative arts since 1900. Opening times and telephone no. as for City Art Gallery. Free.
The John Rylands University Library of Manchester Famous library, dating from 1851, containing over 3,000,000 books, 17,000 manuscripts, extensive archival collections and *c* 600,000 titles in microform. Rare books division in the architecturally distinguished Rylands memorial building in Deansgate, holds regular exhibitions and lectures. Open all year (ex BH and Christmas to 1 Jan), Mon to Fri 9.30 – 5.30, Sat 9.30 – 1. Free. ⚠
The Gallery of English Costume Platt Fields, Rusholme. The famous costume collection displaying the changing styles of everyday clothes and accessories of the last

) years, including contemporary fashion.
e costume library is available to students
request. Open all year. May to Aug Mon to
t 10–6, Sun 12–6; Mar, Apr, Sep and Oct
n to Sat 10–6, Sun 2–6; Nov to Feb Mon
Sat 10–4, Sun 2–4. Free. *(Tel 061-*
4 5217) ✍ B

nchester Museum The University, Oxford
ad. Contains exhibits of archaeology and
ural history including an extensive
ection from Ancient Egypt, rocks,
erals, fossils, coins and native
ftsmanship and huge study collections of
er 8 million specimens. Popular lectures
given on winter Sats. Open all year daily
Sun, 4 Apr, 25, 26 Dec) 10–5 (9, Wed).
e but charge for P in University grounds.
l 061-273 3333)

rth Western Museum of Science and
dustry Grosvenor Street. Steam and
ernal-combustion engines, machine tools,
ctrical exhibits, railway photographs,
er-making, printing and textile machinery,
d equipment among other exhibits.
rking days are held on last Sat of most
nths (ex Jul, Aug, Dec) when the machines
demonstrated. Museum book shop. ⚏
en all year (ex Sun, 4 Apr and several days
Christmas) 10–5. Free. Ch 11 admitted
y if accompanied by an adult. P. *(Tel 061-*
3 6636 for Museum, 061-273 1955 for
seum Education Service) ✍ B

een's Park Art Gallery Harpurhey.
torian and Edwardian paintings, including
ais, Watts and Brangwyn. Paintings by
r Artists. Displays of the Manchester
giment and the 14th/20th King's Hussars.
en Mon to Sat 10–6 (4 Nov to Feb); Sun
6 (4 Nov to Feb) 12–6 May to Aug. Free. ⚠
l 061-205 2121)

itworth Art Gallery University of
nchester, Whitworth Park. Founded 1889
Royal Charter. The principal collections
British water-colours including work by
ke, Turner, the Pre-Raphaelites and
39–45 War Artists; Continental water-
ours including works by Cézanne, Van
gh and Picasso; drawings and prints,
uding examples by leading Renaissance
sters such as Pollaiuolo, Mantegna and
rer, and fine collection of Japanese prints;
tiles, including the Whitworth Tapestry,
signed by Paolozzi 1968; historic wall
ers; and contemporary works of art.
ecial exhibitions for 1980 include, 100
ster Prints in the Whitworth Art collection,
Jan to 26 Apr; Contemporary Swiss
pestries, 1 Mar to 8 Apr; Treasures from
versity of Manchester, late Apr to 28 Jun;
tdoor Sculpture at the Whitworth, Summer
30; Mondriaan and Hague School
awings, 17 May to 12 Jul; Treasures from
State Jewish Museum, Prague, 4 Oct to
Dec. Open all year daily (ex Sun, 4 Apr, 5
y and 25/26 Dec) 10–5 (Thu 10–9). Free.
Tel 061-273 4865) ✍

NNINGTON HALL *Norfolk* Map 9 TG13
lt in 1460 of flint. A moated manor house,
a family home. ⚏ (teas). Gardens open
y to Sep, Thu and Fri 2–5, house by
tten appointment only, Thu (enclose sae).
dens 30p, House 50p. ⚠ *(The Hon Robin*
lpole) ✍ B (gardens)

PLEDURHAM *Berkshire* Map 4 SU67
pledurham House* Elizabethan mansion
in unspoilt village beside River Thames.
lt by Blount family in the 16th C, and
tored by their descendant. Within the
se are great oak staircases, well-

proportioned rooms and moulded ceilings in
white plasterwork, of the late Elizabethan
period. Collection of pictures and family
portraits. River launches from Caversham
Bridge, Reading (4m), when house is open,
(charter bookings arranged for parties).
Riverside picnic park open same days as
house, noon to sunset. Open 6 Apr to 28 Sep
Sat, Sun, BH 2.30–5.30. Admission prices
under review. Party 20+ by arrangement
weekends, Tue, Wed and Thu. Enquiries:
Estate Office, Mapledurham, Reading
RG4 7TR. *(tel Kidmore End 3350)*. *(Mr J J*
Eyston) ✍ B

Mapledurham Watermill Last working corn
and grist mill on the Thames. Wheel, gearing
and stones restored and used for grinding
wholemeal flour which can be purchased.
Open 6 Apr to 28 Sep Sat, Sun and BH
2.30–5.30 also Tue, Wed and Thu 2–4.30.
Party 20+ as Mapledurham House. Visit the
Mill by river launch from Caversham Bridge,
details from the Estate Office as above.

MARAZION *Cornwall* Map 2 SW52
St Michael's Mount Offshore in Mount's Bay,
reached on foot over causeway, or by ferry
during summer only. Well-situated island-
castle, with 14th-C chapel and collection of
armour, pictures, and furniture. Open Nov to
31 Mar Mon, Wed and Fri, guided tours at 11,
12, 2, 3 and 4; 1 Apr to end May Mon, Wed
and Fri 10.30–5.45 (last admission 4.45); Jun
to Oct, Mon to Wed and Fri, guided tours from
10.30–4.45; £1 (ch 50p) Mar to May special
educational visits by prior arrangements, Tue
only. *(Tel 710507)*. *(NT)*. *(NGS)*

MARGATE *Kent* Map 5 TR37
Salmestone Grange Nash Road. A restored
Medieval Monastic Grange 14th-C with
Monk's Kitchen and Crypt-cellar also 'Jewel'
Chapel (1326) with stained-glass windows by
the Australian John Trinick between
1949–59. Open Easter weekend and
thereafter 1 May to 1 Sep Sat 2–5. 10p. Other
times by appointment with the Warden. ⚠
(Tel Thanet 21136) ✍
Tudor House King Street. The oldest
domestic building in Margate dating from
early 16th C, displaying heavily moulded
beams, and an enriched plaster ceiling in an
excellent state of preservation. Housed here
is a small local history museum including a
fine collection of foreign sea shells. Open mid
May to mid Sep, daily (ex Sun) 10–12.30,
2–4.30. Free. ⚠ *(Tel Thanet 25511 ext 333)*

MARKET BOSWORTH *Leicestershire*
Map 4 SK40
Market Bosworth Light Railway 5m NW on
unclass road at Shackerstone Station.
Regular train service from Shackerstone to
Market Bosworth, mainly steam operated.
Extensive railway museum of small relics and
collection of rolling stock on view. ⚏ Easter
to Nov, Sun and BH, ⚠ Enquiries and
bookings *(Tel Atherstone 3966)* ✍

MARKET DEEPING *Lincolnshire*
Map 8 TF11
Rectory Dates from 13th to 14th C and is said
to be oldest inhabited parsonage in country.
Retains original hall, carved beams, and
monks' dormitory. Possibly refectory of
former Abbey. Open any day after 11am
when residents are at home. 25p. ⚠ *(Tel*
342237). *(Mrs Kathleen Davies)* ✍ B

MARKET HARBOROUGH *Leicestershire*
Map 4 SP79
Langton Hall 4½m NW at West Langton off
B6047. Small English country house dating

from 15th and 16th C. Contains fine collection of Chinese furniture and ornaments, also interesting French and English pieces. Garden laid-out in French style. ♨. Open Easter to Oct, Sat, Sun and BH 2–5. 75p (ch 14 and pen 40p), subject to review for 1980. ⚠ *(Tel East Langton 240 or 435)* ♿ B

MARSTON *Lincolnshire* Map 8 SK94
Marston Hall Tudor manor house with early 18th-C interior containing pictures and furniture. Thorold family have held the estate since 14th C and church contains Thorold tombs. Garden with fine trees and gazebo decorated by Barbara Jones. Open on certain Sun in aid of local causes (times to be announced in local press) and at other times by appointment. ⚠ *(Tel Hannington 225). (The Rev H Thorold)* ♿

MARTIN MERE *Lancashire* Map 7 SD41
Wildfowl Trust W of A59 at Burscough Bridge station towards Mere Brow. Comprises a waterfowl garden, wild marsh and mere. The waterfowl garden covers some 40 acres, with pens, lakes and paddocks in which can be seen a large number of tame and flying wildfowl from all parts of the world. The wild marsh consists of 262 acres of wet land on which the habitat has been improved. Here many species of indigenous birds can be seen in their completely natural state, and here also 10–15,000 pink footed geese may settle during the winter months. The mere is a large man-made lake of about 20 acres. Both the wild marsh and the mere are viewable from hides. Also of interest is the main entrance building, the largest log cabin in Britain, constructed of Norwegian log with a grass roof, where the geese are free to graze. ♨. Open all year, daily (ex 24, 25 Dec) 9.30–6.30, or 15 min after dusk (whichever is earlier). Last admission 1 hour before closing. 80p (ch 40p, pen 65)p Party 20+. ⚠ ♿ *(Tel Burscough 895181)*

MARWELL *Hampshire* Map 4 SU52
Marwell Zoological Park Colden Common. Opened in May 1972, it is now established as one of Britain's major wild animal collections. In 100 acres of spacious enclosures, groups of rare animals thrive and breed. These include Siberian Tigers, leopards, snow-leopards, jaguars, lynx, cheetah, Asian lions and many species of deer, antelope, zebra, Przewalski wild horses, camels, giraffes, monkeys and many other species of mammals and birds. More than 1,000 animals from over 100 species. New exhibits constantly being added. Free children's zoo. ♨. Picnic areas. Open all year daily 10–5.30 (or dusk). £1 (ch and pen 60p). Cars £1 extra if brought into park. ⚠ outside park. Party. Prices under revision for 1979. *(Tel Owslebury 206)* **(79)**

MARYPORT *Cumbria* Map 11 NY03
Maritime Museum Shipping Brow, 1 Senhouse Street. Maritime models and artifacts of all kinds. Photographic display illustrating Maryport's history. Open all year, 1 Jun to 30 Sep Mon to Sat 10–5 (closed 1–2 Tue and Thu), Sun 2–5; 1 Oct to 31 May Tue to Sat 10–12, 2–4, (closed Sun and Mon). Free. P. *(Tel 3738)*

MATLOCK *Derbyshire* Map 8 SK36
Riber Castle Fauna Reserve Castle dates from 1862, and fauna reserve of more than 20 acres on 853ft-high Riber Hill contains comprehensive collection of European birds and animals in near-natural surroundings. Breeding colonies of European Lynx. Kittens

can be seen Jun to Sep. Large collection of domestic poultry and rare breeds of bulls, sheep, pigs, cattle and goats. Models of prehistoric animals, model railway, vintage cars, children's playground. Butterfly exhibition. ♨ (licensed) in season, picnic area. Open all year, daily (ex 25 Dec) 10–7 (4, in winter). 70p (ch and pen 35p, ch 5 free. Admission prices under revision for 1980. N dogs except in car park. ⚠ *(Tel 2073)* ♿

MATLOCK BATH *Derbyshire* Map 8 SK25
Peak District Mining Museum The Pavilli The history of the Derbyshire lead industry. The museum illustrates the many facets of industry including geology, lead mining and miners, lead smelting, mining and quarryin today, by means of static and moving displa and an audio-visual programme. Also a unique early 19th-C water pressure pumpin engine – the only one of its kind in the Britis Isles. Open all year (ex 25 Dec) 11–4 (long in season). 60p (ch 16, pen and students 30p). P. *(Tel Matlock 3834)*

MAWNAN SMITH *Cornwall* Map 2 SW72
Glendurgan Beautifully situated gardens near Helford River inlet on road to Helford Passage. Walled garden and also maze. Open Mar to end Sep Mon and Wed (also F Apr to May) 10.30–4.30. 60p *(NT)*

MELBOURNE *Derbyshire* Map 8 SK32
Melbourne Hall 8m S of Derby.
The Derbyshire home of the Marquess of Lothian. Lord Melbourne, the great Prime Minister lived here, and Lady Palmerston inherited it. The contents include an import collection of pictures and antique furniture . One of the most famous formal gardens in Britain. Garden produce on sale. Shop. ♨. Open 5 Apr to 28 Sep, Apr, May, Jun and S Wed, Thu and Sun 2–6. BH weekends Sat Tue also 5 May and BH Mon 11–6. Jul and Aug, daily (ex Mon and Fri). Last admission 5pm. Party 30+. ⚠. For further information contact the Secretary, Tue, Thu and Fri mornings. *(Tel 2502)* ♿ B

MELTON MOWBRAY *Leicestershire*
Map 8 SK71
Melton Carnegie Museum Thorpe End. N museum illustrating past and present life of the area. Open all year (ex 4 Apr, 25, 26 De Mon to Sat 10–5, Sun 2–5. *(Tel 69946)* ♿

MERSHAM *Kent* Map 5 TR03
Swanton Mill The restored mill won the 19 European Architectural Heritage Year Awa Mill can be seen working, with flour on sale Exhibition on top floor. Also water garden. Open Apr to Oct, Sat and Sun 3–6. 30p (ch 20p). Under revision for 1980. *(Tel Aldingt 223 or 01-937 0931)*

MEVAGISSEY *Cornwall* Map 2 SX04
Folk Museum East Quay. Occupying old boatbuilders' workshop dating from 1745, specialises in local crafts, seafaring, agricultural and mining items. Monthly exhibitions on loan from Plymouth Art Galle Open Easter to end of May from 1 Jun to er Sep from 10.30am. Admission prices not y decided for 1980. P (limited) on quay. *(Tel 3568)*
Model Railway British, Continental and American models run through a realistic layout which features urban and rural areas an Alpine ski resort with cablecars and a Cornish china clay pit with refining plant. Other models are on display together with information about the china clay industry . Model shop. Open end May to end Sep 11.

m during High Season); Oct to May, Sun
ly 2–5. 50p (ch 35p). Admission charges
1980 not yet decided. P. *(Tel 2457)* &

CKLETON *Gloucestershire* Map 4 SP14
dcote Manor ½m SE. 17th-C Cotswold
use with fine formal gardens within various
ecies of hedges. ⚑ until end Sep. Gardens
ly open Apr to end Oct, daily (ex Tue and
) 11–8 (no entry after 7pm, or 1 hour before
nset). £1.10. No dogs. *(NT)*
tsgate Court Garden ½m S off A46,
jacent Hidcote NT garden. Magnificently
uated house with fine views and trees. The
rden has many unusal plants and shrubs,
d an exceptional collection of old fashioned
d specie roses including R Filipes
tsgate, the largest rose in England. Open 1
r to 30 Sep Wed, Thu and Sun including BH
6. 70p (ch 20p) ⚠ *(Tel 202) (Mrs D H
nny)*

DDLE CLAYDON *Buckinghamshire*
ap 4 SP72
aydon House Off A413. Entrance by North
ive only. Fine mid 18th-C west façade by Sir
omas Robinson, notable rococo and
inese interior decoration, state rooms with
ghtfoot carvings, Joseph Rose ceiling in
loon, notable staircase, and Florence
ghtingale bedroom, and museum. Concerts
en there at times. Open Apr to end Oct,
ily 2–6 (ex Mon, Fri and Tue following BH,
t open BH Mon) 12.30–6. 90p *(Tel Steeple
aydon 349).* (NT)

DDLEHAM *North Yorkshire* Map 7 SE18
ddleham Castle 12th-C former seat of the
villes, with two-storeyed keep standing
hin 13th-C curtain walls. Open, see inside
nt cover. 15p (ch 16 and pen 5p). ⚠ *(AM)*

DDLESBROUGH *Cleveland* Map 8 NZ42
ptain Cook Birthplace Museum 3m S on
72 at Stewart Park, Marton. Open Oct 1978
mark the 250th anniversary of Cook's birth
Marton in 1728. Situated in spacious rolling
rkland. Other attractions include an aviary
colourful parakeets including many rare
eeds, a conservatory of tropical plants, and
sorted animals and fowl in small paddocks.
Open summer 10–6, winter 9–4. Free.
el 311211)

DHURST *West Sussex* Map 4 SU82
wdray Ruins Ruined mansion, built 1520
d burnt 1793, in which Queen Elizabeth I
yed in 1591. Three-storeyed gatehouse,
ll and chapel are notable. Open most days.
–dusk. 20p. *(Tel 2215)* &

MILDENHALL *Suffolk* Map 5 TL77
Mildenhall Museum Market Place. The
museum illustrates local archaeology,
agricultural implements, local and natural
history. Open all year Wed, Sat and Sun
2.30–4.30. Free. P. *(Tel 712162)*

MILTON *Oxfordshire* Map 4 SU49
Milton Manor House 17th-C house with
18th-C wings and a walled garden. ⚑ by
arrangement. Open Easter then Sat, Sun and
BH till 12 Oct, 2–6. 70p (ch 14 30p). Party. ⚠
*(Tel Abingdon 831287). (Surgeon Capt and
Mrs E J Mockler)* & B

MILTON ABBAS *Dorset* Map 3 ST80
Brewery Farm Museum A country museum
housed in the building of the Old Brewery of
Milton Abbas. Contains agricultural
implements of the past, bygones and a
collection of old photographs. Open all year
daily dawn–dusk. 10p (ch 14 5p). ⚠ *(Tel
880221)* (79)

MILTON LILBOURNE *Wiltshire* Map 4 SU15
Milton Manor Gardens Gardens only open
May to end Oct Wed 2–6. Free. ⚠ Antique
business. *(Tel Pewsey 3344). (Mrs Rupert
Gentle)* &

MINEHEAD *Somerset* Map 3 SS94
West Somerset Railway Steam and railcar
trains run to various points Minehead,
Watchet and Bishops Lydeard. Souvenir
shops at many stations. ⚑ at Minehead.
Services all year. Steam trains in summer
months. Return tickets range from 90p to
£2.50 (reductions for families, parties, ch and
pen). Special coach link between Taunton
(town centre or railway station) and Bishops
Lydeard provided on Sats. ⚠ *(Tel 4996)* &
(24hr min notice)

MINIONS *Cornwall* Map 2 SX27
Hurlers Stone Circle Off B3254. Line of
three prehistoric stone circles with large
round barrow nearby. Accessible at any
reasonable time. Free. *(AM)*

MINSTEAD *Hampshire* Map 4 SU21
Furzey Gardens Eight acres peaceful glades
with winter and summer heathers, flowering
trees and shrubs, many of which are rare,
spring bulbs. Of botanical interest throughout
the year. Also ancient cottage (1560) now
restored, with art and craft gallery, where the
crafts of 50 artists and 100 local craftsmen are
displayed. Open all year daily 10–7 (dusk in
winter). Gardens, cottage and gallery 50p (ch
5–14 20p), Mar to Oct; 30p (ch 5–14 10p),
Nov to Feb. Admission prices for 1980 not yet
decided. Party 30+. ⚠ *(Tel Cadnam 2464).
(Mr H J Cole). (NGS)* & B

MINSTER-IN-THANET *Kent* Map 5 TR36
Minster Abbey One of the oldest inhabited
houses in Kent with some 11th-C work. Now
home of religious order. Gift shop. Open all
year daily (ex Sun) 11–12, also 1 May to 1
Oct, Mon to Fri 2–4.30, Sat 3.30–5. ⚠ &

MINSTER LOVELL *Oxfordshire* Map 4 SP31
Minster Lovell Hall Ruined 15th-C structure
associated with two strange legends
including the Mistletoe Bough Chest.
Accessible any reasonable time. Free. ⚠
(AM)

MINTERNE MAGNA *Dorset* Map 3 ST60
Minterne House 10m N of Dorchester. Large
shrub garden set in a beautiful valley. Many
varieties of Himalayan and Chinese
rhododendrons, magnolias, azaleas and rare
trees. Open Sun and BH in Apr, May and Jun,
also by appointment for parties on weekdays.
2–7. 40p. ⚠ *(Tel Cerne Abbas 370). (Lord
Digby)*

MISTLEY *Essex* Map 5 TM13
Mistley Towers Twin, square porticoed
towers, remaining features of church erected
originally by Robert Adam *c* 1776. Of hall,
built about the same time, only Adam lodges
of 1782 still stand. Towers accessible all
reasonable times. Free. *(AM)*

MONTACUTE *Somerset* Map 3 ST41
Montacute House Elizabethan house, built
1588–1601, from Ham Hill stone by Edward
Phelips. Fine old glass, and panelling.
Permanent collection of Tudor and Jacobean
portraits from the National Portrait Gallery, on
view in Long Gallery. Shop, information
rooms. ⚑ Apr to Sep. Open Apr to Oct, daily
(ex Tue) 12.30–6, last admission to house
5.30. Party by written appointment with the
Administrator. £1.20 (ch 60p). Dogs in car
park only. *(Tel Martock 3289). (NT)*

MORDIFORD *Hereford & Worcester*
Map 3 SO53
Sufton Court Small Paladian mansion
designed by James Wyatt. Completed *c* 1780.
Exquisite mouldings, fireplaces and doors.
Antique china, lace, embroideries and water-
colours. Park and grounds by Humphrey
Repton. ⚑ (home-made teas usually
available, advisable to book 75p). Open 1
May to 30 Sep Sun only and BH Mon
2.30–5.30. 50p (ch half price). ⚠ *(Tel Holme
Lacy 268)* & B

MORECAMBE *Lancashire* Map 7 SD46
Marineland Oceanarium and Aquarium
Stone Jetty, Promenade. During the summer
season there are several dolphin and sea lion
shows daily. On show a unique display of
mink, also penguins, turtles, aligators.

Tropical, fresh and marine fish, cold water,
fresh and marine fish. Open summer daily
10.30 am. Winter months; Europe's No. 1
Aquarium only, open weekends only 11–4.
Admission prices for 1979 not yet decided.
(Tel 414727) **(79)**

MORETON CORBET *Salop* Map 7 SJ52
Castle Triangular group comprising keep o
c 1200, gatehouse altered in 1579, and
notable Elizabethan range of the same date
the work of Sir Andrew Corbet, all damaged
by Parliamentary forces in 1644. Open, see
inside front cover. Free. ⚠ *(AM)*

MORVAH *Cornwall* Map 2 SW43
Lanyon Quoit 4m NW of Penzance, off
B3306. In field to right of unclassified road
beyond Madron. Famous Neolithic sepulch
monument, comprising large granite
capstone balanced on three upright stones
Re-erected during the 19th C. Accessible
regularly. Free. *(NT)*

MORWELLHAM *Devon* Map 2 SX46
Morwellham Open-air Museum Off A390
between Tavistock and Gunnislake. A
riverside tramway going underground into a
ancient copper mine is only one of the many
attractions of Morwellham, once the 'Great
Copper Port in Queen Victoria's Empire'.
Unspoilt country, riverside and woodland
trails, slide shows and other exhibits will hel
you to discover 1,000 years of history. A tru
fascinating experience. Open all year, daily
10–6 (dusk in winter). £1.10 (ch 55p). Party
Under revision for 1980. ⚠ *(Tel Gunnislake
832766)*

MOSELEY *Staffordshire* Map 7 SJ90
Moseley Old Hall Built in Elizabethan time
as half-timbered house, now encased in 19
C brick, with interesting panelled rooms. W
the refuge (hiding hole and bed) of Charles
after Battle of Worcester in 1651. Open Ma
Oct, Wed, Thu, Sat, Sun, BH Mon and Tue
2–5.30 (or sunset), Nov, Wed and Sun
2–5.30. 70p. No dogs. *(NT)*

MONTACUTE
HOUSE

4 miles west of Yeovil,
Somerset

Tudor mansion of glowing Hamstone, containing National Portrait Gallery's
collection of Court Paintings. Cream teas. Lunches in Montacute Village.
See gazetteer for details.

MOTTISFONT *Hampshire* Map 4 SU32

Mottisfont Abbey Mainly 18th-C mansion with portions of former 12th-C priory. Fine Rex Whistler paintings in drawing room. Walled rose garden. Open Apr to end Sep, grounds daily (ex Sun and Mon) 2.30 – 6. House (Whistler Room and Cellarium) Wed and Sat 2.30 – 6. 80p; grounds only 60p. *(NT)*

MOULTON *North Yorkshire* Map 8 NZ20

Moulton hall Manor house rebuilt *c*1650. Fine example of carved wood staircase. Open only by appointment in writing from tenant, *Hon J D Eccles.* Free. *(NT)*

MUCHELNEY *Somerset* Map 3 ST42

Muchelney Abbey 15th- to 16th-C remains of Benedictine Abbey. Open, see inside front cover. 15p (ch 16 and pen 5p). ⚠ *(AM)*

MUCH WENLOCK *Salop* Map 7 SO69

Guildhall Striking half-timbered building dating from 1577, with beautiful oak panelling and furnishings. Open 1 Apr to 30 Sep, Mon, Tue and Thu to Sat 11 – 12.30 and 2.30 – 5, Wed 3 – 5, Sun 2 – 6, BH 10.30 – 12.30, 2.30 – 4.30, and 6 – 8. 20p (ch 16 10p). Party. P. *(Tel 727509)*

Much Wenlock Museum An interpretation of the history of the town and priory, including displays of geology, local natural history, costume and local trades, housed in the old Market hall. Regular special exhibitions and demonstrations. Comprehensive book stand. Open 20 Mar to 1 Oct, Mon to Sat, 11 – 12.30 and 2 – 5, Sun 2 – 6. 15p (ch 5p). Under revision for 1980. P. *(Tel 727773)* ⓕ

Wenlock Priory Remains of 13th-C abbey adjacent to chapter house, lavabo, and transepts. Only abbey ruins are open, see inside front cover. 20p (ch 16 and pen 5p). ⚠ *(AM)*

MULLION *Cornwall* Map 2 SW61

Marconi Memorial Erected in 1937 by Marconi Company to commemorate first morse signal sent across Atlantic in 1901 and received by Marconi himself in Newfoundland. Short-wave beam system was successfully tested here for first time in 1923. Accessible regularly. *(NT)*

MUNCASTER *Cumbria* Map 6 SD19

Muncaster Castle and Bird Garden Seat of Pennington since 13th C. Famous collection of rhododendrons, azaleas, etc, ornamental and tropical birds, bear garden with Himalayan bears, flamingo pool, garden centre. Collection of 16th- and 17th-C furniture, pictures, and embroideries. ⓣ gift shop. Nature Trail. Open from Easter weekend for 1980 season. Grounds daily (ex Fri) 12 – 5, Castle Tue, Wed, Thu and Sun 2 – 5, Castle Tue, Wed, Thu and Sun 2 – 5. Admission prices not yet known. ⚠ *(Tel Ravenglass 614). (Sir W Pennington-Ramsden)* ⓕ

Muncaster Mill 1m NW on A595 by railway bridge. The mill race brings water from the River Mite ¾m to the 13ft overshot water wheel. Milling Room contains three pairs of mill stones, two elevators, flour separators, and sackhoist, all water driven. Newly opened Fish Farm. Flour milled on premises for sale. Open Easter to end Sep, daily (ex Sat) 11 – 6. 20p (ch 10p). Under revision for 1980.

MUNDESLEY *Norfolk* Map 9 TG33

Stow Mill Built in 1780 and in use for grinding corn until about 1920. At one time converted to residential use, but eventually restored in 1961. Open May to Sep. Free. P. *(Tel 720298)*

NANTWICH *Cheshire* Map 7 SJ65

Dorfold Hall 1m W, off A51. Attractive gabled house, dating from 1616, with fine panelling, plaster ceilings, and furniture. Open Apr to Oct Tue only, also BH Mon, at other times by appointment. 2 – 5. 50p (ch 16 25p). ⚠ *(Tel 65245)*

Churche's Mansion Hospital Street. An H-plan half-timbered mansion built in 1577 for Rychard and Margerye Churche. Restoration commenced in 1930 and continues to reveal the original fabric. ⓣ Licensed. Open Apr to Oct 10 – 5.30. 25p (ch 16 20p). ⚠ *(Tel 65933)*

NASEBY *Northamptonshire* Map 4 SP67

Naseby Battle and Farm Museum Purlieu Farm. Contains miniature layout of Battlefield with commentary and relics from the field, village history, farm hand tools and machinery. Vintage Tractors. Open Easter to Sep, Sat and Sun 2 – 6. 35p (ch 16 20p). ⚠ *(Tel Northampton 740241)*

NETHER ALDERLEY *Cheshire* Map 7 SJ87

Alderley Old Mill 15th-C mill, last worked in 1939. Preserves wooden waterwheels and machinery. Open Apr, May, Jun and Oct, Wed, Sun 2 – 5.30. Jul – Sep, daily ex Mon but open BH Mon 2 – 5.30. 50p *(NT)*

NETHER STOWEY *Somerset* Map 3 ST13

Coleridge Cottage Home of Samuel Taylor Coleridge from 1897 to 1800. *The Ancient Mariner* was written here. Open Apr to end Sep, Sun to Thu 2 – 5. 30p. Parties by arrangement with caretaker, *Mrs MacDermaid (Tel 662). (NT)*

NETHER WINCHENDON *Buckinghamshire* Map 4 SP71

Nether Winchendon House Medieval house with Elizabethan and Georgian additions, containing portraits and maps belonging to Sir Francis Bernard, Governor of Massachusetts. Open Thu 2 – 6; Spring and Summer BH 2 – 5.30. Parties 10+ by written appointment May to Aug. £1 (ch 12 and pen 50p). P. *(Tel Hadenham 290101). (Mrs J G C Spencer Bernard)* ⓕ B

NETLEY *Hampshire* Map 4 SU40

Netley Abbey Extensive and beautiful remains of a Cistercian abbey founded in 1239. Open, see inside front cover. 15p (ch 16 and pen 5p). ⚠ *(AM)*

NETTLECOMBE COURT *Somerset* Map 3 ST03

Elizabethan and Georgian house, the ancestral home of the Raleigh and Trevelyan families. Two Adam-type drawing rooms. Open for viewing Mar to Oct Thu, by appointment. 25p to 50p. ⚠ *(Tel Washford 320).* Houses the Leonard Wills Field Centre operated by the Field Studies Council open Feb to Nov. One week residential courses on various topics connected with the countryside are available. Programme of courses available (free) from warden.

NEWARK-ON-TRENT *Nottinghamshire* Map 8 SK85

Newark District Council Museum Local history, archaeology, natural history, and art. Open all year Mon to Sat 10 – 1 and 2 – 5 (closed Thu afternoons). Sun 2 – 5 (Apr to Sep only). Free. P *(Tel 702358)*

NEWBURGH PRIORY *North Yorkshire* Map 8 SE57

Originally an Augustinian Priory with 17th- and 18th-C additions. Wild water garden. ⓣ Open 10 May to 13 Sep, Wed 2 – 5.30, other days for parties by arrangement. 40p (ch 20p), grounds only 15p (ch 5p). ⚠ No coaches up 200yd drive.

NEWBURY *Berkshire* Map 4 SU46
The Museum (Old Cloth Hall) Wharf St. Restored timbered and plastered building, with fine Jacobean woodwork. Now interesting museum with prehistoric finds and Civil War relics. Natural history section. Camera collection, temporary exhibitions. Open all year, weekdays (ex Wed afternoon and BH) 10–12.30 and 1.30–5 (4, Oct to Mar). Free. No dogs. △ *(Tel 30511)* ♿ B

NEWBY HALL AND GARDENS *North Yorkshire* Map 8 SE36
Late 17th-C house with additions and interior by Robert Adam. Contains important collection of classical sculpture and Gobelin tapestries. Gardens cover 25 acres and includes a miniature railway. ☕ Opening dates, times and admission charges for 1979 not yet decided. △ *(Tel Boroughbridge 2583). (R E J Compton Esq)* ♿ **(79)**

NEWCASTLE-UNDER-LYME *Staffordshire* Map 7 SJ84
Borough Museum Brampton Park. Local history, including Royal Charters, ceramics, natural history, dolls and display of firearms. Open all year Mon to Sat 9.30–1 and 2–6 (5.30 Sat), May to Sep, Sun also 2–5.30. Free. △ *(Tel 619705)*
Hobbergate Art Gallery The Brampton Permanent collection of 18th- and 19th-C English water-colours. Travelling exhibitions and picture loan scheme. Open all year Tue to Sat 9.30–1, 2–6. △ *(Tel 611962)*

NEWCASTLE UPON TYNE *Tyne and Wear* Map 12 NZ26
Bagpipe Museum Black Gate, St Nicholas Street. Presented by Mr William Cocks of Ryton, Co Durham, to city's Society of Antiquaries. Among over 100 sets are English, Scottish, Irish, European, and Egyptian pipes, and an English Shepherd's pipe (1690) which may be unique. Other exhibits include old recordings, music and transcripts. Open all year Wed to Sat 12–4. 15p (ch 5p). P (meters). *(Tel 27938)*
Hancock Museum Barras Bridge. One of finest natural history museums in England. Other collections include geological specimens, insects, birds and Bewick drawings. Open all year (ex 4 Apr, 25, 26 Dec, 1 Jan) Mon to Sat 10–5, Sun (from 2 Apr to 24 Sep) 2–5. 20p (ch 10p). P. *(Tel 22359)*
Museum of Antiquities University Quadrangle. The collection has been in course of assembly since 1813, and was opened in its present form in 1960. Valuable collection of Roman and other antiquities, with models, reconstructions, etc. Open all year (ex 4 Apr, 24–26 Dec, and 1 Jan), weekdays 10–5. Free. P (consult University police). *(Tel 28511 ext 3844/3849)* ♿
Science Museum Exhibition Park. Develpment of mining, shipbuilding, engineering in the North East. Models of locally built ships, collieries and their equipment, etc. Extensive electrical engineering collections. One of Stephenson's earliest locomotives is preserved, and also steam yacht 'Turbinia' (1894), pioneer turbine propelled ship. ☕ in park open during summer months. Open all year (ex 13 Apr, 25, 26 Dec, 1 Jan) 1 Apr to 30 Sep Mon to Sat 10–6, Sun 2–5, 1 Oct–31 Mar Mon–Sat 10–4.30, Sun 1.30–4.30. Free. P. *(Tel 815129)* **(79)**

NEWCHAPEL *Surrey* Map 5 TQ34
Mormon Temple Visitors Centre and Gardens Pictures, films, genealogy assistance. Beautiful gardens. Open all year, daily 10–dusk. Free. △ *(Tel Lingfield 833842)* ♿

NEWENT *Gloucestershire* Map 3 SO72
The Birds of Prey Conservation and Falconry Centre Leave Newent by Cliffords Mesne Road. At foot of May Hill, has wide variety of trained birds and an interesting museum. Of special interest are Hawk Walk, aviaries, and falcon flying ground. Courses in falconry are held. Also displays and flying demonstrations. ☕ Open Feb to end Nov, daily (ex Tue) 10.30–5.30 (or dusk); Guided tours and reduced fees for parties of 25 or more. Schools especially welcome. 80p (ch 14 35p), prices subject to alteration and VAT. △ *(Tel 820286)* ♿

NEWPORT *Essex* Map 5 TL53
Mole Hall Wildlife Park Widdington. Partly Elizabethan, with moat crossed by four bridges. Wildlife Park dates from 1948 and was opened to the public 16 years later. Large collection of animals and birds in pools and enclosures can be seen. Picnic area. Open all year (ex 25 Dec) daily 10.30–6. Admission charges for 1980 not yet decided. Party. △ *(Tel Saffron Walden 40400)* ♿

NEWQUAY *Cornwall* Map 2 SW86
Newquay Zoo Trenance Park, on A3075. In over 8 acres of landscape grounds, laid out in 1969, is a fine selection of wild animals, tropical birds in a walk-through aviary, wild fowl, large walking birds, reptiles, seals and pengiun pools, pets' corner and pony rides. Gift shop and ☕. Open all year. 65p (ch and pen 32p, ch 4 free). Opening times and prices under revision for 1980. △ *(Tel 3342)* ♿

NETTLECOMBE COURT
Williton, Taunton
TA4 4HT

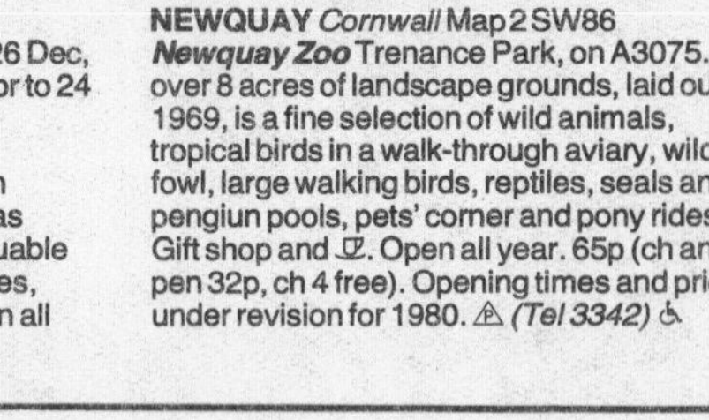

Nettlecombe Court is situated on the edge of the Brendon Hills in North-west Somerset (Grid Reference ST 057378). At present it is leased by the Field Studies Council and offers a wide range of residential week and weekend courses for amateur naturalists and artists. The programme, available from the Centre, includes courses on local history, churches, wild flowers and geology.

NEW ROMNEY *Kent* Map 5 TR02
Romney, Hythe and Dymchurch Railway
Depot of 13½-mile long Romney, Hythe and
Dymchurch railway, the world's smallest
public railway from Hythe through New
Romney to Dungeness. ⚏ at new Romney
and Dungeness stations. Open daily Easter to
end Sep, also weekends in Mar, Oct and Nov.
For times apply for timetable to *The Manager,
Romney, Hythe and Dymchurch Light
Railway Co, New Romney Station, New
Romney, Kent.* Also engine shed and very
large model railway exhibition. Open
whenever train service operates. Admission
prices dependent on journey (ch half price).
⚠ 12p. *(Tel 2353)* ㅎ B

NEWSTEAD *Nottinghamshire* Map 8 SK55
Newstead Abbey Former Priory, founded in
12th C, rebuilt as a house in the 16th and 17th
C, famous for its associations with Lord
Byron, who lived here, including pictures and
furniture. ⚏ (summer only). Open 13 Apr to
30 Sep 2 – 6 (6.30 Sun and BH), conducted
tours on weekdays at 2, 3, 4, and 5, garden
open daily, all year (ex 25 Dec) 10 – dusk.
Admission to grounds and garden 35p (ch
12p and pen coach parties 12p per person).
Additional charge for abbey tour 20p (ch and
pen 5p), coach parties 12p per person. ⚠ *(Tel
Blidworth 2822)* **(79)**

NEWTIMBER *West Sussex* Map 4 TQ21
Newtimber Place Moated 17th- to 18th-C
house with Etruscan-style decorations.
House and gardens open May, Jun, Jul, and
Aug, Thu 2 – 5. 50p (ch 25p). ⚠ *(Tel
Hurstpierpoint 833104). (His Honour Judge
and Mrs John Clay)*

NEWTON ABBOT *Devon* Map 3 SX87
Bradley Manor In deep valley of River
Lemon, 15th-C house with a fine hall and
chapel. Open 9 Apr to Sep, Wed 2–5. 60p. *(NT)*
*New Devon Pottery and Devon
Leathercrafts* Forde Road. Interesting tour to
see pottery and leather manufacture can be
made with guides. Picnic area available. ⚐
Open Easter to Oct, Mon to Fri 9.30–12 and
1.30–5 (last tours 12 and 4.30). Frequent
tours. 40p, joint ticket to visit both factories
50p (accompanied ch 14 free). Party 25+ 35p
single, 45p joint ticket. Reduction for pen to
end of May and all Oct. ⚠ *(Tel 4262)* & **(79)**
NORFOLK WILDLIFE PARK Norfolk
Map 9 TG11
Zoological park of 50 acres, with
comprehensive collection of British and
European mammals in natural surroundings.
Great variety of birds in specially built
aviaries. Rare ornamental pheasant Trust.
The world's largest European collection. ⚐
(licensed). Open all year, daily 10.30–6. £1
(ch 18 50p). Subject to alteration. ⚠ *(Tel
Great Witchingham 274). (Mr Philip Wayre,
Naturalist)* &
NORHAM *Northumberland* Map 12 NT94
Castle Mid 12th-C keep, built by Bishop Hugh
Puiset, with later alterations, and overlooking
River Tweed. Open, see inside front cover.
15p (ch 16 and pen 5p). *(AM)*
NORTHAMPTON *Northamptonshire*
Map 4 SP76
Abington Park Landscaped park,
ornamental gardens and collection of
ornamental and game birds. Seasonal games
facilities including bowls and pitch-and-putt.
Venue of Northampton Show third weekend
in Jul. Within park stands 15th- to 18th-C
house, now a museum. ⚐ (Apr to Oct). Open
all year (ex Sun, Oct to Mar; 24–26 Dec),
weekdays 10–12.30, and 2–6, Sun 2.30–5.
Free. P (street). *(Tel 31454)* & B
Central Museum and Art Gallery Guildhall
Road. Archaeological and geological
exhibits, as well as collections of footwear and
ceramics. Iron age discoveries from nearby
Hunsbury Hill camp are also on display. Open
weekdays 10–6 (closed Sun, 4 Apr, 24, 25,
26 Dec). Free. P. *(Tel 34881 ext 397)* & B
Delapre Abbey 16th- to 19th-C house, with
fine porch, built on site of Cluniac nunnery.
Contains Northamptonshire Record Office
and HQ of Northamptonshire Record Society.
Abbey grounds open all year Oct to Apr,
2.30–4.30; May to Sep 2.30–6. Wall garden,
open May to Sep only during daylight. Certain
parts of the interior shown Thu afternoon
2.30–4.30, Oct to Apr; 2.30–5, May to Sep.
Free. ⚠ &

Eleanor Cross Hardingstone (on southern
outskirts of the city). One of the crosses
erected by Edward I in memory of his dead
Queen Eleanor on her last journey to
Westminster Abbey. Commenced in 1291,
this cross is octagonal in design. Located on
side of road, easily accessible at all times.
NORTHBOROUGH *Cambridgeshire*
Map 4 TF10
Northborough Castle One of the finest
medieval houses in England, built in 1330 by
William de Eyton. Great Hall with original
timbered roof, beautiful windows and stone
carved doorways, also Lady Claypole's
Room, the Solar and Cromwell's Room.
James Claypole was a friend of William Penn
and a signatory of the first Charter of Liberties
to Pennsylvania. David Claypole, of the firm
Dunlap and Claypole, printed the Declaration
of Independence, 1776. Open 1 May to 1 Oct,
Sun 2–6. 20p(ch 5p). ⚠
NORTH CREAKE *Norfolk* Map 9 TF83
Creake Abbey 1m N off B1355. Ruins of the
crossing and eastern arm of the church of a
house of Augustinian canons founded in
1206. Accessible any reasonable time. Free.
(AM)
NORTHIAM *East Sussex* Map 5 TQ82
Brickwall ½m S. Three-gabled, half-timbered
Jacobean house, now a school, dating from
1617 and 1632 with Victorian alterations and
additions. 17th-C stucco ceiling to be seen in
drawing room (only part of house open to
public). Open 30 Apr to 21 May and 4 Jun to 9
Jul, inclusive, Wed and Sat only 2–4. 30p. ⚠
Great Dixter 15th-C half-timbered house with
notable great hall, and fine gardens. Picnics.
Open 1 Apr to 12 Oct also 18/19 and 25/16
Oct. Tue to Sun and BH Mon 2–5; other times
by appointment. £1 (ch 14 30p). Gardens only
50p (ch 15p). Prices are provisional for 1980.
No dogs. ⚠ *(Tel 3160). (Mr Quentin Lloyd)* &
B

NORTH LEIGH *Oxfordshire* Map 4 SP31
North Leigh Roman Villa Excavations of
Roman villa occupied between 2nd and 4th C
and reconstructed late in period. Tessellated
pavement and 2–3ft high wall span. Open,
see inside front cover. Free. ⚠ *(AM)*
NORTH LEVERTON *Nottinghamshire*
Map 8 SK78
Windmill ½m W of village in minor road. In
1813 the local farming community set up a
committee to build the four-sailed tower mill
which has been in use ever since. Steam
threshing tackle. Open Sun and BH 2–5,
other times by appointment. 10p (ch 5p, ch 5
free). ⚠ *(Tel Sturton le Steeple 200)* & **(79)**

NORTHWICH *Cheshire* Map 7 SJ67
Vale Royal Abbey constructed around the
Monastery of 1277, which survives the Abbey
of the same name. Now under restoration and
partly in use as a Special Education Centre.
Beautiful beech-lined drive approach from the
south. Gardens available for picnics on
request. Open Apr to Sep, Sun 2–5. 50p (ch
16 20p). ⚠ 25p. *(Tel Sandiway 882777)*
Weaver Hall London Road. A permanent
exhibition on salt in Cheshire is on show at the
Headquarters of the County Museum
Service, together with a programme of
temporary exhibitions. Open all year (ex
Easter and all Mon also Tue following a BH,
25/26 Dec and 1 Jan) Tue to Sat 10–12, 1–5.
Sun 2–5. Free. Under revision for 1980. ⚠
(Tel 41331/2)
NORTH WOOTTON *Somerset* Map 3 ST54
Wootton Vines North Town House. A
vineyard, set in the foothills of the Mendips,
3m from Wells, with 8,500 vines specially
imported from the Rhine and Alsace. The old
farm buildings house a winery where fresh dry
white wine is made. Visitors can walk in the
vineyards and wines may be purchased direct
from the cellar. Open all year, 2–5 (closed
Tue). ⚠ *(Tel Pilton 359)*
NORWICH *Norfolk* Map 5 TG20
Bridewell Bridewell Alley. Flint-faced late
14th-C merchant house, used as a prison
from 1583 to 1828. Now interesting museum
of local crafts and industries. Open all year (ex
4 Apr, 25, 26 Dec, 1 Jan) weekdays 10–5.
Free.
Norwich Castle Castle Meadow. Restored
12th-C keep with walls refaced 1834 to 1839,
now museum. ♨ (licensed). Conducted tours
of dungeons and battlements (fee payable).
Open all year (ex 4 Apr, 25, 26 Dec, 1 Jan)
weekdays 10–5, Sun 2–5. 45p (28 May to
Sep) other times 20p (ch and pen always
free). ⚠ ৬
City Hall St Peter Street. Opened 1938. On
display are the Civic Plate and Insignia dating
from 1549 and the Council Chamber. Open all
year Mon to Fri 10–4, parties by arrangement
with the *Director of Administration*. Free. P.
(Tel 22233 ext 743) ৬
Royal Norfolk Regiment Museum Brittania
Barracks, Brittania Road. Contains a fine
collection of medals, uniforms and weapons,
paintings, silver and trophies amassed by the
Regiment from 1685–1959. There is also an
excellent library containing books on many
military subjects. Open all year (ex Sat, Sun
and BH) 9–12.30, 2–4.30. Free. ⚠ *(Tel
28455)*
Sainsbury Centre for Visual Arts University
of East Anglia. Now houses Sir Robert and
Lady Sainsbury's private art collection which
was given to the University in 1973. The
collection is indexed under the following
headings: European Art 19th and 20th C;
African Tribal Sculpture; Oceanic Traditional
Sculpture; North American Indian and Eskimo
Art; Middle and South American
Precolumbian Art; Oriental Antiquities;
Egyptian and Western Asiatic Antiquities;
European Antiquities Medieval and later.
Varying other exhibitions during the year. ♨
(restaurant). Open all year Tue to Sun 12–5
(closed Mon). 25p ⚠ *(Tel 56060)* ৬
St Peter Hungate Church Museum Princes
Street, near Elm Hill. Fine church (1460), with
hammer-beam roof and good Norwich
painted glass, now museum of church art and
antiquities. Open all year (ex 4 Apr, 25, 26
Dec, 1 Jan) weekdays 10–5, Free.
Strangers' Hall Charing Cross. Late

medieval merchants' house dating from 1320
and later, with furnished period rooms from
early Tudor to late Victorian. Open all year (ex
4 Apr, 25, 26 Dec, 1 Jan) weekdays only
10–5. 20p, 26 May to Sep (ch free), other
times free. *(Tel 22233 ext 645)*

NOSTELL *West Yorkshire* Map 8 SE41
Nostell Priory Mid 18th-C mansion, built by
Paine in 1733, with Adam wing of 1766,
pictures and Chippendale furnishings,
notable saloon and tapestry room, collection
of old motor cycles. Lake in grounds. ♨ Open
Apr and Oct Wed, Sat, Sun 2–6, May to Sep
daily (ex Fri) 2–6, BH Sun, Mon and Tue
11–6. House, garden and grounds £1;
gardens and grounds only 50p. ⚠ *(NT)*

NOTTINGHAM *Nottinghamshire* Map 8 SK53
Brewhouse Yard Museum Castle
Boulevard. Housed in 17th-C buildings on a
historic site. The museum depicts daily life in
the City, with period rooms and thematic
displays on aspects of post medieval life in the
City. Unusual rock-cut cellars open showing
their uses in the past and recent history. This
museum contains material which can be
touched or operated by the public. Extensions
are planned for 1980. Open all year (ex
Christmas) 10–12 and 1–5. Free. *(Tel
411881 ext 67,48)* ৬ B
Holme Pierrepont Hall 4m E of Nottingham
off A52 1m beyond the National Water Sports
Centre. Early brick Tudor manor house of
medieval design built around 1500 and
contains fine old timbering. Contents are
mostly 17th-C English oak furniture of
regional design. Victorian formal courtyard
garden. Jacob and Soay sheep. ♨ for parties
by appointment. Open Apr and Sep Sun 2–6,
Jun, Jul and Aug Thu and Sun 2–6. Also 6–8
Apr, 26, 27 May, 25, 26 Aug 2–6. Parties
throughout the year by appointment. 50p (ch
25p). Admission prices under revision. ⚠ *(Tel
Radcliffe on Trent 2371)* ৬
Industrial Museum Courtyard Buildings,
Wollaton Park. Housed in 18th-C stable block
are displays illustrating Nottingham's
industrial history and in particular the lace and
hosiery industries, together with exhibits on
the pharmaceutical industry, engineering,
tobacco industry and printing. New
extensions house a mid 19th-C beam
pumping engine in steam last Sun in each
month and BH Mons, and heavy agricultural
machinery. Outside yards display a horse gin
from a local coalmine, Victorian street
furniture, etc. ♨ in park (Apr to Sep). Open all
year Apr to Sep, Mon to Sat 10–7, Sun 2–5;
Oct to Mar, Thu and Sat 10–4.30; Sun
1.30–4.30. Free. P. *(Tel 284602)*
Museum of Costume and Textiles 43–51
Castlegate. Displays include costume from
1730–1885 in furnished room settings of *c*
1790, *c* 1830, and *c* 1855; other rooms of
17th-C costume and embroidery (the Lord
Middleton Collection), map tapestries of
Nottinghamshire, dress accessories from
18th-C to *c* 1960, English, European and
Asian embroidery, hand and machine made
lace; other rooms in preparation. Open all
year (ex 25 Dec) daily 10–5. Free. P. *(Tel
411881)* ৬ B
Castle Museum Mainly 17th C, with much
restored late 13th-C gateway. Now museum
and art gallery. Conducted tours through
underground passages. Open all year (ex 25
Dec) summer 10–5.45, winter 4.45. Grounds
open all year (ex 25 Dec) Mon to Fri 8–dusk,
Sat, Sun, BH Mon 9–dusk. Free, ex Sun, BH
10p. ♨ Apr to Sep. P. *(Tel 411881)* ৬ B

Natural History Museum Wollaton Hall. Housed in imposing Elizabethan mansion by Robert Smythson, dating from 1580–88, and situated in large park with deer. ☕ Open all year (ex 25 Dec), weekdays 10–7 (5.30 Oct and Mar; 4.30 Nov to Feb); Sun, Mar to Oct 2–5; Nov to Feb 1.30–4.30. Free. ⚠ *(Tel 281333)*

NUNEATON *Warwickshire* Map 4 SP39
Nuneaton Museum and Art Gallery Riversley Park. A purpose-built structure, situated in a pleasant public park. It houses a permanent collection of ethnography, archaeology, the George Eliot Collection, and a display of fine miniatures painted by May B Lee (Lady Stott). Changing art exhibitions. From Apr to Jun the Nuneaton Festival of Art is held here. Open all year (ex 4 Apr, 25 Dec), summer Mon to Fri 12–7, Sat Sun 10–7 (closes 5 in winter). Times may be subject to alteration. Free. P. *(Tel 382683)*

NUNEHAM COURTENAY *Oxfordshire* Map 4 SU59
Nuneham House Thames-side Palladian villa (with additions by Brown and Smirke) in a picturesque setting created by 'Capability' Brown with a temple-church by 'Athenian' Stuart. State rooms unfurnished. Open 19, 20, 26–28 Aug, 2, 3 Sep 2–5.30. 40p (ch 20) Admission prices under review for 1979. ⚠ *(Tel Woodstock 811624)* ♿ **(79)**

NUNNEY *Somerset* Map 3 ST74
Nunney Castle Moated structure modelled on French 'Bastille', built by Sir John de la Mere in 1373. Held for king during civil war and surrendered after siege in 1645. Surrounded by one of the deepest moats in England. Open, see inside front cover. Free. *(AM)*

NUNNINGTON *North Yorkshire* Map 8 SE67
Nunnington Hall 16th- to 17th-C house with panelled hall and staircase. Open Apr to end Sep, (ex 4 Apr) Wed to Sun and BH Mon 2–6. 60p *(NT)*

OAKHAM *Leicestershire* Map 4 SK80
Oakham Castle Off Market Place. Preserves splendid Norman hall, with unique collection of presentation horseshoes. Open all year (ex 4 Apr, 25, 26 Dec) Apr to Oct, grounds daily 10–5.30; great hall, Sun and Mon 2–5.30, Tue to Sat and BH 10–1, 2–5.30; Nov to Mar as above but closes 4pm. Magistrates Court in session normally on Mondays. Free. P. *(Tel 3654)* ♿
Rutland County Museum Catmos Street. Local archaeology, especially Roman and Anglo-Saxon, craft tools, local history, Victorian shop. Court yard contains farm wagons and agricultural implements. Open all year (ex 4 Apr and 25, 26 Dec) Apr to Oct, Tue to Sat 10–1 and 2–5, Sun 2–5; Nov to Mar, Tue to Sat 10–1 and 2–5. Mon all year by arrangement. Free. P. *(Tel 3654)* ♿ B

OAKHILL *Somerset* Map 3 ST64
The World of Models at Oakhill Manor Entrance by 'Mendip Inn' on A37 A country estate of 45 acres situated high in the Mendip Hills. The mansion is a fine example of one of England's smaller country houses set in eight acres of delightful gardens. Features one of the world's finest collections of models relating to transport, displayed in a furnished setting. Visitors are transported from the car park on a miniature railway which covers ¾ mile with views of the surrounding hills. ☕ Open 12 Apr to 31 Oct, 12–6. Admission charges for 1980 not yet decided. ⚠ *(Tel 840210)* ♿ B

OAKWELL HALL *West Yorkshire* Map 8 SE22
In Nova Lane, near Birstall Smithies. Elizabethan moated manor house (1583), with Civil War and Brontë connections. It was 'Fieldhead' of Charlotte Brontë's novel *Shirley*. Open Apr to Oct, Tue to Sat 10–6, Sun 1–5; Nov to Mar, Tue to Sat 10–5. Free. ⚠

OKEHAMPTON *Devon* Map 2 SX59
Okehampton Castle ½m S in Castle Lane. Chapel, keep, and hall dating from 11th to 14th C on northern fringe of Dartmoor National Park. Open*, see inside front cover. 15p (ch and pen 5p). ⚠ *(AM)*

OLD WHITTINGTON *Derbyshire* Map 8 SK37
Revolution House Old house, once known as Cock and Pynot (or Magpie) Inn, with 17th-C furnishings. Associated with 1688 revolution. Open 13 Apr to 30 Sep, daily 11–12.30, 2–5 and 6–dusk. Opening times under revision for 1980. Free. ⚠ *(Tel Chesterfield 32088)* ♿

OLNEY *Buckinghamshire* Map 4 SP85
Cowper and Newton Museum House where William Cowper lived from 1768 to 1786, now containing manuscripts of letters and poems, together with many personal possessions. Two small gardens open to visitors to the museum. Open Easter to Oct, Tue to Sat 10–12 and 2–5; Nov to Easter, 2.30–4.30; other times by prior arrangement with Curator. 35p (ch and pen 25p, ch 5 free). Party 10+ *(Tel Bedford 711516)*

ORFORD *Suffolk* Map 5 TM44
Orford Castle On B1084. Castle with three towers, incorporating remarkable 18-sided keep, built by Henry II, c1165. Open, see inside front cover. 20p (ch and pen 5p). ⚠ *(AM)*

ORMESBY *Cleveland* Map 8 NZ51
Ormesby Hall 18th-C mansion, with stables attributed to John Carr of York. Plasterwork, furniture, and 18th-C pictures. Open Apr to end Oct, Wed, Sun and BH Mon 2–6. 60p *(NT)*

ORPINGTON *Gt London* Map 5 TQ46
Priory Museum Church Hill. 13th- to 14th-C clergy house with addition of 15th-C manor house. Now small museum of local interest, and special exhibitions are held during year: Open all year weekdays (ex Thu and Sun) 9–5.30, Sat 9–5. Free. ⚠ *(Tel 31551)* ⚕

OSMOTHERLEY *North Yorkshire* Map 8 SE49
Mount Grace Priory 1m NW. Ruined 14th-C Carthusian Priory, neighboured by 17th-C house. Priory open, see inside front cover. 20p (ch 5p). ⚠ *(AM and NT)*

OSWESTRY *Salop* Map 7 SJ23
Old Oswestry ½m N. Iron age hill-fort, covering 68 acres, with five ramparts and elaborate western portal. Abutted by part of prehistoric Wat's Dyke. Accessible any reasonable time. Free. *(AM)*

OTTERTON *Devon* Map 3 SY08
Otterton Mill A Devon cornmill, mentioned in the Domesday Book, making wholemeal flour by water power. Gallery with a series of exhibitions through the summer. Furniture making, wood turning, pottery, glass engraving, leatherwork and lace-making in our workshops. Shop and ⚐ Open Easter to end Sep, daily, 2–5.30. Workshops and flour shop all the year. Party. ⚠ *(Tel Colaton Raleigh 68521)*

OTTERY ST MARY *Devon* Map 3 SY19
Cadhay ½m from Fairmile, near junction of A30 and B3167. Beautiful and historic house, built 1550. Open 25 and 26 May, then 16 Jul to 28 Aug, Wed and Thu, also 24 and 25 Aug, 2–6. 50p (ch 14 25p). Party. ⚠ *(Tel Ottery St Mary 2432)*. *(Lady William-Powlett)* ⚕ B

OUTWOOD *Surrey* Map 4 TQ34
Old Mill Fine example of post-mill dating from 1665, oldest working mill in England, one of best-preserved in existence. The former smock mill nearby collapsed in 1960. Open 2 Apr to 29 Oct, Sun only 2–6; other days and evening tours by arrangement. 35p (ch 14 15p). P. ⚕

OXBOROUGH *Norfolk* Map 5 TF70
Oxburgh Hall Moated 15th-C and later. Home of Bedingfelds with turreted 80ft gatehouse, and French design parterre garden. Gatehouse, principal rooms and gardens open Apr to 12 Oct, Tue, Wed, Thu, Sat, Sun and BH Mon 2–6 (last admission 5.30). £1. Party 15+. No dogs. *(NT)*

OXFORD *Oxfordshire* Map 4 SP50
Ancient and picturesque University city on rivers Cherwell and Thames, dating back to the 8th C AD. **The University**, the oldest in Britain, probably dates from c1167 and consists of a large complex of colleges built over a period of several centuries, many of which are among the finest buildings of their age. Access to some colleges is restricted to certain times, and details may be obtained from the *Official Information Bureau, Carfax Tower*

Christ Church College Founded in 1525 by Cardinal Wolsey, it has a notable gateway, surmounted by a great octagonal bell tower of 1682, designed by Sir Christopher Wren. The College Art Gallery contains many Old Master paintings, and in the dining-hall are portraits of distinguished former members of the college.

Magdalen College Largely built in the 15th C around the 13th-C St John's Hospital. New building is a fine Georgian addition of 1733.

Merton College Founded in 1264 with parts dating from the 13th to the present century. The library, which is open to the public, dates from the 14th C.

New College A fine complex of Gothic buildings dating from 1380, the work of William Wykeham, Bishop of Winchester 1367–1404. Most of his original work survives, although much has been remodelled and added to. A stretch of the Medieval city wall marks part of the boundary of the gardens.

Trinity College Founded in 1555, and incorporating parts of the old Durham College (established 1380), which previously occupied this site. Features are Kettell Hall, a row of gabled buildings, The Garden Quadrangle, designed by Wren in 1668, and the chapel built by Bathhurst in 1691, which contains lavishly carved wooden reredos, stalls and screen.

The Sheldon Theatre Designed by Sir Christopher Wren, at the request of Sir Gilbert Sheldon, Archbishop of Canterbury, who financed the project, as a theatre for the public ceremonies of the University and a place to house the University Press. Completed in 1664–9, it is based on a Roman theatre and is roughly semicircular in plan.

Ashmolean Museum of Art and Archaeology Beaumont Street. The oldest (1683) museum in the country, housed in C R Cockerell's building of 1845 (with later extensions). Its main exhibits are of an archaeological nature of British, European, Mediterranean, Egyptian and Near Eastern origins. Also exhibited are coins and medals of all countries and periods, located in the Heberden Coin Room; Italian, Dutch, Flemish, French, and English oil paintings; Old Master and modern drawings, water-colours, prints and miniatures; the Hope collection of engraved portraits; European ceramics; English silver; Chinese and Japanese porcelain; painting and lacquer; Tibetan art; Indian sculpture and paintings; Islamic pottery and metalwork; Chinese bronzes; casts from the antique and objects of applied art. Temporary exhibits throughout year. Open all year (ex 24–26 Dec, 1 Jan, 4–6 Apr and during St Giles Fair in early Sep) Mon to Sat 10–4, Sun 2–4. Free. P. *(Tel 57522)* ৬ (by previous arrangement)

Museum of the History of Science Broad Street. Contains the finest collection of early astronomical, mathematical and optical instruments in the world, which are housed in the Old Ashmolean Building, a fine example of 17th-C architecture, originally built to hold the collection of Elias Ashmole. One of the most distinguished parts of the present display is the series of Islamic and European astrolabes, once used for astronomical calculations. Many of the exhibits are artistic as well as scientific, including sun-dials, and three fine orreries which represent the motions of heavenly bodies. Other exhibits include early microscopes, other optical instruments, photographic apparatus, clocks and watches, air-pumps, etc. Of special interest are the penicillin material, H G J Moseley's X-ray spectrometer, and a prototype of Dr C R Burch's ultra-violet reflecting microscope made in 1946. Open all year Mon to Fri (ex Christmas week and week after Easter) 10.30–1, 2.30–4. Free. ⚠ (limited). *(Tel 43997)*

Museum of Modern Art 30 Pembroke Street. Changing exhibitions of 20th-C art by British and international artists. Evening films, lectures, seminars, performances. Book stall. ⌂ Open all year, daily (ex Mon) Tue to Sat 10–5, Sun 2–5. Free. *(Tel 722733)*

Museum of Oxford St Aldates. Permanent displays of the archaeology and history of this famous University City from the earliest times to the present day. Temporary exhibitions. Facilities for parties. Bookshop. Museum assistant available for enquiries on Wed. Open all year (ex 13 Apr, 25–26 Dec) Tue to Sat 10–5. 20p (ch, students and pen 10p). P. *(Tel 815539)* **(79)**

Rotunda Museum of Antique Doll's Houses Grove House, 44 Iffley Turn, next to school. 2m from centre of Oxford, off A423. A collection of over fifty dolls' houses dating from c1700–1886 together with their furnishings, kitchen implements, china, silver, food and dolls' house dolls, which reflect the changes in social life and attitudes throughout the aforementioned period. Open 1 May to mid Sep (Sun only) 2.15–5.15. (At other times for parties of 12+ appointment only). Ch 16 not admitted. 25p. ⚠ ৬ B

University Private Botanic Garden High Street, by Magdalen Bridge. Gardens of great botanical interest, founded in 1621, and oldest in country. Open all year round (ex 4 Apr, 25 Dec), weekdays 8.30–5, Sun 10–12

and 2–6 (4.30 Oct to Apr); greenhouses open daily 2–4. Free. No dogs. P (St Clements car park). *(Tel 42737)* ৬

The *University Arboretum* is at Nuneham Courteney. On A423 just S of the village. 50 acres of Conifers and broad leaf trees. Open May to Oct Mon to Sat 8.30–5. Free. ⚠ limited. No dogs. ৬

PACKWOOD HOUSE Warwickshire Map 7 SP17

13m SE Birmingham on unclass road off A34. Timber-framed 16th- to 17th-C house containing tapestry, needlework, and furniture. Famous for remarkable mid 17th-C yew garden representing Sermon on the Mount. Open Apr to Sep, Wed to Sun, BH Mon 2–7; Oct to Mar (ex 25 Dec), Wed, Sat, Sun, BH Mon 2–5. 85p; garden only 50p. No dogs. *(NT)*

PADIHAM Lancashire Map 7 SD73

Gawthorpe Hall Early 17th-C house built around pele tower, with contemporary ceilings, woodwork, and a minstrel's gallery. Some 19th-C alterations by Sir Charles Barry. In house is the Kay Shuttleworth collection of lace and embroidery. Open 15 Mar to 31 Oct, BH Mon, Wed, Sat, Sun also Tue Jul and Aug, 2–6. 50p (ch 25p). ⚠ *(NT)*

PADSTOW Cornwall Map 2 SW97

Tropical Bird and Butterfly Gardens Fentonluna Lane. Established for years and continues to successfully breed many birds from all corners of the world. Gardens with tropical and sub-tropical plants, many of which are labelled. Heated walk-in Tropical House with free flying birds. Butterfly Exhibition with live flight operating during summer months on sunny days. Open all year (ex 25 Dec) daily 10.30–8 or 1hr before dusk. 80p (ch 3–14 40p, pen 60p). Prices under revision for 1980. ⌂ spring and summer. Dogs allowed on leads. P on B3276. *(Tel 532262)* ৬

PAIGNTON Devon Map 3 SX86

Kirkham House Restored 15th-C house, known as the Priest's House. Open Apr to Sep, weekdays 9.30–7 (5.30, Apr), Sun 2–7 (5.30, Apr). 15p (ch 16 and pen 5p). *(AM)*

Oldway 19th-C house containing replicas of rooms at Palace of Versaille. Picturesque gardens. ⌂ summer. House open May to Sep. Mon to Sat 10–1 and 2.15–5.15, Sun 2.30–5.30; winter Mon to Fri 10–1 and 2.15–5.15 (closed Sat and Sun); closed occasionally for Council purposes. Free. ⚠ *(Tel Torquay 26244 ext 286 for bookings. Paignton 550711 enquiries)*

Torbay Aircraft Museum Higher Blagdon. Off Totnes Road, A385, near Berry Pomeroy. About 2 miles from Paignton Zoo. Features over 18 complete aircraft dating from 1924 to 1954. Comprehensive indoor exhibition of aeronautics. Special exhibition 'The Red Baron and Fighter Aces of World War 1'. Aviation shop and ⌂ licensed (summer only). Open all year (ex 25 and 26 Dec) 10–6 (4 winter). 85p (ch 45p, pen 50p, ch 5 free). Under revision for 1980. ⚠ (75% under cover) *(Tel 553540)* ৬

Torbay and Dartmouth Railway Steam trains run on former Great Western line from Paignton to Kingswear for ferry across to Dartmouth. Model railway exhibition at Paignton station. Gift shop. Open Easter then mid May to end Sep daily. Tel for other dates in season. P in Victoria Park. *(Tel 555872)* ৬

Zoological and Botanical Gardens Totnes Road. In approximately 100 acres of grounds, enhanced with tropical plants and shrubs are extensive collection of animals and birds from all over the world. Among the main attractions are a breeding colony of Lar Gibbons on a large island in a lake, the baboon rock, monkey house, large tropical house, sub-tropical house, aquarium and reptile house. A large collection of peafowl roam the grounds. ☟ Licensed bar. Children's playground. Miniature railway. Open all year, daily (ex 25 Dec) 10–7.30 (5.30 winter). £1.20 (ch 3–14 60p). Party. Admission prices under revision for 1980. ⚠ *(Tel 557479)*

PAINSWICK *Gloucestershire* Map 3 SO80
Painswick House A Georgian Palladian house situated ½m outside the picturesque village. It has some splendid reception rooms and a special feature is the 18th-C Chinese wall paper in the drawing room. ☟ (teas for parties 20+ by appointment). Open Sun Jul, Aug, and Sep 2–6. 50p (ch 14 10p, pen 20p). Parties 20+ can be booked all year. ⚠ limited. *(Tel 813646)* **(79)**

PARCEVALL (PERCIVAL) HALL GARDENS *North Yorkshire* Map 7 SE06
Beautiful gardens of Elizabethan house, in hillside setting east of main Wharfedale valley. ☟. Open Easter to end Sep. 20p ⚠ (5p). *(Tel Burnsall 214)*

PATELEY BRIDGE *North Yorkshire* Map 7 SE16
Niderdale Museum Many rooms depicting historical Dales life. Displays include the Cobbler's shop, Victorian room, also costume, domestic, industrial, farming, geology, apothecaries, medical, religious and photographic sections. Open all year, Easter to Spring BH, Sat and Sun, summer, daily, Oct to Easter Sun only. 2–5. 10p (ch and pen 5p). ⚠ Party. *(Tel Harrogate 711225)*

PEAKIRK *Cambridgeshire* Map 4 TF10
Wildfowl Trust Over 600 ducks, geese and swans of 100 different species in an attractive water garden. Magnificent flock of Chilean flamingoes, trumpeter, black-necked and coscoroba swans, Andean geese and many other rare and unusual waterfowl. Visitor centre, Gift shop, ☟ and picnic facilities. Open daily (ex 24/25 Dec) from 9.30. Party 20+ (evening) ⚠ free. *(Tel Peterborough 252271)* ♿

PENSHURST *Kent* Map 5 TQ54
Penshurst Place On B2176. One of the outstanding stately homes in Britain, and birthplace of Sir Philip Sidney in 1554. The world-famous chestnut-beamed Great Hall is the oldest and finest in England. The state rooms are splendidly furnished and the toy museum is much loved by children. Extensive

Tudor gardens, leisure area includes a venture playground, Countryside Exhibition and nature trail. Open 1 Apr to 5 Oct, daily (ex Mon and Fri), House 2–6; all other facilities – 1 Apr to 30 Jun 12–6, 1 Jul to 5 Oct 11.30–6, BH, all facilities including house, 11.30–6. Grounds £1 (ch 50p), House 50p (ch 25p), Toy museum 10p, Victoria Regina Exhibition 10p; Inclusive ticket for House, Grounds and Exhibitions £1.50 (ch 75p ex BH). ⚠ *(Tel 870307)*. *(Viscount De L'Isle VC KG)*

PENZANCE *Cornwall* Map 2 SW43
Museum of Nautical Art and Man-O-War Display 19 Chapel Street, opposite the Admiral Benbow. Museum has on exhibition the hundreds of 'nautifacts' brought up by the diving teams of Roland Morris from the sunken wrecks of Anson Association Romney Eagle and Colussus. The display of the latter wreck depicting recovery of Lord Hamilton's 2,500-year-old pottery. Man-o'-war display shows full scale section of 1730 warship with four decks including gun-decks and great cabin with guns and men of the period. Open May to Sep 10–1 and 2–4 (also 7–9 in season). 20p (ch 15p). **(79)**

Penlee House, Penzance and District Museum Penlee Park. The Museum takes a look at the history and development of Penzance and Penwith District from earliest man to the 1950s. Open all year, Mon to Sat 12.30–4.30 (ex BH). Free. P. *(Tel 3625)* **(79)**

PETERBOROUGH *Cambridgeshire* Map 4 TL19
Longthorpe Tower Fortified 13th- to 14th-C house, which belonged formerly to the de Thorpe family. Contains some rare wall-paintings of religious and didactic subjects on first floor. Open, see inside front cover. 15p (ch 16 and pen 5p). *(AM)*

Lowlands Farm and Bygone Centre Fenbridge Road, Werrington. 3m NW. 40 acres of farmland with rare breeds of British farm animals. A museum of vintage and veteran cars, and working demonstrations of vintage agricultural machinery and farm work are held. ¾m river frontage for fishing. Country Festival and Game Fair 16 Sep. Open all year daily from 10am. 50p (ch 15 and pen 35p). ⚠ *(Tel 74477)* **(79)**

City of Peterborough Museum and Art Gallery Priestgate. Local geology and archaeology, natural history, Victorian rooms, and articles from former French prisoners' jail at Norman Cross. Paintings mainly of local topographical interest and small collection of ceramics and glass. Temporary exhibitions. Open all year (closed 25, 26 Dec and 4 Apr) Sep to May Tue to Sat, BH 12–5. Jun to Aug Tue to Sat 10–5. Free. P. *(Tel 43329)*

PETWORTH *West Sussex* Map 4 SU92
Petworth House Large, late 17th- to 19th-C
mansion, partly by Salvin, in great park.
Notable picture gallery, 13th-C chapel,
Grinling Gibbons carvings, and grand
staircase probably painted by Laguerre.
Open Apr to end Oct Tue, Wed, Thu, Sat, Sun
and BH Mon 2 – 6. £1.10 Connoisseurs' day
on Tue, extra rooms shown. £1.35. No dogs in
the house. Deer park open all year 9 till
sunset. ⚏ 2.30 – 5.30. *(NT)*

PEVENSEY *East Sussex* Map 5 TQ60
Old Minthouse High Street. Built in 1342 on a
site which is reputed to have been used as a
Norman mint as long ago as 1076. The
interior was considerably altered in 1542 by
Dr Andrew Borde, then court physician to
Henry VIII. It contains 18 rooms, open to the
public, carvings, frescoes, etc. Small
museum. Open all year Mon to Fri 10 – 5, Sat
10 – 1, mid Jul to Sep Sun also BH 11 – 5. 20p
(ch 14 10p). P. *(Tel Eastbourne 762337)* **(79)**
Pevensey Castle 3rd-C Roman fort of Saxon
Shore, with Norman and 13th-C additions,
including keep, curtain wall, and gatehouse.
Open*, see inside front cover. 20p (ch 16 and
pen 5p). ⚠ *(AM)*

PICKERING *North Yorkshire* Map 8 SE78
Beck Isle Museum of Rural Life Georgian
house, once the home of William Marshall, an
authority on agriculture. Museum contains
folk exhibits relating to Pickering and
surrounding area. Open Easter to mid Oct
daily, 10.30 – 12.30, 2 – 5.30, Aug 10.30 – 7.
Open evenings or in winter for parties, by
appointment only. 20p (ch 16 10p). ⚠ *(Tel
73359)* ⚹ B
North Yorkshire Moors Railway 'Moorsrail'
Operates through the heart of the North York
Moors National Park between Pickering and
Grosmont, a distance of 18 miles. Services
operate a week prior to Easter until early Nov.
Loco shed, viewing gallery, gift shop and ⚏ at
Grosmont. Audi-visual Unit, bookshop,
information centre and ⚏ at Pickering
Station. Further details available from
Moorsrail, Pickering Station, North Yorkshire.
⚠ at Grosmont Station and Pickering town.
(Tel (0751) 72508/73535) ⚹
Pickering Castle Large shell keep on mound
between two baileys, the inner of which,
together with keep, is 12th C. Open*, see
inside front cover. 15p (ch 16 and pen 5p). ⚠
(AM)

PITSTONE *Buckinghamshire* Map 4 SP91
Pitstone Windmill Off B488. One of
England's oldest postmills, some of it part of
original structure of 1627. Recently well-
restored and is again fully operative. Open
May to Sep, Suns and BH Mon 2.30 – 6. 15p
(ch 7p). *(NT)*

PLAXTOL *Kent* Map 5 TQ65
Old Soar Manor Part of late 13th-C house
joined to 18th-C farmhouse. Open, see inside
front cover, Apr to Sep only. 15p (ch 16 and
pen 5p). *(NT and AM)*

PLYMOUTH *Devon* Map 2 SX45
City Museum and Art Gallery Drake Circus.
Collections of paintings and drawings,
ceramics (especially Plymouth porcelain),
silver; archaeology and local history; natural
history. Cottonian collection of Old Master
drawings, engravings and early printed
books. Open all year (ex 4 Apr, 25/26 Dec)
weekdays 10 – 6 (8 Fri), Sun 3 – 5. Free. P.
(Tel 68000 ext 4378) ⚹

Elizabethan House 32 New Street. A 16th-C
merchant's house furnished according to
period in Plymouth's historic precinct. Open
all year, weekdays 10 – 1 and 2.15 – 6 (dusk,
Oct to Mar); Apr to Sep, Sun also 3 – 5. Free.
P. *(Tel 68000 ext 2006)* **(79)**
The Merchant's House 33 St Andrews
Street. Large town house of 16th- and early
17th-C, with many period features. Converted
to Museum of Plymouth history up to 1670.
Open all year (ex 4 Apr, 25, 26 Dec)
weekdays 10 – 6, Sun 3 – 5. Free. P. *(Tel
68000 ext 4378)*
Prysten House Off Royal Parade (Main
Street). Old house in city, built 1490, former
Priest's house of St Andrew's Church.
Mayflower Story Room and model of
Plymouth 1620. Herb display. Open Mon to
Sat (ex 4 Apr, 25/26 Dec and 1 Jan also Sun)
10 – 4. 30p (ch 16 15p). ⚠ *(Tel 61414 Mon to
Fri 9.30 – 1)*

Royal Citadel Magnificent entrance
gateway, dated 1670, and designed probably
by Sir Thomas Fitz for stronghold
commenced by Charles II in 1666. The
remaining buildings from the fort include the
Guard House, Governor's House, and
Chapel, the two last-named rebuilt. Open any
reasonable time at the discretion of the
military. Free. *(AM)*
Smeaton Tower The Promenade, Plymouth
Hoe. A former Eddystone Lighthouse now
rebuilt on The Hoe. Open 26 Apr to 4 Oct daily
10.30 – one hour before dusk. 10p. Party. *(Tel
264840)*

PLYMPTON *Devon* Map 2 SX55
Dartmoor Wild Life Park 3m NE at
Sparkwell, north of A38. 25-acre park with
birds and animals of many species. Six deer
species in separate paddocks, and free-flying
waterfowl. Donkeys for children. New monkey
pen. ⚏ and souvenir shop. Open all year,
daily 10 – dusk. Admission prices not
available. ⚠ *(Tel Cornwood 209)*
Saltram House (S of bypass). Tudor house,
refronted in 18th-C, with saloon and dining
room (1768) by Robert Adam;
furniture, carpets and Reynolds portraits.
Shrub garden with 18th-C summer house and
orangery (1773) by Stockman. Open 1 Apr to
Oct, daily 11 – 6, house 12.30 – 6 (last
admission 5.30, house only closed on Mon);
Nov to Mar garden only open, daily during
daylight hours. £1.50. Garden only 90p.
Candlelit evenings 26 Apr, 30 Aug, 27 Sep
and 25 Oct, 8 – 10.30 pm. £2. *(NT and NGS)*

POCKLINGTON *Humberside* Map 8 SE84
*Burnby Hall Gardens and Stewart
Collection* Museum of sporting trophies,
objects of interest from world-wide travels,
and gardens with fine lily ponds. ⚏. Gardens
open all year Mon to Fri 10 – 7, Sat and Sun
2 – 7; museum and café open Easter to late
May, Sat and Sun 2 – 5; end of May to mid Sep
daily then Sat and Sun to end of Sep. 30p (ch
14 5p, pen 20p). Under revision for 1980.
Free. *(Tel 2068 and 2114)* ⚹ B

ENGLAND

Portsmouth 163

POLEGATE *East Sussex* Map 5 TQ50
Polegate Windmill Off A22. A complete
tower-mill dating from 1817 and in use until
some 20 years ago. Tower is 45ft high, and
original applewood machinery and milling
museum are of interest. Open Easter to Oct,
Sun and BH Mon, also Wed in Aug
2.30–5.30. Other times by arrangement. 20p
(ch 14 10p). P (roads round mill). *(Tel
Eastbourne 54845)*

POLPERRO *Cornwall* Map 2 SX25
Museum of Smuggling Talland Street.
Interesting museum of past- and present-day
smuggling activities. Open Easter to 24 Oct,
daily 10–7. 30p. Under revision for 1980.
Dogs on lead only. P.

PONTEFRACT *West Yorkshire* Map 8 SE42
Pontefract Museum Salter Row. Opened
April 1978. Museum of Pontefract history also
temporary exhibitions. Open all year Mon to
Sat 10.30–12.30 and 1.30–5.30. Closed Sun
and BH. Free. *(Tel 77289)*

POOL *Cornwall* Map 2 SW64
Cornish Engines Five original Cornish beam
engines were given to the National Trust in
1967 by Cornish Engine Preservation
Society. Two of these, East Pool and Agar
Mine (on either side of A30), are open 1 Apr to
end Oct, daily 11–1 and 2–6 (last tour 5.30).
50p. There are others for which suitable
arrangements must be made in advance for
visiting: Levant Mine, St Just *(The Manager,
Geevor Mine, Tel St Just 662)*, and South
Crofty Mine, Camborne *(The Manager, Tel
Camborne 3150). (NT)*

POOLE *Dorset* Map 4 SZ09
Guildhall Museum Market Street. The Civic
and social life of Poole during the 18th and
19th C is portrayed in the displays in this fine
example of a two-storey Georgian Market
House. Open all year (ex 1 Jan, 4 Apr, 25/26
Dec) Mon to Sat 10–5, Sun 2–5. 1 Apr to 30
Sep. 15p (ch 5p) combined ticket for all three
museums 35p (ch 10p); 1 Oct to 31 Mar 10p
(ch 5p). P. *(Tel 5323)*
Maritime Museum Paradise Street, Poole
Quay. The displays in the late 15th-C Town
Cellars illustrate Poole's association with the
sea from prehistoric times until the early 20th
C. Admission charges and opening times as
Guildhall Museum. P. *(Tel 5323)*
Poole Park Zoo A small but well-equipped
zoo within the limits of beautiful Poole Park.
Animals at present include wild cat, pumas,
leopards, bears, porcupine and otters. There
is also a monkey house, tropical house,
children's corner and a fine collection of
flamingoes, penguins, parrots and tropical
birds. Gift shop. Open Mar to Oct, 10–6 or
sunset whichever is earlier; Nov to Feb Sat,
Sun, PH and every day during local school
holidays 10–sunset. 45p (ch 15 25p). Party.
All charges subject to alteration for 1980. ⚠
(Tel Parkstone 745296) &
Poole Pottery The Quay. Well-known
pottery, founded in 1873, which has been
producing 'Poole Pottery' since 1921. Craft
section on several floors where making of the
pottery can be seen. Open all year (ex
Christmas week and BH) Tours Mon to Fri
10–12.30 and 1.50–4.15. 35p (ch 15p).
Under revision for 1980. Shop Mon to Sat 9–5
(later in summer also Sun in Aug). P. *(Tel
2866)*
Scaplen's Court High Street. One of the
finest examples of a 15th-C town house to be
seen on the South Coast. The displays
illustrate the development of Poole from

prehistoric times until the 19th C with an
emphasis on archaeological material.
Admission charges and opening times as
Guildhall Museum. P. *(Tel 5323)*

PORCHESTER *Hampshire* Map 4 SU60
Porchester Castle Off A27. 4th-C Saxon
shore fort, with 12th-C keep in one corner and
Assheton's Tower (1367) in another corner.
Parish church (1133) in south-west corner
was church of Augustinian foundation moved
later to Southwick. Open*, see inside front
cover. 25p (ch 16 and pen 10p). ⚠ *(AM)*

PORTLAND *Dorset* Map 3 SY67
Portland Castle Erected originally by Henry
VIII and added to in 17th and 18th C. Open
Apr to Sep, weekdays 9.30–7 (5.30, Apr) Sun
2–7 (5.30, Apr). 15p (ch and pen 5p). ⚠ *(AM)*
Portland Museum 217 Wakeham.
Associated with Thomas Hardy's *The Well-
Beloved* (Avice's Cottage). Now a museum of
local and historical interest. Open May to Sep,
Mon, Wed, Thu, Fri 10–8; Tue and Sat 10–5;
Sun 11–1 and 2–5. Oct to Apr, Tue to Sat
10–1 and 2–5. 10p (ch, students and pen
free). *(Tel Portland 821804)*

PORTSMOUTH *Hampshire* Map 4 SZ69
City Museum and Art Gallery Museum
Museum Road. Formerly military barracks,
now partially art gallery and museum with
furniture, pottery, glass, sculpture, and
paintings. Also local history galleries, and
monthly temporary exhibitions. ⚐ (licensed).
Open all year, daily (ex 25, 26 Dec)
10.30–5.30. 11p (ch and pen 6p). ⚠ & B
Cumberland House Museum Eastern
Parade. Local natural history and an
aquarium. Open all year daily (ex 25, 26 Dec)
10.30–5.30. 11p (ch and pen 6p).
Dickens' Birthplace Museum Old
Commercial Road. Georgian house where
Charles Dickens was born in 1812, now
restored and furnished to illustrate the style of
the period. Prints and portraits are exhibited,
and couch on which Dickens died is displayed
in separate room. Open Mar to Oct daily
10.30–5.30. 21p (ch and pen 11p).
*Eastney Pumping Station and Gas Engine
House* Henderson Road. A fine building
containing Boulton and Watt reciprocal steam
pumps installed in 1887. One operating under
steam at weekends. Adjacent buildings of
1904 houses Crossley gas engines. Open
Apr to Sep, daily 2–6. Weekends 27p (ch and
pen 11p), weekdays 16p (ch and pen 6p). ⚠
Fort Widley Portsdown Hill Road. Fort built in
the 1860s by Lord Palmerston against the
threat of French invasion. Contains a
labyrinth of underground passages,
magazines and gun emplacements.
Commands superb panoramic views. Open
Apr to Sep daily 2–6. Guided tours. 27p (ch
and pen 11p). P.
Point Battery and Round Tower Three-
storeyed building dating back originally to
1485, with later alterations. Once part of 18-
gun battery defending harbour. Good views.
P.
Royal Naval Museum Museum boasts many
fine exhibits connected with Nelson, his
officers, and men, huge panorama of
Trafalgar being outstanding, as are also
ship's figureheads. Displays include
exhibitions on Victorian navy and the history
of Warships and Boats. The McCarthy
collection of Nelson commemorative
material. ⚐ 20p (ch 10p). ⚠ in dockyard. *(Tel
22351 ext 23868)* & B
HMS Victory The Hard. Entry via main
dockyard gate. Nelson's famous flagship,

moored in the harbour until 1922, has since been restored and fitted out to show conditions as at Battle of Trafalgar in 1805. Open 1 Mar to 31 Oct Mon to Sat 10.30 – 5.30, Sun 1 – 5; 1 Nov to end Feb Mon to Sat 10.30 – 4.30, Sun 1 – 4.30. Free. *(Tel 22351 ext 23111)* ⓗ B (by prior arrangement)

PORT SUNLIGHT *Merseyside* Map 7 SJ38
Lady Lever Art Gallery Situated near Mersey estuary in well-known model village, this art gallery displays pictures by famous English Masters in addition to collections of English period furniture, Chinese porcelain, and Wedgwood. Open all year (ex 1 Jan, 4 Apr, 24, 25 and 26 Dec) Mon to Sat 10 – 5, Sun 2 – 5 (subject to revision). Voluntary contribution. ⚠ *(Tel 051-645 3623)* ⓗ B

POWDERHAM *Devon* Map 3 SX98
Powderham Castle Entrance off A379 Exeter/Dawlish road. Seat of Earls of Devon, built between 1390 and 1420, damaged in Civil War and restored and altered in 18th C and 19th Cs. Fine furnishings and portraits. Lovely deer park. ☕ (teas). Open Easter then Sun until mid May, after which, daily (ex Fri and Sat) until end Sep, 2 – 6. £1 (ch 16 and pen 50p). Party 20+. Subject to alteration. *(Tel Starcross 243)* ⓗ B

PRESTON *Lancashire* Map 7 SD52
Harris Museum and Art Gallery The specialist collections cover the fields of fine art, decorative art, archaeology, natural history, and include works by the Devis family, the Newsham Bequest of the 19th C, paintings and sculpture, and the Cedric Houghton Bequest of ceramics. Annual Lancashire Art Exhibition Mar/Apr. Free guided tours by arrangement. ☕ (Mon, Wed and Fri mornings). Open all year Mon to Sat (ex BH) 10 – 5. Free. P. *(Tel 58248)* ⓗ

PRESTWICH *Gt Manchester* Map 7 SD80
Heaton Hall Heaton Park on A665. The finest house of its period in Lancashire and one of the finest in the country. Designed for the Earl of Wilton by James Wyatt in 1772, the house has magnificent decorated interior and commands panoramic views of Manchester. Open all year Mon to Sat 10 – 6 (4 Nov to Feb); Sun 2 – 6 (4 Nov to Feb), 12 – 6 May to Aug. Free. ⚠ *(Tel 061-773 1231)*

PRINCES RISBOROUGH *Buckinghamshire* Map 4 SP80
Princes Risborough Manor 17th-C house with 17th- and 18th-C woodwork. Open Apr to Oct, Wed 2 – 6 (two room only shown). 20p *(NT)*

PRISTON *Avon* Map 3 ST66
Priston Mill Priston Farm. Historic water powered corn mill, driven by a large waterwheel. Dates from Anglo Saxon period. Records in Domesday Book indicate that flour has been milled in this area for over a thousand years. Flour is still ground in the mill today, and is used to make 'Priston Mill Whole Wheat Bread'. Farm shop. Visitors may picnic by mill in fine weather. Open 24 Mar to 31 Oct, Mon to Fri 2.15 – 5, Sat, Sun and BH 11 – 12.45 and 2.15 – 6. Free. Conducted tours with parties 25p per head, (by appointment only.). ⚠ *(Tel Bath 23894)*

PROBUS *Cornwall* Map 2 SW94
County Demonstration Garden and Arboretum Permanent displays of the many aspects of garden layout, plant selection, and effect of weather conditions. Plant, tree and flower propagation. Exhibits of fruit, herbs and vegetables. Emphasis on choosing right foliage, flowers, etc, to suit individual requirements and environment. For special

vents see local press. Open May to Sep,
Mon, Tue, Wed & Fri 2 – 5, Thu 2 – 8, Sun 2 – 6,
Oct – Apr, Thu 2 – 5. 10p (ch 5 free). ⚠ *(Tel
Truro 74282 ext 349)* &

Trewithen Gardens Grampound Road.
Internationally renowned landscaped garden
of camellias, magnolias, rhododendrons and
many rare plants of distinction. Open Mar to
Sep, daily (ex Sun) incl BH 2 – 4.30. Mar to
Jun, 60p (ch 30p, pen 40p); Jul to Sep, 40p
(ch 20p, pen 30p). Nurseries open all year. ⚠
Tel St Austell 882418) & P also **Trewithen
House** An 18th-C Cornish country house built
1720 and lived in continuously by
descendants of the same family. Open Apr to
Jul inclusive, Mon and Tue only 2 – 4.30. £1

PRUDHOE *Northumberland* Map 12 NZ06
Prudhoe Castle On River Tyne, 12th- to
14th-C former stronghold of d'Umfravelles
and Percys. Keep stands in inner bailey, and
notable example of entrance guards outside
bailey. Access to Pele Tard only. Open, see
inside front cover. Closed Wed and Fri. Free
ch 16 not admitted unless accompanied by
an adult). *(AM)*

PUDSEY *West Yorkshire* Map 8 SE23
Fulneck Moravian Museum This museum of
Moravian exhibits and Victoriana dates from
1969 and includes photographs, furniture,
150-year-old fire engine, working hand loom
and spinning wheel. Open 1 Mar to 31 Oct,
Wed and Sat 2 – 5, other times by
appointment only. 10p (ch 3p). ⚠ *(Tel Pudsey
64862)*

PULBOROUGH *West Sussex* Map 4 TQ01
Parham Park 3m SE off A283. Dates from
1577, and great hall, long gallery, and
principal rooms contain fine portraits,
furniture, and needlework. Walled garden,
pleasure grounds, and glasshouses.
Beautiful downland setting. ℘ 3 – 5.15. Open
Apr to 5 Oct 2 – 5.30, Wed, Thu, Sun and
BH. £1 (ch 17 and pen 60p). Gardens open
1 – 6. 25p. Connoisseurs Days 2nd and 4th
Sun in each open month, visitors not guided.
1.20 (ch and pen 60p). ⚠ *(Tel Storrington
2021). (Mr and Mrs P A Tritton)*

PURSE CAUNDLE *Dorset* Map 3 ST61
Purse Caundle Manor Excellent example of
medieval manor house, with great hall and
chamber. Open 5 Mar to 31 Oct, Wed, Thu,
Sun and BH 2 – 5. 75p (ch 13 20p). ⚠ *(Tel
Milborne Port 250400)*

PUSEY *Oxfordshire* Map 4 SU39
Pusey House Gardens Designed 1748 with
new garden terraces added 1935 by Geoffrey
Jellicoe. 20 acres of garden and lake, with
herbaceous borders. Plants for sale. ℘.

Gardens only open 2 Apr to 29 Jun, Wed, Thu
and Sun 2 – 6; 2 Jul to 19 Oct, daily (ex Mon
and Fri) 2 – 6 also BH weekends. 50p (ch 10
free). Prices for 1980 under revision. ⚠ *(Tel
Buckland 222)* &

QUAINTON *Buckinghamshire* Map 4 SP71
Quainton Railway Centre Quainton Station.
Off A41. The largest collection of standard
gauge locomotives in the country including
examples built by Hunslet, Hudswell Clarke
and British Rail (Metropolitan, LNER, LMS,
GWR). Also items of rolling stock including
many built before 1900. ℘ Steam Railway
Galas 5 – 7 and 27 Apr, 24 – 26 May, 29 Jun,
27 Jul, 23 – 25 Aug, 28 Sep and 26 Oct, 10 – 6.
70p (ch and pen 35p), family ticket £1.75. Not
expected to change for 1980. ⚠ &

RADCLIFFE *Gt Manchester* Map 7 SD70
Radcliffe Tower Sandford Street. Remains
of medieval tower once part of a larger hall
occupied by the Radcliffe family. Adjacent to
medieval Parish Church. Open at all times.
Free. P. Enquiries to Bury Museum. *(Tel Bury
4021)* &

RAINTHORPE HALL *Norfolk* Map 5 TM29
Fine medium-sized Elizabethan manor house
of brick and timber. Open by appointment
only. ℘. £1 (ch 50p). ⚠ *(Tel Swainsthorpe
470618). (G F Hastings)* & B

RAMPTON *Nottinghamshire* Map 8 SK77
Sundown Pets Garden Treswell Road.
Caters specially for young children. The
animal and bird enclosures are set amidst
attractive gardens, and there is also a Play
Village, modern playground and a unique life
size 'Toy Jungle'. Tea garden. Open all year
10 – 7 or dusk (closed 25, 26 Dec). 25p (ch 2
free). Admission prices for 1980 not yet
decided. ⚠ *(Tel 274)* &

RAMSEY *Cambridgeshire* Map 4 TL28
Abbey Gatehouse 15th-C Benedictine relic.
open Apr to 12 Oct, daily 10 – 5 (or sunset).
Free. *(NT)*

RAVENGLASS *Cumbria* Map 6 SD09
Ravenglass and Eskdale Railway Narrow
gauge (15in) steam railway established in
1875 to carry iron ore. Now passenger line
with steam and diesel locomotives, open and
saloon coaches. Runs 7 miles from
Ravenglass to Eskdale through beautiful
scenery. Railway Museum at Ravenglass.
Shops and cafés at each end of line. Open 30
Mar to 2 Nov (reduced services at other times,
one train a day during winter, except
Christmas). 7.45 – 6.40 (summer). Return
fare £2 (ch 15 and pen £1.30), subject to
possible increase. ⚠ at each station. *(Tel
226)*

PARHAM Pulborough, West Sussex.

House open Wednesdays, Thursdays, Sundays and Bank
Holidays from Easter Sunday to first Sunday in October.
2pm-5.30pm. Second and fourth Sundays in the month
unguided. Gardens open same days 1pm-6pm. Free Car
Park. Church. Teas in the Big Kitchen. Shop. All enquiries
to the Secretary. Tel: Storrington 2021.

See gazetteer for details.

READING *Berkshire* Map 4 SU77
Museum and Art Gallery Blagrave Street.
noted especially for exceptional collection of
exhibits from Roman Silchester, but there are
also finds from River Thames area, including
splendid Bronze Age torc from Moulsford.
Displays of local natural history. Monthly
changing exhibitions. Open all year Mon to Fri
10–5.30, Sat 10–5 (closed Sun and BH).
Admission free. Station and municipal car
parks within 5 mins. *(Tel 55911 ext 2242)* See
also SILCHESTER, **Calleva Museum**
Museum of English Rural Life The
University. Whiteknights Park, Shinfield Road
entrance. Collection of highly interesting
agricultural, domestic, and crafts exhibits.
Open all year (ex BH) Tue to Fri 10–4.30; Sat
10–1 and 2–4.30. Free. ⚠ *(Tel 85123 ext
475)* & B

RECULVER *Kent* Map 5 TR26
Roman Fort Remains of 3rd-C Roman fort of
the Saxon Shore, on an even older site.
Within its walls stand the towers of a Norman
church, the body of which was destroyed in
1809, the towers being left as a mariners'
landmark. Accessible any reasonable time.
Free. P. *(AM)*

REDCAR *Cleveland* Map 8 NZ62
The Zetland Museum Exhibits include the
oldest lifeboat in the world, pictures, relics,
models, etc, relating to sea rescue on the
North-East coast and to the fishing
communities of North Yorkshire. A marine
aquarium and displays about local marine life.
Open all year Mon to Sat 10–5.30. Closed 4
Apr, 25 Dec and 1 Jan. Free. P. Esplanade
and King Street. *(Tel 71921)*

REDDITCH *Hereford and Worcester*
Map 7 SP06
Forge Mill 2m N of town, off A441. On the site
of the original mill serving Cistercian Abbey at
Bordesley. Present mill converted to needle
scouring between 1728 and 1730. Some
machinery in west wing is original. Open by
appointment only with *Mr J Luty*. ⚠ *(Tel
64412)*

REDRUTH *Cornwall* Map 2 SW64
Tolgus Tin Company Portreath Road. 2m N.
Only remaining Cornish tin steaming works
dating from 1800, retaining original water-
wheels and only surviving set of 12 headed
Cornish stamps still in commercial use.
Objects made of tin sold in Mineral House.
Guided tours around mill. Madame Tussaud's
animals tea party. ⚟ Picnic and children's
play area. Open all year daily 10–6 (later in
season). 85p (ch and pen 55p). Opening
times and admission prices under revision for
1980. Dogs not allowed around tin mill. *(Tel
215171)*

REEDHAM *Norfolk* Map 5 TG40
Pettitts Rural Industries Peacocks,
ornamental pheasants, game birds and
waterfowl on show in garden surroundings
with picnic area. Art of feather craft and
taxidermy usually being demonstrated and
products are on sale, also oven-ready game
and recipes. Conservation literature.
Museum of Reedham. ⚟ spring and summe
Mon to Fri only. Open all year Mon to Fri 9–5
Charges for 1980 not yet known, may also op
Sat and Sun pm. ⚠ *(Tel Freethorpe 243* &

REIGATE *Surrey* Map 4 TQ25
Priory Museum Bell Street. Founded
originally in 1235, house was converted into
Tudor mansion, of which hall fireplace is fine
surviving relic. Palladian stucco of 1779
changed face of building, and painted
staircase by Verrio c1710 is notable example
House now used as school and part is a smal
museum of local history, Victorian toys and
costumes. Special exhibitions for 1980 Sprin
term – History of Reigate Priory. Summer
term – Costume exhibition. Autumn term –
Globe-trotters souvenirs. ⚟ Open Wed in
term-time 2–4.30. Free. P. *(Tel 45065)* &

REIGATE HEATH *Surrey* Map 4 TQ25
Old Windmill 400-year-old mill, converted fo
holding of church services at 3 pm on third
Sun of each month between May and Oct.
Restored in 1964. Accessible all the year,
daily 9–dusk. Free. P. & B

RESTORMEL *Cornwall* Map 2 SX16
Restormel Castle 1 m N of Lostwithiel, off
A390. Comprises circular mound and
gateway c1100, with notable round keep buil
c1200. Rectangular 13th-C chapel *(AM)*
situated nearby. Castle open*, see inside
front cover. 15p (ch 16 and pen 5p). Party
11+. ⚠ *(AM)*

RIBCHESTER *Lancashire* Map 7 SD63
Roman Museum and Fort 5½m NE Preston.

n B6245. Site museum of the Roman Fort of
remetennacum' in an attractive village.
ontains cavalryman's tombstone, coins,
ottery, jewellery, inscriptions and replica of
mous Parade Helmet, the original of which
in the British Museum. Unique collection of
eltic heads. Exposed remains of Roman
anary open to view. Open all year, May to
ug Mon to Sat (ex Fri) 2–5.30; Sep to Nov
d Feb to Apr, Mon to Sat (ex Fri) 2–5; Dec
nd Jan Sat only 2–5. 20p (ch 10p). (Tel 261)
NCHBOROUGH Kent Map 5 TR 36
ort and Museum Roman 'Rutupiae' and
iginal fort of the Saxon Shore. Accessible
ny reasonable time. Free. ⚠ (AM)
CHMOND North Yorkshire Map 7 NZ10
chmond Castle Dates from 11th and 12th
, one of the earliest in England, with massive
urtain walls and splendid rectangular keep
erlooking River Swale. Open*, see inside
ont cover. 20p (ch 16 and pen 5p). P. (AM)
he Green Howards Museum Trinity
quare, Market Place. Covers history of
mous regiment, including many uniforms
ating from 1688, weapons and special VC
xhibition. Runner-up in National Heritage
useum of the Year Award 1975. Open all
ear ex Dec and Jan, 1 Apr to 31 Oct
eekdays 10–4.30, Sun 2–4.30; Nov, Feb
nd Mar Mon to Sat 10–4.30, closed Sun.
0p (ch 10p). Disc P in Market Place. (Tel
133)
CKMANSWORTH Hertfordshire
ap 4 TQ09
oor Park Mansion Fine Palladian mansion
y Leoni, reconstructed in 1727, with Amigoni
nd Thornhill frescoes. Now a golf club
ouse. Open (ex BH) Mon, all year, 10–4.30;
nd 1st Sat in month May to Sep for guided
urs 10–12 and 3–4. Free. ⚠

RIEVAULX North Yorkshire Map 8 SE58
Rievaulx Abbey Magnificent Cistercian
abbey begun about 1132, surrounded by
wooded hills. Earliest large Cistercian nave in
Britain. Extensive, well-preserved, monastic
buildings. Open*, see inside front cover. 40p,
winter 15p (ch 16 and pen 15p, winter 5p). ⚠
(AM)
Rievaulx Terrace The layout includes a fine
terrace providing views towards Ryedale and
the Hambleton Hills. There are two 18th-C
garden temples and some remarkable fresco
paintings by Burnici. Open Apr to Oct (ex 4
Apr) daily 10.30–6 (last admission 5.30). 60p.
⚠ (NT)
RIPLEY North Yorkshire Map 8 SE26
Ripley Castle 16th- and late 18th-C home of
Ingilby family since 1350, with gatehouse
c1450, Cromwellian associations Royalist
armour and weaponry and priest's hiding hole
discovered in 1964. Fine gardens and
grounds. ⚐ Sun and BH 2–6, catering for
parties by arrangement. Castle and gardens
open Easter, May to Sep, Sun and BH (also
Wed and Thu Jul and Aug only) 2–6, gardens
only Sat 2–6. Parties during week by
arrangement. Charges for 1980 not yet
known. ⚠ (Tel Harrogate 770186) ⅄ B
RIPON North Yorkshire Map 8 SE37
Fountains Abbey and Studley Royal
Country Park 3m SW off B6265. Extensive
Deer Park in which to spend several pleasant
hours, deer, specimen trees and lake. Walk
through ornamental gardens with views of
ponds, monuments and temples before
reaching Fountains Abbey, a magnificent
ruined Cistercian Abbey and the 17th-C hall
(hall may be closed during 1980). ⚐ Deer
Park open all year during daylight hours.
Free. Abbey and gardens open all year (ex 25

Dec) from 9.30 to 4.30 Nov to Mar, 5.30 Apr
and Oct, 7.30 May and Sep, 9.30 Jun, Jul,
Aug. Admission, including floodlighting,
Easter to Oct 50p (ch and pen 20p), Nov to
Mar 25p (ch and pen 10p). Floodlighting (not
on Mon) Aug 8.30–11, Sep 8–10.30. 35p (ch
5–16 and pen 10p). ⚠ cars 25, coaches 50.
Opening hours and admission prices under
revision for 1980.
*Wakeman's House, Museum and Tourist
Information Centre* House dates back to
14th C, now a combined tourist information
centre and museum of local and historical
interest. Open Spring BH to late Sep daily
10–6, Sun 12–4. Sat only during winter
10–4. Free.

RIVERFORD FARM *Devon* Map 3 SX76
2½m SE of Buckfastleigh on A384. A 500-acre
mixed Devonshire farm, which is open to the
public on organised visits. An adapted farm
trailer transports visitors around the farm to
see the various farm operations, including
machine milking in the afternoons, and the
livestock. Every afternoon, tour starts at 2.30.
Displays show the three stages of farming
from Tudor to the present day. There are local
crafts and produce on display and for sale. ⚐
(inclusive of price) are served in the Barn at
the end of the tour £1 (ch 75p). Open
Apr–Sep. Party (evening tours), which
includes barn dance and barbecue. ⚠ *(Tel
Staverton 636)* & **(79)**

ROCHE ABBEY *South Yorkshire*
Map 8 SK59
1½m SE Maltby. Cistercian abbey founded in
1147 with walls of north and south transepts
still standing to their full height. Firm
gatehouse lies to north-west of church. Open,
see inside front cover but closed 4.30 Mon
and Tue. 15p (ch 16 and pen 5p). ⚠ *(AM)*

ROCHESTER *Kent* Map 5 TQ76
Rochester Castle Commenced 1087 and
retaining remarkable storeyed keep dating
from 1126 to 1139. Keep open, see inside
front cover but closed all day Tue and Fri pm.
20p (ch and pen 5p). ⚠ *(AM)*
Eastgate House High Street. Elizabethan
house described in Charles Dicken's *Edwin
Drood* and *Pickwick Papers*, now museum of
local history, including Dickens' relics. Also
extensive general collections of arms and
armour and ship models (principally sailing
barges), furniture, Victoriana, toys and dolls
etc. Dickens' Swiss Chalet from Gadshill
stands in grounds. Open all year, daily (ex
Sun) 10–12.30 and 2–5.30. Free. P. *(Tel
Medway 44176)* **(79)**

ROCKBOURNE *Hampshire* Map 4 SU11
Roman Villa Excavation is still in progress on
this site. Museum has unique items of pottery
and jewellery and hoard of 7,717 coins. So far
73 rooms have been uncovered. Open 1 Apr
to 1 Oct, Mon to Fri 2–6, Sat, Sun and BH
10.30–6. Jul and Aug every day 10.30–6.
25p (ch 16 15p). ⚠ *(Tel 445)* &

ROCKINGHAM *Northamptonshire*
Map 4 SP89
Rockingham Castle Elizabethan family
home within walls of Norman royal castle.
Panoramic views of four counties. Fine
paintings, gardens and close associations
with Charles Dickens–a frequent visitor. ⚐
Open Easter to 30 Sep, Thu, Sun, BH Mon
and following Tue 2–6; other days, for parties
by previous appointment. 90p (ch 50p)
subject to alteration. ⚠ *(Tel 770240)*. *(Cmdr
Michael Saunders Watson)*

RODE *Somerset* Map 3 ST85
The Tropical Bird Gardens 17 acres of
grounds planted with trees and shrubs and
dotted with lakes, surround aviaries where
more than 180 species of colourful birds are
kept. During summer months rabbits, guinea
pigs, goats, and donkeys can be seen. Pets
corner of domestic animals with donkey rides
⚐ Easter to mid Oct. Gardens open all year
(ex 25 Dec) summer 10.30–7 (no entry after
6.30) winter 10.30–sunset. 85p (ch 14 45p).
Party 25+. Admission prices for 1980 under
revision. Ch 14 must be accompanied by
adults. Wheelchairs for hire. No dogs. ⚠
(ample). *(Tel Beckington 326, Catering
Beckington 585)* &

ROLVENDEN *Kent* Map 5 TQ83
C M Booth Collection of Historic Vehicles
Falstaff Antiques, 63 High Street. Contains
historic vehicles and other items of transport
interest. The main feature is the unique
collection of Morgan 3-wheel cars dating from
1913, plus the only known Humber tri-car of
1904, a 1929 Morris van, motorcycles,
bicycles, etc. New extension opened 1979.
Open all year (ex 25 Dec and BH) weekdays
10–6 (10–1 Wed), open some Sun. 25p (ch
15 10p). P. *(Tel 234)* &
Great Maythan Hall Large brick mansion,
built by Sir Edwin Lutyens in 1910, and with
fine grounds. Open May to Sep, Wed and Th
2–5. 40p (ch 25p) ⚠ & B

ROMSEY *Hampshire* Map 4 SU32
Broadlands Main entrance on A31 Romsey
by-pass. The home of the late Lord
Mountbatten. Previously the home of the
Victorian Prime Minister, Lord Palmerston,
and long famous as a centre of hospitality for
Royal and distinguished visitors. Classic
Palladian architecture and landscape by
'Capability' Brown. Richly decorated interiors
and fine artworks. Special exhibition
'Mountbatten of Burma' traces Lord
Mountbatten's distinguished career in War
and Peace. Also an audio-visual show which
illustrates events in his life. Picnic area, Gift
shop and ⚐. Open 1 Apr to 28 Sep 10.30–6
(last admission 45 min before closing time).
Closed Mon except Aug, Sep and BH. £1 (ch
5–13 and pen 50p, also disabled). Admissio
prices under revision for 1980. Party 15+. ⚠
(Tel 516878) & B

ROTHBURY *Northumberland* Map 12 NU00
Cragside Victorian house designed for the
first Lord Armstrong by Richard Norman
Shaw–the first house in the world to be lit by
electricity generated by water power.
Contains much of its original furniture. 900
acres Country Park. Open: grounds Apr to
Sep daily 10.30–6, Oct, Wed, Sat and Sun
2–5; house Apr to Sep daily ex Mon, but ope
BH Mon (closed following Tue) 1–6, Oct,
Wed, Sat and Sun 2–5. Country Park only
50p, Country Park and House £1.20. *(Tel
20333)* (NT)

ROTHERHAM *South Yorkshire* Map 8 SK49
Art Gallery Brian O'Malley Library and Arts
Centre, Walker Place. Continuous
programme of temporary exhibitions
including, at times, 19th and 20th-C painting
from the Museum collections and
Rockingham pottery. ⚐ (licensed). Open all
year daily (ex Sun and BH), Mon to Fri 10–6,
Sat 10–5. Free. & *(Tel 65481)* &
Museum Clifton Park. Late 18th-C mansion
reputed by John Carr of York. Contains 18th-
C furnished rooms, family portraits, period
kitchen. Displays of Victoriana, local history,

local Roman antiquities, numismatics, glass and glassmaking, church silver, 19th- and 20th-C paintings; British ceramics, including Rockingham, local geology and natural history. Temporary exhibitions. Open Apr to Sep weekdays (ex Fri) 10–6. Sun 2.30–5. Nov to Mar; weekdays (ex Fri) 10–5. Sun 2.30–4.30. P. *(Tel 65481)* &

ROTTINGDEAN *East Sussex* Map 5 TQ30
The Grange Museum and Art Gallery Early Georgian house, remodelled by Lutyens, now library, art gallery and museum including Kipling exhibits and part of the National Toy Museum. Frequent temporary exhibitions. Open Mon, Tue, Thu, Fri and Sat 10–5, Sun 2–5. Closed Weds and 4 Apr, 25/26 Dec. Free. ⚠ *(Tel Brighton 31004)*

ROUSHAM *Oxfordshire* Map 4 SP42
Rousham House Off A423. Attractive 17th- and 18th-C house near River Cherwell, with Civil War associations, fine pictures, furniture, and notable garden layout by William Kent. Open Wed, Sun and BH Apr to Sep, 2–5.30; gardens only daily, all year, 10–6. Garden 50p, House 75p. These prices are provisional for 1980. Party. ⚠ *(Tel Steeple Ashton 47110)* & B

ROWLANDS GILL *Tyne and Wear* Map 12 NZ15
Gibside Chapel and Avenue Repaired and rededicated in Jul 1966, originally built by James Paine in 1760, one of remaining buildings of 18th-C landscape layout. Open Apr to Sep, daily (ex Tue); Oct and Mar, Wed, Sat, Sun 2–6. Car Park, grounds and chapel 20p. ⚠ *(NT)*

ROYSTON *Hertfordshire* Map 5 TL34
Royston Museum Old Town Hall contains displays and collections of old photographs, paintings and other historical material from the town. Open all year, Sat only 10–4. Free. ⚠ *(Tel Hitchin 4476)* &

RUDDINGTON *Nottinghamshire* Map 8 SK53
Ruddington Framework Knitters Museum Chapel Street. A unique early 19th-C complex of Frame shops and knitters cottages showing the working and domestic conditions of the workers. Illustrates the transition stage between domestic and factory working. Stockingers shop has eleven hand frames and allied equipment. Cottages are part tenanted and part in the process of restoration as Stockingers back-to-back cottage (1850) and hosier's cottage (1900). Open all year by appointment only. 20p. Special openings with machinery working by arrangement. P. *(Tel Nottingham 213287 or 212116)*
Ruddington Village Museum The Hermitage, Wilford Road. The Headquarters of the Ruddington local History and Amenity Society, this museum is housed in the village's oldest buildings with evidence of medieval occupation on the site. Permanent displays of local archaeological and folk material. Changing exhibitions throughout the year. ⚐ as ordered. Open all year (ex BH) Tue 10.30–12. Fri 7.30–9pm. At other times by appointment. 10p P in village *(Tel Nottingham 212116 or 213964)*

RUFFORD *Lancashire* Map 7 SD41
Rufford Old Hall Tudor and later (1662 and 1821), with a fine Great Hall and remarkable woodwork, including a rare example of a movable screen. The Philip Ashcroft museum is contained in a wing. Open Mar to Dec, Tue to Sun and BH Mon (closed Wed in Mar, Oct, Nov and Dec) 1–6 (or sunset). Hall and gardens 80p (ch 40p). *(NT)*

RUNCORN *Cheshire* Map 7 SJ58
Norton Priory Museum Warrington Road, nr Astmoor. Subject of largest excavation carried out by modern methods of any monastic site in Britain. Landscaped remains, standing 12th-C undercroft with beautifully carved passage, an exhibition of objects found by the excavators, surrounded by seven acres of Georgian woodlands. Winner of the 1978 National Archaeological Award. Archaeological excavation in progress Aug. Reconstruction model of Priory, wildlife display in restored summerhouse. Viewing gallery. ⚐ picnic area. Open Apr to Sep Mon, Tue and Wed 1–5, Sat, Sun and BH 1–6. Winter, Sun only 1–4. Special arrangements for parties booked in advance, including guided tour. 30p (ch 16 and pen 15p). *(Tel 69895 or 76531)*

RUSHTON *Northamptonshire* Map 4 SP88
Triangular Lodge Curious three-sided lodge, built 1593–96 by recusant Sir Thomas Tresham in the form of mystical and heraldic symbolism of the figure three. A Latin-inscribed frieze encircles the building. Open, see inside front cover. 15p (ch 16 and pen 5p). *(AM)*

RUSLAND *Cumbria* Map 7 SD38
Rusland Hall The house was built in 1720, and enlarged 1845. it contains many unusual mechanical instruments including a grand piano and a mechanical organ. Varied collection of antiques. Early cinema projectors and photographic equipment. Four acres of landscaped grounds of 18th-C style with peacocks, including rare whites. Demonstrations of mechanical music every afternoon. Open 1 Apr to 30 Sep daily 11–6. 60p (ch 14 40p). ⚠ *(Tel Satterthwaite 276)* &

RYCOTE *Oxfordshire* Map 4 SP60
Rycote Chapel Off B4013. Small well-restored 15th-C chapel, consecrated in 1449 and visited by Princess Elizabeth in the reign of her sister, Mary I, and also by Charles I. Interior contains notable 15th-C benches and 17th-C pews. Barrel roof is noted for gilded star decor cut originally from rare Continental playing cards. Open, see inside front cover. 15p (ch 16 and pen 5p). ⚠ *(AM)*

RYDAL *Cumbria* Map 11 NY30
Rydal Mount Family home of William Wordsworth from 1813 until his death in 1850. Incorporates a pre-1574 farmer's cottage. Now owned by a descendant and containing an important group of family portraits, possessions and books. Lovely setting overlooking Windermere and Rydal Water. The 4½-acre fell garden was landscaped by the poet. ⚐ Open daily Mar to Oct, 10–5.30, Nov to mid Jan, 10–12.30 and 2–4, 40p (pen and students 30p, ch 14 20p). Party. ⚠ *(Tel Ambleside 3002)* **(79)**

RYE *East Sussex* Map 5 TQ92
Lamb House West Street. 18th-C house, home of Henry James from 1898 until his death in 1916. Attractive garden. Three rooms only open 2 Apr to Oct, Wed and Sat 2–6 (last admission 5.30) 40p *(NT)*
Rye Museum Ypres Tower. A 13th-C three-storey fortification. Contains collections of Cinque Port material, medieval and other pottery from the Rye kilns, militaria, shipbuilding, dolls, toys and local history archives. Open Easter–mid Oct daily Mon–Sat 10.30–1, 2.15–5.30, Sun 11.30–1, 2.15–5.30 (last admission half-an-hour prior to closing times). Admission charge. ⚠ *(Tel 3254)*

RYHOPE (Nr Sunderland) *Tyne and Wear*
Map 12 NZ45
Ryhope Engines Museum Twin beam
Engines (1868), restored by Ryhope Engines
Trust. ⚒ when steaming. Bookstall. Open
weekends Easter to end of year – Sat, Sun
2 – 5. Run under steam power 11 – 5, 4 to 7
Apr; 3 to 5 and 24 to 26 May; 23 to 25 Aug;
25/26 Oct. Information about midweek visits
and current charges *(Tel Sunderland
210235)* ⚠

SAFFRON WALDEN *Essex* Map 5 TL53
Saffron Walden Museum Museum built
1834 for display of collections relating to
anthropology, archaeology, natural history
and applied arts. Special exhibition 7 Jun to 6
Jul 'The Furniture Maker's Workshop'. Open
all year (ex 24, 25 Dec and 4 Apr), weekdays
11 – 5 (4 Oct to Mar), Sun and BH 2.30 – 5.
Free. ⚠ *(Tel 22494)*

ST AGNES *Cornwall* Map 2 SW75
Wheal Coates Engine House The engine
house lies on the cliff between St Agnes and
Chapel Porth, and once housed an engine
which provided the essential services of
winding, pumping and ventilation for the mine.
An important relic of the country's industrial
past. *(NT)*

ST ALBANS *Hertfordshire* Map 4 TL10
City Museum Displays collections relating to
natural history and geology of south-west
Hertfordshire. Salaman colllection of tools
and crafts has reconstruction of craftsmen's
shops. Open all year Mon to Sat 10 – 5. Free.
(Tel 64511). (Tourist Information Centre) ⚓
Clock Tower Market Place. Example of early
15th-C curfew tower, which provides fine
views over the city. Open 29 May to mid Sep,
Sat 10 – 5.30, Sun 11 – 5.30. 10p (ch 5p). *(Tel
64511). (Tourist Information Centre)*
Gorhambury House Entry via lodge gates at
St Michael's Church, or at the Pré, on A5. Late
Georgian mansion designed 1777 – 84 in
modified classical style by Sir Robert Taylor.
Chippendale furniture, Grimston portraits,
16th-C enamelled glass, and Francis Bacon
associations. Open May to Sep Thu 2 – 5. 75p
(ch and pen 35p). Party. Admission prices for
1980 under revision. ⚠ *(Tel 54051). (Earl of
Verulam)*
St Albans Organ Museum 326 Camp Road.
Contains a unique collection of automatically
operated organs and other musical
instruments. Records of some of the organs
and other instruments, also books on
mechanical musical instruments can be
purchased. Recitals Sun 2 – 4.15. 40p.
Parties at other times by appointment. *(Tel
52875). (Mr E Cockayne)* ⚓

*The Royal National Rose Society's
Gardens* Chiswell Green Lane. Rose garden
and trial ground for new varieties. Over
30,000 plants in 1,650 varieties. Species
roses, old fashioned roses, modern roses and
roses of the future. ⚒ Open 15 Jun to 30 Sep
(ex BH Mon) Mon to Sat 9 – 5, Sun 2 – 6. 60p
(ch 15 free). Party. Opening hours and
admission charges for 1980 under revision.
⚠ *(Tel 50461)* ⚓
*Verulamium Theatre, Museum and
Hypocaust* St Michael's. Roman theatre,
built AD 140 – 150, used for presentation of
plays and other functions. Superb museum of
Roman finds, including tessellated
pavements near by. Hypocaust, across
parkland, also to be seen. Theatre open Mar
to end Oct, daily 10 – 5; Nov to end Feb 10 – 2.
20p (ch 5p students 10p). Museum open Mar
to end Oct, weekdays 10 – 5.30, Sun 2 – 5.30.
Nov to end Feb, weekdays 10 – 4, Sun 2 – 4.
25p (ch 10p). *(Tel 54051 Theatre; 54659
Museum and Hypocaust)*

ST AUSTELL *Cornwall* Map 2 SX05
Wheal Martyn Museum 2m N on A391.
Open-air site museum of the china clay
industry. Complete clay works of the last
century have been restored; huge granite-
walled settling tanks, working water-wheels
and wooden slurry pump, 220ft pan kiln or
'dry', horse-drawn wagons, two steam
locomotives from the industry and the story of
clay in Cornwall over two centuries shown in
indoor displays. Also short slide and sound
programme for visitors. Working Pottery.
Open 1 Apr to 30 Oct 10 – 6 (last admission 5),
open during winter for Party 12+ by prior
arrangement. Admission prices for 1980 not
yet decided. ⚠ *(Tel Stenalees 850362)*

ST CLEER *Cornwall* Map 2 SX26
Trethevy Quoit Famous example of a
Neolithic tomb, with large slanting capstone.
Accessible any reasonable time. Free. *(AM)*

ST HELENS *Merseyside* Map 7 SJ59
Pilkington Glass Museum On Prescot
Road, A58, 1m from town centre. History of
glass-making from Egyptians to present day,
with some of the finest examples of glass in
world. Various temporary exhibitions
throughout the year. ⚒ Open all year (ex
Christmas and New Year), Mon to Fri 10 – 5
(10 – 9 on Wed Mar to Oct), Sat, Sun and BH
2 – 4.30. Free; parties must book in advance.
P. *(Tel 28882 ext 2499)* ⚓ B

ST IVES *Cambridgeshire* Map 4 TL37
Norris Museum The Broadway. Established
1933 using some 18th-C bricks from a former
granary, containing a comprehensive

collection of Huntingdonshire books, manuscripts, and local artefacts bequeathed to the town. Agricultural tools and bygones in new display area, water-colours of local features, work in bone and straw by French prisoners at Norman Cross. Ice skates – an unusual and comprehensive selection of fenland runners etc. Huntingdonshire lacemaking. Open all year (ex BH and Mon). May to Sep Tue to Fri 10 – 1 and 2 – 5, Sat 10 – 12 and 2 – 5, Sun 2 – 5, Oct to Apr Tue to Fri 10 – 1 and 2 – 4, Sat 10 – 12 only, closed Sun. Free. P. *(Tel 65101)*

ST IVES *Cornwall* Map 2 SW54
Park your car at Lelant Station and take advantage of the park and ride service. The fee includes parking and journeys on the train between Lelant and St Ives during the day.

Barnes Museum of Cinematography
Comprehensive collection of items relating to history of cinematography and photography. Open Jun to Sep Mon – Sat 11 – 1 and 2.30 – 5. 20p (ch 10p). P in town.
The Barbara Hepworth Museum and Sculpture Garden Barnoon Hill. The museum is in the house lived in by Dame Barbara Hepworth from 1949 to her death in 1975. Sculpture by Dame Barbara from 1929 to 1974 is on display in the house and garden. Also to be seen are many photographs, letters and other documents showing the background of the artist's career. Open all year, Mon to Sat (closed Sun, 25, 26 Dec, 1 Jan and 4 Apr), Oct – Mar 10 – 4.30; Apr – Jun and Sep 10 – 5.30; Jul and Aug Mon to Sat 10 – 6.30 also Sun 2 – 6. £1 (ch, students, and pen 50p). P 200 yds. *(Tel 6226)* &

ST KEYNE *Cornwall* Map 2 SX26
Paul Corin Musical Collection Old Mill (St Keyne Station). One of the finest collections in Europe, of automatic musical intruments which includes a rare 1929 German theatre organ by Hupfeld, also organs from fairs, cafés and streets of Holland. Reproducing Player pianos with performances of famous pianists. Orchestrions played in the cafés of Europe and the Americas. Playing daily, Easter week then May to Sep, 10.30–1, 2.30–5; Oct, Mar and Apr, Sun only, 2.30–5. 80p (ch 40p). Party. Admission prices under revision for 1980. ⚠ free. *(Tel Liskeard 43108)* &

ST MAWES *Cornwall* Map 2 SW83
St Mawes Castle Coastal blockhouse erected in 16th C by Henry VIII. Faces Falmouth across Carrick Roads. Open*, see inside front cover. 20p (ch 16 and pen 5p). ⚠ *(AM)*

ST NEOT *Cornwall* Map 2 SX16
Carnglaze Slate Caverns Old slate mine unique in South West England, situated in the beautiful valley of the River Loveny. Half a million tons of slate were mined from these huge caverns. Guided tours of great interest take approx 45 minutes. Temperature underground is 52°F all year round – jacket or cardigan is advisable on hot summer days. Open Easter and BH 10.30–5, Sun 2–5, May and Jun 2–5, 1 Jul to 7 Sep Mon – Fri 10.30–5, Sun 2–5, 8 Sep to 30 Sep 2–5 (closed Sats). 70p (ch 35p, pen 50p). Parties by appointment. Admission prices under revision for 1980. ⚠ *(Tel Dobwalls 20251)*

ST NEWLYN EAST *Cornwall* Map 2 SW85
Lappa Valley Railway The 15in-gauge steam railway runs along part of the old Newquay – Chacewater GWR line. The train makes a round trip of over two miles through scenic countryside, and stops at East Wheal Rose Halt where you can explore the site of a famous old silver and lead mine. Five-acre pleasure area (accessible by the train only), boating lake, play area, book shop and ⚊. Parties catered for. Open Easter week then Weds and Suns only 2–6 until 23 May; 23 May to 30 Jun 11–5, 1 Jul to 7 Sep 10–5.30, 8 Sep to 4 Oct 11–5. 80p (ch and pen 50p, ch 3 free). *(Tel Mitchell 317)*

ST OLAVES *Norfolk* Map 5 TG49
St Olaves Priory Near Fritton Decoy. Remains of small Augustinian priory. Exceptional early example of brickwork dating from late 13th C or early 14th C. Open Apr to Sep at any reasonable time. Free. *(AM)*

ST OSYTH *Essex* Map 5 TM11
St Clere's Hall 1 m SSE on unclass road. Moated on three sides, this Medieval manor house has 16th-C additions and renovations. It is one of the least altered examples of an aisled hall with separately roofed coss-blocks (wings) at either end. Open all year by appointment only. ⚠ *(Tel 243)* & B

SALCOMBE *Devon* Map 3 SX73
Sharpitor ½m SW on unclass road. A modern house with a museum and 6 acres of gardens providing fine views. Museum of local interest. Open 1 Apr to Oct, daily 11–1, 2–6. Museum and gardens 70p, gardens only 50p. *(NT) (NGS)*

SALFORD *Gt Manchester* Map 7 SJ89
Ordsall Hall Museum Taylorson Street. Partly half-timbered manor house with later brick-built wing (1639), includes Tudor Great Hall, Star Chamber with 14th-C features and Victorian farmhouse kitchen. On upper floor are social history displays and temporary exhibitions. Open all year Mon to Sat 10–5, Sun 2–5 (ex 4 Apr, 24–26 Dec, 1 Jan). Free. P (street). *(Tel 061-872 0251)*
Salford Museum and Art Gallery The Crescent, Peel Park. The ground floor displays a period street scene typical of a northern industrial town at the turn of the century. The first floor art galleries house a large collection of works by L S Lowry, as well as a regular series of temporary art exhibitions and displays of decorative arts. Open all year daily (ex 4 Apr, 24, 25, 26 Dec and 1 Jan) 10–6 (Oct–Mar, 10–5) Sun 2–5. Free. ⚠ *(Tel 061-736 2649 and 061-737 7692)*

SALISBURY *Wiltshire* Map 4 SU12
Salisbury and South Wilts Museum St Ann Street. Comprehensive displays of exhibits relating to the history of the city and south Wiltshire. Important prehistoric and medieval collections. Display of ceramics and costumes, and models of Old Sarum and Stonehenge. Open daily (ex Sun) Oct to Apr 10–4; May to Sep 10–5; Sun also in Jul and Aug 2–5 (closed 25, 26 Dec and 13 Apr). 40p (ch 16 and members free, pen and students 20p). Shop on premises for replicas and publications. P. *(Tel Mr P R Saunders, 4465)* & B
Mompesson House Standing in the Cathedral Close, surrounded by gracious period houses, dates from 1701, with splendid panelling and woodwork. Open Apr to end Oct, daily ex Thu and Fri 12.30–6 (sunset if earlier). Closed Nov to end Feb. 70p. *(NT)*

The Lappa Valley Steam Railway
ST NEWLYN EAST, NEAR NEWQUAY, CORNWALL
* Over two-mile return trip through pretty country.
* Boating lake with canoes and paddle boats.
* Putting green.
* Book and gift shop.
* Old forge tea rooms. Cream teas, snacks and home-made cakes.
* Historic engine house and stack of disused East Wheal Rose Silver Lead Mine.
* Picnic and play area.
* Wooded streamside walk.
* Free parking at Benny Halt.
* Open every day during the season. Ring Mitchell 317 for timetables.

ld Sarum 2m N on A345. First probably an
on Age camp, later Roman 'Sorbiodunum'
nd finally site of Norman castle and
athedral town. Foundations of castle and
athedral can be seen, together with small
useum. Open*, see inside front cover. 15p
h 16 and pen 5p). ⚠ *(AM)*

AMLESBURY *Lancashire* Map 7 SD63
amlesbury Hall Restored half-timbered
ouse, administered and preserved by the
amlesbury Hall Trust and the Lancashire
ranch of the Council for the Protection of
ural England. Various exhibitions. ⚏ Open
4 Jan – 18 Dec daily (ex Mon) 11.30 – 5. 35p
h 15 20p). P. *(Tel Mellor 2229 and 2010)*

ANCREED *Cornwall* Map 2 SW42
arn Euny Ancient Village 1m SW. Iron Age
llage site with characteristic Cornish
ogous' (subterranean hiding hole) preserved
ome 66ft in length, with circular chamber.
pen, see inside front cover. 15p (ch 16 and
en 15p) ⚠ *(AM)*

ANDRINGHAM *Norfolk* Map 9 TF62
*andringham House, Grounds and
Museum* Bought by Queen Victoria for the
rince of Wales in 1862, this modern royal
ansion contains paintings of the Royal
amily from 1845, also of members of
uropean Royal Families. Sculpture, china,
rnaments and furniture. ⚏ Open 6 Apr to 25
ep (ex 21 Jul to 9 Aug). Apr Tue, Wed, and
nu. May to Sep daily (ex Fri and Sat) also
pen 6/7 Apr. Admission prices not available.
△ *(Tel King's Lynn 2675)* ⚹
Wolferton Station (down side). On the
andringham Estate, former Royal Retiring
ooms built in 1898 specifically for, and solely
sed by Kings and Queens and their guests
n route for Sandringham, can be seen. Fine
ak panelling, original fittings (some gold
ated). Period railway posters, important
mall railway relics and Edwardian curios
cluding some from Royal train journeys,
ueen Victoria's Travelling Bed (1828). Open
pr to Sep (plus BH), Daily (ex Sat 11 – 1,
–6, Sun 2 – 6. 35p (ch 14 20p). ⚠ *(Tel
ersingham 40674)* ⚹

ANDTOFT *Yorkshire* Map 8 SE70
andtoft Transport Centre 15m E of
oncaster off A18. Developing National
ransport Museum, primarily for the
reservation and operation of trolleybuses,
ut also includes motorbuses and other items
f transport interest, boasting a collection of
ver 50 vehicles from many parts of Britain
nd the Continent. Several trolleybuses are
estored and operate on the centre's own
verhead wiring circuit on 15, 16 Apr; 27, 28

May; 26, 27 Aug; also last weekend in Jun and
Sep. 15p (ch 14 and pen 10p). Special open
day 29 Jun when many interesting vehicles
and items from other collections are on show.
Admission prices under review for 1979. ⚠ ⚹
(79)

SANDWICH *Kent* Map 5 TR35
Guildhall Dates from 1578, since restored.
Contains a collection of local documents,
paintings, and interesting relics. Open all
year, Mon to Fri 10.30 – 12.30 and 2 – 4 (5, Jun
to Oct), subject to Courts being held Tue,
Wed, and Fri each week. 10p (ch 14 with
parents, free; unaccompanied children not
admitted). ⚠ *(Tel 3060 or 2200 or 3044)* ⚹

SAXTEAD GREEN *Suffolk* Map 5 TM26
Windmill Off B1115. Fine 18th-C postmill,
twice altered, the present superstructure
dating from 1854. Open, see inside front
cover, but closed on Sun. 20p (ch and pen
5p). ⚠ *(AM)*

SCARBOROUGH *North Yorkshire*
Map 8 TA08
Scarborough Castle Fortified c1140 by the
Earl of Albemarle and rebuilt with a four-
storeyed keep in 1155 by Henry II. Damaged
in the Civil War and the 1914 – 18 War. Open*,
see inside front cover. 25p (ch 16 and pen
10p). ⚠ *(AM)*
Scarborough Zoo and Marineland
Performing dolphins, penguins, monkeys,
bears and parrots are among the attractions.
Children are provided with free fish to feed the
sealions, and bottles of milk for the young
lambs and goats. ⚏ Open Easter to 31 Oct,
daily 10 – dusk. Admission prices not yet
known. P. *(Tel 64401)* ⚹ **(79)**

SCUNTHORPE *Humberside* Map 8 SE81
Borough Museum and Art Gallery This
regional museum for South Humberside
contains important prehistoric exhibits.
Roman and later archaeology, geology,
natural history and local industry, bygones,
period rooms and Ironstone workers' cottage.
New local history galleries. Continuous
programme of temporary exhibitions. Open
all year, Mon to Sat 10 – 5, Sun 2 – 5. Free on
weekdays; 5p (ch 2½p) on Sat and Sun
afternoon and BH. P. *(Tel 3533)*
Normanby Hall Normanby Park. 5m N on
B1430. A Regency mansion built in 1825 by
Sir Robert Smirke for the Sheffield family.
Displays of costume and Regency furniture.
The house is set in 350 acres of parkland,
lawns and gardens. The stable complex
includes a Countryside Interpretation Centre.
Nature trail. Blacksmith and potter. ⚏ Open
all year, Apr to Oct Mon, Wed, Thu, Fri, Sat

10–12.30, 2–5.30, Sun 2–5.30; Nov to Mar weekdays (closed Sat) 10–12.30, 2–5, Sun 2–5. 20p (ch 10p). ⛺ *(Tel 720215)* ♿ B

SEATON DELAVAL *Northumberland* Map 12 NZ37
Seaton Delaval Hall 1½m NE on A190. Baroque-style 18th-C masterpiece of Vanbrugh, with tall Doric façade flanked by twin wings, one built to house the stables. Paintings and furnishings in the west wing, historical documents and statuary in the restored centre block. Open 1 May to 30 Sep, Wed, Sun, and BH 2–6. 30p (ch and pen 20p). ⛺ *(Tel 481 493). (Lord Hastings)*

SEDBERGH *Cumbria* Map 7 SD69
National Park Centre 72 Main Street. Permanent interpretation centre for the Sedbergh area with displays, books, maps, etc. Open Apr to end Sep, daily mid morning to late afternoon. Free. ⛺ *(Tel 20125)* ♿ B

SEDLESCOMBE *East Sussex* Map 5 TQ71
Nortons Farm Museum and Farm Trail 4½m NW of Hastings on A21. Depicts the 'cart horse era' with a fine display of carts, ploughs and hand tools. The Farm Trail takes visitors round the fruit and arable farm, where cart horses are still used. Picnic area. Open Jun to Sep 9–5. ⛺ *(Tel 471)* **(79)**

SELBORNE *Hampshire* Map 4 SU73
Oates Memorial Library and Museum and the Gilbert White Museum The Wakes. Home of the Rev Gilbert White, pioneer naturalist whose 'Natural History of Selborne' was written here. Galleries concerning the history and natural history of Selborne; galleries devoted to Captain Oates of Antarctica fame and to Frank Oates, explorer of Central Africa. Extensive gardens. Open Mar to Oct, Tue to Sun, BH 12–5.30 (last admission 5, parties outside these dates by arrangement). 45p (ch 16 20p, pen 35p). P. *(Tel 275)* ♿

SELBY *North Yorkshire* Map 8 SE63
Carlton Towers 6m S (A1041). The Duke of Norfolk's Yorkshire home, Carlton Towers was built in 1614 on property owned by the Duke's ancestors since the Norman Conquest. It was remodelled in the 18th and 19th C and now presents a mainly Victorian appearance. The elaborate state rooms are by John Francis Bentley, architect of Westminster Cathedral. Interesting paintings, furniture, silver and heraldry. Exhibitions of family uniforms and coronation robes. Viewing of the Priest's hiding hole. Shop. Picnic area and ☕. Open 5 to 8 Apr incl., 4/5 also 24 to 28 May incl. Thereafter Sat, Sun, Mon and Wed 31 May to end Sep also 26 Aug 1–5 (last admission 4.30). Conducted tours by appointment only Thu evenings. Also 5–8 Apr, 4/5 May. Admission prices not available. ⛺ *(Tel Goole 860243)*

SEVENOAKS *Kent* Map 5 TQ55
Black Charles 2½m SE at Underriver. A Hall House, built about 1400. It has fine panelling and fire-places and other interesting features. The original structure can be easily seen. Open 1 May to 10 Sep for parties by arrangement. 40p (ch 14 25p). ⛺ *(Tel Hildenborough 833036)*
Knole Famous mansion of Sackvilles, one of the largest in England, begun in 1456 by Thomas Bourchier, Archbishop of Canterbury, with many early 17th-C additions. Notable state-rooms with pictures and 17th- and 18th-C furnishings. Cartoon and Brown galleries and vast park. Open Apr to Sep, Wed to Sat and BH Mons 11–5, Sun 2–5; Oct and Nov Wed to Sat 11–4, Sun 2–4. £1.20 (ch 60p). Connoisseurs' day Fri (ex 4 Apr), £1.60, no reduction for children. Last admission one hour before closing. House closed Dec to end Mar. Gardens open 1st Wed in month, May to Sep 50p Park open free to pedestrians. ⛺ £1. *(Tel 53006 for special concessions for cars). (NT)*
Long Barn 2m S at south end of Weald village. 14th-C house, reputed birthplace of William Caxton. Restored by Edwin Lutyens and enlarged by addition of 16th-C barn in 1915 for Sir Harold Nicolson and his wife, Vita Sackville-West, who lived here for 15 years prior to Sissinghurst Castle. Fine beams, fireplaces, old brick paving, small galleried hall with ornamental panelling. Home of the late Charles Lindbergh from 1936–1938. Medium-sized garden, created by Vita Sackville-West; terraced lawns, yew trees and raised herbaceous borders. Open Apr to Sep Wed 2–6. Parties by prior arrangement. 60p (ch 25p). Under revision for 1980. No dogs. *(Tel Weald 282)*

SHAFTESBURY *Dorset* Map 3 ST82
Local History Museum Gold Hill. Small museum of needlework toys, agricultural and domestic items, fans, pottery and finds from local excavations. Fire engine of 1744. Award winner in 'Museum of the Year' award scheme for 1976. Open Easter to end Sep daily 11–5, Sun 2.30–5. 10p (ch 5p). Admission prices under revision for 1980. P. *(Tel 2157)* ♿ B

SHALFORD *Surrey* Map 4 TQ04
Shalford Mill An 18th-C watermill with a small garden, on the River Tillingbourne. Part open on application to 45 The Street. *(NT)*

The Famous Five

of Yorkshire

FIVE HOUSES OVER FOUR CENTURIES

Bramham Park
Burton Constable
Carlton Towers
Sledmere House
Sutton Park

The Famous Five of Yorkshire are a group of Stately Homes within about 40 miles of York, which are still lived in and cared for by their owners.

Each house is fascinating in its own right, but seen as a group they show the changing styles of houses built by wealthy country families over four centuries, from the grace of the sixteenth century to the grandeur of Victorian Gothic.

The Houses stand in grounds varying from the French formal design, to the natural landscaping of Capability Brown. In addition there are lakes, lily ponds, fountains, cascades, rose gardens and nature walks. We hope you will come and share the pleasures of these lovely places with us;

Our voucher scheme allows a substantial saving.

There is a Free Car Park, a Cafeteria and a gift shop at each House and between us we are open every day during the Summer.

BRAMHAM PARK
Wetherby

BURTON CONSTABLE
Sproatley

SUTTON PARK
Sutton on the Forest

CARLTON TOWERS
Selby

SLEDMERE HOUSE
Driffield

See each gazetteer entry for details, and send for the free leaflet and vouchers giving details of opening times, special attractions and booked party rates.

WE LOOK FORWARD TO SEEING YOU!

SHALLOWFORD *Staffordshire* Map 7 SJ82
Izaak Walton's Cottage A restored cottage
where Izaak Walton, the famous angler,
stayed at times during his retirement. There is
a small museum. Open all year, Thu to Sun
10–1, 2–5, also Mons 29 May and 28 Aug. 5p
(ch 3p). ⚠ (in lane). *(Tel Yarnfield 278)*

SHAP *Cumbria* Map 12 NY51
Shap Abbey An abbey of the
Premonstratensian order, dedicated to St
Mary Magdalene, with buildings dating from
1201–Jan 1540, when abbey was dissolved.
Open, see inside front cover. Free. P. *(Tel
670). (AM)* ⓖ
Keld Chapel 1m SW off A6, close to River
Lowther. Small, pre-Reformation building, in
which occasional services are still held. Key
available at cottage in village, see notice on
chapel door. Free. *(NT)*

SHARPTHORNE *West Sussex* Map 5 TQ33
Tanyard A medieval tannery and manor with
16th- and 17th-C additions, set in attractive
walled gardens. Formerly reputed to have
been a royal household where Queen Victoria
once stayed. The main rooms with oak beams
and timbering are on view, displaying large
open fireplaces, furniture, *objets d'art* and
early Victorian photographs typical of the
period. Open 1 May to 30 Sep, Mon and Wed
2–5 (other times by prior appointment). 75p
(ch and pen, no reduction). ⚠ *(Tel 01-
643 5448). (Mr M R Lewinsohn)*

SHEBBEAR *Devon* Map 2 SS40
Alscott Farm Agricultural Museum A
remarkable collection of vintage farm tractors,
ploughs, dairy and household implements,
photographs and information on North
Devon's agricultural past. Special exhibition
of unique scale model of an Edwardian
travelling fair and contemporary photographs
and original circus posters. Open Easter to 30
Sep, daily, 12–dusk. 40p (ch 10p). Party &
coaches welcome. ⚠ *(Tel 206)* ⓖ

SHEFFIELD *South Yorkshire* Map 8 SK38
Abbeydale Industrial Hamlet Abbeydale
Road South. One of the first examples of
industrial archaeology to be preserved and
made accessible to the public. The late 18th-
and early 19th-C steel and scythe works, with
their machinery, show production from the
raw material stage to the finished production.
🍴. Children's Working Days 7 Mar, 3 Oct, 7
Nov. Working Days 8/9 Mar, 4 Oct, 8 Nov.
Craftsman's Fair 14–22 Jun. Open daily (ex
24–26 Dec), Mon to Sat 10–5, Sun 11–5;
open until 8, 26 May to 27 Aug. 30p (ch 15p,
pen free). ⚠ 10p car, 5p m/c, 40p coach. *(Tel
367731)*
Bishops' House Meersbrook Park. A 15th- to
16th-C Yeoman's house, restored as a
museum of local and social history. Open all
year, Wed to Sat 10–5, Sun 11–5, closed
24–26 Dec. 10p (ch 5p). ⚠ *(Tel 57701)* ⓖ
City Museum Weston Park. A regional
museum of geology, natural sciences,
archaeology, and Sheffield area trades,
including cutlery, plate and ceramics. North
Derbyshire antiquities and changing
exhibitions are also featured. Open daily (ex
24–26 Dec), weekdays 10–5, Sun 11–5; 26
May to 25 Aug, weekdays 10–8, Sun 11–8.
Free. *(Tel 27226)*
Shepherd Wheel Whiteley Woods. An early
water-powered cutler's grinding
establishment. Open Wed to Sat (ex 24–26
Dec) 10–12.30 and 1.30–5, Sun 11–12.30
and 1.30–5. Free. *(Tel 367731)* ⓖ

SHEFFIELD PARK *East Sussex* Map 5 TQ4:
On A275. Belonged to King Harold's father
and later was mentioned in Domesday Book.
Basically Tudor, it was remodelled by James
Wyatt 1775–8 for 1st Lord Sheffield. In last
century was famous for the inter-Australian
cricket matches, started by 3rd Lord Sheffielc
whose own team included W G Grace.
Guests to house included Henry VIII, Edward
Gibbon, King Edward VII. Present owners, M
and Mrs P J Radford, purchased property in
1972 and are engaged in restoring and
redecorating over a long period. It is one of th
most beautiful houses in Sussex and the
situation is unrivalled. Open Easter to end
Oct, Wed, Thu, Sun and BH Mons 2–5. 50p
Party 40+. ⚠ *(Tel Danehill 790531)* ⓖ **(79)**

SHEFFIELD PARK GARDEN *East Sussex*
Map 5 TQ42
On A275. Magnificent gardens and a lake-
watered park of nearly 150 acres, laid out
from the 18th to the 20th C; they surround a
house by James Wyatt (see previous entry).
Rhododendrons, azaleas (May to Jun), and
notable trees and shrubs (autumn). 🍴 (not
under NT management). Gardens open Apr
to Sep, Tue to Sat 11–7, Sun 2–7; Oct to 15
Nov, Tue to Sat 11–5, Sun 2–5; BH Mon
11–7. £1. No dogs. *(NT)*

**SHEFFIELD PARK STATION, BLUEBELL
RAILWAY MUSEUM** *East Sussex*
Map 5 TQ42
Off A275. A station of the revived Bluebell
Railway, a former London, Brighton and
South Coast line. Parade Day 11 May, 20th
Anniversary celebrations 3 Aug, Vintage
Sunday 14 Sep. Vintage steam trains run as
follows: weekends throughout the year (Sun
only in Dec, Jan, and Feb); weekends and
Wed in May and Oct, daily Jun to end Sep,
and daily during Easter week. Fares 90p (ch
45p). Party. Under revision for 1980. Part of
the station is a small museum of old railways
relics and records. Open from 10.30am on
days when trains run, on other days open for
limited viewing. ⚠ 20p. 🍴 *(Tel Newick 2370)*
ⓖ

SHERBORNE *Dorset* Map 3 ST61
Sherborne Castle A 16th-C house built by S
Walter Raleigh, home of the Digby family
(17th-C Earls of Bristol) since 1617, with fine
furniture, paintings, porcelain, and items of
historical interest in their natural settings.
Twenty acres of 'Capability' Brown planned
lakeside lawns and pleasure grounds with
cascade and orangery. Old Castle ruins and
Abbey. Varied programme of special events
on most Sundays during summer. Teas and
refreshments in the Gothic Dairy by the lake.
Picnic grounds. Open 5 Apr to end Sep, Thu,
Sat, Sun, and BH Mon 2–6. Admission price
under review. ⚠ *Tel 3182). (Mr S Wingfield
Digby)* ⓖ B
Sherborne Museum, Abbey Gate House
Church Lane. Opened in 1968 and extended
to the second floor in 1970. On show are a
model of the Norman castle, a fine Victorian
dolls' house, local geological and Roman
material, coloured photographs of the
Sherborne missal of 1400, local photographs
from 1850 and other items. Natural history
section. Open 1 Apr to 31 Oct daily (ex Mon)
10.30–12.30 and 3–4.30, Sun 3–5. 1 Nov tc
31 Mar, Tue, Sat and Sun afternoon only. 10
(ch 19 5p). P. *(Tel 2252)*
Sherborne Old Castle This ruined castle
about half a mile east of the town was built by
Roger, Bishop of Salisbury between 1107 an

135. The keep, curtain walls, towers and
gates date from the period. Minor alterations
were carried out by Sir Walter Raleigh in
1592. Open*, see inside front cover. 15p (ch
16 and pen 5p). ⚠ *(AM)*

*Worldwide Butterflies Ltd and
Lullingstone Silk Farm* Compton House.
Entrance on A30 2½m W. Unique example of
butterfly farm in stately home and grounds.
Collections from across the world. Natural
jungle with living exotic butterflies and tropical
palm-house. Also the home of the
Lullingstone Silk Farm which produced
unique English reared silk for the last two
Coronations and the Queen's wedding dress.
Open 1 Apr to 31 Oct, 10–5. £1.10 (ch 16
55p) under revision for 1980. ⚠ *(Tel Yeovil
3608/9)* &

SHERBORNE ST JOHN *Hampshire*
Map 4 SU65
The Vyne ½m NE. A notable early 16th-C
house, showing diaper brickwork, built for the
Sandys family, with additions of 1654 by John
Webb, including the earliest classical portico.
Chapel contains Renaissance glass. Fine
henfold panelling in long gallery. Open Apr to
end Oct, Tue, Wed, Thu, Sat and Sun 2–6
(5.30 Oct). BH Mon 11–1 and 2–6. £1 (ch
10p), gardens only 40p (ch 20p). ⚌ in the Old
Brewhouse 3–5.30. *(NT)*

SHERIFF HUTTON *North Yorkshire*
Map 8 SE66
Sheriff Hutton Castle The ruins of a 12th-C
castle, originally five storeys high with
massive square towers and an extensive
gallery. Strong Royal connections existed
from the 14th century onwards, but from the
time of James I the castle was greatly
neglected. Still an impressive structure, the
highest remaining part is the south west
tower, 100ft high, beneath which there is a
dungeon. Open all year during daylight hours.
⚠ *(Tel 341)* &

SHERINGHAM *Norfolk* Map 9 TG14
Sheringham Hall ½m W of town, off A149.
Regency mansion and park, work of
Humphrey Repton in 1812. Magnificent
rhododendron woods (one mile drive) planted
in the 19th C. Hall open on Fri 2–6, from May
to Sep, only by previous written application to
the Secretary. 25p in aid of charity. Gardens
generally open on five Suns during the year.
25p. Park open all weekdays. 25p per person.
Rhododendron Woods open 1 May to 30 Jun.
25p. ⚠ *(Tel 822074). (Mr T Upcher)* & B
North Norfolk Railway Sheringham Station.
A collection of steam locomotives and rolling
stock, some undergoing or awaiting
restoration. Among the former are several
industrial tank engines and two examples of

ex-Great Eastern Railway main line engines.
Rolling stock includes suburban coaches,
Brighton Belle, Pullmans and directors private
saloons. Model railway. Souvenirs and
bookshop. Museums of railwayana. Steam-
hauled trains to operate weekends, Easter,
Spring Bank Hol, the every Sun and certain
weekdays throughout summer, until Oct. ⚌
Open Easter to mid Oct, daily from 10–5 (or
later). Admission prices under revision for
1980. Party. P. *(Tel 822045)* &

SHILDON *Co Durham* Map 8 NZ22
Timothy Hackworth Museum Soho House,
Hackworth Cottage. A sixteen-room house,
fully renovated, originally the home of
Timothy Hackworth, famous locomotive
engineer and first manager of the Stockton-
Darlington railway. Four of the rooms contain
furniture from the 1830s and the other rooms
hold displays of Hackworth's papers and
personal trivia, Stockton and Darlington
railway items, etc. Timothy Hackworth
original engine shed. Copies of the booklet
'Shildon Urban Rail Trails' available from
museum. Open 1 Apr to 30 Sep 10–6, Wed to
Sun. 15p (ch 15 and pen 10p). ⚠ *(Tel
Spennymoor 816166 ext 385)*

SHIPLEY *West Sussex* Map 4 TQ12
Belloc's Mill King's Mill. A fine example of a
smock mill (1879, restored 1957) in full
working order. Hilaire Belloc, the writer, lived
here from 1906–53. Small exhibition of his
work in mill. Open for conducted tours May to
Oct, first weekend in month 2.30–5.30. 30p
(ch 5–16 15p). Parties at other times by
written appointment to *Mr P J Crowther, West
Sussex RH13 8PJ*. P. *(Tel Coolham 310)*

SHIPTON *Salop* Map 7 SO59
Shipton Hall 6½m SW of Much Wenlock on
B4378. A beautiful Elizabethan Manor house
in picturesque Corvedale setting. Notable
interior plasterwork of 1762 also fine
Georgian stable block. There is an attractive
walled garden, medieval dovecote and old
parish church. ⚌ for parties by arrangement.
Open May to Sep Thu 2.30–5.30; Sun
2.30–5.30 during Aug, also 4, 5, 25, 26 May,
24, 25 Aug. 70p (ch 14 40p). Party. ⚠ *(Tel
Brockton 225). (C R N Bishop Ltd)* & B
(gardens)

SHOREHAM-BY-SEA *West Sussex*
Map 4 TQ20
Marlipins A Norman-and-later flint building
possibly a warehouse, now a maritime and
local history museum. Open May to Sep Mon
to Sat 10–12.30 and 2–5, Sun 2.30–5. ⚠
*(Tel 62994). (Sussex Archaeological
Society)*

Sherborne
Castle

**Built by Sir Walter
Raleigh 1594**

Home of the Digby family (17th-
century Earls of Bristol) since
1617. A fascinating fully-furnished
historic home in a beautiful setting
of lake, woods and parkland with
ruins of the old castle in the background. Described by Alexander
Pope in 1722 as a 'phantasy castle
— so peculiar and of so uncommon

kind that it merits a more particular
description'. Situated 1 mile to the
east of the attractive town of
Sherborne, with its ancient abbey,
Almshouses and 2 castles. For
details of the opening times see the
gazetteer entry.

SHOTTERY *Warwickshire* Map 4 SP15
Anne Hathaway's Cottage The thatched
and timbered Elizabethan cottage, where
Anne Hathaway, who became
Shakespeare's wife, was born. Open all year
(ex 4 Apr, morning, 24–26 Dec), Jun, Jul,
Aug, Sep, weekdays 9–7, Sun 10–6; Apr,
May, Oct, Thu and Sat 9–7, Mon to Wed and
Fri 9–6, Sun 10–6; Nov to Mar, weekdays
9–4.30 Sun 1.30–4.30. 50p (ch school age
20p). Admission prices under revision for
1980. ⚠ P. *(Tel Stratford-upon-Avon
292100)* ♿ B
SHREWSBURY *Salop* Map 7 SJ41
Bear Steps St Alkmund's Square. Recently
restored, timber-framed, 14th-C cottage with
shops and meeting hall. Hall has mid 14th-C
crown-post roof, and buildings of
considerable antiquarian interest. A winner of
European Architectural Heritage Year Award.
Open all year Mon to Sat 10–5. Free. P. *(Tel
52019)* ♿ B
Shrewsbury Castle Castle Gates. A 12th-C-
and-later building, with historic associations,
altered by Thomas Telford after 1780. Open
Easter Sat to Oct, daily 10–5; Oct to Easter,
Mon to Sat 10–4. 22p (ch and pen 11p). P.
(Tel 52019)
Clive House Museum An 18th-C town house
occupied by the 1st Lord Clive during his
period as Mayor of Shrewsbury in 1762. Now
houses a collection of Caughley and Coalport
China, maw tiles, costume, church silver,
Georgian room and the Museum of the 1st
The Queen's Dragoon Guards. Open all year
(ex Sun and BH) Mon 12–1 and 2–6 (4.30 in
winter), Tue to Sat 10–1 and 2–6 (4.30
winter). Free. P in streets. *(Tel 54811)*
Longden Coleham Pumping Station Two
compound beam engines installed in 1900

and worked until 1970, restored to working
order. Open all year Wed to Fri 2–5; other
times by arrangement with Curator. Free. P.
(Tel 54811)
Rowley's House Barker Street. A fine
restored half-timbered house, containing
Roman remains from Wroxeter, and
Shropshire bygones. Geology and prehistory
can be seen by arrangement. Open all year
Mon to Sat (ex Sun and BH) 10–1, 2–5. Free
P. *(Tel 61196)*
SHUGBOROUGH *Staffordshire* Map 7 SJ92
*Shugborough Hall and Staffordshire
County Museum* 5m E of Stafford off A513.
Mansion (NT) built 1693–1810, including
work by Samuel Wyatt. Plasterwork, pictures
fine collection of French furniture,
mementoes of Admiral George Anson
(1697–1762). Notable landscape includes
Chinese House in neo-Grecian style by
James 'Athenian' Stuart. Riverside gardens.
Museum exhibits include social history,
agriculture, crafts, natural history and geolog
in Staffordshire. ⚐ Open Mar to Oct Tue to
Fri, 10.30–5.30, Sat, Sun and BH 2–6.
Entrance to site weekends and BH only 40p
(ch 15p). School parties booked in advance
free. Party 20+. House 60p (ch 25p). Parties
as above. Park Farm 20p (ch 15p), school
parties booked in advance 10p per person. ⚠
free. All details subject to alteration. *(Tel Little
Haywood 881388)* ♿ *(NT)*
SIDMOUTH *Devon* Map 3 SY18
Sidmouth Museum An elegant Georgian
House adjacent parish church. Open 10 days
Easter and from Spring BH to end Sep.
10.30–12.30 and 2.30–4.30 Mon to Sat, and
Sun 2.30–4.30. When closed can be visited
by appointment. 15p (ch school 5p). *(Tel 294
or 2357)* **(79)**

LCHESTER *Hampshire* Map 4 SU66
alleva Museum A small museum dealing
th the Roman town of Calleva Atrebatum,
nich was recently rearranged and updated
include panels of photographs, maps and
her illustrative materials as well as actual
jects excavated here, in order to present a
ief account of life in this Roman town.
ccessible daily from 9 – sunset. Free. P in
ad. *(Tel 700362)* &

LSOE *Bedfordshire* Map 4 TL03
rest Park Gardens Notable 18th-C garden
yout with formal canals and alterations by
apability' Brown. Baroque early 18th-C
nqueting house by Thomas Archer, and
wling Green House by Batty Langley. ℤ.
rounds only open Sat, Sun and BH Mon
–5.30 in Apr; 10 – 7 from May to Sep. 25p
h 16 and pen 10p). △ *(AM)*

NGLETON *West Sussex* Map 4 SU81
eald and Downland Open-Air Museum A
useum of historic buildings from the Weald
d Downland area in Kent, Sussex, Surrey
d Hampshire which have been re-erected
re together with displays of traditional crafts
d rural industries. Exhibits include a 14th-C
use, a 15th-C farmhouse from Kent, a
th-C granary from Littlehampton, 19th-C
uthwater forge, a 19th-C Sussex toll
ttage, the Titchfield market hall, and the
mbrook barn which houses an exhibition of
ilding techniques and materials since
edieval times. Woodland nature trail
cluding special trail for wheelchairs which
e pushed) and picnic area. Open 1 Apr to 30
p daily (ex Mon but incl BH and Mon in Aug)
–5; Oct Wed, Sat, Sun 11 – 5; Nov to Mar
80 Sun 11 – 4. Last admission 1 hr before
sing. 60p (school ch, students and pen
p). Under revision for 1980. Party. △ *(Tel*
8)*

SSINGHURST *Kent* Map 5 TQ73
ssinghurst Castle Garden 1½m NE of
wn. Tudor, with a fine gate tower and moat,
d beautiful gardens, created by the late V
ckville-West, famous for roses in Jun and
'. ℤ May to Sep. Part of castle and the
rdens are open Apr to 15 Oct. Mon to Fri
– 6.30; Sat, Sun, 4 Apr and BH Mon
– 6.30. £1.10 (ch 50p). Party 70p. Shop. No
gs. *(Tel 250).* (NT)

TTINGBOURNE *Kent* Map 5 TQ96
olphin Yard Sailing Barge Museum
own Quay Lane. Original sail loft, forge,
pwrights, also sailmakers and riggers
ls. Models, plans, prints, etc. ℤ. Open
ster to end Oct, Sun also BH Mon 11 – 5.
p (ch 16 and pen 15p). P.

SIZERGH *Cumbria* Map 7 SD48
Sizergh Castle 14th-C pele tower
incorporated in a house dating from the 15th
to 18th C. Tudor great hall, Jacobite relics.
Fine ceilings and panelling. Open Apr to end
Sep; house open Wed and Sun, Thu, 29 May
and all Thu in Jul and Aug 2 – 5.45. Closed BH
Mons. 70p Gardens only 30p. *(NT)*

SKEGNESS *Lincolnshire* Map 9 TF56
Church Farm Museum Farmhouse and
outbuildings restored to show the way of life of
a Lincolnshire farmer at the end of 19th C. The
Bernard Best collection of farm implements
and machinery together with veterinary
equipment are on display. Craftsmen at work
during summer weekends. ℤ (teas
weekends). Open Apr to Oct daily
10.30 – 5.30. 25p (ch 16 and pen 15p). △ *(Tel
66658)*
Skegness Natureland Marine Zoo North
Parade, The Promenade. A modern marine
zoo, specialising in keeping sea lions, seals
and penguins. There is also a tropical house,
aquarium, including a large Fresh Water Fish
Exhibit, and a Floral Palace full of exotic
plants, with tropical birds in free flight. The zoo
also cares for orphan baby seals, that have
been washed up on nearby beaches. Pets
Corner and a Wild Fowl Pool provide
amusement for the children. ℤ. Open all year
(ex 25 Dec), daily 29 May to Oct 10 – 7.30
(10 – 4, Oct to 28 May). Admission charges
not yet decided. P. *(Tel 4345)* &

SKELTON *Cumbria* Map 12 NY43
Hutton-in-the-Forest 17th-C house built
around a 14th-C pele tower, alterations in
18th and 19th Cs by Webster and Salvin. The
house contains contemporary pictures and
furnishings. Gardens include fine specimen
trees and an ornamental lake. ℤ House open
during summer months, details from local
Tourist Information centres. Party. Opening
times and prices under revision for 1980. △
(Tel 207). (Lord Inglewood) & B

SKIDBY *Humberside* Map 8 TA03
Skidby Windmill On A164. Only surviving
example of intact windmill north of Humber
and east of Pennines, this is a well-preserved
mill of 1821 which is being established as an
agricultural museum. Black-tarred tower and
white cap form prominent local landmark.
Open first Sat in May to last Sun in Sep, Sat
10 – 4, Sun 1 – 4.30. Parties at other times by
arrangement. 15p (ch 10p). P. *(Tel Beverley
882255)*

The Weald and Down Open Air Museum
— Singleton

A collection of historic buildings saved from destruction and re-erected at the museum.

Exhibits include a 14th-century house, a 15th-century
farmhouse from Kent, a working Elizabethan treadwheel
from Hampshire, a 19th-century blacksmith's forge and
a wheelwright's shop. The Museum is continuously
developing and buildings are being re-erected by the
Museum's craftsmen. An introductory exhibition housed
in the Hambrook Barn helps the visitor to profit from
his visit. The museum is situated on a magnificent 40
acre site with the woodland nature trail and free parking.
Parties and school visits by appointment only. Details
from Weald and Downland Open Air Museum,
Singleton, Chichester, West Sussex. Tel: Singleton 348.

SKIPTON *North Yorkshire* Map 7 SD95
Craven Museum Town Hall, High Street.
Contains collection dealing especially with
the Craven district. There are important
exhibits of folk life, lead mining and prehistoric
and Roman remains. Open all year, Apr to
Sep Mon, Wed, Thu, Fri 11 – 5, Sat 10 – 12
and 1 – 5, Sun 2 – 5; Oct to Mar, Mon, Wed,
Thu, Fri 2 – 5, Sat 10 – 12 and 1.30 – 4.30.
Free. P. *(Tel 4079)*
George Leatt Industrial and Folk Museum
High Corn Mill, Chapel Hill. Old mill, four
storeys high to which Victorian machinery is
being added and where milling has been
carried out since the 12th C. Two
waterwheels, a turbine of 1912, and a
winnower which took a prize in 1884, are all
operational. Collection of horse traps, carts,
etc. The mill is open most Suns and BH at
visitors own risk 12 – 5; parties at other times
by arrangement only. Free, but possibility of
charge being made. P. *(Tel 2883)* & B
Skipton Castle High Street. Fully-roofed
12th-C and later castle, with picturesque
interior courtyard. Massive gateway and six
14th-C round towers. Besieged for three
years in Civil War. Open all year daily (ex Sun
mornings, 4 Apr, 25 Dec) 10 – 7 (Sun from 2).
Last admission, 6 or earlier sunset. Tours on
the hour, 10, 11, 12, 2, 3, 4. Admission
between tours with illustrated tour sheets in
English, French or German. 45p (ch 18 25p,
ch 5 free). Party. (school) 25p per person. P.
behind nearby Town Hall. *(Tel 2442)*

SLEDMERE *Humberside* Map 8 SE96
Sledmere House Georgian house built in
1751, and enlarged by Sir Christopher Sykes
in 1787. Decorative plasterwork by Joseph
Rose in Adam style. Contents include
Chippendale, Sheraton, and French
furnishings, paintings, porcelain, and antique
statuary. Also unique room decorated with
Turkish tiles. Park and gardens by 'Capability'
Brown include greatly extended lawns with
large water basin and Italian fountain. ☕.
Open 6, 7 Apr then Suns only until mid May;
mid May to 1 Oct daily (ex Mon and Fri)
1.30 – 5.30 (last admission 5) also open BH
Mons. A children's playground is available
free of charge. Opening hours and times also
prices under revision for 1980. ⚠ *(Tel Driffield
86208). (Sir Tatton Sykes)*

SLIMBRIDGE *Gloucestershire* Map 3 SO70
Wildfowl Trust Off A38 and M5, junction 13.
This well-known wildfowl refuge, founded by
and under the direction of Peter Scott, is
famous for its large variety of ducks, geese,
and swans, which can be studied at close
quarters. The collection is the largest in the
world; in the wild area in the winter months

thousands of geese, swans, and ducks are t
be seen. First-class viewing facilities are
available and there are permanent exhibitio
and a tropical house. ☕ licensed. Gift shop.
Exhibition Hall. Picnic area. Open daily (ex
24, 25 Dec) from 9.30 – 5.30 or dusk
whichever is earlier. £1.10 (ch 55p, ch 4 free
pen 85p). Party 20+. ⚠ No dogs. *(Tel
Cambridge, Gloucestershire 333)* &

SMALLHYTHE *Kent* Map 5 TQ82
Smallhythe Place Dame Ellen Terry's form
half-timbered 15th-C home with a museum
and barn theatre. Open Mar to Oct, daily (ex
Tue and Fri) 2 – 6, or dusk. 60p. No dogs. *(N*

SOMERLEYTON *Suffolk* Map 5 TM49
Somerleyton Hall Off B1074. Magnificent
Tudor to Jacobean mansion rebuilt in Anglo-
Italian style in 1846. House contains superb
antique furniture, tapestries, pictures.
Heritage Display and Grinling Gibbons
carvings. There are 12 acres of grounds with
famous maze, nature trail and miniature
railway. ☕ Open Easter to end Sep, Thu, Su
and BH 2 – 6; Tue and Wed also in Jul and
Aug. Admission prices not yet decided. No
dogs. ⚠ *(Tel Lowestoft 730224). (Lord and
Lady Somerleyton)* &

SOUTHAMPTON *Hampshire* Map 4 SU41
Art Gallery Civic Centre, Commercial Road
Collections include 18th to 20th-C English
paintings, Continental Old Masters of 14th t
18th C. Modern French paintings, including
the impressionists and a small collection of
sculpture and ceramics. Of special interest
are paintings and drawings of the 'Camden
Town Group'. There is also a regular
programme of temporary exhibitions. Open
all year (ex Mon, 4 Apr, 25 Dec), Tue to Sat
11 – 5.45, Sun 2 – 5. Free. *(Tel 23855 ext 76:*
& (by arrangement)
Bargate Guildhall Museum High Street. Th
medieval North gate of the city. Its upper floo
once a guildhall, contains a museum of loca
interest and also other exhibits. Open all yea
(ex Mon, 4 Apr, 25, 26 Dec) Tue to Sat 11 – 1
and 1 – 5, Sun 2 – 5. Free. *(Tel 22544)*
Southampton Zoo The Common. An
attractively laid-out zoo, with a
comprehensive collection of animals and
birds. ☕. Open daily 10 – 6. 50p (ch 25p)
subject to alteration. P in Cemetery Road.
(Tel 556603) &
Spitfire Museum Kingsbridge Lane.
Contains the Spitfire Mk 24 and the Seaplan
S6A which made world speed record in 192
Other exhibits, models and photographs of
the famous aircraft designer R J Mitchell.
Aviation history covering the era 1914 to

954. Winner of 1976 Tourist Award. Open all
ear Tue to Sat 10–4.30, Sun 2–5. 30p (ch
4 10p). ☝ *(Tel 35830)* ⅋

udor House Museum St Michael's Square.
restored, half-timbered, 16th-C house,
ontaining a museum of antiquarian and
istorical interest. Open all year (ex Mon) Tue
Sat 11–5, Sun 2–5. Free. ☝ *(Tel 24216)*

Vool House Maritime Museum Bugle
treet, this 600-year-old building, once wool
varehouse, has buttressed stone walls and
ld roof timbering. Houses an interesting
aritime museum. Open all year (ex Mon)
ue to Sat 11–1 and 2–5, Sun 2–5. Free. ☝
Tel 23941)

OUTHEND-ON-SEA *Essex* Map 5 TQ88
listoric Aircraft Museum Aviation Way, ½m
ff A127, on western boundary of Southend
irport. Aircraft on view include Flying Flea to
lackburn Beverley, and there are also
ircraft engines, and miscellaneous
quipment. ⚑ Open 1 Jun to 30 Sep, daily
0–6; Oct to May, Sat and Sun 11–6. 50p (ch
4 25p, ch 5 free, pen 10p). Under revision for
980. ☝ *(Tel 545881)* ⅋

rittlewell Priory Museum Priory Park
north side of town). A restored 12th-C
luniac Priory, preserving the refectory,
rior's chamber, cellars, and cloister garth.
he nave, south transept with side chapels,
nd lines of the chapter house are now laid
ut in a new garden. The 19th-C wing
ontains a museum of antiquities and also
atural history exhibits appertaining to south-
ast Essex. ⚑ during summer. Open all year
ex 4 Apr, 25, 26 Dec) 1 Apr to 30 Sep
eekdays 10.30–5.30 (closed 1–2), Sun
–5.30; 1 Oct to 31 Mar weekdays only
0.30–4.30. 10p (ch 5p). Party (school
arties weekdays). P. *(Tel 42878)* ⅋ B

outhchurch Hall Southchurch Hall Close.
arly 14th-C timber-framed manor house,
entral hall open to roof. Restored, equipped
nd furnished as a medieval manor house
ith a small Tudor wing and an exhibition
om. Open all year, weekdays 2–5.30, Sat
1–5.30, Sun (Apr to Sep only) 2.30–5.30
losed 4 Apr, 25, 26 Dec). Organised parties
y appointment weekdays 10–12.30. 10p (ch
>). P (limited) in adjacent streets. *(Tel
7671)* ⅋

OUTH HARTING *West Sussex* Map 4 SU71
ppark 1m S on B2146. A notable
edimented, red brick mansion, designed by
alman c1690 with interior decoration of
750, including original wallpapers and
urtains. Beautiful downland setting and
ews. Open Apr to Sep, Wed, Thu, Sun, and
H Mon 2–6. All visitors guided on Wed. £1.
JT)

OUTH MOLTON *Devon* Map 3 SS72
astle Hill 3½m W on A361. A seat of the
ortescue family. Palladian mansion built
729–1740. Fine 18th-C furniture,
pestries, porcelain and pictures.
rnamental garden, large shrub and
oodland garden and arboretum. Open Apr
Oct by appointment for conducted tours by
e owner for parties of 12 or more. £1 per
ead. Garden only, 30p, can be seen any time
y telephoning Estate Office. ☝ *(Tel Filleigh
36)* ⅋

outh Molton Museum A part of the
uildhall, a stone-fronted building c1743,
ith an open, arcaded ground floor, and a
lastered upper floor. Open all year Mon to
at 11–12.30 and 2.30–4.30 summer (Sat
orning only in winter). Free. P. *(Tel 2501)* ⅋

SOUTHPORT *Merseyside* Map 7 SD31
Atkinson Art Gallery Lord Street. Exhibits
include mainly 20th-C oil paintings and
sculpture; 19th-, 20th-C water-colours,
drawings and prints. Also an active visiting
exhibition programme. The Art Gallery and
Southport Arts Centre form a complex where
the visual arts, theatre, film, music and other
media are available to visitors. ⚑. Open all
year daily (ex Sun) Mon, Tue, Wed, Fri 10–5,
Thu and Sat 10–1. Free. P. *(Tel 33133 ext
129)*

Botanic Gardens Museum Churchtown.
Situated in public park. Exhibits include
collections of local history; natural history;
18th-, 19th-C collection of china; a display of
the local shrimping industry; and a rare
example of an early dug-out canoe from the
nearby Martin Mere. Also Ainsdale National
Nature Reserve display reconstructed
Victorian parlour and Cecily Bate collection of
dolls. Temporary exhibitions of local or topical
interest. ⚑. Open all year Tue to Sat and BH
Mon (closed Mon and 4 Apr, 25 Dec, 1 Jan
also Fri following BH Mon) May to Sep 10–6
(5 Oct to Apr), Sun 2–5. Free. ☝ *(Tel 27547)*

Model Village and Model Railway The
Promenade. Set amidst a variety of trees,
shrubs and plants, this model village opened
in 1957, comprises some 250 models,
hundreds of figures, and over 1,000ft of model
railway, all constructed on a scale of 1:12. The
residential buildings display a wide range of
architectural styles from Tudor to
Contemporary. Other features include a
country residence, football stadium, Norman
castle, stone gorge with rock climbs and lake
with waterfalls spanned by a 30ft suspension
bridge. ⚑ and covered area overlooking
grounds. Open 1 Mar to 31 Oct, 9 until 1 hour
before dusk. 50p (ch and pen 25p). Party.
Subject to alteration. P. *(Tel 42133)* ⅋

Steamport Transport Museum Derby Road.
Now houses ex-British Rail locomotives, as
well as several industrial locomotives. 1000ft
of standard guage track, laid by museum
members, connects the museum to the British
rail system. Also on display are local buses.
Southport tramcars, traction engines and
commercial vehicles in what is planned to
become the largest preservation centre of its
type in North West England. Steam
locomotives 'Steam-ups' summer Suns and
BH. ⚑ Open Jun to mid Sep inclusive 1–5
weekdays (11–5 Jul and Aug also weekends
May to Sep); Oct to Apr weekends only 2–5.
Party 20+. 40p (ch 20p). Special events and
BH 50p (ch 25p). Rides Brake Van
(steamdays) 10p. Prices under revision for
1980. ☝ *(Tel 30693, enquiries)* ⅋

Southport Zoo Princes Park. A varied
collection, within an area of 2½ acres,
surrounded by flowers. Several of the animals
breed in captivity, including a rare breeding
group of Mandrills. Other attractions include
leopards, bears, large Indian otters,
wallabies, giant Seychelle tortoise, duck and
flamingo pools, and assorted aviaries. New
aquarium, reptile house, alligator beach and
mandrill house. ⚑ Open all year (ex 25 Dec).
10–dusk. 50p (ch 15 25p). Party. Subject to
revision. P. *(Tel 38102)* ⅋

SOUTHSEA *Hampshire* Map 4 SZ69
Castle Clarence Esplanade. Military and
naval museum within a castle by Henry VIII in
1539 which recalls fortifications of port and
history of regiments of the garrison. Contains
permanent exhibition of the *Mary Rose* which
sank in 1545 and displays of local
archaeology. Lighthouse dates from 1828.

Open 10.30 – 5.30 daily (ex 25 and 26 Dec). 16p (ch and pen 6p . ⚠ (weekend charge). ♿ B

Royal Marines Museum Eastney. A chronological history of the Royal Marines from 1664 to the present day. Specialist displays of uniforms, badges, Royal Marines' bands and medals, including the complete collection of 10 Royal Marines' VCs. Museum is established in the original Royal Marine Artillery Officers' Mess, a superb example of Victorian architecture, and retaining original mouldings and fireplaces. Souvenir shop. Open all year (ex 1 – 15 Jan, 25 and 26 Dec) Mon to Fri 10 – 4.30 Sat and Sun 10 – 12.30. Free. ⚠ *(Tel Portsmouth 22351 ext 6132)* ♿ *(with assistance of Warder staff)*

SOUTH WALSHAM *Norfolk* Map 9 TG31
The Fairhaven Garden Trust The gardens, developed over the past 30 years, contain a beech walk with spring flowers, rhododendrons, a water garden and fish pond. The King Oak is said to be 900 years old. The Bird Sanctuary may be visited at certain times by arrangement with the Warden. Open 2nd Sun in Apr to last Sun in Sep, Thu, Sat, Sun and BH 2 – 6. 40p (ch 12 and pen 20p). ⚠ Gates close, all cars must be out of the car park by 6 pm. *(Tel 449)* ♿

SOUTHWOLD *Suffolk* Map 5 TM57
Southwold Museum Bartholomew Green. Formerly known as Dutch Cottage Museum, contains relics of Southwold light railway and also illustrations of local history, including archaeology, fossils, prints, and bygones. Open 29 May to end of Sep, Tue, Wed, Fri 2.30 – 4.30, also Sun in Aug and spring and summer BH other times by appointment. Free. P.

SPALDING *Lincolnshire* Map 8 TF22
Ayscoughfee Hall and Gardens Restored 15th-C house, now museum of ornithology. 🎦 during summer. Open all year, weekdays 8 to ½hr after sunset (5 in winter), Sun from 10 am. Free. P. *(Tel 5468)* ♿
Springfields Gardens Unique 25-acre spring flower spectacle on eastern outskirts of the town (A151). More than a million bulbs, with lawns, lake and glasshouses. Recently opened Summer Rose Gardens with over 12,500 rose bushes in 100 varieties. 🎦 Flower parade 10 May. Exhibition of floats 10 – 14 May. Spring gardens open Apr to mid May, Summer gardens open mid Jun to end Sep daily 10 – 6 both seasons. Spring 80p (ex 10/11 May £1). Summer 50p (ch free). ⚠ *(Tel 4843)* ♿

SPEKE *Merseyside* Map 7 SJ48
Speke Hall Grand example of 16th-C half-

timbering, with interior courtyard, Great hall, 16th- and 17th-C plasterwork, and Mortlake tapestries. 🎦 (parties only). Open Apr to end of Sep Mon to Sat 10 – 5, Sun 2 – 7 and BH 10 – 7; Oct to Mar (ex 1 Jan, 4 Apr, 24 – 27 Dec) Mon to Sat 10 – 5, Suns 2 – 5 (last visitor ½hr before closing). 40p (ch 20p). Party. All details subject to alteration. ⚠ *(NT and Merseyside County Museums)* ♿ B

SPETCHLEY *Hereford and Worcester* Map 3 SO85
Spetchley Park Fine gardens and park, surrounding early 19th-C mansion. Worcestershire's only deer park, with red and fallow deer, lake with wildfowl. Gardens cover 30 acres and include many unusual trees and shrubs. 🎦 Sun only. Gardens only shown 1 Apr to 31 Oct, Mon to Fri 11 – 5, Sun 2 – 6; BH Mons 11 – 6. Other days by appointment. Garden Centre within gardens open same hours, also weekdays in winter. Admission prices not yet decided. Party 25+. *(Tel 213)*. *(Major R J G Berkley TD MFH)*

SPROATLEY *Humberside* Map 8 TA13
Burton Constable Hall 1½m N. Elizabethan house, built 1570 with 18th-C state rooms and 200 acres of parkland landscaped by 'Capability' Brown including 4 acres of lawns and gardens and 22 acres of lakes. 🎦 picnic grounds by lake. Caravan and camping park. Seasonal fishing. Open 5 to 7 Apr incl, then Sat and Sun, then daily (ex Mon and Thu) but open BH Mon, to 24 May to 28 Sep 12 – 5. Admission prices not yet decided. ⚠ *(Tel Skirlaugh 62400)*. *(Mr & Mrs J Chichester Constable)*.

STAFFORD *Staffordshire* Map 7 SJ92
Museum and Art Gallery The Green. Display of local history and changing temporary art exhibitions. Open all year Tue to Sat 10 – 5. Free

STAGSDEN *Bedfordshire* Map 4 SP94
Stagsden Bird Gardens A breeding centre of rare pheasants, waterfowl and old breeds of poultry and other birds. Also a fine collection of shrub roses. Picnics allowed. 🎦 Open all year daily (ex 25 Dec) 11 – 7 or dusk 60p (ch 15 30p). ⚠ *(Tel Oakley 2745)* ♿

STAINDROP *Co Durham* Map 12 NZ12
Raby Castle Principally 14th-C, work of the Nevilles, with 18th- and 19th-C alterations. Fine pictures from English, Dutch and Spanish schools, also gardens of about 10 acres. 🎦 Open Easter to end Sep; Easter weekend including Tue; Wed and Sun Apr to Jun also 5 – 8 May and Spring BH weekend'

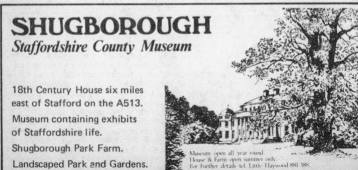

SHUGBOROUGH
Staffordshire County Museum

18th Century House six miles east of Stafford on the A513.

Museum containing exhibits of Staffordshire life.

Shugborough Park Farm.

Landscaped Park and Gardens.

Museum open all year round.
House & Farm open summer only.
For further details tel. Little Haywood 881 388.

ncluding Tue; daily (ex Sat) Jul to end Sep.
–5. £1 (ch and pen 60p). Under revision for
980. △ *(Tel 60202). (The Lord Barnard TD)*

TALHAM *Norfolk* Map 9 TG32
Sutton Wind Mill 2m SE on unclass road.
The tallest wind mill in the country with nine
doors plus the cap floor. Built in 1789 the
milling machinery is complete and there is
access to all floors including the top outside
stage. A working fantail and many other
interesting items are on display. Open 6 Apr to
0 Sep daily 9.30–6. 30p (ch 15 15p). △ *(Tel
1195)*

TAMFORD *Lincolnshire* Map 4 TF00
Brewery Museum A 19th-C brewery in
attractive stone buildings and with equipment
made from four tons of copper and brass.
Production ceased in 1974 and the museum
opened in 1978. Antique beer engine still in
use in the refreshment room. ☕ (also
censed). Opening times not yet decided. 55p
(ch 18 and pen 40p). P. *(Tel 52186)* ঙ B
Browne's Hospital Broad Street. Ancient
almshouses, founded c1483 by William
Browne, wool merchant. Fine medieval
stained glass in Chapel and Audit room. Open
all year, daily 10–5. Free. P (in North Street
and Broad Street). *(Tel 3746)*
Stamford Museum A new museum, opening
spring 1980, of the history of Stamford. The
display includes the clothes of Daniel
Lambert. Temporary exhibitions are also
housed here. Open Tue to Sat (closed Sun
and Mon). Admission times and prices not yet
decided. *(Tel 55611)* ঙ B

TANSTED MOUNTFITCHET *Essex*
Map 5 TL52
Windmill Red-brick tower-mill of 1787
restored 1966), with machinery and
furnishings intact. 65ft high and has been
used as Scouts Headquarters. Open 2.30–7
n first Sun in month from Apr to Oct, every
Sun in Aug. Also on Easter, May, Spring and
ate Summer BH (Sun and Mon). 15p (ch 14
5p). Other times by telephone application to
committee secretary. △ *(Tel Bishop's
Stortford 813159)*

TANTON LEES *Derbyshire* Map 8 SK26
Nine Ladies Stone Circle Off B5057
approached via Birchover village. Stone circle
n Stanton Moor. Dates back probably to late
Bronze Age and incorporates nine stones.
Accessible all reasonable times. Free. *(AM)*

TAPLEFORD *Leicestershire* Map 8 SK81
Stapleford Park Off B676. Old wing dating
from 1500 and restored in 1633 has exterior
decoration of exceptional interest. The
mansion, extended in 1670, contains
interesting furnishings, tapestries and
pictures. Miniature steam passenger railway
and liners SS Northern Star and Southern
Cross. Children's amusements. Picnic area.
Garden centre. ☕ (licensed). Teas at Hall.
Open 6 Apr to 28 Sep BH Mon and Tue
following; Sun only Apr; Sun and Wed only
May and Sep; Sun, Tue, Wed and Thu in Jun,
Jul, Aug. 1.30–6.30. £1.05 (ch 55p). △ *(Tel
Wymondham 229 or 245)* ঙ B

TEETON *North Yorkshire* Map 8 SE43
Teeton Hall Gatehouse 14th-C fortified
gatehouse from medieval manor house,
displaying remarkable series of 53 grotesque
and heraldic carved corbels supporting
parapets and chimneys. Open any
reasonable time (exterior only). Free. *(AM)*

STEVENAGE *Hertfordshire* Map 4 TL22
Stevenage Museum St George's Way. This
Museum, in the undercroft of the parish
church of St George, tells the Story of
Stevenage from the present day back to
earliest times. Also geology, natural history,
and live exhibits. Open all year 10–5. Free. P.
(Tel 54292) ঙ

STEVENTON *Oxfordshire* Map 4 SU49
Priory Cottages Former monastic buildings
converted into attractive timbered cottages,
one of which contained the Great Hall. South
cottage open Wed Apr to Sep 2–6; Oct to Mar
2–5. Free. *(NT)*

STICKLEPATH *Devon* Map 2 SX69
**Sticklepath Museum of Rural Industry and
Finch Foundation Trust** Once corn mill and
cloth mill known as Manor Mills, later
converted to edge-tool factory and grinding
house. Among the exhibits are two water-
powered 'tilt' hammers, unique in West
Country, and other machinery driven by three
separate water-wheels. Demonstrations of
machinery and water-wheels in motion on Sat
and Sun, or by appointment: apply to
Secretary. Many examples of hand-made
agricultural tools and equipment. Open all
year, daily 11–6. 40p (ch 16 15p). △ *(Tel 352
or 286)* ঙ B

STOKE BRUERNE *Northamptonshire*
Map 4 SP74
Stoke Park Pavilion Twin 17th-C pavilions,
attributed to Inigo Jones, remains of Stoke
Park, burnt in 1884 and subsequently rebuilt.
Exteriors of pavilions and gardens shown Jun
to Aug, Sat and Sun 2–6. 30p (ch 8 20p). △
(Tel Roade 862172). (Mr R D Chancellor) ঙ
(79)
Waterways Museum Former corn mill,
situated near a flight of locks on the Grand
Union Canal, now converted into a museum
of items recording the fascinating canal story
of over two centuries. There is an old narrow
boat on show. Canal-side inn and hump-back
bridge near by. Open all year, incl BH. In
winter from second Mon in Oct to Mon before
24 Mar 10–4 (closed Mon also 25, 26 Dec); in
summer, daily (10–6. Enquiries to Curator.
40p (ch 25p). Admission prices under revision
for 1980. △ *(Tel Northampton 862229)*

STOKE-ON-TRENT *Staffordshire*
Map 7 SJ84
Chatterley Whitfield Mining Museum Nr
Tunstall. Guided tours of the underground
workings showing the development of mining
technology from earliest times. Colliery
lamphouse, exhibitions and steam winding
engines also open. Museum shop and ☕.
Open Tue to Fri 9.30–4.30. Weekends and
BH 10–5. Closed Mon. Admission prices for
1980 not yet decided but approx
£1.25–£1.50. △
Ford Green Hall Ford Green Road,
Smallthorne. A black and white timber-framed
yeoman farmer's house with brick-built
additions. originally built for the Ford family
during the 16th-C and contains 16th-, 17th-
and 18th-C English furniture. Guided tours by
resident custodian (approx 1–1½hrs). Open
all year (ex Tue and Fri) 1 Apr to 30 Sep Mon,
Wed, Thu and Sat 10–12.30 and 2–5.30 (5, 1
Oct to 31 Mar), Sun all year 2–5. Closed Tue
and Fri. △ limited. *(Tel 534771)*
Gladstone Pottery Museum Uttoxeter
Road, Longton, 2m SE of Stoke-on-Trent, on
A50. A Victorian pottery, still complete with
old warehouses, workshops and four bottle
ovens. Old traditional skills may be seen in

action in this living and working museum of
British pottery. Historical, Tile and Colour
galleries. Winner of the 1976 Museum of the
Year Award. Visitors may buy wares
produced here, also new quality china shop
and large teapots display. Open all year
weekdays (ex Mon, Oct to Mar and 25 Dec)
10.30–5.30 (9pm Wed, Apr to Sep, for
booked parties). 90p (ch 16, students and pen
45p). ⚠ *(Tel 319232 or 311378)*
The Mitchell Spitfire Museum Bethesda
Street, Hanley. Modern glass-domed building
houses museum, which includes a Spitfire, to
commemorate R J Mitchell, the famous
aircraft designer who came from this area.
Open all year (ex Sun). Mon to Sat 9–12.30,
1–5.30. ⚙
Spode Museum and Factory Church Street.
Works museum contains examples of 18th- to
20th-C Spode pottery. Visitors's shop. Tours
of factory arranged Mon to Fri by appointment
at 10.15 and 2.15. 50p. Admission to museum
free, but strictly by prior appointment only. Ch
12 not admitted. ⚠ *(Tel 46011)* **(79)**
Trentham Gardens On SW edge of town, on
A34. 700 acres of gardens and woodland
include rose and Italian gardens, rock and
peat block gardens, shrubs, and
demonstration blocks. Many acres converted
to spring shrub and bulb gardens. Tree and
shrub nursery. Garden centres. Swimming
pool, boats, and miniature railway. ⚓ Open all
year daily (ex 25 Dec) dawn to dusk.
Individual, family and group rates. Fishing.
Full catering facilities. Admission charges for
1980 not yet decided. ⚠ *(Tel 657341 or
657225)* ⚙

STOKESAY *Salop* Map 7 SO48
On A49 near Craven Arms.
Stokesay Castle Oldest fortified manor
house in England with additions in 13th C.
Open 7 Apr to 28 Sep 10–6 (last admission
5.30); Mar and Oct 10–5 (last admission
4.30). Closed Tue also Nov, Dec, Jan, Feb. All
enquiries to the Custodian. 50p (ch 15 25p).
⚠ *(Sir Philip and Lady Magnus-Allcroft)*

STOKE-SUB-HAMDON *Somerset*
Map 3 ST41
Stoke-sub-Hamdon Priory 15th-C Ham-Hill
stone house, once a chantry, retaining
original screens and part of Great Hall. Open
all year, daily 10–6. Free. *(NT)*

STONEHENGE *Wiltshire* Map 4 SU14
Prehistoric monument dating from two
periods. The encircling ditch, bank, and
Aubrey holes are late Neolithic. The stone
circles, consisting of sarsen stones around
horseshoe of trilithons encompassing the

blue stones, with an altar stone, are probably
of early Bronze Age date. Two of the fallen
stones were re-erected in 1958. ⚓ Open daily
Mar, Apr, Oct 9.30–5.30; May to Sep 9.30–7
Nov to Feb 9.30–4.30p (ch 16 and pen 15p).
(AM)

STONOR *Oxfordshire* Map 4 SU78
Stonor House and Park 4m NW of Henley-
on-Thames on B480. The house is the home
of Lord and Lady Camoys and the Stonor
family and has been occupied by
descendants for the past eight hundred years
Built over many centuries from c1190, the
house contains examples of some of the
earliest domestic architecture in Oxfordshire
It has rooms with beautiful stained and
painted glass windows with interesting
heraldic designs, family pictures, good
furniture and tapestries, and important Italian
sculpture and drawings. The beautiful
gardens on the hillside behind the house have
commanding views of the Park. Open 6 Apr t
30 Sep Wed, Thu, Sun and BH 2–5.30. £1 (c
12 60p, pen 80p). ⚠ *(Tel Turville Heath 587)*

STOURBRIDGE *West Midlands* Map 7 SO9
Glass Collection Council House, Mary
Stevens Park. A collection of local products,
and glass from all parts of the world, from
1630 to the present day. Lectures given by
arrangement with Curator. Open all year Mon
to Fri 10–5. Free. P. *(Tel Dudley 55433)* ⚙ E
Hagley Hall SSE at Hagley. 18th-C Palladia
house, the family home of the Lyttletons,
completed by George, 1st Baron Lyttleton in
1760. Renowned for the fine Rococo
plasterwork by Francesco Vassali. Family
portraits, 18th-C furniture and Lyttleton
papers are also on view. The park, in
existence since the reign of Edward III, was
re-landscaped in the 18th C. Lunch and teas
daily (in house). House and Park open daily
17 May to 31 Aug, 12–5. £1.10 (ch 13 50p,
pen 80p). ⚠ *(Tel Hagley 882408)* ⚙ B

STOURHEAD *Wiltshire* Map 3 ST73
Stourhead House and Pleasure Gardens
At Stourton (B3092). 18th-C house by Colin
Campbell, with paintings and Chippendale
furniture. There are notable mid 18th-C lake-
watered grounds laid out by Henry Hoare,
which show contemporary garden temples,
forming one of Europe's most famous layout
The trees and shrubs are magnificent, many
being rare varieties. The estate covers more
than 2,500 acres. Shop and information roor
House open Apr, Sep and Oct, Mon, Wed, S
and Sun 2–6 or sunset if earlier; May to end
Aug daily (ex Fri) 2–6; gardens open all year
daily 8–7 (or sunset). Last admissions ½hr

efore stated closing time. House £1,
ardens 80p; Nov to Mar 40p(ch, reduced
ates). Party 15+ (should be booked two days
advance). *(Tel Bourton [Dorset] 348).* No
ogs. *(NT)*

TOWE *Buckinghamshire* Map 4 SP63
Rowe House Landscape Gardens Fine
8th-C mansion, now a public school. The
plendid grounds, with statuary and garden
mples by William Kent and James Gibbs. ♀
pen 24 Mar to 22 Apr and 15 Jul to 9 Sep,
ily 1 – 6. 45p (ch and pen 25p). Opening
nes and prices under revision for 1980. ⚠
el Buckingham 3164) ♿

TOWMARKET *Suffolk* Map 5 TM05
useum of East Anglian Life Medieval
arn, collections of horse-drawn vehicles,
gricultural tools and implements, craft tools
id domestic items. 14th-C aisled hall, 18th-
smithy, watermill and mill house. Country
alk down the centuries-old Crowe Lane and
ong the river bank to mill. Open 1 Apr to 31
ct, Mon to Sat 11 – 5, Sun 2 – 5. 50p (ch 30p,
en 40p). Admission prices under revision for
980. ♀ Sun and BH, Jun, Jul, Aug 3 – 5.
arty. ⚠ *(Tel 2229)* ♿

TRACEY ARMS WINDPUMP *Norfolk*
ap 5 TG40
iven to the County Council by Lady Stracey.
s a drainage mill and was restored in 1960.
urther major repairs were completed by the
orfolk Windmills Trust in 1974, and a special
xhibition of the Trust's work is a permanent
ature. Open May to Sep (other times by
ppointment) 9 – dusk (or as displayed). 10p
h 14 and pen 5p). P. (limited). *(Tel Norwich
1122 ext 5224)*

STRATFIELD SAYE *Hampshire* Map 4 SU66
Stratfield Saye House Built in the reign of
Charles I and presented to the Great Duke in
1817, since when it has been the family home
of the Dukes of Wellington. Contains a unique
collection of paintings, prints, furniture and
relics of the first Duke. In the grounds are the
American, Rose and Walled gardens, also the
grave of Copenhagen, the Duke's favourite
charger. Open daily (ex Fri) from 30 Mar to 28
Sep, 11.30 – 5. Party. ⚠ *(Tel Turgis Green
602)* ♿

STRATFORD-UPON-AVON *Warwickshire*
Map 4 SP15
Hall's Croft Old Town. Tudor house with
walled garden, former home of
Shakespeare's daughter, Susanna.
Exhibition: 'Dr John Hall and the medicine of
his time'. Open all year (ex 4 Apr, am, 24 – 26
Dec) Apr to Oct, weekdays 9 – 6, Sun 2 – 6;
Nov to Mar weekdays only 9 – 4. 30p (ch
school age 15p). Admission prices under
revision for 1980. P. *(Tel 292107)* ♿ B
Harvard House High Street. An ornate half-
timbered house, dating from 1596, the former
home of the mother of John Harvard, who
founded Harvard University in the USA. Open
Apr to Sep, weekdays 9 – 1 and 2 – 6, Sun
2 – 6; Oct to Mar, weekdays 10 – 1 and 2 – 4.
40p (ch 17 20p). ⚠ *(Tel 4507)*
Louis Tussaud's Waxworks 60 Henley
Street. Open all year daily. 1 May to end Aug
9.30 – 6.30 (5.30 winter). 50p (ch and pen
25p, students 30p). *(Tel 5880)*
Model Car Museum Ely Street. International
collection of 19,000 miniatures from 40
countries representing all forms of transport,
especially motor vehicles, displayed in

historical settings. Includes interesting collection of tram cars and unique collections of model cars from Japan, Israel, and South America. Open all year daily 9–5.30. 50p (ch 5 free). ⚠ (limited). P. *(Tel 2233)* ⅃
New Place Chapel Street. Foundations of the house (destroyed in 1759), where Shakespeare spent the last five years of his retirement and died in 1616. Picturesque Knot garden, an Elizabethan replica. Ancient mulberry tree in the Great Garden of new Place. Furniture and local history exhibits in adjacent Nash's House. Open all year (ex 4 Apr, am, 24–26 Dec) Apr to Oct, weekdays 9–6, Sun 2–6; Nov to Mar, weekdays only 9–4. 30p (ch school age 15p). Admission prices under revision for 1980. P (street). *(Tel 292325)*
Royal Shakespeare Theatre Picture Gallery and Museum Waterside. The gallery contains portraits of Shakespeare, and famous Shakespearian actors and actresses, in addition to numerous other theatrical relics. Open, daily Apr to Oct, weekdays 10–1, 2–6, Sun 2–6; Nov, weekdays 10–1, 2–4, Sun 2–4, Dec to Mar, Sat 10–4, Sun 2–4. 25p (ch 10p) subject to alteration. P. *(Tel 3693)* **(79)**
Shakespeare's Birthplace Henley Street. A half-timbered house, the birthplace of the poet in 1564. Contains numerous exhibits. Open all year (ex 4 Apr, am, 24–26 Dec) Apr to Oct weekdays 9–7 (6, Mon, Tue, Wed and Fri in Apr, May and Oct), Sun 10–6; Nov to Mar weekdays 9–4.30, Sun 1.30–4.30. 50p (ch school age 20p). Admission prices under revision for 1980. *(Tel 4016-8)*
Stratford-upon-Avon Motor Museum 1 Shakespeare Street. Housed in a former church and school, 100 yards from Shakespeare's birthplace, a charming Victorian building in which the vintage cars and motorcycles are displayed in a unique setting of the Roaring Twenties – the Golden Age of Motoring. The museum specialises in exotic sports and grand touring cars, many of which have been rescued from India and magnificently restored. In addition to the cars you will also find the fashions, music and décor of the Twenties. Displays include a fascinating collection of period enamel signs, road signs, motor clubs badges from throughout the world and numerous early motoring items of historic and nostalgic interest; typical Twenties roadside garage, picture gallery, picnic garden and speciality shop. Open all year daily (ex 25 Dec), Mar to Sep 10–6.30, Oct to Feb 10–5.30. 75p (ch accompanied by parents, free, teenagers and pen 50p). Opening times and admission prices under revision for 1980. *(Tel 69413)* ⅃ B

STREET *Somerset* Map 3 ST43
Street Shoe Museum C & J Clark Ltd, High Street. The museum is housed in the oldest part of the factory of C & J Clark Ltd. The museum contains shoes from Roman times until 1950, Georgian shoe buckles, caricatures and engravings of shoemakers, costume illustrations and fashion plates, shoe machinery from 1860s until 1920, shoes and showcards from 1850 to 1950 produced by C & J Clark, and 19th-C documents and photographs illustrating the early history of the firm from the founding in 1825 by Cyrus Clark. Open May to Oct inclusive Mon to Sat 10–1 and 2–4.45; winter months by appointment only. Free. ⚠ limited. P. *(Tel 43131)*

STROUD *Gloucestershire* Map 3 SO80
Stroud and District Museum Lansdown. The exhibits cover geology, archaeology, local crafts, industrial archaeology, including local mills and houses, and farmhouse household equipment. A full-length model of the dinosaur Megalosaurus is on display. Open all year (ex Sun, 1 Jan, 4 Apr and 3 days at Christmas) Mon to Fri 10.30–5, Sat 10.30–1 and 2–5. Free. P (roadside). *(Tel 3394)* ⅃

STUDLEY *Oxfordshire* Map 4 SP51
Studley Priory Hotel Off B4027. Original Priory founded 12th C and sold after Dissolution to John Croke, whose descendants owned it for over 300 years. West range was altered to form Elizabethan manor, which received 17th- and 19th-C additions. Fine stone doorways and early panelling. Used to portray home of Sir Thomas More in film, *A Man for all Seasons*. Studley priory is now a hotel, open all year, but visitors most welcome.

SUDBURY *Derbyshire* Map 7 SK13
Sudbury Hall A very fine brick-built 17th-C house, the former home of the Lords Vernon with plasterwork ceilings, murals by Laguerre and some Grinling Gibbons' carving, Museum of Childhood. Open Apr to Oct, Wed, Thu, Fri Sat, Sun, and BH Mons 1–5.30 or sunset. £1.10. *(NT)*

SUDBURY *Suffolk* Map 5 TL84
Gainsborough's House Half-timbered house with Georgian façade, birthplace of Thomas Gainsborough, now an art gallery and museum. Open all year (ex 25, 26 Dec) Tue to Sat 10–12.30, 2–5, Sun 2–5. 30p (ch students and pen 15p). P. *(Tel 72958)*

SUFFOLK WILDLIFE PARK Suffolk Map 5 TM58
A world-wide selection of animals, birds, ⚐

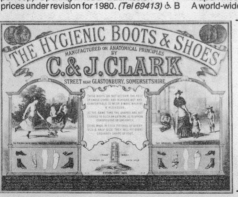

hop. Wheelchairs available for disabled. pen Mar to Oct, daily 10–6. Admission harges not yet decided. Picnic areas; ⚠ eparate park for cars bringing dogs. *(Tel owestoft 740291)* & **(79)**

ULGRAVE *Northamptonshire* Map 4 SP54 *ulgrave Manor* Off B4525. 16th-C manor ouse and garden, famous for its Washington ssociations. There are portraits, ontemporary furniture, and the Washington rms carved in the main doorway. Open all ear, ex Jan. 1 Apr to 30 Sep, daily (ex Wed) 0.30–1, 2–5.30 (4, after 30 Sep). 50p (ch in chool parties 25p). ⚠ *(Tel 205)*

UNDERLAND *Tyne and Wear* lap 12 NZ35 *rindon Close Museum* Grindon Lane. dwardian period rooms, including chemist's

shop and dentist's surgery. Open all year (ex Christmas, 1 Jan, and 4 Apr), Mon, Wed and Fri 9.30–12, 1–7.30; Tue and Thu closes 5; Sat 9.30–4. Summer Sun 2–5. Free. ⚠ *(Tel 284042)*

Museum and Art Gallery Borough Road. On display are examples of local lustre-ware pottery, a collection of 15th- to 19th-C silver, models of Sunderland-built ships, archaeology, natural history, local history, period rooms and 19th- and 20th-C paintings. ⚼ Open all year daily (ex Christmas, 1 Jan and 4 Apr). Mon to Fri 9.30–6, Sat 9.30–4, Sun 2–5; BH Mon 10–5. Free. P. *(Tel 41235)* &

Monkwearmouth Station Museum North Bridge Street. Land transport museum in classical station of 1848 designed by Thomas Moore of Sunderland. The booking office,

platform area and footbridge have all been
restored and there is an outdoor area with
rolling stock. Displays inside the museum
deal with transport in North East England.
Open all year (ex Christmas, 1 Jan and 4 Apr),
Mon to Sat 10–6, Sun 2–5. Free. ⚠ *(Tel
77075)* &

SUTTON-AT-HONE *Kent* Map 5 TQ57
St John's Jerusalem Garden A fine 13th-,
16th-, and 18th-C house, once the home of
the Kentish historian, Edward Hasted. Only
the walls and former chapel of the original
buildings remain. The River Darenth borders
the garden. Gardens and former chapel
shown Apr to Oct, Wed 2–6. 20p. *(NT)*

SUTTON CHENEY *Warwickshire*
Map 4 SP39
Battlefield of Bosworth Centre 7m NE of
Nuneaton on unclass road. Historic site of
battle in 1485. The Centre includes an
exhibition, model room, replica flags, shields
and figures also film theatre. There is also a
Battle Trail which guides visitors around the
area where the battle actually took place.
Picnic areas. Open Easter to Oct, Mon to Sat
2–5, Sun and BH 1–6. 40p (ch 25p). Party (all
year). ⚠ cars 20p, mini-coaches 50p,
coaches £1. Opening hours, dates and
admission prices not available for 1980. *(Tel
Market Bosworth 290429)*

SUTTON-ON-THE-FOREST *North Yorkshire*
Map 8 SE56
8m N of York, on B1363 or Helmsley Road.
Sutton Park A medium-sized garden, with a
temple and woodland walks, terraces, border
and rose gardens, a lily pond, and Georgian
ice house. The house dates from 1730 and
contains a collection of antique furniture and
pictures. ⚌ (open 2–5.30). Souvenir shop
with some antiques. Open 4, 6/7, 13, 20 Apr
then 27 Apr to 28 Sep Sun, Tue, Wed, Thu
and all BH Mon 2–6. Special openings by
arrangement, apply to Administrator. House
and Gardens 80p (ch 25p), Coach parties 65p
per person. Gardens only 40p (ch 20p).
Prices under revision for 1980. *(Tel
Easingwold 810249)* & B *(NGS)*

SWAINSHILL *Hereford and Worcester*
Map 3 SO44
The Weir Dates from 1784, with fine views of
the River Wye and the Welsh hills. Spring
gardens only open 25 Mar to 15 May, daily (ex
Sat;) 16 May to Oct, Wed and BH Mon 2–6.
20p. *(NT)*

SWALLOWFIELD *Berkshire* Map 4 SU76
Swallowfield Park 18th-C remodelling of
house built in 1689 designed by William
Talman. Special features include Baroque
door case or gateway, oval stucco decorated
vestibule containing the Arms of the
Clarendon family (c1700) and bold and cove
ceiling mouldings in the Main Hall and
Drawing Room. Gardens including a Walled
Garden of about 4 acres containing a variety
of flowering shrubs and roses and many fine
specimens of interesting trees. Open May to
Sep Wed and Thu 2–5 40p (ch 25p) ⚠ *(Tel
Reading 883815)* & B *(gardens)*

SWARTHMOOR *Cumbria* Map 7 SD27
Swarthmoor Hall Elizabethan and later, the
former home of George Fox, founder of the
Quakers. The house is now administered by
the Society of Friends. Open mid Mar to mid
Oct, Mon, Tue, Wed and Sat 10–12 and 2–5;
Thu and Sun by arrangement only (closed
Fri); mid Oct to mid Mar by appointment only.
Free. ⚠ *(Tel Ulverston 53204)* & B

SWINDON *Wiltshire* Map 4 SU18
Great Western Railway Museum Faringdo
Road. Interesting collection of locomotives
and other exhibits pertaining to the Great
Western Railway. Locomotives include the
historic 'City of Truro', and there is also a
Brunel room. Recent additions include a
model, made 1847–48, of the broad gauge
locomotive 'Iron Duke'. Open all year (ex 4
Apr 25, 26 Dec), weekdays 10–5, Sun 2–5.
27p (ch and pen 13p). Under revision for
1980. Party 20+ P. *(Tel 26161 ex 562)* also
Railway Village House Adjacent GWR
museum. Refurbished as it was at turn of
century. Hours as museum above. 11p (ch
and pen 5p). Party.
Jefferies Museum Coate Farm, off A345.
Birthplace in 1848 of Richard Jefferies, the
nature writer, and is now museum exhibiting
literature relating to local wildlife written by
Jefferies and Alfred Owen Williams. Open all
year, Wed Sat and Sun, 2–5. Free. ⚠ *(Tel
26161 ex 563)*
Town Museum Bath Road. Contains small
collections of items of local interest and an ar
gallery, where visiting exhibitions alternate
with pictures by 20th-C artists including
Moore, Piper, Sutherland, Grant, Bevan and
Lowry, from the permanent collections. Ope
all year (ex 4 Apr, 25, 26 Dec) weekdays
10–6, Sun 2–5. Free. P. *(Tel 26161 ext 560,*

SWINFORD *Leicestershire* Map 4 SP57
Stanford Hall 1m E. William and Mary hous
on River Avon, built 1690, with antique
furniture and paintings, and replica of Percy
Pilcher's flying machine of 1898. Old forge
and walled rose garden; motor cycle and car
museum; working crafts centre weekends;
nature trail. ⚌ Fishing. Open Easter to end o
Sep, Thu, Sat, Sun 2.30–6; Easter, Spring
and Late Summer BH Mons and Tue 12–6.
Conducted tours. Admission prices under
review for 1980. ⚠ *(Tel 250)*. *(Lord and Lad*
Braye)

TADCASTER *North Yorkshire* Map 8 SE44
The Ark Museum Kirkgate. Old restored
timbered house, now museum of pubs and
brewing. Open all year, Tue, Wed, and Thu
2–4. Free. P. *(Tel 833085)*. *(Mrs Brewster)*
(79)

TAMWORTH *Staffordshire* Map 4 SK20
Tamworth Castle Museum Norman keep
and tower, 15th-C banqueting hall, and 17th-
C apartments with fine woodwork, period
furniture and painted heraldic frieze. The
building houses a small local history museur
Restoration is in progress and sections of
building may be closed. Pleasure grounds,
swimming pools. Open all year (ex 25 Dec
and Fri Oct to Mar) Mon to Sat 10–6 (5 winte
Sun 2–6 (5 winter). Admission prices under
revision for 1980 and will depend upon how
much is open. ⚠ (free on Sun) adjoining
castle entrance. *(Tel 3561 ext 294)*

TARLETON *Lancashire* Map 7 SD42
Leisure Lakes Boating lakes set in 90 acres
of picturesque woodland and heath setting
with picnic areas and pleasant walks. The
sandy beaches are ideal for children. ⚌.
Open Apr to end of Sep 8–8. 25p (ch 20p).
Sun and BH £1 per car, including all
passengers. Caravans welcome for the day.
⚠ *(Tel Hesketh Bank 3446)* &

TATTERSHALL *Lincolnshire* Map 8 TF25
Tattershall Castle The mid 15th-C, 100ft-
high brick keep of a fortified house, well-
restored. The Marquess of Curzon recovere
the stone Gothic fireplaces in 1911. Open all

year Mon to Sat (ex 13 Apr, 25/26 Dec)
11–6.30 (11–1 and 2–6.30, Oct to Mar) or
sunset, Sun 1–6.30 (or sunset). 60p *(NT)*
Dogdyke Steam Pumping Station Bridge
Farm. The only known land drainage beam
engine with scoop wheel worked by steam in
its original setting. The low pressure 16hp
double acting separate condenser beam
engine (1855) is capable of moving 25 tons of
water per minute. Also 1940 diesel engined
centrifugal pump still in use. Open 6 Apr and
first Sun in month May to Oct, 2–5. 50p (ch
and pen 25p) or £1 per car including
passengers. ⚠ *(Tel Coningsby 42495)*
TATTON *Cheshire* Map 7 SJ78
Tatton Park 3½m from M6, junction 19;
entrance by Rostherne Lodge on Ashley
Road; 1½m NE of junction of A5034 with A50.
Late 18th-C mansion by Samuel and Lewis
Wyatt. Fine collection of paintings, furniture,
china, and silver. Tenants' Hall museum
contains State Coach, veteran cars, sporting
trophies, and curiosities. 50 acres of
ornamental gardens; 1,000 acres of parkland,
including lake or mere, one mile long.
Historical trails. ⚲ Open daily (ex Mon but
open BH Mon). 18 May to 1 Sep: House 1–5
(Sun and BH 12–5), gardens 11–5.30 (Sun
and BH 11–6). 1 Apr to 17 May and 3 Sep to
12 Oct: House 1–4 (5 Sun and BH), garden
12–4.30 (11–5 Sun and BH). 14 Oct to 12
Apr 1981 House closed ex Sun to 16 Nov and
from 2 Mar 1–4. Gardens 1–4 (12–4 Sun
and BH). House 60p (accompanied ch 30p);
garden only 30p (accompanied ch 15p);
Parkland 60p incl ⚠ (incl NT members).
Winter, parkland open daily (ex Mon and 25
Dec) times variable. Entrance by Knutsford
Lodge, ⚠ 25p (incl NT members). Opening
times and prices are provisional and subject
to revision for 1980. An additional charge may
be made at times of special events. Dogs in
park on leads only. ♿ B *(NT)*

TAUNTON *Somerset* Map 3 ST22
Taunton Castle containing Somerset County
Museum. Partly 12th-C structure, associated
with Judge Jeffreys' 'Bloody Assize' of 1685.
Somerset County Museum which contains
exhibits of local archaeology, natural history,
geology, glass, ceramics, bygones, costume
and dolls, also houses the ***Somerset Military
Museum*** containing relics of the Somerset
Light Infantry from 1685–1959 when the
regiment was amalgamated with the Duke of
Cornwall's Light Infantry. Exhibits include
Jellalabad campaign of 1842, and a large
collection of uniforms, medals, etc; the
Yeomanry and Militia also being well
represented. Open all year (ex BH), 1 Apr to
30 Sep, Mon to Sat (closed Sun) 10–5; 1 Oct
to 31 Mar, Tue to Sat 10–5 (closed Sun and
Mon). 35p (ch 10p) ⚠ *(Tel 3451 ext 286)* ♿ B
Hestercombe Gardens 3m N of Taunton, off
A361 near Cheddon Fitzpaine. Late 19th-C
house, now the headquarters of the Somerset
Fire Brigade. The gardens, originally planned
in 1905 by Sir Edwin Lutyens and Gertrude
Jekyll, are at present being restored to their
original planting. Pools and borders and
terraces with fine views. Gardens open 25
May, 29 Jun and 27 Jul 2–6 and every Thu,
May to Sep 12–5. Free. ⚠ *(Tel 87222/3)*
Post Office Telecommunications Museum
38 North St. Exhibits include manual
exchange (1900), an automatic exchange
(1929), and many smaller items. Oldest
telephone is dated 1877, and section of first
transatlantic telegraph cable (1857) is
displayed. Open Sats, 1.30–5, other times by
arrangement, special service for schools.
Free. P. *(Tel 3391)*

Not just a stately home...

. . . . but a thousand acres
of beautiful parkland and meres perfect for walks and picnics,
swimming and sailing, fishing and horse riding.
Magnificent gardens with a Japanese temple.
A family museum with veteran cars and a fire engine.
Carriage rides, exciting trails, wild deer
and lots, lots more besides.
Just off the M6 and M56 at Knutsford, Cheshire.
Park and gardens open all the year. House, April to October.
All closed Mondays except during August and on Bank Holidays.
Telephone Knutsford (0565) 3155 — 52748
for information and opening hours.

Tatton Park
so many things to so many people

Cheshire County Council

TEIGNMOUTH *Devon* Map 3 SX97
Aqualand The Den. Specialises in Tropical
Marine Fish, but also has Tropical Freshwater
Fish and a fine exhibition of Local Marine Life.
Shell shop. Open daily Easter to Oct 10–6.
30p (ch 15 20p, ch 5 accompanied free, pen
15p). P. *(Tel 3383)*. Also Model Railway
exhibition 'N' gauge. Situated below
Aqualand. Open as above. 30p (ch 15 20p, ch
5 accompanied, free, pen 15p). *(79)*

TEMPLE SOWERBY *Cumbria* Map 12 NY62
Acorn Bank Garden Walled and herb
gardens, with spring bulbs and herbaceous
plants are open Apr to end of Oct, daily (ex
Mon) 10–5.30. 30p. No dogs. *(NT)*

TENTERDEN *Kent* Map 5 TQ83
Town Station Principal station of Britain's
first Light Railway, the Kent and East Sussex
Railway, constructed by Col H F Stephens at
turn of the century and reopened with steam
trains in 1974. Some 18 steam locomotives
(earliest built 1872, others from USA and
Norway) are in various stages of restoration.
Train services run to Wittersham Road.
Wealden Pullman specials, using Pullman
Bar Car 'Barbara' (built 1926) operate on Sat
evenings May to Oct. The station, shop,
carriage and wagon yards open all year. ⚏
(when trains operate). Trains operate every
weekend and BH, Easter to end Oct, also
Wed Jun and Jul, daily 12 Jul to 31 Aug Sun
only Nov and Dec. Fares: Day return 90p (ch
15 45p) Rover ticket £1.25 (ch 15 65p) Under
revision for 1980. ⚠ *(Tel 2943)* ♿

TETBURY *Gloucestershire* Map 3 ST89
Chavenage 2m NW. Elizabethan house
(1576) with later additions, containing some
17th-C stained glass, furniture and tapestries.
Open May to Sep, Thu, Sun and BH 2–6. £1
(ch 50p). ⚠ *(Tel 52329). (Mr D Lowsley
Williams)*

THETFORD *Norfolk* Map 5 TL88
Ancient House Museum White Hart Street.
An early Tudor timbered house with
collections illustrating Thetford and Breckland
life, history and natural history. Open all year
(ex 4 Apr, 25, 26 Dec, 1 Jan) Mon to Sat 10–5
(closed Mon 1–2), Sun 2–5. Free. P. *(Tel
2599)*
Thetford Castle One of the original motte
and bailey castles, at 80ft, perhaps the largest
still in existence. This represents the earliest
form of castle, before masonry was added.
Accessible any time. Free.
Thetford Priory Extensive remains of
Cluniac monastery founded at beginning of
12th C. The 14th-C gatehouse of priory
stands to its full height. Open*, see inside
front cover. 10p (ch 16 and pen 5p). ⚠ *(AM)*

Warren Lodge 2m NW of town, on B1107.
There are remains of a two-storey hunting
lodge in 15th-C flint with stone dressings.
Open Mon to Fri only 9–4.15 (closed
weekends and BH). Free. *(AM)*

THORESBY *Nottinghamshire* Map 8 SK67
Thoresby Hall A great Dukeries mansion, in
the heart of Sherwood Forest, dating from
1864–75, the architect being Salvin. This is
the only Dukeries mansion still occupied by
descendants of the original owners open to
the public. Fine state apartments and
terraces. Adventure woodland and paddling
pool. ⚏ House open 2–5. Telephone for
details of opening dates and admission
prices. ⚠ *(Tel Mansfield 823210). (Countess
Manvers)*

THORNBURY *Devon* Map 2 SS30
Devon Museum of Mechanical Music Mill
Leat. On unclassified road 5m NE of
Holsworthy. A fascinating collection of old
mechanical musical instruments from a tiny
music box to an eight-ton fairground organ.
The variety between these two extremes is
bewildering. All instruments are played for the
visitor and the curator demonstrates how they
work and shows the various mechanisms that
operate them. Continuous demonstrations.
Special concerts on the fairground organ to
be announced. ⚏ in the farm house. Open
Easter to Oct, daily 2–5. Admission prices for
1980 not yet decided. ⚠ *(Tel Milton Damerel
378 and Shebbear 483)* ♿

THORNTON *Humberside* Map 8 TA11
Thornton Abbey Displays a magnificent
example of a 14th-C gateway approached
across a dry moat spanned by a long bridge,
with arcaded walls and circular towers. Open,
see inside front cover but closes 4.30 Mon
and Tue. 15p (ch 16 and pen 5p). ⚠ *(AM)*

THURNHAM *Lancashire* Map 7 SD45
Thurnham Hall 5m S Lancaster on A588.
Dating from 13th C, the major part being
16th-C. The Great Hall contains fine
Elizabethan plaster work, Jacobean panelling
and fine Jacobean staircase, Priest Room
and Priest Hide. 19th-C private chapel. The
tour includes slide lecture on restoration, also
at the Hall the Turin Shroud exhibition. Shop
and ⚏. Open Easter to 31 Oct daily (ex Sat)
2–5.30. Admission charges not available at
time of going to press. Party. ⚠ *(Tel
Lancaster 751766)*

THURSFORD GREEN *Norfolk* Map 9 TF93
The Thursford Collection 6m NE
Fakenham. The collection includes
Showman's engines, traction engines,
ploughing engines, steam wagons, steam
rollers, 2ft gauge steam railway. Wurlitzer

cinema organ, fairground organs, dance and cafe organs, street and barrel organs and barrel pianos, also farm machinery. Midsummer musical evenings Tue at 8pm through summer on Wurlitzer cinema organ by the country's leading Organists. Sauages Venetian Gondola switchback ride. Picnic area and children's play area. ☕ Open all year 1 May to 31 Oct daily 2–5.30, 1 Nov to 30 Apr Sun only 2–5.30. Admission prices for 1980 not yet decided. ⚠ *(Tel Fakenham 3836 or Thursford 238)* ♿

TILBURY *Essex* Map 5 TQ67
Thurrock Riverside Museum Civic Square. Illustrates the history of the River Thames and the people of its riverside in the Borough of Thurrock. Ship and barge models, photographs, etc. Open daily (ex Sun and Mon) Tue, Sat 10–5, Wed, Fri 10–8, Thu 10–12 (closed 1–2 each day). Free. *(Tel 79216)* ♿
Tilbury Fort Dates from the reign of Henry VIII and was the scene of the review by Queen Elizabeth I of the army raised to resist the Spanish Armada. Later altered and restored. Open, see inside front cover. 25p (ch 16 and pen 10p). ⚠ *(AM)*

TILFORD *Surrey* Map 4 SU84
Old Kiln Agricultural Museum Reeds Road. Collection of farm implements and machinery of the past, and examples of the crafts and trades allied to farming. Larger exhibits are displayed in the pleasant garden and woodland surroundings, covering some ten acres. Smithy, wheel-wright's shop, hand tools, etc, are housed in the old farm buildings. Arboretum. Picnic area. Open 1 Apr to 30 Sep, Wed, Sat and Sun 12–6. 50p (ch 14 25p). ⚠ *(Tel Frensham 2300)* ♿

TINTAGEL *Cornwall* Map 2 SX08
Tintagel Castle Remains of a mid 13th-C castle, later abandoned and divided by subsequent erosion into two portions. There are also some remains of a Celtic monastery dating from the 5th C to the 9th C. Open*, see inside front cover 30p. Winter 15p (ch 16 and pen 15p, winter 5p). *(AM)*
Old Post Office A former 14th-C manor house, with a hall and an ancient slate roof. Open 1 Apr to end Oct, weekdays 11–1, 2–6 (or sunset), Sun 2–6; Dec, Jan, Feb. Key from caretaker (closed Nov). 50p (incl guide book) (ch 15p). P. *(NT)*

TINTINHULL *Somerset* Map 3 ST51
Tintinhull House Modern formal garden surrounding an attractive 17th-C house, with fine pedimented façade. Open Apr to Sep, Wed, Thu, Sat and BH Mons 2–6. 70p *(NT)*

TISBURY *Wiltshire* Map 3 ST92
Pythouse A late Palladian mansion, with family portraits. Shown May to end of Sep. Wed and Thu 2–5. 40p. P. *(Tel 0210)*

TITCHFIELD *Hampshire* Map 4 SU50
Titchfield Abbey Also known as 'Place House'. The surviving picturesque gatehouse of a 13th-C abbey converted into a mansion by the Earl of Southampton, Lord Chancellor of England, during the 16th C and showing fine Tudor chimneys. Open, see inside front cover. 15p (ch 16 and pen 5p). ⚠ *(AM)*

TIVERTON *Devon* Map 3 SS91
Tiverton Castle Historic fortress of Henry I founded 1106. Notable medieval gatehouse, clock museum, Joan of Arc gallery and Chapel of St Francis. Open Easter then mid May to mid Sep, daily (ex Fri and Sat) 2.30–5.30. 70p (ch and pen 40p). Party 15+. Prices are under revision for 1980. Private visits by arrangement. ⚠ *(Tel 3200)*
Tiverton Museum St Andrew Street, near Town Hall. Here is a comprehensive folk museum housed in a restored 19th-C school and comprising numerous local exhibits, a Victorian laundry, two water-wheels, costume gallery and an industrial gallery covering the Grand Western Canal, natural history and wartime rooms. Agricultural section includes a collection of farm wagons and a complete smithy. Now one of the outstanding West Country folk museums. Loan exhibitions are changed monthly. A large railway gallery houses the GWR locomotive No. 1442 and other railway relics. Entrance from public car park. Open all year Mon to Sat 10.30–1 and 2–4.30 (ex BH). Free. P. *(Tel 56295 and 2446)* ♿

TOLLAND *Somerset* Map 3 ST13
Gaulden Manor 1 m E of Tolland Church. Small historic manor originating from the 12th C. Unique plaster ceiling in Great Hall with oak screen leading to former chapel. Past home of the Turberville family, immortalised by Thomas Hardy, and of the Wolcotts of the USA. Herb garden, bog garden, gift shop. Plants for sale. ☕ (teas) in old stables. Open 6/7 Apr then 4 May to 7 Sep, Thu, Sun and BH 2–6. Admission to house and garden probably 70p (ch 13 30p). Garden only 30p. ⚠ *(Tel Lydeard St Lawrence 213)* ♿ B

TONBRIDGE *Kent* Map 5 TQ54
Tonbridge Castle Late 12th-C curtain walls, with a ruined shell keep and a round-towered early 14th-C gatehouse. Nature trail through Castle grounds 10p. Grounds open daily 7.30–dusk; castle open weekends only May, Jun and Jul, daily Aug, 10.30–4.30. Grounds

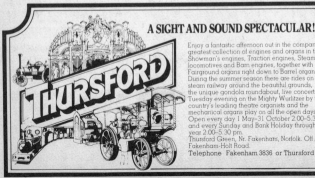

free; castle 30p (ch and pen 20p). Ch 12 must
be accompanied. Opening times and
admission prices under revision for 1980. P.
(Tel 353241) ⬄ B

TONG *West Yorkshire* Map 8 SE23
Tong Hall This 18th-C house built by Sir
George Tempest is an early example of
'Queen Anne' domestic architecture. Open
from Easter to Oct, Sat, Sun and BH 2 – 6.
Educational services. ⚠ *(Tel Leeds
852356)*

TOPSHAM *Devon* Map 3 SX98
Topsham Museum 25 The Strand. This
small museum, which is located in the sail-loft
of one of the beautiful old Dutch-gabled 17th-
C houses that are a feature of this little port,
depicts its history and trade through the
centuries. Open all year, Mon, Wed, Sat 2 – 5.
Free. ⚠ *(Tel 3244)*

TORPOINT *Cornwall* Map 2 SX45
Antony House 2m NW off A38. Fine, largely
unaltered mansion of 1711 – 21 in brick and
stone, with early 19th-C porte-cochère by Sir
William Carew and panelled rooms with
portraits and old furniture. House open 1 Apr
to Oct, Tue, Wed, Thu and BH 2 – 6. £1. *(NT)*

TORQUAY *Devon* Map 3 SX96
Aqualand Beacon Quay. The largest
Aquarium in the West Country which
specialises in tropical marine fish. There is
also a splendid exhibition of local marine life,
as well as tropical freshwater fish and a pair of
Otters from Asia. Open Apr, May, Sep and
Oct daily 10 to dusk; Jun to Aug daily 10 – 10.
40p (ch 14 and pen 20p). Party. ⚠ *(Tel
24439)* ⬄
Babbacombe Model Village Situated in four
acres of beautiful, miniature landscaped
gardens, this attractive example of a model
village contains over 400 models and 1,200ft
of model railways. Open all year, daily (ex 25
Dec); Easter to Oct 9 – 10; Nov to Mar 9 – 5.
80p (ch 40p, pen 60p). Under revision for
1980. Party. ⚠ *(Tel 38669)* ⬄
Natural History Society Museum 529
Babbacombe Road. Founded in 1844.
Exhibits include finds from Kent's Cavern and
other caves in South Devon; local
archaeological material. Open all year daily
(ex Sun, 4 Apr and Christmas period)
10 – 4.45. 25p (ch and pen 10p, ch 5 free). ⚠
(Tel 23975)
Torre Abbey Mansion The Kings Drive. An
18th-C house with interesting pictures and
furniture. Abbey ruins and Tythe Barn
(Spanish Barn) nearby. House open Apr to
Oct daily 10 – 1 and 2 – 5.30, winter parties by
appointment. 15p P (pen free). *(Tel 23593)*

TOTNES *Devon* Map 3 SX86
Totnes Castle A ruined 13th- and 14th-C
castle with a shell keep and curtain walls.
Open*, see inside front cover. 15p (ch 16 and
pen 5p). ⚠ *(AM)*
Elizabethan House 70 Fore Street. Four-
storey, restored, partly half-timbered, gabled
house, dating from c1575, with notable
interior features and a cobbled courtyard.
Now a museum of furniture, domestic objects,
toys, dolls, costumes and archaeology.
Computer exhibition. Open Mar to Oct, Mon to
Sat only 10.30 – 1 and 2 – 5.30. (Reduced
hours in winter.) 15p (ch 16 10p). Under
revision for 1980. ⚠ *(Tel 863821, winter
862147)*
Guildhall Off High Street. Gabled and
colonnaded 16th-C building, now housing
council chamber (in use since 1624). Relics
on show include Saxon coins minted locally.
Open Easter to Sep, Mon to Fri 9.30 – 1 and
2 – 5, Oct to Mar, by appointment. 10p (ch 5p,
school parties £1). P. *(Tel 862147)*
Totnes Motor Museum The Quay. Private
collection of vintage, sports and racing cars,
most of which are currently raced and cover a
50-year span of motoring. Engines,
motorbikes and motormania are also
displayed. Souvenir shop. Open Easter to
Oct, daily 10 – 6. 75p (ch 30p). Prices for 1980
under review. ⚠ *(Tel 862777)*

TRELISSICK GARDEN *Cornwall*
Map 2 SW83
4m S of Truro, on B3289. A beautiful
woodland park at the head of Falmouth
Harbour, growing rhododendrons and sub-
tropical plants. Large shrub garden. Plants
available at shop. ⚏ in Trelissick Garden
Barn 11 – 6. Gardens shown Mar to end of Oct
Mon to Sat 11 – 6; Sun 2 – 6. £1 *(NT) (NGS)*

TRERICE *Cornwall* Map 2 SW85
Off A3058. A picturesque Elizabethan House,
displaying unusual curly gables, rebuilt in
1571. There are contemporary fireplaces and
plaster ceilings. ⚏ 2 – 5.30. Open 1 Apr to end
Oct daily 11 – 6 (last admission 5.30) £1 *(NT)
(NGS)*

TREWINT *Cornwall* Map 2 SX28
Wesley's Cottage near Altarnun. Small 18th-
C Methodist shrine, well-restored in 1950.
John Wesley came here six times between
1744 and 1762. Annual Wesley Day service is
held. Also Sun services in summer.
Interesting testaments and period furnishings
are on display. Wesley Day celebrations 24
May. Open all year, daily 9 – dusk. Free. ⚠
Caution necessary when leaving owing to
restricted visibility on road. *(Tel Pipers Pool
561) (79)*

TRING *Hertfordshire* Map 4 SP91
The Zoological Museum A branch of the
British Museum (Natural History) specialising
in mounted specimens of animals, shells,
birds, eggs, and butterflies. Open all year (ex
1 Jan, 4 Apr, 5 May, 24–26 Dec), Mon to Sat
10–5, Sun 2–5. Free. P. *(Tel 4181)* B

TROUTBECK *Cumbria* Map 7 NY40
Townend Fine 17th-C yeoman's house,
containing carved woodwork and furnishings
of the Browne family. Open Wed only Mar
then Apr to Oct daily (ex Mon and Sat but
open BH Mon) 2–6 (or sunset). 60p (ch 30p).
(NT)

TRURO *Cornwall* Map 2 SW84
County Museum and Art Gallery River
Street. An exceptionally interesting display
illustrating the history of the county. The
mineral collection is world-famous. Unusually
fine collections of pottery and porcelain,
pewter, old-master drawings, Japanese
ivories and lacquer-work. Open all year, (ex
BH) 9–1, 2–5. Free. P. *(Tel 2205)*

TUNBRIDGE WELLS *Kent* Map 5 TQ53
Tunbridge Wells Museum and Art Gallery
Civic Centre. Old prints, local bygones,
natural history, geology, Wealden prehistory,
and Tunbridge ware. Collections of Victorian
paintings; toys and dolls. Temporary
exhibitions in art gallery. Open Mon to Sat
10–5.30. Closed Suns, BH and Tue after
Spring and Summer BH also 5 April. Free. P.
(Tel 26121 ex 171)

TUTBURY *Staffordshire* Map 8 SK22
Tutbury Castle Ruined 14th-C stronghold.
Mary Queen of Scots was twice imprisoned
here for a total of seven years. Picnic
grounds, putting green. Fêtes in May, Jun and

Jul. Café and banquet hall. Open all year (ex
25 and 26 Dec) 10–6. 20p (ch 5p). Coach
parties welcome. ⚲ ⚠ *(Tel Burton on Trent
812129)* **(79)**

PKF

TWYCROSS ZOO PARK *Leicestershire*
Map 4 SK30
Collection of all kinds of animals, especially
noted for the range of primates, including
gorillas, orang-utans and chimpanzees.
Modern reptile house. Wild animals include
giraffes, elephants, camels, lions, and tigers.
Numerous exotic birds. ⚲ and picnic areas,
only Tea Bar open during winter months.
Open all the year (ex 25 Dec) daily 10–4 (6 in
summer). £1 (ch 50p subject to alteration.
Party. ⚠ (10p). *(Tel Tamworth 880250)*

TYNEMOUTH *Tyne and Wear* Map 12 NZ36
Tynemouth Priory and Castle A 16th-C ruin,
with the towers, gatehouse, and keep erected
to defend the nearby 11th- to 13th-C Priory.
Open*, see inside front cover. 15p (ch 16 and
pen 5p). ⚠ *(AM)*

UCKFIELD *East Sussex* Map 5 TQ41
Beeches Farm 1½m W of town on Isfield road.
16th-C farmhouse with gardens, lawns,
sunken garden, borders, and yew trees. Wide
views. Gardens open all year, daily 10–5;
house open by appointment only, conducted

our 50p. Admission to gardens 15p (ch 12 7p). ⚠ *(Tel 2391). (Mrs V Thomas)* ♿ B
Horsted Place Gardens The gardens were redesigned and landscaped in the 1960s by Geoffrey Jellicoe around the Victorian Gothic mansion, surrounded by undulating countryside and woodland. Victorian garden, rose borders, rhododendrons, shaded walks, bleached limes and laburnum tunnel. Fragrant flowers and herbs are given special emphasis. Open Apr to 29 Sep, Wed, Thu and Sun 2–6, (house not open to the public except by special arrangement). 40p (ch 14 20p, party). Under review for 1980. ⚠ *(Tel Isfield 315)* ♿

UFFINGTON *Oxfordshire* Map 4 SU38
Castle and White Horse Situated on the ancient Ridgeway at a height of more than 700ft on the Berkshire Downs. The castle is a defensive Iron Age hill fort and below is a cut in the chalk the famous White Horse, believed to be contemporary. Both accessible any reasonable time. Free. ⚠ *(AM)*

ULEY *Gloucestershire* Map 3 ST79
Uley Tumulus 1m N. Known also as Hetty Pegler's Tump, this long barrow 120ft by 85ft, has a chamber approached by means of a deep forecourt. The chamber forms part of a gallery grave and was excavated in 1821 and 1854. Accessible any reasonable time. 10p (ch 16 and pen 5p). *(AM)*

ULVERSTON *Cumbria* Map 7 SD27
Cumbria Crystal Lightburn Road. using a fine full-lead crystal, the factory specialises in glassware based on 18th-C design. Goblets, decanters, candlesticks, tankards and many other items are made by traditional hand-blown and hand cutting techniques. Visitors welcome in factory, but large parties by appointment. Open all year, factory Mon to Fri 8–12, 12.30–4, Sat 8–11, closed Sun; shop and showroom Mon to Fri 9–12, 12.30–5.30, Sat and Sun 9–12. Free. P. *(Tel 54400)* ♿

UPMINSTER *Gt London* Map 5 TQ58
Tithe Barn Agricultural and Folk Museum Hall Lane. 15th-C thatched timber building contains large selection of old agricultural implements, craft and farm tools, domestic bygones and items of local interest, over 1,200 exhibits in all. Open first full weekend of each month. Apr to Oct 11–1 and 2.15–5.30. Free. ⚠ *(Tel 29614)* ♿

UPNOR *Kent* Map 5 TQ77
Upnor Castle A restored castle of 1561, designed originally as a River Medway blockhouse. A number of interesting relics have been preserved. Queen Elizabeth I reviewed the fleet here in 1581. Open, see inside front cover but closed all day Wed and Fri pm. 20p (ch 16 and pen 5p), ⚠ *(AM)*

UPPERMILL *Lancashire* Map 7 SD90
Saddleworth Museum High Street. Part of an old wooden mill converted into a museum with exhibits of local historical interest. Fine model of the Roman fort at Castleshaw and two working hand looms which show the history of weaving. Extension under construction will house new art gallery and provide full facilities for ♿. Open all year Sat, Sun and Wed 2.30–5. Free (charge for admission under review). ⚠ *(Tel Saddleworth 2273 day, 3884 evening).* ♿

UPPER SLAUGHTER *Gloucestershire* Map 5 SP12
Manor House One of the finest Elizabethan houses in Gloucestershire. Grade I listed building, restored in 1973. Mainly Elizabethan, it has a remarkable 15th-C vaulted chamber surviving from an earlier religious foundation, plus an ornamental entrance porch of the Jacobean period. Home of the Slaughter family for 500 years. Open May to Sep inclusive, Fri 2–6. 40p. *(Tel Bourton-on-the-Water 20927)*

UPTON CRESCENT *Salop* Map 7 SP69
Upton Cressett Hall Elizabethan manor house, gatehouse and gardens in beautiful countryside. Fine plasterwork, brickwork and panelling. 14th-C Great Hall. Open May to end Oct, Thu 2.30–5.30 and 25 Aug. Parties at other times by appointment. 50p ⚠ *(Tel Morville 307)*

UPTON HOUSE *Warwickshire* Map 4 SP34
7m NW of Banbury on A422. 17th-C house with fine collection of paintings, porcelain, tapestries and furniture. Terraced garden. Open Apr to Sep, Mon to Thu 2–6 (last admission to house 5.30) and some weekends in May and Aug. £1.10, garden only 60p. *(NT)*

WADDESDON *Buckinghamshire* Map 4 SP71
Waddesdon Manor 6m NW Aylesbury, gates on A41. French Renaissance-style château built in 1874–1889 for Baron Ferdinand de Rothschild by Destailleur. Rich in French decorative art of 17th and 18th Cs, Royal furniture, Sèvres and Meissen porcelain, Savonnerie carpets, fine paintings and personal mementoes of the family. New exhibition room in 1980. ☕ Open 26 Mar to 26 Apr, Oct, Wed to Sun 2–6; 4 Apr and BH Mons 11–6 (closed Wed after BH). Sun, grounds open from 11.30am. House and grounds incl 4 Apr £1.30, other Fri £1.50 (extra rooms shown). Grounds and Aviary only 60p (ch 25p). Play area for young ch. Ch 12 not admitted to house. ⚠ *(NT)*

WAKEFIELD *West Yorkshire* Map 8 SE32
Wakefield Art Gallery Wentworth Terrace. Good collection of modern paintings and sculpture including works by Henry Moore, Barbara Hepworth, Jacob Epstein, Graham Sutherland, Ben Nicholson etc. Regular programme of temporary exhibitions. Open all year, Mon to Sat 12.30–5.30, Sun 2.30–5.30 (closed BH). Free. P. *(Tel 75402)*
Wakefield Museum Wood Street. Specialises in collections of local interest, including archaeology, costume, period rooms. Waterton Collection of natural history specimens. Temporary exhibitions. Open all year weekdays, 12.30–5.30, Sun 2.30–5.30 (closed BH). Free. P. *(Tel 61767)*

WALL *Staffordshire* Map 7 SK10
Roman Remains Remains of baths and posting stations (most complete in Britain), and a museum of excavated finds from the Roman station of 'Letocetum' at the junction of Watling Street and Ricknield Street. Open, see inside front cover but closed Mon and Tue. 15p (ch 16 and pen 5p). ⚠ *(NT and AM)*

WALSINGHAM *Norfolk* Map 9 TF93
Walsingham Abbey Grounds Contain site of the Shrine of Our Lady and the remains of an Augustinian Priory including the gatehouse, crypt, refectory and East Window Arch. The Abbey Grounds are open Apr to Sep. Wed Apr; Wed, Sat & Sun May to Jul and Sep also Mon, Wed, Fri, Sat and Sun Aug and BH Easter to Sep. 20p (ch 10p). P. *(Tel 259)* ♿
Shirehall Museum Almost perfect 18th-C courtroom with its original fittings, including prisoner's lock-up. The museum contains

items illustrating the history of Walsingham, including a new display on the History of Pilgrimage. Open daily May to Sep 10–12 and 2–4, Oct Sat and Sun only. 10p (ch and pen free). P. *(Tel 510)*

WALTHAM ABBEY *Essex* Map 5 TL30
Waltham Abbey Gatehouse, Bridge and entrance to Cloisters This example of a gatehouse is 14th-C and has separate carriage and pedestrian entrances. Harold's Bridge is attributed to the 14th C. Cloister entrance dates from 12th C. Open at any reasonable time. Free. In the historic Norman and later Abbey Church nearby is an undercroft museum. ⚠ *(AM)*

WALWICK *Northumberland* Map 12 NY97
Chesters Roman Fort and Museum ½m E. Roman Fort designed for a garrison of 500 cavalry. Extensive ruins of bath house. Museum houses Clayton collection of items excavated from local forts such as 'Cilurnum'. Open*, see inside front cover. 40p, winter 15p (ch 16 and pen 15p, winter 5p). ⚠ *(AM)*

WANDLEBURY RING *Cambridgeshire*
Map 5 TL45
On the summit of the low Gog Magog Hills, this hill fort comprises a double rampart and ditch, 1,000ft in diameter; about 110 acres of the hills have been protected by the Cambridge Preservation Society. Open daily without charge but donations are welcome. Parking.

WANSFORD *Cambridgeshire* Map 4 TL09
Nene Valley Railway Standard-gauge steam railway running over five miles through Nene Park, between Wansford and Orton Mere, Peterborough. Having many steam locomotives, it offers a unique spectacle of British, French, Danish, German, Swedish and Norwegian locomotives and stock on the same railway. ⚐ Greene King bar car also lunch (reservations advisable) and tea every Sun in Wagons-Lit restaurant car. Open Apr to Sep, Sat, Sun also mid week during Jun, Jul and Aug. Also open for Christmas Specials every Sat and Sun during Dec. ⚠ For further information and reservation contact the General Manager. *(Tel Stamford 782854)*

WANTAGE *Oxfordshire* Map 4 SU48
Wantage Museum Civic Hall, Portway. A small museum with displays on the landscape history of the Vale of the White Horse and the growth of the town of Wantage. Museum Keeper available for enquiries on Wed. Open all year Wed 2–5, Sat 10–12.30 and 2–5 (closes 4.30 Oct to Mar). Free. P. *(Tel 66838)* ⚐

Kingstone Lisle Park 4½m W off B4507. The home of Captain and Mrs Leopold Lonsdale. The central part of the mansion was built in 1677 and the wings were added in the 19th C. It has a magnificent flying staircase and an interesting collection of 17th- and 18th-C glass. Also on display are letters which belonged to Field Marshal Lord Raglan, Commander-in-Chief of the Crimea. ⚐ (by arrangement). Open Apr to Sep by appointment only, market garden also open. £1 (less than 5 min £5). Party 15+ 80p per person. ⚠ Further information write to: The Secretary, Kingstone Lisle Park, Wantage. *(Tel Uffingtoni223)*

WARDOUR *Wiltshire* Map 3 ST92
Wardour Castle Built by James Paine in 1768, and restored in 1960 for Cranborne Chase School. Contains a notable stairway with two semi-circular flights. Open Jul to Sep

Mon, Wed, Fri, Sat 2.30–6.35p (ch 14 20p). Party 12+. Under revision for 1980. ⚠ *(Tel Tisbury 870464)*
Wardour Old Castle Built in 1392 by John Lord Lovel, with additions by Robert Smythson after 1570. Damaged after the Civil War. Open*, see inside front cover. 15p (ch 16 and pen 5p). ⚠ *(AM)*

WARKWORTH *Northumberland*
Map 12 NU20
Warkworth Castle Built between 11th- and 14th-C with a gatehouse and a great keep, probably built by the 1st Earl of Northumberland. Old bridge over River Coquet and rare bridge tower. Open Apr to Sep only, see inside front cover. 20p (ch 16 and pen 5p). ⚠ *(AM)*
Warkworth Hermitage Interesting 14th-C hermitage with a small chapel cut in solid rock. Access by rowing boat from nearby Castle. Open, see inside front cover, Apr to Sep only. 15p (ch 16 and pen 5p). P (at Castle).

WARNHAM *West Sussex* Map 4 TQ13
The Warnham War Museum 1m NE on east of A24. Private collection of World War II vehicles, uniforms, badges, medals, equipment, tracked and amphibious vehicles, set in ten acres of woodland. ⚐ (licensed). Open all year (ex 25 Dec) daily 1 Oct to Easter 10–4; Easter to 30 Sep 10–6. 50p (ch 5–14 25p). Party. ⚠ *(Tel Horsham 65607)* ⚐ *(79)*

WARRINGTON *Cheshire* Map 7 SJ68
South Lancashire Regiment (PWV) Regimental Museum Peninsula Barracks, Orford. Military museum of South Lancashire Regiment from 1717 onwards, containing historical records, uniforms and accoutrements, arms, badges, and medals. Open all year Mon to Fri 9–12.30, 2–4.30. Free. ⚠ limited. *(Tel 33563)*

WARWICK *Warwickshire* Map 4 SP26
Warwick Castle Off Castle Hill. Famous 14th-C and later castle, overlooking the River Avon. Guy's Tower (1394) and Caesar's Tower (1356) between which is an imposing gatehouse. Exhibition areas include the Great Hall, State rooms, Dungeon and Torture display, Armoury, Clocktower and Barbican, Guy's Tower and Ghost Tower. Peacocks and peacock gardens. Special events on Sunday afternoons (April to October). Children's adventure area. Picnic areas. Souvenir shops. Licensed restaurant (all year). ⚐ (Mar to Sep). Medieval Banquets throughout the year. Open all year (ex 25 Dec) 10–5.30 (4.30 Nov to Feb). Admission prices not yet decided. ⚠ *(Tel 45421)* ⚐ B
Lord Leycester's Hospital West Gate. Lovely, half-timbered building, built in 1383, and adapted for its present use by the Earl of Leycester in 1571. It is still an almshouse for ex-servicemen and their wives. Guildhall Chapel, Regimental Museum of Queen's Own Hussars. ⚐ Easter to Sep. Open all year 10–5.30, summer; in winter 10–4 (closed Suns, 4 Apr and 25 Dec). Last admission ½hr before closing. 40p (ch 14 20p). Party 20+. ⚠ *(Tel 42797)*
Warwick Doll Museum Oken's House, Castle Street. Half-timbered Elizabethan house, the 16th-C birthplace of Thomas Oken, a benefactor of the town. Now a doll museum containing the Joy Robinson Collection of antique and period dolls, and toys. Open daily 10–6. Sun 11–5. 30p (ch 15p). Admission prices under revision for 1980. P. *(Tel 42843)*

St John's House Junction of A429 and A445
east of town. Fine 17th-C house, with gardens
and notable wrought-iron gates, rebuilt by the
Stoughton family on the site of an old hospital.
It is now a branch of the County Museum
(crafts, costume, and musical instruments),
and includes the museum of the Royal
Warwickshire Regiment on the first floor.
Open weekdays (ex Tue) 10–12.30 and
1.30–5.30, Sun (May to Sep only) 2.30–5.
Regimental museum open weekdays (ex
Tue) 10–12.30, 2–4.30 (4 Fri), Sat 1.30–5,
Sun 2.30–5 (May to Sep only). Free. P in St
Nicholas Park. *(Tel 43431 ext 2132; for
Regimental Museum, 41653)*

WASHAWAY *Cornwall* Map 2 SX07
Pencarrow House 1m N on unclass road.
Georgian mansion *c*1770. The interior
contains interesting architectural features,
including an impressive Inner Hall with
marbled pillars and a cantilever staircase; a
music room with a Rococo ceiling; and many
fine 18th-C paintings by Reynolds, Devis,
Scott, Raeburn, Wilson etc, together with
English, French and Oriental furniture and
china. There are 35 acres of woodland
gardens with arrowed trails. Plant shop.
Picnic area, ⊡. Open Easter to end Sep, Tue,
Wed, Thu, Fri, Sun 1.45–5.30, BH Mon and 1
Jul to 10 Sep 11.30–5.30, (last tour of house
5). Gardens and plant shop open 15 Mar to
end Sep daily. Admission charges not yet
decided. ⚠ *(Tel St Mabyn 369)* ⅃ B

WASHFORD *Somerset* Map 3 ST04
Bardon Manor 2m SW of Watchet, off
B3190. Unspoilt and reputedly haunted 14th-
C manor house with Saxon fireplace in main
hall, and cockpit. Historical associations with
famous Bardon Papers connected with Mary,
Queen of Scots. Exhibition of paintings and
handicrafts by West Country artists. ⊡. Open
Jun to Sep, daily 10.30–5.30. 20p (ch 14 and
pen 10p). ⚠ *(Tel 217)*
Cleeve Abbey Ruined 13th-C Cistercian
house noted for gatehouse, dormitory, and
refectory with traceried windows, timber roof,
and wall paintings. Open*, see inside front
cover. 15p (ch 16 and pen 5p). ⚠ *(AM)*

WASHINGTON *Tyne and Wear* Map 12 NZ35
Washington Old Hall Mainly early 17th-C,
the seat of the Washington family, now
restored as a museum. Open, Mar to Oct,
daily (ex Tue) 1–6 (or sunset). Nov to Feb,
Sat and Sun 2–5. 50p (ch 25p). *(NT)*
The Wildfowl Trust A waterfowl park on the
N bank of the River Wear. 103 acres with a
comprehensive collection of the world's
waterfowl in attractive landscaped
surroundings, including a refuge of 70 acres
for wild birds, which can be viewed from a
number of public hides. Attractive log cabin
visitor centre, souvenir and natural history
bookshop, inside viewing gallery giving
excellent view over part of main collection
area. Lecture theatre where free natural
history films shown most days. ⊡ weekends
and daily Jul and Aug. Open all year (ex 24/25
Dec) daily 9.30–6.30 (9 Jun, Jul and Aug).
Last admission 1 hour before closing. 65p (ch
4–15 30p, ch 4 free, pen 50p). Party 20+
(educational tours may be arranged). P. *(Tel
465454)* ⅃

WEDNESBURY *West Midlands* Map 7 SO99
Sandwell Art Gallery and Museum
Holyhead Road. Collection of English and
Continental 19th-C oil paintings and water-
colours and also a collection of various
applied arts. Frequent temporary exhibitions.

Open all year (ex BH) Mon, Tue, Wed, Fri
10–5. Thu, Sat, 10–1. Free. P. *(Tel 021-556
0683)*

WEETING *Norfolk* Map 5 TL78
Weeting Castle A ruined 11th-C fortified
manor house, situated in a rectangular
enclosure, and preserving slight remains of a
three-storeyed cross-wing. Open any
reasonable time. Free. ⚠ *(AM)*

WELLAND *Hereford and Worcester*
Map 3 SO74
Little Malvern Court c 1380, on foundations
dating from 1171. Originally part of monastic
buildings, probably reconstructed by Bishop
Alcock in 1480 when extensive repairs to the
Priory Church were carried out. North wing
built about 1500. Adjacent Priory Church has
14th-century stained glass, carved rood-
screen, misericords and hatchments. Prior's
Hall and associated rooms only open Easter
to end Sep, Wed 2.30–5.30. 30p. P. *(Tel
Hanley Swan 257)*

WELLING *Gt London* Map 5 TQ47
Danson Park Lake watered park, designed
originally by 'Capability' Brown, with rock and
water gardens, and recreational facilities. ⊡.
Gardens open all year, daily Mon to Fri
7.30–dusk (4.30 winter) Sat and Sun 9–dusk
(4.30 winter). Free. P. 10p weekends and BH
Apr to Sep. Free weekdays and Oct to Mar.
(79)

WELLS *Somerset* Map 3 ST54
Bishop's Palace The early part of the Palace,
the Bishop's Chapel and the ruins of the
banqueting hall date from the 13th C. The
Undercroft remains virtually unchanged from
this date. The first floor has former State
Rooms with Long Gallery containing portraits
of former Bishops. Ringed with fortifications
and a moat, access is gained through a 14th-
C Gatehouse. The moat is fed by St Andrew's
Well from which the City derives its name.
⊡(Aug only). Open Easter and then May to
Oct Suns (Thu, Grounds only), Aug daily 2–6.
35p (ch 14 20p); Grounds only 25p (ch 14
15p); special rate Aug only 40p (ch 14 25p). ⚠
(Tel 78691) ⅃ B
Wells Museum This museum illustrates the
history and natural history of the caves in the
Central Mendip area. Open all year. Apr to
Sep 10–6, Oct to Mar 2–4.30, Sun Jun to Sep
2.30–5.30. Closed 24–26 Dec. 10p (ch 16
5p). P. (limited in street). *(Tel 73477)* **(79)**

WELNEY *Norfolk* Map 5 TL59
The Wildfowl Trust 800-acre popular
wildfowl refuge on the Ouse Washes. Winter
home of vast numbers of migratory swans,
geese and ducks; in spring, alive with nesting
mallard, redshank, snipe, ruff, black-tailed
godwit etc. Spacious observatory, a series of
hides and, in winter, a floodlit lagoon
containing hundreds of Bewick's swans.
Open all year daily (ex 24, 25 Dec) 10–5. 50p
(ch 16 25p, pen 40p). Escorted visits at 10 and
2 (weekends only) 60p (ch 16 30p, pen 50p).
Party 20+. Evening visits for parties only
1 Nov to 1 Mar commencing 7pm. 60p (ch
30p, pen 50p). Overnight accommodation
available. ⚠ *(Tel Ely 860711)* ⅃ **(79)**

WEMBWORTHY *Devon* Map 2 SS60
Ashley Countryside Collection Ashley
House. 1½m NW on unclass rd. Signposted on
A377 at Eggesford Station and on B3220 at
Winkleigh. A unique collection of 45 breeds of
British sheep including all the rare breeds.
Fleeces exhibition, and 1,000 items of the Ox,
Horse and open fireplace era. Wheelwrights',

Coopers, Blacksmiths' and Country Craftsmen's tools and workshops. Mainly under cover. Picnic area. Open Easter to Oct Mon, Wed, Sat and Sun also BH and daily (ex Thu) in Aug 10 – 6. 50p (ch 12 25p). Under revision for 1980. ⚠ *(Tel Ashreigney 226)* ♿

WENDRON *Cornwall* Map 2 SW63
Poldark Mining and Wendron Forge
Stretching over three acres is a major collection of antique machines around the only underground tin mine workings in Cornwall open to the public. A forty-foot high beam engine runs daily in the summer, and the licensed restaurant contains a five-ton working waterwheel. Open Easter to 1 Nov daily 10 – 6 (sunset in Jul and Aug). £1 (ch 10 50p and pen 70p). ⚠ *(Tel Helston 3531 or 3173)* ♿ B

WEST BROMWICH *West Midlands* Map 7 SP09
Oak House Oak Road. Half-timbered 16th-C house, displaying furniture, and furnishings in the Jacobean style. Open all year, May to Sep, weekdays 10 – 5 (1, Thu); Sun 2.30 – 5; Oct to Apr weekdays 10 – 1. Free. P. *(Tel 021-553 0759)*

WESTBURY-ON-SEVERN *Gloucestershire* Map 3 SO71
Westbury Court Garden A unique example of a 17th-C water garden layout, with angle pavillions, the earliest survivor of its kind in England. They have for many years lain derelict, but were given a government grant for repairs and have been taken over by the National Trust. Open May to Sep, daily (ex Mon and Tue but open BH) 11 – 6; Apr and Oct, Sat and Sun only. 60p (ch 30p). No dogs. *(NT)*

WESTCLIFF-ON-SEA *Essex* Map 5 TQ88
Beecroft Art Gallery Station Road. Specialises in traditional and contemporary British art, but also has works from the Continental schools. A special gallery devoted to the development of Southend and scenes of the Thames Estuary. Temporary exhibitions every month. Open all year, daily, weekdays 10.30 – 5.30. Sun 2 – 5.30. Free. P. (limited). *(Tel Southend-on-Sea 47418)*

WESTERHAM *Kent* Map 5 TQ45
Quebec House A 16th- to 17th-C house, once the home of General Wolfe. Open 2 – 30 Mar, Sun only 2 – 6. Apr to Oct daily (ex Thu and Sat) 2 – 6. 60p (ch 30p). *(NT)*
Squerryes Court Dates from 1681, associated with General Wolfe, to whom cenotaph stands. Much of interior shown, with fine pictures, china, tapestries, and period furniture. Very attractive grounds with lake, spring bulbs, azaleas and rhododendrons. Open 1 Mar to 29 Oct, Wed, Sat, Sun, BH Mon 2 – 6 (last entry to house 5.30). House and grounds 80p (ch 14 40p); Grounds only 40p (ch 14 20p). Party (ex Sun). ⚠ *(Tel 62345)*. *(J St A Warde)* ♿ B

WEST HOATHLY *West Sussex* Map 5 TQ33
West Hoathly Priest's House 15th-C house, now a small interesting folk museum. Open weekdays (ex Fri) 11 – 5.30, Sun 2 – 5; Easter to end of Sep. 20p (ch 10p). ⚠ *(Tel Sharpthorne 810479)*. *(Sussex Archaeological Society)*

WEST MALLING *Kent* Map 5 TQ65
St Leonard's Tower The surviving part of the former castle or fortified manor house belonging to Bishop Gundulph. Open any reasonable time. Free. *(AM)*

WESTONBIRT *Gloucestershire* Map 3 ST88
Westonbirt Arboretum Includes splendid
examples of rare specimen trees, and was
founded originally by Robert Stayner Halford
in 1829. Now incorporated in a 600-acre
Forestry Commission estate. ⚲ Apr to Oct.
Accessible daily 10 – 8 or sunset (whichever is
earlier) all the year. Free. ♿ 80p. Under
revision for 1980. *(Tel 220). (The Forestry
Commission)* &

WESTON PARK *Staffordshire* Map 7 SJ81
A fine mansion of 1671, built by Lady
Wilbraham. Notable collection of pictures,
furniture, and tapestries. Disraeli letters on
show. The home of the Earls of Bradford for
300 years. Fine gardens and vast parklands
by 'Capability' Brown. Three lakes, pets
corner, and woodland adventure playground
and aquarium. Garden centre, studio pottery.
Special exhibitions and events. ⚲. Open
Easter to end Sep daily (ex Mon and Fri) but
open BH, House 2 – 6 (last admission 5.30).
Park 11 – 7.30 (last admission 5.30). School
parties 1 May to 31 Jul weekdays from 10am.
Admission prices not available. Party. ♿ *(Tel
Weston-under-Lizard 207 or 385). (The Earl
of Bradford)* &

Hilton Valley Railway On A5 near village of
Weston-under-Lizard. Narrow-gauge railway
which operates five steam and three diesel
locomotives. Moving from Hilton and opening
early 1980. Information from Hilton Valley
Railway Ltd, Hem Manor, Shifnal, Salop TF11
9PT.

WESTON RHYN *Salop* Map 7 SJ23
Tyn-y-Rhos Hall 2m W near Bron-y-Garth on
unclass road. Small manor house, seat of the
Phillips family for over three hundred years.
Fully furnished in the style of the late 19th-C.

Many interesting items including a painting of
Charles I, believed to be of Van Dyke school,
also worthy of note is the family chapel within
the house. Open 1 May to 15 Sep Wed, Thu,
Sat and Sun 2.30 – 6. 60p (ch and pen 30p). ♿
(Tel Chirk 7898)

WESTON-SUPER-MARE *Avon* Map 3 ST36
Woodspring Museum Burlington Street.
The museum is housed in the old workshops
of the Edwardian Gaslight Company. Around
a central courtyard are displays of the
Victorian Seaside Holiday, an old chemist's
shop, a dairy and a gallery of wildlife in the
district. Other exhibits include Mendip
minerals and mining, archaeology, costume
jewellery, toys, dolls, transport from penny
farthing to Weston Autogyro, cameras, the
Dentist in 1900, and a Steep Holm display.
Changing exhibitions are held in the Art
Gallery. ⚲. Open all year (ex 4 Apr, 25 Dec, 1
Jan) Mon to Sat 10 – 1, and 2 – 5. Free. ♿
roadside (1hr). *(Tel 21028)*

WESTON UNDERWOOD *Buckinghamshire*
Map 4 SP85
Flamingo Gardens and Zoological Park
1,000 birds of 200 different species, including
flamingos, cranes, pelicans, penguins,
Scarlet Ibis, owls, waterfowl, and birds of
prey, emanating from many countries.
Mammals include Llamas, Wallabies, Black
Buck, Big Horn sheep, dwarf Zebu. ⚲. Open
Wed, Thu, Sat, Sun and BH 2 – 8, from 4 Apr
to end Sep. £1 (ch 14 50p, pen 60p). Party
15+. Prices under rivision for 1980. ♿ *(Tel
Bedford 711451)* &

WEST TARRING *West Sussex* Map 4 TQ10
Parsonage Row Cottages High Street (at
West Worthing). A group of three late 15th-C
houses, fine examples of medieval close-

WESTON PARK

The 17th-century home of the Earl and Countess of Bradford contains
a treasury of beautiful objects including an exceptional art collection.
**Located in 1,000 acres of picturesque wooded parkland on the
Shropshire/Staffordshire border.**
Woodland adventure playground — aquarium — studio pottery —
garden centre — Collection of British Wildlife — pony rides — nature
and architectural trails.
Catering Facilities. Picnic in peaceful surroundings.
Open Easter till the end of September (see entry for specific dates and
times).
For further information write or telephone: The Old Stables, Weston
Park, Shifnel, Shropshire. Tel: Weston-under-Lizard 207 or 385.
Access is easy — head for Weston-under-Lizard on the A5, 6 miles
west of Junction 12 on the M6.

timbering construction, which are known as the Thomas-à-Becket cottages. They now house a small folk museum of bygones. Open 1 Apr to 31 Oct, Tue to Sat 2.15–5; other times by appointment with the Custodian. 15p (ch 10p). P. *(Tel Worthing 36385)*

WESTWOOD *Wiltshire* Map 3 ST85
Westwood Manor A beautiful 15th- to 17th-C house showing fine Jacobean plasterwork. Modern topiary garden. Open Apr to Sep, Wed 2.30–6. 70p *(NT)*

WEST WYCOMBE *Buckinghamshire*
Map 4 SU89
West Wycombe Park Rebuilt for Sir Francis Dashwood, c1765, probably built by Robert Adam, and situated in a fine park containing garden temples by 'Capability' Brown and Humphrey Repton. Notable furnishings and painted ceilings. House and grounds open Jun, Mon to Fri; Jul and Aug, every day (ex Sat) 2.15–6. £1.40. Grounds only 60p *(NT)*. *(NGS)*
West Wycombe Caves Built between 1748 and 1752. The caves are said to have been used as a meeting place for the Hell Fire Club. The entrance to the caves is half way up West Wycombe Hill, and consists of a large forecourt with flint walls, from which a brick tunnel leads into the caves. The many halls and chambers include the Labyrinth, Hall of Statues, Treasure Chamber and the Inner Temple. ♫ Open daily 1 Mar to 28 May and 9 to 29 Sep, 1–6pm, 29 May to 8 Sep daily 11–6. Sat and Sun 30 Sep to 25 Feb 12–4. £1 (ch and pen 50p). Party. ⚠ *(Tel High Wycombe 24411)*

WEYHILL *Hampshire* Map 4 SU34
The Hawk Conservancy Weyhill Wildlife Park A specialist collection of hawks, falcons, eagles, owls, vultures etc. Open daily, including Sun, from 10.30. 1 Mar to 9 Nov. 90p (ch 14 40p) ch must be accompanied by an adult. 1979 prices under revision for 1980. No dogs or pets. *(Tel 2252)*

WEYMOUTH *Dorset* Map 3 SY67
Museum of Local History Westham Road. An illustrated survey of the history of Weymouth and Portland, including local transport, and links with visits of King George III (1789–1805). Collections include special section of 'Household bygones', with occasional temporary exhibitions. Open all year. Summer: Mon, Wed, Thu, Fri 10–8, Tue and Sat 10–5; Winter: Tue to Sat 10–1 and 2–5. Closed Sun and Mon in winter. 10p (ch, students and pen free). P. *(Tel 74246)* ♿

WHALLEY *Lancashire* Map 7 SD73
Whalley Abbey The Abbey ruins are in delightful gardens reaching down to the river. Open all year daily 10–dusk. 20p (ch 13 10p). Party 30+ (school ch only). ⚠ *(Tel 2268)*

WHIPSNADE *Bedfordshire* Map 4 TL01
Whipsnade Park Zoo Open-air zoo situated on edge of Chilterns. Over 2,000 animals and birds can be seen in near natural surroundings in the 500-acre park. Children's zoo, water mammals exhibit displaying dolphins. ♫ Open daily (ex 25 Dec) 10–7 or sunset if earlier. Admission not yet know for 1980. ⚠ Cars may drive round the zoo at an extra charge. A Zoo Train operates in the park according to demand. Steam Railway runs through White Rhino enclosure, Apr to Oct. *(Tel 872171)* ♿

WHITBY *North Yorkshire* Map 8 BN81
Whitby Abbey Considerable remains of fine church dating from 13th C. Damaged by shell fire during the 1914–18 War. Open*, see inside front cover. 20p (ch 16 and pen 5p). ⚠ *(AM)*
Whitby Museum Pannett Park. Museum portrays the history of the town. Next door is the Pannett Art Gallery; both are open 1 May to 30 Sep daily, Mon to Sat 9.30–5.30, Sun 2–5; 1 Oct to 30 Apr Mon, Tue, Thu and Fri 10.30–1, Wed and Sat 10.30–4, Sun 2–4; Easter weekend: Fri, Sat and Mon 10.30–4, Sun 2–4; BH: normal opening times. Closed 25, 26 Dec and 1 Jan. 20p (ch 16 15p) subject to review for 1980. P. *(St Hilda's Terrace)*. *(Tel 2908)* ♿

WHITEHAVEN *Cumbria* Map 11 NX91
Whitehaven Museum and Art Gallery Market Place. Lower gallery devoted to changing exhibitions, approximately 20 per year, very diverse subjects. The upper gallery features local history including geology, coal and iron mining, archaeology, ship building, Whitehaven made pottery. Slide/tape shows usually featured in lower gallery. Open Mon to Sat 10–5 (closed Sun and BH). Free. P (street; multi-storey 5p). *(Tel [0946] 3111 ext 289)*

WHITNEY-ON-WYE *Hereford and Worcester* Map 3 SO24
Brilley: Cwmmau Farmhouse Early 17th-C timber-framed and stone-tiled farmhouse. Picnics only by previous arrangement. Open 5, 6, 7 Apr; 24, 25, 26 May; 23, 24, 25 Aug 2–6; other times by previous written appointment with *Mr S M Joyce*. 20p *(NT)*

WHITTINGHAM *Northumberland* Map 12 NU00
Callaly Castle, Gardens and Grounds 2m W. Entrance by west lodge only. 17th-C

mansion incorporating 13th-C tower, with later (notably 18th-C) alterations and additions. Interesting pictures and furnishings and fine saloon with 18th-C plasterwork. ⬠ Sun and BH. Open 23 May to 28 Sep, Sat and Sun also BH 2.15–5.30; other days on application to the Estate Office, Callaly, Alnwick. 50p (ch 15 25p). Subject to alteration. Party 20+. No dogs. ⚠ *(Tel 663)*. *(Major A S C Browne DL)* ⬠ B

WHTTINGTON *Staffordshire* Map 7 SK10
Whittington Barracks, Staffordshire Regiment Museum An interesting museum displaying details of the Regiment's battle honours; captured trophies, weapons old and new, uniforms past and present, and a special display of medals. Open Mon to Fri 9.30–4.30; Sat, Sun, and BH by appointment only. *(Tel the Curator, Major M K Beedle MBE, Tel 433333 ext 240 or 229)*. Free. ⚠ (limited.) ⬠

WICHENFORD *Hereford and Worcester* Map 3 SO76
Dovecote 17th-C half-timbered, black and white dovecote. Open daily until sunset. 10p *(NT)*

WILDERHOPE *Salop* Map 7 SO59
Wilderhope Manor Off B4371. A fine 16th-C house, with 17th-C plaster ceilings. Views of Corvedale. Leased to Youth Hostels Association. Open Apr to end of Sep, Wed and Sat, Oct to Mar Sat only, 2–4.30. 50p *(NT)*

WILDFOWL TRUST
see **Arundel, Caerlaverock** (Scotland), **Martin Mere, Peakirk, Slimbridge Washington** and **Welney.**

WILMCOTE *Warwickshire* Map 4 SP15
Mary Arden's House The picturesque, half-timbered, Tudor birthplace of Shakespeare's mother. Farming museum in barns. Open all year (ex 24–26 Dec, 4 Apr, am, and Sun Nov to Mar) Apr to Oct, weekdays 9–6, Sun 2–6; Nov to Mar, weekdays only 9–4.30 (ch 15p). Admission prices under revision for 1980. ⚠ *(Tel Stratford-upon-Avon 293455)*

WILMINGTON *East Sussex* Map 5 TQ50
Priory Remains of a 13th-C Benedictine foundation now housing an agricultural museum. Open mid Mar to mid Oct, weekdays (ex Tue) 11–5, Sun 2–5. 25p (ch 15p). ⚠ *(Tel Alfriston 870537)*. *(Sussex Archaeological Society)*

WILTON *Wiltshire* Map 4 SU03
Wilton House A magnificent 16th- to 19th-C house by Inigo Jones, Holbein, and James Wyatt, of great historical and architectural interest. It contains a world-famous collection

of paintings, furniture, and sculpture, in state apartments, including the great double and single 'cube' rooms. Exhibition of 7,000 miniature model soldiers. Unparalleled settings of lawns and Cedars of Lebanon. 21/22 Jun 'The Wonderful World of Wood'. ⬠ (and licensed). Open 10 Apr to 7 Oct, Tue to Sat and BH 11–6, Sun 2–6 (last admission always 5.30) (closed Mon). £1 (ch 15 and pen 50p). Party. Garden centre open. ⚠ *(Tel 3115)*. *(Earl of Pembroke)* ⬠ B

WIMBORNE MINSTER *Dorset* Map 4 SZ09
Merley Bird Gardens 1½m S off A349. Large outdoor aviaries in three acres of lawns and gardens enclosed by wall dating from 1750. Colouring of the birds can be studied while they are in full flight. Children's pets corner, mini-golf, and children's rides. ⬠ Open all year daily 10.30–6.30, tea-room closes 5.30. Admission prices not yet decided. Children must be accompanied by adults. No dogs or radios. ⚠ *(Tel 3790)* ⬠ **(79)**
Model Town Superb 1/10th scale model of town built from genuine materials. Beautiful garden stocked with miniature trees and fish. Rare 10½in gauge 'Beyer Garret' locomotive, 20ft length, weight 3 tons, on display. Open daily 1 Mar to 31 Nov 9–6, high season 9–9. 30p (ch 14 15p, ch 3 free). P. *(Tel 886950)* ⬠
Priest's House Museum It contains a number of exhibits of local interest including Roman objects also section devoted to rural implements. Open 7 Apr to Sep weekdays only 10.30–12.30 and 2.30–4.30. Other dates as announced locally. Special exhibition at Christmas. Museum and garden 10p (ch 3p). ⚠ *(Tel 882533)* ⬠

WIMPOLE HALL *Cambridgeshire* Map 4 TL35
8m SW of Cambridge at junction of A14 and A603. Large 18th-C country mansion. The interior has the Lord Harley's library, long gallery, Soane's yellow drawing room and Chapel painted by Thornhill. The Park was landscaped by such eminent gardeners as 'Capability' Brown, Repton and Sanderson Miller. ⬠ Open 1 Apr to 12 Oct, Tue, Wed, Thu, Sat and Sun also BH Mon 2–6 (last admission 5.30). £1. Party 15+. Wheelchairs available. *(NT)*

WINCHCOMBE *Gloucestershire* Map 4 SP02
Belas Knap 2m S. Well-known long barrow, 170ft by 60ft, with pair of side chambers in centre of mound and two others at south end. Dates probably from c2000 BC, and was excavated in 1863 and 1929–30. Accessible at all reasonable times. Free. *(AM)*
Sudeley Castle and Gardens Mainly 15th-C building with part 12th-C and 19th-C restoration. Magnificent art collection, fine

furniture and costume exhibitions. Tomb of Queen Katherine Parr in Chapel. Extensive grounds with large collection of waterfowl. Large children's playground with 3-storey replica Castle. Picnic area. ♌ (licensed). Open 1 Mar to 31 Oct daily. Grounds from 11 am. Castle and exhibitions 12–5.30, BH Sun and Mon from 11 am. £1.25 (ch 50p, pen £1.05). Party 20+. Admission prices under revision for 1980. Enquiries to the Secretary. ⚠ *(Tel 602308). (The Dent-Brocklehurst Family Trust)* ⅋ B

WINCHELSEA *East Sussex* Map 5 TQ91
Winchelsea Museum Located in the restored 14th-C court hall, it contains collection illustrating the history of the Cinque Ports. In addition there are maps, documents and archaeological specimens. Open May to Sep, weekdays 10.30–12.30 and 2.30–5.30, Sun 2.30–5.30. 50p (ch 14 10p) subject to alteration. ⚠

WINCHESTER *Hampshire* Map 4 SU42
Avington Park 3m E. 17th-C mansion built largely of red brick with state rooms and fine ballroom. In wooded park in attractive Itchen valley. ♌ Sun and BH. Open May to end Sep, Sat, Sun and BH 2.30–5.30 (parties at other times by arrangement). 40p (ch 10 20p) (prices may be subject to increase). ⚠ *(Tel Itchen Abbas 202). (Major J B Hickson)* ⅋ B
Winchester Castle Castle Avenue, off High Street. The surviving portion of the castle, a notable great hall of 1235, with Purbeck marble colums. At the west end is the legendary Round Table of King Arthur and his knights, their names painted in 1522. Henry III was born in the castle in 1207. Open all year (ex 4 Apr and 25 Dec) Mon to Fri 10–5, also Apr to Sep Sat and BH 10–6 and Sun 2–6, Oct to Mar Sat and Sun 10–5, BH 10–5. Free (contributions). No dogs. P (multi-storey). *(Tel 4411 ext 569)* ⅋
Winchester City Museum The Square. Contains a well-laid out display relating to the archaeology and history of the city and also of central Hampshire. Open Mon to Sat 10–5, Sun 2–5 (4 winter). Closed 4 Apr, 25, 26 Dec, 1 Jan. Free. ⚠ *(Tel 68166 ext 269)*
Winchester College College Street. One of England's oldest public schools, founded by William of Wykeham in 1382. Of special interest is the chapel, and during school terms, Fromond's chantry and the cloisters, which are accessible weekdays 10–6 (Sun 2–6) in summer; 10–4 (Sun 2–4) in winter. Free. Guided tours (ex Sun mornings) 11, 2 and 3 (also 4.30 May to Aug), subject to alteration. 40p (ch 16 20p). Under revision for 1980. *(Tel 64242)* ⅋
Guildhall Picture Gallery High Street. On show are local topographical views. Temporary exhibitions are held during the year. Open during exhibitions, Tue to Sat 11–5, Sun and Mon 2–5, all year. Free. P (charge) in Central car park. *(Tel 68166 ext 269)* ⅋
Hospital of St Cross S of city, off St Cross Road. Founded originally in 1136, and extended by Cardinal Beaufort in 1446. This is the oldest charitable institution in Britain still functioning. The Wayfarer's dole of bread and ale is given at the Porter's lodge, between 9.30 and 5; 10–12 and 2–3.30 in the winter. Brother's hall, old kitchen, and 12th-C church. Open Apr to Sep 9–12.30 and 2–5; Oct to Mar 10–12.30 and 2–3.30. 25p (ch and pen 10p). Party. (A guide is always available). ⚠ *(Tel 2888)*

Serle's House Southgate Street. A fine Baroque-style 18th-C house, now incorporating the Royal Hampshire Regiment museum and memorial garden. Open Mon to Fri 10–12.30 and 2–4. Closed BH. Free. *(Tel 61781 ext 261)*
Westgate Museum High Street. The medieval west gate of the city, containing exhibition of arms and armour. Open (ex 4 Apr, 25/26 Dec and 1 Jan) Mon to Sat 10–5, Sun 2–5 (4 winter), 10p (ch 5p). Party (school). ⚠ *(Tel 68166 ext 269)*
Wolvesey Castle College Street. Remains of a 12th-C bishop's castle, incorporating parts of the great hall, keep, and gatehouse. Adjacent stands the fine Palace (1684) of Bishop Morley. The interior of the castle has been closed since 1967 owing to archaeological excavation, which has now revealed a 12th-C hall larger than any in England after Westminster Hall (London). *(AM)*

WINDERMERE *Cumbria* Map 7 SD49
(see also BOWNESS ON WINDERMERE)
Lake District National Park Centre On A591. 19th-C house in 32 acres of garden and woodland on the eastern shore of Lake Windermere. National Park Visitor Centre with audio-visual displays, films and information room. Special family events during school hols. ♌ Picnic areas. Open 18 Mar to 12 Nov daily from 10 (closing time varies with season). 50p (ch 18 25p). ⚠ *(Tel 2231)* ⅋
Steamboat Museum Bayrigg Road. Unique collection of Victorian and Edwardian vessels, typical of the steam era on the lakes, housed in covered dock and kept in working order. Other boats and exhibits illustrate the development of navigation on the lake. Museum shop. Picnic area. ♌. Open Easter to Oct, Mon to Sat 10–5, Sun from 2 pm. Admission prices for 1980 not available. ⚠ (Coaches by appointment). *(Tel 5565)*

WINDSOR *Bershire* Map 4 SU 97
Savill Garden (Windsor Great Park) (Reached via Wick Lane, Englefield Green, near Egham). Very beautiful woodland gardens with flowering shrubs and rare flowers. ♌ (licensed). Open from 1 Mar to 31 Oct daily 10–6. 60p (ch and pen 40p). Party 20+, subject to alteration. ⚠ *(Tel 60222)* ⅋
Windsor Guildhall High Street. Built in 1689 and attributed to Wren. It contains an interesting exhibition of local historical and archaeological items, a collection of royal portraits and also old charters and documents. Generally open 4 Apr to mid/end Sep, daily 1.30–4.30. 15p (ch 10p) subject to alteration. *(Tel Maidenhead 33155)*
Windsor Castle A restored Norman royal castle with 19th-C additions for George IV by Wyatville. Precincts open daily (ex 16 Jun) 1 Jan to 15 Mar and 26 Oct to 31 Dec 10–4.15; 16 Mar to 30 Apr and 1 Sep to 25 Oct 10–5.15; 1 May to 31 Aug 10–7.15. Free.
St George's Chapel all enquiries to Chapter Clerk *(Tel 65538)*
State Apartments Open daily 1 Jan to 15 Mar and 26 Oct to 31 Dec (ex 1 Jan, 7–31 Dec and Sun) 10.30–3; 1 May to 31 Aug and 1 Sep to 25 Oct (ex 1/2 May and 2–27 Jun) Mon to Sat 10.30–5, Sun 1.30–5; closed 16 Mar to 30 Apr. Opening times cannot be guaranteed as Castle is always subject to closure, sometimes at very short notice. 45p (ch 5–15 and pen 30p) until 15 Mar. From 3 May 60p (ch 5–15 and pen 30p). Some rooms closed.

Queen Mary's Dolls House Open daily 1 Jan
to 15 Mar and 26 Oct to 31 Dec (ex 1 Jan,
25–27 Dec and Sun) 10.30–3; 16 Mar to 30
Apr (ex 4 Apr and Sun) 10.30–5; 1 May to 31
Aug and 1 Sep to 25 Oct (ex 16 Jun) Mon to
Sat 10.30–5, Sun 1.30–5. 20p (ch 5–15 and
pen 10p) until 2 May. From 3 May 30p (ch and
pen 10p).
Exhibitions of Drawings Open daily. Times
and prices as above. ⚠
Household Cavalry Museum Combermere
Barracks. One of the finest military museums
in Britain. Uniforms, weapons, horse
furniture, and armour of the Household
Cavalry from the Monmouth Rebellion (1685)
to the present day. A series of terrain models
depicts the Life Guards and Royal Horse
campaigns. Open all year Mon to Fri (ex BH)
10–1 and 2–5 also Sun Apr to end Aug 10–1
and 2–4. Free. *(Tel 68222 ext 203)*
Windsor Safari Park and Seaworld (SW of
town on B3022). Drive-in zoo where wild
animals including giraffes, lions, tigers,
baboons and cheetahs can be seen. Dolphin
and killer whale shows in the Seaworld
complex. Children's farmyard. Picnic area.
⚲. Open from 31 Mar daily 10–7 (or dusk if
earlier). Last admission 5 pm. Inclusive
charge £2 (ch and pen £1). party. Under
revision for 1980. *(Tel 69841)* ⚹
Valley Gardens (Windsor Great Park) Near
Virginia Water. An area of some 300 acres
noted especially for an outstanding range of
rhododendrons, camellias, magnolias and
other woodland trees and shrubs. Peak
period is Apr, May and Jun but something to
be seen all year. Open all year but adjoining
car park open only for 6 to 8 weeks in spring
when a charge is made. 60p per car.

WING *Buckinghamshire* Map 4 SP82
Ascott 19th-C mansion housing notable
works of art – including French and
Chippendale furniture and Oriental porcelain.
Fine gardens. Open Apr to Sep, Wed, Sat,
and BH Mon 2–6; Suns Jul and Aug 2–6.
House and garden £1.40. Garden only 80p
(ch 40p). *(NT) (NGS)*

WINSLOW *Buckinghamshire* Map 4 SP72
Winslow Hall Built in 1700 by Sir William
Lowndes the Hall was almost certainly
designed by Wren. It retains most of its
original features and has recently been
restored and redecorated. 18th-C English
furniture, Chinese art and some fine clocks
and pictures. Gardens. Open Jul to Sep daily
(ex Mon) 2.30–5.30. 60p (pen 30p, ch 16
free). P. *(Tel 2323)* ⚹ B

WINSTER *Derbyshire* Map 8 SK26
Market House Stone-built 17th- or 18th-C

market house in main street of village. Open
Apr to 30 Sep, Wed, Sat, Sun, BH Mon 2–6
(or sunset). Free. *(NT)*

WISBECH *Cambridgeshire* Map 5 TF40
Wisbech and Fenland Museum Situated
near the site of the former castle and
containing fine collection of ceramics and
objets d'art, coins, glass, and pottery from
Celtic, Roman, and Saxon England, in
addition to Fenland life and birds, and objects
associated with Thomas Clarkson, famous for
his work in abolishing the slave trade. Open
all year. Tue to Sat 10–1, 2–5 (4, winter).
Free. ⚠ *(Tel 3817)*
Peckover House On the north bank of the
River Nene, and dating from 1722. Interior
Rococo decoration in plaster and wood. The
garden is a delightful and colourful example of
Victorian planting. Open Apr to 12 Oct, Tue,
Wed, Thu, Sat, Sun, and BH Mons 2–5; Nov
to Mar, prior arrangement must be made with
Custodian. No dogs. 70p. *(NT) (NGS)*

WISLEY *Surrey* Map 4 TQ05
Wisley Gardens The famous and extensive
garden of the Royal Horticultural Society.
Information centre. Plant sales centre. Shop.
⚲ Mar to Oct. Open all year (ex 25 Dec), Feb
to Oct weekdays 10–7 or sunset (whichever
is earlier), Sun 2–7 or sunset; Jan, Nov and
Dec weekdays 10–4.30, Sun 2–4.30 or
sunset. 90p (ch 14 45p). ⚠ *(Tel Ripley 2234
or 2235)* ⚹

WOBURN *Bedfordshire* Map 4 SP93
Woburn Abbey and Wild Animal Kingdom
Junction B528 and A418. A palatial 18th-C
mansion, designed by Holland and Flitcroft,
with State apartments and pictures. Private
apartments shown BH and when the family
are not in residence. Stands in a 3,000–acre
park famous for its rare collection of wild life.
Souvenir shops, pottery, art galleries. Open
all year. 1 Nov to 3 Apr, Abbey 11.30–5.15
(last entry 4); Park 11–3. 4 Apr to 31 Oct,
Abbey Mon to Sat, 11.30–5.30 (last entry
4.45), Sun 11.30–6 (last entry 5.15); Park
Mon to Sat 10.30–4.30, Sun 10–5. Angling in
season. The Wild Animal Kingdom is a game
reserve with lions, tigers, monkeys, giraffe,
elephants, dolphinarium, pets corner, Sky
ride, and Safari Boat trips. ⚲ Open daily
throughout the year 10–dusk (fog and other
weather permitting). ⚹

WOLVERHAMPTON *West Midlands*
Map 7 SO99
Bantock House Museum Bantock Park,
Merridale Road. This 19th-C house contains
important collections of English enamels
japanned tin and papier-mâché products of
the Midlands. Also shown are early Worcester

porcelain pottery, local history, and English and foreign dolls. Open all year Mon to Fri 10-7; Sat 10-6, Sun 2-5 (ex 1 Jan, 4 and 6 Apr, and 25, 26 Dec). Free. ⚠ *(Tel 24548)* ♿ B

Bilston Museum and Art Gallery Mount Pleasant, Bilston. Houses a large collection of fine English painted and transfer print enamels from 18th and 19th C. Also iron and steel artifacts (traps, jewellery, plated ware) relating to the industrial history of the area. Collection of local and Staffordshire pottery. Permanent collection of Victorian oil paintings and periodic travelling exhibitions. Open all year, Mon to Sat 10-5. Free. P (roadside). *(Tel 42097)*

Central Art Gallery Lichfield Street. 18th- and 19th-C English water-colours and oil paintings including works by Bonington,

Fuseli, Gainsborough, Zoffany and Wilson. Modern prints and drawings, including works by Warhol, Hamilton, John Salt, Caulfield, Rosenquist, Lichtenstein etc. Fine Oriental collections and full programme of temporary exhibitions. Open all year, Mon to Sat 10-6. Free. P. *(Tel 24549)*

Wightwick Manor 19th-C house with a collection of pre-Raphaelite works of art, including Morris fabric and de Morgan ware. Terraced gardens. Open all year (ex 25, 26 Dec and 1 Jan also Feb). Thu, Sat, and BH Sun and Mon 2.30-5.30. Also each Wed 2.30-5.30 from May to Sep. House 70p (ch 15p). Sat (extra rooms) 80p, students 30p; gardens only 20p. No children under 12. *(NT)*

WOODHENGE Wiltshire Map 4 SU14 Consisted formerly of six concentric rings of timber posts within a ditch. Positions of the

posts are marked by concrete pillars. Discovered accidentally by aerial reconaissance in 1925. Accessible at all reasonable times. Free. ▲ *(AM)*

WOODSTOCK *Oxfordshire* Map 4 SP41
Oxfordshire County Museum Located in the 16th- to 18th-C Fletcher's House. Newly completed exhibitions tell the story of Oxfordshire from the earliest times to the present day. ⚑ Bookshop and gardens. Open all year (ex 13 Apr, 25, 26 Dec) May to Sep Mon to Fri 10 – 5, Sat 10 – 6, Sun 2 – 6; Oct to Apr Tue to Fri 10 – 4, Sat 10 – 5, Sun 2 – 5. 20p (ch students and pen 10p). *(Tel 811456)* **(79)**
Blenheim Palace Started 1705 by Vanbrugh for first Duke of Marlborough, palatial baroque-style mansion in Henry Wise and 'Capability' Brown lake-watered park. Fine furnishings, china, and pictures and terraced water gardens below Long Library. Sir Winston Churchill born here in 1874, and buried in 1965 in village churchyard of Bladon on southern fringe of park. Launch trips on Lake. Narrow-gauge steam railway in grounds normally operates daily throughout the season. Garden centre. ⚑ (licensed). Charity cricket 25 May, Horse Show 26 May, opening times likely to alter for the events. Palace open 17 Mar to 31 Oct 11.30 – 5. Admission prices on application. Garden centre open daily, 9 – 5. *(Tel 811325)*. *(The Duke of Marlborough)* ₺

WOOKEY HOLE *Somerset* Map 3 ST54
Wookey Hole Caves and Mill The great cave of Wookey Hole through which the river Axe flows was inhabited for 650 years from 250BC to AD400 – 'an outpost of the Celtic territories during the Roman occupation'. Tunnel through to new caverns containing steel bridges high above waters of River Axe. A small museum includes coins, pottery, tools of late Celtic and Roman British periods. Madame Tussaud's store room and the unique Lady Bangor's Fairground Collection are housed in the mill. The old machinery used for making paper by hand, the original purpose of the mill, has now been restored to provide a working exhibition about hand-made paper. ⚑ Picnic area. Open daily (ex 25 Dec) Apr to Sep 10 – 6, Oct to Mar 10 – 4.30. £1.60 (ch 16 and pen 90p). Party 20+. ▲ *(Tel Wells 72243)* ₺ B (Mill)

WOOLSTHORPE *Lincolnshire* Map 8 SK92
Woolsthorpe Manor A fine stone-built 17th-C house, the birthplace in 1642 of Sir Isaac Newton (room shown). Open Apr to end Oct, Mon, Wed, Fri, Sat and BH 11 – 12.30 and 2 – 6. 70p (ch 35p). *(NT)*

WORCESTER *Hereford and Worcester* Map 3 SO85
The Commandery Sidbury. A large late 15th-C timber framed building with later additions. Fine Great Hall with hammerbeam roof. Displays of furniture, civil war material, local history from Roman times to the 20th C. Crafts, tools and industry. One small room with religious wall paintings of *c*1500. ⚑. Open Tue to Sat 10.30 – 5, Sun (1 Apr to 30 Sep) 2.30 – 5. Open BH Mons. 30p (ch 16 and pen 10p). P. *(Tel 355071)*
City Museum and Art Gallery Foregate Street. Contains items of archaeology, geology and natural history. Also collections of the Worcestershire Yeomanry Cavalry, Worcestershire Regiment and Stewards Chemist's Shop. Open all year Mon, Tue, Wed, Fri 9.30 – 6, Thu, Sat 9.30 – 5. Free. P. *(Tel 25371)*

Elgar's Birthplace Museum Crown East Lane, Lower Broadheath. 3m W of Worcester off A44 (to Leominster). Cottage where Sir Edward Elgar was born in 1857, now a museum displaying scores, photographs, letters and personalia. Open all year, daily (ex Wed) 1.30 – 6.30 (4.30 winter). 40p (ch 14 15p) subject to alteration. Parties by arrangement with Curator. *(Tel Cotheridge 224)*
Guildhall High Street. A notable, restored 18th-C building (1723 – 31) built by Thomas White, a local architect, with wings added later. Paintings and armour on show. Open all the year Mon to Fri 9 – 5. Free. *(Tel 23471)*
Dyson Perrins Museum of Worcester Porcelain Severn Street. The Dyson Perrins Museum has the finest collection of Worcester china in the world, comprising examples from the foundation of the factory by Dr John Wall, in 1751, to the present day. ⚑. Open all year Mon to Fri 10 – 1 and 2 – 5 also Sat Apr to Sep (closed BH). Free. Tours of works Mon to Fri by prior arrangement. Connoisseurs' tours twice daily. ▲ *(Tel 20272 and 23221)* ₺
Hawford Dovecote 3m N on A449. 16th-C half-timbered dovecot. Open daily until sunset. 10p. *(NT)*
Tudor House Friar Street. 500-year-old timber-framed house, once an inn, with a squint, and an ornate plaster ceiling. Opened 1971 as museum of local life. Features period room settings and open displays. Large exhibits displayed in yard at rear. Open all year, Mon to Sat (ex Thu and Sun) 10.30 – 5. Free. P. *(Tel 25371)*

WORKINGTON *Cumbria* Map 11 NY02
Helena Thompson Museum Park End Road. Museum containing collection of costumes, glass, ceramics, and other interesting exhibits. Museum and grounds open all year Tue to Sat 10 – 12 and 2 – 4. Free. *(Tel 62598)*

WORKSOP *Nottinghamshire* Map 8 SK57
Worksop Museum Memorial Avenue. Historical displays, bygones, Victoriana, birds and butterflies, and items of local archaeological interest. Open daily Mon to Sat (ex Thu) 10 – 4. Free. ▲ *(Tel 5531)* ₺
Worksop Priory Church and Gatehouse Remarkable 14th-C double archway with large upper room which from 1623 housed earliest elementary school in county. Elaborate façade with statues, and 15th-C wayside shrine and chapel. Church has unique 12th-C Transitional nave, with 20th-C additions of east end and central tower. Contains 14th-C scroll iron-work on doors in South porch. 13th-C Lady Chapel. Church open every day (ex Mon) 10 – 12, 2 – 5. Gatehouse open by application to church verger. Free. P. *(Tel 2180)*

WORTHING *West Sussex* Map 4 TQ10
Worthing Museum and Art Gallery Chapel Road. Archaeology, geology, history of Worthing. Large costume collection. Open all year Mon to Sat, 10 – 7 (summer), 10 – 5 (winter). Free. P. *(Tel 204226)* ₺

WOTTON UNDERWOOD *Buckinghamshire* Map 4 SP61
Wotton House and Pavilions Dating from 1690 – 1714 and the only house almost identical to Buckingham House prior to its becoming Buckingham Palace. Landscaped by 'Capability' Brown 1757 – 1760. Restored by Sir John Soane, 1820. Notable Tijou and Robinson wrought iron. Open Jun to end Sep

Wed 2–6 (last tour 5). 50p (ch 12 not
admitted). Parties by arrangement. Guided
tours by Curator *Mrs P Brunner*. ⚠ *(Tel Brill
363). (Mrs D Gladstone)* **(79)**
WRAWBY *Humberside* Map 8 TA00
Wrawby Postmill The last surviving example
of its type in Lincolnshire, built *c*1780 and
restored to working order in the 1960s. Wide
views. Descriptive illustrated booklet 35p.
Open 5 and 26 May, 29 Jun, 27 Jul and 25
Aug, 1–6. 20p (ch and students 10p ch 5
free). Under revision for 1980. ⚠ *(Tel Brigg
53699)* ⚠ B

WROXETER *Salop* Map 7 SJ50
Roman Town Remains of the Roman town of
'Viroconium' dating probably from AD
140–150, including public baths and a
colonade. Open*, see inside front cover
(closed, however, between 1–2). 20p (ch 16
and pen 5p): ⚠ *(AM)*

WROXHAM *Norfolk* Map 9 TG31
Beeston Hall 3m NE off A1151. 18th-C
mansion in Gothic style with Neo-Classical
interiors. Descendants of the Preston family
have resided here since 1640. ⚇ (teas).
Open, 6 Apr to 14 Sep Fri, Sun and BH Mon,
2–5.30. 70p (ch 30p, pen 50p). ⚠ *(Tel
Horning 630771)* ⚠

YEALMPTON *Devon* Map 2 SX55
Kitley Caves Floodlit caves and lime kilns
situated on the banks of the picturesque River
Yealm. ⚇. Open Easter, then 28 May to 30
Sep daily 10–5. 20p (ch 16 15p). ⚠ 30p. *(Tel
202)* **(79)**

YELVERTON *Devon* Map 2 SX56
Paperweight Centre Buckland Terrace, Leg-
O'Mutton. Exhibition of over 800
paperweights. Beautiful antique and modern
glass, Millefiori, faceted, diamond-cut dated
and signed 'investment' paperweights, many
for sale (from £1 to £500). Open week before
Easter to end Oct, Mon to Sat 10–5. Free. ⚠
(Tel 4250) ⚠

YEOVIL *Somerset* Map 3 ST51
Yeovil Museum Hendford Manor Hall. Local
history and archaeology, and specialised
collections of costumes and firearms. Open
all year Mon to Sat (ex Thu) 9.30–1 and 2–5.
Free. P. *(Tel 5171, Sat only 24774)*

YEOVILTON *Somerset* Map 3 ST52
Fleet Air Arm Museum and Concorde 002
A collection of more than 40 historic aircraft,
ship and aircraft models, paintings and
photographs with many other memorabilia of
the Royal Naval Air Service and the Fleet Air
Arm tell the story of the development of
aviation at sea from 1903. The museum
premises have been extended and a new
display is being created. Concorde 002 is in a
new exhibition hall where the development of

passenger supersonic flight is to be
graphically portrayed. ⚇. Open daily (ex
24/25 Dec) Mon to Sat 10–5.30, Sun
12.30–5.30 (dusk in winter). Picnic area,
flying viewing area and ⚠ are free. Coaches
and caravans welcome. *(Tel Ilchester 840551
ext 521)* ⚠ B

YORK *North Yorkshire* Map 8 SE65
Borthwick Institute of Historical Research
St Anthony's Hall, Peasholme Green.
Originally a late 15th-C Guildhall, it has
served in turn as poor-house, hospital,
armoury, and Blue-Coat school. Now the
Borthwick Institute of Historical Research,
with a collection of ecclesiastical archives. It is
part of York University. Exhibition of
documents throughout the year. Hall open
Mon to Fri 9.30–1 and 2–5. Closed
Christmas, Easter, week before late Summer
BH and first full week in Oct. Free. P. *(Tel
59861 ext 274)*
City Art Gallery Exhibition Square. An
outstanding collection of European and
British paintings. Particularly known for the
Lycett Green collection of Old Masters, but
also includes paintings and drawings by York
Artists, notably William Etty, R A, and modern
stoneware pottery. Provisional, for 1980,
Festival Exhibition June 'Turner in Yorkshire'.
Open all year (ex 1 Jan, 4 Apr, 25/26 Dec)
Mon to Sat 10–5, Sun 2.30–5. Free. P. *(Tel
23839)* ⚠ B
Guildhall by River Ouse, off Coney Street. A
15th-C building, restored after severe
damage during the 1939–45 war. Hall with
notable timbered roof. Underground passage
leading to the River. Open May to Oct Mon to
Thu 9–5, Fri 9–4.30, Sat 10–5, Sun 2–5;
Nov to Apr Mon to Thu 9–5, Fri 9–4.30,
closed Sat and Sun, also closed 1 Jan, 4 Apr,
25/26 Dec. Free. ⚠ *(Tel 59881)* ⚠ B
King's Manor Exhibition Square. Former
home of Abbot of St Mary's Abbey, later
stopping place of James VI of Scotland on
way to become James I of England, and of
Charles I at time of Civil War. Much altered in
early 17th C, and finally restored to become
part of University in 1964. Open all year, daily
(ex 25 Dec) 9–5 Free. ⚠ *(Tel 59861)* **(79)**
Merchant Adventurer's Hall Fossgate. A
medieval guildhall, dating from 1357–68 to
Tudor times, with the major part dating from
the 15th C. Belonged to the wealthy and
influential Company of the Merchant
Adventurers. Open (ex when Hall is being
used for functions) weekdays Apr to Oct
10–4.30 (4 Nov to Mar). Closed 1 Jan, 4 Apr,
25/26 Dec and Suns. Open all other BH. 30p
(ch 16 and pen 15p). P in Piccadilly. *(Tel
54818)* i ⚠

National Railway Museum Leeman Road. The museum, which is part of the Science Museum, illustrates the history and development of British railway engineering, including the social and economic aspects. Collection contains some 25 locomotives from the Agenoria of 1829 including Mallard and a fully sectioned rebuilt Merchant Navy class 4-6-2. Some twenty items of rolling stock as well as signalling equipment and permanent way items. Small exhibits feature models of locomotives (many working) and rolling stock. Also variety of railway equipment and material, including uniforms, station furniture, nameplates, bridge models and other categories of relics associated with the past 150 yrs of railways in the UK. Also displays and reference collections of paintings, posters, drawings and films. Reference library service provided by appointment. Lecture theatre seating eighty, is incorporated in the building and an Education programme of lecture/demonstrations is available. Please apply for details. Shop with railway books, postcards, slides, etc. ⬙ Open all year except Jan, 4 Apr, May Day, 24–26 Dec and some other public holidays (contact Museum for details). Mon to Sat 10–6; Sun 2.30–6. Free. ⬙ *(Tel 21261)* ⬙

Treasurer's House Chapter House Street. Mainly 17th- and 18th-C with fine paintings, furniture, and a sunken garden. Open Apr to 1 Oct, daily (ex 4 Apr) 10.30–6. 70p *(NT)*

York Castle Off Tower Street, Clifford's Tower, a two-storeyed 13th-C keep, built on an 11th-C motte raised by William the Conqueror. Open*, see inside front cover. 25p (ch 16 and pen 10p). ⚠ *(AM)*

York Castle Museum Tower Street. An outstanding folk museum of Yorkshire life based on the Kirk collection of bygones and including period rooms, a cobbled street, domestic and agricultural equipment, early crafts, costumes, toys, Yorkshire militaria, an Edwardian street and a water-driven corn mill. Open all year (ex 25/26 Dec and 1 Jan) Apr to Sep, Mon to Sat 9.30–6, Sun 10–6; Oct to Mar, Mon to Sat 9.30–4.30, Sun 10–4.30. 70p (ch 30p). *(Tel (0904) 53611)* ⬙ B

The York Story The Heritage Centre, Castlegate. Britain's finest Heritage Centre, set up in 1975 to interpret the social and architectural history of the City of York. The exhibition, which includes many notable pieces by modern artists and craftsmen, is equipped with audio-visual units and a film theatre showing life in the historic core of the city today. A Heritage 'Walk Around York' is available, guiding visitors to the major buildings in the city. Open all year (ex 1 Jan, 25/26 Dec) Mon to Sat 10–5; Sun 1–5. 30p (ch 15p). *(Tel (0904) 28632)* ⬙ B

Yorkshire Museum and Gardens Museum Street. The museum contains Roman, medieval, geological and natural history collections. In the gardens are the ruins of St Mary's Abbey. Near by stands the Roman Wall, multangular tower, and St Leonard's Hospital. Museum open Mon–Sat 10–5, Sun 1–5. Hospitium open Mon–Sat 10–5 in summer only. Gardens open daily. 30p (ch 15p). Under revision for 1980. Closed 25/26 Dec. P. *(Tel 29745)* ⬙

ZENNOR *Cornwall* Map 2 SW43

Wayside Cottage Folk Museum A small wayside museum illustrating Cornish life and archaeology, including household, farming, and mining equipment. Cottage kitchen and open hearth on show. Open daily, May to Oct 9.30–dusk. Free. P. *(Tel St Ives 6945)* ⬙ B

ISLE OF MAN

BALLAUGH *Isle of Man* Map 6 SC39
Curraghs Wild Life Park Variety of British
and foreign wild life. Otter exhibit. ℒ Open
Easter then 1 May to 28 Sep, daily 10–6. 50p
(ch 15 25p). Party 25+. Admission prices
under revision for 1980. ⚠ *(Tel Sulby 323)* &

CASTLETOWN *Isle of Man* Map 6 SC26
Castle Rushen 14th-C stronghold with
remains of earlier structure. State
apartments, Norman keep flanked by 14th-C
towers. Clock given by Queen Elizabeth I in
1597. ℒ Open all year, 1 May to 30 Sep Mon
to Sat 10–7, Spring BH to 2nd Sun Sep also
Sun 10–1; 1 Oct to 30 Apr Mon to Fri 10–5,
Sat 10–12 noon. 25p (ch 16 and pen 10p).
Admission prices under revision for 1980. P.
(Tel 3326)
Nautical Museum Includes 18th-C Manx
yacht 'Peggy'. Quayle Room and Cabin
Room are interesting. Open mid May to late
Sep, Mon to Sat 10–1 and 2–5, Sun 2–5.
Small admission charge. Under revision for
1980. P. *(Tel Douglas 5522)*

CREGNEASH *Isle of Man* Map 6 SC16
Manx Open-Air Folk Museum Comprises
group of traditional Manx cottages (some
thatched), including crofter-fisherman's
home, farmstead, loom-shed with hand loom,
lathe shed with treadle lathe, and smithy.
Open mid May to late Sep, Mon to Sat 10–1
and 2–5, Sun 2–5. Small admission charge.
Under revision for 1980. ⚠ *(Tel Douglas
5522)* & B

DOUGLAS *Isle of Man* Map 6 SC37
Manx Museum Items illustrate island's
archaeology, history, natural history, folk life,
and art. Also National Reference Library.
Open all year (ex 25/26 Dec and 1 Jan, 4 Apr
and am 5 Jul), Mon to Sat 10–5. Free. ⚠ *(Tel
5522)*

LAXEY *Isle of Man* Map 6 SC48
Laxey Wheel The Big Wheel 'Lady Isabella',
72½ft in diameter, was constructed in order to
keep the lead mines free from water. Open
Easter weekend then 1 May to 30 Sep. 20p
(ch and pen 10p). Under revision for 1980. P.
(Tel Douglas 26262)

PEEL *Isle of Man* Map 6 SC28
Peel Castle On St Patrick's Isle, facing Peel
Bay. The Curtain wall and buildings range
from the 10th to 19th-C. The Gatehouse
featured prominently as a location for Sir
Walter Scott's novel *Peveril of the Peak*.
Open Easter weekends then 1 May to 30 Sep.
20p (ch and pen 10p). Opening times and
admission prices under revision for 1980. P.
(Tel Douglas 26262)

RAMSEY *Isle of Man* Map 6 SC49
'The Grove' Rural Life Museum On west
side of Andreas Road. A Victorian House with
a display of early agricultural equipment in the
outbuildings. ℒ Open mid May to late Sep
Mon to Fri 10–5, Sun 2–5 (closed Sat). Small
admission charge. Under revision for 1980. ⚠

SNAFELL MOUNTAIN *Isle of Man*
Map 6 SC38
Murray's Museum The Bungalow. Junction
A14 and A18. Contains an interesting
collection of veteran and vintage motor cycles
dating from 1902 to 1950, in addition to
ancient arms and musical instruments and
hundreds of bygones of yesteryear. ℒ Open
May to end Sep, daily 10–6. 40p (ch 15 15p).
Under revision for 1980. ⚠ *(Tel Laxey 719)*

ISLES OF SCILLY

TRESCO *Isles of Scilly*
Cromwell's Castle Round-towered
stronghold of 1651, altered after Civil War,
and again in 18th-C. Open at all reasonable
times; access is by motor boat from St Mary's.
Free. *(AM)*
King's Charles's Castle Coastal defence
fortress built during reign of Henry VIII and
added to in Civil War times. Accessible at any
reasonable time by motor boat from St
Mary's. Free. *(AM)*
Tresco Abbey Gardens and Museum The
modern abbey stands on the site of the former
10th-C abbey. Remarkable terraced gardens
with sub-tropical plants. ℒ (Apr to Oct).
Gardens open all year. Mon to Sat from 10–4
Abbey open Apr to Oct. The Valhalla museum
of ships' figureheads is open as gardens.
£1.30 (Apr to Sep) 30p (Oct to Mar). Under
review for 1980. Access is by motor boat from
St Mary's. *(Tel Scillonia 22849)*. *(R A Dorrien-
Smith)*

ISLE OF WIGHT

ARRETON *Isle of Wight* Map 4 SZ58
Arreton Manor Early 17th-C manor house,
situated to S of ridge of Arreton Down. Some
fine panelled rooms with contemporary
furniture. A collection of old toys, including
dolls and doll's houses, and a folk museum.
ℒ (10–5.45). Open one week before Easter
to last week Oct, Mon to Sat 10–6, Sun 2–6;
60p (ch 5 to 14 25p, pen party 25+ 40p each).
Admission prices under revision for 1980. P
(car and coach). *(Tel Arreton 255)*. Also
*Pomeroy Museum and the National
Wireless Museum* where the Pomeroy
Regency Dolls' House together with modern
dolls, baby gowns, etc, are exhibited. *(Count
Slade de Pomeroy)* & B
*Robin Hill Country Park and Zoological
Park* Robin Hill, Downend. Over 100
interesting species of mammals, birds,
reptiles and insects, in over 80 acres of down
and woodland. Also large tropical Jungle
House, 10-acre walk-through enclosure,
breeding colony of monkeys. Pony, donkey
and Argocat rides in high season. Nature trail
commando-styled assault course, also
Continental 'TRIMM' course and playground.
Mini dodgems. Radio-controlled model boats
and armoured tanks. Several rooms of
excavated Roman villa exposed to view.
Water gardens and picnic areas. Gift shop. ℒ
(licensed). Barbecue lunches daily in high
season, evening barbecues five nights a
week 10 Jul to 1 Sep (licensed). Open Mar to
Nov 10–6 (high summer 10–dusk). 70p (ch
40p). Under review for 1980. ⚠ *(Tel 430)* &

BEMBRIDGE *Isle of Wight* Map 4 SZ68
Bembridge Windmill Off B3390. Built
c1700, in use until 1913, last windmill on
island. Stone-built tower mill with wooden cap
and machinery. Open Apr to end Sep. Mon to
Sat 10–5, Sun 11–6. 25p (ch 15p). *(NT)*
Maritime Museum Sherborne Street.
Situated in the centre of the village close to
the harbour and sandy beaches. Six galleries
devoted to our nautical past, designed to
interest the whole family. Included is a unique
collection of ship models, also early diving
equipment. Gift shop. Open Easter to Oct
daily 10–5.30; Oct to Christmas weekends
only. 40p (ch 15 20p, pen 30p). School parties
and groups welcome. ⚠ *(Tel 2223/2576)*

BLACKGANG *Isle of Wight* Map 4 SZ47
Blackgang Chine Opened as scenic
gardens in 1843, covering some 20 acres,
including much natural cliff scenery. The
grounds are floodlit by approximately 5,000
lamps, until 10 pm on summer evenings.
Attractions include a museum of local and
nautical interest, water gardens, model
village, nursery land, smuggler's cave,
smuggler's Galleon, Jungleland, crooked
house, maze, hall of mirrors and other
amusements. ⚲ (licensed). Open Jun to Sep
daily 10–10; Apr, May and Oct 10–5. 60p (ch
45p). Under revision for 1980. ⚠ *(Tel Niton
730330)* &

BRADING *Isle of Wight* Map 4 SZ68
Lilliput Museum High Street. Cottage
Museum contains a comprehensive private
collection of over 600 old dolls, with some
houses and toys. Dolls shop. Open mid Mar to
mid Oct daily 10–5 (10 pm during high
season). Admission charges not yet known.
Party. P. *(Tel 231)*
Morton Manor Built in 1680 and furnished
with period furniture. Beautiful terraced
landscaped gardens with ornamental duck
pond. ⚲ (in old-world thatched cottage).
Open from Whitsun, Mon to Fri 11–6, Sun
2–6 (closed Sat). 50p (ch 20p, pen 30p). ⚠
Tel Sandown 406168)
Osborn-Smith's Wax Museum On A3055.
Cameos of Island history, with authentic
costume, wax figures, period furniture and
harmonious settings cleverly brought to life
with the added realism of sound, light and
motion. Displayed in the oldest house on the
island dated c1228. Gift shop. Open all year
daily 10–10 (5 Oct to Apr). Party. ⚠ *(Tel 286)*
& B
Roman Villa Includes mosaic pavements
and hypocaust. ⚲ Open Easter to end Sep,
Mon to Sat 10–5.30, Sun 10.30–5.30. 25p
(ch 18 15p, pen 20p) ⚠ *(Tel during season
Sandown 406223)*

CALBOURNE *Isle of Wight* Map 4 SZ48
Watermill and Rural Museum On B3401.
17th-C mill. Water wheel and Mill stones still
in use. Open Apr to Oct, daily 10–6. 40p (ch
15 20p, ch 5 free, pen 30p). Under review for
1980. *(Tel 227)* & B

CARISBROOKE *Isle of Wight* Map 4 SZ48
Carisbrooke Castle On B3401. 12th-C and
later building, once the prison of Charles I. It
houses the Isle of Wight Museum. ⚲ Open,
see inside front cover, museum closes Oct to
Easter. Open Sun am Apr to Sep. 70p, winter
25p (ch 16 and pen 30p, winter 10p). ⚠ 5p
m/cycles 2½p). *(AM)*

COWES *Isle of Wight* Map 4 SZ49
Maritime Museum and Public Library
Beckford Road. Ship models, photographs,
paintings, books, etc, showing the island's
maritime past. Open all year, Mon to Fri
9.30–6, Sat 9.30–5 Free. P. *(Tel 293341)* &
Curds and Whey Dottens Farm, Baring
Road. A cheese farm which gives talks on
cheese making twice daily during the
summer. Shop selling own cheese also other
English and Continental cheeses. Talks
11.30 and 2.30 weekdays Easter to Sep. 10p.
⚠ (limited), P. *(Tel 292466)*

EAST COWES *Isle of Wight* Map 4 SZ59
Barton Manor Gardens and Vineyard 20-
acre gardens, grounds and lake with 5-acre
vineyard. Winery, wine tasting, ⚲ and home
produce shop. Open Sun and BH Mon from
Easter to end May, then daily (ex Fri and Sat)
to end Sep 2–6. 50p (ch 15p, pen 35p). Prices
include guide leaflet. ⚠ *(Tel Cowes 292835)*
Norris Castle 18th-C castle designed by

James Wyatt and built for Lord Henry
Seymour. Great Georgian castle containing
furniture and curiosities, weapons, armour,
sculpture, pictures and tapestries collected
from around the world over four centuries.
Queen Victoria's bedroom and the German
Emperor's Bath can be seen. Superb views of
the Solent yachting scene from the park. ⚲
Open 4–7 Apr, then Sat, Sun and Mon 17
May to 5 Sep also daily during Cowes Week,
11–5. These dates may be altered without
notice. ⚠ *(Tel Cowes 293434)* & B

GODSHILL *Isle of Wight* Map 4 SZ58
Model Village Old Vicarage Gardens. Well
laid out interesting model village, many
establishments with thatched roofs. Under
construction is a model of the model part of
which is on show. Open Apr to Sep Mon to Sat
10–5.30, Sun 2–5.30. P. *(Tel 270)* &
Natural History Collection Coral View.
British and tropical butterflies, some 30,000
tropical sea shells, a marine and tropical
aquarium and exhibitions of precious and
semi-precious stones. Replicas of the Crown
Jewels on display. Open daily 1 Apr to
Whitsun 10–6. Whitsun to end Sep, Sun to Fri
10–9.30, Sat 10–6. 15p (ch 9 free, 10–14
and pen 10p). P. *(Tel 333)* &

HAVEN STREET *Isle of Wight* Map 4 SZ58
Isle of Wight Steam Railway Former LSWR
tank engine (1891), also IWCR loco No. 11 of
1878 which worked on island, and two other
tank engines on show. Also rolling stock,
including ex-LBSC and SEC coaches, and
19th-C goods wagons. Steam train rides
through 2 miles of unspoilt countryside.
Refreshments available. Trains run Sun May
to Sep and Easter, also Thu Jul and Aug
11–5.30. Admission prices not yet available.
⚠ *(Tel Wooton Bridge 882204)* &

NEWPORT *Isle of Wight* Map 4 SZ48
Roman Villa Avondale Road. Villa built
towards end of 2nd C AD and discovered in
1926. Baths in good state of preservation and
several mosaic floors. Open Apr to Sep, Sun
to Fri 10.30–5.30 15p (ch 5p). P. (streets
only) *(Tel 522324/524541)*

NEWTOWN *Isle of Wight* Map 4 SZ49
Old Town Hall Restored 18th-C building.
Open Apr to end May, Wed, Sun and BH Mon,
Jun, Jul and Sep Wed, Thu, Sat and Sun also
daily Aug 2.30–5.30. 20p (ch 10p). *(NT)*
OSBORNE HOUSE *Isle of Wight* Map 4 SZ59
19th-C house, once Queen Victoria's home,
and where she died. State apartments, Swiss
Cottage and museum open 11–5, Mon to Sat
from 7 Apr to beginning of Oct (open at 10am
in Jul and Aug). Opening times subject to
extension. 70p (ch 16 and pen 30p). ⚠ 10p.
(AM)

ST CATHERINE'S LIGHTHOUSE *Isle of
Wight* Map 4 SZ47
Situated at St Catherine's Point, 136ft above
the sea. Open all year. Mon to Sat only from
1pm to one hour before dusk, weather and
other conditions permitting at visitors own
risk. Free. Cars not allowed within ½m except
on business. *(Tel Niton 730284)*

ST LAWRENCE *Isle of Wight* Map 4 SZ57
Tropical Bird Park Old Park. Over 400 exotic
birds in unique walk-through aviaries and
around the ornamental lake. ⚲ (tea garden).
Open all year, daily, Easter to Oct 10–6 and
Oct to Easter 12–4. Prices are approximate.
50p (ch 14 30p and pen 40p). ⚠ *(Tel Ventnor
852583)*

SANDOWN *Isle of Wight* Map 4 SZ58
Museum of Isle of Wight Geology This
museum, situated in the local library, houses

a collection of fossils and exhibits of the island's geology. Open all year Mon to Sat 10–5 (ex BH). Free. ⚠ *(Tel 4344)*

SEAVIEW *Isle of Wight* Map 4 SZ69
Flamingo Park Bird Sanctuary Oakhill Road, Springvale. Island's largest bird sanctuary, set in lovely countryside overlooking the Solent, with hundreds of waterfowl which feed from the hand; geese, swans, flamingos, peacocks, cranes and pheasants. British and foreign bird house and pets corner. Suitable for both young and old. Gifts and ⚏. Open Easter to end May 2–6; Jun to Sep 10.30–6 Mon to Sat, Sun only 2–6. 70p (ch and pen 50p). Under revision for 1980. ⚠ *(Tel 2153)* & (reduced rate).

SHANKLIN *Isle of Wight* Map 4 SZ58
Shanklin Chine A natural gorge of great scenic beauty, with a main waterfall of over 40ft. Although it now contains, amongst other attractions, an aviary, kiddy rides and a Victorian sea water bath, it differs very little from its original state. Open Easter to Sep from 9.30; 1 to 16 Oct 10.30–3.30. Floodlit at night end May to Sep. 30p (ch 14 10p, pen 20p). P (200yds). *(Tel Framfield Sussex 279)*

SHORWELL *Isle of Wight* Map 4 SZ48
Yafford Water Mill Farm Park Situated in attractive surroundings with a large mill pond, meandering stream and collection of waterfowl. The 19th-C water-mill contains much of the original machinery–still in use until a few years ago–there is also a collection of farm implements, wagons and tractors. Rare breeds survival centre. Children's playground. ⚏ Open Easter to Oct, 10–6, Sun 2–6. 50p (ch and pen 30p). Under revision for 1980. Parties by arrangement. ⚠ *(Tel Brightstone 740610)* &

VENTNOR *Isle of Wight* Map 4 SZ57
Museum to the History of Smuggling Botanic Gardens. Said to be the only museum in the world showing methods of smuggling over a 700-year period to the present day. ⚏ (licensed). Open daily Easter to end Sep 10–5; Jun to Aug also 7.30–9 in the evening. 30p (ch 7–14 and pen 10p, accompanied ch 7 free). Admission to gardens free. ⚠ *(Tel 853677)* & B

WROXALL *Isle of Wight* Map 4 SZ57
Appuldurcombe House Erected in 1710 on site of earlier house, roofless shell of mansion designed in classical style standing in ornamental grounds. Unoccupied since 1904. Open*, see inside front cover. 15p (ch 16 and pen 5p). *(AM)*

YARMOUTH *Isle of Wight* Map 4 SZ38
Fort Victoria Country Park Sconce Point. ½m W. Remains of Fort built in 1853 to protect the western approach to Portsmouth. Now being developed as a Country Park with picnic and barbecue facilities and nature trail. Spectacular views of the Solent. ⚏ Jun to Sep. Park open all year daily. *(Tel Newport 524031 ext 162)*.
Yarmouth Castle A Tudor castle, built by order of Henry VIII. Repaired in 1609 and 1632. Open, see inside front cover but closed Fri and Sat. 20p (ch 16 and pen 5p). *(AM)*

CHANNEL ISLANDS

GUERNSEY

FOREST
Occupation Museum Contains the largest exhibition of authentic Occupation relics to be found in the Channel Islands, including a

tableau of an 'Occupation Kitchen', 'Bunker rooms' and a new section on horse transport. Special tours arranged to explore the underground fortifications. ⚏. Open Apr, Sun and Thu 2–5.30 May to Oct daily 10–12.30, 2–6. 30p (ch 14 25p). ⚠ *(Tel Guernsey 38205)*

ST ANDREW
The German Military Underground Hospital and Ammunition Store La Vassalerie. The largest structural reminder of the German occupation of the Channel Islands. A concrete maze of about 75,000 sq ft, which took slave workers 3½ years to construct, at the cost of many lives. It was designed to accommodate 500 patients but could in emergency have housed three or four times that number. The hospital was only used for about 6 weeks for German wounded brought over from France soon after D-Day, but the ammunition store, which was larger than the hospital, was packed tight with thousands of tons of ammunition during its nine months of use. Most of the equipment has been removed, but there are still some signs of previous use such as the central heating plant, some hospital beds and cooking facilities. Open 1 Apr to 8 May, Thu and Sun 2–5; 9 May to 30 Sep, daily 10–12, 2–5; Oct Thu and Sun 2–5. 30p (ch 15 10p). Under revision for 1980. ⚠ *(Tel Guernsey 39100)* &

ST PETER PORT
Castle Cornet An ancient castle with buildings dating from the 13th to 20th C and scene of many battles. During the Civil War it was garrisoned by the Royalist governor of the island, Sir Peter Osborne, and although the island's people sympathised with Cromwell it was not until 15 Dec 1651 that this last Royalist stronghold surrendered to Parliamentarian forces. In 1940 it was taken over by German troops and adapted to the needs of modern warfare. Today it is maintained as an ancient monument and houses the Spencer collection of uniforms and badges the Museum of Guernsey's own 201 Squadron Royal Air Force, the Royal Guernsey Miltia Museum, a Maritime Museum, Art Gallery and Armoury. Open Apr to Oct, daily 10.30–6. Guided tours 10.45. 40p (ch 5 10, pen 15p). Joint ticket with Candie Museum and Fort Grey 90p. P. *(Tel Guernsey 21657)*
Fort Grey Built as part of the Island's defences against Napoleon on the site of an ancient castle. It has recently been restored and opened as a maritime museum, featuring the wrecks on the treacherous Hanois Reef nearby. Open May to Sep daily 10–12.30, 2–6. 25p (ch 10p, pen 15p). P. *(Tel Guernsey 65036)*
Guernsey Museum and Art Gallery Candie Gardens. Opened in 1978, it is the Island's first purpose-built museum. The exhibition depicts the story of the Island and its people. It includes an audio-visual programme in the museums own theatre and paintings in the Art Gallery. Special exhibitions are featured during the winter. Museum shop. Museum tea room with excellent views. Open all year daily 10.30–5.30 (winter hours may be shorter). 40p (ch 10p, pen 15p). Joint ticket with Castle Cornet and Fort Grey 90p. *(Tel Guernsey 26518)* &
Hauteville House Maison de Victor Hugo, 38 Hauteville. Built *c*1800 and brought by Victor Hugo, the great French writer, in 1856 who lived there until 1870 and returned in 1872, 1875 and 1878, the house contains a fine

collection of china, paintings and tapestries
and the decoration and furniture is much as it
was. Open 1 Apr to 30 Sep, daily (ex Thu
afternoons, Sun and BH) 10 – 12, 2 – 4.30.
Open once a day at 10.30 for 1 guided tour
during closed season or by appointment. 30p
(ch 10p, students and Party 10+, 20p per
person, school parties free). P. *(Tel Guernsey
21911)*

SAUMAREZ PARK
Folk Museum Centred on a courtyard of
buildings, depicting a traditional kitchen,
bedroom and cartroom. One room contains a
costume display, together with a range of
sewing machines, prams, pushchairs, and
samplers. A dairy has been laid out with a
large toolroom overhead, and another
building exhibits carts and ploughs, including
a 'grande charrue' and other farm
implements. A recent addition is a cider barn
with apple crusher and press. The museum is
entirely voluntary and is organised by the
National Trust of Guernsey. Open Easter to
mid Oct daily 10 – 12.30, 2 – 5.30. 30p (ch 15p,
free if accompanied). Under revision for 1979.
P. *(Tel Guernsey 55384)* ₰ **(79)**

JERSEY

*GERMAN MILITARY UNDERGROUND
HOSPITAL* Tunnelled out of solid rock by
Russian slave labour, during the German
occupation of 1940 – 1945. It was only ever
half completed, but over a period of 2½ years
4,000 tons of rock were removed and 4,000
tons of concrete were used to line the massive
galleries and walls. Light and sound effects
tell the story of Jersey during the invasion,
occupation and liberation, and photographs
of war personalities, events, newspaper
articles and German leaflets line the walls.
The Museum and Exhibition of Occupation
Relics includes an excellent collection of
authentic German firearms, daggers, officers'
badges and awards. Open 12 Mar to 5 Nov,
daily 10 – 6, winter season Thu and Sun only,
2.30 – 5. 60p (ch 15 20p). Prices under
revision for 1980. ⚠ *(Tel Jersey Central
42963)* ₰

GOREY
Mont Orgueil Castle Situated on a rocky
headland, on a site of fortification dating back
to the Iron Age and possibly Neolithic times.
The Castle, one of the best preserved
examples in Europe of the medieval
concentric castle, dates from the 12th to 13th
C. A series of tableaux with commentary tells
the history of the building. ⚏ and souvenir
shop. Open Mar to Oct, daily 9.30 – 6. 30p (ch
6 10p). Under revision for 1979. P. *(Tel
Jersey Central 53292)* **(79)**

LA HOUGIE BIE
The Jersey Museum Prehistoric burial
mound containing Neolithic tomb,
surmounted by Medieval chapels.
Underground shelter containing German
Occupation Museum. Agricultural museum.
Railway exhibition in original guard's van of
Jersey Eastern Railway. Archaeology and
geology museum. Pleasant grounds. Open
Mar to Oct, Tue to Sun 10 – 5 (other times by
appointment). 40p (ch and pen 20p). Party. ⚠
Tel Jersey 53823 or 22133) ₰

ST AUBIN'S
Elizabeth Castle Built off L'Islet rock about a
mile from shore in St Aubin's Bay. This old
fortress is steeped in history dating back to
the Elizabethan period when it was named
Fort Isabella Bellissima by Sir Walter Raleigh.
⚏ and souvenir shop. Open Mar to Oct daily

9.30 – 6. 30p (ch 10p) which includes entry to
the tableaux with commentary, Militia
museum and German bunkers. These prices
do not include fares on the service to the
castle. Opening times and prices under
revision for 1979. *(Tel Central 23971)* **(79)**

ST HELIER
*The Jersey Museum and Barreau Art
Gallery* Pier Road. Local collections relating
to history, maritime biology, natural history,
coins and medals, silver, postal service, law
and order, photography, shipping and sport.
Lillie Langtry displays. Victorian pharmacy
and four period rooms. Art gallery. All in large
Georgian house. Open Feb to Dec Mon to Sat
10 – 5. 40p (ch and pen 20p). P 200yds. *(Tel
Jersey 22133)*. ₰ B

ST MARY'S
Fantastic Gardens Tropical gardens, where
natural systems of growth and flowering are
presented in miniature, around replicas of
shrines and other architectural structures.
Past beliefs, customs, and myths of Islam,
India, China, Japan and Mexico are explained
on plaques, also the many ways man has
used the plants for drugs, fibres, dyes,
flavourings, cosmetics, etc. ⚏ Open 1 May to
6 Oct Mon to Fri 10 – 6. 50p (ch 20p, must be
accompanied and remain with adult).
Admission prices under revision for 1980.
Party. ⚠ *(Tel Central 81585, enquiries may
be made during the closed season)* ₰

ST OUEN
Battle of the Flowers Museum La Robeline,
Mont des Corvées. Contains exhibits which
have appeared in the Jersey Battle of Flowers
over the last 13 years. The tableaux executed
in Harestails and Marram grass, represent
scenes of wild and tame animals from all over
the world. Open Easter to 30 Nov. daily 10 – 5.
40p (ch 20p). ⚠ *(Tel Jersey West 82408)* ₰

ST PETER
Jersey Motor Museum Contains fascinating
collection of motor vehicles from the early
1900s, together with Allied and German
Military vehicles of World War Two, a Jersey
Steam Railway Section and Aero Engines
etc. Also pre-war Jersey AA Box and
collection of AA badges of all periods. ⚏
(licensed). Open Mar to Oct daily 10 – 5. 40p.
Under revision for 1980. (ch 10p). ⚠ *(Tel
Jersey 82966)* ₰
St Peter's Bunker At junction of A12 and
B41. An exhibition of Nazi German equipment
and Occupation relics, housed in an actual
German bunker, including uniforms, motor
cycles, equipment, weapons, documents,
photographs, various newspaper cuttings,
badges, awards and insignia. This six-
roomed bunker accommodated thirty-three
men, and could be air and gas sealed in case
of attack. One of the rooms contains an actual
reconstruction with original bunk beds, other
furniture, a store and rifle rack as well as
figures of soldiers asleep and on duty. ⚏
Open 20 Mar to 31 Oct, daily 10 – 5. 40p (ch
10p). Under revision for 1980. ⚠ *(Tel Jersey
81048)*

TRINITY
Zoological Park Founded in 1959 by Gerald
Durrell it became the headquarters of the
Jersey Wildlife Preservation Trust in 1963. Its
purpose is to breed animals critically
endangered in the wild. Families include
gorilla, orang-utan, spectacled bear, giant
tortoise, serval cat, white-eared pheasant and
numerous others. Open all year, daily (ex 25
Dec) May to Sep 10 – 6 (5 winter). £1 (ch and
pen 50p) ⚠ *(Tel Central 61949)* ₰
(wheelchairs available).

The National Trust

in Wales invites you to visit

ABERCONWY HOUSE

PLAS NEWYDD

ERDDIG

BODNANT GARDEN

PENRHYN

CHIRK CASTLE

POWIS CASTLE

FURTHER INFORMATION FROM
THE REGIONAL INFORMATION OFFICER, THE NATIONAL TRUST,
DINAS, BETWS-Y-COED, GWYNEDD TEL: 069-02-636

WALES

P.K.FRY.

ABERCRAVE *Powys* Map 3 SN81
Dan-yr-Ogof and Cathedral Showcaves
3m N on A4107. The longest and largest
showcaves in Britain contain some of the
largest stalactites and stalagmites in the
country. Guided tours of passages. ⚐
(licensed). Shops. Caravan and tent park.
Children's model Dinosaur Park (additional
charge). Open Easter to 31 Oct daily from 10;
for winter opening please telephone.
Admission prices not yet decided. ⚠ *(Tel 284
or 693 or 648)*

ABERGAVENNY *Gwent* Map 3 SO21
Abergavenny Museum The Castle.
Antiquities, rural craft tools, Welsh kitchen,
saddler's shop, costumes and exhibits of local
history Open all year, Mar to Oct, Mon to Sat
11–1, 2–5, Sun 2.30–5; Nov to Feb Mon to
Sat only 11–1, 2–4. 12p (ch and pen 7p). P
(in Castle Street). *(Tel 4282)*
Abergavenny Castle Remains of 12th-C
stronghold; walls, towers, and gateway. Open
daily 11–dusk. Free. Car park as above.

ABERGWILI *Dyfed* Map 2 SN42
Carmarthen Museum Old Bishop's Palace.
Local prehistoric, Roman and medieval
displays also folk material, military history and
costume. Cheese and butter making, local
pottery and temporary exhibitions. Open all
year Mon to Sat 10–4.30. Free. ⚠ *(Tel
Carmarthen 31691)*

ABERYSTWYTH *Dyfed* Map 6 SN58
Aberystwyth Castle Remains of 12th- to
13th-C castle on promontory which forms
good viewpoint. Open at all times. Free.
National Library of Wales Penglais Hill.
Granted Royal Charter of Incorporation in
1907, and one of Britain's six copyright
libraries, it is housed in imposing building of
1911–16, added to in 1931, 1937, 1955, and
1971. Large number of books in all
languages, musical publications, prints,
drawings, and old deeds; specialises in
Welsh and Celtic literature. Exhibitions of
pictures from certain collections; Central Hall.
Special exhibitions between May and Oct.
Library open all year (ex Christmas and
Easter), reading rooms Mon to Fri 9.30–6,
Sat until 5 pm. Free. ⚠ *(Tel 3816/9)* &
Vale of Rheidol Light Railway Only steam
railway operated by British Rail with 3 engines
and 16 passenger coaches (1ft 11½in-gauge).
Opened in 1902. Runs between Aberystwyth
and Devil's Bridge (11¾m) passing through
some of the finest scenery in Wales. Operates
Easter to Oct. Journey time (each direction)
one hour. Reduced fares for children and
morning times, for details telephone
Aberystwyth station. ⚠ *(Tel 612377)*

ARTHOG *Gwynedd* Map 6 SH61
Ty'n-y-Coed Peaceful woodland grounds,
with triple waterfall and peacocks. Champion
Welsh Farm ponies bred here. Welsh
craftshop. Woodland shrubs at their best mid
May to mid Jun. ⚐ in ancient Welsh kitchen.
Open (grounds only) 15 Apr to 15 Oct,
weekdays 10.30–5.30, Sun 12.30–5.30, last
tickets 5. 30p (ch 12 15p) subject to alteration.
⚠ No dogs during peacock breeding season,
otherwise on lead only. *(Tel Fairbourne 208)*.
(Dowager Viscountess Chetwynd)

BANGOR *Gwynedd* Map 6 SH57
Bangor Museum and Art Gallery
(University College of North Wales) Ffordd,
Gwynedd. The museum portrays history of
North Wales, collections of furniture, crafts,
costumes, maps, ceramics, and both Roman
and prehistoric antiquities. Exhibitions

illustrating history of the Menai Bridge and
Tubular Bridge and smaller items on Conwy
Bridge. Open all year (ex Sun and BH)
10.30–4.30. Free. P. Attendant always on
duty to deal with enquiries. *(Tel 51151 ext
437)*. The Gallery stages exhibitions of
sculpture and paintings each year changing
at approximately monthly intervals. Open
weekdays (ex BH) 10.30–5. Free. *(Tel 3368*
Penrhyn Castle 1m E, at junction A5 & A55.
The 19th-C furnished castle is an
outstanding, well preserved example of neo-
Norman architecture situated with superb
views in lovely grounds, walled garden.
Industrial railway museum, exhibition of doll
and a natural history display. Shop. ⚐ Open
Apr to 26 Oct daily. Apr, May and Oct 2–5,
Jun to Sep and all BH weekends 11–5. £1.2
(ch 60p). Party 20+. *(NT)*

BEAUMARIS *Gwynedd* Map 6 SH67
Beaumaris Castle Moated castle begun
1295 by Edward I and completed in 1323,
perhaps finest concentrically planned
stronghold in Britain. Retains original small
dock for shipping. Open*, see inside front
cover. 35p, winter 20p (ch 16 and pen 17p,
winter 10p). ⚠ *(AM)*
The Tudor Rose 32 Castle Street. One of th
few ancient monuments in Wales of the 15th
C. A half-timbered building with a fine
example of a hall of that period at the rear.
Upstairs has a minstrel gallery which offers a
view of the barrel braced ceiling and the hall
below. Hendrik Lec bought and restored the
property in 1945 and there is a continually
changing exhibition of both his and his sons'
paintings, drawings and prints. Open 1 Jul to
15 Sep, daily, 10.30–1, 2–5.30 (out of
season by request). 10p (ch 14 and pen 5p).
P. *(Tel 810203)*

BETWS-Y-COED *Gwynedd* Map 6 SH75
Conwy Valley Railway Museum Old Good
Yard. Houses displays covering the whole
railway scene with special reference to
standard and narrow-gauge lines in North
Wales. The smaller exhibits are in a purpose
built museum and there is a collection of
standard-gauge vehicles and large exhibits
on the site. ⚐ Open daily, Easter to 28 Sep
and weekends in Oct. BH weeks and summe
months 10.30–5.30. Spring and Autumn
2–5. 40p (ch 16 and pen 25p). Prices under
review for 1980. ⚠ Access and toilets for
wheelchair-bound visitors. *(Tel 568)* &

BLAENAU FFESTINIOG *Gwynedd*
Map 6 SH64
Gloddfa Ganol Ffestiniog Mountain Tourist
Centre. the centre is situated on the site of th
'world's largest slate mine' where the old min
workings, massive machinery and the skill o
the slate craftsmen is displayed. A museum
and gallery tell the story of the slate industry
while a fairy grotto and play area provide
amusement for the children. Also panoramic
walks. ⚐ (licensed). Land Rover conducted
tours. Craft shop. Open Easter to Oct
daily 10–5.30. 75p (ch 14 35p). Prices for
1980 under review. ⚠ *(Tel 664)* &
Llechwedd Slate Caverns Slate mine in
which rock formations, open quarries, and
slate chambers can be seen. Slate splitting
demonstrated in reconstructed mill.
Accessible by means of specially designed
cars hauled by battery-operated locomotive
Exhibitions of Victorian mining, photographs
quarry tramway and 'Slate Heritage'. Audio-
visual presentation of the history of slate ove
the last 1700 years. Temperature in caverns
about 55°F. ⚐ gift shop. Open Mar to Oct,

aily 10–6 (last trains 5.15 pm); 80p (ch 16
5p and pen 60p). Party 20+ (ex Aug). Prices
r 1980 under review. ⚠ *(Tel 306)* &

RECON *Powys* Map 3 SO02
recknock Museum Captain's Walk.
rchaeological and local historical exhibits,
lk life and decorative arts; natural history;
eology. Open all year Mon to Sat 10–5.
ree. ⚠ *(Tel 4121/2)* &

4th Regiment Museum The Barracks.
luseum of South Wales Borderers and
lonmouthshire Regiment, granted Freedom
* the Borough in 1948. Regiment was raised
1689 and has been awarded 23 VCs, of
hich 15 are displayed. Three rooms devoted
relics, photographs and medals. Special
ulu War display. Open all year (ex 25, 26
ec) daily 9–1 and 2–5; Oct to 31 Mar closed
at and Sun. 10p. P (limited). *(Tel 3111 ext
40)* & B

RIDGEND *Mid Glamorgan* Map 3 SS97
ewcastle Small ruined, 12th-C and later
ronghold, with rectangular tower, richly
arved Norman gateway to S side, and
assive curtain walls enclosing polygonal
ourtyard. Open Apr to Sep, weekdays 10–7,
un 2–7; Oct to Mar, weekdays 10–dusk,
un 2–dusk. Free. *(AM)*

RONWYDD ARMS *Dyfed* Map 2 SN42
wlli Railway ½m along B4301 from junction
th A 484. Only standard-gauge steam
assenger railway in South Wales. Welsh
aft centre, riverside picnic area at end of line
:wmdwyfran – no road access). ⚟
ookshop and ⚠ at Bronwydd Arms. Usually
pen Sat and Sun from 28 Jun to 21 Sep also
H Sun and Mon 6/7 Apr, 4/5 and 25/26
ay, 25 Aug, with special enthusiasts

weekend 27/28 Sep. Return fare 50p (ch 14
and pen 30p). Provisional dates and prices for
1980. Time tables are available from Great
Western Chambers, Angel Street, Neath,
West Glamorgan. *(Tel Neart 2191)* & B

BRYN-CELLI-DDU *Gwynedd* Map 6 SH57
Excavated in 1865, and again 1925–29,
prehistoric circular cairn covering passage
grave with polygonal chamber. Open, see
inside front cover. Free. *(AM)*

CAERLEON *Gwent* Map 3 ST39
Amphitheatre On A449. Roman
amphitheatre, with accommodation for 6,000
people from legionary fortress dated AD
80–100. Excavated from 1849 onwards.
Open*, see inside front cover. 15p (ch 16 and
pen 7p). ⚠ *(AM)*
Legionary Museum A branch of the National
Museum of Wales containing the principal
objects from the fortress of the Second
Augustan Legion. Open all year, daily (ex 24
to 26 Dec, 1 Jan and May Day) weekdays
9.30–5.30 (6, May to Sep; 4, Nov to Feb). Sun
2–5 (6, May to Sep; 4 Nov to Feb). Free. P (by
entrance to Roman amphitheatre) *(Tel 462)*
&

CAERNARFON *Gwynedd* Map 6 SH46
Caernarfon Castle Begun by Edward I in
1283, and completed in 1323, includes
polygonal angle towers, notable Eagle Tower,
and extensive town walls. Birthplace of
Edward II, first Prince of Wales, and site of
investiture in 1969 of present Prince of Wales.
Open*, see inside front cover. 55p. 55p (ch
25p (ch 16 and pen 20p, Oct to Mar 12p). ⚠
(AM)
Segontium Roman Fort and Museum
Branch archaeological gallery of the National
Museum of Wales. Remains of Roman fort of

'Segontium', and museum of excavated relics. Open Mon to Sat from 9.30, Sun from 2pm. Closes 4 Nov to Feb, 5.30 Mar, Apr and Oct, 6 May to Sep. Closed 1 Jan, 4 Apr, 5 May and 24–26 Dec. Free. *(AM)*

CAERPHILLY *Mid Glamorgan* Map 3 ST18
Caerphilly Castle On A469. A concentrically planned castle, begun in 1268 by Gilbert de Clare and completed 1326. One of the largest in Wales with extensive land and water defences. Open*, see inside front cover. 20p (ch 16 and pen 10p). ⚠ *(AM)*

CALDICOT *Gwent* Map 3 ST48
Caldicot Castle, Museum and Countryside Park On B4245. Norman castle, started in 1100 by Fitzwalter and completed in 1396 by Thomas Woodstock, with many interesting features including a local history museum exhibiting rural crafts, costume etc. The Woodstock Tower now houses an art exhibition. Open 1 Mar to 31 Oct, Mon to Fri 11–12.30, 1.30–5, (6 Sat and BH), Sun 1.30–6. 18p (ch and pen 7p) Park open all year. ⚠ *(Tel 420241)*

CAPEL GARMONG *Gwynedd* Map 6 SH85
Burial Chamber Off A496. Long barrow with covering mound and false portal. Excavated in 1926 revealing examples of neolithic pottery. Accessible at all reasonable times. Free. *(AM)*

CARDIFF *South Glamorgan* Map 3 ST17
Cardiff Castle Castle Street. Roman and Norman, with 12th-C keep, and 1861 additions including state apartments and curtain walls built on visible remains of Roman Wall. Conducted tours Mar, Apr and Oct, weekdays 10–12.30 and 2–4 (castle closes 5), Sun 10–12, 2–4; May to Sep daily, 10–12.40 and 2–5, Sun 10–12.30, 2–5 (castle closes 6); Nov to Feb 11–3 (castle

---

Amgueddfa Genedlaethol Cymru: Caerdydd
National Museum of Wales: Cardiff

An impressive building of Portland stone, the Museum is conveniently situated in the centre of Cardiff. Although the emphasis of its permanent collections is on themes relating to Wales from earliest times, it does not restrict itself to these interests alone. It includes, for example, an exceptional collection of modern European painting and sculpture which has helped the Museum to earn its international status. Within a few miles of Cardiff, the National Museum also has branch galleries — the art gallery at Turner House, Penarth and the archaeological gallery at the Legionary Museum, Caerleon. The Welsh Folk Museum is situated at nearby St Fagans, and the new Welsh Industrial and Maritime Museum is now open in Cardiff's dockland. Other branch museums include the North Wales Quarrying Museum, Llanberis and the Segontium Roman Fort Museum, Caernarfon in Gwynedd, the Museum of the Woollen Industry, Dre-fach Felindre, the Graham Sutherland Gallery, Picton Castle, Haverfordwest and Amgueddfa'r Hen Gapel, Tre'r Ddôl in Dyfed.

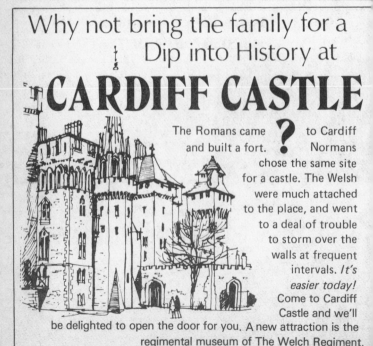

loses 4). The castle is closed occasionally
or special functions. P (in Sophia Gardens
and city centre). Further information from
Technical Services Dept, Hodge House, St
Mary Street. (Tel 31033 ext 716)

National Museum of Wales Cathays Park.
Collections and exhibitions in archaeology,
geology, botany, zoology industry and art, ⬔
open all year, daily (ex 24 to 26 Dec, 1 Jan
and 4 Apr and May Day) weekdays 10–5 (6,
Apr to Sep), Sun 2.30–5. Free. (Tel 397951)

Welsh Industrial and Maritime Museum
Bute Street. A branch museum of the National
Museum of Wales. Working exhibits tell the
story of motive power and the roles played by
a variety of machines over two centuries of
intense industrial production and progress in
Wales. Open all year, daily (ex 24–26 Dec, 1
Jan, 4 Apr and May Day) weekdays 10–5 (6,
Apr to Sep), Sun 2.30–5. Free. (Tel 371805)

CARDIGAN Dyfed Map 2 SN14
Wildlife Park Coedmore Estate. Entrance S
of River Teify near Cilgerran Village. The park
specialises in European animals, especially
of Wales past and present, incorporated in an
unusually diverse area of 250-acres of natural
habitats. Animal enclosures, nature trails,
wildlife sanctuary also slate and lime
industrial archaelogy. Craft shop and ⬔.
Coracle fishing demonstrations on most PH
and every weekend Jul and Aug. Open all
year, daily 10–6. 75p (ch 14 and pen 35p). ⚠
(Tel Llechryd 662) ♿ (most parts ex trails)

CARREG CENNEN CASTLE Dyfed
Map 3 SN61
Spectacularly sited hill-side ruin, originally
native Welsh stronghold, rebuilt in late 13th C.
Remarkable passage lit by loopholes cut into
side of cliff. Open*, see inside front cover. 15p
(ch 16 and pen 7p) ⚠ (AM)

CHEPSTOW Gwent Map 3 ST59
Chepstow Castle Earliest documented
masonry castle, begun 1067–71 by William
Fitz-Osborn. Fortified Port Wall. Royalist
stronghold during Civil War, later garrisoned
by Parliamentarians and dismantled in 1690.
Open*' see inside front cover. 25p (ch 16 and
pen 12p). ⚠ (AM)
Chepstow Museum Board School, Bridge
Street. Exhibitions of all aspects of Chepstow,
the lower Wye Valley and surrounding area.
The wine trade and salmon fisheries
exhibition is of special note. Free children's
worksheet available. Open 1 Mar to 31 Oct
Mon to Sat 11–1, 2–5, Sun 2–5. 12p (ch and
pen 7p). P (at castle). (Tel 5981)

CHIRK Clwyd Map 7 SJ23
Chirk Castle off the A5, ½m from Chirk
Village. (1½m driveway) Unique example of
Marcher fortress, completed in 1310, with
State rooms providing examples of 16th,
17th, 18th and early 19th-C decorations. ⬔.
Open 5 Apr to 26 Oct Wed, Thu, Sat and Sun
2–5; Jun to Sep Wed and Thu 11–5. All BH
weekends 11–5. £1 (ch 50p). Party 20+.
(managed by NT on behalf of Secretary of
State for Wales).

CILGERRAN Dyfed Map 2 SN24
Cilgerran Castle Off A484. In picturesque
setting above River Teifi, Norman to 13th-C
castle reduced to ruins during Civil War, and
subject of well-known paintings by Peter de
Wint and Richard Wilson. Open, see inside
front cover. 15p (ch 16 and pen 7p). Under
revision for 1980. (AM)

COITY Mid Glamorgan Map 3 SS98
Coity Castle 12th- to 16th-C stronghold with
hall chapel and three-storeyed round tower.
Open, see inside front cover. 15 (ch 16 and
pen 7p). (AM)

COLWYN BAY Clwyd Map 6 SH87
Welsh Mountain Zoo and Botanic Gardens
Animals and flora of all types in area of great
beauty. Daily displays of Falconry (free-flying
birds of prey). Penguin pool with underwater
observation. ⬔ Open all year Apr to Oct
9.30–7; Oct to Mar 10–4. £1 (ch 3–14 50p,
ch 3 free) Party. ⚠ Special toilets for
wheelchair visitors. (Tel 2938 catering
30891) ♿

CONWY Gwynedd Map 6 SH77
Aberconwy At junction of Castle Street and
High Street. Medieval house that dates from
the 14th-C, now houses the Conwy
Exhibition, depicting the life of the borough
from Roman times to the present day. Shop.
Open 1 Apr to 30 Sep, 10–5.30 daily (ex Wed
in Apr, May. Oct to Mar by appointment. 30p
(ch 12p). Party. (Tel 2246) (NT)
Conwy Castle A magnificent linear plan
fortress built 1283–89 by Edward I. Also
extensive town walls, originally with 27
towers, and old and new road bridges. Open*,
see inside front cover. Castle 35p, winter 20p
(ch 16 and pen 20p, winter 10p). Walls (open,
see inside front cover, May to Sep only) 17p
(ch 16 and pen 10p). ⚠ (AM)
Conwy Visitor Centre Off Lancaster Square.
For the whole family, a fascinating journey
through Conwy's colourful past, illustrated on
film and in displays. Welsh craft and
bookshop. Open, Jun to Sep, daily 10–9.30
(5.30 Sun); Oct to Dec and Mar to May

10–5.30 (closed Sun also Jan and Feb). 50p (ch and pen 30p). P.
Plas Mawr High Street. Finest example in Great Britain of an Elizabethan town house. It is in practically the same condition as when it was built (1570–1580), by Robert Wynne. Art exhibitions all year (closed mid Dec to mid Jan), ⚏ (2–5). Open daily 10–5.30 (4.30 Oct to Mar). 25p (ch 10p, pen 15p). Party ⚿ *(Tel 3413)*
'Smallest House' So-called 'Smallest House in Great Britain', on quay, with mid Victorian Welsh cottage interior. Open Easter to Oct 10–6 (10–9 in Aug). 5p. Under revision for 1980.

CORRIS *Gwynedd* Map 6 SH70
Railway Museum In village, 300 yds from A487. Museum in century-old railway building with photographs of operation of Corris narrow-gauge railway from 1890–1948. Items connected with railway are constantly added, and some old wagons are on show on short length of track. Children's playground nearby. Open BH week ends and Tue to Fri Jul and Aug 1–5.30, and as advertised on local posters during the holiday season. Free. ⚠ ⚿

CRICCIETH *Gwynedd* Map 6 SH43
Criccieth Castle 13th-C fortress, rebuilt with two baileys and notable gatehouse. Remains of keep, and wide views over Snowdonia. Open*, see inside front cover. 20p (ch 16 and pen 10p). *(AM)*

CWMCARN *Gwent* Map 3 ST29
Scenic Forest Drive Operated by Forestry Commission in Ebbw Forest. A 7-mile drive through mountain forest with spectacular views of the surrounding countryside and the Bristol Channel; picnic places; adventure play areas; forest and mountain walks. Open daily, Easter to Aug 11–8; Sep to Oct 11–6. 50p. Coaches by appointment. ⚠ *(Tel Newbridge 244223)* ⚿

CYMMER *West Glamorgan* Map 3 SS89
Welsh Miners Museum and Afan Argoed Country Park Set in the wooded, picturesque Afan Valley 2½m W on A4107. The museum is housed in the Countryside Centre. By entering simulated coal faces, viewing pit gear, examining miners' equipment, the visitor will experience the harsh realities of 'coal getting' and understand the effects it had on the communities of South Wales. The Countryside Park has forest walks and trails also picnic areas. ⚏ and Countryside Centre adjoin the parking area. Open Easter to end Sep 10.30–6; 12–5 winter weekends. Park open daily during daylight hours. Free. ⚠ *(Tel 7175)* ⚿

CYMMER ABBEY *Gwynedd* Map 6 SH71
Remains of the church of a small early 13th-C Cistercian monastery. Open 9–sunset. 10p (ch 16 and pen 5p). ⚠ *(AM)*

DENBIGH *Clwyd* Map 6 SJ06
Denbigh Castle Built 1282–1333, with gatehouse preserved, and fine viewpoint. Open*, see inside front cover. 20p (ch 16 and pen 10p). ⚠ *(AM)*
Town Walls and Leicester's Church Remains of walls include one of the gateways, and ruined church, 'Leicester's Folly', which was planned to become cathedral of the diocese, in place of St Asaph after the Reformation. Open, see inside front cover. 10p (ch 16 and pen 5p). *(AM)*

DOLWYDDELAN *Gwynedd* Map 6 SH75
Dolwyddelan Castle Restored rectangular 12th-C keep, with 13th-C curtain walls, the supposed birthplace of Llewelyn the Great. Open all year, weekdays 9.30–7 (5.30, Mar, Apr, Oct; 4, Nov to Feb), Sun 9.30–4. 15p (ch 16 and pen 7p). ⚠ *(AM)*

DRE-FACH FELINDRE *Dyfed* Map 2 SN33
Museum of the Woollen Industry A branch of the National Museum of Wales administered by the Welsh Folk Museum. It occupies part of a working mill, the Cambrian Mills. Its collection of textile machinery dates back to the 18th C and the exhibition traces the development of the industry from the Middle Ages to the present day. Open 1 Apr to 30 Sep, Mon to Sat 10–5 (ex May Day). Free. P. ⚿

DRYSLWYN *Dyfed* Map 2 SN52
Dryslwyn Castle Ruined, 13th-C, native Welsh stronghold on a lofty mound, important for its part in the struggles between the Welsh and English in the 13th C. Accessible at any time. Free. ⚠ *(AM)*

EWLOE *Clwyd* Map 7 SJ26
Ewloe Castle Remains of native Welsh castle in Ewloe woods, near where Henry II was defeated in 1157. Open Oct to Feb any reasonable time without charge; Mar to Apr 9.30–5.30, Sun 2–5.30; May to Sep 9.30–7 Sun 2–7. 10p (ch 16 and pen 5p). *(AM)*

FLINT *Clwyd* Map 7 SJ27
Flint Castle Ruined late 13th-C castle, erected by Edward I, with circular detached keep surrounded by moat. Open, see inside front cover. 10p (ch 16 and pen 5p). ⚠ *(AM)*

FORT BELAN *Gwynedd* Map 6 SH46
Napoleonic fort and private dock built around 1775. Featuring maritime museum, old forge pleasure flights and sea cruises also miniature steam railway. Pottery, Gift shop,

and cannon firing. Open May to Sep daily
10–5. 65p (ch 30p, and pen 55p). ⚠ *(Tel
Llanwnda 830220)* &

GROSMONT *Gwent* Map 3 SO42
Grosmont Castle Ruined Marcher
stronghold, rebuilt in 13th C by Hubert de
Burgh, on hill above Monnow Valley. One of
three 'tri-lateral' castles of Gwent. Open at all
reasonable times. Free. *(AM)*

HARLECH *Gwynedd* Map 6 SH35
Harlech Castle Built 1283–90 by Edward I,
and captured by Owain Glyndwr in 1404,
rectangular fortress on concentric plan, with
notable gatehouse. Wide views of Snowdonia
and Lleyn peninsula across Tremadoc Bay.
Open*, see inside front cover. 35p, winter 20p
(ch 16 and pen 20p, winter 10p). ⚠ *(AM)*
Old Llanfair Slate Quarries Man-made
caverns, previously blasted out of the hills in
the search for slate, through which guided
tours are given today. For the safety of visitors
authentic quarrymen's helmets are provided.
The mine, although underground, is for the
first part lit by daylight, while further on it is
illuminated, where the varying thicknesses of
the layers of slate may be seen. On emerging
from the mine, there is a splendid view of
Cardigan Bay. ⚏ Slate souvenir shop. Open
Easter to mid Oct, daily 10–5.30 (parties by
arrangement throughout the year). 50p (ch 15
20p, pen 35p). P. *(Tel 247)* **(79)**

HAVERFORDWEST *Dyfed* Map 2 SM91
*Haverfordwest Castle, Museum, Art
Gallery, and Record Office* Ruined 12th-C
stronghold, slighted after Civil War, converted
in 18th and early 19th C, used as a jail until
1820, when new county jail was built, later
became police HQ and recently converted to
museum and art gallery. Museum open all
year Mon to Sat (ex 13 Apr 25, 26 Dec, 1 Jan)
summer 10–5.30, winter 11–4. Record
Office open all year Mon to Thu 9–4.45, Fri
9–4.15. Castle ruins open all times during
daylight, at visitors' own risk. Free. P. *(Tel
3708, Records Office 3707)*

HAWARDEN *Clwyd* Map 7 SJ36
Hawarden Old Castle Remains of 14th-C
castle twice besieged during civil wars of 17th
C, and visited by Henry VII. Castle and
ornamental gardens open Easter to mid Sep
Sat, Sun, BH 2–5.30. Admission to castle and
ornamental gardens 20p (ch 16, 10p). Full
garden openings for charities, 2–6 on one
Sun in Apr, May and Jun. Use garden centre
park on A55.

KIDWELLY *Dyfed* Map 2 SN40
Kidwelly Castle 12th-C fortress with
additions of following two centuries, and

curious circular ovens of great size. Chapel
dating from c1400. Open*, see inside front
cover. 20p (ch 16 and pen 10p). ⚠ *(AM)*

LAMPHEY *Dyfed* Map 2 SN00
Lamphey Palace Ruined 13th-C Palace of
the Archbishops of St David's Later portion
added by Bishop Gower. Open, see inside
front cover. 15p (ch 16 and pen 7p). ⚠ *(AM)*

LLANALLGO *Gwynedd* Map 6 SH48
Din Lligwy Ancient Village 1 m NW off
A5205. Remains of 4th-C village, with two
circular and seven rectangular buildings
encircled by pentagonal stone wall. Open all
reasonable times. Free. *(AM)*

LLANBERIS *Gwynedd* Map 6 SH56
Dolbadarn Castle Native Welsh stronghold,
with a three-storeyed 13th-C round tower
(AM). Open Mar, Apr, Oct 9.30–5.30, Sun
2–5.30; May to Jun 9.30–7, Sun 2–7; Jul to
Sep 9.30–7, Sun 11–7; Nov to Feb 9.30–4.
Sun 2–4. 10p (ch and pen 5p). ⚠ (limited).
(AM)
Lake Railway Llyn Padarn. Narrow-gauge
railway operated by steam trains. Four-mile
journey commencing from and returning to
Gilfach Ddu, adjacent to the North Wales
Quarrying Museum and the centre of the
Padam County Park. Railway line was
formerly used to carry slate from the Dinorwic
Quarries to Port Dinorwic. The steam
locomotives date from 1889 to 1948; coaches
built specially for railway. Souvenir shop. ⚏
Trains run frequently, every day, from Easter
to end Sep (10.30–6 in peak season). Return
fare 80p (ch 40p) subject to alteration.
Party–apply to Commercial Manager. ⚠ 20p,
coaches free. Toilet facilities for disabled
persons. *(Tel 549)* &
North Wales Quarrying Museum ½m off
A4086. Contains original workshop
machinery for servicing quarries and to
maintain machinery and rolling stock.
Foundry mill with machinery and famous
Dinorwic 54ft water wheel. Also machinery
from other redundant Welsh quarries. Open
daily Easter to Sep (ex May Day) 9.30–7. 25p
(ch 16 and pen 12p). *(AM)* &
Snowdon Mountain Railway First opened in
1896, the only rack and pinion steam railway
in Britain (2ft 7½in gauge).
Locomotives built by Swiss Locomotive
Works at Winterthur. Climbs 4⅞ miles to
summit of Snowdon providing views of North
Wales, Anglesey and Cardigan Bay. Shops
and ⚏ at Base station (including Welsh Craft
Shops). ⚏ and shop at summit. Open early
Apr to early Oct, daily from 9. Fares not yet
available, details available from General
Manager. ⚠ *(Tel 223)* & (not at summit)

LLANDRINDOD WELLS Powys Map 3 SO06
Llandrindod Wells Museum Archaeological
exhibits, and objects excavated from Roman
Camp at Castell Collen to north of town.
Paterson Doll Collection is on show. Victorian
Spa gallery with period costume and 19th-C
chemist's equipment. Temporary exhibitions
are displayed. Open all year, Mon to Fri (ex
BH) 10–12.30 and 2–5. Sat 10–12.30 (May
to Sep only) Free. P. *(Tel 2212)*

LLANELLI Dyfed Map 2 SN50
*British Steel Corporation, Trostre Works
Museum* Trostre works cover 270 acres and
are Britains largest tinplate works. Exhibits
include model of handmill for producing
tinplate, actual handmill equipment, and
documents relating to industry. Parties of
limited numbers catered for on application.
Free. ⚠ (Limited) *(Tel 2260)* ⅋ B
Parc Howard Art Gallery and Museum
Situated in a pleasant park, and containing a
permanent collection of paintings. Llanelli
pottery and museum exhibits. From Mar to
Oct, a programme of exhibitions of paintings,
porcelain, sculpture, etc, is in operation. ⚟
May to Oct. Open all year Nov to Mar 10–4;
Apr to Oct 10–7. Free. *(Tel 3538)*

LLANFAIR CAEREINION Powys
Map 6 SJ10
*Welshpool & Llanfair Light (Steam)
Railway* (2ft 6in gauge). Open between
Llanfair Caereinion and Sylfaen (5½ miles).
Includes Austrian and Colonial locomotives.
⚟ at Llanfair Stn. Open at weekends from
Easter to Oct and daily from early Jun to early
Sep. Trains from Llanfair at 2.15 and 4.15,
also at 11.15 during daily running period.
Fares for 1980 not yet decided. ⚠ at Llanfair
and Castle Caereinion Stations. *(Tel 441)* ⅋

LLANGOLLEN Clwyd Map 7 SJ24
Llangollen Station Situated alongside the
river Dee in the centre of the town. Great
Western Railway Station restored, with steam
locomotives and rolling stock on display.
International Eisteddfod week 2–6 Jul and
most BH. ⚟ and railway shop. Open all year
Sat and Sun 10–5 also weekdays in tourist
season. Passenger service may operate
during 1980, please check. Steam days 10p,
non steam days free. P. *(Tel 860951)* ⅋
Plas Newydd Butler Hill. Former home of
well-known 'Ladies of Llangollen' in 18th C.
Oak carvings, panelling, and leather-work.
Exhibition room, attractive grounds. Open 1
May to 30 Sep, Mon to Sat 10–7.30, Sun
11–4. 15p (ch 14 10p) subject to alteration. ⚠
(limited) *(Tel 860234)*
Valle Crucis Abbey Abbey founded in 1201
for Cistercian monks by Madog ap Gruffydd
Prince of Powys. The remaining buildings
date mainly from 13th C. Open*, see inside
front cover. 15p (ch 16 and pen 7p). ⚠ *(AM)*

LLANGYBI Gwynedd Map 6 SH44
St Cybi's Well Rectangular structure, known
also as Ffynnon Gybi, with dry-stone structure
covering adjacent pool. Interior has wall
niches, and the corbelled beehive vaulting of
Irish type is unique in Wales. Open all
reasonable times. Free. *(AM)*

LLANIDLOES Powys Map 6 SN98
Old Market Hall Half-timbered building,
standing on open arches, with museum on
upper floor. Open Easter, and Spring BH to 30
Sep, daily 11–1 and 2–5. Free. P.

LLANRHIDIAN West Glamorgan
Map 2 SS49
Weobley Castle 12th- to 14th-C fortified

manor house above Gower marshland. Open
Apr to Sep, weekdays 10–7, Sun 1–7; Oct to
Mar 10–4, Sun 1–4. 15p (ch 16 and pen 7p).
⚠ *(AM)*

LLANRUG Gwynedd Map 6 SH56
Bryn Bras Castle and Grounds 1½m SE on
A4086. Early Victorian Romanesque castle
which is a delightful lived-in home with
extensive grounds of natural beauty,
including stream, waterfalls, pools,
hydrangeas, rhododendrons, woodland
walks, and panoramic, ½m-mountain walk. ⚟
Open Spring BH to end Sep, daily (ex Sat),
1–5 (10.30–5 mid Jul to end Aug). 70p (ch 15
35p). Party. ⚠ *(Tel Llanberis 210)*. *(Mr R D
Gray-Williams and Mrs M Gray-Parry)*

LLANRWST Gwynedd Map 6 SH86
Forest Information Centre Operated by
Forestry Commission in Gwydyr Forest to
interpret the forest as part of the landscape,
as a form of land use, as a traditional industry,
as a habitat for wildlife and as a place for
recreation and relaxation. 12 forest trails in
the vicinity, one starting from the centre. Open
daily, Easter to 30 Sep 10–4.30. Free. ⚠ 20p.
(Tel 640578)
Gwydyr Castle Historical royal residence,
magnificently furnished, from the Tudor
period. Beautiful grounds with more than 50
peacocks and many tropical birds. ⚟ Open
Easter to second week in Oct, daily (ex Sat)
10.30–5.30. 75p (ch 12 35p). Under revision
for 1980. ⚠ *(Tel 640261)* ⅋ B
Gwydyr Uchaf Chapel Former private
chapel of Gwydyr Castle (see above), and
dating from 1673, noted for rare Welsh
painted roof of the period. Open all year, any
reasonable time. 15p (ch 16 and pen 7p).
(AM)
Tu Hwnt I'r Bont Stone cottage, formerly
courthouse and restored partly by local
subscription, now let as tea-room. Open
Easter to end of touring season, daily (ex
Mon). Regret no parties. Free. *(NT)*
*Llanrwst Transport Group Museum and
Transport Workshop* Goods Warehouse,
Station Yard. Exhibition of items of transport
interest including two railway wagons, diesel
shunting locomotives, scammel three-
wheeler lorries, single-decker bus and
smaller railway exhibits. Open 1st Sun of
each month 10–4.30. Free. ⚠ (limited)
additional P nearby. *(Tel Deganwy 82394)*
(79)

LLANSTEPHAN Dyfed Map 2 SN31
Llanstephan Castle Remains of 11th- to
13th-C stronghold on west side of Towy
estuary. Accessible all reasonable times.
Free. *(AM)*

LLANTHONY Gwent Map 3 SO22
Llanthony Priory Augustinian foundation, c
1108, most of present structure being 12th- or
13th-C and including western towers, north
nave arcade, and south transept. Former
chapter house and western range have been
converted to secular use, and former Priest's
House is now hotel. The Honddu valley
scenery in Black Mountains is very
picturesque but roads are narrow, especially
continuing northwards towards lofty Gospel
Pass leading to Hay-on-Wye. Open all
reasonable times. Free. ⚠ *(AM)*

LLANTILIO CROSSENNY Gwent
Map 3 SO31
Hen Gwrt Rectangular enclosure of medieval
house which is still surrounded by wet moat.
Open any reasonable time. Free. *(AM)*

LLANTWIT MAJOR *South Glamorgan* Map 3 SS96
Town Hall Originally 12th- and largely 17th-C medieval courthouse and market, known once as the 'Church loft'. Retains original plan and comprises two storeys. Curfew bell (1320) now in church. Drama weeks May and Nov. Local art exhibition Jul. Horticultural Show Aug. Open all year Mon to Fri 9–4. Sat and Sun by appointment. Free. ⚠ *(Tel 3707)*

LLANUWCHLLYN *Gwynedd* Map 6 SH82
Bala Lake Railway Narrow-gauge railway running 4½ miles from Llanuwchllyn station, alongside Bala Lake to Bala. 3 ex-Dinorwic quarry steam engines built between 1889 and 1903 also diesel locomotives. Llanuwchllyn Station buildings date from 1867 and the original GWR signal box with 21 lever double twist frame installed in 1896 may be seen there. Also large selection of slate wagons and a gunpowder van. There are also early and later pattern Lancashire and Yorkshire railway signals in use. ⚏ Shop. Open Easter to 23 Oct daily 9–6 (weekends only after 30 Sep). 90p return (ch 45p return). 2 adults and 2 ch £2.30. Under revision for 1980. ⚠ *(Tel 666 or Bala 520226)* ＆

LLANVAPLEY *Gwent* Map 3 SO31
Rural Crafts Museum Exhibitions of 500 items of farm and rural craft tools and implements and other domestic and rural bygones. Open Feb to Nov Sun 3–6 (or dusk). Large or small parties wishing to view on other days *Tel Llantilio 210*. 20p (ch and pen 5p). ⚠ (very limited) otherwise on verge.

LLANVIHANGEL CRUCORNEY *Gwent* Map 3 SO32
Llanvihangel Court Tudor house, with interior remodelled in 1560. Interesting furnishings, yew staircase, and portraits. Attractive gardens. ⚏ Open every BH Sun and Mon (ex winter) and first, third and fifth Sun in Jun and every Sun in Jul and Aug 2.30–6. 50p (ch 15 10p). ⚠ *(Tel Crucorney 217)*. *(Col and Mrs Somerset Hopkinson)*

LLANYSTUMDWY *Gwynedd* Map 6 SH43
Lloyd George Museum David Lloyd George, famous Liberal Prime Minister, was educated in the village and died at the house of Ty Newydd in 1945. Museum has relics and mementos of his life. Open end May to 30 Sep, Mon to Fri 10–5. 20p (ch 15 and pen 10p) may be subject to increase. ⚠ *(Tel Criccieth 2654)* ＆

LLAWHADEN *Dyfed* Map 2 SN01
Llawhaden Castle Ruined 13th-C fortified residence of Bishops of St David's. Open, see inside front cover. 15p (ch 16 and pen 7p). *(AM)*

LOUGHOR *West Glamorgan* Map 2 SS59
Loughor Castle Slight remains of castle, originally Norman, but several times rebuilt by the Welsh to defend a river ford. Accessible all reasonable times. Free. *(AM)*

MACHYNLLETH *Powys* Map 6 SH70
Centre for Alternative Technology An old slate quarry overlooking Snowdonia National Park, a working demonstration independent of mains services, showing the possibilities of living with only a small share of the earth's dwindling resources, and creating a minimum of pollution and waste. Research, low energy studies, monitoring of equipment, housing, horticulture. Demonstrations of windpower, solar energy and vegetable growing. Salad lunches in summer. Open daily (ex Christmas), 10–5 (or dusk in winter). 80p (ch and pen 40p, students 60p). ⚠ *(Tel 2400)* ＆

MAESGWM *Gwynedd* Map 6 SH72
Forest Information Centre Operated by Forestry Commission in Coed-y-Brenin to interpret the forest as part of the landscape, as a form of land use, as a traditional industry, as a part of the local community, as a habitat for wild life, and as a place for recreation and relaxation. Includes a display of machinery from local gold mines. Open Easter to Oct, daily 10–5 (7, Jul and Aug). Admission and ⚠ 20p. Under revision for 1980. *(Tel Ganilwyd 210)* ＆

MANORBIER *Dyfed* Map 2 SS09
Manorbier Castle Mainly 13th-C, including chapel, hall and gatehouse, with 16th-C additions. Birthplace of 12th-C historian, Giraldus Cambrensis. Life-size wax figures in various parts of the castle. Open for a week at Easter then Whitsun to 30 Sep, daily 11–6. 25p (ch 10p). P. *(Tel 394)* **(79)**

MARGAM *West Glamorgan* Map 3 SS88
Margam Country Park E of junc 38 M4. 840 acres with large herd of fallow deer, rhododendron gardens, romantic buildings and remains, Margam Orangery (the largest building of its kind in Britain). Gymkhana, horse trials, pony and carriage events, band concerts, archery competitions. Waymarked walks. Adventure playground. Boating, riding, putting and fishing. ⚏ Open all year 1 Apr to 30 Sep Tue to Sun 10.30–8 (no entry after 6.30); 1 Oct to 31 Oct Tue to Sun 10.30–one hour before dusk; 1 Nov to 31 Mar Wed to Sun 10.30–one hour before dusk. 30p (ch and pen 15p, ch 5 and reg disabled free). ⚠ free. *(Tel Port Talbot 87626)* ＆ B

Stones Museum Small collection of Early Christian and pre-Norman carved stones and crosses. Adjacent to Margam churchyard. Open all year, Wed, Sat and Sun 2–5 (4, Nov to Feb). 15p (ch 16 and pen 7p). ⚠ *(AM)*

LLOYD GEORGE MUSEUM
LLANYSTUMDWY

Situated in the pleasant country village of Llanystumdwy, 1½ miles from Criccieth on the main Pwllheli road is the Lloyd George Museum. In the natural setting of his home village, near to his grave on the banks of the River Dwyfor, the life story of the famous world statesman is depicted in photographs, documents and mementoes of his career.
Open Spring Bank Holiday to end of September. 10am-5pm. Mon. to Fri.

MENAI BRIDGE *Gwynedd* Map 6 SH57
Museum of Childhood Water Street. The
exhibits, many of which are rare and valuable
illustrate the habits and interests of children
and families spanning 150 years. They
include children's saving boxes; dolls;
educational toys and games; pottery and
glassware depicting and used by children;
early clockwork toys, including trains, cars
and aeroplanes; music boxes; polyphons;
magic lanterns and an art gallery full of
paintings and prints of children, as well as
early samplers and needlework pictures
worked by children. Open Easter to end of
Oct, daily 10 – 6, Nov to Apr consult
curator. 50p (ch 35p pen 40p ch 6 free). P.
(Tel 712498)
Tegfryn Art Gallery Cadnant Road. A private
gallery, standing in its own pleasant grounds
near to shores of the Menai Straits, exhibits
paintings by contemporary, prominent artists
including many from North Wales. Pictures
may be purchased. Open all year daily 10 – 1,
2 – 6. Free. ⚠ *(Tel 712437)*. &

MERTHYR TYDFIL *Mid Glamorgan*
Map 3 SO00
Cyfarthfa Castle Museum and Art Gallery
Built by William Crawshay in 1825 the
collections cover paintings, ceramics, coins
and medals, silver and other *objets d'art*,
natural history and local history, also a small
Welsh kitchen. Open weekdays 10 – 1 and
2 – 6 (5 Oct to Mar) Sun 2 – 5. Free ex Sun and
BH 5p. Closed 4 Apr, 5 May, 25/26 Dec and 1
Jan. *(Tel 3112)*
Garwnant Forest Centre 5m N of Merthyr
Tydfil off A470. The centre provides
information about, and has an exhibition
featuring, the forests in the Brecon Beacons.
Parking and picnic places close by with
associated forest walks. Open Easter to 30
Sep weekdays 10.30 – 4 (also 4 – 6pm Wed
and Thu in Jul and Aug), BH 12 – 6. Open Sat
and Sun Apr and Sep 2 – 4; May 2 – 5; Jun, Jul
and Aug 2 – 6. Other times, phone for opening
details. Free ⚠ *(Tel 3060)* &

MONMOUTH *Gwent* Map 3 SO51
Monmouth Castle and Great Castle House
12th-C castle keep, birthplace of Henry V.
Great Castle House built by 1st Duke of
Beaufort in 1673. Exterior only freely
accessible any reasonable time. ⚠ *(AM)*
Monmouth Museum (Nelson Collection and
Local History Centre). Collections of Nelson
relics and mementoes. Local history centre of
Monmouth. Open all year weekdays,
10.30 – 1 and 2.15 – 5.15. Sun 2.15 – 5.15; Jul
and Aug, weekdays 10 – 6, Sun, 2.15 – 5.15.
Admission to local collection free; Nelson
collection 20p (ch and pen 7p). P. (Glendower
Street) 5p. *(Tel 3519)*

MUMBLES *West Glamorgan* Map 2 SS68
Oystermouth Castle Ruined gatehouse,
chapel, and great hall of 13th- to 14th-C date.
Former stronghold of Braose family. Small
park, open Jun, Jul and Aug 11 – 5.30, other
months Mon to Fri 11 – 3.30. 11p (ch 16 5p).
Under revision for 1980. P. *(Tel Swansea
50821 ext 2815)*

NEATH *West Glamorgan* Map 3 SS79
Neath Abbey Ruins of Cistercian (originally
Savignac) abbey founded by Richard de
Grainville in 1130. Open, see inside front
cover. 15p (ch 16 and pen 5p). ⚠ *(AM)*
Penscynor Wild Life Park Interesting bird
garden. New extension into forestry land. Gift
shops. Open all year (ex 25 Dec). Daily 10 – 6.
Admission prices not yet decided. 🍽 No dogs
⚠ *(Tel 2189)* &

NEWCASTLE EMLYN *Dyfed* Map 2 SN34
Felin Geri Mill 2m N on unclass road off
B4333 at Cwmcoy. The last watermill in
Wales using the original means of production
to grind stone ground wholemeal flour on a
regular commercial basis. Built in the 16th C.
Visitors are shown all stages of production.
There is also a mill museum and a water
powered saw mill. Shop and bakery. 🍽. Open
Easter to end Oct, Mon to Fri, 10 – 5.30, Sat
and Sun 10 – 4. 40p (ch 16 20p). ⚠ *(Tel
710810)*

NEWPORT *Dyfed* Map 2 SN04
Pentre Ifan Burial Chamber 3m SE.
Remains of this chamber comprise capstone
and three uprights with semi-circular
forecourt at one end. Excavated 1936–37
when found to be part of vanished long
barrow. Open all reasonable times. Free.
(AM)

NEWPORT *Gwent* Map 3 ST38
Museum and Art Gallery John Frost Square.
Archaeology and history of Gwent including
Roman finds from Caerwent and Pontypool
Japanned ware, section on Chartist
movement of 1838–40. Natural history and
geology. Open all year (ex BH) Mon to Fri
10–5.30. Sat 9.30–4. Free. ⚠ *(Tel 840064)*
&

Tredegar House Former home of the Morgan
family. Finest Restoration house in Wales,
with part of the early 16th-C hall block
surviving. Extensive grounds, farm, boating
lake. ⬛ (licensed). Grounds open daily
8–sunset. House and farm open 2 Apr to 25
Sep Wed to Sun and BH 2–6. Grounds free;
House 25p (ch 15p). Under revision for 1980.
(Tel 62275).

Whitson Zoological Park Whitson Court.
Set in the grounds of an 18th-C house
designed by John Nash. Among the exhibits
are bears, monkeys, baboons, lions,
macaws, and pheasants. There is also an
aquarium set in the cellars of the house. ⬛
Open Apr to Sep daily 10–6. 30p (ch 16 and
pen 20p). Party 20+. Guided tours for school
parties. Under revision for 1979. ⚠ *(Tel
72515)*. & **(79)**

PKF

OGMORE *Mid Glamorgan* Map 3 SS87
Ogmore Castle On River Ogmore, with inner
and outer wards, and early 12th-C three-
storeyed stone keep preserving hooded
fireplace. West wall 40ft high, and dry moat
around inner ward. Open, see inside front
cover. Free. *(AM)*

PEMBROKE *Dyfed* Map 2 SM90
Pembroke Castle Impressive 12th- to 13th-C
fortress by river bank, with 80ft-high round
keep, work of Earl of Pembroke. Open all year
Easter to 30 Sep, Mon to Fri 10–7, Sat 10–6,
Sun 11–7; Oct to Easter, Mon to Sat 10.30–5
(closed Sun and 25 Dec). Castle gates close
½hr before stated closing times. 20p (ch 10p).
P. *(Tel 4585)*. &

PEMBROKE DOCK *Dyfed* Map 2 SM90
Pembrokeshire Motor Museum A number
of vintage and veteran cars and motorcycles
in Garrison Theatre. Several early bicycles
can also be seen. Costumes of early motoring
period on display. Early children's toys and
replica of garage of the Twenties. Items of
local historical interest. Open 29 May to 30
Sep, Sun to Fri 10–6. 50p (ch 17 25p). ⚠ *(Tel
Pembroke 3279)* &

PENARTH *South Glamorgan* Map 3 ST17
Turner House Small art gallery holding
temporary exhibitions of pictures and *objets
d'art* from the National Museum of Wales and
other sources. Open all year, weekdays (ex
Mon, 1 Jan, 4 Apr, May Day and 24–26 Dec
but open BH Mon 11–12.45 and 2–5, Sun
2–5. Free. P. *(Tel 708870)*

PENARTH FAWR *Gwynedd* Map 6 SH43
Off A497. Part of house, built probably in early
15th-C, preserving hall, buttery, and screen.
Open any reasonable time. Free. *(AM)*

PENHOW *Gwent* Map 3 ST49
Penhow Castle The oldest inhabited castle in
Wales was originally a small border fortress.
The first home in Britain of the famous
Seymour family, one of whom was living in the
Castle in 1129. The building presents a
fascinating picture of life from the 12th to
19th-C, 12th-C ramparts (with view of three
counties), 15th-C Great Hall with
reconstructed screen and minstrels' gallery,
17th-C kitchen, also Victorian house-keeper's
room. Gift and publication shop. ⬛ by
arrangement. Open Easter to Sep, Wed to
Sun (closed Mon and Tue) 10–6. 65p (ch 14
and pen 35p). Guided tours, party, evening
visits by arrangement. Educational facilities.
⚠ *(Tel 400800)* & B

PENMACHNO *Gwynedd* Map 6 SH75
Tŷ Mawr 2m NW at head of Gwybernant
Valley. The birthplace of Bishop William
Morgan c1541–1604, the first translator of
the Bible into Welsh. ♨ Open 4 Apr to 26 Oct
daily (ex Sat) 10–6. 10p. Party by
appointment *(Mrs Roberts, Ty Mawr,
Gwybernant, Dolwyddelan, Gwynedd).*
Approach roads unsuitable for large coaches.
(Tel 213). (NT)

PENMON *Gwynedd* Map 6 SH68
Dovecote Off B5109. Dovecote dates from
c1600 and is square with domed vault and
hexagonal cupola. Open all reasonable
times. Free. *(AM)*

PICTON *Dyfed* Map 2 SN01
*Picton Castle Grounds and Graham
Sutherland Gallery* Castle **NOT** open. The
gallery is in a building in a courtyard close to
the castle, 300yds from car park. On display,
oil paintings, water-colours, works in mixed
media, lithographs, etchings and aquatints.
The extensive grounds provide walks through
shrub gardens and woodland. Grounds open
1 Apr to 30 Sep (ex Mon & Fri) 10.30–6. 50p
(ch 10p). ⚠ *(Tel Rhos 201)* ♿ Graham
Sutherland Gallery Easter to end Sep (ex May
Day) daily (ex Mon & Fri, but open BH Mon)
10.30–12.30, 1.30–5.30. Oct to Easter Sat
and Sun 2–5. Free. ⚠ 50p. *(Tel Rhos 296)* ♿

PLAS NEWYDD *Gwynedd* Map 6 SH56
On A4080 1m SW Llanfairpwll. 18th-C house
by James Wyatt in unspoilt position adjacent
to Menai Strait; magnificent views to
Snowdonia; fine spring garden. Rex
Whistler's largest wall painting. Military
museum. Shop. ♨ Open 4 Apr to 26 Oct, daily
(ex Sat, but open BH Sat) 12.30–5.30 (last
admission 5 pm). £1 (ch 50p). Gardens only
50p (ch 25p). Party 20+. No dogs. *(Tel
Llanfairpwll 714795).* (NT)

PLAS-YN-RHIW *Gwynedd* Map 6 SH22
Off B4413. 16th-C house with Georgian
features and attractive woodlands, on lower
slopes of Mynydd Rhiw with views across
Porth Neigwl. Gardens with flowering shrubs
and trees, stream, and waterfall. Open strictly
by appointment only. No room for coaches.
(Tel Rhiw 219). (NT)

PLWMP *Dyfed* Map 2 SN35
*West Wales Farm Park (Parc Fferm Gorlle
win Cymru)* Blaenbed Isaf 1m S. 60 acres of
farmland devoted to the display or breeding
groups of old British breeds of farm animals
and poultry. Many rare species are displayed.
Beautiful views of Welsh coastline from the
top of the Park. Tractor and trailer rides

operate around the Park in peak season.
Picnic sites, children's play area, pets corner,
nature trail. ♨ Open 15 May to 30 Sep daily
10–6. 75p (ch 14 40p). Party. ⚠ *(Tel
Rhydlewis 317)*

PONTERWYD *Dyfed* Map 6 SN78
Bwlch Nant-Yr-Arian Forest Visitor Centre
3m W
Operated by the Forestry Commission in
Rheidol to interpret the forest as a part of the
landscape, form of land use, traditional
industry, part of local community, habitat for
wildlife, and as a place for recreation and
relaxation. Picnic areas and forest walks in
the vicinity. Open Easter to Oct 10–5 (7, Jul
and Aug). 10p. ⚠ ♿
Llywernog Silver-Lead Mine A mid 19th-C
water-powered silver-lead mine located in the
midst of the Welsh mountains. Restored to
provide interpretive facilities for the bygone
mining industry of the region. Way-marked
trail system (the miner's trail), museum,
audio-visual unit, underground drift mine and
working machinery. Collections include the
last Cornish Roll Crusher in Wales, jiggers,
buddles and many water-wheels and other
items. Regular working days at the Smithy,
Horse-gin and Ore Jigger. ♨ Open Easter to
Sep; Easter to 30 Jun 11–4.30; Jul and Aug
10–6; Sep 11–4. 65p (ch 15 35p, pen 55p).
⚠ *(Tel 620).* Stout footwear recommended.

PORTHMADOG *Gwynedd* Map 6 SH53
Festiniog Railway Historic narrow-gauge
railway which originally carried slate from
mines at Blaenau Ffestiniog to the sea at
Porthmadog, with trucks running down from
the quarries by gravity. Steam locomotives
were introduced in 1863 and passengers
were carried soon afterwards. Line closed in
1946 but re-opened by enthusiasts to operate
between Porthmadog and Tanygrisiau with
bus connection to Blaenau Ffestiniog. Steam
locomotives including unique Fairlie type
articulated locomotive. Observation and
licensed Buffet cars on trains. Daily service
Mar to Nov. Also 26 Dec to 1 Jan and
weekends Feb and Mar. ⚠ Timetable and
fares on request. *(Tel 2384)* ♿ (Special
arrangements on trains if notified in advance)
Ffestiniog Railway Museum Located in
Harbour Station, includes old four-wheeled
hearse converted from Quarryman's coach,
historic slate waggon, model steam engine
(1869), and maps and diagrams illustrating
history of the well-known narrow-gauge
railway. ♨ Open Feb to Dec all weekends and
Mar to Nov when train service is operating.
See entry above. Free. ⚠ *(Tel 2384)* ♿

PORTMEIRION *Gwynedd* Map 6 SH53
Gwylt Gardens Wild gardens with some 20 miles of woodland paths, famous for rhododendrons, azaleas and a variety of sub-tropical flora. Open Apr to Oct daily 9.30–5.30. 75–95p (ch 14 20p). Under revision for 1980. Party 20+. ⚐ *(Tel Penrhyndeudraeth 228)* ⅍ B

RAGLAN *Gwent* Map 3 SO40
Raglan Castle Mainly 15th-C, and noted for 'Yellow Tower of Gwent'. Built by Sir William ap Thomas, and destroyed during the Civil War. Long Gallery, added by Lord Worcester, was 126ft long. Castle has own bowling green. Open*, see inside front cover. 20p (ch 16 and pen 10p). ⚐ *(AM)*

RHOOSE *South Glamorgan* Map 3 ST06
Wales Aircraft Museum Cardiff (Wales) Airport. Opened in 1977, the privately-operated museum is situated adjacent to the airport. At least 18 aircraft, including a Viscount air liner, can be inspected. Aircraft engines and aviation related items, photographs, models and historical items. Children can sit in the airport Fire Engine which is on display. ⚐ (licensed) at airport terminal. Open all year Sun 10.30–7 or dusk if earlier, or by arrangement. 30p (ch 14 and pen 15p, ch 6 free). Under revision for 1980. P. *(Tel Cardiff 29880 or 562780)*

RHUDDLAN *Clwyd* Map 6 SJ07
Bodrhyddan Hall 1½m E on A5151. 17th-C house (part earlier), with armour, furniture, and notable pictures, and in fine grounds. ⚐ Open Jun to end Sep, Tue, Thu 2–5.30. 50p (ch 14 25p). ⚐ *(Tel 590414). (Col the Lord Langford)* ⅍ B

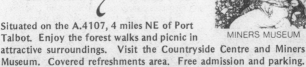

Rhuddlan Castle Begun 1277 by Edward I, to a 'diamond' plan and showing round towers, gatehouses, and 9ft-thick curtain walls. Open*, see inside front cover. 15p (ch 16 and pen 7p). ⚠ *(AM)*

ST DAVID'S *Dyfed* Map 2 SM72
Bishop's Palace Extensive remains of the principal residence of Bishops of St David's. Dates from 13th C, with fine architectural detail. Open*, see inside front cover. 20p (ch 16 and pen 10p). *(AM)*

ST FAGAN'S *South Glamorgan* Map 3 ST17
Welsh Folk Museum Open-air branch museum of the National Museum of Wales, exhibits including 16th-C St Fagan's Castle and gardens, woollen mill complete with machinery, old Welsh farmhouses, tannery and tollgate from mid Teifi, chapel from Vale of Teifi, and North Wales quarryman's cottage. ⚲ Open all year (ex 24–26 Dec, 1 Jan and May Day). Apr to Sep Mon to Sat 10–6, Sun 2.30–6 Oct to Mar 10–5, Sun 2.30–5. 10p (ch 16 5p, pen free). Sun from 2.30, admission free for pre-arranged school parties. ⚠ *(Tel Cardiff 569441)* ♿

ST FLORENCE *Dyfed* Map 2 SN10
Manor House Wildlife and Leisure Park Set in 12 acres of delightful wooded grounds and gardens. Collections of birds, tropical and freshwater fish; animal collection includes apes, monkeys, otters, deer, in a picturesque setting of flowers, plants and trees. Pets corner, adventure playground. Children's amusements and rides. Model railway exhibition. Radio-controlled models. Free flight exhibitions of birds of prey. Open from Easter to Sep daily, 10–6. Admission prices for 1980 not yet decided. No dogs. ⚠ *(Tel Carew 201)* ♿

ST HILARY *South Glamorgan* Map 3 ST07
Old Beaupré Castle 1m SW. Ruined manor house, rebuilt in 16th C, with notable Italianate gatehouse and porch. Porch is three storeyed and displays Basset arms. Open any reasonable time (ex Sun). Free. *(AM)*

ST NICHOLAS *South Glamorgan* Map 3 ST07
Dyffryn Gardens 72 acres of gardens including rare trees and shrubs. ⚲. Open daily 31 Mar to 20 May and Sep, also weekends Oct; 21 May to 31 Aug 10–7. Plant houses close 1 hour earlier. Closed occasionally for special occasions. 30p (ch and pen 15p). Party 12+. ⚠ *(Tel Cardiff 593328)* ♿

St Lythan's Burial Chamber Isolated burial chamber which comprises three upright blocks and a capstone. It dates from *c*2000 BC. Open all reasonable times. Free. *(AM)*

Tinkinswood Burial Chamber A notable example of a long cairn, with a forecourt leading to a massively roofed chamber, rectangular in shape, with revetted walls. When excavated (1914–15) remains of human skeletons, animal bones, and pottery of *c*2000 BC were found. Accessible all reasonable times. Free. *(AM)*

SCOLTON *Dyfed* Map 2 SM92
Scolton Manor Museum and Country Park Late Georgian country mansion set in 40 acres of grounds, specially rich in fine trees and ornamental shrubs. A 'tree trail' and a nature trail are provided. The mansion, stable block and large exhibition hall provide for a comprehensive display of the history and natural history of Pembrokeshire. Picnic sites. Free ⚠ *(Tel Haverfordwest 3708)*.

SKENFRITH *Gwent* Map 3 SO42
Skenfrith Castle 7m NW of Monmouth, on
B4521. 13th-C Marcher keep within a towered
curtain wall, the work of Hubert de Burgh. One
of three 'trilaterial' castles of Gwent. Open at
all reasonable times. Free. *(AM and NT)*

STRATA FLORIDA ABBEY *Dyfed*
Map 3 SN76
Remains of church and cloister of Cistercian
abbey founded in 1164. Open, see inside
front cover. 15p (ch and pen 7p). ⚠ *(AM)*

SWANSEA *West Glamorgan* Map 3 SS69
Glynn Vivian Art Gallery and Museum
Alexandra Road. Contains works of British
and French masters, and contemporary
British artists; also collections of Continental
and Swansea porcelain and pottery. Various
exhibitions to be held through the year. Open
all year (ex 25, 26 Dec and 1 Jan), weekdays
10.30 – 5.30. Free. P. *(Tel 55006)* &
Maritime and Industrial Museum South
Dock. Contains complete working woollen
mill in continuous production. Displays
relating to the industry and the Port of
Swansea and its environs. Transport exhibits,
steam locomotives which run on some Sats
throughout season. Open all year (ex 25, 26
Dec, 1 Jan) weekdays 10.30 – 5.30. Free. P.
(Tel 55006 and 53051) &
***University College of Swansea and Royal
Institution of South Wales Museum***
Victoria Road. Founded in 1835, the museum
contains finds of local interest including
Roman and other archaeological remains,
birds, Swansea of Nantgarw china, and a
reproduction of a 19th-C Gower kitchen.
Exhibits include display of Lower Swansea
Valley. Open all year (ex 4 Apr and
Christmas/New Year week). Mon to Sat
10 – 5. 15p (ch 16 and students 10p, if
accompanied by adult, ch 5 free, pen 10p). ⚠
(Tel 53763)

TALLEY *Dyfed* Map 2 SN63
Talley Abbey The abbey was founded
towards the end of the 12th C probably by
Rhys ap Gruffydd, for Premonstratensian
canons. Open, see inside front cover. 15p (ch
16 and pen 7p). ⚠ *(AM)*

TAL-Y-CAFN *Gwynedd* Map 6 SH77
Bodnant Garden 8m S of Llandudno on
A470. Entrance ½m along Eglwysbach road.
Among the finest gardens in the country, with
magnificent collections of shrubs and trees.
Fine views of Snowdonia. ☞ Apr to Sep.
Open 15 Mar to 31 Oct daily 10 – 5. 80p (ch
40p). Party 20+. No dogs, prams or
pushchairs. (ex guide dogs and invalid
wheelchairs). *(NT)*

TENBY *Dyfed* Map 3 SN10
St Catherine's Island Situated on a small
island fortress off Tenby beach which is only
accessible on foot for about six hours a day at
low tide. Open Whit to 30 Sep daily 10 – dusk
(depending on tide). Admission prices not
available for 1980.
Tenby Castle 13th-C ruins comprising keep
and walls. Also extensive remains of 14th-C
town walls, with later alterations including
partly rebuilt gateway known as the 'Five
Arches'. Open all times. Free.
Tenby Museum Notable collections of
geological specimens, seashells, and cave
deposits, illustrative of Tenby district and the
country generally. Picture gallery, topography
and other works of art. Open Jun to Oct, daily
10 – 6, Nov to May, daily 10 – 4. 15p (ch 5p). P.
(Tel 2809)
Tudor Merchant's House Quay Hill. Good
example of gabled 15th-C architecture,
ground floor of which is now National Trust
Information Centre, with exhibition of Tudor
period. Open 14 Apr to Sep, Mon to Fri 10 – 1
and 2.30 – 6, Sun 2 – 6. 20p (ch 10p). No dogs.
P. *(NT)*

TINTERN *Gwent* Map 3 SO50
Tintern Abbey Extensive remains of a fine
13th-C church founded for monks of the
Cistercian Order in 1131. Open*, see inside
front cover. 20p (ch 16 and pen 5p). ⚠ *(AM)*

TONGWYNLAIS *South Glamorgan*
Map 3 ST18
Castell Coch Restored 13th-C castle,
triangular in plan, with round towers at angles,
in Taff-side setting. Open*, see inside front
cover. 35p (ch and pen 17p); winter 20p (10p).
⚠ *(AM)*

TRE'R DDOL *Dyfed* Map 6 SN69
Yr Hen Gapel Off A487. A branch museum of
the National Museum of Wales, administered
by the Welsh Folk Museum. The museum
portrays 19th-C religious life in Wales. Open
Apr to Sep, Mon to Sat 10 – 5 (ex 4 Apr and
May Day). &

TRETOWER *Powys* Map 3 SO12
Tretower Court and Castle Remains of a
14th- to 15th-C Welsh fortified manor house,
with nearby ruined Norman and 13th-C
castle, noted for its cylindrical keep. Open,
see inside front cover. 15p (ch 16 and pen 7p).
⚠ *(AM)*

TYWYN *Gwynedd* Map 6 SH50
Narrow-Gauge Railway Museum This
interesting small museum is located in the
Talyllyn Railway Wharf station yard, Neptune
Road. A number of locomotives and wagons
are on display. ☞ Open Easter to Oct, Mon to

Fri 10 – 5, Sat and Sun, 11 – 5. Closes at 6 Jul
and Aug. Nov to Mar by arrangement. 15p (ch
14 5p) subject to revision. P. *(Tel 710472)* &
Talyllyn Railway The oldest 2ft 3in gauge
railway in the world. Steam operated. Built
1865 and became first railway to be saved by
a voluntary preservation society. Runs 7¼
miles, from Tywyn to Nant Gwernol. ⏣
Regular daily (ex Oct) services Easter to Oct.
Timetables available. Fares for return journey
£1.40 (ch 15 70p, pen £1), subject to revision.
P. *(Tel 710472)* & (limited)

WELSHPOOL *Powys* Map 7 SJ20
Powis Castle On S edge of Welshpool,
pedestrians' access from High Street (A490),
cars 1m along main road to Newton A483 take
signposted route to Waterloo. Medieval castle
with late 16th-C plasterwork and panelling,
contents include paintings, tapestries, early
Georgian furniture and relics of Clive of India,
early 18th-C terraced garden and woodland
garden. Shop. ⏣ Open 5 to 7 Apr then 1 May
to 28 Sep, Wed to Sun, Castle 2 – 6, garden
1 – 6. Castle and garden open each BH Mon
11.30 – 6 (last admission 5.30). Castle and
garden £1.10 (ch 60p). Castle only 70p (ch
30p), garden only 70p (ch 30p). Children not
admitted unless accompanied by an adult. ⚠
(Tel Welshpool 2554). (NT)
Powysland Museum Opened in 1874, the
museum illustrates the social history of the
Powysland region through archaeological,
domestic, agricultural and craft material. It
contains many notable items such as Iron Age
shield, a model of a guillotine and a fine
collection of hatchments. Open all year,
Easter week, then Jun to Sep Mon to Fri
11 – 1, 2 – 5, Sat 2 – 4.30; other times as
summer opening but closed Wed. Free. P.
(Tel 3001) & *(please ring)*

WHITE CASTLE *Gwent* Map 3 SO41
An impressive 12th- to 13th-C Marcher
stronghold situated on a hill, with a gatehouse
and towers, erected by Hubert de Burgh.
Open, see inside front cover. 15p (ch 16 and
pen 7p). ⚠ The finest of the trio of 'trilateral'
castles in Gwent. See **Grosmont** and
Skenfrith Castles. *(AM)*

WOLVESNEWTON *Gwent* Map 3 ST49
**Wolvesnewton Folk Museum and Craft
Centre** 1½m off B4235 at Llangwm. Late 18th-
C cruciform barn housing a collection of
unusual and entertaining items used in
everyday life from the reign of Queen Victoria
onwards. Also agricultural implements, a
Victorian bedroom, Doulton pottery, a
medical section, Victorian lithographs and
photographs, children's toys and games.
Mementoes of two world wars. Craft
workshops, gift shop, antiques showroom, ⏣
(licensed). Entertainment evenings, one-day
craft courses, exhibitions, work sheets for
children. Open Easter to 30 Sep daily 11 – 6, 1
Oct to Easter Sun 2 – 5.30. 40p (ch 20p).
Under revision for 1980. Special
arrangements for parties. ⚠ &

WONASTOW *Gwent* Map 3 SO41
Tre-Owen Four-storeyed manor house
dating from mid 16th-C, now farm. Contains a
notable staircase. Open May to Aug, by
appointment only. 40p (ch 15 30p, open 20p).
⚠ Apply to the owner, *Mr R H Wheelock. (Tel
Dingestow 224)*

WREXHAM *Clwyd* Map 7 SJ35
The Doll and Toy Museum Ruabon Road.
Housed in detached residence, built in 1830,
is a large collection of Georgian, Victorian and
Edwardian dolls, miniature furniture including
beds and cradles. All in lovely settings.
Mechanical toys, rocking horses, money
boxes, birds' eggs, over 3,500 items. A
display of Victorian suits, dresses, furs, fans
and lace. Garden. Play and picnic area. Open
daily (ex Nov) 10.30 – 6. 35p (ch 25p). ⚠ *(Tel
52623)* &
Erddig 1m S. Late 17th-C house with 18th-C
additions and containing much of its original
furniture. Garden restored to its 18th-C formal
design. The range of domestic out-buildings
include laundry, bakehouse, sawmill and
smithy, all in working order. ⏣ Open 4 Apr to
26 Oct, Agricultural museum 5 Jul to 26 Oct.
Daily (ex Mon but open BH Mon). 12 – 5.30
(last admission to house 4.30, Oct 3.30).
£1.20 (ch 60p). Outbuildings and garden only
60p (ch 30p). Agricultural museum 50p (ch
25p). *(NT)*

SCOTLAND

P.K.Fry

Ancient Monuments
For monuments in the care of the Secretary of State for Scotland, opening times and entry fees are under review and changes may be made during the current year.

ABERDEEN Grampian *Aberdeenshire* Map 15 NJ90
Aberdeen Art Gallery and Museums
Schoolhill. Scottish art from 16th C to present day, with outstanding collection of 20th-C painting. Water-colours, print-room, and art library; contemporary sculpture and decorative arts; special exhibitions and events throughout the year. ☑ Open all year (ex 25, 26 Dec and 1, 2 Jan) Mon to Sat 10 – 5 (8 Thu) Sun 2 – 5. Free. P. *(Tel 53517)*. ら
Cruickshank Botanic Gardens University of Aberdeen. First developed at the end of the 19th C, the 7 acres of mature garden include rock and water gardens, a heather garden, collections of spring bulbs, gentians and alpine plants and, under glass, succulent plants. There are also extensive collections of trees and shrubs, of both horticultural and botanical interest. Open all year Mon to Fri 9 – 5; also Sat and Sun May to Sep 2 – 5. Free. *(Tel 40241 ext 340 or 348)* ら
James Dun's House 61 Schoolhill. 18th-C house used as a museum for children with a programme of changing exhibitions. Open all year (ex 25, 26 Dec and 1, 2 Jan) Mon to Sat 10 – 5. Free. P. *(Tel 22234)*
Provost Ross's House Shiprow. Due to open in 1980 as a maritime museum. Contact Aberdeen District Council for details.

Provost Skene's House Guestrow. A 17th-C house restored as a museum of local history and social life. Furnishings, panelling, and plaster ceilings of 17th and 18th C. Local bygones. ☑ Open all year (ex 25, 26 Dec and 1, 2 Jan) Mon to Sat 10 – 5. 10p (ch 12 and pen 2p). P. *(Tel 50086)*.

ABERDOUR Fife *Fife* Map 11 NT18
Aberdour Castle A 14th- to 17th-C stronghold, still partly roofed. Fine circular dovecote and gardens. Open Apr to Sep, weekdays 9.30 – 7, Sun 2 – 7; Oct to Mar, weekdays 9.30 – 4, Sun 2 – 4. 15p (ch 7p). ⚠ *(AM)*
Inchcolm Abbey Remains of an Augustinian Abbey, founded *c*1123 by Alexander I which are situated on a green island in the Firth of Forth, S of Aberdour. The monastic buildings thought to be the best preserved in Scotland, include a fine 13th-C octagonal Chapter House. In the original choir a fine example of a 13th-C wall painting was discovered, depicting a funeral procession of clerics. Open, see inside front cover. 15p (ch 7p). No boat service at present. *(Tel Dalgety Bay 823332) (AM)*

ABERLADY Lothian *East Lothian* Map 12 NT47
Myreton Motor Museum A collection of historic motor cars and motorcycles from 1896, cycles from 1863 and commercial vehicles. Many famous and obscure makes, latest addition is a rapidly expanding collection of historic British military vehicles. Largest motor museum in Scotland. Open Easter to Oct, daily 10 – 6; Oct to Easter, Sat and Sun 10 – 5. 50p (ch 16 10p) (subject to review). ⚠ *(Tel 288)* ら
See also under **Dunbar**.

ABERNETHY Tayside *Perthshire* Map 11 NO11
Abernethy Round Tower 11th- or 12th-C

Round Tower, 74ft high, one of only two examples on Scottish mainland, the other being at Brechin (Angus). Pictish symbol stone stands near by. Open, see inside front cover. Apply to Custodian. Free. *(AM)*

ALFORD Grampian *Aberdeenshire* Map 15 NJ51
Alford Valley Railway Narrow gauge passenger railway located in Haughton Park. 1½ miles of track through nature trails and historic battlefield. Diesel traction with possible addition of steam-hauled trains. Open 1 May to 9 Sep, Sat, Sun, BH and PH 1 – 7. 70p return fare (ch and pen 35p, ch 3 free) ⚠ *(Tel Cruden Bay 410 and Alford 2045)* ら

ALLOWAY Strathclyde *Ayrshire* Map 10 NS31
Burns Cottage Thatched cottage, built in 1757, now museum, birthplace in 1759 of Robert Burns. ☑ Open all year, Apr to mid Oct Mon to Sat 9 – 7, Sun, Mar, Apr, May, Sep, Oct 2 – 7, Jun, Jul and Aug 11 – 7. Closing time 7 or dusk if earlier. P. (100 yds) Also **Burns Monument**. Built in 1823 to a design by Thomas Hamilton Junior with fine examples of sculptures of characters in Burns' poems by a self-taught artist, James Thorn. Open as cottage. Admission to both properties 30p (ch and pen 15p). Admission prices under revision for 1980. P. *(Tel 41215 for cottage or 41321 for monument)*. ら

ANNAN Dumfries and Galloway *Dumfriesshire* Map 11 NY16
Kinmount Gardens Gardens and signed woodland walks of ½hr, 1 hr and 2hr duration. Rhododendrons and azaleas in May and Jun. Picnic area. Open 1 Apr to 1 Oct 9 – 5. 25p (ch 10, 10p). ⚠ *(Tel Cummertrees 207)*

ANSTRUTHER Fife *Fife* Map 12 NO50
The Scottish Fisheries Museum St Ayles. A 14th- to 18th-C group of buildings around a cobbled courtyard. Contains fishing boats and gear, fisherman's house *c*1900, a marine aquarium and a Lecture Hall for special displays. Awarded Architectural Heritage Year Award in 1975. ☑ Open Apr to Oct, Mon to Sat 10 – 12.30 and 2 – 6, Sun 2 – 5; Nov to Mar, daily (ex Tue) 2 – 5. 40p (ch and pen 20p). ⚠ *(Tel 310628)*

ARBROATH Tayside *Angus* Map 12 NO64
Arbroath Abbey Remains of a Tironensian Monastery founded in 1176 by William the Lion, King of Scotland. Considerable portions of the cruciform abbey remain, and the Abbot's house has been restored as a museum. Open, see inside front cover. 20p (ch 10p). *(AM)*
Art Gallery Hill Terrace. General art collection with emphasis on local artists. Also collection of pastels and watercolours by J W Herald. Occasional travelling exhibitions. Open all year (ex Public and Local Hols) Mon to Fri 9.30 – 6, Sat 9.30 – 5. Free. P. *(Tel 72248)*
Signal Tower Museum Ladyloan. Collection of local history and natural history. Open all year Mon to Sat 9.30 – 1 and 2 – 5. Free. ⚠ *(Tel 75598)*.

ARDCLACH Highland *Nairnshire* Map 14 NH94
Ardclach Bell Tower Two-storeyed 14ft-square tower, with upper floor containing fireplace and shot hole. Belfry on side gable built to house the bell formerly used as a warning, or for church services. Built probably in 17th C. Assessible on application to key keeper. Free. *(AM)*

ARDFERN Strathclyde *Argyll* Map 10 NM80
Argyll Wildlife Park Lunga Reserve.
Presented in a natural setting on a small hill
with an area of old Caledonian Oak woodland
and marshland. Visitors will find birds,
mammals, trees, plants etc, formerly or
currently native to Scotland. Education and
Conservation are primary objectives with
guided tours provided whenever possible.
Open Easter to Sep daily, 11–5. 80p (ch 40p).
Party

ARDWELL Dumfries and Galloway
Wigtownshire Map 10 NX14
Ardwell House Gardens Country house
gardens and grounds with flowering shrubs
and woodland walks. House not open to ·
public. Gardens open March to Oct 10–6.
Voluntary donations. ⚠

AUCHINDRAIN Strathclyde *Argyll*
Map 10 NN00
Open-Air Museum A folk life museum on
ancient Communal-tenancy farm. Original
18th and 19th-C buildings being restored and
furnished. Traditional crops and livestock,
also a display centre. Picnic area and craft
shop. ⚲ (Egon Roney listed). Open Easter to
30 Sep (other times by appointment), Mon to
Sat 10–6, Sun 2–6. 45p (ch 20p). Admission
prices under review for 1980. ⚠

AUCHINLECK Strathclyde *Ayrshire*
Map 11 NS52
*Auchinleck Boswell Museum and
Mausoleum* Church Hill off A76. The Boswell
Museum was the family seat of the Boswells
whose most famous member was James
Boswell 1740–1795. The Biographer of Dr
Johnson, author of the *'Tour of the Hebrides'*
etc. The old parish church, of which a portion
dates back to *c* 900AD, is where the family
worshipped and is now the museum
containing books, manuscripts, portraits,
china and etc of Boswelliana. Attached to the
north wall is the Mausoleum where five known
generations of Boswells are buried. 10th
Annual Boswell dinner 22 Aug. Open Aug and
Sep 10–12, 2–4, (evenings by appointment)
Sun 2–4. Free. ⚠ P (coaches). Curator at
131 Main Street. *(Tel Cumnock 20757)* ⚿ B

AUCHTERARDER Tayside *Perthshire*
Map 11 NN91
Strathallan Aircraft Collection The
collection includes various vintage aircraft
including, Hurricane, Harvard, Hudson, Tiger
Moth, Anson, Mosquito and Lancaster,
collected from all over the world. Air display
proposed 12/13 Jul. Open daily 10–5 (or
dusk during winter months). 80p (ch 30p).
Party. ⚠ *(Tel 2545)* ⚠

AULDEARN Highland *Nairnshire*
Map 14 NH95
Boath Doocot A circular 17th-C doocot, or
dovecot. The standard of Charles I was raised
here, in the battle of Auldearn in 1645. Doocot
itself closed. 10p. Battle plan on display
outside. *(NTS)*

AYR Strathclyde *Ayrshire* Map 10 NS32
Tam O'Shanter Museum This is considered
to be the point where Tam O'Shanter's
memorable ride commenced. The house now
contains relics belonging to Robert Burns.
Open Apr to Sep Mon to Sat 9.30–5.30; Oct
to Mar Mon to Sat 12–4, also Sun Jun, Jul and
Aug 2.30–5. 21p (ch 10p).

BALERNO Lothian *Midlothian* Map 11 NT16
Malleny Garden Off Bavelaw Road. A
delightfully personal garden, with shrub roses
and shaped yews. Open 1 May to 30 Sep daily
10–dusk. 30p (ch 15p). ⚠ ⚿ *(NTS)*

BALLATER Grampian *Aberdeenshire*
Map 15 NO39
McEwan Gallery 1m NW on A939. Built by
the Swiss artist Rudolf Christian in 1902. All
paintings in the main gallery are for sale.
Open all year, Mon to Sat 10–6, Sun 2.30–5.
Free. ⚠ *(Tel 429)* ⚠

P.R.F.

BALLOCH Strathclyde *Dunbartonshire*
Map 10 NS38
Balloch Castle Park Situated on the shore of
the loch, with large area of grassland, suitable
for picnics and surrounded by extensive
woodlands. Views of the Loch from the Castle
terrace (c1800). Walled garden. Nature trail.
Open all year daily. Park 8 to dusk; garden
10–9 (4.30 winter). Free.
Cameron Loch Lomond 1m NW. Drive in
your car amongst different species of bears,
bison, yak and deer which roam freely in the
acres of parkland. Other attractions include
the children's zoo, waterfowl sanctuary,
landscaped gardens, adventure playground,
children's assault course, giant slide, paddle
boats, canoes, trampolines etc. Lochside
picnic and play areas, ⚲ and shops. Also
Cameron House, home of the Smolletts of
Bonhill. Contains artifacts and documents
collected by the family for over 300 years,
including 'Whisky Galore' room, Staffordshire
pottery collection, fine porcelain, pictures,
furniture, armour, Oriental curios, nursery
with children's toys and books. Tobias
Smollett Museum. Open Easter to Sep, daily,
10.30–6. Entrance off unclass road on
lochside. £2.50 per car and occupants.
Cameron House extra. 50p (ch 25p).
Kennels. ⚠ *(Tel Alexandria 57211)*

BALMACARA Highland *Ross and Cromarty*
Map 14 NG82
Visitor Centre Situated in magnificent stretch
of West Highland mountainous scenery,
including Five Sisters of Kintail and Beinn
Fhada. Self-guided and guided walks from
Balmacara on the Kyle to Plockton Peninsula.
Ranger Naturalist Service. Woodland Garden
open all year, daily. Kiosk open 1 Jun to 30
Sep, Mon to Sat 10–1 and 2–6. Woodlands
20p (ch 10p). *(Tel 207). (NTS)*

BALMORAL Grampian *Aberdeenshire*
Map 15 NO29
Balmoral Castle Grounds The Highland
residence of Her Majesty the Queen.
Beautiful Deeside forest setting. In the
absence of the Royal Family, the grounds
only are open from 1 May to 31 Jul, daily (ex
Sun) 10–5. ♎ 35p (ch 10p). Donations to
charities from charges. P (400 yds). *(Tel
Crathie 334)* ♿ (cars for ♿ allowed to enter by
separate entrance)

BANCHORY Grampian *Kincardineshire*
Map 15 NO69
Banchory Museum Council Chamber.
Exhibition of local history and bygones. Open
Jun to end Sep daily (ex Thu) 2–5, Sat
10–12. *(Tel Peterhead 2554)* ♿

BANFF Grampian *Banffshire* Map 15 NJ66
Duff House ½m S, access from bypass south
of the town. Designed by William Adam for
William Duff (later Earl of Fife). The main
block was roofed in 1739, but proposed wings
were never built. Although incomplete it ranks
among the finest works of Georgian Baroque
architecture in Britain. An exhibition,
illustrating the history of the house can also be
seen. Open Apr to Sep. Mon to Sat 9.30–7,
Sun 2–7. 15p (ch 7p). *(AM)*
Banff Museum Exhibition of British birds set
out as an aviary. Local history also costumes
on show. Open Jun to end Sep, Wed, Fri, Sat,
Sun 2–5. Free. P. *(Tel Peterhead 2554)*

BANNOCKBURN Central *Stirlingshire*
Map 11 NS89
Bannockburn Monument This is the
Borestone Site, by tradition King Robert the
Bruce's command post before the battle
(1314). Bruce is commemorated by a bronze
equestrian statue. Rotunda and site always
open. Visitor centre and historical exposition
in sound and colour, open 4 Apr to 30 Sep,
Mon to Sat 10–6 (7, Jul and Aug); also Sun
Jul and Aug 11–7. Admission to exhibition
65p (ch 30p). ♎ 10p. *(Tel 2664). (NTS)*

BATHGATE Lothian *West Lothian*
Map 11 NS96
***Cairnpapple Hill Sanctuary and Burial
Cairn*** 2m N. Monumental temple, in the form
of a stone circle and ditch, of several dates in
the prehistoric period, notably the second
millenium BC. It was recently excavated and
laid out. Open Apr to Sep, weekdays 9.30–7.
Sun 2–7; closed 1½ days per week. 15p (ch
7p). *(AM)*

BEAULY Highland *Inverness-shire*
Map 14 NH54
Beauly Priory Founded in 1230, one of three
houses of the Valliscaulian Order founded in
Scotland. Only the church remains, a long
narrow building comprising aisleless nave,
transepts and chancel. This is the burial place
of the Mackenzies of Kintail and contains the
fine monument of Sir Kenneth Mackenzie.
Open, see inside front cover. Closed Sat and
Sun. 15p (ch 7p). *(AM)*

BENMORE Strathclyde *Argyll* Map 12 NS18
Benmore Younger Botanic Garden
Woodland and garden on a grand scale,
featuring conifers, rhododendrons, azaleas,
and many other shrubs. ♎ (teas). Open from
Apr to Oct, daily 10–6. 10p (ch and pen 5p).
♿ 5p. Under revision for 1980. *(Tel 036-
985 261)* ♿

BERRIEDALE Highland *Caithness*
Map 15 ND12
Langwell A residence of the Duchess of
Portland, which has fine gardens showing
plant growth in exposed areas. The gardens
only are shown 2–7. Dates for 1980 not
available. 20p (ch 12 and pen 10p). ♿ 20p. ♎
(Tel Barrock 275) ♿

BETTYHILL Highland *Caithness*
Map 14 NC76
Strathnaver Museum Fine stone-built, white
harled building, formerly a church, in an area
of outstanding beauty. It contains a
magnificent pitch pine canopied pulpit dated
1774, a fine collection of home-made
furnishings, domestic and farm implements
and Gaelic books. The churchyard contains a
carved stone known as the Farr Stone dating
back to the 10th-C. Open 1st week in Jun to
end Sep, Mon to Sat 2–5. 30p (ch 10p).
Provisional dates for 1980. P. ♿

BIGGAR Strathclyde *Lanarkshire*
Map 11 NT03
Gladstone Court Museum Entrance by 113
High Street. Interesting museum which
portrays an old-world village street, housed in
century-old coachworks with modern
extension. On display are reconstructed old
shops, complete with fascinating signs and
adverts, a bank, telephone exchange,
photographer's booth, etc. Archive material
on Thomas Blackwood Murray, founder of
Albion Motors. The museum owns an early
Albion Tipper Lorry and organises a
commemorative run for vintage and veteran
vehicles annually in mid Aug. Work has
started on an open-air development which will
include a Gas Works (1839) and other
industrial agricultural buildings. The 17th-C
Covenanter's Farmhouse of Greenhill is
currently being rebuilt at the open-air site.
Museum shop. Open Easter to 31 Oct, daily
(ex Sun morning and local holidays)
10–12.30, 2–5; other times by appointment.
40p (ch 20p, ch 8 free). P. *(Tel 20005)* ♿

BLAIR ATHOLL Tayside *Perthshire*
Map 14 NN86
Blair Castle Of 13th-C origin, altered in the
18th-C, and later given a castellated exterior.
There are Renaissance-style furnishings,
paintings, Jacobite relics, china, and arms
displayed in 32 rooms. It is the home of the
Duke of Atholl. ♎. Open Easter weekend,
each Sun and Mon in Apr, afterwards daily,
from first Sun in May to second Sun in Oct,
Mon to Sat 10–6, Sun 2–6; no admission
after 5.30pm. Prices under revision for 1980.
Party. ♿ *(Tel 355)* ♿

BLAIR DRUMMOND Central *Perthshire*
Map 11 NS79
Scotland's Safari Park Exit 10 off M9, A84
between Doune and Stirling. Features, free in
natural surroundings, wild animals, including
lions, giraffes, buffalo, ankole, eland, zebras,
camels, elephants, monkeys and
chimpanzees, Siberian tiger reserve. Also
pets corner, boat safari, aquatic mammal
show and Astra glide (extra charges).
Amusement and picnic areas. ♎ (Licensed).
Kennels at entrance. Open mid-Mar to end of

SCOTLAND

Oct, daily from 10am. Prices not available for 1980. ⚠ petrol station *(Tel Doune 456)* ⅋

BLANTYRE Strathclyde *Lanarkshire*
Map 11 NS65
The David Livingstone Centre with 'The Livingstone Memorial'. The birthplace of David Livingstone in 1813 containing personal relics, tableaux and working models. The 'Africa Pavilion' with exhibition describing life in modern Africa and 'Shuttle Row (Social History) Museum'. ⚏ (Apr to Sep). Picnic area. Gardens. Open all year Mon to Sat 10–6, Sun 2–6. 45p (ch and pen 25p). ⚠ *(Tel 823140)* ⅋ B

BOAT OF GARTEN Highland *Inverness-shire* Map 14 NH91
Strathspey Railway The Station. Steam railway covering the five miles from Boat of Garten to Aviemore, a twenty-minute journey. Trains can also be boarded at Aviemore where the station is under construction. Open 17 May to 28 Sep Sat and Sun, also Tue, Wed and Thu 1 Jul to 28 Aug. Family fares, party bookings. Basic return fare £1. ⚠ at Boat of Garten; P 600 yds at Aviemore. *(Tel 692)* ⅋

BO'NESS Central *West Lothian* Map 11 NS98
Kinneil House Situated in a public park, and preserving 16th- and 17th-C wall paintings. Open, see inside front cover. 15p (ch 7p). ⚠ *(AM)*
Kinneil Museum Situated in the 17th-C stable block of Kinneil House, part of a complex of renovated buildings. The ground floor houses regularly changing temporary exhibitions, while the main display on the first floor illustrates the industrial heritage of Bo'ness. Lecture room for educational purposes. Open all year May to Oct, Mon to Sat 10–12 and 1–5. Nov to Apr, Mon, Wed and Fri 10–12 and 1–5. Sat 1–5. Free. ⅋ B

BOTHWELL Strathclyde *Lanarkshire*
Map 11 NS75
Bothwell Castle An impressive, ruined 13th- to 15th-C stronghold. Open Oct to Mar (ex Thu pm and all day Fri); Apr to Sep open all week. Entrance to castle is at Uddington Cross by traffic lights. 15p (ch 7p). ⚠ *(AM)*

BRAEMAR Grampian *Aberdeenshire*
Map 15 NO19
Braemar Castle A picturesque castle, built in 1628; purchased by the Farquharson of Invercauld in 1731. Largely rebuilt in 1748, spiral stone staircase leading to the principle rooms. Situated near the River Dee. *Son et Lumière* late Aug/early Sep. Open May to early Oct, daily 10–6. 60p (ch 13 25p). Provisional for 1980. ⚠ *(Tel 219)*. *(Capt AAC Farquharson of Invercauld)*

BRODIE CASTLE Grampian *Morayshire*
Map 14 NH95
6m E of Nairn, off A96. Largely rebuilt after being burned down in 1645 and with additions of the 18th and 19th centuries. Contents include fine furniture, porcelain and paintings. Opening Jun (provisional date) to 30 Sep, Mon to Sat 11–6, Sun 2–6. 85p (ch 40p). *(To check details Tel Udny 352)*. *(NTS)*

BROUGHTON Borders *Peeblesshire*
Map 11 NT13
Broughton Place Built on the site of a much older house and designed by Sir Basil Spence in 1938, the house is in the style of a 17th-C Scottish tower house. The drawing room and main hall are open to the public and contain paintings by living British artists for sale. The gardens, which are occasionally

open under Scotland's Gardens Scheme, afford fine views of the Tweeddale hills. Open, Easter to end Sep daily (ex Wed) 10.30–6. Free. ⚠ *(Tel 234)* ⅋ B

BRUAR Tayside *Perthshire* Map 14 NN86
Clan Donnachaidh (Robertson) Museum
A newly founded small museum for items of historical interest, documents, books and pictures associated with the Clan Donnachaidh, one of whose early chiefs fought for King Robert the Bruce. There is an interesting craft room. Open Easter to 15 Oct, Mon to Sat 10–5.30, Sun 2–5.30. At other times by arrangement with the curator. Clan gathering 3rd Sat in Jan. Clan items for sale. ⚠ *(Tel Clavine 264, or Curator's residence Clavine 222)* ⅋

BUCKIE Grampian *Banffshire* Map 15 NJ46
Buckie Museum and Peter Anson Gallery
Maritime museum opened in 1973 containing exhibits relating to the fishing industry in the Moray Firth area from mid 19th C to the present day. Mr Peter Anson donated his collection of 400 pictures of fishing vessels, from the earliest times to modern dual purpose craft, to the museum. Open May to Sep, Mon 2–5, Tue to Sat 10–12.30, 2–5. Free. ⚠ *(Tel 31150)* ⅋

BURGHEAD Grampian *Moray* Map 15 NJ16
Burghead Museum 16–18 Grant Street. Illustrates the archaeology of the Laich of Mory from 2500 BC–1300 AD. Open Tues 5.30pm–8.30pm, Thu 2–5, Sat 9.30–12.30. Free. ⚠ *(Tel Forres 73701)*

CAERLAVEROCK Dumfries and Galloway *Dumfriesshire* Map 11 NY06
Caerlaverock Castle A famous medieval stronghold, besieged by Edward I in 1300. Mainly 14th to 15th-C, with a Renaissance wing of 1638. Open, see inside front cover. 25p (ch 12p). ⚠ *(AM)*
Wildfowl Trust Outstanding hide facilities, observation towers, and observatory, providing impressive views of the magnificent flocks of barnacle, and pink-footed geese, and the large number of wigeon, pintail, etc, that spend most of the winter in the refuge. Open 1 Sep to 15 May (ex 24, 25 Dec). Guided tours 11 and 2 daily. 65p (ch 35p, pen 55p). ⚠ Party 20+ *(Tel Glencaple 200)*

CAIRNDOW Strathclyde *Argyll* Map 10 NN11
Strone House Gardens featuring rhododendrons, azaleas, conifers and daffodils. The tallest tree in Britain, measuring 190ft, is located within the gardens. Picnic area. Open 1 Apr to 30 Sep, 9–9. 30p (ch and pen free). ⚠ 20p *(Tel 284)* *(Rt Hon the Lord Glenkinglas PC)*.

CALLANDER Central *Perthshire*
Map 11 NN60
Kilmahog Woollen Mill At one time thriving woollen mill, famous throughout the district for hand-woven blankets and tweed. Part of the old structure can be seen, also an old water wheel which has been preserved and is still in working order. Woollens can be purchased in the store. Open all year Mon to Fri 9–8, Sat and Sun 9–6. ⚠ *(Tel 30268)* ⅋

CARDONESS CASTLE Dumfries and Galloway *Kirkcudbrightshire* Map 11 NX55
A late 15th-C stronghold, overlooking Fleet Bay, once home of the McCullochs of Galloway. Notable fireplaces. Open from Apr to Sep, weekdays 9.30–7 (Sun 2–7); from Oct to Mar 9.30–4 (Sun 2–4). 20p (ch 10p). ⚠ *(AM)*

CARNASSERIE CASTLE Strathclyde *Argyll*
Map 10 NM80
Built in the late 16th C by John Carswell, first
Protestant Bishop of the Isles, who translated
into Gaelic and published Knox's *Liturgy* in
1567. It was taken and partly destroyed in
Argyll's rebellion of 1685, and consists of a
towerhouse, with a courtyard built on to it.
Open, see inside front cover. Free. *(AM)*

CARRADALE Strathclyde *Argyll*
Map 10 NR83
Carradale House Off B879. Overlooks the
lovely Kilbrennen Sound. Beautiful gardens,
with flowering shrubs, mainly rhododendrons,
best visited Apr to Jun. Plants, vegetables
and shrubs for sale. Open from Apr to end of
Sep. 20p (ch 12 free). ⚠ *(Tel 234)* &

CARRBRIDGE Highland *Inverness-shire*
Map 14 NH92
Landmark Europe's first 'visitor' centre, with
an exhibition on the history of Strathspey, a
multi-screen programme in the auditorium
showing in sound and vision the story of The
Highlands from the last Ice Age to the present
day, and evening film shows. Also craft and
bookshop, ⚐, nature trail, with picnic area,
open-air sculpture park. Open summer
9.30–10.30, winter 9.30–5. Admission to
Exhibition and Auditorium 60p (ch 30p). ⚠ &

CARSLUITH CASTLE Dumfries and
Galloway *Kirkcudbrightshire* Map 11 NX45
A roofless 16th-C tower house on Wigtown
Bay. A previous owner was the last abbot of
Sweetheart Abbey. Entry free on application
to Custodian. Open, see inside front cover.
(AM)

CASTLE DOUGLAS Dumfries and Galloway
Kirkcudbrightshire Map 11 NX76
Threave Castle Follow A75 SW to Bridge of
Dee (3m) then take unclass rd to N. Standing
on an islet in the River Dee, this lonely castle,
erected by Archibald the Grim in the 14th C, is
four storeys in height, with round towers
guarding the outer wall. It was dismantled by
the Covenanters in 1640. Open Apr to Sep,
weekdays 9.30–7, Sun 2–7 Oct to Mar
weekdays 9.30–4, Sun 2–4. 20p (incl ferry)
(ch 10p). Access to castle is by rowing boat.
(AM)
Threave Gardens 1½m SW. Fine gardens
noted for daffodils in Apr and May, and
rhododendrons in May and Jun. Walled
garden and glasshouses. Open all year, daily
9–sunset, walled garden and glasshouses
9–5. (The house is NTS School of
Gardening). Visitor centre open 1 Apr to 31
Oct. 75p (ch 35p). *(Tel 2575). (NTS)*

CASTLES GIRNIGOE AND SINCLAIR
Highland *Caithness* Map 15 ND35
Two adjacent ruined castles of the Sinclairs,
in a striking rock setting at Noss Head.
Girnigoe is 15th-C and Sinclair dates from the
early 16th-C. After *c*1697 both castles were
abandoned. They can be seen at any time.
Free.

CASTLE KENNEDY Dumfries and Galloway
Wigtownshire Map 10 NX15
Castle Kennedy Gardens Situated 3m E of
Stranraer on A75. 17th-C and later gardens,
with a fine collection of rhododendrons,
azaleas, magnolias and other shrubs.
Situated on peninsula between two lochs, the
gardens offer a choice of walks. ⚐. Open 1
Apr to 26 Sep, daily (ex Sat) 10–5. 50p (ch 16
20p). Garden centre adjoining gardens. ⚠
(Tel Stranraer 2024) &

CAUSEWAYHEAD Central *Stirlingshire*
Map 11 NS89
Wallace Monument 220ft-high tower erected
in 1869, in which Sir William Wallace's
famous two-handed sword is preserved. No
fewer than seven battlefields are visible from
the summit of the monument, in addition to a
wide panoramic view towards the Highlands.
There is a Hall of Heroes. Audio-visual
system on life of Wm Wallace. ⚐ & souvenirs.
Open all year Nov to Jan 10–4, Oct and Feb
10–5, Sep and Mar 10–6, Apr and Aug 10–7,
May to Jul 10–8. 15p (ch and pen 10p). Under
revision for 1980. Party. P at foot of Abbey
Craig. *(Tel Stirling 2140)*

CAWDOR Highland *Nairnshire* Map 14 NH84
Cawdor Castle Home of the Thanes of
Cawdor since the early 14th C. Home of the
present Earl of Cawdor, with its drawbridge,
its ancient tower built around a tree, and its
freshwater well inside the house, is a glorious
reminder of Scotland's colourful and often
bloody history. Nature trails, pitch and putt. ⚐
(licensed). Open 1 May to 30 Sep daily
10–5.30 (last admission 5 pm). Provisional
prices for 1980, £1.25 (ch 16 and pen 65p)
subject to alteration. Party 20+ £1 (ch 50p). ⚠
(Tel 615) &

CLACKMANNAN Central
Clackmannanshire Map 11 NS99
Clackmannan Tower A fine 14th- and 15th-C
tower house, battlemented and turreted, and
at one time moated. Now under repair and not
open, but can be closely viewed from outside.
(AM)

CLAVA CAIRNS Highland *Inverness-shire*
Map 14 NH74
Situated on the south bank of the River Nairn,
this group of burial cairns has three concentric
rings of great stones. They are of late neolithic
or early Bronze Age. Open regularly. Free.

COLDSTREAM Borders *Berwickshire*
Map 12 NT84
Dundock Wood 1½m W on A697. Magnificent
display of rhododendrons and azaleas (mid
May to end of Jun depending on season). It is
also a large bird sanctuary. The wood and
grounds are open at all times. Estate
interpretation centre in Hirsel House grounds.
Nature walks. Admission by collecting box. ⚠
(Tel 2345 and 2439) &

COLPY Grampian *Aberdeenshire*
Map 15 NJ63
Williamston House Attractive gardens, with
a lochan. Ancient St Michael's Well nearby.
Gardens open Jun to Sep, 10–7 daily. 20p
(ch 5p) by collection box at garden entrance.
Garden produce and plants for sale. Teas
available by prior arrangement. ⚠ *(Tel Colpy
227). (Cdr M S L Burnett)*

COMRIE Tayside *Perthshire* Map 11 NN72
Museum of Scottish Tartans Occupies an
18th-C building situated in the centre of town
on the A85. The collection is the most
comprehensive in the world of books,
pictures, prints, maps and manuscripts
relating to the history and development of
Tartans and Highland Dress. Specialised
library, and research collection of over 1,300
specimens of Tartans, and a unique system
(Sindex) which records details of every known
tartan. Open all year, summer Mon to Sat
10–1, 2–5, Sun 2–5; winter weekdays
10.30–12.30, 2–4 (closed Sun). 35p (ch and
pen 20p). Party. Under revision for 1980. P.
(Tel 779) &

CORGARFF Grampian *Aberdeenshire*
Map 15 NJ20
Corgarff Castle 16th-C tower, which was besieged in 1571, and is associated with the Jacobite Risings of 1715 and 1745. Later it became a military barracks. Open Apr to Sep, weekdays 9.30–7, Sun 2–7. 15p (ch 7p). ⚠ *(AM)*

CORSOCK Dumfries and Galloway *Kirkcudbrightshire* Map 11 NX77
Corsock House Gardens Specialising in a fine show of species rhododendrons, woodland walks, and a water garden. Also classical temples and bridge. View of the valley of the River Urr. Open 2.30–5.30, each Sun in May; other times by appointment. May to Sep. 30p. ⚠ *(small). (Mr F L Ingall)*

CRAIGIEVAR Grampian *Aberdeenshire*
Map 15 NJ50
Craigievar Castle Unaltered tower house, built 1610 to 1626, with a notable Renaissance ceiling. Perhaps the most characteristic example of the true Scottish Baronial period. It enjoys a lovely setting between the valleys of the Dee and the Don. Castle open 1 May to 30 Sep, 2–7 daily (ex Fri), last visitors 6.15. Grounds open all year, 9.30–sunset. Castle 80p (ch 40p), school parties 35p; grounds by donation. *(Tel Lumphanan 635). (NTS)*

CRATHES Grampian *Kincardineshire*
Map 15 NO79
Crathes Castle and Gardens A picturesque 16th-C structure noted for its magnificent painted ceilings and famous gardens. Castle open May to Sep, Mon to Sat 11–6, Sun 2–6; (last admission 5.15). Gardens and grounds open daily all the year from 9.30 to dusk. Castle only, 75p (ch 35p); gardens only 40p (ch 20p); grounds and cars 60p, minibuses £1.50, coaches £5, May to Sep only. *(Tel 525). (NTS)*

CREETOWN Dumfries and Galloway *Kirkcudbrightshire* Map 11 NX45
Creetown Gem Rock Museum and Art Gallery Largest private collection in Great Britain with many of the exhibits collected by the proprietors on their world travels. Also extensive collection of walking sticks and drinking mugs. Lapidary workshops open to view. Craft shop and lapidary requirements for sale. Open daily 9.30–6. 20p (ch 7 free, ch 7–16 5p). ⚠ *(Tel Creetown 357)* ♿

CRICHTON Lothian *Midlothian* Map 11 NT36
Crichton Castle A 14th- to 16th-C castle, notable for the Earl of Bothwell's Italianate wing. Open weekdays (ex Fri from Oct to May), summer 9.30–7; winter 9.30–4; Sun, summer 2–7; winter 2–4. 15p (ch 7p). *(AM)*

CRIEFF Tayside *Perthshire* Map 11 NN82
Innerpeffray Library 4½m SE of B8062. A late 18th-C building, housing Scotland's second oldest library founded in 1691 (the oldest library founded in 1683 is at Kirkwall, Orkney). Accessible all year weekdays (ex Thu) 10–1 and 2–5 (4, Nov to Feb), Sun all year 2–4. 30p (ch 10p). ⚠ *(Tel 2819)*

CROMARTY Highland *Ross and Cromarty*
Map 14 NH76
Hugh Miller's Cottage House *c*1711 birthplace in 1802 of Hugh Miller, the geologist. Open 1 May to 30 Sep, Mon to Sat 10–12 and 1–5; Jun to Sep also Sun 2–5. 40p (ch 20p). *(Tel 245). (NTS)*

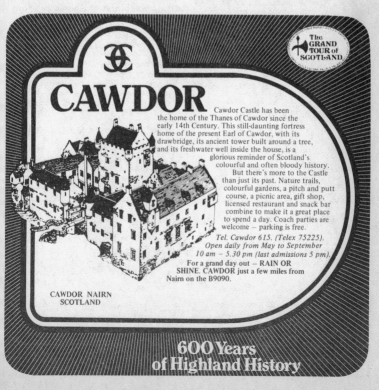

CULLODEN MOOR Highland *Inverness-shire* Map 14 NH74
Culloden Battlefield The Cairn, built in 1881, recalls the famous battle of 1746, when 'Bonnie' Prince Charles Edward Stuart's army was routed by the Duke of Cumberland's forces. Near the Graves of the Clans is the Well of the Dead, and also the Cumberland Stone. The battle fought around Old Leanach Farmhouse, now a museum. Site always open. There is also a Trust Visitor Centre and exhibition open 4 Apr to mid Oct Mon to Sat 9.30–6.30, Sun 2–6.30, except Jun to end Aug Mon to Sat 9.30–9.30, Sun 2–6.30. Admission to Visitor Centre and museum (includes audio-visual exhibition in centre and parking). 65p (ch 30p). Party 20+ 45p (ch 15p). ⚠ *(Tel 607)*. *(NTS)*

CULROSS Fife *Fife* Map 11 NS98
Abbey Cistercian monastery founded by Malcolm, Earl of Fife in 1217. The choir is still used as the parish church and parts of the nave remain. Fine central tower, still complete, bears the arms of abbot Masoun (1498–1513). Open, see inside front cover. Free. *(AM)*
Culross Palace Dated 1597 and 1611, and noted for the painted rooms and walled gardens. Open, see inside front cover. 25p (ch 12p). *(AM)*
Dunimarle Castle Part of this castle is now a museum, with valuable paintings, silver, books, and rare items of furniture, once belonging to Napoleon. Open 1 Apr to 31 Oct, daily 11–6. 40p (ch 14 20p). ⚠ *(Tel Newmills 229)* ⅙ B

CULZEAN CASTLE Strathclyde *Ayrshire* Map 10 NS21
18th-C castle, in a fine Firth of Clyde setting of 500 acres. The castle was designed by Robert Adam and contains fine plaster ceilings, a splendid central staircase, and a circular drawing room. There is a collection of portraits of the Kennedys, Earls of Cassillis, and Marquesses of Ailsa. Guest flat presented to the late General Eisenhower. Open 1 Apr to 30 Sep, daily 10–6 (last admission 5.30). Oct daily 10–4. £1 (ch 50p), party 75p per person, schools 50p per person. Jul and Aug £1.20 (ch 60p). No party reduction. *(Tel Kirkoswald 236)*. *(NTS)*

CULZEAN COUNTRY PARK Strathclyde *Ayrshire* Map 10 NS21
565 acres including 1783 walled garden, camellia house, orangery, swan pond, aviary. The home farm buildings by Robert Adam have been converted into a Reception and Interpretation Centre. Park open all year. Centre 1 Apr to end Sep daily 10–6; Oct daily 10–4. Admission charges not yet decided. *(NTS)*

CUPAR Fife *Fife* Map 11 NO31
Hill of Tarvit Mansion House and Garden 2m S off A916. A mansion house remodelled in 1906 by Sir Robert Lorimer, with a notable collection of furniture, tapestries and paintings. Open 4 to 7 Apr, then 1 May to 30 Sep daily (ex Fri) 2–6, last admission 5.30. Gardens and grounds (ex arable land) open all year 10–dusk. House and gardens 85p (ch 40p); gardens only 30p (ch 15p). *(Tel 3127)*. *(NTS)*

DOLLAR Central *Clackmannanshire* Map 11 NS99
Castle Campbell and Dollar Glen 1m N. 15th-C tower with 16th- and 17th-C additions, in a picturesque Ochil Hills setting above the Dollar Glen, providing splendid views. Open, see inside front cover. 20p (ch 10p). ⚠ *(Castle AM and Glen NTS)*

DORNIE Highland *Ross and Cromarty* Map 14 NG82
Eilean Donan Castle Stands at the meeting-point of Lochs Duich, Alsh, and Long. Connected to the mainland by a causeway. This Seaforth fortress, erected originally in 1220, was destroyed in 1719, after being held by Jacobite troops, and was restored in 1912. Beautiful mountain setting. Open Easter to end Sep, daily 10–6. 30p. P. *(Tel 202)*. *(Mr J D H MacRae)*

DOUNE Central *Perthshire* Map 11 NN70
Doune Castle 14th-C stronghold, well restored, with two fine towers and associations with Bonnie Prince Charlie and Scott's *Waverley*. It stands on the banks of the River Teith. Open 1 Apr to 31 Oct, daily 10–6 (ex Thu in Apr and Oct). 40p (ch 20p). Under revision for 1980. ⚠ 5p. *(Tel 203)*. *(Earl of Moray)*
Doune Motor Museum Situated 9m NW of Sterling on A84. Approximately 35 cars on display. Motor Racing Hill Climbs held in Apr, Jun and Sep. Picnic area, tourist shop and garden centre. Open 1 Apr to 31 Oct, daily. Admission prices not available. ⚠ Telephone for information. *(Tel 203)* ⅙

DRUMCOLTRAN TOWER Dumfries and Galloway *Kirkcudbrightshire* Map 11 NX86
A 16th-C tower house, three-storeys in height and built to an oblong plan, with a projecting tower or wing. Standard hours, apply to key keeper. Free. *(AM)*

DRUMNADROCHIT Highland *Inverness-shire* Map 14 NH53
Urquhart Castle Historic, mainly 14th-C castle overlooking Loch Ness, destroyed before the 1715 Rising and possibly built originally by the Lords of the Isles. Open, see inside front cover. 25p (ch 12p). *(AM)*

DRYBURGH Borders *Berwickshire*
Map 12 NT53
Dryburgh Abbey One of the famous Border
group of monasteries founded by David I. The
ruins are of great beauty and occupy a lovely
situation in a horseshoe bend of the River
Tweed. Within the church are the graves of Sir
Walter Scott and Earl Haig. Open, see inside
front cover. 25p (ch 12p). ⚥ *(AM)*

DUFFTOWN Grampian *Banffshire*
Map 15 NJ33
Balvenie Castle Mainly 15th- and 16th-C, the
ancient home of the Comyns, preserving a
remarkable iron 'yett'. Open, see inside front
cover. 15p (ch 7p). ⚥ *(AM)*
Dufftown Museum The Tower. Small local
history museum. Civic regalia. Mortlach Kirk
material. Open Jun to Sep daily 10–5 (7 Jul
and Aug). Free. ⚥
Glenfiddich Distillery N of town, off A941.
Situated by the 'Robbie Dubh' or 'Black
Robert' stream, this distillery was founded in
1886 by Major William Grant in the heart of the
Speyside country. A visitor's Reception
Centre houses a bar and a Scotch whisky
museum. Gift shop. Open 8 Jan to 23 Dec.
Trained guides give tours Mon to Fri 9–5.
Free. ⚥ *(Tel 375)*

DUFFUS Grampian *Moray* Map 15 NJ16
Duffus Castle Off B9012. Motte and bailey
castle, with 8-acre bailey surrounding rebuilt
15th-C hall and 14th-C tower, now split into
two halves. Open all reasonable times. Free.
⚥ *(AM)*

DUMBARTON Strathclyde *Dunbartonshire*
Map 10 NS37
Dumbarton Castle Atop 240ft high rock, with
ancient gateway preserved. Associations
with Mary, Queen of Scots. Open, see inside
front cover. 20p (ch 10p). *(AM)*

DUMFRIES Dumfries and Galloway
Dumfriesshire Map 11 NX97
Burns House Robert Burns died in this house
in 1796. In the house are displayed memorials
and personal relics of the poet. Open all year,
29 Mar to 30 Sep Mon to Sat 10–1, Sun 2–7,
1 Oct to 28 Mar Mon to Sat 10–12 and 2–5.
10p (ch 5p). P. *(Tel 5297)*
Burns Mausoleum St Michael's Churchyard.
Situated here is the tomb of the poet, the
mausoleum being in the form of a Grecian
temple. Here also are buried Jean Armour,
Burns' wife, and their five sons. A sculptured
group depicts the Muse of Poetry throwing her
cloak over Burns at the plough. Opens as
Burns House by arrangement with Curator. P.
(Tel 5297)

Dumfries Museum and Camera Obscura
The Observatory, Church Street. Large
collection of local history, archaeology,
geology, local birds and animals. The Old
Bridge House branch museum (on the Old
Bridge) contains period rooms portraying the
local way of life in the past. Open all year (Old
Bridge House 1 Apr to 30 Sep only) Mon to
Sat 10–1, 2–5 (ex Tue), Sun 2–5 Apr to Sep
only. Museum and Old Bridge House free.
Camera Obscura. 15p (ch 5p). P. *(Tel 3374)*
Lincluden College Originally the site of a
Benedictine nunnery, founded by Uchtred,
Lord of Galloway in 1164. This was
suppressed at the end of the 14th C by
Archibald the Grim, 3rd Earl of Douglas, who
established in its place a college of eight
secular canons under a provost. The present
remains are that of the collegiate church,
dating from the early 15th C and the provost's
house, dating from the 16th C. Open, see
inside front cover. 15p (ch 7p). *(AM)*

DUNBAR Lothian *East Lothian* Map 12 NT67
Myreton Motor Museum Castle Park. A
branch of the museum founded at Aberlady. A
collection of historic motor cars from 1896,
motorcycles from 1903, cycles from 1863 and
commercial vehicles. Many famous and
obscure makes. Tractors, farm machinery
and horse-drawn vehicles. Open Easter to
Oct, daily 10–6. 40p (ch 14 10p), subject to
alteration. ⚥ *(municipal)*. *(Tel 62365)* ⚥

DUNBEATH Highland *Caithness*
Map 15 ND12
Laidhay Croft Museum Late 18th- to early
19th-C Caithness-type longhouse with
dwelling, byre and stable under one roof and
detached winnowing barn. All thatched and
furnished in typical croft style. Open Easter to
30 Sep daily 9–6. 30p (ch 14 and pen 15p). ⚥
⚥

DUNBLANE Central *Perthshire*
Map 11 NN70
Keir 2m S off B824. Beautiful gardens
featuring rhododendrons, shrubs,
herbaceous borders, and water gardens,
which will be open 3 Apr to end of Oct, Tue,
Wed, Thu 2–6. 40p. ⚥ *(Tel 822200)*. *(Mrs W
J Stirling of Keir)* ⚥

DUNDEE Tayside *Angus* Map 11 NO43
Barrack Street Museum Ward Road.
Shipping and industrial exhibits relating
especially to local ships built at or associated
with Dundee. There are also art and
photographic exhibitions. Open from Mon to
Sat 10–5.30; closed Sun. P. *(Tel 25492 & 3
ext 17 or 27866 for educational services)*

Broughty Castle and Museum Broughty Ferry. 4m E. 15th-C castle rebuilt as an estuary fort in the mid 19th C. Displays relating to former Burgh of Broughty Ferry, whaling, natural history of the Tay, arms and armour, also Ecology Gallery. Open all year, Mon to Sat (ex Fri) 10 – 1 and 2 – 5.30; Sun (Jun to Sep only) 2 – 5. Free. ⚠

Museum and Art Gallery Albert Square. Covers in depth local archaeology, history, natural history, and geology. There is a display devoted to the works of Mary Slessor, the missionary. The Art Gallery portrays the principal British and European masters. Open from Mon to Sat 10 – 5.30; closed Sun. Free. P. ⚅

Claypotts Broughty Ferry. 4m E. Claverhouse of Dundee's castle, of unusual appearance, built between 1569 and 1588, showing angle towers with crowstepped gables. Open, see inside front cover (ex to Apr 1980). 15p (ch 7p). *(AM)*

Mills Observatory Situated in Balgay Park the observatory, erected in 1935, is equipped with a 10in Cooke refracting telescope, and two 4in Terrestrial telescopes. Open Apr to end of Sep, Mon to Fri 2 – 7, Sat 2 – 5; Oct to Mar, Mon to Fri 2 – 10, Sat 2 – 5. Closed Sun and public hols. 5p (ch 2p). Family Party 8p. ⚠ ⚅ B

Orchar Art Gallery Beach Cresent, Broughty Ferry. 4m E. The gallery displays oil-paintings and water-colours mostly by Scottish artists of the 19th C. Among the etchings are 36 by Whistler. Open Mon to Sat (ex Fri) 10 – 1 and 2 – 5; Sun Jun to Sep only 2 – 5. Free. ⚠ *(Tel 77337)*

St Mary's Tower Kirk Style, Nethergait. A 15th-C bell tower or steeple containing a magnificent peal of bells also displays relevant to the Tower. Open Easter to Oct, daily (ex Fri) 1 – 5, Sun 2 – 5. 5p (ch 2p). Family Party 8p. P. *(Tel 25492/3 ext 16)*

Spalding Golf Museum Camperdown Park. The museum in Camperdown House portrays the history of golf through three centuries and includes an iron club of c1680. ⚌ available at Camberdown House. Open Mon to Thu and Sat 1 – 5 (closed Fri), also Sun Easter to Oct 2 – 5. Free. ⚠ ⚅

DUNDONNELL Highland *Ross and Cromarty* Map 14 NH18
Dundonnell House 2m SE. An 18th-C house, noted for its fine gardens, featuring Chinese, Japanese, and other rare plants and shrubs. Collection of exotic birds. Teas available on open days. Times and dates published by Scotland's Garden scheme and in the press. ⚠ *(Tel 206)*. *(Messrs Alan, Neil and Alastair Roger)*

DUNDRENNAN Dumfries and Galloway *Kirkcudbrightshire* Map 11 NX74
Dundrennan Abbey The remains of a Cistercian house founded by David I and Fergus Lord of Galloway in 1142. Here Mary Queen of Scots spent her last night on native soil before seeking shelter in England. Open, see inside front cover. 20p (ch 10p). *(AM)*

DUNFERMLINE Fife *Fife* Map 11 NT08
Andrew Carnegie Birthplace Junction of Moodie Street and Priory Lane. The cottage in which the great philanthropist was born in 1835. Personal relics, presentation caskets. Roll of Honour of Carnegie Hero Fund Trust displayed in a memorial Hall. Open May to Aug, Mon to Sat 11 – 1 and 2 – 7, Sun 2 – 6; Sep to Apr Mon to Sat 11 – 1 and 2 – 5, Sun 2 – 6. Street P. *(Tel 24302 or 23638)* ⚅

Dunfermline Abbey Benedictine house founded by Queen Margaret and the foundations of her church remain beneath the present Norman nave. The site of the choir is now occupied by a modern parish church, at the east end of which are remains of St Margaret's shrine dating from the 13th C. King Robert Bruce is buried in the choir and his grave is marked by a modern brass. Guest house was a Royal palace where Charles I was born. Situated in Pittencrieff Park. Open, see inside front cover. Free. *(AM)*

Dunfermline Museum Viewfield Terrace. Interesting and varied displays of local history, domestic bygones and damask linen. Periodic special exhibitions. Open 1 Apr to 30 Sep Mon to Sat (ex Tue) 11 – 5, Sun 1 – 5; Oct to 31 Mar Wed to Sat 11 – 5, Sun 1 – 5. Free. ⚠ *(Tel 21814)*

Pittencrieff House Museum Situated in a rugged glen, with lawns, hothouses, and gardens, overlooked by the ruined 11th-C Malcolm Canmore's tower. Fine 17th-C mansion house, with costume and art galleries. Views of Forth estuary and Dunfermline Abbey. Open May to Sep Mon to Sat (ex Tue) 11 – 5; Sun 1 – 5. ⚠ *(Tel 21814)*

DUNKELD Tayside *Perthshire* Map 11 NO04
Loch of Lowes Wild Life Reserve Variety of wild life. Great crested grebes and other waterfowl in natural surroundings can be watched through high powered binoculars from observation hide. Exhibition and slide programme in visitor centre. Open Apr to Sep daily 10 – 7 Apr, May and Sep; 10 – 8.30 Jun to Aug. Hide open all times. Free. Special arrangements for parties booked in advance. ⚠ limited. *(Tel 337, Apr to Sep, or Ballinluig 267 Oct to Mar)*

Trust Visitor Centre 'Little Houses' dating from the rebuilding of village after the Battle of Dunkeld in 1689. Restoration undertaken by NTS and Perth County Council who received a Saltire Society award in 1958. Visitor Centre open 4 Apr to 30 Sep 10 – 6, Sun 2 – 6. Free. *(Tel 460)*. *(NTS)*

DUNS Borders *Berwickshire* Map 12 NT75
Jim Clark Room This room in Newtown Street contains motor racing trophies won by the famous driver Jim Clark, who was killed in Germany in 1968. Included are the two world Championship trophies of 1963 and 1965 and other Grand Prix awards. Clark was the only Honorary Burgess of Duns and his parents gifted the trophies to the town. Open Apr to Sep Mon to Sat 10 – 1, 2 – 6, Sun 2 – 6. 30p (ch 16 15p). Parties during winter by special arrangement. Jim Clark Memorial Rally Jul. Under revision for 1980. P.
Manderston 1½m E off A6105. A fine Edwardian house with magnificent State Rooms and extensive domestic offices, all completed in 1905, emphasising a high standard of workmanship. Stables, marble dairy, gardens, woodland garden and lakeside walks. ⚌ Open 18 May to 18 Sep, Sun and Thu 2 – 5.30, also Scottish and English BHs. Charges not available. ⚠ *(Tel 3450)* ⚅

EASDALE Strathclyde *Argyll* Map 10 NM71
An Cala Garden Featuring cherry trees, azaleas, roses, water and rock gardens. Tea available in village. Open mid Apr to mid Sep Mon and Thu 2 – 6. 20p (ch 5p). Dogs admitted if on lead. ⚠ *(Mrs H I Blakeney)* ⚅ main garden.

EAST FORTUNE Lothian *East Lothian* Map 12 NT57

Museum of Flight East Fortune Airfield. (A Royal Scottish Museum Outstation). The airship base from which the R34 set out in July 1919 to make the first double crossing of the Atlantic, now displays the history of aircraft and rockets. Working exhibits which visitors may operate. Exhibits include Supermarine *Spitfire* Mk 16, De Havilland *Sea Vampire*, and Hawker *Sea Hawk*. Open Jul and Aug daily 10–4, also open days yet to be decided. Free. ⚠ *(Tel 031-225 7534)* ⚠ ⅏

EAST LINTON Lothian *East Lothian*
Map 12 NT57
Hailes Castle 1m SW on unclass rd. An old castle or fortified manor house of the Gourlays and Hepburns, with a 16th-C chapel, dismantled by Cromwell in 1650. Open, see inside front cover. 15p (ch 7p). ⚠ *(AM)*

Preston Mill This is the sole working water-mill to survive on the River Tyne, perhaps the only functioning example in Scotland. Conical roof, projecting wind vane and red pantiles. Open all year, Mon to Sat 10–12.30 and 2–7.30; closes at 4.30 pm Oct to Mar. 40p (ch 20p). Phantassie Doocot, a short walk away, once held 500 birds. *(Tel 426)*. *(NTS)*

ECCLEFECHAN Dumfries and Galloway *Dumfriesshire* Map 11 NY17
Carlyle's Birthplace A characteristic late 18th-C Scottish artisan's house, where Thomas Carlyle was born in 1795. Collection of manuscripts and personal relics. Open 4 Apr to 31 Oct, daily (ex Sun) 10–6. 25p (ch 10p). *(Tel 666)*. *(NTS)*

EDINBURGH Lothian *Midlothian*
Map 11 NT27
Acheson House, Scottish Craft Centre A fine 17th-C mansion in the Royal Mile, opposite Canongate Church. Headquarters of the Scottish Craft Centre. Open daily (ex Sun and PH) 10–5. Free. P.

Canongate Tolbooth Dates from 1591 and shows a curious projecting clock. The J Telfar Dunbar Tartan Collection is on show. Special exhibitions throughout the year. Open Jun to Sep, Mon to Sat 10–6, and also Sun 2–5 during Festival; Oct to May 10–5. Free. ⚠ *(Tel 031-556/5813)*

Craigmillar Castle 14th-C stronghold associated with Mary, Queen of Scots, and also the Earl of Mar. Notable 16th- and 17th-C apartments. Open Apr to Sep, weekdays 9.30–7, Sun 2–7; Oct to Mar 9.30–4, Sun 2–4. Closed 1½ days per week Oct to Mar. 20p (ch 10p). ⚠ *(AM)*

Edinburgh Castle An historic stronghold, famous for the Crown Room, Banqueting Hall, Scottish United Services Museum, St Margaret's Chapel (faced by Mons Meg, a 15th-C cannon) and the impressive Scottish National War Memorial. Open Nov to Apr, weekdays 9.30–5.05, Sun 12.30–4.20; May to Oct, weekdays 9.30–6, Sun 11–6 (subject to Tattoo requirements). Last admissions 45 min before closing. Admission May to Oct, 40p (ch 16 20p); Nov to Apr 25p (ch 16 12p); War Memorial and precincts free. ⚠ *(AM)*

Edinburgh Zoo The Scottish National Zoological Park. Set in 80 acres of grounds, this zoo is one of the finest in Europe, containing a superb collection of animals, fish, birds and reptiles. Also magnificent panoramic views of Edinburgh and surrounding countryside. ☟ (also licensed). Open all year, summer 9–7 (Sun opens 9.30) or dusk winter). £1.20 (ch 15 and pen 60p). Party application to *Bookings Officer,*

Zoological Park, Murrayfield, Edinburgh EH12 6TS. (Tel 031-334 9171) ⚠ ⅏

George Heriot's School Lauriston Place. Dates from 1628 and was founded by George Heriot, the 'Jingling Geordie' of Sir Walter Scott's *Fortunes of Nigel.* Open Mon to Fri (ex BH) 9.30–4.30. Free. ⅏ B

The Georgian House 7 Charlotte Square. Lower floors open as typical Georgian House, furnished as it might have been by first owners, showing domestic surroundings and reflecting social conditions of that age. Open 4 Apr to 26 Oct, Mon to Sat 10–5, Sun 2–5. 1 Nov to 31 Jan Sat 10–4.30, Sun 2–4.30. (Closed 20/21 and 27/28 Dec). 75p (ch 35p) (includes audio-visual shows). *(Tel 031-226 5922). (NTS)*

Gladstone's Land 483 Lawnmarket. Built in 1620, contains fine examples of tempera painting on the walls and ceiling and is furnished as a typical 17th-C home. Ground floor includes shop front and goods of the period. Open 4 Apr to 26 Oct, Mon to Sat 10–5, Sun 2–5; 1 Nov to 31 Jan, Sat 10–4.30, Sun 2–4.30. (Closed 20/21 and 27/28 Dec). 50p (ch 25p). *(NTS)*

Holyroodhouse At E end of Canongate. Historic Royal Palace of 16th and 17th C, built by Sir William Bruce, and associated with Mary, Queen of Scots, and also Prince Charles Edward. The picture gallery and the state apartments are outstanding. Ruined 13th-C nave of former Abbey church. Open from Nov to Apr, Mon to Fri 9.30–5.15, Sat 11–4; from May to Oct, weekdays 9.30–6, Sun 11–5.15 (last entry 45 mins before closing time). Closed when occupied by the Royal Family, and also for 10 days, probably in late spring (see Press), during the Lord High Commissioner's visit. Also closed about 2 weeks before and 1 week after visit. 45p (ch and pen 20p) from May to Oct. Nov to Apr 30p (ch and pen 15p). All details subject to review. ⚠ *(AM)*

Huntly House Canongate. Dates from 1570. It is now the interesting City Museum of local history, containing among other things, collections of silver, glass and pottery. Open Jun to Sep, Mon to Sat 10–6; Oct to May 10–5. During Festival period Sun 2–5. Free.

John Knox's House High Street, 15th-C house, preserving old wooden galleries. Built by the goldsmith to Mary Queen of Scots. Open weekdays only 10–5. 25p (ch 15p).

Lady Stair's House Off Lawnmarket. Restored house, dating from 1622. Museum, with literary relics of Robert Burns, Sir Walter Scott and Robert Louis Stevenson. Open Jul to Sep, Mon to Sat 10–6; Oct to May 10–5 (during Festival period, Sun 2–5). Free. ⚠

Museum of Childhood 38 High Street. Children's life in the past. Open Jun to Sep, Mon to Sat 10–6, Oct to May 10–5, also during Edinburgh's Festival period on Sun 2–6. 30p (ch 15 10p). ⚠

National Gallery of Scotland The Mound. One of the most distinguished of the smaller galleries in Europe, containing collections of Old Masters, Impressionists and Scottish paintings including: Raphael's *Bridgewater Madonna,* Constable's *Dedham Vale,* and masterpieces by Titian, Velasquez, Raeburn, Van Gogh and Gauguin. Drawings, water-colours and original prints by Turner, Goya, Blake, etc (shown on request Mon to Fri 10–12.30 and 2–4.30). Postcards and colour slides on sale at the gallery shop. Museum open daily, Mon to Sat 10–5, Sun 2–5 (Mon to Sat 10–6 [Sun 11–6] during Festival). Free. P (meters). *(Tel 031–556 8921)* ⅏

National Museum of Antiquities of Scotland 1 Queen Street. Extensive collections and national treasures from all parts of Scotland covering the prehistoric, Roman and later periods and illustrating everyday life and history. Open Mon to Sat 10–5 (6 during Festival) Sun 2–5 (11–6 during Festival). Free. P (meters). *(Tel 031–556 8921 ext 35)*

Outlook Tower Castlehill. This tower contains a fine *camera obscura*, which has operated since 1892. A guide gives a 15-minute tour of the city and its surroundings. Scottish Book and Craft shop. Open all year 9.30–6.30; winter 9.30–4.30. 50p (ch 30p). Notable view. *(Tel 031–226 3709)*

Parliament House East of George IV Bridge. Dates from 1639, but façade was replaced in 1829. Hall has a fine hammer-beam roof. The Scottish Parliament met there before the Union of 1707. ⚲ Open Mon to Fri 10–4.

Register House East end of Princes Street. designed by Robert Adam, it was founded in 1774. Headquarters of the Scottish Record Office and the repository for National Archives of Scotland. Summer exhibition Jul to Sep. Open all year (ex certain PH) Mon to Fri 9–4.45; Sat 9–12.30 (Historical search room only). Free. ⚠ *(Tel 031–556 6585)* &

Royal Botanic Garden Inverleith Row. Famous garden, noted especially for the rhododendron collection, rock garden, and new exhibition hall. ⚲ (Apr to Sep) The garden is open Feb to Oct, 9 to 1 hr before sunset Mon to Sat, Sun 11 to 1 hr before sunset; Nov to Jan, Mon to Sat 9–sunset, Sun 11–sunset; plant houses open 10–5 and exhibition hall open 11–5 (during Festival period open on Sun from 10am). Free. ⚠ Sorry, no animals. &

also Scottish National Gallery of Modern Art Inverleith House, Botanic gardens Temporary home since 1960 of the National Gallery's collection of 20th-C painting, sculpture and graphic art. Among many modern masters represented are Derain, Picasso, Giacometti, Magritte, Henry Moore and Barbara Hepworth. Some sculpture is displayed in the garden immediately surrounding the Gallery. Print room and library also open to the public (closed for lunch). ⚲ Open all year, Mon to Sat 10–5, Sun 2–5 (10–6, Sun 11–6 during Festival, closes at sunset during winter). Free. P. *(Tel 031–332 3754)*

Royal Scottish Museum Chambers Street. The most comprehensive display in Britain under one roof comprising the decorative arts, natural history, geology (minerals and fossils), and technology. Colliery locomotive of 1813, many scale-model locomotives, models of ships. Aeronautics, space flight, science and Victorian engineering. Lectures, gallery talks and films at advertised times. Special exhibitions. ⚲ (Mon to Sat 10–4) Open weekdays 10–5, Sun 2–5. Free. P (meters). &

Scottish National Portrait Gallery Queen Street. Striking red Victorian building containing portraits of men and women who have contributed to Scottish history. The collection includes such popular figures as Mary Queen of Scots, James VI and I, Burns, Sir Walter Scott and Ramsay MacDonald. Many other artists, statesmen, soldiers and scientists are portrayed in all media, including sculpture. Collections also illustrate the development of Highland dress. Open all year, Mon to Sat, 10–5, Sun 2–5 (10–6, Sun

11–6 during Festival). Free. P (meters). *(Tel 031–556 8921)* &

West Register House Charlotte Square. The former St George's church, designed by Robert Reid in the Greco-Roman style in 1811. Auxiliary repository for the Scottish Record Office and houses its museum. Open all year (ex PH) Mon to Fri 9–4.45. Free. ⚠ &

EDZELL Tayside *Angus* Map 15 NO56
Edzell Castle 16th C, and associated with Mary, Queen of Scots, preserved walled garden from 1604. Open, 9.30–4.30 Mon to Fri only. 15p (ch 7p). *(AM)*

ELGIN Grampian *Moray* Map 15 NJ26
Elgin Museum The museum conserves and displays the heritage of Elgin and Moray. It contains a world-famed collection of fossils of the Old Red Sandstone. Open 15 Mar to 15 Oct, Mon to Sat (ex Tue, but open Tue during Jul and Aug) 10–12.30 and 2–5; 16 Oct to 1 Mar, Wed and Sat 10–12. 20p (ch 5p) Under revision for 1980. ⚠

Pluscarden Abbey 6m SW on unclass road The original monastery was founded by Alexander II in 1230. Restorations and reconstruction took place in the 14th and 19th C, and the Abbey has been re-occupied by the Benedictines since 1948. Open daily 5am–8.30pm. Free. ⚠ *(Tel Dallas 257)* & B

ELLISLAND FARM Dumfries and Galloway *Dumfriesshire* Map 11 NX98
In this farm on the west bank of the Nith, Robert Burns composed *Tam O'Shanter* and other poems and songs. Material associated with the poet is on display. Burns lived here from 1788 to 1791. No restriction on times of visiting and admission is free. ⚠ (limited). &

FALKIRK Central *Stirlingshire* Map 11 NS87
Falkirk Museum Temporary exhibitions on until further notice. Open all year Mon to Sat 9–5. Free. P. *(Tel 27703)*

Rough Castle One of the most remarkable Roman military sites in Britain, situated on the Antonine, or Roman Wall. It covers one acre with double ditches and defensive pits. Excavations revealing a bathhouse and other buildings made in 1903. Accessible at any reasonable time. Free. ⚠ *(AM)*

Scottish Railway Preservation Society Wallace Street Depot. Fine collection of restored steam locomotives and vintage rolling stock. Engines in steam on certain weekends. ⚲ Open all year (ex Christmas and New Year) Sat and Sun 11–5. 15p (ch 1 and pen 10p), prices increased on 'steam' days. ⚠ *(Tel 20790)* **(79)**

FALKLAND Fife *Fife* Map 11 NO20
Falkland Palace and Gardens Historic former hunting palace of Stuart Kings and Queens, situated below the Lomond Hills. The mid 16th-C buildings include a notable courtyard façade. Chapel Royal and apartments restored. Royal tennis court of 1539, second oldest extant. Visitor Centre. Palace and Gardens open 1 Apr to 31 Oct, Mon to Sat 10–6; Sun 2–6. Last visitors to Palace 5.15. Admission to Palace and gardens £1 (ch 50p); gardens only 50p (ch 25p). Parties 75p (school parties 35p). ⚠ 10 *(Tel 397)*. (NTS)

FETTERCAIRN Tayside *Kincardineshire* Map 15 NO67
Fasque Home of the Gladstone family since 1829, the large mansion reflects the life of the original owner, Sir John Gladstone, and of subsequent generations and their families. Four times Prime Minister, William Gladstone, lived at Fasque from 1830 to

1851. Also illustrated is the life and work of the many servants who contributed to the running of the household. Collection of agricultural and other local machinery. Extensive parkland with red deer and Soay sheep. Open May to Sep incl, daily 1.30–5.30 (last entry 5). 75p (ch 40p, pen 60p) subject to review. ⚠ *(Tel 201)* & B

FINTRY Central *Stirlingshire* Map 11 NS68
Culcreuch Castle Castle dates from 1320 to 1460. ⚐ Open 1 May to 30 Sep. Sun 12.30 Piper's Cold table lunch. Sun 2.30 to 6 Castle and gardens 60p (ch 30p). Fri 8.30 Ceilidh £1.20. Sat 8.30 Country dance £1.20. ⚠ *(Tel 228). (Hercules Robinson of Culreuch)* & B

FORRES Grampian *Moray* Map 14 NJ05
Falconer Museum Tolbooth Street. Items relating to Hugh Falconer; fossil fish; natural history; ethnography; weaponry and Culbin archaeological finds. Open May to Sep, daily 10–5 (7 Jul and Aug). Free. P. *(Tel 73701)* & B
Nelson Tower Located on Cluny Hill, within Grant Park, overlooking Forres. The Tower was erected in 1806 by the survivors of the battle of Trafalgar and offers magnificent views of Moray Firth, Black Isle and inland mountains. Key available from Forres Tourist Information Centre at Falconer Museum (£1 deposit). Open mid May to end Sep. Daily 10–6. *(Tel 72938)*
Suenos' Stone A notable 20ft high monument, with a sculptured cross on one side and groups of warriors on the reverse. Accessible at all times. Free. *(AM)*

FORT AUGUSTUS Highland *Inverness-shire* Map 14 NH30
Great Glen Exhibition History and traditions of people of the Great Glen, rare maps and prints. Latest information on the search for Loch Ness Monster. Evening audio-visual shows. Four buildings on site. Open Jun to Sep, Mon–Sat 10–6. Sun 2–6. 30p (ch 15 15p). P. &

FORT GEORGE Highland *Inverness-shire* Map 14 NH75
Fort George As 18th-C fort, visited by Dr Johnson and Boswell in 1773. Open Apr to Sep, weekdays 9.30–7, Sun 2–4; Oct to Mar 9.30–4, Sun 2–4. 25p (ch 12p). P. *(AM)*
Also Queen's Own Highlanders Museum Housed in the fort, exhibits include period uniforms, silver and medals. The Georgian garrison church dates from 1768. Open Apr to Sep weekdays 10–6.30, Sun 2–6. Oct to Mar, weekdays 10–4, Sun 2–6.30; closed 1, 2 Jan, 25, 26 Dec and PH. *(Tel Ardersier 2274 ext 47)*

FORT WILLIAM Highland *Inverness-shire* Map 14 NN17
Inverlochy Castle Well-preserved example of a 13th-C and later stronghold, famous for the battle fought nearby in 1645, when Montrose defeated the Campbells. Now under repair and interior not accessible, but may be viewed from the outside. Free. *(AM)*
West Highland Museum A museum of local and particularly Jacobite interest, including an exhibition about the '45 rising with the well-known 'secret portrait' of Prince Charles Edward Stuart. Relics from the former fort, archaeology, wildlife, geology, and folk exhibits. Open mid Jun to mid Sep, 9.30–9; Oct to May 9.30–1, 2.15–5. Closed Sun. 20p (ch 10p)

GAIRLOCH Highland *Ross-shire* Map 14 NG87
Gairloch Heritage Museum Achtercairn. A converted farmstead now houses the

museum which relates the way of life in the typical West Highland parish of Gairloch from the earliest times to the 20th century. Open-air display area in front of building. ⚐ Open 19 May to 30 Sep daily (ex Sun) 10–1 and 2–4. 20p (ch 10 10p). P 50yds. *(Tel Badachro 243)*

GALASHIELS Borders *Selkirkshire* Map 12 NT43
Bernat Klein Exhibition Waukrigg Mill. This exhibition is intended to show the sequence, the thought process and the stages between the conception of a design idea and its realisation as a finished product. The exhibition consists of approximately 100 paintings, sketches, photographs, patterns and other objects, specially selected from Bernat Klein's work for the purpose. It also shows the relationship between the countryside in which the designer lives and works and the designs which he and those working with him, produce. Open all year daily 10–4. Free. ⚠ *(Tel 2764). (Mrs Jennifer Mellor)* &

GLAMIS Tayside *Angus* Map 15 NO34
Glamis Castle The ancestral seat of the Earl of Strathmore and Kinghorne, family home of Her Majesty Queen Elizabeth, The Queen Mother and birthplace in 1930 of HRH Princess Margaret. Mainly late 17th-C but with an older tower. The drawing room ceiling of 1621 and the painted panels in the chapel are notable. Open 1 May to 1 Oct Mon to Thu and Sun 1–5, also Fri from 1 Jul. £1 (ch 40p, pen 80p). Grounds only, half-price. Prices subject to review for 1980. ⚠ *(Earl of Strathmore and Kinghorne)* & B
Angus Folk Museum Kirkwynd Cottages. Row of restored 17th-C cottages, now housing the Angus Folk Collection of agricultural and domestic equipment and cottage furniture etc. Open 1 May to 30 Sep, daily 1–6 (last admission 5.30) and on request. 45p (ch 20p). *(NTS)*

GLASGOW Strathclyde *Lanarkshire* Map 11 NS56
Bellahouston Park Ibrox. 171 acres of parkland only 3 miles from the city centre. Site of the Empire Exhibition of 1938. Sunken garden and rock garden. Multi-purpose Sports Centre situated at west end of park, with all-weather Athletic Centre adjacent and nursery ski slope. ⚐ in Sports Centre. Open daily 7–dusk. Free. ⚠ at ski slope and sports centre. &
Botanic Garden Off Great Western Road. Established in 1817, it contains an outstanding collection of plants. The Kibble Palace open 10–4.45 (4.15 in winter), is a unique glasshouse with, among others, a famous collection of tree ferns. The main glasshouse open Mon to Sat 1–4.45 (4.15 in winter), Sun 12–4.45 (4.15 in winter), contains numerous tropical and exotic plants. The 40 acres of gardens include systematic and herb gardens, and a chronological border. Open daily 7–dusk. Free. ⚠ *(Tel 041–334 2422)* &
Crookston Castle Probably 13th C, with an earlier defensive ditch. Visited by Mary Queen of Scots, and Darnley in 1565. Open, see inside front cover. 15p (ch 7p). *(AM)*
Glasgow Art Gallery and Museum Kelvingrove Park, Italian, Flemish, Dutch, French and British paintings representing the finest civic art collection in Great Britain. Collections of pottery, porcelain, silver, sculpture, arms and armour. Plus archaeology, ethnography, natural history, etc, and selections from the world famous

Visit

Glasgow Museums & Art Galleries

Art Gallery and Museum, Kelvingrove, 041-334 1134

Museum of Transport, Albert Drive, 041-423 8000

Haggs Castle, St. Andrews Drive, 041-427 2725

People's Palace, Glasgow Green, 041-554 0223

Pollok House, Pollokshaws Road, 041-632 0274

St. Enoch's Exhibition Centre, St. Enoch's Square, 041-221 6454

Open daily 10 am — 5 pm, Sundays 2 pm — 5 pm.

Burrell Collection. ☕ Open Mon to Sat 10–5, Sun 2–5. Closed 25 Dec and 1 Jan. Free. ⚠ *(Tel 041–334 1134)* ♿

Greenbank Clarkston. Off A726 on southern outskirts of the city. Small garden at which has been established a Gardening Advice Centre, particularly suitable for the owners of small gardens. Lectures, demonstrations etc. Garden open all year daily 10–5. Advice centre open all year Mon–Fri 10–5, also Sat and Sun 1 Apr to 31 Oct, 2.30–5. 40p (ch 20p). *(NTS)*

Haggs Castle 100 St Andrew's Drive. Built in 1585, the castle is a museum created for children. The theme is exploration of time – particularly the last 400 years since the castle was built. Activities in the adjacent workshop allow visitors to become practically involved in the past. Open all year (ex 25 Dec and 1 Jan) Mon to Sat 10–6.15, Sun 2–5. Free. *(Tel 041–427 2725)*

Hunterian Museum The University of Glasgow. The museum is named after the 18th-C surgeon, Dr William Hunter, who bequeathed his own collections to the University. The geological, archaeological, ethnographical, numismatic and historical collections are exhibited in the main building of the University. The Hunterian Art Gallery is expected to open in 1980. *(Tel 041–339 8855 ext 7431* for information). Open all year Mon to Fri 9–5, Sat 9–12. Free. ⚠ *(Tel 041–339 8855 ext 221)* ♿ B

Linn Park Cathcart. Southern outskirts of Glasgow. Comprises more than 200 acres of pine, deciduous woodland, and riverside walks. Britain's first public park nature trail (1965) features many varieties of flowers, trees, and insects. Children's zoo. Collection of British ponies and Highland cattle. There is also a ruined 14th-C castle, with a Mary Queen of Scots historical plaque. ☕ at Golf Clubhouse. Open daily 7–dusk. Free. ⚠ ♿

People's Palace Glasgow Green. Contains a fascinating visual record of the history and life of the City. In addition to items illustrating prehistoric and medieval Glasgow, there are interesting relics of Mary, Queen of Scots, the Battle of Langside, the Tobacco Lords of the 18th C, and the history of the music hall. Fine examples of Glasgow craftsmanship, particularly pottery, are on view, and there are special displays illustrating the social and domestic life. A wide range of pictures brings to life people and places of note. Open Mon to Sat 10–5, Sun 2–5. Free. ⚠ *(Tel 041–554 0223)*

Pollock Park 361 acres, formerly a private estate containing an extensive collection of flowering shrubs and trees in a natural setting. Display rose garden, nature trails, jogging track. Open daily 7–dusk. Demonstration an(display garden open daily 10–4. Demonstrations held fortnightly, Sat mornings. Free. Also **Pollock House** situate(within the grounds, a William Adam building (1752), containing the famous Stirling-Maxwell Collection of Spanish and other paintings, works by William Blake, silver, furniture, etc. ☕ Open all year Mon to Sat 10–5, Sun 2–5. Free. ⚠ *(Tel 041–632 0274 restaurant 041–649 7547)*

Provan Hall Auchinlea Road, E4. 15th-C house, once mansion of lands of Provan. Wel restored, and considered most perfect example of a simple pre-Reformation house remaining in Scotland. For information on opening hours contact Glasgow District Council, Parks Dept. *(NTS)*

Ross Hall Park Crookson. Beautifully kept gardens with artificial ponds featuring a variety of aquatic plants and stocked with fish Extensive heather and rock gardens. Garden and woodland nature trails. Open Apr to Sep, daily 1–8; Oct to Mar, daily 1–4. Free. ⚠ *(Te 041–882 3554)* ♿

Rouken Glen Park Thornliebank. Fine park with lovely walks through the glen, waterfall at head of the glen is a noted beauty spot. Large walled garden. Boating on picturesque loch. ☕ Open daily 7–dusk. Free. ⚠ *(Tel 041–638 1077)* ♿

Transport Museum Albert Drive, near Eglinton Toll. A life-size presentation of land transport, showing the development of the bicycle, horse-drawn vehicles, tramcars, Scottish motor cars from vintage to present day and railway locomotives, also the Clyde room with an outstanding collection of ship modes. ☕ Open Mon to Sat 10–5, Sun 2–5. Free. ⚠ *(Tel 041–423 8000)* ♿

Victoria Park Whiteinch. This park has the best known fossilized tree stumps of the prehistoric Coal Age period, discovered in 1887, and housed in the Fossil Grove building. Open Mon to Sat from 8am (Sun from 10am). The park has extensive carpet bedding depicting centennial events. Open daily 7–dusk. Free. P. ♿

GLENAPPS Strathclyde *Ayrshire* Map 10 NX08

Castle Gardens Daffodils, azaleas, rhododendrons, flowering shrubs, terraces, lily ponds, herbaceous borders. Open May to Aug incl, daily (ex Sat). ☕ 30p (ch 12 15p) Party ⚠ *(Rt Hon Earl and Countess of Inchcape)* ♿

GLENCOE Highland *Argyll* Map 14 NN15

Glencoe and North Lorn Folk Museum Housed in two heather-thatched cottages,

ne of cruck construction, in main street of
Glencoe. Macdonald relics, local domestic
and agricultural exhibits, and Jacobite relics
costume and embroidery. Open mid May to
end Sep, Mon to Sat 10–5.30. 15p (ch 10p)
Under revision for 1980. P.

Glen Coe Visitor Centre Situated at north
end of Glen Coe close to site of 1692
massacre. Ranger-Naturalist service
available. Open 4 Apr to mid May and mid Sep
to mid Oct daily 10–5; mid May to mid Sep,
daily 10–7. 10p including ⚠. *(NTS)*

GLENELG Highland *Inverness-shire*
Map 14 NG81
Glenelg Brochs Reached by way of the
steep and winding Marn Rattachen pass, off
A87. Situated in Glen Beag, on a byroad.
Remains of two brochs, known as Dun Telve
and Dun Troddan. Probably of Iron Age date,
some 30ft in height, and showing well-
preserved walls, galleries, and courts.
Picturesque Highland setting. Accessible at
all reasonable times. Free. *(AM)*

GLENFINNAN Highland *Inverness-shire*
Map 14 NM98
Monument Erected in 1815 to commemorate
the Highlanders who followed Prince Charles
Edward in 1745. Plaques on retaining wall
give a dedication in English, Gaelic, and Latin.
The monument stands in a superb setting of
mountains at the head of Loch Shiel. Visitor
Centre. Open daily 4 Apr to 31 May 9.30–6;
Jun to Aug 9.30–8; Sep to mid Oct 9.30–6.
10p (ch 15p) including ⚠ *(Tel Kinlocheil 250)*.
(NTS)

GLENGOULANDIE DEER PARK Tayside
Perthshire Map 14 NN75
8m NW of Aberfeldy on B846. A fine herd of
red deer, Highland cattle, endangered
species and other birds and animals live in the
park in surroundings as like their natural
environment as possible. Pets must not be
allowed out of cars. Picnic area. Shop. Open 1
Apr to 30 Sep daily 9 – two hours before
sunset. 20p (ch 10p), cars £1. ⚠ *(Tel
Kenmore 306)* ⚠

GLENLIVET Grampian *Banffshire*
Map 15 NJ12
Glenlivet Distillery Off B9136 12m SW of
Dufftown (via B9009 and B9008). The
reception centre contains an exhibition of
ancient artefacts used in malting, peat cutting
and distilling. Shop. Open May to Sep, Mon to
Fri 10–4. Free. ⚠ *(Tel 202 or Lhanbryde 251)*
79)

GLENLUCE Dumfries and Galloway
Wigtownshire Map 10 NX15
Glenluce Abbey 2m NW of the village. A
Cistercian house founded in 1192 by Roland,
Earl of Galloway. The ruins occupy a site of
great beauty and are themselves of much
architectural interest and distinction. Open,
Apr to Sep, see inside front cover. Closed 1½
days per week. Oct to Mar Sat and Sun pm.
15p (ch 7p). ⚠ *(AM)*

GOGAR Lothian *Midlothian* Map 11 NT17
Suntrap Gogarbank. 1½m S off Gogar Moor-
Mansfield road. Small garden containing a
Gardening Advice Centre, with lecture hall,
glass-houses, demonstrations etc, adapted
to help owners of small gardens. Garden
open all year, daily 9 – dusk. Advice Centre
open all year, Mon to Fri 9–5 (1 Mar to 31 Oct,
also Sat and Sun 2.30–5). 30p (ch
accompanied by adult 15p). *(Tel 031-
339 7283)* ⚠ *(NTS)*

GOLSPIE Highland *Sutherland* Map 14 NH89
Dunrobin Castle 1m NE. The ancient seat of
the Earls and Dukes of Sutherland. Much of
the interior is open to the public and contains a
wide variety of furniture, paintings and
exhibits. Museum with many antique exhibits
of local and general interest within the
grounds. Magnificent formal gardens. ⚐
Open 1 May to 30 Sep daily Mon to Sat
10.30–5.30, Sun 1–5.30. £1 (ch 50p) subject
to alteration. Party. ⚠ *(Tel 377) (Countess of
Sutherland)* ⚑ B

GORDON Borders *Berwickshire*
Map 12 NT64
Mellerstain House 3m S on unclass road.
Adam house with fine plaster ceilings, period
furniture and pictures. Terraced gardens and
lake. Historic Vehicle display 8 Jun. ⚐ Open
4 – 7 Apr then 1 May to 30 Sep, Mon to Fri and
Sun 1.30–5.30 (last admission 5). 80p (ch 14
40p, pen 60p). ⚠ Dogs must be on a lead.
(Lord Binning)

GREENOCK Strathclyde *Renfrewshire*
Map 10 NS27
Mclean Museum and Art Gallery 9 Union
Street. A museum displaying exhibits relating
to local history, ethnography, natural history,
geology, and shipping, including river
steamers (paddle), cargo vessels. There are
also relics of James Watt. Inverclyde art
exhibition last week in Feb and Mar;
Greenock Art Club exhibition in Sep/Oct.
Open all year, Mon to Sat 10–5 (closed Sat
1–2). Free. P. *(Tel 23741)*

HAMILTON Strathclyde *Lanarks*
Map 11 NS75
Hamilton District Museum Muir Street.
Collections of local history and crafts,
paintings and early photographs, farming,
horse and motor transport and period kitchen,
all housed in late 17th-C inn with 18th-C
Assembly Hall with musicians gallery. Also
the Regimental Museum of the Cameronians,
Scottish Rifles. Open all year daily (ex Sun)
Mon to Fri 10–12 and 1–5, Sat 10–5. Free.
⚠ *(Tel 283981)*

HAWICK Borders *Roxburghshire*
Map 12 NT51
Museum and Art Gallery Wilton Lodge. The
museum contains exhibits of natural history,
local history, hosiery trade, archaeology,
geology, coins and medals. The Art Gallery
has exhibitions throughout the year. Open all
year, Apr to Oct Mon to Sat 10–5 (2–5 Sun)
Nov to Mar Mon to Sat 10–4 (closed Sun).
20p (ch 16 10p) under review. P. *(Tel 3457)*

HERMITAGE Borders *Roxburghshire*
Map 12 NY59
Hermitage Castle An old Douglas
stronghold, mainly 14th-C, well-restored, with
Mary, Queen of Scots associations. Open,
see inside front cover. 20p (ch 10p). ⚠ *(AM)*

HUNTLY Grampian *Aberdeenshire*
Map 15 NJ53
Agricultural Museum 3½m SE. Opened in
1972; this museum contains an interesting
collection of about 450 items of farm and
farmhouse equipment, including farm
implements, horse and cattle equipment,
butter- and cheese-making utensils, corn
dollies and many hand-tools. Sales dept,
selling farm and country antiques. 'Farming
Yesteryear' Field Days 26, 27 May with old
horse implements, steam powered threshing
mill and other items. Open daily at all
reasonable times. Collections in aid of Royal
Scottish Agricultural Benevolent Institution.
⚠ *(Tel Drumblade 231)*

Huntly Castle Formerly Palace of Strathbogie, dates largely from 1602, with elaborate heraldic embellishments. Open, see inside front cover. 20 (ch 10p). △ *(AM)*
Huntly Museum The Square. Local history and changing special exhibitions every year. Governed by North East of Scotland Library Committee. Open all year (ex Mon) Tue to Sat 10–12, 2–4. Free. *(Tel Peterhead 2554)*

INNERLEITHEN Borders *Peebleshire* Map 11 NT33
Traquair House 1m S on B709. Scotland's oldest inhabited, and most romantic house, dating back to the 10th C. Twenty-seven English and Scottish Kings have stayed here. Rich in association with Mary, Queen of Scots, and the Jacobite Risings. Contains a fine collection of historical treasures, many recently discovered. Unique 18th-C brewhouse licensed to sell own beer. Woodland walks, 5 craft workshops. Craft Fair 16/17 Aug (please check dates). Gift shop, Antiques and Bric a Brac. ⚏ Open 5 to 13 Apr, then remaining Sun in Apr; thereafter daily 1 May to 5 Oct, 1.30–5.30. Also Jul and Aug only 10.30–5.30 (last admission 5). △ *(Tel 830323). (Mr P Maxwell Stuart)* ঙ B

INVERARAY Strathclyde *Argyll* Map 10 NN00
Inveraray Bell Tower The 126ft tower was planned in 1914, and the ring of ten bells were hung in the great bell chamber in 1931. From the roof of the tower is an excellent view. Exhibition of vestments and campanology and there will be a 'ring-in' daily during Inveraray Week at the end of July. Open Spring BH to 30 Sep, Mon to Sat 10–1, 2–5, Sun 2–5. 25p (ch and pen 10p). △
Inveraray Castle A fine mansion of the late 18th-C by Robert Mylne and Roger Morris. The great hall and armoury, staterooms, tapestries and furniture are of note. The ancestral home of the Dukes of Argyll. Shop. ⚏ Open Apr to 28 Jun daily (ex Fri) 10–12.30 and 2–6; 29 Jun to 30 Sep, weekdays 10–6, Sun 2–6 (last admission 5.30). £1 (ch 15 and pen 50p). Admission prices under revision for 1980. △ *(Tel 2203)*

INVERESK Lothian *Midlothian* Map 11 NT37
Inveresk Lodge Garden New garden featuring numerous varieties of plants for small gardens. Garden only shown all the year, Mon, Wed and Fri 10–4.30, on Sun 2–5 when house is occupied. 30p (ch accompanied by adults 15p). *(NTS)*

INVERNESS Highland *Inverness-shire* Map 14 NH64
Abertarff House Church Street. The town house of Lord Lovat, built in 1593, it is now the headquarters of An Comunn Gaidhealach. It has a stone turnpike staircase and contains an exhibition of the origins and history of the Gaels, a sales point for Gaelic books and records and English books on the Highlands. Open all year, Mon to Fri 9–5 (9–1 Wed, 9–4.30 on Fri, 10–1 Sat). Free. *(Tel 31226)*

INVERTROSSACHS Central *Perthshire* Map 11 NH50
Nature reserve in extremely fine setting beside Loch Venachar. Open May to Aug by prior appointment only. 50p (ch 25p). △ *(Tel Callander 30010)* ঙ

INVERURIE Grampian *Aberdeenshire* Map 15 NJ72
Inverurie Museum Town House, Thematic displays changing 4- or 6-monthly. Permanent local history and archaeology exhibition. Reserve collections may be

viewed by appointment. Established in 1884, this museum is now governed by the North East Scotland Library Service Committee. Open all year, Mon to Fri 2–5, Sat 10–12. Free. *(Tel Peterhead 2554)*

IRVINE Strathclyde *Ayrshire* Map 10 NS34
Eglinton Castle and Gardens Irvine Road Kilwinning. Late 18th-C castle, built for 13th Earl of Eglinton. Castle ruin set in a 12-acre garden. Site of the famous Eglinton Tournament of 1839. Always open. Free. △ *(Tel 74166)*

JEDBURGH Borders *Roxburghshire* Map 12 NT62
Jedburgh Abbey One of the four famous border monasteries founded by Davi I. The remains of the church are mostly Norman or Transitional. Also small museum, containing many carved fragments of medieval work and some important monuments from the Anglian period. Open, see inside front cover Apr to Sep. During Oct to Mar closed 1½ days per week. 25p (ch 12p) △ *(AM)*
The Castle Jail This is the former county prison, dating from 1820–3, on the site of the medieval castle, demolished in 1409. There were three blocks, used for different categories of prisoners. Possibly the last surviving example of its kind. A small museum is also open to visitors. Open Apr to Sep, Mon to Sat 10–12, 1–5, Suns 1–5. 10p (ch 16 5p) P. *(Tel Hawick 3457)*
Mary Queen of Scots House A historic and picturesque bastle house built in the early 16th C. Now a museum with exhibits relating to the Queen and to the earlier story of Jedburgh and district. Open Mar to Oct daily 10–5.30. 20p (ch 16 10p). △

KELLIE CASTLE AND GARDENS Fife *Fife* Map 12 NO50
Fine example of the domestic architecture of the Scottish lowlands. The mainly 16th- and 17th-C building probably assumed its present dimensions in 1606. Notable plasterwork and panelling painted with 'romantic' landscapes. Audio-visual show. Open 4 Apr to 30 Sep, daily (ex Fri) 2–6; gardens 4 Apr to 30 Sep, daily 10–dusk. Admission to castle and gardens 85p (ch 40p); gardens only 30p (ch accompanied by an adult 15p). Party 20+ (55p each). *(Tel Arncroach 271). (NTS)* ঙ (gardens)

KELSO Borders *Roxburghshire* Map 12 NT73
Kelso Abbey Little but the abbey church remains, and that only in imposing fragments which are almost wholly of Norman and Transitional work. The best preserved portion is the north transept. Open see inside front cover. Free. *(AM)*

KEMNAY Grampian *Aberdeenshire* Map 15 NJ71
Castle Fraser 2½m SW on unclass rd. This castle is considered by many to be the most spectacular of the Castles of Mar. The massive Z-plan castle, with splendid architectural embellishments was begun about 1575 by the sixth laird, Michael Fraser, and incorporates an earlier castle. It was completed in 1636. An exhibition tells the story of 'The Castles of Mar'. Open 1 May to 30 Sep Mon to Sat 11–6, Sun 2–6 (last admission 5.15). Garden and grounds open all year 9.30–sunset. Castle 80p (ch 40p), school parties 35p; grounds by donation. △ *(NTS)*

KILBARCHAN Strathclyde *Renfrewshire* Map 10 NS46

Weaver's Cottage An early 18th-C craftsman's house, formerly used by weavers. Looms, weaving equipment, domestic utensils. Open 1 May to 31 Oct, Tue, Thu, Sat and Sun 2–5. 40p (ch 20p). *(NTS)*

KILCHRENAN Strathclyde *Argyll* Map 10 NN02

Ardanaiseig 3m NE at end of unclass road. The gardens have azaleas, rhododendrons, are shrubs and trees. Splendid views across Loch Awe. Open 1 Apr to 31 Oct, daily 10–8. 0p (ch 16 free). ⚠ *(Mr and Mrs J M Brown)*

KILDRUMMY Grampian *Aberdeenshire* Map 15 NJ41

Kildrummy Castle A splendid, ruined, 13th-fortress, with an imposing gatehouse and notable 15th- to 16th-C additions. Gallantly defended by Sir Nigel Bruce in 1306. Open, see inside front cover. 15p (ch 7p). ⚠ *(AM)*

Kildrummy Castle Garden Trust Two of the trustees are the Professors of Forestry and Botany, University of Aberdeen. At foot of the medieval castle lies the Water garden running under a copy of the 14th-C Brig O'Balgownie. Facing south is the shrub bank. The ancient quarry from which the ruins were built, contains a variety of alpines and shrubs from overseas. Festival 8 Jun 1.30–5. Plants for sale. Open 1 Apr to 31 Oct, daily, 9–5. 25p (ch p). ⚠ 10p (inside Hotel gates). (Coaches 0p by appointment). *(Tel 264, 277 and 288)*

KILLIECRANKIE Tayside *Perthshire* Map 14 NN96

Trust Visitor Centre Situated close to site of 1689 battle where Jacobite army, led by Bonnie Dundee', routed King William's troops. Battle display. Open 4 Apr to 30 Sep, Mon to Sat 10–6; Sun 1–6; 1 Jul to 31 Aug, Mon to Sat 9.30–6, Sun 1–6. 20p (ch 10p). ⚠ *(Tel 233). (NTS)*

KILMARNOCK Strathclyde *Ayrshire* Map 10 NS43

Burns Museum Outstanding Burns memorial, including 1st Kilmarnock edition of 1786, original manuscripts (including *Tam o'Shanter, Cottar's Saturday Nigh* etc). Burns' letters and works, and McKie Burns Library. Panoramic views towards Arran from Tower. Open May to Sep daily 1–5 Oct to Apr Sat and Sun 1–5. 3p. *(Tel 26401)*

Dean Castle Dean Road. Fortified tower built 1350 with lower keep, Great Hall and Upper Hall in perfect condition. Exhibitions of European arms and armour, early keyboard and other musical instruments. Palace has Long Gallery, kitchen and tower in equally good condition. Restoration shows Dean Castle as it was in 14th-15th C. 42 acres of gardens and nature trail. Concerts of period music and other historical performances. 🚻. Open mid May to mid Sep, Mon to Fri 2–5, Sat and Sun 10–5 (organised parties throughout the year by arrangement). Free. P. *(Tel 26401)*

Dick Institute Elmbank Avenue. The museum contains exhibits of geology (including fossils), small arms, shells, ethnography, numismatics, and archaeological specimens. The art gallery (paintings and etchings) and the library (Ayrshire and Burns printed books, etc) are of interest. Open My to Sep, Mon, Tue, Thu and Fri 10–8 (Wed and Sat until 5pm); Oct to Apr 10–5. Free. ⚠ *(Tel 26401)* ♿

KILMARTIN Strathclyde *Argyll* Map 10 NR89

Dunadd Fort 3m S, A816. A prehistoric hill-fort incorporating walled enclosures. It was once the capital of the ancient Scots kingdom of Dalriada. Accessible at all reasonable times. Free. *(AM)*

KILMORY Strathclyde *Argyll* Map 10 NR77

Castle Sween 2½m N. Lonely ruin, situated on the rocky western coast of Knapdale, probably one of the earliest stone castles in Scotland dating from the mid 12th C. The castle was destroyed by Sir Alexander Macdonald in 1647. Open at all times. Free. *(AM)*

KILMUN Strathclyde *Argyll* Map 10 NS18

Kilmun Arboretum and Forest Plots A large collection of conifer and broadleaved tree species planted in plots and specimen groups. Established by the Forestry Commission in 1930, and now extending to 100 acres on a hillside overlooking the Holy Loch. Open all year during daylight hours. Entrance and car park at Forestry Commission District Office, Kilmun, from which an illustrated guide book is available.

KILSYTH Strathclyde *Stirlingshire* Map 11 NS77

Colzium House Partly a museum, with attractive walled garden, and associated with Montrose's victory over the Covenanters in 1645. Recreational facilities include pitch and putt and a football field in grounds. House open Mon, Tue, Wed, Fri, Sun 2–5 and 7–dusk (ex when booked for private functions), grounds open at all times. Free. ⚠ *(Tel 823110)*

KINCRAIG Highland *Inverness-shire* Map 14 NH80

Highland Wild Life Park Native animals of Scotland past and present, including wolves, bears, reindeer, wildcat and European Bison. Open daily 1 Mar to first Sun in Nov 10–6 (or

1½ hrs before dusk if earlier). ♨, picnic site, shop, children's park and temporary caravan park. £3 per car (prices subject to review for 1980). Kennels for pets at entrance. ♿ *(Tel 270)* ♿

KINGUSSIE Highland *Inverness-shire* Map 14 NH70
Highland Folk Museum Contains an interesting display of Highland crafts and furnishings; a farming museum; reconstructed Hebridean mill, and primitive 'black house' set in 6 acres of garden. Picnic garden. Open all year Apr–Oct, Mon to Sat 10–6, Sun 2–6; Nov to Mar Mon to Fri 10–3. 45p (ch 4–13 10p) subject to review for 1980. ♿ *(Tel 307)* ♿

KINNESSWOOD Tayside *Kinross-shire* Map 11 NO10
Michael Bruce Cottage and Museum The Loan. The cottage birth-place of Michael Bruce (1746–67), the gentle poet of Loch Leven, where his father once operated a loom. Now a Michael Bruce museum displaying family relics. Annual commemoration service 1st Sun in Jul at 6 pm. Open on application to *Mr T Buchan, The Garage, Drummond Place*. Free. ♿ *(Tel Cowdenbeath 510832)*

KINROSS Tayside *Kinross-shire* Map 11 NO10
Kinross House Gardens Dates from 1685 to 1692, from designs by Sir William Bruce. Gardens only open May to Sep daily 2–7. 30p (ch 10p). Admission prices under review for 1980. ♿ *(Tel 63467)* ♿
Loch Leven Castle Castle Island. From this historic, ruined, 15th-C and earlier island stronghold in the River Dee, Mary Queen of Scots escaped in 1568, after a year's imprisonment, Scott's novel *The Abbot* describes the event. Erected by Archibald the Grim in the 14th C, it is four storeys in height, with round towers guarding the outer wall. It was dismantled by the Covenanters in 1640. Open Apr to Sep 10–6. Sun 2–6. Free. Ferry Charge 25p (ch 12p). *(AM)*

KINTORE Grampian *Aberdeenshire* Map 15 NJ71
Balbithan House 2½m NE. A fine 17th-C house, with an interesting garden, situated near the River Don. Contains small museum with collection of Scottish kitchen antiques. Also gallery of original flower and landscape water-colours, all for sale. Nursery garden with plants for sale. Open May to Sep. 50p (ch 16 10p). Admission prices under revision for 1980. ♿ To view please *Tel 2282 (Mrs McMurtrie)*

KIRKBEAN Dumfries and Galloway *Dumfriesshire* Map 11 NX95
Arbigland Garden 1m SE adjacent to Paul Jones cottage. The gardens and dower house of this mansion have been evolving through three centuries. Paul Jones the US Admiral worked here under his father, who was the gardener in the 1740s. Woodland, water and formal gardens arranged around a sandy bay. ♨ Shop. Open 1 May to 30 Sep, Tue, Thu and Sun 2–6. Charges not available. Parties by prior arrangement. ♿ *(Tel 213)*

KIRKCALDY Fife *Fife* Map 11 NT29
Industrial Museum Forth House, 100yds from main museum. Collection of horse-drawn vehicles, blacksmith's forge etc. Open May to Sep, Mon to Sat 2–5, other times by arrangement. ♿
John McDouall Stuart Museum Rectory Lane, Dysart. A memorial to the Scottish explorer, John McDouall Stuart

(1815–1866), who was the first man to cross Australia from south to north during the years 1861–2. Museum of the Year award winner 1978. Open May to Sep daily 2–5; other times by arrangement. Opening times and days under revision for 1980. Free. P 100yds. *(Tel 60732)*
Museum and Art Gallery War Memorial Grounds. Next to Kirkcaldy station. General museum concerning the surrounding area, its history, natural history and archaeology. Collection of local pottery, including the famous Wemyss Ware, other decorative arts and a collection of Scottish Art, which includes works by William McTaggart and Peploe. Temporary exhibitions throughout the year. Open all year (ex Local Hols) Mon to Sat 11–5, Sun 2–5. Free. ♿ *(Tel 0592 60732)*
Ravenscraig Castle A prominent ruined structure, founded in 1460, and perhaps the first castle designed for defence with firearms. The ashlar masonry is notable. Open, see inside front cover. 15p (ch 7p). *(AM)*

KIRKCUDBRIGHT Dumfries and Galloway *Kirkcudbrightshire* Map 11 NX65
Broughton House An 18th-C house, noted for the collection of pictures by E A Hornel, a library, and an attractive garden. Open Apr to Oct daily 11–1 and 2–5; Nov to Mar, Sat, Sun and Mon 2–4 only. 30p (ch 14 to 18 15p; ch 1 accompanied free).
Maclellan's Castle A notable, ruined structure from 1582. Open, see inside front cover. 20p (ch 10p). ♿ *(AM)*
Stewarty Museum A museum displaying objects connected with Galloway, including firearms, domestic and agricultural implements, and a good natural history section. Open Easter to mid Oct, Mon to Sat 10–1, 2–5. 30p (ch 14 10p). P (street). *(Tel 30797)*

KIRKOSWALD Strathclyde *Ayrshire* Map 10 NS20
Souter Johnnie's Cottage A thatched 18th-C cottage, the former home of the village cobbler, John Davidson, the original Souter Johnnie of Burns' 'Tam O'Shanter'. Life-size figures of the Souter and his friends in the garden. Open 4 Apr to 30 Sep. Sat to Thu 12–5, other times by appointment. 30p (ch accompanied by adults 15p). *(Tel 243)*. *(NTS)*

KIRRIEMUIR Tayside *Angus* Map 15 NO35
Barrie's Birthplace A small house at 9 Brechin Road containing personal mementoes of Sir James Barrie, who was born here in 1860. Open 1 May to 30 Sep, weekdays 10–12.30 and 2–6, Sun 2–6; or by arrangement. 40p (ch accompanied by adult 20p). *(Tel 2646)*. *(NTS)*

KNOCKANDO Grampian *Moray* Map 15 NJ14
Tamdhu Distillery Visitors are able to see the complete process of whisky being made. Open 1 May to 29 Sep, Mon to Fri 10–4. Free. ♿ *(Tel Carron 221)*. *(The Highland Distilleries Co Ltd)*

LANGBANK Strathclyde *Renfrewshire* Map 10 NS37
Finlaystone Estate 1m W. Gardens, garden centre and woodland walks and jogging trail. Open all year Mon to Sat 9–5, Sun 2–5. ♨ May to Aug, Sat and Sun 2–5. Woodlands 30p (ch 20p). House with doll and Victorian collections open to parties by arrangement. ♿ *(Tel 285/235)* ♿ B

LARGS Strathclyde *Ayrshire* Map 10 NS25
Skelmorlie Aisle A splendid example of a Renaissance monument, erected by Sir

obert Montgomery of Skelmorlie in 1636, tands in an aisle, formerly the north transept f the old church of Largs, and is the only ortion now preserved. The monument, vhich is built in stone, consists of a gallery aised above a partially sunk burial chamber. Open Apr to Sep (see inside front cover), Oct o Mar on application to custodian. 15p (ch p). *(AM)*

AURISTON CASTLE Lothian *Midlothian* Map 11 NT27

In NW outskirts of Edinburgh, 1m E of Cramond. A late 16th-C mansion, with urniture and antiques, displaying English and rench styles. Associated with John Law, the arly 18th-C broker. Open Apr to Oct, daily ex Fri) 11 – 1 and 2 – 5; from Nov to Mar, Sat nd Sun daily 2 – 4. 45p (ch 15 20p). Grounds 1 – dusk, free. ⚠ *(Tel 031-336 2060)*

AWERS Tayside *Perthshire* Map 11 NN64 *Mountain Visitor Centre* On slopes of Perthshire's highest mountain, 3,984ft, noted or variety of Alpine flowers, and species of irds to be seen. Centre includes exhibition nd self-guided and guided trails. Open 4 Apr o 25 May, Mon to Sat 11 – 4, Sun 10 – 5.30; 26 May to 30 Sep, daily 10 – 5.30. 30p (ch 10p). ⚠ *(Tel Killin 397)*. *(NTS)*

INLITHGOW Lothian *West Lothian* Map 11 NS97

Blackness Castle 4½m NE. A 15th-C tower nd later stronghold, formerly a Covenanters' rison and at one time used as a powder magazine. Massive 17th-C artillery mplacements. Open, see inside front cover. 0p (ch 10). ⚠ *(AM)*

House of The Binns 4m E off A904. A 15th-C nd later house, with 17th-C plaster ceilings. General Tam Dalyell raised the Royal Scots Greys here in 1681. Panoramic viewpoint in rounds. Open 5/6 Apr, then 1 May to 30 Sep aily (ex Fri) 2 – 5.30. Parkland 10 – 7. 75p (ch 5p). Members of Royal Scots Dragoon Guards, successors to Royal Scots Greys dmitted free when in uniform. *(NTS)*

Jnlithgow Palace A fine, but ruined 15th- nd 16th-C structure, associated with Mary, Queen of Scots (born here in 1542), and also ith Prince Charles Edward. Chapel, great all, and quadrangle fountain are notable. Open, see inside front cover. 25p (ch 12p). ⚠ *(AM)*

OCHAWE Strathclyde *Argyll* Map 10 NN12 *Cruachan Power Station* 3m W off A85, near Pass of Brander. This important power station f the North of Scotland Hydro-electric Board umps water from Loch Awe to a spectacular igh level reservoir up on Ben Cruachan. The tation is open to the public from 9 – 5. 50p (ch 1 – 16 20p; ch 10 accompanied, free) and a

minibus service into the underground station is provided for touring motorists during the summer. Under revision for 1980. ⚠

Kilchurn Castle 1½m E on A85. Dates from 1440, with additions of the 16th and 17th C, in a beautiful mountain setting at the north-east extremity of Loch Awe. Closed for repair but can be seen at close quarters. Free. *(AM)*

LOCHCARRON Highland *Ross and Cromarty* Map 14 NG83

Strome Castle 3m SE. A fragmentary ruin of the Macdonalds of Glengarry, blown up by Kenneth Mackenzie of Kintail in 1602. There are wide views across the Inner Sound to Scalpay, Raasay and the Coolins of Skye. Accessible at all reasonable times. *(NTS)*

LOCHTY Fife *Fife* Map 12 NO50 *Lochty Private Railway* Steam trains run on Sun from Lochty to Knightsward, hauled by the restored War Department Tank Locomotive No. 16. Train includes ex LNER Observation Coach, part of pre-war 'Coronation Express'. There are regular services Jun to Sep, Sun from 2 – 5. Return fare 45p (ch 14 20p). ⚠

LOCHMABEN Dumfries and Galloway *Dumfriesshire* Map 11 NY08

Rammerscales 3m S off B7020. Contains a fine circular staircase, elegant public rooms, and a long library at the top of the house. There are Jacobite relics and links with Flora Macdonald. Also a small collection of works by modern artists. Picnic areas in grounds which have fine views over Annandale. Open 5 Jun to 16 Sep every Tue and Thu and alternate Suns (otherwise by appointment) 2 – 5. 50p (ch 14 25p). ⚠ *(Tel 361)*

LUSS Strathclyde *Dunbartonshire* Map 10 NS39

Rossdhu House 3½m S. Historic home of the Chiefs of Clan Colquhoun on the banks of Loch Lomond. Lochside walks, picnic area and bathing beach. Craft and gift shop ⌾. Open Easter weekend, then May to mid Oct, daily 10.30 – 5 (last admission). Admission to house and grounds 85p (ch 45p); Grounds only 65p (ch and pen 35p) subject to review. ⚠ *(Tel 231)*

MARYPARK Grampian *Banffshire* Map 15 NJ13

Glenfarclas Distillery 1m W. One of the finest Highland Malt whiskies is produced here. There is an exhibition, museum, craft shop and visitor centre. Open all year (ex 25 Dec, 1 and 2 Jan) Mon to Fri 9 – 4.30. Free. ⚠ *(Tel Ballindalloch 257)*

MAUCHLINE Strathclyde *Ayrshire* Map 11 NS42

National Burns Memorial and Cottage Homes The memorial tower of 1896 stands

north of the town on the Kilmarnock road and has a Burns museum containing many relics of the poet. ☞ Open most of the year 9–6. 15p (ch 10p). ⚠ *(Tel Ayr 50213)*

MAYBOLE Strathclyde *Ayrshire* Map 10 NS20

Crossraguel Abbey 2m SW. A cluniac monastery founded by Duncan, Earl of Carrick in 1244. The remains of the abbey are very extensive and of high architectural distinction. They consist of the church, claustral buildings, outer court with an imposing castellated gatehouse and abbot's house. Open, see inside front cover. 15p (ch 7p). ⚠ *(AM)*

MELROSE Borders *Roxburghshire* Map 12 NT53

Abbotsford House 2m W off A6091. 19th-C mansion on the River Tweed. Built by Sir Walter Scott; this is where he died. Contains his library and a collection of historical relics. ☞ Open 20 Mar to 31 Oct, Mon to Sat 10–5 Sun 2–5. 70p (ch 16 35p). Party 60p (ch 30p). (subject to alteration). ⚠ *(Tel Galashiels 2043). (Mrs P Maxwell-Scott)* ⓖ

Melrose Abbey Probably the most famous ruin in Scotland, owing much of its modern fame to the glamour given to it by Sir Walter Scott. This was a beautiful Cistercian abbey, repeatedly wrecked during the wars of Scottish independence and notably by Richard II in 1385. Most of the ruins belong to the 15th-C reconstruction. The heart of Robert the Bruce was discovered buried here some 20 years ago, and was reburied in front of the altar. Open see inside front cover. 25p (ch 12p). ⚠ Also **Abbey Museum** housed in 15th- to 16th-C former Commendator's House, containing carved stones, etc, and situated in the abbey grounds. Details as above. *(AM)*

Priorwood Gardens Special garden with flowers for drying. Visitor centre and shop, picnic area adjacent to Melrose Abbey. Open 4 Apr to mid Oct Mon to Sat 10–6, Sun 1.30–5.30; mid Oct to 24 Dec Mon 2–5.30, Tue to Sat 10–5.30. Free. *(Tel 2555). (NTS)*

MENSTRIE Central *Clackmannanshire* Map 11 NS89

Menstrie Castle 16th-C fortress now restored partly as modern flats. It was the birthplace in 1657 of Sir William Alexander, the founder of Nova Scotia. The Nova Scotia Commemoration Rooms devised and furnished by the NTS are shown May to Sep, Wed, Sat, and Sun 2.30–5 and on application to caretaker in castle. Free. *(NTS and Clackmannan District Council)*

METHLICK Grampian *Aberdeenshire* Map 15 NJ83

Haddo House 2m SE. Designed by William Adam in 1731 and replaces a previous building called the Place of Kellie. Much of the interior is 'Adam Revival' of about 1880, and the contents of this stately yet homely house are unique in their variety and appeal. Open 1 May to 30 Sep, Mon to Sat 11–6, Sun 2–6 (last visitors 5.15). 85p (ch 40p). House closed 10/11 May. *(NTS)*

MEY Highland *Caithness* Map 15 ND27

Castle of Mey Gardens Dates from 1606 and is now a home of Her Majesty Queen Elizabeth, the Queen Mother. Fine views across the Pentland Firth towards the Orkneys. ☞ Gardens only shown. Opening dates for 1980 not available. 20p (ch 12 and pen 10p). ⚠ 20p. *(Tel Barrock 275)* ⓖ

MILNATHORT Tayside *Kinross-shire* Map 11 NO10

Burleigh Castle A 16th-C tower house, with courtyard enclosure and roofed angle tower, dating from 1582. Open, see inside front cover. Key with keeper at farm opposite. Free *(AM)*

MINARD Strathclyde *Argyll* Map 10 NR99

Crarae Gardens Woodland garden, with rhododendrons, eucalyptus, rare trees, and shrubs, in a Highland glen. Open 1 Mar to end of Oct, daily from 8 am. 50p (ch 16 free) by collecting box. ⚠ *(Tel Furnace 284). (Sir Ilay Campbell of Succoth Bt)*

MOFFAT Dumfries and Galloway *Dumfriesshire* Map 11 NT00

Ladyknowe Mill Small weaving unit, skirtmaking department where garments can be seen in process. Showroom for sale of woollens, tweeds and tartans. Scottish gifts and souvenirs. ☞ Open all year, mid Mar to end Oct daily 9–5, Nov to mid Mar Mon to Fri 9–5. Free. ⚠ *(Tel 20134)* ⓖ

MONIAIVE Dumfries and Galloway *Dumfriesshire* Map 11 NX79

Maxwelton House Stronghold of Earls of Glencairn until 1611, and later birthplace of Annie Laurie. Fascinating house, recently restored, covering 500 years of architectural whims. Own chapel, and museum of ancient domestic appliances. Annie Laurie's boudoir and other rooms in the house open May to Sep Wed and Thu afternoon 2–5, also 4th Sun in month. 60p (ch 10 20p). No dogs. ⚠ *(Tel 384). (Maxwelton House Trust)*

MUCHALLS Grampian *Kincardineshire* Map 15 NO89

Muchalls Castle 17th-C castle, with fine fireplaces and plaster ceilings. Open May to Sep, Tue and Sun 3–5. 30p (ch 10p, babies free). No dogs. ⚠ *(Tel Newtonhill 30217). (Mr and Mrs M A Simpson)*

MUSSELBURGH Lothian *Midlothian*
Map 11 NT37
Pinkie House A fine Jacobean building of
1613 and later, incorporating a tower of 1390.
Fine painted ceiling in the long gallery. The
house now forms part of the well-known
Loretto School. Open every Tue 2–4. Party.
& *(Tel 031-665 2825)*

MUTHILL Tayside *Perthshire* Map 11 NN81
Drummond Castle Gardens 1m N. Beautiful
formal gardens. Open (gardens only) 1 Apr to
30 Sep, Wed and Sun 2–6. 40p (ch 20p).
Under revision for 1980. & *(Tel 257)*. *(The
Grimsthorpe and Drummond Castle Trust
Ltd)*

NEW ABBEY Dumfries and Galloway
Kirkcudbrightshire Map 11 NX96
Sweetheart Abbey One of the most beautiful
monastic ruins in Scotland, built for the Lady
Devorgilla of Galloway, in memory of her
husband John Balliol, in 1273. In 1289 the
lady was buried in front of the high altar with
the 'sweet heart' of her husband resting on
her bosom. Open, see inside front cover. 20p
(ch 10p). & *(AM)*

NEWTONMORE Highland *Inverness-shire*
Map 14 NN79
Clan Macpherson House and Museum A
museum containing interesting relics of the
'forty-five', including the 'black chanter' of the
Clan Chattan (1395), the Green Banner and
the Charmed Sword, etc. Open May to Sep,
Mon to Sat 10–12 and 2–6. Free (donation).
& *(Tel 332)* &

NORTH BERWICK Lothian *East Lothian*
Map 12 NT58
North Berwick Museum School Road. Small
museum in former Burgh school with sections
on local history, archaeology, shipping, and
natural history (especially birds). Open Jun
and Sep weekends only; Jul and Aug daily,
Mon to Sat 10–1, 2–5, Sun 2–5 (subject to
review). Free. & *(Tel 3470)*
Tantallon Castle 2m E on A198. A famous
14th-C stronghold of the Douglases facing
towards the lonely Bass Rock from the rocky
firth of Forth shore. Nearby earthworks of
16th- and 17th-C date. Open, see inside front
cover. 25p (ch 12p). *(AM)*

OBAN Strathclyde *Argyll* Map 10 NM83
Dunstaffnage Castle 3m N on Peninsular. A
ruined four-sided 13th-C Campbell
stronghold, showing a gatehouse, two round
towers, and walls 10ft thick. Once the prison
of Flora MacDonald. Open, see inside front
cover. Free. & *(AM)*
Macdonald's Mill ½m S of centre of Oban, on
A816. Exhibition of the Story of Spinning and
Weaving, and demonstrations of this ancient
Scottish industry. Also showroom containing
modern products. Vending machines. Open
Mar to Oct Mon to Fri 9–7.30, Sat 9–5;
demonstrations Mon to Fri only. Free. & &

OLD DAILLY Strathclyde *Ayrshire*
Map 10 NX29
Bargany Gardens 4m NE on B734 from
Girvan. Woodland walks; snowdrops,
bluebells and daffodils in profusion. Fine
display of azaleas and rhododendrons round
lily pond in May and Jun. Autumn colours.
Many fine ornamental trees. Plants for sale.
Picnic area. Gardens open 1 Feb to 31 Oct
daily 10–7 (4 in winter). Contribution box. &
(buses by arrangement). *(Tel 227)* &

OLD DEER Grampian *Aberdeenshire*
Map 15 NJ94
Deer Abbey The remains of the Cistercian
Abbey, founded in 1219, include the southern
claustral range, the Abbot's House and the
infirmary. The famous Book of Deer, compiled
in the former Celtic monastery on a different
site, is now in the University Library at
Cambridge. The ruins are accessible Apr to
Sep, weekdays 9.30–7, Sun 2–7. 15p (ch
7p). & *(AM)*

OLDMELDRUM Grampian *Aberdeenshire*
Map 15 NJ82
Glengarioch Distillery Distillery Road.
Distillation of Scotch Whisky and horticultural
unit using waste heat from the distillery. Open
all year ex Jul and Aug. Telephone for times.
Free. & *(Tel 2706)*

PAISLEY Strathclyde *Renfrewshire*
Map 11 NS46
Paisley Museum and Art Galleries High
Street. Contains collections illustrating local
industrial and natural history of Paisley and
district. World-famous collection of Paisley
shawls. Art collection with emphasis on 19th-
C Scottish artists. Open all year (ex Sun and
PH) Mon, Wed, Thu and Fri 10–5, Tue 10–8,
Sat 10–6. Free. & *(Tel 041-889 3151)*

PALNACKIE Dumfries and Galloway
Kirkcudbrightshire Map 11 NX85
Orchardton Tower A rare example of a
circular late 15th-C tower, built originally by
John Cairns. Open, see inside front cover, on
application to the Custodian. Free. *(AM)*

PATHHEAD Lothian *Midlothian* Map 11 NT36
Prestonhall A late 18th-C mansion designed
by Robert Mitchell. Set in parkland with
beautiful old trees. Open all year by
appointment only. 75p house, garden and
park. & *(Tel Ford [Midlothian] 320309)*.
(Major J D Callander MC)

BARGANY

Bargany, Girvan, Ayrshire
Captain N Dalrymple-Hamilton R.N.

Route B734 from Girvan 3 miles

Visitors welcomed to this private garden, open daily from 10am-7pm,
February 1 to October 31. Free-will contribution box by the car park.
Picnic areas. Paths through fine woodlands, shrub gardens, rock garden
and walled garden. May/June azaleas, rhododendrons, spectacular
sight round lily pond. Spring display of snowdrops, wild hyacinth,
daffodils, cherry blossom. Bus parties by arrangement with owner.
Tel: Old Dailly 227.

PEEBLES Borders *Peebleshire*
Map 11 NT23
Kailzie 2½m SE on B7062. Extensive grounds
with fine old trees, Burnside walk with bulbs,
rhododendrons and azaleas. Walled garden
with herbaceous and shrub rose borders.
High class pottery. Waterfowl pond, Art
gallery. ⚲ 2.30–5 Jun to Sep. Open Easter to
end of Oct daily 10–6.30. 35p. ⚠ *(Tel 20007)*
&

Neidpath Castle On the river Tweed. The
earliest known owners of the lands of
Neidpath were the Frasers. The land passed
to the Hays of Yester, ancestors of the Earls
and Marquises of Tweeddale, about 1310
when Mary, daughter of Sir Symon Fraser
married Sir Gilbert de Haya. Construction of
the Castle apparently began during the 14th
C. After the battle of Dunbar in 1650, Lord
Yester garrisoned the castle against
Cromwellian forces, surrendering in
December 1650. Purchased by the first Duke
of Queensbury in 1686. Has passed through
several heirs to the present Lord Wemyss'
Trust. Open 12 Apr to 14 Oct, Mon to Sat
10–1 and 2–6, Sun 1–6, subject to
availability of staff. 30p (ch 5–14 10p). Dogs
on leads only. ⚠

PENCAITLAND Lothian *East Lothian*
Map 12 NT46
Winton House Dates from 1620, with 19th-C
additions, a fine example of Scottish
Renaissance architecture, with beautiful
plaster ceilings, pictures, furnishings, and
unique carved stone chimneys. Associations
with King Charles I and Sir Walter Scott.
Terraced garden. Open to parties by prior
written or telephone appointment from *Sir
David Ogilvy Bt (Tel 349222)*. Admission to
house and gardens 700p (provisional price for
1980) reduction for children. ⚠

PERTH Tayside *Perthshire* Map 11 NO12
Branklyn Garden on Dundee Road, A85.
Has been described as the finest garden of its
size in all Britain. Little more than two acres, it
is noted for its collection of rhododendrons,
shrubs and alpine plants. Open 1 Mar to 31
Oct, daily 10–sunset or by arrangement. 50p
(ch 25p). ⚠ 5p. *(Tel 25535). (NTS)*
The Black Watch Regimental Museum
Balhousie Castle, Hay Street. Treasures of
the 42nd/73rd Highland Regiment from
1725–1979 including painting, silver, colours
and uniforms. Open May to Oct Mon to Fri
10–12 and 2–4.30 (Nov to Apr 3.30). Free. ⚠
(Tel 26287 ext 3)
Elcho Castle 5m SE on S bank of River Tay.
A well-preserved 16th-C stronghold, with

wrought-iron window grilles. Open from Apr t
Sep, weekends 9.30–7, Sun 2–7; from Oct t
Mar. weekdays 9.30–4, Sun 2–4. 15p (ch 7)
⚠ *(AM)*
Fair Maid's House North Port. Situated near
the historic North Inch where the battle of the
Clans was fought in 1396. It was built near the
former Dominican monastery and in the 14th
C became the home of Simon Glover, a
glovemaker, whose daughter Catherine was
the heroine of Sir Walter Scott's *Fair Maid of
Perth*. The house was a guildhall for over 150
years. It was renovated in the 19th C and is
now a centre for Scottish Crafts and Antiques
A recently uncovered wall is said to be the
oldest visible wall in Perth. Open all year Mon
to Sat 10–5. P. *(Tel 25976)*
Huntingtower Formerly known as Ruthven
Castle. A castellated 15th- and 16th-C
structure, with a painted ceiling. Famous as
the scene of the so-called 'Ruthven Raid' of
1582. Open, see inside front cover. 15p (ch
7p). *(AM)*
Perth Museum and Art Gallery George
Street. Purpose-built in 1935 to house
collections of fine and applied art, social &
local history, natural history, archaeology etc
Special events monthly, holiday activities for
schoolchildren. Open all year, Mon to Sat
10–1 and 2–5, Sun 2–4. Free, ⚠ *(Tel Perth
32488)* &

PETERCULTER Grampian *Aberdeenshire*
Map 15 NJ80
Drum Castle 3m W. The oldest part, the gre
square tower – one of the three oldest tower
houses in Scotland – dates from the late 13th
C. A charming mansion was added in 1619,
with characteristic features of the period,
enclosing a quadrangle. In 1323 King Rober
the Bruce gave a charter of the Royal Forest
of Drum to William de Irwin. This family
connection remained unbroken until the
death in 1975 of Mr H Q Forbes Irvine, who
bequeathed the castle and over 400 acres of
land to the Trust. Open 1 May to 30 Sep Mon
to Sat 11–6, Sun 2–6; (last visitors 5.15). 75
(ch 35p). Grounds open all year 9.30–sunse
(by donation). ⚠ 10p. *(Tel Drumoak 204)*.
(NTS)

PETERHEAD Grampian *Aberdeenshire*
Map 15 NK14
Arbuthnot Museum and Art Gallery A
museum specialising in local exhibits,
particularly those relating to the fishing
industry; includes also Arctic and whaling
specimens. British coin collection. Open Mo
to Fri 10–12 and 2–5 (4.30 Fri), Sat 2–5.
Free. *(Tel 2554)*

The Fair Maid's
House

The Fair Maid's House, home of the
legendary Fair Maid of Perth, is a perfect
setting to view a wide selection of Scottish
Crafts and Curios and Antiques.
Open daily 10-5pm (except Sunday).
Visitors welcome.

Fair Maid's House, North Port, Perth, Scotland. Tel: 25976

SCOTLAND

Rhynie 251

PITCAPLE Grampian *Aberdeenshire*
Map 15 NJ72
Pitcaple Castle Built in the 15th C, a castle owned by the Leslies and Lumsdens. Many historical associations and family relics. Still lived in as a home. Visitors welcomed Apr to Sep during reasonable hours if convenient. Large parties at other times by prior appointment. 50p (ch 16 25p). ⚠ *(Tel 204).* *(Capt and Mrs Burges-Lumsden of Pitcaple)*

PITLOCHRY Tayside *Perthshire*
Map 14 NN95
Faskally Wayside Centre 2m NW. Incorporates woodland/lochside parking, picnic facilities, children's play area and nature trail. Open May to Sep daily 8–7.50. ⚠ 20p per vehicle. *(Tel Killiecrankie 223)*
Pitlochry Power Station Dam and Fish Pass There is a permanent definitive exhibition of hydro electricity at Pitlochry Power Station, with audio-visual presentation. The Power Station is not open, but there is a viewing gallery in exhibition area. Fish Pass observation chamber open during daylight hours. ⚐ Exhibition open Easter to Oct daily 10–6 (8.30 Jul an Aug, ex Mon). 15p (ch 5p, free if accompanied). Under revision for 1980. ⚠ (limited).

PITMEDDEN Grampian *Aberdeenshire*
Map 15 NJ82
Pitmedden A fine late 17th-C garden, now re-created. Sundials, pavilions, and fountains. Elaborate floral desings. Gardens only open all year, daily 9.30–dusk. 40p (20p). Grounds by donation. *(Tel Udny 445).* *(NTS)* ₷
Tolquhon Castle 2m NE off B999. A late 16th-C quadrangular mansion, now roofless. and enclosing an early 15th-C tower. Fine gatehouse and courtyard. Open, see inside front cover. 15p (ch 7p). ⚠ *(AM)*

POLMONT Central *Stirlingshire*
Map 11 NS97
Westquarter Dovecot This notable example of a Scottish dovecot is dated 1647 and carries the arms of Sir William Livingstone. The exterior can be seen regularly. *(AM)*

POOLEWE Highland *Ross and Cromarty*
Map 14 NG88
Inverewe Remarkable gardens, full of interest and beauty from Mar to Oct (at their best May to early Jun), and containing rare and sub-tropical plants. They were commenced in 1862 by Osgood Mackenzie. Magnificent mountain background, Loch Maree lies to south. ⚐ (open Apr to Sep). Open daily (incl Sun), all the year, 9–9 (or dusk if earlier). Visitor centre, 1 Apr to mid Oct 10–6.30 or dusk if earlier, Sun 1–6.30 or dusk if earlier. 95p (ch 45p), adult parties 55p per person. ⚠ 10p. *(Tel 229). (NTS)* ₷

PORT GLASGOW Strathclyde *Renfrewshire*
Map 10 NS37
Newark Castle Dates from the 16th and 17th C, preserving a courtyard and hall; the hall carries an inscription of 1596. Fine turrets and remains of painted ceilings. Once a home of the Maxwells. Open, see inside front cover. 5p (ch 7p). ⚠ *(AM)*

PORT LOGAN Dumfries and Galloway *Wigtownshire* Map 10 NX04
Logan Botanic Garden An annexe of the Royal Botanic Garden in Edinburgh. Notable garden containing a wide range of plants from the warm temperate regions of the world. ⚐ Open Apr to 30 Sep, daily 10–5. ⚠ Car and passengers 30p. No animals. Under revision for 1980. *(Tel 077–686 231)* ₷

PORT OF MENTEITH Central *Perthshire*
Map 11 NN50
Inchmahome Priory The 13th-C ruins of the church and cloisters of an Augustinian house, founded by Walter Comyn in 1238. Famous as the retreat of the infant Mary, Queen of Scots, in 1543. The ruins are situated on an island in the Lake of Menteith and are open Apr to mid-Nov, weekdays 9.30–7, Sun 2–7. Ferry subject to cancellation in adverse weather conditions. Advisable to check 25p (ch 12p) *(Tel Stirling 62421).* ⚠ At ferry. *(AM)*

QUEENSFERRY (South) Lothian *West Lothian* Map 11 NT17
Hopetoun House 2m W on unclass road. residence of the Marquess of Linlithgow MC. Scotland's greatest Adam mansion. Magnificent reception rooms, pictures, furnishings, and spacious grounds. Red and fallow deer and St Kilda sheep. Nature trail. Views of Forth Road Bridge. ⚐ (lunch, tea). Open 27 Apr to 22 Sep, daily 11–5.40. £1 (ch and pen 50p) Subject to review for 1980. ⚠ ₷ B
William Sanderson and Son 27 The Loan. Blending and bottling plant where VAT 69 and The Antiquary de Luxe Whiskies are prepared for United Kingdom and all export markets. Open all year (ex for Edinburgh statutory holidays, first two weeks in Jul and Christmas week), for conducted tours. Mon to Fri at 10 and 2. No tour Fri afternoons. Visits by prior appointment only. Free. ⚠ (limited). P. *(Tel 031-331 1500)*

QUEEN'S VIEW Tayside *Perthshire*
Map 14 NN85
Tummel Forest Centre Exhibits show changes in Tummel Valley since Queen Victoria's visit in 1866. Included are a diorama, a model of a Highland Clachan in the forest, which has recently been excavated and partly restored. Slides and sound show. Information desk. Forest walks. Picnic areas. Regular access. Open Easter to Sep 9–6. Free. ⚠ ₷ B

REAY Highland *Caithness* Map 14 NC96
Dounreay United Kingdom Atomic Energy Authority Exhibition 2m NE. Scale models, charts, and panels, relating to the fast reactor and nuclear energy generally housed in a former airfield control overlooking the plant, conspicuous for its 135ft sphere and the Prototype fast reactor. Limited number of afternoon tours to the reactor. Tickets from Thurso Tourist Information Centre. Open May to Sep, daily 9–4. Free. ⚠ *(Tel Thurso 2121 ext 656)*

RHU Strathclyde *Dunbartonshire*
Map 10 NS28
Glenarn A woodland garden with a remarkable collection of rhododendron species and hybrids, also Chilean and Australasian shrubs and trees. Open 1 Apr to 30 Jun, daily, dawn to dusk. 40p (ch 15p). P (roadside). ₷

RHYNIE Grampian *Aberdeenshire*
Map 15 NJ42
Druminnor Castle 1½m SE. This 15th-C castle was a former home of the Forbes family, and incorporates a small museum of local household, garden and ancient utensils. The building has been restored and preserves a hall fireplace of 1660. Open May to Sep Wed 2.30–5.30. 50p (ch 30p). ⚠ *(Tel 248). (Andrew Forbes)* **(79)**
Leith Hall and Garden 3½m NE on B9002. A house built round a courtyard, with Jacobite

relics and a fine rock garden. The earliest part dates from 1650. Open 1 May to 30 Sep, Mon to Sat 11–6, Sun 2–6 (last visitors 5.15). Gardens and grounds open all year 9.30–sunset. House 75p (ch 35p), school parties 25p per person. Gardens and grounds by donation. *(Tel Kennethmont 216). (NTS)* & B

ROTHES Grampian *Moray* Map 15 NJ24
Glen Grant Distillery Established 1840. The whisky produced here is regarded as one of the best, as well as being sold as a single Glen Grant Malt in bottle. Traditional malt whisky methods of distillation are used together with the most modern equipment. Reception, Shop and Hospitality Bar. Open Easter to mid Oct 10–4. Free. ⚠ *(Tel 243 or 327)*

RUTHWELL Dumfries and Galloway *Dumfriesshire* Map 11 NY16
Ruthwell Cross Off B724. One of Europe's most famous carved crosses resting in the Parish Church in an apse built specially for it. The date is probably 8th-C and the 18ft-high cross is richly carved with Runic characters showing the earliest form of English in Northumbrian dialect. Free. Key of church obtainable from the *Key Keeper, Kirkyett Cottage, Ruthwell. (AM)*
Henry Duncan Museum First Savings Bank founded here in 1810. Interior set in period furnishings around a peat fire and contains many early savings bank documents, four lock security kist, collection of home savings banks from Great Britain and abroad, International Money Corner etc. Personal pencil drawings. Open daily. Free. ⚠ *(Tel Clarencefield 640)* &

ST ANDREWS Fife *Fife* Map 12 NO51
Castle Ruined 14th-C stronghold where Cardinal Beaton was murdered in 1546. Captured by the French fleet in the following year. Open, see inside front cover. 25p (ch 12p). *(AM)*

ST VIGEANS Tayside *Angus* Map 12 NO64
St Vigeans Museum A notable collection of more than 40 sculptured stones dating from early Christian and medieval periods, including the well-known inscribed Drosten Stone. They are housed in a cottage museum. Open Apr to Sep, Fri to Mon only 9.30–7; Oct to Mar, 9.30–4. 15p (ch 7p). *(AM)*.

SALTCOATS Strathclyde *Ayrshire* Map 10 NS24
North Ayrshire Museum A museum located in the ancient former Parish Church, with interesting old churchyard gravestones. Exhibits portray local historical items, and early 19th-C interiors. Open mid Apr to Oct Mon to Sat (ex Wed) 10–4. ⚠ *(Tel 64174)* &

SCONE Tayside *Perthshire* Map 11 NO02
Scone Palace Home of Earl of Mansfield in town famous in Scottish history as the 'Royal City of Scone'. A seat of government in Pictish times, the home of the Stone of Destiny until 1296 when Edward I removed it to Westminster Abbey; Scottish kings were crowned at Scone until 1651. A religious centre for more than 1,000 years. Present palace, largely rebuilt in 1803, incorporates part of the earlier 1580 palace. Fine collection of French furniture, china, 16th-C needlework, including bed hangings worked by Mary, Queen of Scots, ivories and *objets*

d'art. The Pinetum has one of the finest collections of rare conifers in the country, and the woodland garden displays rhododendrons and azaleas. ⚠ (licensed). Open end Apr to 1st week Oct, Mon to Sat 10–6, Sun 2–6. No admission after 5.30 pm. Admission to house, grounds and pinetum. Opening times and prices under revision. ⚠ *(Rt Hon the Earl of Mansfield)*

SELKIRK Borders *Selkirkshire* Map 12 NT42
Bowhill 2½m off A708. For many generations the Border home of the Scots of Buccleuch. The house contains an outstanding collection of pictures, porcelain and furniture, Monmouth's saddlery and relics, Sir Walter Scott's proofs and portraits. Special Wilkie exhibition. Adventure woodland play area and pony trekking. ⚠ (afternoon teas). Open 5, 6 and 7 Apr; May, Jun and Sep, Sat, Sun, Wed and Thu; Jul and Aug daily (ex Fri) 2–6 (last entry 5.15). Admission prices not yet decided P. *(Tel 20732)* &
Halliwells House Private museum of old ironmongery housed in a close of mid 17th-C cottages and stables. Open May to Sep, weekdays 9.30–11, 2–4. P. *(79)*
Selkirk Museum Ettrick Terrace. Occupies first floor of former Town Jail, built in 1803, and includes items of local history, craft tools, flags, photographs, Common-Riding items, mementoes of local celebrities including Sir Walter Scott, Mungo Park and Andrew Lang. Open Jun to late Sep, Mon–Fri 2–5. Free. P 30yds. *(Tel Selkirk 20096)*

STIRLING Central *Stirlingshire* Map 11 NS79
Cambuskenneth Abbey Founded in 1147 by David I, this abbey was the scene of Bruce's important parliament of 1326. It is also the burial place of James III and his wife. Open Apr to Sep weekdays 9.30–7, Sun 2–7. 15p (ch 7p). *(AM)*
Stirling Castle Upper Castle Hill. A historic 13th-C and earlier structure. The Renaissance additions of the 16th C are notable. Queen Victoria's lookout and the Ladies' Rock are viewpoints. Open Apr, May and Sep 9.30–6.15, Sun 11–6; Jun, Jul and Aug 9.30–8, Sun 11–7; Oct, Mar 9.30–4, Sun 1–4. 1 Apr to 30 Sep 30p (ch 15p); 10 Oct to 31 Mar 25p (ch 12p). ⚠ *(AM)*
Landmark Scotland's second Landmark Centre, with exhibition and shop in restored old building overlooking River Forth near castle. Multi-screen presentation of the history of Stirling Castle. ⚠ Open all year, daily summer 9–8, winter 9–5. Theatre and exhibition 60p (ch 30p). P. *(Tel 62517)* &
Mar's Wark Broad Street. A partly ruined Renaissance mansion, with a gatehouse enriched by sculptures. Built by the Regent Mar in 1570. Open at all times. Free. *(AM)*
The Museum of the Argyll and Sutherland Highlanders Situated in King James V Palace of Stirling Castle and contains fine collection of regimental silver and plate, colours, pipe banners, painting and items of uniform. Also collection of medals, covering period from Waterloo to present day, including a number of Victorian crosses. Open 1 Apr to 31 Oct, Mon to Sat 10–6, Sun 12–6 (closes at 4 in Oct). Free. ⚠

STOBO Borders *Peeblesshire* Map 11 NT13
Dawyck Arboretum 2m SW. 8m SW Peebles. Impressive gardens, noted for collections of trees and shrubs. House not shown. Arboretum open daily from Easter to end Sep, 10–5. ⚠ &

STONEHAVEN Grampian *Kincardineshire*
Map 15 NO88
Dunnottar Castle 1½m S off A92. On a
headland facing North Sea, dates from late
14th to 16th C. Besieged by Montrose in
1645. The Scottish regalia were kept here for
safety in the 17th C. Open all year (ex Sats in
Winter) Mon to Sat 9 – 6, Sun 2 – 5. 30p (ch 15
10p). ⚠ *(Tel 62173)*
Stonehaven Tolbooth Once a 16th-C
storehouse of the Earls Marischal, later used
as a prison. Restored and re-opened in 1963
by the Queen Mother; fishing and local history
museum. Open from Jun to Sep, daily (ex
Tue) 2 – 5 Sat 10 – 12. Free. ⚐ ⚠ *(Tel
Peterhead 2554)* ⚹

TARBOLTON Strathclyde *Ayrshire*
Map 10 NS42
Bachelors' Club A 17th-C house, taking its
name from the society which Robert Burns
and his friends founded there in 1780. Period
furnishings. Contains a small museum. Open
1 Apr to 30 Sep daily 10 – 6, other times by
appointment. 30p (ch 15p). *(Tel 424)*. *(NTS)*

THORNHILL Dumfries and Galloway
Dumfriesshire Map 11 NX89
Drumlanrig Castle 3½m NW. 17th-C castle in
pink stone with 15 lead cupola turrets.
Celebrated collection of paintings, Louis XIV
furniture, silver and Bonnie Prince Charlie
relics. Woodland walks and picnic spots.
Open 5, 6 and 7 Apr, then Sat, Sun, Wed and
Thu in May and Jun and BH Mon 12.30 – 5
(last entry 4.30). Daily Jul and Aug 11 – 5 (last
entry 4.30), ground incl adventure woodland
open till 6pm. Party. Admission prices not yet
decided. ⚠ *(Tel 30248)* ⚹

TARFSIDE Tayside *Angus* Map 15 NO57
The Retreat 1m E. Former shooting lodge,
with museum of local country life and
handicrafts. Shop. ⚐ Beautiful glen setting.
Open from Easter to 1 Jun, Sun only, 2 – 6;
from Jun to end of Sep, daily 2 – 6. 30p (ch 12
15p) subject to alteration. ⚠

TOMINTOUL Grampian *Banffshire*
Map 15 NJ11
Tomintoul Museum The Square.
Reconstructed farm kitchen. Cobbler's and
harness displays. Jun to Sep 10 – 6 (7 Jul and
Aug). Free. ⚠ *(Tel 285)*

TONGLAND Dumfries and Galloway
Kirkcudbrightshire Map 11 NX65
Tongland Tour Visitors can see part of the
SSEB Galloway hydro-electricity scheme. It
includes a visit to the dam and power station
at Tongland. A fish ladder is an attraction to
the tour. Also small exhibition at the
Portakabin reception area. Open Jul to Sep.
Mon to Sat 9 – 5 by appointment only. Free. ⚠
people wishing to make the tour are picked up
by bus in Kirkcudbright, and later returned.
(Tel Kirkcudbright 30144)

TORPHICHEN Lothian *West Lothian*
Map 11 NS97
Torphichen Preceptory This was the
principal seat of the knights of St John. The
central tower and trancepts of their church still
remain. The west tower is of Romanesque
date; and the nave, now the parish church,
was rebuilt in the 18th C. Open, see inside
front cover, ex Wed and alternate Fri when
closed all day. 15p (ch 7p). *(AM)*

TORRIDON Highland *Ross and Cromarty*
Map 14 NG85
Trust Visitor Centre Situated at junction of
A896 and Diabeg road amid some of
Scotland's finest scenery. Audio-visual

presentations on wild life and static display at
nearby Mains of the life of the red deer, also
collection of live animals; both open 1 Jun to
30 Sep, Mon to Sat 10 – 6, Sun 1 – 6.
Programme of walks available on request.
Admission to Deer Museum 20p (ch 10p),
audio-visual display 20p (ch 10p). *(NTS)*

TRANENT Lothian *East Lothian*
Map 12 NT47
*Prestongrange Historical Site and Mining
Museum* Site with around 800 years of coal
mining history, the centre piece of which is a
Cornish beam engine – the only one
left in Scotland. Its five-storey building is
scheduled as an industrial Monument and
contains plans and documents. The former
power house is now an exhibition hall. Mining
artefacts on show. Outside are two colliery
shunting locomotives, one of which can be
seen working on first Sun in month, and a
100-year-old steam navvy. Around the site
the foundations of many old engines have
been exposed. Open Mon to Fri 9 – 4.30, Sat
by arrangement, Sun Apr to Oct incl
(volunteers at work). ⚠ Enquiries to *David
Spence, Hon Curator, 24 Woodlands Grove,
Edinburgh EH15 3PD (Tel 031 – 661 2718)* or
*Mr G B Duncan, Director, Physical Planning,
East Lothian District Council, Haddington*.

TURRIFF Grampian *Aberdeenshire*
Map 15 NJ75
Craigston Castle 4m NE off B9105. Early
17th-C, and little altered since its construction
by John Urquhart. Remarkable wood
carvings. Viewable by written permission
from *Bruce Urquhart, Turriff. (Tel King
Edward 228)*
Delgatie Castle 2m E off unclass rd. The
12th- to 16th-C, with turnpike stair of 97 steps,
groined and painted ceilings, arms, armour,
pictures and furnishings. Oldest archery
meeting in Scotland dating back to 1584, held
1st Sat in Jul. Open by previous arrangement
at any date or time. 50p. ⚠ 25p. *(Capt Hay of
Hayfield)*.

UDDINGSTON Strathclyde *Lanarkshire*
Map 11 NS66
Calderpark Zoo Birds, mammals, and
reptiles housed in spacious new enclosures
and buildings. Other attractions include
ample picnic sites, souvenir shop, and
children's shows. ⚐ Open all year, daily 9 – 5
(or 7, depending on season). 85p (ch and pen
40p, ch 3 free). Party. ⚠ *(Tel 041 – 771 1185)*

WALKERBURN Borders *Peeblesshire*
Map 11 NT33
Scottish Museum of Wool Textiles
Tweedvale Mill. Museum contains a variety of
objects connected with the Scottish woollen
industry. Also demonstrations of hand
spinning and hand weaving. Open all year
Mon to Fri 10 – 5; weekends by arrangement.
Demonstrations Easter to Oct. 20p (ch 16 and
pen 10p). ⚠ *(Tel 281)* ⚹

WANLOCKHEAD Dumfries and Galloway
Dumfriesshire Map 11 NS81
Museum of Scottish Lead Mining On B797
at N end of Mennock Pass. Conserves,
displays and interprets the physical and
documentary history of lead mining in
Scotland. Indoor museum and library. 1½-mile
Visitor Walkway links a variety of mining and
social structures including mine-head,
pumping, ore preparation and smelting sites,
lades, tramways and old cottages. Open
Easter to end Sep daily 11 – 5. 25p (ch 10p).
⚠ *(Tel Leadhills 387)*

WEST KILBRIDE Strathclyde *Ayrshire*
Map 10 NS24
Hunterston Castle 2½m NW on unclass road
near coast. 15th-C Peel Tower with five
rooms furnished on show to the public. Walled
garden. Opening dates and times not yet
decided. 40p (ch 16 10p). ⚠ *(Tel West
Kilbride 823–151)*

WHITHORN Dumfries and Galloway
Wigtownshire Map 10 NX44
Whithorn Priory First Christian church in
Scotland, founded by Fergus, Lord of
Galloway in the 12th C. The ruins are scanty,
and their chief feature of interest is the fine
Norman doorway of the nave. The museum
preserves a notable group of early Christian
monuments, including the Latinus stone
dating from the 5th C. Open, see inside front
cover. 15p. (ch 7p). *(AM)*

WICK Highland *Caithness* Map 15 ND34
Castle of Old Wick A four-storeyed, ruined
square tower, known also as Castle Oliphant,
probably of 12th-C date. Besieged in 1569 by
the Master of Caithness. Accessible except
when adjoining rifle range is in use. Free.
(AM)

SCOTTISH ISLANDS

ARRAN, ISLE OF Strathclyde *Bute*
Map 10 NS03
BRODICK CASTLE Part dates from the 13th
C, with extensions of 1652 and 1844. The
former stronghold of the Dukes of Hamilton
contains a wonderful art collection.
Outstanding gardens. Open 4 to 30 Apr, Mon,
Wed and Sat 1–5,; 1 May to 30 Sep Mon to
Sat 1–5 Sun 2–5. Gardens open daily all
year 10–5. Castle and gardens 85p (ch 40p).
Gardens only 50p (ch 25p). Party rates, castle
and gardens 70p (ch 35p). ⚑ May to Sep,
Mon to Sat 10–5, Sun 1–5 (no lunches on
Sun). ⚠ 10p. (Tel Brodick 2202). *(NTS)*

BRODICK
Rosaburn Heritage Museum Set in part of a
former croft farm, the museum illustrates the
changing way of life of the island's
inhabitants. Features include a working
blacksmith's shop, a cottage furnished in
early 1920's style, a stable block with six
horses and several coaches and an open air
display of old farm equipment. Open Easter to
Sep daily (ex Sat). 25p (ch 15p). ⚠ *(Tel
Brodick 2140/2401)*

BUTE, ISLE OF Strathclyde *Bute*
Map 10 NS06

ROTHESAY
Rothesay Castle 13th-C moated castle, with
lofty curtain walls, defended by drum towers
enclosing a circular courtyard. Open, see
inside front cover, Sun 2–4. 20p (ch 10p).
(AM)
The Bute Museum Contents are all from the
county of Bute. Natural history room contains
exhibits of birds, mammals and items from the
seashore. History room has varied collections
of recent bygones including models of Clyde
steamers. There is a collection of early
Christian crosses. Prehistoric section
contains flints and pots from two recently
excavated neolithic burial cairns. Details of
nature trails on the island are on sale. Open all
year, Apr to Sep 10.30–12.30, 2.30–4.30,
Oct to Mar 2.30–4.30. Sun Jun to Sep
2.30–4.30. 20p (ch and pen 10p). P (street).

GIGHA, ISLE OF Strathclyde *Argyll*
Map 10 NR64
ARDMINISH
Achamore Unique garden of azaleas and
rhododendrons, created by the late Sir James
Horlick Bt. Open all year 10–sunset. 40p (ch
and pen 20p). P. *(Tel Gigha 254)*. *(D W N
Landale)*

GREAT CUMBRAE ISLAND
Strathclyde *Bute* Map 10 NS15
MILLPORT
Museum of the Cumbraes Garrison House.
The museum tells the story of life on and
around the Cumbraes and features many old
photographs and objects. Also photographs
of some of the steamers which achieved fame
on the Millport run. Open during summer
months Tue to Sat 10–4.30 or at other times
by appointment. Free. P 150yd. *(Tel 741)*

MULL, ISLE OF Strathclyde *Argyll*
Map 10 NM73
CRAIGNURE
Duart Castle The restored ancestral home of
the Macleans which dates from 1250 is in a
splendid setting by Duart Point, overlooking
the Sound of Mull and Firth of Lorne. ⚑ (teas)
Open May to Sep, Mon to Fri 10.30–6; in
addition Jul and Aug Sat and Sun. 40p (ch
20p). P. 5p *(The Rt Hon the Lord Maclean KT
GCVO KBE)* frequent motor launch service
from Oban direct to Castle pier and steamer to
Craignure.
Torosay Castle and Gardens 19th-C house
containing family portraits, wildlife pictures, a
superb collection of Stags' 'Heads' (antlers)
and the huge head of a prehistoric Irish elk,
dug out of a bog in Co Monaghan. Victorian
library and archive rooms with family

Achamore Gardens   Isle of Gigha   Argyll

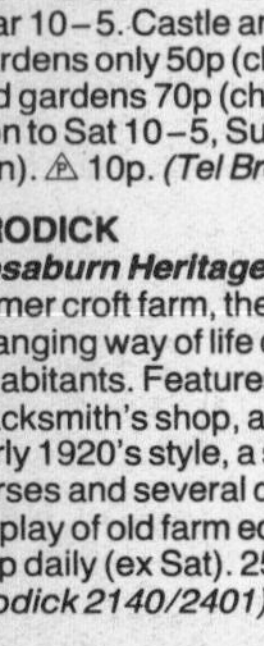

The celebrated and unique rhododendron and azalea gardens, extending to 50 acres, were created by the late Sir James Horlick between 1947-73. He left the plant collection to the National Trust for Scotland and the gardens are open to the public all the year round.
The exquisite small Island of Gigha, 3 miles off the coast of Kintyre, is easily accessible by passenger ferry from TAYINLOAN and by Caledonian-MacBrayne car ferry from Kennacraig (6 miles south of Tarbert, Loch Fyne).
The island has an excellent and attractive hotel and the Mansion House of ACHAMORE, in the centre of the Garden itself, is comfortably furnished for letting as a whole, or as two separate flats; for family holidays, or as a small conference centre.
For details: Write to Gigha Enterprises, Isle of Gigha, Argyll, Scotland (Tel: for bookings, Gigha Hotel — Gigha (058 35) 254).

scrapbooks and photographs covering the last 100 years. 11 acres of Italian gardens and grounds with Venetian statues and a plantation of Australian gum trees and many other Gulf Stream shrubs. ⫿ (teas). Open 15 May to early Oct daily 11–5 (last entry). £1 (ch, students and pen 40p, accompanied small ch free). Gardens only (when house not open) half price in 'Honesty Box'. Dogs in garden only. ⚠ *(Tel 421)*

DERVAIG Map 13 NM45
The Old Byre Visitor Centre Torra Chlachainn. 1m S off B8073. Converted with skill and imagination the centre provides a vivid reconstruction of the past life of the crofters at the time of the clearances. Authentic cottage interiors with life-size figures and animals. 1978 winner of special Certificate of Commendation in BTA 'Come to Britain Trophy' competition. 1979 awarded 1st prize in 'Museum of the year award for Scotland'. Audio-visual presentations every half-hour. Gift stall. ⫿. Open 1 May to 30 Sep Mon to Fri 10.30–5, Sun 2–5 (exhibition closes at 5.30 daily). 50p (ch 12 25p). Under revision for 1980. ⚠ *(Tel 229)*

ORKNEY ISLANDS Map 16 HY22
DOUNBY
The Brough of Birsay 6m NW. Ruined Romanesque church consisting of nave chancel and semicircular apse, with claustral buildings on north side. Adjacent to the ruins are remains of Viking dwellings which have been unearthed and are not conserved. Open, see inside front cover. (Closed on Mon in winter). Crossing by foot except at high water (no boat). 15p (ch 7p). *(AM)*
Click Mill NW of town, off B9057. Example of one of the rare old Ocadian horizontal water-mills, in working condition. Open at all times. Free. *(AM)*
Skara Brae 4m SW. A notable collection of well-preserved Stone Age dwellings, engulfed in drift sand, including stone furniture and fireplace. The most remarkable survival of its kind in Britain, much of it was first discovered in 1850 after a layer of sand was disturbed by a gale. Open, see inside front cover. 20p (ch 10p). *(AM)*

FINSTOWN HY31
Maeshowe Chambered Cairn Britain's finest megalithic tomb, of Neolithic date (c 1800 BC). Masonry in a remarkable state of preservation, showing Viking carvings and runes. Open, see inside front cover. Apply to key-keeper at nearby farmhouse. 20p (ch 10p). *(AM)*

Standing Stones 3m SW on A965. Remains of stone circle, second millenium BC. Nearby is the Ring of Brogar, of c 1600 BC, consisting of a splendid circle of upright stones with a surrounding ditch. Open at any reasonable time. Free. *(AM)*

KIRKWALL HY41
Bishop's Palace A ruined palace dating originally from the 12th C. Round tower built by Bishop Reid with addition of c 1600 by Patrick Stewart, Earl of Orkney. Open, see inside front cover. Apply custodian of Earl Patrick's Palace. 15p (ch 7p). *(AM)*
Earl Patrick's Palace Built c 1607 by Patrick Stewart, Earl of Orkney, and considered one of the finest Renaissance buildings in Scotland. Although roofless, much still remains. The oriel windows are notable. Accessible, see inside front cover ex Oct to Mar Mon to Sat 9.30–dusk, Sun 2–dusk. 15p (ch 7p) (incl Bishop's Palace). *(AM)*
Tankerness House Broad Street. Dating from the 16th C, this is one of the finest vernacular town houses in Scotland. It is now a museum of Orkney history with growing archaeological and folk life collections. Special exhibitions. Open all year, Mon to Sat 10.30–1, 2–5. Free. P. *(Tel 3191)*

STROMNESS HY20
Stromness Museum Alfred Street. The museum occupies the former Town Hall and was founded by the Orkney Natural History Society in 1837. Deals mainly with Orkney maritime and natural history, notably in bird and shell collections. There is also a New Stone Age collection. Special exhibition of Orkney interest each summer. Open 11–12.30 and 1.30–5 (from 10.30am in Jul and Aug). Closed Sun, Thu afternoon and local holidays also 3 weeks Feb–Mar. 10p (ch 3p). ⚠ *(Tel 850025)*
Stromness Art Centre The Pier Arts Centre. Collection housed in warehouse building on its own stone pier. Also galleries for visiting exhibitions and children's work. Arts library and reading room in adjacent house. Open all year 11–12.30 and 1.30–5, Thu 11–1, Sun 2–5. Free. P 50yds. *(Tel Stromness 850209)*

WESTRAY HY44
Noltland Castle Near Westray. Situated on an island in the north-west of the group, this early 15th-C ruined castle suffered several sieges and was finally destroyed in 1746. The fine hall, vaulted kitchen, and notable winding staircase are the main features of interest. Open at all reasonable times on application to custodian. Free. *(AM)*

TOROSAY CASTLE, Isle of Mull

The only house and garden in private occupation open daily to the public in the six Highland crofting Counties.

Early Scottish Baronial house by the leading Victorian architect David Bryce with French Chateau south aspect and plenty of light overlooking Italian terraced gardens laid out by Sir Robert Lorimer. Statue walk with 19 life-sized figures by Antonia Bonazza, late 18th-century Venetian. Sheltered water-garden with shrubs that flourish in Gulf-stream climate.

House refurbished to Edwardian taste with family portraits by Sargent, Poynter, de Laszlo and, more recently, Carlos Sancha etc. Wildlife pictures by Landseer, Thorburn, Lodge and Sir Peter Scott. Photographic displays of the final epoch in sail, life in the Antarctic and evidence for the Loch Ness Monster. One hundred years of family scrap books to browse over.

Vistas over Firth of Lorne to Ben Cruachan and up Appin coast to Ben Nevis 40 miles distant.

"An atmosphere lost elsewhere" (Visitor's Book 1978).

Please see Gazetteer for details of opening times and admission charges.

SHETLAND ISLANDS Map 16 HU

MOUSA ISLAND HU42
Mousa Broch Best preserved Pictish drystone tower in Scotland. Rises to a height of 40ft and is exceptionally complete. Reached by boat from Leebotton, on Mousa Sound. Open, see inside front cover. Apply keeper. Free. *(AM)*

SCALLOWAY HU33
Scalloway Castle Erected by Patrick Stewart, Earl of Orkney, *c* 1600, and designed on the 'two-stepped' plan. Open, see inside front cover, on application to the Custodian. Free. *(AM)*

SUMBURGH HU30
Jarlshof Prehistoric Site Remarkable Bronze Age, Iron Age, Viking, and Medieval settlements. The 17th-C Laird's House is the 'Jarlshof' of Scott's novel *The Pirate*. The remains are accessible, see inside front cover. 20p (ch 10p). *(AM)*

SKYE, ISLE OF Highland *Inverness-shire* Map 13 NG

ARMADALE NG60
Clan Donald Centre Situated ½m N of pier in the recently-restored north wing of Armadale Castle, the Seat of the Macdonalds, a building dating from the early 18th C, although main part, now derelict, was built in 1815. Flora Macdonald was married from Armadale in 1750. Also famous arboretum, over 300 years old, and sheltered woodland gardens overlooking the Sound of Sleat. ⏛ Museum and shop. Centre open Easter end Oct, 10–5.30; gardens always open. 30p (ch 10p). Party. P. *(Tel Ardvasar 227)* &

COLBOST NG24
The Skye Black House Folk Museum On B884. Typical 19th-C house of the area containing implements and furniture of bygone days, with peat fire burning throughout the day. A replica of an illicit whisky still can be seen behind the museum. Open Easter to 31 Oct daily 10–7. 35p (ch 10–16 10p). ⚠ *(Tel Glendale 291)*

DUNVEGAN NG24
Dunvegan Castle 13th-C and later. Historic and romantic home of the Chief of Macleod since the 13th C. Pit dungeon and famous 'fairy' flag. ⏛ Shop. Open Easter to mid Oct, Mon to Sat 2–5; late May to Sep 10.30–5.

80p (ch 14 40p, pen 50p) under revision for 1980. P. 10p. *(John Macleod of Macleod)*. *(Tel 206)*

GLENDALE NG15
Skye Watermill On the shores of Loch Pooltiel, a 200-year-old grain mill and kiln, recently restored to full working order. ⏛. Open Easter to 31 Oct, Mon to Sat 10–7. 30p (ch 10p, ch 6 free, pen 15p). ⚠ *(Tel 223)*

KILMUIR NG24
Skye Cottage Museum The museum consists of three 100-year-old thatched cottages giving excellent coverage to the croft house of that period. It shows a fine selection of implements, tools, etc used by the men and women of the Highlands and a very interesting collection of old letters, papers and pictures are on display. Open 15 May to 30 Sep Mon to Sat 9–6. 30p (ch 15p). ⚠ *(Tel Duntulm 270)* & **(79)**

WESTERN ISLES

BARRA, ISLE OF Outer Hebrides
Western Isles *Inverness-shire* Map 13 NL

CASTLEBAY NL69
Kisimul Castle Facing Castlebay, an early 15th-C island stronghold, the historic home of the MacNeils of Barra. Open May to end Sep, Sat and Wed. Free. Accessible by boat from Castlebay, ferry charge 50p (ch 25p). *(The MacNeil of Barra XLV)*

LEWIS, ISLE OF Outer Hebrides
Western Isles *Ross and Cromarty* Map 13 NB
ARNOL NB34
Black House Museum Good example of traditional Hebridean dwelling. Retains many of its original furnishings. Open Apr to Sep, weekdays 9.30–7; Oct to Mar, weekdays 9.30–4. 15p (ch 7p). ⚠ *(AM)* &

CALLANISH NB23
Callanish Standing Stones Unique collection of megaliths comprising an avenue 27ft in width, with 19 standing stones, terminating in a 37ft-wide circle containing 13 additional stones. Other stones, burial cairns, and circles in the near vicinity. Accessible at all times. Free. ⚠ *(AM)*

CARLOWAY NB24
Dun Carloway Broch Well-preserved broch, or Pictish tower, about 30ft in height, one of the finest in the Western Isles. Accessible at all times. Free. ⚠ *(AM)*

P.K.F.

Grant-aided Properties

The following buildings have been given a grant by the Historic Buildings Council for England and are either open by appointment or for a total of 30 days a year. We suggest you contact places direct for further information. The majority of these establishments will be found within the guide.

AVON
Bath – Guildhall; Pump Room
Bristol – Kings Weston House;
 Manor House, Bishopsworth;
 Theatre Royal
Dodington House
Twickenham Court

BEDFORDSHIRE
Elstow – Whitbread Cottages
Old Warden – Swiss Garden,
 Old Warden Park;
 Warden Abbey
Ridgmont – Old Saints Church

BERKSHIRE
Bray – Monkey Island Hotel
Burchetts Green – Bee House, Hall Place
Uffington – Tom Brown's School
Windsor – Canon Cloisters; 2 The Cloisters
Wraysbury – King John's Hunting Lodge

BUCKINGHAMSHIRE
Brill – Boarstall Tower
Hartwell House (Grecian Temple)
High Wycombe – 1/3 Church St,
 2 White Hart St
Stowe – Garden, Buildings; School
West Wycombe Park – Garden, Buildings

CAMBRIDGESHIRE
Brampton – Samuel Pepys' House
Buckden Palace
Burghley House
Ely – The Almondry
Kimbolton Castle
Peterborough – Thorpe Hall
Soham – Downfields; Windmill
Wimpole Hall
Wisbech – Peckover House

CHESHIRE
Adlington Hall
Combermere Abbey
Handorth Hall
Haslington Hall
Little Morton Hall
Lyme Park
Styal – Quarrybank Mill
Tatton Park – Old Hall

CORNWALL
Cotehele House
Lanhydrock House
Poundstock – Guildhouse

CUMBRIA
Appleby – Red House
Carlisle – Deanery Tower
Drumburgh Castle
Grasmere – Dove Cottage
Kirkoswald – The College
Levens Hall
Preston – Patrick Hall

DERBYSHIRE
Bridlingcote Hall
Hardwick Hall
Melbourne Hall
Sudbury Hall
Whitwell Hall

DEVON
Bishop's Nympton – South Yarde
Castle Drogo
Compton Castle
Gidleigh – West Chapple
Lawrence Castle
Saltram House
Tiverton Castle
Torquay – Torre Abbey Chapel

DORSET
Bloxworth House
Sherborne – School; The Slype

DURHAM
Bishop Auckland Castle
Bowes Museum – The Lodges
Durham – Church of St Mary le Bow

ESSEX
Brightlingsea – Jacobes Hall
Clovile Hall
Dunmow Great – The Clock House
Finchingfield – Spains Hall
Laindon – All Saints Church
Layer Marney Tower
Little Coggeshall – Abbey Mill
St Osyth's Priory
Steeple Bumpstead – Moat Hall

GLOUCESTERSHIRE
Berkeley – Temple of Vaccina, The Chantry
Cheltenham – Pittville Pump Room
Dyrham Park
Elmore Court
Minchinhampton – Old Market House
Painswick Post Office
Tetbury – Chavenage House
Uley – Stout's Hill
Westonbirt School – Italian Garden

HAMPSHIRE
Basing – Tithe Barn
Beaulieu – Palace House
Breamore House
Charford Manor
Ringwood – Greyfriars
Stockbridge – Marsh Court

HEREFORD & WORCESTER
Abberley Hall
Besford Court
Clodock – Ty Mawr Farm
Eastnor Castle
Eye Manor
Hereford – The Old House
Lower Maescoed – Old Court Farm
Middle Littleton – Tithe Barn
Moccas Hall
Staunton – Red House, Pillows Green
Upton Bishop – Tedgewood Farm
Weobley – Corner Hall
Worcester – Guildhall

HERTFORDSHIRE
Ashridge College
Berden Hall
Berkhamsted – Court House
Knebworth House
Ware – Place House

HUMBERSIDE
Beverley – The Friary
Burton Constable Hall
Hull – Old Grammar School
Ulceby – Wootton Hall

ISLE OF WIGHT
Haseley Manor, Arreton

KENT
Betteshanger House
Canterbury – Poor Priests' Hospital
Cobham Hall
Cowden – Bassetts Farm
Gravesend – New Tavern Court
Hadlow Castle (tower)
Herne Windmill
Knole House
Lenham – Honeywood House
Maidstone – Douglas Lodge, Old College;
    Stonewall Hunton
Rolvenden – Great Maythem

LANCASHIRE
Borwick Hall
Hoghton Tower
Longridge – Dun Cow Rib Farm
Stoneyhurst College – The Pavilions

LEICESTERSHIRE
Leicester – Belgrave Hall
Medbourne Manor
Shenton Hall
Stanford Hall
Wymondham Windmill

LINCOLNSHIRE
Alford Windmill
Aubourn Hall
Boston – Rochford Tower
Culverthorpe Hall
Harlaxton Manor
Harrington Hall
Somerton Tower

LONDON (GREATER)
Camden – Keat's House, Hampstead
    Perceval House, Hampstead
Enfield – Tudor Grammar School
Hammersmith – Fulham Palace
    Kelmscott House, Upper Mall
Hovering – Oretons, Rainham Road
    Hornchurch
Hounslow – Beaufort House
    Great Conservatory, Syon Park
Islington – Hoxton Hall, Hoxton St, N1
    St George's Elizabethan Theatre N7
Merton – Eagle House, London Rd, Mitcham
Richmond upon Thames – Garrick's Temple,
    Hampton
    Sir Richard Burton's Tomb, Mortlake
    White Lodge, Richmond Park
Sutton – Little Holland House, Carshalton
Tower Hamlets – Whitechapel Art Gallery
Waltham Forest – Water House, Forest Rd,
    Walthamstow
Westminster – 100 Bayswater Rd, W2
    Deans Yard, SW1
    84 Margaret St, W1

MANCHESTER (GREATER)
Bramall Hall

MERSEYSIDE
Liverpool – Oriel Chambers, Water St
Speke Hall

NORFOLK
Felbrigg Court
Heydon Hall

King's Lynn – King's Staithe Mews; Lattice
    House; Town Hall
Langley Hall (Chedgrave Lodges)
Norwich – Bacon House
Oxburgh Hall
Sutton – Wort's Mill

NORTHAMPTONSHIRE
Apelthorpe Hall
Geddington – The Old Forge
Kettering – Carey Mission House
Little Oakley Church
Newton – Church of St Faith
Northampton – Halsilrigg Manor
Oakley Hall
Southwick Hall
Upton Hall

NORTHUMBERLAND
Bamburgh Castle
Beaufort Castle
Cragside Hall
Lindisfarne Castle
Woodburn – Church of St Mary the Virgin

NOTTINGHAMSHIRE
Clumber Park
Holme Pierrepont Hall
Keyworth – The Barn
Worksop – Manor Lodge

OXFORDSHIRE
Aynhoe Park
Blenheim Palace
Cottisford – Old Manor House
Cuddesdon
Fawley Court
Mapledurham – Chagey Court
    Old Manor House; Mill
Oxford – Great Tower, Magdalen College;
    51 Holywell St; Keble College;
    St Paul's; Bell Tower, Christchurch
Wheatley – Shotover House, The Temple
Woodstock – The Manor

SALOP
Adcote School
Attingham Park
Bentham Hall
Condover Hall
Ellesmere – Adcote School
Market Drayton – The Old House;
    41 Shropshire St
Pitchford Hall

SOMERSET
Croscombe – Old Baptist Chapel
Dunster Castle
East Coker – Hymorford House
Forde Abbey
Frome – Blue House Almhouses
Tintinhull House
West Compton House

STAFFORDSHIRE
Alton Towers
Barlaston Hall
Blithfield Hall
Broughton Hall
Brund Mill
Chillington Hall
Oakley Hall
Pillaton Old Hall
Stafford – Ancient High House
Stoke-on-Trent – The Roundhouse, Etruria
Tixall Park – Gatehouse

SUFFOLK
Bentley Hall
Bury St Edmunds – Unitarian Chapel
Friston Mill
Hadleigh – The Deanery Tower
Ickworth House
Ixworth Abbey
Melford Hall
Pakenham – Newe House; Watermill

SURREY
Farnham – Castle, New Place
Thames Ditton – Newlands

SUSSEX (EAST)
Forest Row – Kidbrooke Park
Hove – Goldstone Pumping Station
Northiam – Brickwall
St Leonards – Clock House

SUSSEX (WEST)
Arundel Castle
Chichester – See House, Chapel, The Palace
Petworth House

TYNE AND WEAR
Newcastle upon Tyne – Blackfriars; Old
    Assembly Room
South Shields – Old Town Hall

WARWICKSHIRE
Baddesley Clinton
Compton Wynyates – The Windmill
Coombe Abbey
Honington Hall
Stoneleigh Abbey

Warwick – Elizabethan House;
    Lord Leycester Hospital;
    Northgate House

WEST MIDLANDS
Birmingham – St Mary's Convent
Moseley Old Hall

WILTSHIRE
Bradford-on-Avon – Barton Farm;
    St Olave's;
    Silver St House
Constable Burton Hall
Corsham – Warden's House, Hungerford
    Almhouses
Devizes – Brownston House
Malmesbury – Abbey House
Marlborough – Saints Peter and Paul
Swindon – Railway Accident Hospital

YORKSHIRE (NORTH)
Arncliffe Hall
Beningsbrough Hall
Carlton Towers
Castle Howard
Duncombe Park
Kiplin Hall
Old Scriven, Home Farmhouse
Richmond – Old Station Buildings
Rievaulx Abbey
Skipton – High Corn Mill
York – Treasurer's House

YORKSHIRE (SOUTH)
Hickleton Hall
Sheffield – Oakes Park

Follow the Country Code
and preserve your heritage

Guard against all risk of fire

Leave all gates as you find them (which usually
means fastening them)

Keep dogs under proper control

Keep to the paths across farm land

Avoid damaging fences, hedges and walls

Leave no litter

Safeguard water supplies

Protect and do not disturb wild life

Protect wild plants and trees (do not take specimens)

Go carefully on country roads

Respect the life of the countryside

INDEX

This is not a fully comprehensive index. Establishments with the same name as the town or village will not be found in the index but in their alphabetical order in the Country concerned.

Stately Homes, Museums, Castles and Gardens in Britain

Your suggestions

In an effort to make this Guide as varied and interesting as possible, we have given this page to you. Please fill in this form if you know of any building or place of interest that does not appear in this book and which you feel merits our attention.

BLOCK LETTERS PLEASE

Name of building or place of interest:......................................

....

Address: ....

....

Reason for your suggestion: ....

....

....

....

....

....

....

....

Your name:...

Your address: ....

....

Membership No: ....

Please send to:

> **The Automobile Association**
> **Publications Research Unit**
> **Fanum House, Basingstoke,**
> **Hants RG21 2EA**

Your views

Please take this opportunity to tell us what you think of our Guide.

Send your completed form to:
The Automobile Association
Publications Research Unit
Fanum House, Basingstoke,
Hants RG21 2EA

BLOCK LETTERS PLEASE

Name ....

Address ....

....

Membership No. ....

Comments ....

....

....

....

....

....

....

....

....

....

....

....

....

....

....

....

We will take your suggestions and views into consideration but are unable to enter into any correspondence.